theories of *Personality*

Fourth Edition

Jess Feist

McNeese State University

Gregory J. Feist

College of William and Mary

Boston, Massachusetts   Burr Ridge, Illinois   Dubuque, Iowa
Madison, Wisconsin   New York, New York   San Francisco, California   St. Louis, Missouri

theories of *Personality*

McGraw·Hill
*A Division of The **McGraw·Hill** Companies*

THEORIES OF PERSONALITY, 4/E

Cover and part opener image: *Abstrakter Kopf* by Alexej von Jawlensky, © Superstock
Library of Congress Catalog Card Number: 97-73326

2 3 4 5 6 7 8 9 0 QPD/QPD 0 9 8

ISBN: 0-697-27565-5

Editorial director: Jane E. Vaicunas
Sponsoring editor: Mickey Cox
Marketing manager: James Rozsa
Senior project manager: Kay J. Brimeyer
Production supervisor: Mary E. Haas
Designer: Lu Ann Schrandt
Photo research coordinator: Carrie K. Burger/Laura Fuller
Compositor: Shepherd, Inc.
Typeface: 10/12 Novarese Book
Printer: Quebecor, Inc.

http://www.mhhe.com

Contents

Preface

What makes people behave as they do? Are people ordinarily aware of what they are doing, or are their behaviors the result of hidden, unconscious motives? Are some people naturally good and others basically evil, or do we all have potential to be either good or bad? Is human conduct largely a product of nature, or is it shaped mostly by environmental influences? Can people freely choose to mold their personality, or is their life determined by forces beyond their control? Are people best described by their similarities, or is uniqueness the dominant characteristic of humans? What causes some people to develop disordered personalities, whereas others seem to grow toward psychological health?

These questions have been asked and debated by philosophers, scholars, and religious thinkers for several thousand years, but most of these discussions were based on personal opinions, which were colored by political, economic, religious, and social considerations. Then, near the end of the 19th century, some progress was made in humanity's ability to organize, explain, and predict its own actions. The emergence of psychology as the scientific study of human behavior marked the beginning of a more systematic approach to the study of human personality.

Early personality theorists, such as Sigmund Freud, Carl Jung, and Alfred Adler, relied mostly on clinical observations to construct models of human behavior. Although their data were more systematic and reliable than those of earlier observers, they continued to rely on their own individualized way of looking at things, and thus they arrived at different conceptions of the nature of humanity.

Later personality theorists tended to use more empirical studies to learn about human behavior. They developed tentative models, tested hypotheses, and then reformulated their models. In other words, they applied the tools of scientific inquiry and scientific theory to the area of human personality. Science, of course, is not divorced from speculation, imagination, and creativity, all of which are needed to formulate theories. Each of the personality theorists discussed in this book has evolved a theory based both on empirical observations and on imaginative speculation. Moreover, each theory is a reflection of the personality of its creator.

Thus, the different theories discussed in these pages are a reflection of the unique cultural background, family experiences, and professional training of their originators. The usefulness of each theory, however, is not evaluated on the personality of its author but on its ability to (1) generate research, (2) offer itself to falsification, (3) integrate existing empirical knowledge, and (4) suggest practical answers to everyday problems. Therefore, we evaluate each of the theories discussed in this book on the basis of these four criteria, as well as on (5) its internal consistency and (6) its simplicity. In addition to these six criteria, some personality theories have fertilized other fields, such as sociology, education, psychotherapy, advertising, management, mythology, counseling, art, literature, and religion.

THE FOURTH EDITION

Theories of Personality, fourth edition, provides a comprehensive coverage of 23 of the most influential theorists of personality. It emphasizes normal personality, although we have also included brief discussions on abnormality and methods of psychotherapy when appropriate. Because each theory is an expression of its builder's unique view of the world and of humanity, we include extended biographical information on each theorist so that you will have an opportunity to become acquainted with both the theory and the theorist.

NEW FEATURES

Readers familiar with earlier editions of *Theories of Personality* will note several new features in this fourth edition. First, we have presented the chapters in a somewhat different order, with Jung preceding Adler, and Erikson following the other psychodynamic theorists. Also, we have included the ideas of John Bowlby in the object relations chapter, which now comes before chapters on Horney, Fromm, Sullivan, and Erikson. This reorganization was designed to give the reader clearer chronological and topical perspective of the psychodynamic theories. In addition, we introduce Skinner's behavioral analysis with short discussions on E. L. Thorndike's law of effect and John B. Watson's revolutionary views on scientific psychology.

Second, we have included a little more biographical information on Freud, Jung, Adler, Klein, Horney, Sullivan, Erikson, Skinner, Rotter, Mischel, Allport, Rogers, and May with the hope that this information will help you better understand these theorists' own personalities.

Third, we have included additional discussions on: (1) the psychology of science; (2) Freud's early therapeutic technique and seduction theory in relation to repressed and recovered memories; (3) Jung's Number 1 and Number 2 personalities; (4) Adler's notion of dreams and a summary table of Adlerian birth order traits; (5) Horney's recently published ideas on feminine psychology; (6) Skinner's view of science; (7) Bandura's newly developed concept of collective efficacy; (8) Rotter's locus of control scale; (9) Mischel's new cognitive-affective personality system and his recent emphasis on affective responses; (9) Eysenck's conception of psychoticism (P) and his view of the diathesis-stress model of illness; (10) Allport's visit with Freud and the true identity of Glenn and Isabel, the couple with whom "Jenny" exchanged letters; (11) a recently published paper by Rogers; (12) the Personal Orientation Inventory that measures Maslow's concept of self-actualization; and (13) the current frequency of research studies related to the various theories of personality.

Fourth, we have reorganized several chapters to facilitate a smoother flow of information and included several new tables that summarize key ideas. In addition, we have completely revised the sections on related research to include not only a structure for understanding key research concepts, but a sampling of results from recent empirical studies. We believe that personality theories are more than interesting templates through which people can search for explanations of human nature. They are also dynamic entities that spawn much of the ongoing psychology research, and our update of this research is intended to keep the reader current with important studies on personality.

FAMILIAR FEATURES

Although the fourth edition of *Theories of Personality* contains many new features, it continues to emphasize the strong and unique features of earlier editions, namely, instructive chapter introductions, extended biographical data, a lively writing style, thought-provoking concepts of humanity as seen by each theorist, structured evaluations of each theory, informative chapter summaries, and annotated suggested readings. As with previous editions, the fourth edition is based on original sources and the most recent formulation of the theory. Early concepts and models are included only if they retained their importance in the later theory or if they provided vital groundwork for understanding the final theory.

COVERAGE

The fourth edition of *Theories of Personality* is divided into six broad areas, beginning with the *introductory remarks* found in Chapter 1. The so-called *psychodynamic theorists* are discussed in Part Two—Chapters 2 to 9. Freud, the original personality theorist, heads this list. The others—Jung, Adler, Klein, Mahler, Kernberg, Kohut, Bowlby, Horney, Fromm, Sullivan, and Erikson—all tended to emphasize unconscious determinants of behavior and all, in one way or another, were influenced by Freud.

Part Three presents the *behavioral and cognitive learning theories*. Included in this group are Skinner's radical behavioral approach, Bandura's cognitive learning theory, Rotter's social learning theory, and Mischel's cognitive social learning theory.

In Part Four, we discuss the *dispositional theories*, including the trait and factor theories of Cattell and Eysenck as well as the personal disposition theory of Allport. However, Allport's emphasis on the uniqueness of personality gives his theory a strong humanistic complexion.

Part Five contains the *humanistic/existential theories* of Kelly, Rogers, Maslow, and May. Kelly's unique theory, however, almost defies classification.

Finally, in Part Six we summarize the major theorists' concepts of humanity, present a concise evaluation of the different theories (including their current ability to generate research), and speculate about future directions in personality theory.

WRITING STYLE

Although this fourth edition of *Theories of Personality* explores difficult and complex theories, we use clear, concise, and comprehensible language as well as an informal writing style. The book is designed for undergraduate students and should be understood by those with a minimum background in psychology. However, we have tried not to oversimplify or violate the theorist's original meaning. We have made ample comparisons between and among theorists where appropriate and have included many examples to illustrate how the different theories can be applied to ordinary day-to-day situations. A glossary at the end of the book contains definitions of technical terms used throughout—many from the view of a particular theorist. The same terms also appear in **boldface** and are defined within the text.

INSTRUCTIONAL AIDS

Besides an end-of-book glossary, we have supplied other features to aid both the student and the instructor. These include:

Chapter outlines orient readers to each chapter by previewing major topics to be discussed. Chapter overviews introduce readers to the general tone of the theory. Near the end of each presentation is a chapter summary, written to give just enough detail for a quick review of important topics. Finally, each chapter closes with several suggested readings along with a short description of each. We chose these books and articles for their readability, content, and interest level. They direct readers in further study.

INSTRUCTOR'S MANUAL

Accompanying this text is an instructor's manual with learning objectives, a lecture outline, teaching suggestions, essay questions, and a test bank of multiple-choice items. The *learning objectives* are designed to provide instructors with concepts that should be important to the student. The *lecture outline* is intended to help busy instructors organize lecture notes and grasp quickly the major ideas of each chapter. With some general familiarity with a particular theory, instructors should be able to lecture directly from the lecture outline. *Teaching suggestions* reflect class activities and paper topics that we have used successfully with our students.

We have included three or four essay questions and answers for instructors who prefer this type of student evaluation. For those who prefer multiple-choice questions, we have provided a *test bank* with more than 1,400 items, each marked with the correct answer. Computerized versions of the test bank are also available. See your sales representative for further information.

STUDY GUIDE

Students who wish to organize their study methods and enhance their chances of achieving their best scores on class quizzes may acquire the study guide that accompanies the fourth edition of *Theories of Personality*. This study guide includes learning objectives and chapter summaries. In addition, it contains a variety of test items, including fill-in-the blank, true/false, multiple-choice, and short answer questions. The study guide is available through your college bookstore.

ACKNOWLEDGMENTS

Finally, we wish to acknowledge our gratitude to the many people who have contributed to the completion of this book. Joanne Durand, Leslye Quinn, and Patrick Moreno supplied materials and encouragement; Linda Brannon unselfishly completed the instructor's manual for *Health Psychology: An Introduction to Behavior and Health*, third edition, allowing the senior author to receive partial credit for that publication while beginning work on the present text. The people at McGraw-Hill, formerly Brown and Benchmark, provided much professional assistance, which has made this a better book. Special thanks to Steven Yetter, Ted Underhill, Linda Falkenstein, Megan Rundel, Kris Queck, Kay J. Brimeyer, and Karen Dorman.

The fourth edition has benefited from the insightful suggestions of its reviewers as well as from comments by reviewers of the first three editions. We hereby acknowledge our indebtedness to William Arndt (University of Missouri, Kansas City), Drew Arnold (Keuka College), James Barger (Missouri Western State College), John Brockway (Davidson College), Clinton E. Browne (Liberty University), Ana Mari Cauce (University of Washington), Calvin Claus (National College of Education), W. Grant Dahlstrom (University of North Carolina), Boice Daugherty (East Carolina University), Lenore E. DeFonso (Indiana University—Purdue University at Fort Wayne), Richard E. Dowell, Jr. (Lycoming College), David A. F. Haaga (American University), Cooper Holmes (Emporia State University), Ralph W. Hood, Jr. (University of Tennessee–Chattanooga), Deborah Huntley (Wichita State University), Charles Johnston (University of Nebraska–Lincoln), Gary King (Rose State College), Alfred Kornfeld (Eastern Connecticut State University), Phil Lau (DeAnza College), Paul Lewan (Green River Community College), Alan J. Lipman (Rutgers University), Mariam London (Northern Arizona University), Samuel Lotegelvaki (Concordia University), John McBrearty (Temple University), Joseph McCormack (Washburn University), Kathleen McCormick (Ocean County College), Eugene McCown (Northwest Missouri State College), Diane Mello-Goldner (Pine Manor College), Lesly Morey (Vanderbilt University), Richard Pasework (University of Wyoming), Joseph Philbrick (California State Polytechnic, Pomona), James Pullen (Central Missouri State University), Kathryn Ryan (Lycoming College), Alice Scheuer (University of Hawaii–Manoa), Kendell C. Thornton (South Dakota State University), Keith Thrasher (Rose State College), Terence J. Tracey (University of Illinois–Champaign), Robert H. Williams (Maple Woods Community College), Brian Yates (American University), and Edward Yellinek (Wilson College).

We are also indebted to the following personality theorists for their kindness in taking time to discuss appropriate sections of the manuscript: Albert Bandura, Raymond B. Cattell, Hans J. Eysenck, Carl R. Rogers (deceased), Julian B. Rotter, and B. F. Skinner (deceased).

Finally, we thank Mary Jo and Erika for their patience and understanding during the course of this project.

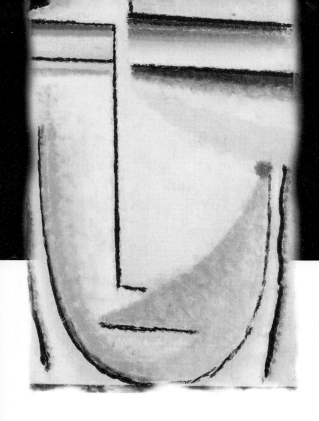

Chapter

1

Introduction to Personality Theory

hy do people behave as they do? Do people have some choice in shaping their own personality? What accounts for similarities and differences among people? What makes people act in predictable ways? Why are they unpredictable? Do hidden, unconscious forces control people's behavior? What causes mental disturbances? Is human behavior shaped more by heredity or by environment? Is society or biology a stronger influence on human personality? For centuries, philosophers, theologians, and other thinkers have asked these questions as they pondered the nature of human nature, or wondered whether humans have a basic nature.

Until relatively recent times, great thinkers made little progress in finding satisfactory answers to these questions. A little more than 100 years ago, however, Sigmund Freud began to combine philosophical speculations with a primitive scientific method. As a neurologist trained in science, Freud began to listen to his patients to find out what hidden conflicts lay behind their assortment of symptoms. "Listening became, for Freud, more than an art; it became a method, a privileged road to knowledge that his patients mapped out for him" (Gay, 1988, p. 70).

Freud's method gradually became more scientific as he formulated hypotheses and checked their plausibility against his clinical experiences. From this combination of speculation and clinical evidence, Freud evolved the first modern theory of personality. Later, a number of other men and women developed theories of personality—some based largely on philosophical speculation, others mainly on **empirical** evidence, but all used some combination of the two. Indeed, this chapter shows that a useful theory should be founded on *both* scientific evidence and controlled, imaginative speculation.

Psychologists have come to a better understanding of human behavior, in part, because a number of personality theorists have (1) made controlled observations of behavior and (2) speculated on the meaning of those observations. Those theorists widely recognized as having made significant contributions to our present understanding of personality include Sigmund Freud, Carl Jung, Alfred Adler, Melanie Klein, Margaret Mahler, Otto Kernberg, Heinz Kohut, John Bowlby, Karen Horney, Erich Fromm, Harry Stack Sullivan, Erik Erikson, B. F. Skinner, Albert Bandura, Julian Rotter, Walter Mischel, Raymond Cattell, Hans Eysenck, Gordon Allport, George Kelly, Carl Rogers, Abraham Maslow, and Rollo May. The theories of personality formulated by these people are the topic of this book.

WHAT IS PERSONALITY?

Psychologists differ among themselves as to the meaning of personality. Most agree the word "personality" originated from the Latin **persona,** which referred to a theatrical mask worn in Greek drama by Roman actors before the birth of Christ. A persona (mask) was used to project a false appearance to others; that is, the role one plays in life. This surface view of personality, however, is not an acceptable definition. When psychologists use the term "personality," they are referring to what one really is, not to mere surface appearance.

Nevertheless, personality theorists have not agreed on a single definition of personality. Indeed, they have evolved unique and vital theories because they lack agreement as to the nature of humanity, and because each sees personality from an individual reference point. The personality theorists discussed in this book have had a variety of backgrounds. Some were born in Europe and lived their entire lives there; others were born in Europe, but migrated to other parts of the world, especially the United States; still others were born in North America (the United States and Canada) and have

No two people, not even identical twins, have exactly the same personality.

remained there. Many have been influenced by early religious experiences; others have not. Most, but not all, have been trained in either psychiatry or psychology. Many have drawn on their experiences as psychotherapists; others have relied more on empirical research to gather data on human personality. Although they have all dealt in some way with what we call personality, each has approached this global concept from a different perspective. Some have tried to construct a comprehensive theory; others have been less ambitious and have dealt with only a few aspects of personality. Few personality theorists have formally defined personality, but all have had their own view of it.

Although no single definition is acceptable to all personality theorists, we can say that **personality** is a pattern of relatively permanent traits, dispositions, or characteristics within the individual that give some measure of consistency to that person's behavior. These traits may be unique, common to some group, or shared by the entire species, but their pattern is different for each individual. Thus everyone, although like others in some ways, has a unique personality.

WHAT IS A THEORY?

The word "theory" has the dubious distinction of being one of the most misused and misunderstood words in the English language. Some people contrast theory to truth or fact, but such an antithesis demonstrates a fundamental lack of understanding of all three terms. In science, theories are tools used to generate research and organize observations, but neither truth nor fact has a place in a scientific terminology.

THEORY DEFINED

A scientific **theory** is *a set of related assumptions from which, by logical deductive reasoning, testable hypotheses can be drawn.* This definition needs further explanation. First, a theory is *a set of* assumptions. A single assumption can never fill all the requirements of an adequate theory. A single assumption, for example, could not serve to integrate known facts, something a useful theory should do.

Second, a theory is a set of *related* assumptions. Isolated assumptions could not generate meaningful hypotheses. Neither would they be internally consistent—a criterion for a useful theory.

A third key word in the definition is *assumptions*. The components of a theory are not proven facts in the sense that their validity has been absolutely established. They are, however, accepted *as if* they were true. This is a practical step, taken so that useful research can be conducted and further theory building can proceed.

Fourth, *logical deductive reasoning* is used by the researcher to formulate hypotheses. The tenets of a theory must be stated with sufficient precision and logical consistency to permit scientists to deduce clearly stated hypotheses. The hypotheses are not components of the theory, but flow from it. It is the job of an imaginative scientist to begin with the general theory and, through deductive reasoning, arrive at a particular hypothesis that can be tested. If the general theoretical propositions are illogical, they remain sterile and incapable of generating hypotheses. Moreover, if a researcher uses faulty logic in deducing hypotheses, the resulting research will be meaningless and will make no contribution to the ongoing process of theory construction.

The final part of the definition includes the qualifier *testable*. Unless a hypothesis can be tested in some way, it is worthless. The hypothesis need not be tested immediately, but it must suggest the possibility that scientists in the future might develop the necessary means to test it.

WHAT A THEORY IS NOT

People sometimes confuse theory with philosophy, or idle speculation, or hypothesis, or taxonomy. Although theory is related to each of these concepts, it is not the same as any of them.

Not a Philosophy

First of all, a theory is not a philosophy, which is a much broader term. Philosophy means love of wisdom, and philosophers are people who pursue wisdom through thinking and reasoning. Philosophers are not scientists; they do not ordinarily conduct controlled studies in their pursuit of wisdom. Philosophy encompasses several branches, one of which is **epistemology,** or the nature of knowledge. Theory relates most closely to this branch of philosophy, because it is a tool used by scientists in their pursuit of knowledge.

Theories do not deal with "oughts" and "shoulds." Therefore, a set of principles about how one should live one's life cannot be a theory. Such principles involve values and are the proper concern of philosophy. Although theories are not free of values, they are built on scientific evidence that has been obtained in a relatively unbiased fashion. Thus, there are no theories on why society should help homeless people or on what constitutes great art.

Philosophy deals with what ought to be or what should be; theory does not. Theory deals with broad sets of if-then statements, but the goodness or badness of the outcomes of these statements is beyond the realm of theory. For example, a theory might tell us that if children are brought up in isolation, completely separated from human contact, then they will not develop human language, exhibit parenting behavior, and so on. But this statement says nothing about the morality of such a method of child rearing.

Not Idle Speculation

Second, a theory is not mere armchair speculation. Although theories involve speculation, they must never be totally separated from empirical observation. They are closely tied to science and are based on scientifically gathered data.

What is the relationship between theory and science? **Science** is the branch of study concerned with observation and classification of data and with the verification of general laws through the testing of hypotheses. Theories are useful tools employed by scientists to give meaning and organization to observations. In addition, theories provide fertile ground for producing testable hypotheses. Without some kind of theory to hold observations together and to point to directions of possible research, science would be greatly handicapped.

Theories are not useless fantasies fabricated by impractical scholars fearful of soiling their hands in the machinery of scientific investigation. In fact, theories themselves are quite practical and are essential to the advancement of any science. Speculation and empirical observation are the two essential cornerstones of theory building, but speculation must not run rampantly in advance of controlled observation.

Not a Hypothesis

Although theory is a narrower concept than philosophy, it is a broader term than hypothesis. A good theory is capable of generating many hypotheses. A **hypothesis** is an educated guess or prediction specific enough for its validity to be tested through the use of the scientific method. A theory is too general to lend itself to direct verification, but a single comprehensive theory is capable of generating thousands of hypotheses. Hypotheses, then, are more specific than the theories that give them birth. The offspring, however, should not be confused with the parent.

Of course, a close relationship exists between a theory and a hypothesis. Using *deductive reasoning*, a scientific investigator can derive testable hypotheses from a useful theory and then test these hypotheses. The results of these tests—whether they support or contradict the hypotheses—feed back into the theory. Using *inductive reasoning*, the investigator then alters the theory to reflect these results As the theory grows and changes, other hypotheses can be drawn from it, and when tested they in turn reshape the theory.

Not a Taxonomy

A **taxonomy** is a classification of things according to their natural relationships. Taxonomies are essential to the development of a science because without classification of data, science could not grow. Mere classification, however, does not constitute a theory. Even a combination of several taxonomies—each with several complex subsystems—does not produce a theory. Unlike theories, taxonomies are not generative. They are dynamic only in the sense that new systems can be added to them; they cannot produce testable hypotheses.

THEORY AND OBSERVATIONS

What is the relationship between theory and observations? A useful theory has a mutual and dynamic interaction with observations. This relationship generally

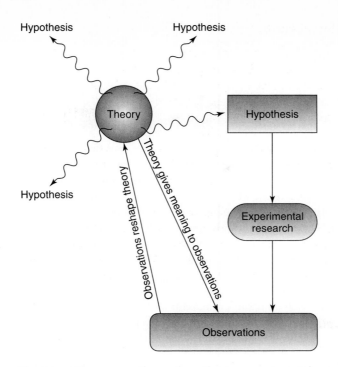

Figure 1.1 The interaction among theory, hypotheses, experimental research, and observation.

proceeds in the following manner. *Theories* generate a number of *hypotheses* that can be experimentally investigated. The results from the subsequent experimental research, called *observations*, then flow back into the theory and restructure it so that additional hypotheses can be generated. This cyclic relationship is shown in Figure 1.1. As the theory changes and grows, it extends its utility to a wider range of possible perceptions. More hypotheses can be tested and additional observations made, which in turn reshape and enlarge the theory even more. This cyclic effect continues for as long as the theory proves useful. When a theory is no longer able to explain related observations or to generate additional research, it is set aside in favor of a better one, not because it has been disproven, but because it has ceased to be useful.

WHY DIFFERENT THEORIES?

If theories of personality are truly scientific, why do we have so many different ones? The very nature of a theory allows the theory builder to make speculations from a particular point of view, and each of the theorists discussed in this book has had his or her unique perspective. Theorists must be as objective as possible when gathering data, but their decisions as to what data are collected and how these data are interpreted are personal ones. Theories are not immutable laws; they are built, not on proven facts, but on assumptions that are subject to individual interpretation.

All theories are a reflection of their authors' personal backgrounds, childhood experiences, philosophy of life, interpersonal relationships, and unique manner of looking at the world. Because observations are colored by the individual observer's frame of reference, it follows that there may be many diverse theories. Nevertheless, divergent theories can be useful. The usefulness of a theory depends on its ability to integrate known observations and to generate research, not on its agreement with some other established theory.

THEORISTS' PERSONALITIES AND THEIR THEORIES OF PERSONALITY

Because personality theories grow from theorists' own personalities, a study of those personalities is appropriate. In recent years a subdiscipline of psychology called **psychology of science** has begun to look at personal traits of scientists. The psychology of science studies both science and the behavior of scientists; that is, it investigates the impact of an individual scientist's psychological processes and personal characteristics on the development of her or his scientific theories and research (Feist, 1993, 1994; Feist & Gorman, 1996; Gholson, Shadish, Neimeyer, & Houts, 1989). In other words, the psychology of science examines how scientists' personalities, cognitive processes, developmental histories, and social experience affect the kind of science they conduct and the theories they create. Indeed, a number of investigators (Hart, 1982; Johnson, Germer, Efran, & Overton, 1988; Polanyi, 1958; Zachar & Leong, 1992) have demonstrated that personality differences influence one's theoretical orientation as well as one's inclination to lean toward the "hard" or "soft" side of a discipline.

A full understanding of theories of personality rests on information regarding the historical, social, and psychological worlds of each theorist at the time of his or her theorizing. Because we believe that personality theories reflect the theorist's personality, we have included a substantial amount of biographical information on each major theorist. Indeed, personality differences among theorists account for fundamental disagreements between those who lean toward the quantitative side of psychology (behaviorists, social learning theorists, and trait theorists) and those inclined toward the clinical and qualitative side of psychology (psychoanalysts, humanists, and existentialists).

Although a theorist's personality partially shapes his or her theory, it should not be the sole determinant of that theory. Likewise, your acceptance of one or another theory should not rest only on your personal values and predilections. When evaluating and choosing a theory, you should acknowledge the impact of the theorist's personal history on the theory, but you should ultimately evaluate it on the basis of scientific criteria that are independent of that personal history. Some observers (Feist & Gorman, 1996) have distinguished between *science as process* and *science as product*. The scientific process may be influenced by the personal characteristics of the scientist, but the ultimate usefulness of the scientific product is and must be evaluated independently of the process. Thus, your evaluation of each of the theories presented in this book should rest more on objective criteria than on your subjective likes and dislikes.

WHAT MAKES A THEORY USEFUL?

What are the objective criteria for evaluating a scientific theory? Scientists use several standards to establish the usefulness of a theory, and we evaluate each of the theories presented in this book on the basis of the following six criteria.

A Theory Should Generate Research

Perhaps the most important criteria of a useful theory is its ability to stimulate and guide further research. Without an adequate theory to point the way, many of our present empirical findings would have remained undiscovered. In astronomy, for example, the planet Neptune was discovered because the theory of motion generated the hypothesis that the irregularity in the path of Uranus must be caused by the presence of another planet. Useful theory provided astronomers with a road map that guided their search for and discovery of the new planet.

A useful theory will generate two different kinds of research: *descriptive research* and *hypothesis testing*. Descriptive research, which is carried out in order to expand an existing theory, is concerned with the measurement, labeling, and categorization of the units employed in theory building. Descriptive research has a symbiotic relationship with theory. On one hand, it provides the building blocks for the theory, and on the other, it receives its impetus from the dynamic, expanding theory. The more useful the theory, the more research generated by it; the greater the amount of descriptive research, the more complete the theory.

The second kind of research generated by a useful theory, hypothesis testing, leads to an indirect verification of the usefulness of the theory. A useful personality theory will generate many hypotheses that, when tested, add significantly to our understanding of human personality.

A Theory Should Be Falsifiable

For a theory to generate meaningful research, it must be **falsifiable;** that is, it must be precise enough to suggest research that may either support or fail to support its major tenets. If a theory is so vague and general that both positive and negative research results can be interpreted as support, then that theory is not falsifiable and ceases to be useful. Falsifiability, however, is not the same as false; it simply means that negative experimental outcomes should be able to refute the theory and force the theorist to either discard or modify it.

A falsifiable theory is accountable to experimental results. Figure 1.1 depicts a circular and mutually reinforcing connection between theory and research; each forms a basis for the other. Science is distinguished from nonscience by its ability to reject ideas that are not supported empirically even though they seem logical and rational. For example, Aristotle argued quite logically that lighter bodies fall at slower rates than heaver bodies. Although his argument may have agreed with "common sense," it had one problem: It was empirically wrong.

Theories that rely heavily on unobservable transformations in the unconscious are exceedingly difficult to either verify or falsify. For example, Freud's psychoanalytic theory suggests that many of our emotions and behaviors are motivated by unconscious tendencies that are directly opposite of the ones we express. For instance, unconscious hate might be expressed as conscious love, and so forth. Transformations of this sort hamper falsification of much of psychoanalytic theory, because alternative explanations can too readily be given to the same set of observations. If the results of a study reveal a particular finding, then that finding can be interpreted as support for Freud's theory. But if the study reveals the opposite findings, then this too can be seen as support for the same theory. Later, we will see that Freud's theory is not the only one that has problems with falsification. All theories must be evaluated on their ability to be confirmed or disconfirmed.

A Theory Should Organize Data

A useful theory should also be able to organize observations. Without some organization or classification, observations made from research would remain isolated and meaningless. Unless observations are organized into some intelligible framework, a scientist is left with no clear direction to follow in the pursuit of further knowledge. Intelligent questions cannot be asked unless observations have some order. Without intelligent questions, further research is severely curtailed.

A useful theory of personality must be capable of integrating what is currently known about human behavior and personality development. It must be able to shape as many bits of information as possible into a meaningful arrangement. If a personality theory does not offer a reasonable explanation of at least some kinds of behavior, its usefulness is extremely questionable. On the other hand, a theory must be falsifiable, so that personality theorists cannot not force opposing observations of behavior into their theory. When theorists become compelled to offer their theory as an explanation for all personality, they risk mistaking theory for truth. The theory then ceases to be viable and rigor mortis sets in.

A Theory Should Guide Action

A fourth criterion of a useful theory is its ability to guide the practitioner over the rough course of day-to-day problems. For example, parents, teachers, business managers, and psychotherapists are confronted continually with an avalanche of questions for which they try to find workable answers. Good theory provides a structure for finding many of those answers. Without a useful theory, practitioners would stumble in the darkness of trial and error techniques; with a sound theoretical orientation, they can discern a suitable course of action.

For the Freudian analyst and Rogerian counselor, answers to the same question would be very different. To the question, How can I best treat this patient? the psychoanalytic therapist might answer along these lines: If psychoneuroses are caused by childhood sexual conflicts that have become unconscious, then I can help this patient best by delving into these repressions and allowing the patient to relive the experiences in the absence of conflict. To the same question, the Rogerian therapist might answer: If people need empathy, unconditional positive regard, and congruence to grow psychologically, then I can best help this client by providing an accepting, nonthreatening atmosphere. Notice that both therapists constructed their answers in an *if-then* framework, even though the two answers call for very different courses of action.

Also included in this criterion is the extent to which the theory stimulates thought and action in other disciplines, such as art, literature (including movies and television dramas), law, sociology, philosophy, religion, education, business administration, and psychotherapy. Most of the theories discussed in this book have had some influence in areas beyond psychology. For example, Freud's theory has recently prompted research on recovered memories, a topic very important to the legal profession. Also, Jung's theory is of great interest to many theologians and has captured the imagination of popular writers such as Joseph Campbell and others. Similarly, the ideas of Adler, Erikson, Skinner, Maslow, Rogers, May, and other personality theorists have sparked interest and action in a broad range of scholarly fields.

A Theory Should Be Internally Consistent

A theory can be useful only if its components are logically compatible. For example, the language of a theory must be consistent; that is, the same term must not have two separate meanings nor be applied in more than one way. Also, one tenet of the theory cannot be opposed to another tenet.

A good theory will include a taxonomy that is logical and that has been systematically constructed. It will use concepts and terms that have been clearly and operationally defined and used only in consonance with those definitions. An **operational definition** is one that defines units in terms of specific operations to be carried out by the observer.

An internally consistent theory cannot offer opposing answers to the same question. Also, it does not force incompatible observations into a framework where they do not fit. Its limitations of scope are carefully defined and it does not offer explanations that lie beyond that scope.

A Theory Should Be Parsimonious

When two theories are equal in their ability to generate testable hypotheses, to be falsified, to give meaning to observations, and to guide the practitioner, the simpler one is preferred. This is the law of **parsimony.** In fact, of course, two theories are never exactly equal in these abilities, but, in general, simple straightforward theories are more useful than ones that bog down under the weight of complicated concepts and esoteric language.

In building a theory of personality, it is usually more desirable to begin on a limited scale and avoid sweeping generalizations that attempt to explain all of human behavior. That was the course of action followed by most of the theorists discussed in this book. For example, Freud began with a theory based largely on hysterical neuroses and, over a period of years, gradually expanded it to include more and more of the total personality.

As simple models evolve into larger theories, the theorist's basic assumptions concerning the nature of humanity become more and more evident. Each of the theorists discussed in this book has an identifiable *concept of humanity*.

DIMENSIONS FOR A CONCEPT OF HUMANITY

Personality theories differ, not merely in terminology, but on basic issues concerning the nature of humanity. Each personality theory reflects its author's assumptions of humanity. These assumptions rest on several broad dimensions that separate the various personality theorists. We use six of these dimensions as a framework for viewing each theorist's concept of humanity.

The first dimension is *determinism vs. free choice.* Are people's behavior and personality determined by forces over which they have no control? Can we choose to be what we wish to be? Is our behavior partially free and partially determined? Although the dimension of determinism vs. free will is more philosophical than scientific, the position theorists take on this issue shapes their way of looking at people and colors their concept of humanity.

A second issue is one of *pessimism vs. optimism*. Are people doomed to live miserable, conflicted, and troubled lives, or can they change and grow into psychologically healthy, happy, fully functioning human beings? In general, personality theorists who believe in determinism tend to be pessimistic (Skinner was a notable exception), whereas those who believe in free choice are usually optimistic.

A third dimension for viewing a theorist's concept of humanity is *causality vs. teleology*. Briefly, **causality** holds that behavior is a function of past experiences, whereas **teleology** is an explanation of behavior in terms of future goals or purposes. Do people act as they do because of what has happened to them in the past, or do they act because they have certain expectations of what will happen in the future?

A fourth consideration that divides personality theorists is their attitude toward *conscious vs. unconscious determinants of behavior*. Are people ordinarily aware of what they are doing and why they are doing it, or do unconscious forces impinge upon them and drive them to act without awareness of these underlying forces?

The fifth question is one of *biological vs. social influences on personality*. Are people mostly creatures of biology, or are their personalities shaped largely by their social relationships? A more specific element of this issue is heredity vs. environment; that is, are personal characteristics more the result of heredity, or are they environmentally determined?

A sixth issue is *uniqueness vs. similarities*. Is the salient feature of people their individuality, or is it their common characteristics? Should the study of personality concentrate on those traits that make people alike, or should it look at those traits that make people different?

These and other basic issues that separate personality theorists have resulted in truly different personality theories, not just differences in terminology. We could not erase the differences among personality theories by adopting a common language. The differences are philosophical and deep-seated. Each personality theory reflects the individual personality of its creator, and each creator has a unique philosophical orientation, shaped in part by early childhood experiences, birth order, gender, training, education, and pattern of interpersonal relationships. These differences help determine whether a theorist will be deterministic or a believer in free choice, pessimistic or optimistic, adopt a causal explanation or a teleological one. They also help determine whether the theorist emphasizes consciousness or unconsciousness, biological or social factors, uniqueness or similarities of people. These differences do not, however, negate the possibility that two theorists with opposing views of humanity can be equally scientific in their data gathering and theory building.

RESEARCH IN PERSONALITY THEORY

Earlier we saw that theories and observations have a cyclic relationship: Theory gives meaning to observations, and observations result from experimental research designed to test hypotheses generated by the theory. Not all observations, however, flow from experimental research. Each of us makes many observations every day. To observe simply means to notice something, to pay attention.

You have been observing human personalities for nearly as long as you have been alive. You notice that some people are talkative and outgoing; others are quiet and reserved. You may have even labeled such people as extraverts and introverts. Are these labels accurate? Is one extraverted person like another? Does an extravert always act in a talkative, outgoing manner? Can all people be classified as either introverts or extraverts?

In making observations and asking questions, you are doing some of the same things psychologists do, that is, observing human behaviors and trying to make sense of these observations. However, psychologists, like other scientists, try to be *systematic* so that their *predictions* will be consistent and accurate.

To improve their ability to predict, personality psychologists have developed a number of assessment techniques, including personality inventories. Much of the research reported in the remaining chapters of this book has relied on various assessment procedures, which purport to measure different dimensions of personality. For these instruments to be useful they must be both reliable and valid. The **reliability** of a measuring instrument is the extent to which it yields consistent results. If a personality inventory is reliable, a person should score about the same on two different administrations of that instrument.

Personality inventories may be reliable and yet lack validity or accuracy. **Validity** is the extent to which an instrument measures what it is supposed to measure. In determining validity, test scores are compared to an independent or outside criterion. For example, a personality inventory designed to measure extraversion and introversion must first be able to differentiate people into an extraverted category and an introverted category. Next, people scoring high in the extraverted direction must be the ones judged by some other criterion to be extraverted, and those scoring in an introverted direction must be independently identified as introverts.

Most of the early personality theorists did not use standardized assessment inventories. Although Freud, Adler, and Jung all developed some form of projective tool, none of them used the technique with sufficient precision to establish its reliability and validity. However, the theories of Freud, Adler, and Jung have spawned a number of standardized personality inventories as researchers and clinicians have sought to measure units of personality proposed by those theorists. Later personality theorists, especially Rotter, Cattell, and Eysenck, have developed and used a number of personality measures and have relied heavily on them in constructing their theoretical models.

Chapter Summary

Personality is one of the most fascinating topics in psychology. Nearly everyone is interested in personality, although fewer people might be attracted to the concept of theory. The term "personality" comes from the Latin *persona*, or the mask that people present to the outside world. Psychologists, however, tend to see personality as including much more than a mask, more than outward appearance. To them, personality includes all those relatively permanent traits or characteristics that render some consistency to a person's behavior.

A *theory* is defined as a set of related assumptions from which testable hypotheses can be drawn. Theory should not be confused with philosophy, idle speculation, hypothesis, or taxonomy, although it is related to each of these terms.

Six criteria determine the usefulness of a scientific theory: (1) Does the theory generate research? (2) Is it falsifiable? (3) Does it organize knowledge? (4) Does it suggest practical solutions to everyday problems? (5) Is it internally consistent? and (6) Is it simple or parsimonious?

Each personality theorist has had either an implicit or explicit *concept of humanity*, and each theorist's view of human nature can be discussed from six perspectives: (1) determinism vs. free choice, (2) pessimism vs. optimism, (3) causality vs. teleology, (4) conscious vs. unconscious determinants, (5) biological vs. social factors, and (6) uniqueness vs. similarities in people.

Suggested Readings

Eysenck, H., & Wilson, G. D. (1976). *Know your own personality*. New York: Barnes and Noble Books.

This popular book was written to help students of personality learn how they score on various standard personality tests. If you are curious to know what kind of person you are, take a look at this book.

Maslow, A. (1966). *The psychology of science*. New York: Harper & Row.

A well-known psychologist argues that the limits of science should be expanded beyond the traditional bounds of reductionistic and mechanistic methods.

McCain, G., & Segal, E. M. (1988). *The game of science* (5th ed.). Pacific Grove, CA: Brooks/Cole.

This consistently popular book presents a very readable and interesting account of some of the new developments in science, including a look at the role of scientific theory.

Stanovich, K. E. (1996). *How to think straight about psychology* (4th ed.). Glenview, IL: Scott, Foresman.

In this small book, Keith Stanovich clears up many popular misconceptions about psychology in general and theory in particular. He also includes basic methods used in psychological research.

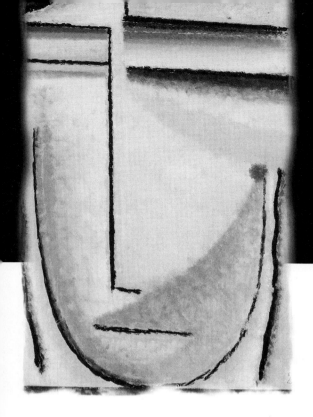

Freud

Chapter

Freud: Psychoanalysis

2

Sigmund Freud's contributions to personality theory have been both substantial and controversial. Freud's theory, **psychoanalysis,** is not only the most comprehensive of all personality theories, but it has generated the greatest amount of critical interest—both positive and negative.

What makes Freud's theory so interesting? First, the twin cornerstones of psychoanalysis, sex and aggression, are two subjects of continuing popularity. Second, the theory was spread beyond its Viennese origin by an ardent and dedicated group of followers, many of whom romanticized Freud as a nearly mythological and lonely hero. Third, Freud's heavy emphasis on unconscious motivation allows several opposing explanations for the same observed behaviors.

Freud's contributions to our understanding of humanity provide a logical starting point in any discussion of personality theories. Besides originating a comprehensive theory of personality, Freud founded a theory of mental disorders as well as a theory and technique of psychotherapy. These three concerns—normal personality, abnormal development, and psychotherapy—cannot be separated. Each complements and supplements the other two. The present discussion focuses on the first. Abnormal personality and psychotherapy are partially explored to elucidate Freud's theory of personality.

Freud's understanding of human personality was based on his experiences with patients, his analysis of his own dreams, and his vast readings in the various sciences and humanities. These experiences provided the basic data for the evolution of his theories. To him, theory followed observation, and his concept of personality underwent constant revisions during the last 50 years of his life. Evolutionary though it was, Freud insisted that psychoanalysis could not be subjected to eclecticism, and disciples who deviated from his basic ideas soon found themselves personally and professionally ostracized by Freud.

Although Freud regarded himself primarily as a scientist, his definition of science would be somewhat different from that held by most psychologists today. He relied more on deductive reasoning than on rigorous research methods, and he made observations subjectively and on a relatively small sample of patients, most of whom were from the upper middle and upper classes. He did not quantify his data, nor did he make observations under controlled conditions. He utilized the case study approach almost exclusively, typically formulating hypotheses after the facts of the case were known.

BIOGRAPHY OF SIGMUND FREUD

Freud was born either on March 6 or May 6, 1856, in Freiberg, Moravia, which is now part of the Czech Republic. (Scholars disagree on his birth date—the first date was but 8 months after the marriage of his parents.) Sigmund was the firstborn child of Jacob and Amalie Nathanson Freud, although his father had two grown sons, Emanuel and Philipp, from a previous marriage. Jacob and Amalie Freud had seven other children within 10 years, but Sigmund remained the favorite of his young indulgent mother, which may have partially contributed to his lifelong optimism and self-confidence (Jones, 1953, Vol. 1). A scholarly, serious-minded youth, Freud did not have a close friendship with any of his younger siblings. He did, however, enjoy a warm, indulgent relationship with his mother, leading him in later years to observe that the mother/son relationship was the most perfect, the most free from ambivalence of all human relationships (Freud, 1933/1964) .

Freud's earliest playmates were his half-nephew, John, and his half-niece, Pauline. John was about a year older and Pauline a little younger than Sigmund. One of Freud's earliest memories was of him and John taking away a bouquet of flowers from Pauline and causing the young girl to run away in tears (Vitz, 1988).

When Sigmund was three, the two Freud families left Freiberg. Emanuel's family and Philipp moved to England, while the Jacob Freud family moved first to Leipzig and then the following year to Vienna. The Austrian capital remained Sigmund Freud's home for nearly 80 years, until 1938 when the Nazi invasion forced him to emigrate to London, where he lived until his death on September 23, 1939.

When Freud was about a year old his mother gave birth to a second son, an event that was to have a significant impact on Freud's psychic development. Sigmund was filled with hostility toward his brother and harbored an unconscious wish for his death. When the boy died at 8 months of age, Sigmund was left with feelings of guilt at having caused his brother's death. Only in later years was Freud able to understand not only that the death wish for a sibling was common in young children but also that his wish did not actually cause his brother's death. This discovery during middle age purged Freud of the guilt he had carried into adulthood and, by his own analysis, contributed to his later psychic development (Freud, 1900/1953).

Freud was drawn into medicine, not so much out of love for medical practice but out of an intense curiosity concerning human nature (Ellenberger, 1970). He entered the University of Vienna Medical School in 1873, but when he graduated in 1881, he had no intention of practicing medicine. He preferred instead to do research in physiology. To pursue his career, however, he was dependent on his father and friends for financial support. After his graduation, he remained at the university's Physiological Institute, conducting research and doing some teaching.

Freud might have continued his work indefinitely had it not been for two factors. First, he believed (probably without justification) that, as a Jew, his opportunities for academic advancement would be limited. Second, his father became less able to provide financial aid. Reluctantly, Freud turned from his laboratory to the practice of medicine. He worked for 3 years in the General Hospital of Vienna, becoming familiar with the practice of various branches of medicine, including psychiatry and nervous diseases (Freud, 1925/1959).

In 1885, he received a traveling grant from the University of Vienna and decided to study in Paris with the famous French neurologist Jean-Martin Charcot. He spent 4 months with Charcot from whom he learned the hypnotic technique for treating **hysteria,** a disorder typically characterized by paralysis or the improper functioning of certain parts of the body. It was through hypnosis that Freud became convinced of the psychogenic origin of hysterical symptoms.

While still a medical student, Freud developed a close professional association and a personal friendship with Joseph Breuer, a well-known Viennese physician 14 years older than Freud and a man of considerable scientific reputation. Breuer taught Freud about *catharsis*, the process of removing hysterical symptoms through "talking them out." While using catharsis, Freud gradually and laboriously discovered the *free association* technique, which soon replaced hypnosis as his principal therapeutic technique.

From as early as adolescence, Freud literally dreamed of making some monumental discovery and also of achieving fame (Newton, 1995). His first opportunity to gain recognition came in 1884–1885 and involved his experiments with cocaine. Freud believed he had achieved an important breakthrough with his work with cocaine and was led to proclaim the wonderful virtues of that drug. After taking cocaine himself without any harmful effects, Freud praised it as a near panacea as well as an effective anesthetic (Byck, 1974). However, he was doomed to disappointment when his associate,

1905/1953c, 1905/1960). These publications gave Freud some local prominence in scientific and medical circles. Soon a small group of local physicians began to meet in Freud's home to discuss psychological issues. Then, in the fall of 1902, five of these men—Freud, Alfred Adler, Wilhelm Stekel, Max Kahane, and Rudolf Reitler—formed the Wednesday Psychological Society, with Freud as discussion leader. In 1908 the name of the organization was changed to the Vienna Psychoanalytic Society.

In 1910 the International Psychoanalytic Association was founded with Carl Jung of Zürich as president. Freud was attracted to Jung because of his keen intellect and also because he was neither Jewish nor Viennese. Between 1902 and 1906, all 17 of Freud's disciples had been Jewish (Kurzweil, 1989), and Freud was interested in giving psychoanalysis a more cosmopolitan flavor. Although Jung was a welcome addition to the Freudian circle and had been designated as the "Crown Prince" and "the man of the future," he, like Adler and Stekel before him, eventually quarreled bitterly with Freud and left the psychoanalytic movement. The seeds of disagreement probably were sown when Freud and Jung, along with Sandor Ferenczi, traveled to the United States in 1909 to deliver a series of lectures. To pass the time while traveling, Freud and Jung interpreted one another's dreams, a potentially explosive practice that eventually led to the end of their relationship in 1913 (McGuire, 1974).

The years of World War I were difficult for Freud. He was cut off from communication with his faithful followers, his psychoanalytic practice dwindled, his home was sometimes without heat, and he and his family had little food. After the war, despite advancing years and pain suffered from 33 operations for cancer of the mouth, he made important revisions in his theory. The most significant of these were the elevation of the death instinct to a level with the life instinct; the inclusion of repression as one of the defenses of the ego; and the clarification of the female Oedipus complex.

Freud's personal life had many highlights: his marriage to Martha Bernays in 1886 after a long engagement; the birth of their six children between 1887 and 1895; his trip with Jung to the United States in 1909 to speak at Clark University; his achievement of worldwide recognition; the Goethe prize for literature that he won in 1930; and finally, at age 82, his emigration to England after the Nazis had marched into Austria.

What personal qualities did Freud possess? A more complete insight into his personality can be found in Clark (1980), Ellenberger (1970), Gay (1988), Isbister (1985), Jones (1953, 1955, 1957), Macmillan (1991), Newton (1995), Roazen (1993), Sulloway (1992), and Vitz (1988). Above all, Freud was a sensitive, passionate person. He had the capacity for intimate, almost secretive relationships. While still a young student, he and a close friend, Edward Silberstein, formed a Spanish society with the purpose of learning that language, but also with the effect of solidifying a close union—one that distrusted others and viewed the world with suspicion. Similar relationships were repeated throughout Freud's life. He could reveal intimate aspects of his personality to those who were close to him while, at the same time, feel persecuted by others. He seemed to have needed these intense relationships, which were both exclusive and somewhat distrustful in attitude toward the outside world. His passionate nature is revealed in his correspondence with his intimates (Freud, 1960, 1985; McGuire, 1974).

Freud was also an exceptionally gifted writer. He knew several foreign languages fluently, but he was a master of the German tongue. He was an excellent translator, having translated the English political philosopher, John Stuart Mill, and the French psychiatrist, Jean-Martin Charcot, among several others. Freud also possessed an intense intellectual curiosity; unusual moral courage, demonstrated by his daily self-analysis; extremely ambivalent feelings toward his father and other father figures; the tendency to hold grudges disproportionate to the alleged offense; a burning ambition, especially during his earlier years; strong feelings of isolation even while surrounded by many followers; and an intense and somewhat irrational dislike of America and Americans, a feeling that became more intense after his trip to the United States in 1909.

Why did Freud have such a disdain for Americans? Perhaps the most important reason is that he rightly believed that Americans would trivialize psychoanalysis by trying to make it popular. In addition, he had several experiences during his trip to the United States that were foreign to a proper bourgeois Viennese gentleman. Paul Roazen (1993) mentioned a number of events that seem almost humorous but were sufficient to make Freud's visit more unpleasant than it might have been. First, Freud experienced stomach problems throughout his visit, probably because the drinking water did not agree with him. In addition, he found it peculiar that American cities did not provide public restrooms on street corners; several Americans addressed him by his first name while challenging him to defend his theories; and one person unsuccessfully tried to prevent Freud from smoking his cigar in a no-smoking area. Moreover, when Freud, Ferenczi, and Jung went to a private camp in western Massachusetts, they were greeted by a barrage of flags of Imperial Germany, despite the fact that none of them were German and each had reasons to dislike Germany. Also at camp, Freud, along with the others, sat on the ground while the host grilled some steaks over charcoal, a custom Freud deemed to be both savage and uncouth.

LEVELS OF MENTAL LIFE

Freud's greatest contribution to personality theory is his exploration of the unconscious and his insistence that people are motivated primarily by instinctual forces of which they have little or no awareness. To Freud mental life is divided into two levels, the **unconscious** and the **conscious.** The unconscious, in turn, has two different levels, the unconscious proper and the **preconscious.** In Freudian psychology the three levels of mental life are used to designate both a process and a location. The existence as a specific location, of course, is merely hypothetical and has no real existence within the body. Yet, Freud spoke of *the* unconscious as well as unconscious processes.

THE UNCONSCIOUS

The unconscious contains all those drives, urges, or instincts that are beyond our awareness, but that nevertheless motivate most of our words, feelings, and actions. Although we may be conscious of our overt behaviors, we often are not aware of the mental processes that lie behind them. For example, a woman may know that she is attracted to a man but not fully understand all the reasons for the attraction, some of which may even seem irrational.

Because the unconscious is not available to the conscious mind, how can one know if it really exists? Freud felt that its existence could be proved only indirectly. To him the unconscious is the explanation for the meaning behind dreams, slips of the tongue, neurotic symptoms, and certain kinds of forgetting, called *repressions*. Dreams serve as a particularly rich source of unconscious material. For example, Freud believed that childhood experiences can appear in adult dreams even though the dreamer has no conscious recollection of these experiences.

Unconscious processes often enter into consciousness but only after being disguised or distorted enough to elude censorship. Freud (1917/1963) used the analogy of a guardian or censor blocking the passage between the unconscious and preconscious and preventing undesirable anxiety-producing memories from entering awareness. To enter the conscious level of the mind, these unconscious images first must be sufficiently disguised to slip past the primary censor, and then they must elude a final censor that watches the passageway between the preconscious and the conscious. By the time these memories enter our conscious mind, we no longer recognize them for what they are; instead, we see them as relatively pleasant, nonthreatening experiences. In most cases, these images have strong sexual or aggressive motifs, because childhood sexual and aggressive behaviors are frequently punished or suppressed. Punishment and **suppression** often create feelings of anxiety, and the anxiety in turn stimulates *repression* of sexual and aggressive fantasies. **Repression** is the forcing of unwanted, anxiety-ridden experiences into the unconscious as a defense against the pain of that anxiety.

Not all unconscious processes, however, spring from repression of childhood events. Freud believed that a portion of our unconscious originates from the experiences of our early ancestors that have been passed on to us through hundreds of generations of repetition. He called these inherited unconscious images our **phylogenetic endowment** (Freud, 1917/1963, 1933/1964). Freud's notion of phylogenetic endowment is quite similar to Carl Jung's idea of a collective unconscious (see Chapter 3). However, one important difference exists between the two concepts. Whereas Jung placed primary emphasis on the collective unconscious, Freud relied on the notion of inherited dispositions only as a last resort. That is, when explanations built on individual experiences were not adequate, Freud would turn to the idea of collectively inherited experiences to fill in the gaps left by individual experiences. Later we will see that Freud used the concept of phylogenetic endowment to explain several important concepts, such as the Oedipus complex and castration anxiety.

Unconscious drives may appear in consciousness, but only after undergoing certain transformations. A person may express either erotic or hostile urges, for example, by teasing or joking with another person. The original instinct (sex or aggression) is thus disguised and hidden from the conscious minds of both persons. The unconscious of the first person, however, has directly influenced the unconscious of the second. Both people gain some satisfaction of either sexual or aggressive urges, but neither is conscious of the underlying motive behind the teasing or joking. Thus the unconscious mind of one person can communicate with the unconscious of another without either person being aware of the process.

Unconscious, of course, does not mean inactive or dormant. Instincts in the unconscious constantly strive to become conscious, and many of them succeed, although they may no longer appear in their original form. Unconscious ideas can and do motivate the individual. For example, a son's hostility toward his father may masquerade itself in the form of ostentatious affection. In an undisguised form, the hostility would create too much anxiety for the son. His unconscious mind, therefore, motivates him to express hostility indirectly through an exaggerated show of love and flattery. Because the disguise must successfully deceive the person, it often takes an opposite form from the original feelings, but it is almost always overblown and ostentatious. (This mechanism, called a *reaction formation*, is discussed later in the section titled Defense Mechanisms.)

THE PRECONSCIOUS

The preconscious level of the mind contains all those elements that are not conscious but can become so quite readily (Freud, 1933/1964). The contents of the preconscious come from two sources, the first of which is conscious perception. What a person perceives is conscious for only a transitory period; it quickly passes into the preconscious when the focus of attention shifts to another idea. These ideas that alternate easily between being conscious and preconscious are largely free from anxiety and, in reality, are much more similar to the conscious images than to unconscious urges.

The second source of preconscious content is the unconscious. According to Freud, ideas can slip past the vigilant censor and find their way into the preconscious, albeit in a disguised form. Some of these ideas never become conscious because if we recognized them as derivatives of the unconscious, we would experience increased levels of anxiety. Therefore, our final censor represses these anxiety-ladened ideas back into the unconscious. Other ideas from the unconscious do gain admission to consciousness, but only because their true nature is cleverly disguised through the dream process, a slip of the tongue, or an elaborate defensive measure.

THE CONSCIOUS

Consciousness, which plays a relatively minor role in psychoanalytic theory, can be defined as those mental elements in awareness at any given point in time. It is the only level of mental life directly available to us.

Ideas can reach consciousness from two different directions. The first is from the **perceptual conscious** system, which is turned toward the outer world and acts as a medium for the perception of external stimuli. In other words, what we perceive through our sense organs, if not too threatening, enters into consciousness (Freud, 1933/1964).

The second source of conscious elements is from within the mental structure and includes nonthreatening ideas from the preconscious as well as menacing but well-disguised images from the unconscious. As we have seen, these latter elements escaped into the preconscious by cloaking themselves as harmless images and evading the primary censor. Once in the preconscious, they are capable of coming under the eye of consciousness by avoiding a final censor. By the time they reach the conscious system, these ideas are greatly distorted and camouflaged, often taking the form of neurotic symptoms or dream images.

In summary, Freud (1917/1963, pp. 295–296) compared the unconscious to a large entrance hall in which many diverse, energetic, and disreputable people are milling about, crowding one another, and striving incessantly to escape to a smaller adjoining reception room. However, a watchful guard protects the threshold between the large entrance hall and the small reception room. This guard, or doorkeeper, has two methods of preventing undesirables from escaping from the entrance hall. He can either turn them back at the door, or he can throw out those people who earlier had clandestinely slipped into the reception room. The effect in either case is the same; the menacing, disorderly people are prevented from coming into view of an important guest who is seated at the far end of the reception room behind a screen. The meaning of the analogy is obvious. The people in the entrance hall represent unconscious mental excitations. The small reception room is the preconscious and its inhabitants represent preconscious ideas. People in the reception room (preconscious) may or may not come into view of the important guest who, of course, represents the eye of consciousness. The doorkeeper who guards the threshold between the two rooms is the primary censor that prevents unconscious ideas from becoming preconscious and renders preconscious ideas unconscious by throwing them back.

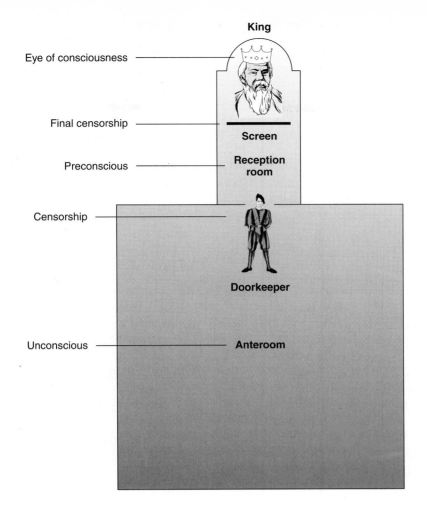

Figure 2.1   Levels of mental life.

The screen that guards the important guest is the final censor, and it prevents many, but not all, preconscious elements from reaching consciousness. The analogy is presented graphically in Figure 2.1.

PROVINCES OF THE MIND

For nearly 2 decades, Freud's only model of the mind was the topographic one we have just outlined, and his only portrayal of psychic strife was the conflict between conscious and unconscious forces. Then, during the 1920s, Freud (1923/1961a) introduced a three-part structural model. This division of the mind into three provinces did not supplant the topographic model, but it helped him explain mental images according to their functions or purposes.

To Freud, the most primitive part of the mind was *das Es*, or the "it," which is almost always translated into English as **id;** a second division was *das Ich*, or the "I," translated as **ego;** and a final province was *das Über-Ich*, or the "above-I," which is rendered into English as **superego.** These provinces or regions have no territorial

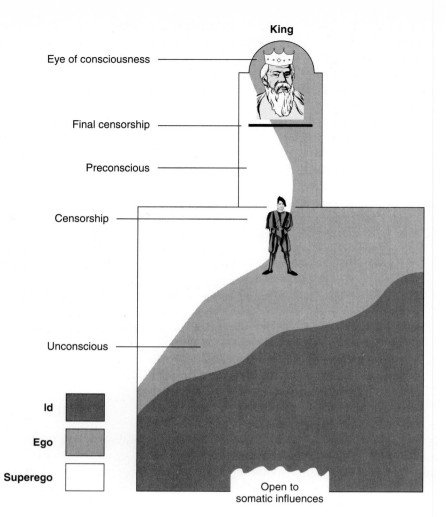

King

Eye of consciousness

Final censorship

Preconscious

Censorship

Unconscious

Id

Ego

Superego

Open to
somatic influences

***Figure* 2.2**   Levels of mental life and provinces of the mind.

existence, of course, but are merely hypothetical constructs. They interact with the three levels of mental life so that the ego cuts across the various topographic levels and has conscious, preconscious, and unconscious components, whereas the superego is both preconscious and unconscious. Figure 2.2 shows the relationship between the provinces of the mind and the levels of mental life.

Id

At the core of personality and completely unconscious to the individual is the psychical region called the id, a term derived from the impersonal pronoun meaning "the it," or the not-yet-owned component of personality. The id has no contact with reality, yet it strives constantly to reduce tension by satisfying instinctual desires. Because its sole function is to seek pleasure, we say that the id serves the **pleasure principle.**

The newborn baby may be seen as a personification of an id unencumbered by restrictions of ego and superego. The baby seeks gratification of needs without regard for what is possible or what is proper, sucking when the nipple is either present or absent. Gaining pleasure in either case, the infant receives nutrition only in the former. The extranutritional sucking continues because the id-dominated infant is not in contact with reality. It fails to realize that thumb-sucking behavior cannot sustain life. Because the id has no direct contact with reality, it is not altered by the passage of time or by the experiences of the person. Childhood wish impulses remain unchanged in the id for decades (Freud, 1933/1964).

Besides being unrealistic and pleasure seeking, the id is illogical and can simultaneously entertain incompatible ideas. For example, a man may have an unconscious wish for the death of his wife, while at the same time desiring sex with her. Or he may consciously love his father, while unconsciously wishing to destroy him.

Another characteristic of the id is lack of morality. Because it cannot make value judgments or distinguish between good and evil, the id is not immoral, merely amoral. All of the id's energy is spent for one purpose—to seek pleasure without regard for what is proper or just (Freud, 1923/1961a, 1933/1964).

In review, the id is primitive, chaotic, inaccessible to consciousness, unchangeable, amoral, illogical, unorganized, and filled with energy received from the instincts and discharged for the satisfaction of the pleasure principle.

As the region that houses the instincts (primary motivators), the id operates through the **primary process.** Because it blindly seeks to satisfy the pleasure principle, its survival is dependent on the development of a **secondary process** to bring it into contact with the external world. This secondary process functions through the ego.

Ego

The ego, or I, is the region of the mind in contact with reality. It grows out of the id during infancy and becomes a person's only source of communication with the external world. It is governed by the **reality principle,** which it tries to substitute for the pleasure principle of the id. As the sole region of the mind in contact with the external world, the ego becomes the decision-making or executive branch of personality. However, because it is partly conscious, partly preconscious, and partly unconscious, the ego can make decisions on each of these three levels. For instance, a woman may choose to behave in an excessively neat and orderly fashion with a recollection that this behavior has previously been rewarded, yet she may not understand the reasons for her choice. Thus, her decision takes place in all three levels of mental life.

When performing its cognitive and intellectual functions, the ego must take into consideration the incompatible, but equally unrealistic, demands of the id and the superego. In addition to these two tyrants, the ego must serve a third master—the external world. Thus, the ego constantly tries to reconcile the blind claims of the id and superego with the realistic demands of the external world. Finding itself surrounded on three sides by divergent and hostile forces, the ego reacts in a predictable manner—it becomes anxious. It then uses repression and the other *defense mechanisms* to defend itself against anxiety by preventing threatening elements from reaching consciousness (Freud, 1926/1959a).

According to Freud (1933/1964), the ego becomes differentiated from the id when a baby learns to distinguish itself from the outer world. While the id remains unchanged, the ego continues to develop; while the id insists on unrealistic and unrelenting demands for pleasure, the ego must be realistic; while the id provides a person with energy, the ego must furnish the control. In comparing the ego to the id, Freud used the analogy of a person on horseback. The rider checks and inhibits the greater strength of the horse but is ultimately at the mercy of the animal. Sometimes the rider permits the horse free rein to avoid falling off. Similarly, the ego checks and inhibits id impulses, but it is more or less constantly at the mercy of the stronger but more poorly organized id. The ego has no strength of its own but borrows energy from the id. In spite of this dependence on the id, the ego sometimes comes close to gaining complete control, for instance, during the prime of life of a psychologically mature person.

As children begin to experience parental rewards and punishments, they learn what to do to gain pleasure and avoid pain. This is an ego function, in as much as very young children are still exclusively concerned with self. As they reach the age of five or six, they identify with their parents and begin to learn what they should and should not do. This is the origin of the superego.

SUPEREGO

In Freudian psychology, the superego, or above-I, is the moral or ethical province of personality. It is guided by the **moralistic** and **idealistic principles** as opposed to the pleasure principle of the id and the realistic principle of the ego. The superego grows out of the ego, and like the ego, it has no energy of its own. However, the superego differs from the ego in one important respect; it has no contact with the outside world and therefore is unrealistic in its demands for perfection (Freud, 1923/1961a).

The superego has two subsystems, the **conscience** and the **ego-ideal.** Freud did not clearly distinguish between these two functions, but in general, the conscience results from experiences with punishments for improper behavior and tells us what we *should not do*, whereas the ego-ideal develops from experiences with rewards for proper behavior and tells us what we *should do*. A primitive conscience comes into existence when a child conforms to parental standards out of fear of loss of love or approval. Later, during the Oedipal phase of development, these ideals are internalized through identification with the mother and father. (We discuss the Oedipus complex in a later section.)

A well-developed superego acts to control sexual and aggressive impulses through the process of *repression*. It cannot produce repressions by itself, but it can order the ego to do so. The superego watches closely over the ego, judging its actions and intentions. Guilt is the result when the ego acts, or even intends to act, contrary to the moral standards of the superego. Feelings of inferiority will arise if the ego is unable to meet the superego's standards of perfection. Guilt, then, is a function of the conscience; inferiority feelings stem from the ego-ideal (Freud, 1933/1964).

The superego is not concerned with the happiness of the ego. It strives blindly and unrealistically toward perfection. It is unrealistic in the sense that it does not take into consideration the difficulties or impossibilities faced by the ego in carrying out its orders. Not all its demands, of course, are impossible to fulfill, just as not all demands of parents and other authority figures are impossible to fulfill. The superego, however, is like the id in that it is completely ignorant of, and unconcerned with, the practicability of its requirements.

Freud (1933/1964) pointed out that the divisions between the different regions of the mind are not sharp and well-defined. The development of the three divisions varies widely in different individuals. For some, the superego does not grow after childhood; for others, the superego may dominate the personality at the cost of guilt and inferiority feelings. For yet others, the ego and superego may take turns controlling personality, which results in extreme fluctuations of mood and alternating cycles of self-confidence and self-deprecation. In the healthy individual, the id, ego, and superego are well integrated and operate in harmony and with a minimum of conflict. Figure 2.3 shows the

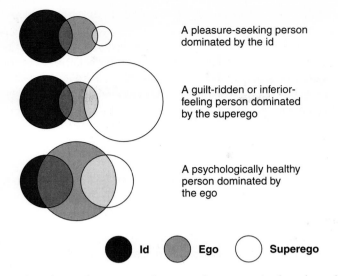

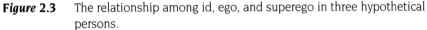

Figure 2.3   The relationship among id, ego, and superego in three hypothetical persons.

relationships among id, ego, and superego in three hypothetical persons. The first person, with a dominating id and a weak ego, has a superego so feeble that it is not capable of counterbalancing the incessant demands of the id. The second person, with strong feelings of either guilt or inferiority and a weak ego, will experience many conflicts because the ego cannot arbitrate the strong but opposing demands of the superego and the id. The third person, with an ego that has incorporated many of the demands of the id and nearly all those of the superego, is a psychologically healthy individual, one who is in control of both the pleasure principle and the moralistic principle.

DYNAMICS OF PERSONALITY

Levels of mental life and provinces of the mind refer to the *structure* or composition of personality; but personalities also *do* something. Thus, Freud postulated a *dynamic*, or motivational principle, to explain the driving forces behind people's actions. To Freud, people are motivated to seek pleasure and to reduce tension and anxiety. This motivation is derived from psychical and physical energy that springs from the instincts.

INSTINCTS

Freud used the German word "Trieb" to refer to a drive or a stimulus within the person. This term is usually translated as **instinct,** but it might more properly be called "drive" or "impulse." An instinct, then, is an internal drive or impulse that operates as a constant motivational force. As an internal stimulus it differs from external stimuli in that it cannot be avoided through flight.

According to Freud (1933/1964), the many individual instincts can all be grouped under two major drives: the **life instinct,** generally called Eros or sex, and the **death instinct,** sometimes known as destruction or aggression. Instincts originate in the id, but they come under the control of the ego. Each instinct has its own form of psychic energy. The force by which the life or sexual instinct works is called **libido;** the psychic energy of the death instinct was never named.

Every instinct is characterized by an impetus, a source, an aim, and an object. An instinct's *impetus* is the amount of force it exerts; its *source* is the region of the body in a state of excitation or tension; its *aim* is to seek pleasure by removing that excitation or reducing the tension; and its *object* is the person or thing that serves as the means through which the aim is satisfied (Freud, 1915/1957a).

The Sexual Instinct

The aim of the sexual instinct is to bring about pleasure within a person by removing the state of sexual excitation. This pleasure, however, is not limited to genital pleasure. Freud believed that the entire body is invested with libido. Besides the genitals, the mouth and anus are especially capable of producing sexual pleasure and are called **erogenous zones.** The ultimate aim of the sexual instinct (reduction of sexual tension) cannot be changed, but the path by which the aim is reached can be varied. It can take either an active or a passive form, or it can be temporarily or permanently inhibited (Freud, 1915/1957a). Because the path is flexible and because sexual pleasure stems from organs other than the genitals, much behavior originally motivated by Eros is difficult to recognize as sexual behavior. To Freud, however, all pleasurable activity is traceable to the sexual instinct.

The flexibility of the sexual *object* or person can bring about a further disguise of Eros. The erotic object can easily be transformed or displaced. Libido can be withdrawn from one person and placed in a state of free-floating tension, or it can be reinvested in another person, including the self. For example, an infant prematurely forced to give up the nipple as a sexual object may substitute the thumb as an object of oral pleasure.

Freud called the sexual instinct conservative because the power of its drive is essential to perpetuate the species. Eros can also be called conservative because it protects individual life. For example, the infant, dominated by the pleasure principle, sucks from the nipple in order to gain sexual pleasure, but, at the same time, it acquires the nourishment that is essential to life.

Eros manifests itself in many ways, including narcissism, love, sadism, and masochism. The last two also possess generous components of the death instinct.

Narcissism
During early infancy a child is primarily self-centered, with its libido invested almost exclusively in its own ego. This condition, which is universal, is known as **primary narcissism.** As the ego develops, the child usually gives up much of its primary narcissism and develops a greater interest in others. In Freud's language, narcissistic libido is then transformed into object libido. During puberty, however, adolescents often redirect the libido back to the ego and become preoccupied with personal appearance and other self interests. This pronounced **secondary narcissism** is not universal, but a moderate degree of self-love is common to nearly everyone (Freud, 1914/1957).

Love
A second manifestation of Eros is love, which develops when the libido is invested in an object or person other than self. A child's first sexual interest is the person who cares for it, generally the mother. During infancy a child of either sex experiences sensual love for the mother. Overt sexual love for members of one's family, however, ordinarily is repressed, which brings a second type of love into existence. Freud called this second

kind of love aim-inhibited love because the original aim of reducing sexual tension is inhibited or repressed. Aim-inhibited love continues throughout a lifetime, with a person loving parents, brothers, and sisters in a nonsexual way.

Obviously, love and narcissism are closely interrelated. Narcissism, of course, involves the love of self, whereas love is often accompanied by narcissistic tendencies, as when a person loves someone who serves as an ideal or model of what that person would like to be.

Sadism and Masochism

Two other instincts that are also intertwined are sadism and masochism. Not only are they inseparable, one from another, but they are interwoven with the life instincts—narcissism and love—as well as being strongly endowed with psychic energy from the death instinct (Freud, 1933/1964).

Sadism is the instinct manifested when sexual pleasure is attained from inflicting pain or humiliation on another person. Carried to an extreme, it is considered a sexual perversion, but in moderation sadism is a common need and exists to some extent in all sexual relationships. It is perverted when the sexual aim of erotic pleasure becomes secondary to the destructive aim (Freud, 1905/1953c).

Masochism, like sadism, is a common need, but it becomes a perversion when Eros becomes subservient to the destructive instinct. Masochists experience sexual pleasure from suffering pain and humiliation inflicted either by themselves or by others. Because masochists can provide self-inflicted pain, they do not depend on another person for the satisfaction of masochistic needs. Sadists, on the other hand, must seek and find another person on whom to inflict pain or humiliation. In this respect, they are more dependent than masochists on other people.

Sadism and masochism serve as cornerstones to the two-instinct theory. They demonstrate the workings of the sexual instinct and the destructive instinct in combination.

The Destructive Instinct

When Freud (1920/1955a) first elevated the death instinct to the level of Eros in *Beyond the Pleasure Principle*, he did so tentatively and with some caution. With time, however, the destructive instinct became more and more a dogma despite the fact that it was not generally accepted by Freud's close followers.

The aim of the destructive instinct, according to Freud, is to return the organism to an inorganic state. Because the ultimate inorganic condition is death, the final aim of the death instinct is self-destruction. As with the life instinct, the death instinct is flexible and the object of destruction is generally transformed from self to others. It then goes under a pseudonyn—**aggression.**

The aggressive tendency is present in everyone and is the explanation for wars, atrocities, religious persecution, and murder, as well as malicious gossip, sarcasm, and humiliation. The death instinct also explains the need for the barriers that people have erected to check aggression. For example, commandments like "Love thy neighbor as thyself" are necessary, Freud believed, to inhibit the strong, though usually unconscious, drive to inflict injury on others. These precepts are actually *reaction formations*. They involve the repression of strong hostile impulses and the overt and obvious expression of the opposite tendency.

Throughout our lifetime, life and death instincts constantly struggle against one another for ascendancy, but at the same time, both must bow to the reality principle, which represents the claims of the outer world. These demands of the real world prevent a direct, unopposed fulfillment of either sex or aggression, create conflict and anxiety, and relegate many sexual and aggressive desires to the realm of the unconscious.

ANXIETY

As important as they are, instincts must share the center of Freudian dynamic theory with the concept of **anxiety.** In defining anxiety, Freud (1933/1964) emphasized that it is a felt, affective, unpleasant state, accompanied by a physical sensation that warns the person against impending danger. The unpleasantness is often vague and hard to pinpoint, but the anxiety itself is always felt.

Only the ego can produce or feel anxiety, but the id, superego, and the external world each are involved in one of the three kinds of anxiety that Freud identified. The ego's dependence on the id results in neurotic anxiety; its dependence on the superego produces moral anxiety; and its dependence on the outer world leads to realistic anxiety.

Neurotic anxiety is defined as apprehension about an unknown danger. The feeling itself exists in the ego, but it originates from id impulses. People may experience neurotic anxiety in the presence of a teacher, employer, or some other authority figure because they earlier felt unconscious feelings of destructiveness against one or both of their parents. During childhood these feelings of hostility were often accompanied by fear of punishment, and this fear became generalized into unconscious neurotic anxiety.

A second type of anxiety, **moral anxiety,** stems from the conflict between the ego and the superego. After we establish our superego, usually by the age of five or six, we may experience anxiety as an outgrowth of the conflict between our realistic needs and the dictates of our superego. Moral anxiety, for example, would result from sexual temptations if we believe that yielding to the temptation would be morally wrong. It may also result from the failure to behave consistently with what we regard as morally right, for example, failing to care for our aging parents or adequately supporting our children.

Realistic anxiety, also known as objective anxiety, bears a close resemblance to fear. This third type of anxiety is defined as an unpleasant, nonspecific feeling involving a possible danger. For example, we may experience realistic anxiety while driving in heavy, fast-moving traffic in an unfamiliar city, a situation fraught with real, objective danger. However, realistic anxiety is different from fear in that it does not involve a specific fearful object. We would experience fear, for example, if our car suddenly began sliding out of control on an icy highway.

These three types of anxiety are seldom clear-cut or easily separated. They often exist in combination, as when fear of water, a real danger, becomes disproportionate to the situation and hence precipitates neurotic anxiety as well as realistic anxiety. This situation indicates that an unknown instinctual danger is connected with the external one.

Anxiety serves as an ego-preserving mechanism because it signals us that some danger is at hand (Freud, 1933/1964). For example, an anxiety dream signals our censor of an impending danger from the instincts, which allows us either to awaken and stop dreaming or to better disguise the manifest level of the dream. The ego, constantly vigilant for signs of threat and unpleasantness, is alerted to potential danger by the experience of anxiety. This signal then stimulates us to mobilize for either flight or defense.

Anxiety is also self-regulating because it precipitates repression, which in turn, reduces the pain of anxiety (Freud, 1933/1964). If the ego had no recourse to defensive behavior, the anxiety would become intolerable. Defensive behaviors, therefore, serve a useful function by protecting the ego against the pain of anxiety.

DEFENSE MECHANISMS

Freud first elaborated on the idea of **defense mechanisms** in 1926 (Freud, 1926/1959a), and his daughter Anna further refined and organized the concept (A. Freud, 1946). Although defense mechanisms are normal and universally used, when carried to an extreme they lead to compulsive, repetitive, and neurotic behavior. Because we must expend psychic energy to establish and maintain defense mechanisms, the more defensive we are the less psychic energy we have left to satisfy id impulses. This, of course, is precisely the ego's purpose in establishing defense mechanisms—to avoid dealing directly with instinctual demands and to defend itself against the anxiety that accompanies them (Freud, 1926/1959a).

The principal defense mechanisms identified by Freud include repression, reaction formation, displacement, fixation, regression, projection, introjection, and sublimation.

REPRESSION

The most basic defense mechanism, because it is involved in each of the others, is *repression*. Whenever impulses from the id become too threatening, anxiety is intensified to the point at which the ego can no longer tolerate it. To protect itself, the ego represses the instinct; that is, it forces the unwanted feeling into the unconscious (Freud, 1926/1959a). In many cases the repression is then perpetuated for a lifetime. For example, a girl may repress her hostility for a younger sister, or a boy may repress his sexual feelings for his mother, because these impulses create too much anxiety.

No society permits a complete and uninhibited expression of sexual and aggressive instincts. When children have their hostile or sexual behaviors punished or otherwise suppressed, they learn to be anxious whenever they experience these impulses. Although this anxiety seldom leads to a complete repression of aggressive and sexual drives, it often results in their partial repression.

What happens to these impulses after they have become unconscious? Freud (1933/1964) believed that several possibilities exist. First, the impulses may remain unchanged in the unconscious. Second, they could force their way into consciousness in an unaltered form, in which case they would create more anxiety than the person could handle, and the person would be overwhelmed with anxiety. A third and much more common fate of repressed instincts is that they find expression in a displaced or disguised form. The disguise, of course, must be clever enough to deceive the ego. Repressed drives may disguise themselves as physical symptoms, for example, sexual impotency in a man troubled by sexual guilt. The impotency prevents the man from having to deal with the guilt and anxiety that would result from normal enjoyable sexual activity. Repressed drives may also find an outlet in dreams, slips of the tongue, or one of the other defense mechanisms.

REACTION FORMATION

One of the ways in which a repressed impulse may show itself is through adopting a disguise that is directly opposite its original form. This defense mechanism is called a **reaction formation.** Reactive behavior can be identified by its exaggerated character and by its obsessive and compulsive form (Freud, 1926/1959a). An example of a reaction formation can be seen in a girl who deeply resents and hates her mother.

Because she knows that society demands affection toward parents, such conscious hatred for her mother would produce too much anxiety. To avoid painful anxiety, the girl concentrates on the opposite impulse—love. Her "love" for her mother, however, is not genuine. It is showy, exaggerated, and overdone. Other people may easily see the true nature of this love, but the girl must deceive herself and cling to her reaction formation, which helps conceal the anxiety-arousing truth that she unconsciously hates her mother.

DISPLACEMENT

Reaction formations, Freud believed, are limited to a single object; for example, people with reactive love shower affection only on the person toward whom they feel unconscious hatred. They do not generalize that kind of love to other people. In **displacement,** however, people can redirect their unacceptable urges onto a variety of objects or people so that the original impulse is disguised or concealed (Freud, 1926/1959a). For example, a woman who is angry at her roommate may displace her anger onto her employees, her pet cat, or a stuffed animal. She remains friendly to her roommate, but unlike the workings of a reaction formation, she does not exaggerate or overdo her friendliness.

Throughout his writings, Freud used the term "displacement" in several ways. In our discussion of the sexual instinct, for example, we saw that the sexual object can be displaced or transformed onto a variety of other objects, including one's self. Freud (1926/1959a) also used displacement to refer to the replacement of one neurotic symptom for another; for example, a compulsive urge to masturbate may be replaced by compulsive hand washing. Displacement also is involved in dream formation, as when the dreamer's destructive urges toward a parent are placed onto a dog or wolf. In this event, a dream about a dog being hit by a car might reflect the dreamer's unconscious wish to see the parent destroyed. (We discuss dream formation more completely in the section on dream analysis.)

FIXATION

Psychical growth normally proceeds in a somewhat continuous fashion through the various stages of development. The process of psychologically growing up, however, is not without stressful and anxious moments. When the prospect of taking the next step becomes too anxiety-provoking, the ego may resort to the strategy of remaining at the present, more comfortable psychological stage. Such a defense is called **fixation.** Technically, fixation is the permanent attachment of the libido onto an earlier, more primitive stage of development (Freud, 1917/1963). Like other defense mechanisms, fixations are universal. People who continually derive pleasure from eating, smoking, or talking may have an oral fixation, whereas those who are obsessed with neatness and orderliness may possess an anal fixation.

REGRESSION

Once the libido has passed a developmental stage, it may, during times of stress and anxiety, revert back to that earlier stage. Such a reversion is known as **regression** (Freud, 1917/1963). Regressions are quite common and can be seen readily in children.

For example, a completely weaned child may regress to demanding a bottle when a baby brother or sister is born. The attention given to the new baby poses a threat to the older child. Regressions are also frequent in older children and in adults. A common way for adults to react to anxiety-producing situations is to revert to earlier, safer, more secure patterns of behavior and to invest their libido onto more primitive and familiar objects. Under extreme stress, one adult may adopt the fetal position, another may return home to mother, and still another may react by remaining all day in bed, well covered from the cold and threatening world. Regressive behavior is similar to fixated behavior in that it is rigid and infantile. Regressions, however, are usually temporary, whereas fixations demand a more or less permanent expenditure of psychic energy.

PROJECTION

When an internal, instinctual impulse provokes too much anxiety, the ego may reduce that anxiety by attributing the unwanted impulse to an external object, usually another person. This is the defense mechanism of **projection,** which can be defined as seeing in others unacceptable feelings or tendencies that actually reside in one's own unconscious (Freud, 1915/1957b). For example, a woman may consistently interpret the actions of older men as attempted seductions. Consciously, the thought of sexual intercourse with older men may be intensely repugnant to her, but buried in her unconscious is a strong erotic attraction to these men. In this example, the young woman deludes herself into believing that she has no sexual feelings for older men. Although this projection erases most of her anxiety and guilt, it permits her to maintain a sexual interest in men who remind her of her father.

An extreme type of projection is **paranoia,** a mental disorder characterized by powerful delusions of jealousy and persecution. Paranoia is not an inevitable outcome of projection but simply a severe variety of it. According to Freud (1922/1955), a crucial distinction between projection and paranoia is that paranoia is always characterized by repressed homosexual feelings toward the persecutor. Freud believed that the persecutor is inevitably a former friend of the same sex, although sometimes the person may transfer his or her delusions onto a person of the opposite sex. When homosexual impulses become too powerful, the persecuted paranoiac defends himself by *reversing* these feelings and then projecting them onto their original object. The transformation proceeds as follows. Instead of saying, "I love him," the paranoid person says, "I hate him." Because this also produces too much anxiety, he says, "He hates me." At this point, he has disclaimed all responsibility and can say, "I like him fine, but he's got it in for me." The central mechanism in all paranoia is projection with accompanying delusions of jealousy and persecution.

INTROJECTION

Whereas projection involves the placing of an unwanted impulse onto an external object, **introjection** is a defense mechanism whereby people incorporate positive qualities of another person into their own ego. For example, an adolescent girl may introject or adopt the mannerisms, values, or lifestyle of a movie star. Such an introjection allows the girl to inflate her sense of worth and to keep feelings of inferiority to a minimum. People always introject characteristics that they see as valuable and that will permit them to feel better about themselves.

Freud (1926/1959a) saw the resolution of the Oedipus complex as the prototype of introjection. During that time the young child introjects the authority and values of one or both parents—an introjection that sets into motion the beginning of the super-ego. When children introject what they perceive to be their parents' values, they are relieved from the work of evaluating and choosing their own beliefs and standard of conduct. As children advance through the latency period of development (approximately ages 6 to 12), their superego becomes more personalized; that is, it moves away from a rigid identification with parents. Nevertheless, people of any age can reduce the anxiety associated with feelings of inadequacy by adopting or introjecting the values, beliefs, and mannerisms of other people.

SUBLIMATION

Each of the above defense mechanisms serves the individual by protecting the ego from anxiety, but each is of dubious value from society's viewpoint. According to Freud (1917/1963), one mechanism—sublimation—helps both the individual and the social group. **Sublimation** is the repression of the genital aim of Eros by substituting a cultural or social aim. The sublimated aim is expressed most obviously in creative cultural accomplishments such as art, music, and literature, but more subtly, it can be manifested in all human relationships and all social pursuits. Freud (1914/1953) believed that the art of Michelangelo, who found an indirect outlet for his libido in painting and sculpting, was an example of sublimation. In most people, sublimations combine with direct expression of Eros and result in a kind of balance between social interests and personal pleasure. Most of us are capable of sublimating a part of our libido in the service of higher cultural values, while at the same time retaining sufficient amounts of the sexual instinct to pursue individual erotic pleasure.

In summary, all defense mechanisms protect the ego against anxiety. They are universal in that everyone engages in defensive behavior to some degree. Each defense mechanism combines with repression, and each can be carried to the point of psychopathology. Normally, however, defense mechanisms are beneficial to the individual and harmless to society; in fact, sublimations are usually beneficial to society.

STAGES OF DEVELOPMENT

Although Freud had little firsthand experience with children (including his own), his developmental theory is almost exclusively a discussion of early childhood. To Freud, the first 4 or 5 years of life, or the **infantile stage,** is the most crucial for personality formation. It is followed by a 6- or 7-year period of **latency** during which time little or no sexual growth takes place. Then at puberty there is a renaissance of sexual life, and the **genital stage** is ushered in. Psychosexual development eventually culminates in **maturity.**

INFANTILE PERIOD

One of Freud's (1905/1953c, 1923/1961b) most important assumptions is that infants possess a sexual life and go through a period of pregenital sexual development during the first 4 or 5 years after birth. At the time Freud originally postulated the existence of

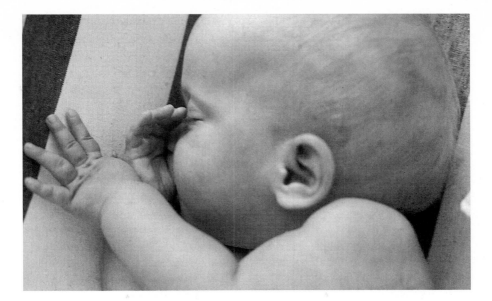

Infants satisfy oral needs one way or another.

infantile sexuality, the concept, though not new, was met with some resistance. Today, however, nearly all close observers accept the idea that children delight in pleasure gained through the erogenous zones, show an interest in the genitals, and even manifest sexual excitement. Childhood sexuality differs from adult sexuality in that it is not capable of reproduction and is exclusively autoerotic. With both children and adults, however, the sexual instinct can be satisfied through organs other than the genitals. The mouth and anus are particularly sensitive to erogenous stimulation (Freud, 1933/1964).

Freud (1917/1963) divided the infantile stage into three phases according to which of the three primary erogenous zones is undergoing the most salient development. The oral phase begins first and is followed by the anal phase and the phallic phase in that order. The three infantile stages overlap, with earlier phases continuing after the onset of later ones.

Oral Phase

Because the mouth is the first organ to provide the infant with pleasure, Freud's first infantile stage of development is the **oral phase.** The infant obtains life-sustaining nourishment through the oral cavity, but beyond that, it also gains pleasure through the act of sucking.

The sexual aim of *early oral* activity is to incorporate or receive into one's own body the instinctual object-choice, that is, the nipple. During this *oral-receptive* phase, the infant feels no ambivalence toward the pleasurable object and its needs are usually satisfied with a minimum of frustration and anxiety. As the baby grows older, however, feelings of frustration and anxiety are more likely to be experienced as a result of scheduled feedings, increased time lapses between feedings, and eventual *weaning*. These anxieties are generally accompanied by feelings of ambivalence toward the love object (mother), and by the increased ability of the budding ego to defend itself against the environment and against anxiety (Freud, 1933/1964).

The infant's defense against the environment is greatly aided by the emergence of teeth. At this point the baby passes into a second oral phase, which Freud (1933/1964) called the *oral-sadistic* period. During this phase the baby responds to others through such diverse means as biting, cooing, closing the mouth, smiling, and crying. The child's first autoerotic experience is thumb sucking, which it uses as a defense against anxiety. Thumb sucking satisfies the sexual, but not the nutritional, needs of the infant.

As the child grows older, the mouth continues to be an erogenous zone, but by the time a person becomes an adult, oral needs can be gratified in a variety of ways, including sucking candy, chewing gum, biting pencils, overeating, smoking cigarettes, "chewing out" other people, and making biting, sarcastic remarks.

Anal Phase

The aggressive instinct, which during the first year of life takes the form of oral sadism, reaches a fuller development during the second year when the anus emerges as a sexually pleasurable zone. Because this period is characterized by satisfaction gained through aggressive behavior and through the excretory function, Freud (1933/1964) called it the *sadistic-anal phase* of development, but current psychoanalysts simply refer to it as the **anal phase.** This phase is divided into two subphases, the early anal and the late anal.

During the *early anal period*, children receive satisfaction by destroying or losing objects. At this time the destructive nature of the sadistic instinct is stronger than the erotic one, and children often behave aggressively toward their parents for frustrating them with *toilet training*.

Then when children enter the *late anal period*, they sometimes take a friendly interest toward their feces, an interest that stems from the erotic pleasure of defecating. Frequently, children will present their feces to the parents as a valued prize (Freud, 1933/1964). If their behavior is accepted and praised by their parents, then they are likely to grow into generous and magnanimous adults. On the other hand, if their "gift" is rejected in a punitive fashion, children may adopt another method of obtaining anal pleasure—withholding the feces until the pressure becomes both painful and erotically stimulating. This mode of narcissistic and masochistic pleasure lays the foundation for the **anal character**—people who continue to receive erotic satisfaction by keeping and possessing objects and by arranging them in an excessively neat and orderly fashion. Freud (1933/1964) hypothesized that people who grow into anal characters were, as children, overly resistant to toilet training, often holding back their feces and prolonging the time of training beyond that usually required. This anal eroticism becomes transformed into the **anal triad** of *orderliness*, *stinginess*, and *obstinacy*, which typifies the adult anal character.

Not all anal erotic impulses are transformed into these three adult character traits. Some are more completely repressed and emerge in the form of neurotic symptoms, and others find expression during the phallic and genital periods of development. Freud (1933/1964) believed that, for girls, anal eroticism is carried over into penis envy during the phallic stage and can eventually be expressed by giving birth to a baby. He also believed that in the unconscious, the concepts of penis and baby—because both are referred to as a "little one"—mean the same thing. Also, feces, because of its elongated shape and because it has been removed from the body, is indistinguishable from baby, and all three concepts—penis, baby, and feces—are represented by the same symbols in dreams (Freud, 1917/1955b).

No basic distinction exists between male and female psychosexual growth during either the oral stage or the sadistic-anal phase. Children of either gender can develop an active or a passive orientation. The active attitude often is characterized by what Freud (1933/1964) considered the masculine qualities of dominance and sadism, whereas the passive orientation is usually marked by the feminine qualities of voyeurism and masochism. However, either orientation, or any combination of the two, can develop in both girls and boys.

Phallic Phase

At approximately age 3 or 4, the child enters into a third stage of infantile development—the **phallic phase,** a time when the genital area becomes the leading erogenous zone. This stage is marked for the first time by a dichotomy between male and female development, a distinction that Freud (1925/1961) believed to be due to the anatomical differences between the sexes. Freud (1924/1961, p. 178) took Napoleon's remark that "History is destiny" and changed it to "Anatomy is destiny." This dictum underlies Freud's belief that physical differences between males and females account for many important psychological differences.

Masturbation, which originated during the oral stage, now enters a second, more crucial phase. During the phallic stage, masturbation is nearly universal, but because parents generally suppress these activities, children usually repress their conscious desire to masturbate by the time their phallic period comes to an end. Just as earlier experiences with weaning and toilet training help shape the foundation of psychosexual development, so, too, does a child's experience with the *suppression of masturbation* (Freud, 1933/1964). The child's experience with the Oedipus complex, however, plays an even more important role in personality development during the phallic phase.

Male Oedipus Complex

Freud (1925/1961) believed that preceding the phallic stage an infant boy forms an *identification* with his father; that is, he wants to *be* his father. Later the boy develops a sexual desire for his mother; that is, he wants to *have* his mother. These two wishes do not appear mutually contradictory to the underdeveloped ego, so they are able to exist side by side for a time. When the boy finally recognizes their inconsistency, he gives up his identification with his father and retains the stronger feeling—the desire to have his mother. The boy now sees his father as a rival for the mother's love. He desires to do away with his father and to possess his mother in a sexual relationship. This condition of rivalry toward the father and incestuous feelings toward the mother is known as the simple male **Oedipus complex.** The term is taken from the Greek tragedy by Sophocles in which Oedipus, King of Thebes, is destined by fate to kill his father and marry his mother.

Freud (1923/1961a) believed that the bisexual nature of the child (of either sex) complicates this picture. Before a young boy enters the Oedipus stage, he develops, to some degree, a feminine disposition. During the Oedipal period, therefore, his feminine nature may lead him to display *affection toward his father* and express *hostility toward his mother*, while at the same time, his masculine tendency disposes him toward hostility for father and lust for mother. During this ambivalent condition, known as the *complete Oedipus complex*, affection and hostility coexist because one or both feelings may be unconscious. Freud believed that these feelings of ambivalence in a boy play a role in the evolution of the **castration complex,** which for boys takes the form of **castration anxiety** or the fear of losing the penis.

To Freud (1905/1953c, 1917/1963, 1923/1961b), the castration complex begins after a young boy (who has assumed that all other people, including girls, have genitals like his own) becomes aware of the absence of a penis on girls. This awareness becomes the greatest emotional shock of his life. After a period of mental struggle and attempts at denial, the young boy is forced into the conclusion that the girl has had her penis cut off. This conclusion may be reinforced by parental threats to castrate or otherwise punish him for his sexual behaviors. Thus, the boy is forced to conclude that the little girl has been punished for masturbation or for seduction of her mother by having her penis removed. The threat of castration now becomes a dreaded possibility. This castration anxiety cannot long be tolerated. The boy represses his impulses toward sexual activity, including his fantasies of carrying out a seduction of his mother.

Prior to his sudden experience of castration anxiety, the little boy may have "seen" the genital area of little girls or his mother, but this sight does not automatically instigate the castration complex. Castration anxiety bursts forth only when the boy's ego is mature enough to comprehend the connection between sexual desires and the removal of the penis.

Freud believed that castration anxiety was present in all boys, even those not personally threatened with the removal of their penis or the stunting of its growth. According to Freud (1933/1964), a boy does not need to receive a clear threat of castration. Any mention of injury or shrinkage in connection with the penis is sufficient to activate the child's phylogenetic endowment. As we have seen, *phylogenetic endowment* is capable of filling the gaps of our individual experiences with the inherited experiences of our ancestors. Ancient man's fear of castration supports the individual child's experiences and results in universal castration anxiety. Freud (1933/1964, p. 86) stated: "It is not a question of whether castration is really carried out; what is decisive is that the danger threatens from the outside and that the child believes in it." He went on to say that "hints at . . . punishment must regularly find a phylogenetic reinforcement in him."

Once his Oedipus complex is dissolved or repressed, the boy surrenders his incestuous desires, changes them into feelings of tender love, and begins to develop a primitive superego. He may identify with either the father or the mother, depending on the strength of his feminine disposition. Normally identification is with the father, but it is not the same as pre-Oedipal identification. The boy no longer wants to be his father; instead, he uses the father as a model for determining right and wrong behavior. He introjects or incorporates the father's authority into his own ego, thereby sowing the seeds of a mature superego. The budding superego takes over the father's prohibitions against incest and ensures the continued repression of the Oedipus complex (Freud, 1933/1964).

Female Oedipus Complex

The phallic phase takes a different and more complicated path for girls than the one it follows for boys. To understand it, we must realize that for girls the castration complex, which takes the form of penis envy, *precedes* the Oedipus complex. The opposite is true with the boy, for whom the castration complex (castration anxiety) follows and breaks up the Oedipus complex.

Differences between boy's and girl's Oedipus complexes are due to anatomical differences between the sexes (Freud, 1925/1961). Like the boy, the pre-Oedipal girl assumes that all other children have genitals similar to her own. Soon she discovers that boys not only possess different genital equipment, but apparently something extra. She becomes envious of this appendage, feels cheated, and desires to have a penis. This experience of **penis envy** is a powerful force in the formation of the girl's personality. Unlike castration anxiety in boys, which is quickly repressed, penis envy may last for years in one form or another. Freud (1933/1964) believed that penis envy is often expressed as a wish to be a boy or a desire to have a man. Almost universally, it is carried over into a wish to have a baby, and eventually it may find expression in the act of giving birth to a baby, especially a boy.

Preceding the castration complex, a girl establishes an identification with her mother similar to that developed by a boy, in that she fantasizes being seduced by her mother. These incestuous feelings, according to Freud (1933/1964), are later turned into hostility when the girl holds her mother responsible for bringing her into the world without a penis. Her libido is then turned toward her father who can satisfy her wish for a penis by giving her a baby, an object that to her has become a substitute for the phallus. The desire for sexual intercourse with the father and accompanying feelings of hostility for the mother are known as the female **Oedipus complex.** Incidentally, Freud (1920/1955b, 1931/1961) objected to the term *Electra complex*, sometimes used by others when referring to the female Oedipus complex, because it suggests a direct parallel between male and female development during the phallic stage. Freud believed that no such parallel exists and that differences in anatomy determine different courses in male and female sexual development after the phallic stage.

Not all girls, however, transfer their sexual interest onto their father and develop hostility toward their mother. Freud (1931/1961, 1933/1964) suggested that when pre-Oedipal girls acknowledge their castration and recognize their inferiority to boys, they will rebel in one of three ways. First, they may give up their sexuality—both the feminine and the masculine dispositions—and develop an intense hostility toward their mother; second, they may cling defiantly to their masculinity, hoping for a penis and fantasizing being a man; and third, they may develop normally; that is, they may take their father as a sexual choice and undergo the simple Oedipus complex that we have been discussing. A girl's choice is influenced in part by her inherent bisexuality and the degree of masculinity she developed during the pre-Oedipal period.

The simple female Oedipus complex is resolved when a girl gives up masturbatory activity, surrenders her sexual desire for her father, and identifies once again with her mother. However, the female Oedipus complex is usually broken up more slowly and less completely than the male's. Because the superego is built from the relics of the shattered Oedipus complex, Freud (1924/1961, 1933/1964) believed that the girl's superego is usually weaker, more flexible, and less severe than the boy's. The reason the girl's superego is not as strict as the boy's is traceable to the difference between the sexes during their Oedipal histories. For boys, castration anxiety follows the Oedipus complex, breaks it up nearly completely, and renders unnecessary the continued expenditure of psychic energy on its remnants. Once the Oedipus complex is shattered, energy used to maintain it is then free to establish a superego. For girls, however, the Oedipus complex *follows* the castration complex (penis envy) and, because girls do not experience a threat of castration, they experience no traumatic sudden shock. The female Oedipus complex is only incompletely resolved by the girl's gradual realization that she may lose the love of her mother and that sexual intercourse with her father is not forthcoming. Her libido thus remains partially expended to maintain the castration complex and its relics, thereby blocking some psychic energy that might otherwise be used to build a strong superego (Freud, 1931/1961). The simple male and female Oedipus complexes are summarized in Table 2.1.

Freud presented his views on the female Oedipus complex more tentatively than he did his ideas regarding the male phallic stage. Nevertheless, his views on feminine development have been criticized as being sexist and uncomplimentary to women (Balmary, 1979/1982; Brannon, 1996; Chodorow, 1989, 1991, 1994; Irigaray, 1986; Krausz, 1994). Although Freud framed these views in a tentative and provisional manner, he

Table 2.1 *Parallel Paths of the Simple Male and Female Phallic Phases*

Male Phallic Phase	Female Phallic Phase
1. *Oedipus complex* (sexual desires for the mother; hostility for the father)	1. *Castration complex* in the form of *penis envy*
2. *Castration complex* in the form of *castration anxiety* shatters the Oedipus complex	2. *Oedipus complex* develops as an attempt to obtain a penis (sexual desires for the father; hostility for the mother)
3. *Identification* with the father	3. Gradual realization that the Oedipal desires are self-defeating
4. Strong *superego* replaces the nearly completely dissolved Oedipus complex	4. *Identification* with the mother
	5. Weak *superego* replaces the partially dissolved Oedipus complex

defended them stubbornly and uncompromisingly. When some of his followers objected to his harsh view of women, Freud became even more rigid in his position and insisted that psychological differences between men and women could not be erased by culture because they were the inevitable consequences of anatomical differences between the sexes (Freud, 1925/1961).

Despite his steadfast public position, Freud privately was uncertain that his views on women represented a final answer. One year after his pronouncement that "anatomy is destiny," he expressed some doubts, admitting that his understanding of girls and women was incomplete. "We know less about the sexual life of little girls than of boys. But we need not feel ashamed of this distinction; after all, the sexual life of adult women is a 'dark continent' for psychology" (Freud 1926/1959b, p. 212).

Then in 1933, he concluded his final essay on femininity with these words:

> That is all I had to say to you about femininity. It is certainly incomplete and fragmentary and does not always sound friendly. But do not forget that I have only been describing women in so far as their nature is determined by their sexual function. It is true that that influence extends very far, but we do not overlook the fact that an individual woman may be a human being in other respects as well. If you want to know more about femininity, enquire from your own experiences of life, or turn to the poets, or wait until science can give you deeper and more coherent information. (Freud, 1933/1964, p. 135)

Throughout his career, Freud often proposed theories without much clinical or experimental evidence to support them. He would later come to see most of these theories as established facts, even though he possessed no intervening substantiating evidence. For as long as he lived, however, he remained doubtful of the absolute validity of his theories on women.

LATENCY PERIOD

Freud believed that, from the 4th or 5th year until puberty, both boys and girls go through a period when psychosexual development is at a standstill. This period in the child's life, the **latency stage,** is brought about partly by the suppression of the sexual instinct and partly by organic factors that owe their existence to prehistoric people.

Freud (1913/1953) suggested that the Oedipus complex and the subsequent period of sexual latency could possibly be explained by the following hypothesis. Early in human development a group of brothers, denied the rights to have sexual relations with their mother or sisters, joined together and killed the father. Because they felt affection as well as hostility toward the father, they were left with strong feelings of guilt, which subsequently caused them to develop strong negative attitudes about sexual relations with members of the family and to repress their hostility toward their father. Later, when they became fathers, they suppressed sexual activity in their own children whenever it became noticeable, probably around age three or four. When this suppression became complete, it led to a period of sexual latency. After this experience was repeated in different families, clans, or totems over a period of many generations, it became an active, though unconscious force in the individual's psychosexual development. This prohibition of sexual activity, then, is part of our phylogenetic endowment and is one possible explanation for the latency period.

Continued latency is reinforced through constant suppression by parents and teachers and by internal feelings of shame, guilt, and morality. The sexual instinct, of course, still exists during this period, but its aim has been inhibited. The sublimated libido now shows itself in social and cultural accomplishments, such as school work and the development of friendships. During this time children form groups or cliques, an impossibility during the infantile period when the sexual drive was completely autoerotic.

GENITAL PERIOD

Puberty signals a reawakening of the sexual aim and the beginning of the *genital period*. During puberty the diphasic sexual life of the person enters a second stage, which has certain basic differences from the infantile period (Freud, 1923/1961b). First, adolescents give up autoeroticism and direct their sexual energy toward another person instead of toward themselves. Second, reproduction now becomes a possibility. Third, although penis envy may continue to linger, the vagina finally obtains the same status for girls that the male organ had for them during infancy, so that boys see the female organ as a sought-after object rather than a traumatic threat. Fourth, the entire sexual instinct takes on a more complete organization, and the component instincts that had operated somewhat independently during the early infantile period gain a kind of synthesis during adolescence; thus the mouth, anus, and other pleasure-producing areas take an auxiliary position to the genitals, which now attain supremacy as an erogenous zone.

This synthesis of Eros, the elevated status of the female genital organ, the reproductive capacity of the life instinct, and its direction outward rather than onto the self, represent the major distinctions between infantile and adult sexuality. In several other ways, however, Eros remains unchanged. It may continue to manifest itself in sublimated forms; it may be repressed; or it may be expressed in masturbation or other sexual acts. The subordinated erogenous zones also continue as vehicles of erotic pleasure. The mouth, for example, retains many of its infantile activities, perhaps dropping thumb sucking but possibly adding smoking or prolonged kissing.

MATURITY

The genital period begins at puberty and continues throughout the individual's lifetime. It is a stage attained by everyone who reaches physical maturity. In addition, Freud alluded to but never fully conceptualized a period of *psychological maturity*, a stage attained after a person has passed through the earlier developmental periods in an ideal manner. Unfortunately, this seldom happens because we have too many opportunities to develop pathological disorders or neurotic predispositions.

Although Freud never fully conceptualized the notion of psychological maturity, we can draw a sketch of psychoanalytically mature individuals. Such people would have a balance among the structures of the mind, with their ego controlling their id and superego but, at the same time, allowing for reasonable desires and demands (see Figure 2.3). Therefore, their id impulses would be expressed honestly and consciously, with no traces of shame or guilt, and their superego would move beyond parental identification and control, with no remnants of antagonism or incest. Their ego-ideal would be realistic and congruent with their ego, and, in fact, the boundary between their superego and their ego would become nearly imperceptible.

Consciousness would play a more important role in the behavior of mature people, who would have only minimal need to repress sexual and aggressive urges. Indeed, most of the repressions of psychologically healthy individuals would emerge in the form of sublimations rather than neurotic symptoms. Because the Oedipus complex of mature people is completely or nearly completely dissolved, their libido, which was formerly directed toward parents, would be released to search for both tender and sensual love. In short, psychologically mature people would come through the experiences of childhood and adolescence in control of their psychic energy and with their ego functioning in the center of an ever-expanding world of consciousness.

CHILDHOOD SEDUCTION: FACT, FALLACY, OR FANTASY?

Freud's psychoanalytic theory rests largely on his conception of a universal Oedipus complex in which the young child desires a sexual relationship with one parent while experiencing feelings of hostility toward the other parent. Freud's idea of the Oedipus complex is so central to his overall theory that his daughter Anna, in a 1981 letter to Freudian critic Jeffery Masson, stated that if her father had not replaced the seduction theory with the Oedipus theory, "there would have been no psychoanalysis afterwards" (Masson, 1984, p. 113).

As we saw in our account of Freud's biography, prior to his belief that young children possess incestuous wishes toward their parents, Freud had held the opposite view; that is, he believed that neurotic symptoms resulted from the seduction of children by adults. Freud (1896/1962) summarized his seduction theory in these words:

> I therefore put forward the thesis that at the bottom of every case of hysteria there are *one or more occurrences of premature sexual experience*, occurrences which belong to the earliest years of childhood but which can be reproduced through the work of psycho-analysis in spite of intervening decades. I believe that this is an important finding, the discovery of a *caput Nili* [source of the Nile] in neuropathology. (p. 203)

However, in his famous letter of September 21, 1897, to Wilhelm Fliess, Freud repudiated his seduction theory, giving four reasons why he could no longer believe in his once-treasured theory. First, he said, the seduction theory had not enabled him to successfully treat even a single patient. Second, a great number of fathers, including his own, would have to be accused of sexual perversion because hysteria was quite common even among Freud's siblings. Third, Freud believed that the unconscious mind could probably not distinguish reality from fiction, a belief that later evolved into the Oedipus complex. And fourth, he found that the unconscious memories of advanced psychotic patients almost never revealed early childhood sexual experiences (Freud, 1985).

R. A. Powell and Douglas Boer (1994) have offered a fifth reason why Freud abandoned the seduction theory. These authors claimed that Freud came to realize that he had used highly suggestive and even coercive tactics in eliciting memories of seduction from his patients and that he lacked clear evidence that these memories were real. Further, Powell suggested that "some of Freud's patients did produce memories of abuse while others did not, yet in each case, Freud believed he had obtained strong evidence of seduction" (R. A. Powell, personal communication, September 6, 1994).

FREUD'S EARLY THERAPEUTIC TECHNIQUE

Prior to his use of the rather passive psychotherapeutic technique of free association, Freud had relied on a much more active approach. In *Studies on Hysteria* (Breuer & Freud, 1895/1955), Freud described his technique of extracting repressed childhood memories:

> I placed my hand on the patient's forehead or took her head between my hands and said: 'You will think of it under the pressure of my hand. At the moment at which I relax my pressure you will see something in front of you or something will come into your head. Catch hold of it. It will be what we are looking for.—Well, what have you seen or what has occurred to you?'
>
> On the first occasions on which I made use of this procedure . . . I myself was surprised to find that it yielded me the precise results that I needed. (pp. 110–111)

Indeed, such a highly suggestive procedure was very likely to yield the precise results Freud needed, namely the confession of a childhood seduction. Moreover, while using both dream interpretation and hypnosis, Freud told his patients to expect that scenes of childhood sexual experiences would come forth (Freud, 1896/1962).

In an autobiography written nearly 30 years after he abandoned his seduction theory, Freud (1925/1959) stated that under the pressure technique, most of his patients reproduced childhood scenes in which they were sexually seduced by some adult. When he was obliged to recognize that "these scenes of seduction had never taken place, and that they were only phantasies which my patients had made up or which I *myself had perhaps forced upon them* [italics added], I was for some time completely at a loss" (p. 34). He was at a loss, however, for a very short time. Within days after his September 21, 1897, letter to Fliess, he concluded that "the neurotic symptoms were not related directly to actual events but to phantasies. . . . I had in fact stumbled for the first time upon the *Oedipus complex*" (Freud, 1925/1959, p. 34).

The Oedipus complex, of course, was a direct contradiction to the seduction theory in that it placed the origin of most parental seductions within the mind of the child and not in reality. In time, Freud became more and more strongly convinced that neurotic symptoms were related to childhood *fantasies* rather than to material reality. In his autobiography, he expressed relief that he had corrected the "error" that would have had fatal consequences for psychoanalysis and wondered how anyone could have believed that childhood seductions were so common (Freud, 1925/1959).

Many observers now believe that the seduction theory was not an error, and that Freud went astray when he attributed the fault of seduction to the child rather than to the parent. Marie Balmary (1979/1982) stated that psychoanalysis got off the right track when Freud repudiated the seduction theory and thus set psychological reality above physical reality. Hannah Lerman (1986) took a standard Freudian view of the Oedipus complex and rejected it as inferior to the original theory as an explanation for neurotic symptoms. She cited evidence from Kinsey that 25% of women had some sexual encounter with an adult by the time they were 13 years old, and that 80% of the time, the adult was a relative or family friend.

Jeffery Masson (1984) claimed that psychoanalysis took a wrong turn when Freud abandoned the seduction theory. By shifting the emphasis from actual child sexual abuse to the inner world of childhood fantasies, "Freud began a trend away from the real world that . . . is at the root of the present-day sterility of psychoanalysis and psychiatry throughout the world" (p. 144). Actually, Freud never completely abandoned his seduction theory; he always retained some belief in real sexual trauma as a source of neurosis (Freud, 1925/1959).

RECENT INTEREST IN RECOVERED MEMORIES

In more recent years, the question of repressed and recovered memories of childhood sexual abuse has generated a great amount of publicity in both professional and popular media (Crews, 1995; Esterson, 1993; Kelley & Kelley, 1994; Robinson, 1993; Webster, 1995). The increasing number of adult children who have accused their parents of sexually abusing them as children has led to some parents establishing the False Memory Syndrome Foundation. As parents began to oppose adult children and their therapists, some observers were led to wonder if these reports of childhood sexual trauma were true or false. The question of whether memories of childhood sexual trauma are either true or false, however, does not exhaust all possibilities.

Janice Haaken (1995) has argued that many such reports are neither fact nor fallacy—they are fantasies. To Haaken, fantasy is an area between the real and the imaginary. Fantasy should not be paired against reality; rather, it is an intrapsychic reconstruction of a blend of wishes and behavior. People have a need for fantasy and myth. (See Rollo May's ideas on myth in Chapter 18.) Haaken pointed out that "the capacity to fantasize provides access to the mythic dramas that underlie both social reality and psychopathology" (p. 194). Haaken further suggested that fantasy can be a means of escaping childhood trauma and that "incestuous longings and what is actually acted out (i.e., overt incest) may converge at various points along a continuum of experience" (p. 195).

Haaken, of course, has acknowledged the seriousness of actual sexual abuse of children. She contended, however, that therapists must evaluate their female clients' reports of sexual trauma in terms of a broad picture of family dynamics. "When the history includes a father with poor impulse control, lack of empathy, and sexualized interactions with the daughter, the emergence of recovered memory of sexual abuse is consistent with this larger clinical picture" (Haaken, 1995, p. 192). This situation, however, must be distinguished from other narratives in which a woman has no conscious memory of abuse and is able to recall such memories only after a therapist probes for themes of childhood sexual trauma. Recently, therapists have become polarized, tending to favor one position or the other, but Haaken counseled therapists to avoid the twin errors of attributing reports either to imagination or to real experiences. "Just as Freudian analysts once saw Oedipal conflict everywhere, many contemporary therapists schooled in trauma theory now see sexual abuse everywhere" (p. 196).

Some researchers, such as Elizabeth Loftus (1993), have questioned the concept of repression as well as the accuracy of many recovered memories. Loftus contended that many therapists have unwittingly planted suggestions of abuse by telling clients that most people with their symptoms were sexually or physically abused as children. Other therapists have used dream interpretation or hypnosis to uncover repressed memories of childhood sexual abuse. Indeed, Loftus's description of current therapists' behavior is strikingly similar to the technique used by Freud more than a century ago. Like Freud, these therapists "have a tendency to search for evidence that confirms their hunches rather than search for evidence that disconfirms. It is not easy to discard long-held beliefs, in part because we are eager to verify those beliefs" (p. 530). Loftus, like Haaken, does not deny the reality of most reports of childhood sexual abuse, and her own research (Loftus, Polonsky, & Fullilove, 1994) has found that more than half the women in treatment for substance abuse reported memories of childhood sexual trauma. Loftus (1993, 1994) argued that memories of childhood sexual abuse, like any other memory, are filled with inaccuracies and that the recent publicity on recovered memories of childhood sexual abuse is partially responsible for triggering confabulated memories. (We discuss recent research on recovered memories in the section on related research, but first we examine the applications of psychoanalytic theory to dreams, unconscious slips, and psychotherapy.)

APPLICATIONS OF PSYCHOANALYTIC THEORY

Freud was an innovative speculator, probably more concerned with theory building than with treating sick people. He spent much of his time conducting therapy, not only to help patients, but to gain the insight into human personality necessary to expound psychoanalytic theory. These insights came, in part, from his work with dream analysis, unconscious slips, and other experiences with psychotherapy.

DREAM ANALYSIS

In interpreting dreams Freud felt that the **latent content** is more important than the **manifest content.** The latent content of a dream refers to its unconscious material whereas the manifest content is the surface meaning or the conscious description given by the dreamer. The basic assumption of Freud's dream analysis is that nearly all dreams are *wish fulfillments*. Some wishes are obvious and are expressed through the manifest content, as when a person goes to sleep hungry and dreams of eating large quantities of delicious food. Most wish fulfillments, however, are expressed in the latent content and only dream interpretation can uncover that wish.

The exception to the rule that dreams are wish fulfillments is found in patients suffering from traumatic neuroses, whose dreams are often filled with repetitions of traumatic experiences. These dreams, which obey the principle of **repetition compulsion** rather than wish fulfillment, often occur with battle-weary soldiers who repeatedly dream of frightening or traumatic experiences (Freud, 1920/1955a, 1933/1964).

Freud believed that dreams are formed in the unconscious and originate as attempts by unconscious wishes to become conscious. To do this, the wishes must slip past both the primary and the final censors (refer again to Figure 2.1). Even during sleep these guardians maintain their vigil, forcing unconscious psychic material to adopt a disguised form. The disguise can operate in two basic ways.

First, the dream content can be distorted through either condensation or displacement. *Condensation* refers to the fact that the manifest dream content is not as extensive as the latent level, indicating that the unconscious material has been abbreviated or condensed before appearing on the manifest level. *Displacement* means that the dream image is replaced by some other idea only remotely related to it (Freud, 1900/1953). Condensation and displacement of content both take place through the use of symbols. Certain images are almost universally represented by seemingly innocuous figures. For example, the phallus may be symbolized by elongated objects such as sticks, snakes, or knives; the vagina often appears as any small box, chest, or oven; parents appear in the form of the president, a teacher, or one's boss; a woman may be represented by a room, with an open room standing for a sexually promiscuous woman and a closed room an unobtainable one; sexual intercourse can be disguised as ascending or descending steep inclines like ladders or stairs, and castration anxiety can be expressed in dreams of growing bald, losing teeth, or any act of cutting (Freud, 1900/1953, 1901/1953, 1917/1963).

Second, dreams can deceive the dreamer through the inhibition and reversal of affect. Strong negative emotions, which ordinarily would result in feelings of unpleasantness if allowed to become conscious, might be completely inhibited. The dreamer, though faced with a fearful or anxiety-provoking situation, feels nothing during the dream. The deceptive nature of the manifest content is also illustrated by the reversal of the affect into its opposite. Deeply felt unconscious hostility can be transformed into love by the workings of the dream. The dreamer is fooled into believing that hate is love or that joy is sorrow, as when one mourns the death of a parent whose extinction would be welcomed by the primitive unconscious (Freud, 1900/1953, 1915/1957a, 1917/1963).

After its content has been distorted and its affect inhibited or reversed, the dream appears in its manifest form and may be recalled by the dreamer. The manifest content nearly always relates to conscious or preconscious experience of the previous day (Freud, 1900/1953). Only the latent content, however, has any psychoanalytic importance.

In interpreting dreams, Freud (1917/1963) ordinarily followed one of two methods. The first was to ask patients to relate their dream and all their associations to it, no matter how unrelated or illogical these associations seemed. Freud believed that such associations revealed the unconscious wish behind the dream. If the dreamer was unable to relate association material, Freud used a second method—dream symbols—to discover the unconscious elements underlying the manifest content. The purpose of both methods (associations and symbols) was to trace the dream formation backward until the latent content was reached. Freud (1900/1953, p. 608) believed that dream interpretation was the most reliable approach to the study of unconscious processes and referred to it as the "royal road" to the unconscious.

Anxiety dreams offer no contradiction to the rule that dreams are wish fulfillments. The explanation is that anxiety belongs to the preconscious system whereas the wish belongs to the unconscious. Freud (1900/1953) reported three typical anxiety dreams: the embarrassment dream of nakedness, dreams of the death of a beloved person, and dreams of failing an examination.

In the embarrassment dream of nakedness, the dreamer feels shame or embarrassment at being naked or improperly dressed in the presence of strangers. The spectators usually appear quite indifferent, although the dreamer is very much embarrassed. The origin of this dream is the early childhood experience of being undressed in the presence of adults. In the original experience, the child feels no embarrassment but the adults often register disapproval. Freud believed that wish fulfillment is served in two ways by this dream. First, the indifference of the spectators fulfills the infantile wish that the witnessing adults refrain from scolding. Second, the fact of nakedness fulfills the wish to exhibit oneself, a desire usually repressed in adults but present in young children.

Dreams of the death of a beloved person also originate in childhood and are wish fulfillments. If a person dreams of the death of a younger person, the unconscious is expressing the wish for the destruction of a younger brother or sister who was a hated rival during the infantile period. When the deceased is an older person, the dreamer is fulfilling the Oedipal wish for the death of a parent. If the dreamer feels anxiety and sorrow during the dream, it is because the affect has been reversed. Dreams of the death of a parent are typical in adults, but they do not mean that the dreamer has a present wish for the death of that parent. These dreams were interpreted by Freud as meaning that, as a child, the dreamer longed for the death of the parent, but the wish was too threatening to find its way into consciousness. Even during adulthood the death wish ordinarily does not appear in dreams unless the affect has been changed to sorrow.

A third typical anxiety dream is failing an examination in school. According to Freud (1900/1953), the dreamer always dreams of failing an examination that has already been successfully passed, never one that was failed. These dreams usually occur when the dreamer is anticipating a difficult task. By dreaming of failing an examination already passed, the ego can reason, "I passed the earlier test that I was worried about. Now I'm worried about another task, but I'll pass it too. Therefore, I need not be anxious over tomorrow's task." The wish to be free from worry over a difficult job is thus fulfilled.

In summary, Freud believed that dreams are motivated by wish fulfillments. Their latent content is formed in the unconscious and usually goes back to childhood experiences, although the manifest content often stems from experiences of the previous day. The interpretation of dreams serves as the "royal road" to the unconscious, but dreams should not be interpreted without the dreamer's associations to the dream. Latent material is transformed into manifest content through the dream work. The dream work achieves its goal by the processes of condensation, displacement, and inhibition of affect. The manifest dream may have little resemblance to the latent material, but accurate interpretation reveals the hidden connection by tracing the dream work backward until the unconscious images are revealed.

FREUDIAN SLIPS

Freud believed that many everyday slips of the tongue or pen, misreadings, and incorrect hearings as well as the misplacing of objects and the temporary forgetting of names or intentions are not chance accidents but reveal the person's unconscious intentions. In writing of these faulty acts, Freud (1901/1960) used the German *Fehlleistung*, or "faulty function," but James Strachey, one of Freud's translators, invented the term **parapraxes** to refer to what many people now simply call "Freudian slips."

Parapraxes or unconscious slips are so common that we usually pay little attention to them and deny that they have any underlying significance. Freud, however, insisted that these faulty acts have meaning; they reveal the unconscious intention of the person: "They are not chance events but serious mental acts; they have a sense; they arise from the concurrent actions—or perhaps rather, the mutually opposing action—of two different intentions" (Freud, 1917/1963, p. 44). One opposing action emanates from the unconscious, the other from the preconscious. Unconscious slips, therefore, are similar to dreams in that they are a product of both the unconscious and the preconscious, with the unconscious intention being dominant and interfering with and replacing the preconscious one.

The fact that most people strongly deny any meaning behind their parapraxes was seen by Freud as evidence that the slip, indeed, had relevance to unconscious images

Freud's consulting room.

that must remain hidden from consciousness. A young man once walked into a convenience store, became immediately attracted to the young woman clerk, and asked for a "sex-pack of beer." When the clerk accused him of improper behavior, the young man vehemently protested his innocence. Examples such as this can be extended almost indefinitely. Freud provided many in his book, *Psychopathology of Everyday Life* (1901/1960). In all parapraxes, the intentions of the unconscious supplant the weaker intentions of the preconscious, thereby revealing the true purpose of the ego.

Psychotherapy

The primary goal of psychoanalytic therapy is to uncover repressed memories. "Our therapy works by transforming what is unconscious into what is conscious, and it works only in so far as it is in a position to effect that transformation" (Freud, 1917/1963, p. 280). More specifically, the purpose of psychoanalysis is "to strengthen the ego, to make it more independent of the superego, to widen its field of perception and enlarge its organization, so that it can appropriate fresh portions of the id. Where id was, there ego shall be" (Freud, 1933/1964, p. 80).

To bring unconscious images to consciousness, Freud (1900/1953, 1905/1953b) utilized two techniques—free association and dream analysis. With **free association,** patients are required to verbalize every thought that comes to their mind, no matter how irrelevant or repugnant it may appear. The purpose of free association is to arrive at the unconscious by starting with a present conscious idea and following it through a train of associations to wherever it leads. The process is not easy and some patients never master it.

For this reason, dream analysis remained a favorite therapeutic technique with Freud. In interpreting dreams, Freud would ask patients to reveal a dream and all thoughts associated with it. In addition to asking for the dreamer's associations, Freud used symbolism to interpret dreams. Although he would suggest possible meanings of symbols, patients had to accept the interpretation and to make additional associations to the dream images. Whether associations and symbols were used individually or in combination, the resulting interpretation usually (but not always) revealed latent content that was sexual in nature.

In order for analytic treatment to be successful, libido previously expended on the neurotic symptom must be freed to work in the service of the ego. This takes place in a two-phase procedure. "In the first, all the libido is forced from the symptoms into the transference and concentrated there; in the second, the struggle is waged around this new object and the libido is liberated from it" (Freud, 1917/1963, p. 455). The transference situation is vital to psychoanalysis. **Transference** refers to the strong sexual or aggressive feelings, positive or negative, that patients develop toward their analyst during the course of treatment. Transference feelings are unearned by the therapist and are merely transferred to her or him from patients' earlier experiences, usually with their parents. In other words, patients feel toward the analyst the same way they previously felt toward one or both parents. As long as these feelings manifest themselves as interest or love, transference does not interfere with the process of treatment but is a powerful ally to the therapeutic progress. Positive transference permits patients to more or less relive childhood experiences within the nonthreatening climate of the analytic treatment. However, **negative transference** in the form of hostility must be recognized by the therapist and explained to patients so that they can overcome any **resistance** to treatment (Freud, 1905/1953a, 1917/1963). Resistance, which refers to a variety of unconscious responses used by patients to block their own progress in therapy, can be seen as a positive sign because it indicates that therapy has advanced beyond superficial material.

Several limitations of psychoanalysis were noted by Freud (1933/1964). First, not all old memories can or should be brought into consciousness. Second, treatment is not as effective with **psychoses** or with constitutional illnesses as it is with the various transference neuroses such as phobias, hysterias, and obsessions. A third limitation, by no means peculiar to psychoanalysis, is that a patient, once cured, may later develop another neurosis. Recognizing these limitations, Freud felt that psychoanalysis could be used in conjunction with other therapies. However, he repeatedly insisted that it could not be shortened or modified in any essential way.

When analytic treatment is successful, patients no longer suffer from debilitating symptoms, they use psychic energy to perform ego functions, and they have an expanded ego that includes previously repressed experiences. They do not experience a major personality change, but they do become what they might have been under the most favorable conditions.

RELATED RESEARCH

In Chapter 1 we stated that useful theories must (1) generate research, (2) be falsifiable, (3) organize known data, (4) guide action, (5) be internally consistent, and (6) be parsimonious. Throughout the book, we present a brief section on current research that relates to each theory and discuss the falsifiability of that theory. We also discussed in Chapter 1 the reciprocal relationship between theory and research. A useful theory must be supported by scientific research, and at the same time, that theory should generate hypotheses and determine the direction taken by research. So for each theory, we ask, Does research support its key assumptions?

Freud's thinking has had an enormous influence on 20th century culture, but are his ideas upheld by scientific research? Perhaps Freud's most controversial and enduring theory is that of a universal Oedipus complex, and this theory has probably received much empirical attention, even if the evidence has sometimes been indirect. In particular, two bodies of empirical research are relevant to Freud's idea of the Oedipus complex. First, and most direct, is research on the possibility that subliminal activation of Oedipal conflict may influence our behavior. Second, and more indirect, is the recent explosion of work on repressed memories.

SUBLIMINAL ACTIVATION OF THE OEDIPUS COMPLEX

One example of research related to psychoanalytic theory is the work on subliminal perception and activation of Oedipal conflict conducted by Lloyd Silverman and his associates (Silverman, 1983, 1985; Silverman, Ross, Adler, & Lustig, 1978; Silverman & Weinberger, 1985; Weinberger & Silverman, 1990). This research has been carried out with clinical and psychiatric participants as well as with college students.

Research in Silverman's laboratory generally uses a design in which participants are exposed for 4 milliseconds to stimuli intended to activate symbiotic-like fantasies. The most effective of such stimuli, especially with men, has been the message, "Mommy and I are one," accompanied by a picture of a man and woman merged at the shoulders. Silverman & Weinberger (1985) reviewed research that showed consistent effects for this subliminal message in a variety of situations. Male schizophrenic patients exposed repeatedly to the "Mommy and I are one" message showed greater improvement than those exposed to no subliminal message or to different messages. Female schizophrenic patients, however, showed no improvement to this message, but they did show decreased pathology after being exposed to a "Daddy and I are one" message.

Silverman and Weinberger (1985) also reviewed studies that found that the "Mommy and I are one" message was effective in helping people to stop smoking, quit drinking, increase assertiveness, reduce personality disorders, decrease phobic reactions, and develop better eating habits. In addition, Thorton, Igleheart, and Silverman (1987) found that male heroin addicts who received this message reported greater reduction in heroin and other drug use, more effectiveness at work, and increased number of pleasant dreams involving women than did a control group that received the message "People are walking." Weinberger and Silverman (1990) argued that such research demonstrates that psychoanalysis is scientifically testable and that the results of their studies show that activated unconscious symbiotic-like fantasies produce a therapeutic effect in a wide variety of circumstances. They further suggested that the "Mommy and I are one" message may be effective because it reduces anxiety, gratifies dependency needs, or helps patients see their therapist as warm, accepting, and empathic—characteristics that Carl Rogers (see Chapter 16) regarded as necessary for therapeutic change.

Silverman has also applied this research paradigm to nonclinical participants, namely college men engaged in competitive dart throwing (Silverman et al., 1978). Rather than subliminally activating a symbiotic oneness with a parent of the other sex, this study attempted to induce Oedipal conflict with the same-sex parent (fathers). The logic of the study was that Oedipal conflict can be intensified or alleviated by presenting subliminal messages that either condemn or sanction men's competition with their father. To *intensify* the Oedipal conflict, Silverman and his associates presented college men with a 4-millisecond subliminal message that verbally condemned competition with one's father ("Beating Dad is wrong"). At the same time, they showed a visual image of father and son figures depicting negative expressions toward one another. To *alleviate* the Oedipal conflict, the reseachers presented a subliminal message that verbally sanctioned competition ("Beating Dad is OK"), while showing a visual image of father and son figures smiling at one another. As Freudian theory would have predicted, when participants were exposed to the condemning message ("Beating Dad is wrong"), their dart-throwing scores were significantly lower than when they were exposed to the sanctioning message ("Beating Dad is OK").

As interesting and compelling as these findings on subliminal activation may be, the authors caution that the findings should be viewed as "only *consistent* with the psychoanalytically based formulation that has been cited rather than as *corroborating* it" (Silverman et al., 1978, p. 343). These findings are also consistent with cognitive theories as well (see Kunzendorf, Jesses, Dupille, & Butler, 1991 for a cognitive theory explanation). Furthermore, some researchers have failed to replicate Silverman's findings (Kothera, Fudin, & Nicastro, 1990) or have pointed out the inconsistencies and lack of exact replication in Silverman's own research (Balay & Shevrin, 1988).

REPRESSED MEMORIES AND THE SEDUCTION HYPOTHESIS

As we previously discussed, some writers have recently questioned the objectivity of Freud's therapeutic technique as well as his switch from his seduction hypothesis to a belief that his patients were unconsciously fantasizing childhood sexual relationships with their parents (see section on Childhood Seduction: Fact, Fallacy, or Fantasy?). Recently, much controversy and some empirical research have centered around the degree to which children are likely to repress memories of actual trauma and then suddenly recall it later in life, often not until adulthood. The recall of repressed memories, however, does not establish the authenticity of the event. Such recollections of childhood abuse suggest three possibilities: (1) The accounts are objectively real (fact); (2) they are therapeutically induced (fallacy); or (3) they are subjectively fantasized (fantasy). The question of fact, fallacy, or fantasy presents current researchers with many of the same problems that surrounded Freud's seduction hypothesis.

The first problem is the frequency of repressed abuse. Loftus (1993) looked at three different studies and found that anywhere between 18% and 59% of therapy patients who had been sexually abused during childhood said that there was a period when they did not remember the abuse at all. This wide range of patients who claimed that they had repressed memories of childhood abuse may be due to ambiguities in how the question was asked and/or interpreted. Loftus's own research (Loftus, Polonsky, & Fullilove, 1994) found that more than 80% of women who had reported childhood sexual abuse had remembered the abuse throughout their whole lives. This study suggests that only a small number of women who had been sexually abused repress and then recover memories of the abuse.

A second problem revolves around the accuracy of repressed and recovered memories. Some therapists have claimed that verifying the authenticity of their patients' memories is not their concern (lawyers would obviously disagree). If patients claim they were abused, these therapists argue, then they were abused. In *The Courage to Heal*, a pioneering book on incest, Ellen Bass and Laura Davis (1988, p. 22) told their readers that "so far, no one we've talked to thought she might have been abused, and then later discovered that she hadn't been. The progression always goes the other way, from suspicion to confirmation. If you think you were abused and your life shows the symptoms, then you were." On the other hand, Loftus (Loftus, 1993; Loftus & Ketcham,

1994) and others have argued that therapists who seek confirmation of their own prior beliefs often plant these memories in the minds of their patients and then unwittingly create a self-fulfilling prophecy through their expectations that such reports will be forthcoming.

Because of this inherent uncertainty of clinical claims, we have to look for evidence about repressed or false memories from the laboratory. We can determine experimentally the extent to which false memories can be induced by having family members or other people tell participants about an event that in fact did not happen, for example, getting lost in a shopping mall. If participants later claim to "remember" this event, then we have evidence that false memories can be created. This is precisely what Loftus and her colleagues have attempted to do. If researchers can induce such false memories of mildly traumatic events in a laboratory setting, then it seems reasonable that therapists can induce memories of highly traumatic events in a clinical setting. What does the experimental evidence show?

In one laboratory situation, a subject and a family member play "Remember that time when . . . " (Loftus, 1993). In this scenario the family member sometimes tells a true story and sometimes an untrue story. The untrue story always consists of the participant being lost in a shopping mall at the age of five. In one case Chris, a 14-year-old boy, was told by an older brother that he had become lost in a shopping mall, and after some panic he was found being led by an older man who might have been wearing a flannel shirt. As early as 2 days after the "implanted memory," Chris began to have very specific recollections of being lost. These recollections actually became more elaborate until 2 weeks after receiving the implanted memory, Chris reported:

> I was with you guys for a second and I think I went over to look at the toy store, the Kay-bee toy and uh, we got lost and I was looking around I thought, "Uh-oh. I'm in trouble now." You know. And then I . . . I thought I was never going to see my family again. I was really scared you know. And then this old man, I think he was wearing a blue flannel, came up to me . . . he was kind of old. He was kind of bald on top . . . he had like a ring of gray hair . . . and he had glasses. (p. 532)

Clearly, these are very vivid, clear, and elaborate recollections. They seem quite real, but it turns out they are false memories. When Chris was told that the story of him being lost was made up, he had trouble believing it and continued to insist that he had specific memories of being lost.

In another real-life situation, Ulrich Neisser and Nicole Harsh (1992) asked people the day after the 1986 space shuttle *Challenger* explosion how they learned of the news. Participants were then contacted 3 years later and asked the same question again, and although they had very vivid memories, none of them remembered the event entirely accurately relative to what they said the morning after the accident. Others who reported very concrete, vivid pictures had essentially none of the details correct. Loftus and her colleagues (Garry, Loftus, & Brown, 1994) have labeled such faulty memories the "misinformation effect."

What implications do created or false memories have for Freud's seduction hypothesis? Clearly, the implications are indirect, but the research on repressed and recovered memories lends support to Freud's idea that adult recollections can be tainted by memory biases and distortions and that "misinformation" can lead to false memories. Such evidence can be seen as support for Freud's abandonment of the seduction hypothesis because it opens the possibility that his patients might have unintentionally distorted and falsified their memories of childhood seduction. On the other hand, this research calls into question Freud's own therapeutic techniques, that is, his practice of putting his hands on his patients' foreheads and imploring them to recall repressed events, a practice almost certain to lead to the memories Freud was seeking.

CRITIQUE OF FREUD

In criticizing Freud, we must first ask, Was Freud a scientist? Although he repeatedly insisted that he was primarily a scientist and that psychoanalysis was a science, Freud's definition of science needs some explanation. When he called psychoanalysis a science, he was attempting to separate it from a philosophy or an ideology; he was not claiming that it was a natural science. The German language and culture of Freud's day made a distinction between a natural science (*Naturwissenschaften*) and a human science (*Geisteswissenschaften*). Unfortunately, James Strachey's translations in the *Standard Edition* make Freud seem to be a natural scientist. However, other scholars (Federn, 1988; Holder, 1988) believe that Freud clearly saw himself as a human scientist, that is, a humanist or scholar, and not a natural scientist.

Bruno Bettelheim (1982, 1983) was also critical of Strachey's translations. He contended that the *Standard Edition* and other English translations used precise medical concepts and misleading Greek and Latin terms instead of the ordinary, often ambiguous German words that Freud had chosen. Such precision tended to render Freud more scientific and less humanistic than he appears to the German reader. To Bettelheim, for instance, psychoanalytic therapy should be seen as a spiritual journey into the depths of the soul (translated by Strachey as "mind") and not a mechanistic analysis of the mental apparatus.

As a result of Freud's 19th century German view of science, many contemporary writers regard his theory-building methods as untenable and rather unscientific (Crews, 1995, 1996; Esterson, 1993; Macmillan, 1991; Sulloway, 1992; Webster, 1995). His theories were not based on experimental investigation but rather on subjective observations that Freud made of himself and his clinical patients. These patients were not representative of people in general but came mostly from the middle and upper classes.

Despite these limitations, Freud developed the most comprehensive and most widely known of all personality theories. This widespread reputation of psychoanalysis is due largely to Freud's gifts as a writer, the comprehensiveness of his psychoanalytic theory, his acceptance of unconscious motivation, and finally, his heavy emphasis on sex and aggression. For nearly a century his theory has been honored and condemned, glorified and vilified, praised and disparaged.

Apart from this widespread popular and professional interest, the question remains: Was Freud scientific? Present opinions differ on this issue. Paul Kline (1984) argued that Freud used free association as the database for exploring the unconscious and that his methods were consistent with proper scientific practice. But even Robert Holt (1989), a strong supporter of Freud, cautioned that Freud's ideas should not be taken as absolute truth, but as beginning points in our understanding of human personality.

Other writers, such as Marie Balmary (1979/1982), Nancy Chodorow (1994), Hannah Lerman (1986), Jeffery Masson (1984), and Paul Vitz (1988), have criticized Freud for adopting a male-oriented theory and for allowing many of his personal biases to influence his theories. These writers generally found Freud to have been unscientific and to have been greatly influenced by his own unconscious needs, especially those springing from the early periods of his life. Their criticisms are consistent with those of

Karl Popper (1963), who regarded psychoanalysis as a pseudo-science, and with those of Hans Eysenck (1990b), who claimed that it was not a science at all but simply a way of interpreting events. Freud's own description of science permits much room for subjective interpretations and indefinite definitions:

> We have often heard it maintained that sciences should be built up on clear and sharply defined basic concepts. In actual fact no science, not even the most exact, begins with such definitions. The true beginning of scientific activity consists rather in describing phenomena and then in proceeding to group, classify and correlate them. Even at the stage of description it is not possible to avoid applying certain abstract ideas to the material in hand, ideas derived from somewhere or other but certainly not from the new observations alone. (Freud, 1915/1957a, p. 117)

Perhaps Freud himself left us with the best description of how he built his theories. In 1900, shortly after the publication of *The Interpretation of Dreams*, he wrote to his friend Wilhelm Fliess confessing that "I am actually not at all a man of science, not an observer, not an experimenter, not a thinker. I am by temperament nothing but a conquistador—an adventurer . . . with all the curiosity, daring, and tenacity characteristic of a man of this sort" (Freud, 1985, p. 398).

Although Freud at times may have seen himself as a conquistador, he also believed that he was constructing a scientific theory. How well does that theory meet the six criteria for a useful theory that we enumerated in Chapter 1?

We have seen that, despite serious difficulties in testing Freud's assumptions, researchers have conducted studies that relate either directly or indirectly to psychoanalytical theory. Westen (1990) has presented an extensive review of much of this research. Because of this current activity, we have rated Freudian theory high in its ability to *generate research*. Second, a useful theory should be *falsifiable*. Because much of the research evidence consistent with Freud's ideas can also be explained by other models, Freudian theory is nearly impossible to falsify. Thus, we rate psychoanalysis very low on its ability to generate falsifiable hypotheses.

A third criterion of any useful theory is its ability to *organize knowledge* into a meaningful framework. Unfortunately, the framework of Freud's personality theory, with its emphasis on the unconscious, is so loose and flexible that seemingly inconsistent data can coexist within its boundaries. Compared with other theories of personality, psychoanalysis ventures more answers to questions concerning why people behave as they do. But only some of these answers come from scientific investigations—most are simply logical extensions of Freud's basic assumptions. Because many psychologists no longer accept most of these assumptions, psychoanalysis receives only a moderate rating on its ability to organize knowledge.

Fourth, a useful theory should serve as *a guide for the solution of practical problems*. Because Freudian theory is unusually comprehensive, many psychoanalytically trained practitioners rely on it to find solutions to practical day-to-day problems. However, psychoanalysis no longer dominates the field of psychotherapy, and most present-day therapists use other theoretical orientations in their practice. Nevertheless, those who do believe in basic Freudian theory rely on psychoanalytic principles in their work with patients as well as their dealings with people outside of therapy. Overall, psychoanalysis receives a low rating as a guide to practice.

The fifth criterion of a useful theory deals with *internal consistency*, including operationally defined terms. Psychoanalysis is an internally consistent theory, if one remembers that Freud wrote over a period of more than 40 years and gradually altered the meaning of some concepts during that time. However, at any single point in time, the theory generally possessed internal consistency, although some specific terms were used with less than scientific rigor.

Does psychoanalysis possess a set of operationally defined terms? Here the theory definitely falls short. Such terms as id, ego, superego, conscious, preconscious, unconscious, oral stage, sadistic-anal stage, phallic stage, Oedipus complex, latent level of dreams, and many others are not operationally defined; that is, they are not spelled out in terms of specific operations or behaviors. Investigators must originate their own particular definition of most psychoanalytic terms. This, of course, can lead to chaos, with different researchers defining the same term in different ways.

Sixth, psychoanalysis is not a simple or *parsimonious* theory, but considering its comprehensiveness and the complexity of human personality, it is not needlessly cumbersome.

CONCEPT OF HUMANITY

In Chapter 1 we outlined several dimensions for a concept of humanity. Where does Freud's theory fall on these various dimensions?

The first of these is *determinism vs. free choice*. On this dimension Freud's views on the nature of human nature would easily fall toward determinism. Freud believed that most of our behavior is determined by past events rather than molded by present goals and that we have little control over our present actions because many of our behaviors are rooted in unconscious strivings that lie beyond our present awareness. Although we usually believe that we are in control of our own lives, Freud believed that, in reality, we have little control over the forces that shape our personality.

Adult personality is largely determined by childhood experiences—especially the Oedipus complex—that have left their residue in the unconscious mind. Freud (1917/1955a) held that humanity in its history has suffered three great blows to its narcissistic ego. The first was the rediscovery by Copernicus that the earth is not the center of the universe; the second was Darwin's discovery that humans are no different from the other animals; the third, and most damaging blow of all, was Freud's own discovery that we are not in control of our own actions or, as he stated it, "the ego is not master in its own house" (Freud, 1917/1955a, p. 143).

A second and related issue is *pessimism vs. optimism*. Again, psychoanalytic theory must be regarded as essentially pessimistic. According to Freud, we come into the world in a basic state of conflict, with life and death forces operating on us from opposing sides. The innate death wish drives us incessantly toward self-destruction or aggression, while the life instinct causes us to seek blindly after pleasure. The ego experiences a more or less permanent state of conflict, attempting to balance the contradictory demands of the id and superego while at the same time making concessions to the external world.

Underneath a thin veneer of civilization, we are savage beasts with a natural tendency to exploit others for sexual and destructive satisfaction. Antisocial behavior lies just underneath the surface of even the most peaceful person, Freud believed. Worse yet, we are not ordinarily aware of the reasons for our behavior nor are we conscious of the hatred we feel for our friends, family, and lovers.

A third approach for viewing humanity is the dimension of *causality vs. teleology*. Basically, Freud believed that our present behavior is mostly shaped by past causes rather than by our goals for the future. We do not move toward a self-determined goal but, instead, are helplessly caught in the struggle between Eros and the death instinct.

These two conservative instincts force us to compulsively repeat primitive patterns of behavior. As adults, our behavior is one long series of reactions. We constantly attempt to reduce tension; to relieve anxieties; to repress unpleasant experiences; to regress to earlier, more secure stages of development; and to compulsively repeat behavior that is familiar and safe.

On the dimension of *conscious vs. unconscious*, psychoanalytic theory obviously leans heavily in the direction of unconscious motivation. Freud believed that everything from slips of the tongue to religious experiences is the result of a deep-rooted desire to satisfy sexual or aggressive instincts. These motives make us slaves to our unconscious. Although we are aware of our actions, Freud believed that the motivations underlying those actions are deeply embedded in our unconscious and are frequently quite different from what we believe them to be.

A fifth dimension is *biology vs. culture*. As a physician, Freud's medical training disposed him to see human personality from a biological viewpoint. Yet Freud (1913/1953, 1985) frequently speculated about the consequences of prehistorical social units and about the consequences of an individual's early social experiences. Because Freud believed that many of our infantile fantasies and anxieties are rooted in biology, we rate him low on social influences on personality.

Sixth is the issue of *uniqueness vs. similarities*. On this dimension, psychoanalytic theory takes a middle position. Our evolutionary past gives rise to a great many similarities among people. Nevertheless, our individual experiences, especially those of early childhood, shape each of us in a somewhat unique manner and account for many of the differences among personalities.

Chapter Summary

The personal traits and experiences of Sigmund Freud permeate and color nearly all aspects of psychoanalytic theory. Freud's character is clearly stamped on the concepts that make up his personality theory. First among these concepts are the three *levels of mental life*—the *unconscious*, *preconscious*, and *conscious*. Freud's exploration of the unconscious mind, including his own, ranks as one of his greatest contributions to our understanding of human personality. Many years after his original investigation of these three levels of mental life, Freud postulated three *provinces of the mind*—the *id*, *ego*, and *superego*. These three regions of personality overlap with, but are not the same as, the three levels of the mind. The id is a completely unconscious, chaotic "cauldron full of seething excitations" (Freud, 1933/1964, p. 73), serving the *pleasure principle* and completely out of contact with reality. The ego is the executive branch of personality, and as the only province of the mind in contact with the real world, it serves the *reality principle*. The superego, which serves the *moral and idealistic principles*, begins to evolve after the resolution of the Oedipus complex, around ages 4 to 6.

The two great *instincts* or drives in Freudian psychology are *sex* and *aggression*. These urges are often punished during childhood and, as a result, become repressed. Nevertheless, a sufficient number of these threatening impulses remain to produce anxiety within the ego. To protect itself against the pain of anxiety, the ego initiates a number of *defense mechanisms*, the most basic of which is *repression*.

Freud suggested three major *stages of development*—*infancy*, *latency*, and a *genital period*. The infantile stage lasts from birth to about ages 4 to 6 and is characterized by the child's first psychosexual experiences. It is the most crucial of the stages in the sense that the foundation for future personality structure is formed then. Infancy is divided into three subphases—*oral*, *anal*, and *phallic*, the last of which is accompanied by the *Oedipus complex*. Following the infantile stage is a period of psychosexual latency that lasts until puberty, at which time the genital stage begins. The genital stage signals the onset of a second, or mature, stage of sexuality. This is the final stage conceptualized by Freud, although psychoanalytic concepts suggest a hypothetical period of psychological maturity.

Both *dreams* and "*Freudian slips*" are disguised means of expressing unconscious impulses. Also, both ordinarily express some hidden wish. Freud used dreams along with *free association* in psychotherapy for the purpose of uncovering portions of the patient's unconscious, thus alleviating neurotic conflicts and symptoms.

Psychoanalytic theory, with its heavy emphasis on such nebulous concepts as the unconscious, presents many difficulties for scientific research. Some present-day researchers and psychotherapists use psychoanalytic concepts to organize knowledge and to treat patients, but most practitioners now view Freud's theory as having very limited practical value. Moreover, psychoanalysis is only moderately parsimonious and is deficient in its use of operationally defined terms.

The Freudian *view of humanity* is essentially pessimistic and deterministic. According to Freud, people must perpetually struggle to balance the sexual and aggressive instincts of the id with the realistic demands of the ego and the restrictive prohibitions of the superego. People are seldom aware of the forces underlying their behavior and, for the most part, have little control over their lives.

Suggested Readings

Freud, S. (1952). An *autobiographical study*. (J. Strachey, Trans.). New York: Norton. (Original work published 1925).
> Freud's own story of his life and work up to 1925. For a more objective account, the reader may wish to supplement this brief autobiography with the writings of such modern "revisionists" as Ellenberger (1970), Gay (1988), Macmillan (1991), Newton (1995), or Sulloway (1992).

Freud, S. (1966). *The complete introductory lectures on psychoanalysis*. (J. Strachey, Trans.). New York: Norton. (Original works published 1917, 1933).
> The best single-volume introduction to the central ideas of psychoanalysis by Freud himself, this book contains Freud's *Introductory Lectures*, first delivered at the University of Vienna from 1915 to 1917, and his *New Introductory Lectures*, which were never delivered, but which contain all the major changes that Freud made in his theory after World War I.

Gay, P. (1988). *Freud: A life for our time*. New York: Norton.
> Although not an easy book to read, Gay's comprehensive, scholarly work is "must" reading for the serious Freud student.

Jacobs, M. (1992). *Sigmund Freud*. London: Sage.
> A readable and brief overview of Freud's life, theory, and therapy, this book also includes a critique of psychoanalysis as a science.

Roazen, P. (1993). *Meeting Freud's family*. Amherst, MA: University of Massachusetts Press.
> Beginning in the mid-1960s, Roazen has interviewed many of Freud's former friends and followers as well as three of his children, including his daughter Anna. The result is an intriguing look at the personal side of Freud.

Jung

An early colleague of Freud, Carl Gustav Jung broke from orthodox psycho-analysis to establish a separate theory of personality called **Analytical Psychology,** which rests on the assumption that occult phenomena can and do influence the lives of all of us. Jung believed that each of us is motivated not only by repressed experiences but also by certain emotionally toned experiences we have inherited from our ancestors. These inherited images make up what Jung called the *collective unconscious.* The collective unconscious includes those elements that we have never experienced individually but which have come down to us from our ancestors.

Some elements of the collective unconscious become highly developed and are called *archetypes.* The most inclusive archetype is the notion of self-realization, which can only be achieved by attaining a balance between various opposing forces. Thus, Jung's theory is a compendium of opposites. People are both introverted and extraverted; rational and irrational; male and female; conscious and unconscious; and pushed by past events while being pulled by future expectations.

Jung saw all people as having both an introverted and an extraverted attitude. If a person relies mostly on conscious introversion, then extraversion is largely uncon-scious. If the extraverted attitude is highly developed on a conscious level, then the introverted attitude remains unconscious. This chapter looks with some detail into the long and colorful life of Carl Jung and uses fragments from his life history to illustrate his concepts and theories. Jung's notion of a collective unconscious makes his theory one of the most intriguing of all conceptions of personality.

BIOGRAPHY OF CARL JUNG

Carl Gustav Jung was born on July 26, 1875, in Kesswil, a town on Lake Constance in Switzerland. His paternal grandfather, the elder Carl Gustav Jung, was a prominent physician in Basel and one of the best-known men of that city. A local rumor suggested that the elder Carl Jung was the illegitimate son of the great German poet, Goethe. Although the elder Jung never acknowledged the rumor, the younger Jung, at least sometimes, believed himself to be the great-grandson of Goethe (Ellenberger, 1970).

Jung's parents were Paul Jung, a minister in the Swiss Reformed Church, and Emilie Preiswerk Jung, the daughter of a theologian. In fact, eight of Jung's uncles were pastors, so both religion and medicine were prevalent in his family. Jung's mother's fam-ily had a tradition of spiritualism and mysticism, and his maternal grandfather, Samuel Preiswerk, was a believer in the occult and often talked to the dead. He kept an empty chair for the ghost of his first wife and had regular and intimate conversations with her. Quite understandably, these practices greatly annoyed his second wife. His grand-daughter Helene Preiswerk (Jung's first cousin) was also a medium and the subject of Jung's medical dissertation on the occult phenomenon. Thus, Jung's interest in spiritu-alism and the occult was acquired as part of a family tradition (Ellenberger, 1970).

Jung's parents had three children, an older son, who lived only 3 days, and a daughter 9 years younger than Carl. The girl was never an important rival of Carl's and did not play a prominent role in his life; thus Carl's early life was that of an only child.

Jung (1961) described his father as a sentimental idealist, with strong doubts about his religious faith. He saw his mother as having two separate dispositions. On one hand, she was realistic, practical, and warm-hearted, but on the other, she was unstable, mystical, and clairvoyant. Carl identified more with this second side of his mother, which he called her No. 2 personality (Alexander, 1990). At age 3, Jung was separated from his mother, who had to be hospitalized for several months. This separation deeply troubled young Carl and for a long time after, he felt distrustful whenever the words "love" or "mother" were mentioned.

Jung was an emotional and sensitive child who felt deeply attached to both parents. His parents' frequent disagreements greatly troubled young Carl because he disliked having to take sides. His mother compounded this confusion by treating him as an adult. She confided in him by telling him things she could not reveal to her husband. Despite her attempts to drive a wedge between the boy and his father, Carl retained a deep affection for both parents.

Before Carl's fourth birthday his family moved to a suburb of Basel. It is from this period that his earliest dream stems. This dream, which was to have a profound effect on his later life and on his concept of a collective unconscious, will be recounted later.

During his school years, Jung gradually became aware of two separate aspects of his self, and he called these his No. 1 and No. 2 personalities. At first he saw both personalities as parts of his own personal world, but during midadolescence he became aware of the No. 2 personality as a reflection of something other than himself—an old man long since dead. At that time Jung did not fully comprehend these separate powers, but in later years he recognized that No. 2 personality had been in touch with feelings and intuitions that No. 1 personality did not perceive. In *Memories*, *Dreams*, *Reflections*, Jung (1961) wrote of his No. 2 personality:

> I experienced him and his influence in a curiously unreflective manner; when he was present, No. 1 personality paled to the point of nonexistence, and when the ego that became increasingly identical with No. 1 personality dominated the scene, the old man, if remembered at all, seemed a remote and unreal dream. (p. 68)

Between his 16th and 19th years, Jung's No. 1 personality emerged as more dominant and gradually "repressed the world of intuitive premonitions" (Jung, 1961, p. 68). As his conscious, everyday personality prevailed, he could concentrate on school and thoughts of a career.

Jung's first choice of a profession was archeology, but he was also interested in philology, history, philosophy, and the natural sciences. Despite a somewhat aristocratic background, Jung had limited financial resources (Noll, 1994). Forced by lack of money to attend a school near home, he enrolled in Basel University, which, however, did not have an archeology teacher. Having to select another field of study, Jung chose natural science because he dreamt twice of making important discoveries in the natural world (Jung, 1961). His choice of a career eventually narrowed to medicine. That choice was narrowed further when he read that psychiatry deals with subjective phenomena. Immediately, Jung became aware that psychiatry was the only possible goal for him (Singer, 1994).

While Jung was still in medical school his father died. Carl then became the head of the family, which at the time included his mother and sister. After completing his medical degree from Basel University in 1900, he became a psychiatric assistant to Eugene Bleuler at Burghöltzli Mental Hospital in Zürich, possibly the most prestigious psychiatric teaching hospital in the world at that time. During 1902–1903, Jung studied for 6 months in Paris with Pierre Janet, successor to Charcot. When he returned to Switzerland in 1903, he married Emma Rauschenbach, a young woman from a wealthy Swiss family. Two years later, while continuing his duties at the hospital, he began teaching at the University of Zürich.

Jung had read Freud's *The Interpretation of Dreams* (Freud, 1900/1953) soon after it appeared, but he was not much impressed with it (Singer, 1994). When he reread the book a few years later, he had a better understanding of Freud's ideas and was moved to begin interpreting his own dreams. By 1906, the two men had begun a steady correspondence (see McGuire & McGlashan, 1994 for the Freud/Jung letters), and the following year Freud invited Jung to Vienna. Immediately, both Freud and Jung developed a strong mutual respect and affection for one another, talking for 13 straight hours during their first meeting (Kerr, 1993). Freud's respect for the younger man led him to groom Jung as his successor and to select him as first president of the International Psychoanalytic Association. In 1909, Jung and Freud were invited to deliver a series of lectures at Clark University in Worcester, Massachusetts. Together with Sándor Ferenczi, another psychoanalyst, the two men journeyed to America, but during their trip an underlying tension between Jung and Freud slowly began to simmer. This personal tension was not diminished when the two now-famous psychoanalysts began to interpret one another's dreams, a pastime likely to strain any relationship. In *Memories, Dreams, Reflections,* Jung (1961) claimed that Freud was both unable to interpret Jung's dreams and unwilling to give Jung the details of his personal life, which Jung needed in order to interpret one of Freud's dreams. According to Jung's account, when asked for intimate details, Freud protested, "But I cannot risk my authority!" (p. 158) At that moment, Jung concluded, Freud indeed lost his authority. "That sentence burned itself into my memory, and in it the end of our relationship was already foreshadowed" (p. 158).

Back in Europe, personal as well as theoretical differences gradually became more intense, and the friendship between Freud and Jung began to cool. In 1913 the two men terminated their personal correspondence, and the following year Jung resigned his presidency and shortly afterward withdrew his membership in the International Psychoanalytic Association (Brome, 1978).

Jung's break with Freud may have related to events not discussed in *Memories, Dreams, Reflections* (Jung, 1961). In 1907, Jung wrote to Freud of his "boundless admiration" for him and confessed that his veneration "has something of the character of a 'religious' crush" and that it had an "undeniable erotic undertone" (McGuire, 1974, p. 95). Jung continued his confession, saying: "This abominable feeling comes from the fact that as a boy I was the victim of a sexual assault by a man I once worshiped" (p. 95). Jung was actually 18 years old at the time of the sexual assault and saw the older man as a fatherly friend in whom he could confide nearly everything. Alan Elms (1994) contended that Jung's erotic feelings toward Freud—coupled with his early experience of the sexual assault by an older man he once worshipped—may have been one of the major reasons why Jung eventually broke from Freud. Elms further suggested that Jung's rejection of Freud's sexual theories may have stemmed from his ambivalent sexual feelings toward Freud.

The years immediately following the break with Freud were filled with loneliness and self-analysis for Jung. From December of 1913 until 1917, he underwent the most profound and dangerous experience of his life—a trip through the underground of his own unconscious psyche. Marvin Goldwert (1992) referred to this time in Jung's life as a period of "creative illness," a term Henri Ellenberger (1970) had used to describe Freud in the years immediately following his father's death (see Chapter 2). Jung's period of "creative illness" was both similar to and different from Freud's self-analysis. Both men began their search for self while in their late 30s or early 40s; Freud as a reaction to the death of his father, Jung as a result of his split with his spiritual father, Freud. Both underwent a period of loneliness and isolation and both were deeply changed by the experience. However, differences also existed. Freud's self-analysis, though not as intense as Jung's, nevertheless lasted longer and became part of his daily routine for the remainder of his life. Freud was filled with outward activity and wrote his first great book, *The Interpretation of Dreams* (Freud, 1900/1953) during the early phase of his self-analysis.

In contrast, Jung published little during the time of his self-analysis and, instead, turned his creative energies inward and became acquainted with what he termed his collective unconscious psyche. During the period of his self-analysis, Jung suspended the formulation of new theoretical concepts and treated his patients by simply listening to and learning from them.

Although his journey into the unconscious was dangerous and painful, it was also necessary and fruitful. By using dream interpretation and active imagination to force himself through his underground journey, Jung eventually was able to create his unique theory of personality. During this period he wrote down his dreams, drew pictures of them, told himself stories, and then followed these stories wherever they moved. Through these procedures he came to an acquaintanceship with his *personal* unconscious. (See Jung, 1979, for a collection of many of his paintings during this period.) Prolonging the method and going more deeply, he came upon the contents of the *collective* unconscious—the archetypes. He heard his anima speak to him in a clear feminine voice; he discovered his shadow, the evil side of his personality; he spoke with the old wise man and the great mother archetypes; and finally, near the end of his journey, he achieved a kind of psychological rebirth called *individuation* (Jung, 1961).

Although he traveled widely in his study of personality, Jung remained a citizen of Switzerland, residing in Küsnacht, near Zürich. He and his wife, who was also an analyst, had five children, four girls and a boy. Jung was a Christian, but not a church-goer. His hobbies included wood carving, stone cutting, and sailing his boat on Lake Constance. He also maintained an active interest in alchemy, archeology, gnosticism, Eastern philosophies, history, religion, mythology, and ethnology.

In 1944, he became professor of medical psychology at the University of Basel, but poor health forced him to resign his position the following year. After his wife died in 1955 he was mostly alone, the "old wise man of Küsnacht." He died on June 6, 1961, in Zürich, 3 weeks short of his 86th birthday. At the time of his death his reputation was worldwide, extending beyond psychology. Jung is popularly regarded as one of the great thinkers of the 20th century (Brome, 1978).

LEVELS OF THE PSYCHE

Jung, like Freud, based his personality theory on the assumption that the mind, or psyche, has both a conscious and an unconscious level. Unlike Freud, however, he strongly asserted that the most important portion of the unconscious springs, not from personal experiences of the individual, but from the distant past of human existence. The psyche, therefore, can be divided into the *conscious* and the *unconscious*, the latter being subdivided into the *personal unconscious* and the *collective unconscious*.

THE CONSCIOUS

According to Jung, **conscious** images are those that are sensed by the ego, whereas unconscious elements have no relationship with the ego. Jung's notion of the **ego** is more restrictive than Freud's. Jung saw the ego as the center of consciousness, but not the core of personality. Ego is not the whole personality, but must be completed by the more comprehensive *self*, the center of personality that is largely unconscious. In a psychologically healthy person, the ego takes a secondary position to the unconscious self (Jung, 1951/1959a). Thus, consciousness plays a relatively minor role in Analytical

Psychology, and an overemphasis on expanding one's conscious psyche can lead to psychological imbalance. Healthy individuals are in contact with themselves and the outer world, of course, but they also allow themselves to experience their unconscious self and thus to achieve *individuation*, a concept we discuss later.

THE UNCONSCIOUS

The **unconscious,** that part of the psyche that adds depth and completeness to personality, refers to all psychic processes that are not related to the ego. Unconsciousness includes all previously conscious images that have been repressed or have merely fallen below the threshold of consciousness. In addition, it comprises those psychic elements that have never been conscious. Many of these elements form the seeds of future consciousness, but some images are not capable of becoming conscious.

The Personal Unconscious

The **personal unconscious** embraces all repressed, forgotten, or subliminally perceived experiences of one particular individual. Our personal unconscious is formed by our individual experiences and is therefore unique to each of us. Our personal unconscious contains repressed infantile memories and impulses, forgotten events, and experiences originally perceived below the threshold of our consciousness. Many of these images can be recalled easily, some remembered with difficulty, and still others are beyond the reach of consciousness. This concept of the personal unconscious differs little from Freud's view of the unconscious and preconscious combined (Jung, 1931/1960b).

Contents of the personal unconscious are called **complexes.** A complex is an emotionally toned conglomeration of associated ideas. For example, a person's experiences with "Mother" may become grouped around an emotion-ladened core so that a person's mother, or even the word *mother*, sparks an emotional response that blocks the smooth flow of thought. Complexes are largely personal, but they may also be partly derived from humanity's collective experience. In the above example, the mother complex comes not only from one's personal relationship with mother but also from the entire species' experiences with mother. In addition, the mother complex is partly formed by a person's conscious image of mother. Thus complexes may be partly conscious and may stem from both the personal and the collective unconscious (Jung, 1928/1960).

The Collective Unconscious

In contrast to the personal unconscious, which results from individual experiences, the **collective unconscious** has roots in the ancestral past of the entire species. It represents Jung's most controversial, and perhaps his most distinctive, concept. The physical contents of the collective unconscious are inherited and pass from one generation to the next as psychic potential. Our distant ancestors' experiences with universal concepts such as God, mother, water, earth, and so forth have been transmitted through the generations so that people in every clime and time have been influenced by our primitive ancestors' primordial experiences (Jung, 1937/1959).

The contents of the collective unconscious do not lie dormant but are active and influence a person's thoughts, emotions, and actions. The collective unconscious is responsible for people's many myths, legends, and religious beliefs. It also produces universal or "big dreams," that is, dreams that have meaning beyond the individual dreamer and are filled with significance for all people (Jung, 1948/1960b).

The collective unconscious does not refer to inherited ideas but rather to our innate tendency to react in a particular way whenever our experiences stimulate a biologically inherited response tendency. For example, a young mother may unexpectedly react with love and tenderness to her newborn infant, even though she previously had negative or neutral feelings toward the fetus. The tendency to respond was part of the woman's innate potential or inherited blueprint, but such innate potential needs an individual experience before it will become activated. Humans, like other animals, come into the world with inherited predispositions to act or react in certain ways if their present experiences touch upon these biologically based predispositions. For example, a man who falls in love at first sight may be greatly surprised and perplexed by his own reactions. His beloved may not resemble his conscious ideal of a woman, yet something within him moves him to be attracted to her. Jung might suggest that the man's collective unconscious contained biologically based impressions of woman and that these impressions were activated when the man first saw his beloved.

How many biologically based predispositions do humans have? Jung said that we have as many of these inherited tendencies as we have typical situations in life. Countless repetitions of these typical situations have made them part of our biological constitution. At first, they are *"forms without content, representing only the possibility of a certain type of perception or action"* (Jung, 1954/1959b, p. 48). With more repetition these forms begin to develop some content and to emerge as *archetypes*.

Archetypes

Archetypes are ancient or archaic images that derive from the collective unconscious. They are similar to complexes in that they are emotionally toned collections of associated images. But whereas complexes are individualized and make up the contents of the personal unconscious, archetypes are generalized and form the contents of the collective unconscious.

Archetypes should also be distinguished from **instincts.** Jung (1948/1960a) defined an instinct as an unconscious physical impulse toward action and saw the archetype as the psychic counterpart to an instinct. Both archetypes and instincts impel a person to action and in both cases the person remains unconscious of the true motives behind the action. In *Man and His Symbols* (1964), written in English shortly before his death, Jung attempted to clarify the relationship between instincts and archetypes.

> What we properly call instincts are physiological urges, and are perceived by the senses. But at the same time, they also manifest themselves in fantasies and often reveal their presence only by symbolic images. These manifestations are what I call the archetypes. (p. 69)

In summary, instincts are unconsciously determined physiological drives, whereas archetypes are unconsciously determined psychological images and are the manifestations of the instincts. Both instincts and archetypes influence behavior and help shape personality; both are biologically determined.

Archetypes *"are not inherited ideas, but mentally expressed instincts*, forms and not contents" (Jung, 1976, p. 188). Archetypes have a biological basis but originate through the repeated experiences of our early ancestors. The potential for countless numbers of archetypes exists within each person, and when a personal experience corresponds to the latent primordial image, the archetype becomes activated, affecting one's personal life.

The archetype itself cannot be directly represented, but, when activated, it expresses itself through several modes, primarily dreams, fantasies, and delusions. During his midlife encounter with his unconscious, Jung had many archetypal dreams and fantasies. He frequently initiated fantasies by imagining that he was descending into a deep cosmic abyss. He could make little sense of his visions and dreams at that time, but later, when he began to understand that dream images and fantasy figures were actually archetypes, these experiences took on a completely new meaning (Jung, 1961).

Dreams are the main source of archetypal material, and certain dreams offer what Jung considered proof for the existence of the archetype. These dreams produce motifs that could not have been known to the dreamer through personal experience. The motifs often coincide with those known to ancient people or to natives of contemporary aboriginal tribes. Jung presented a vivid illustration in one of his earliest dreams, which took place before his fourth birthday. He dreamed he was in a meadow when suddenly he saw a dark rectangular hole in the ground. Fearfully, he descended a flight of stairs and at the bottom encountered a doorway with a round arch covered by a heavy green curtain. Behind the curtain was a dimly lit room with a red carpet running from the entrance to a low platform. On the platform was a throne and on the throne was an elongated object that appeared to Jung to be a large tree trunk.

> It was a huge thing, reaching almost to the ceiling. But it was of a curious composition: it was made of skin and naked flesh, and on top there was something like a rounded head with no face and no hair. On the very top of the head was a single eye, gazing motionlessly upward. (Jung, 1961, p. 12)

Filled with terror, the young boy heard his mother say, "Yes, just look at him. That is the man-eater!" This frightened him even more and jolted him awake.

Jung thought often about the dream, but 30 years would pass before the obvious phallus became apparent to him. An additional number of years were required before he could accept the dream as an expression of his collective unconscious rather than the product of a personal memory trace. In his own interpretation of the dream, the rectangular hole represented death; the green curtain symbolized the mystery of Earth with her green vegetation; the red carpet signified blood; and the tree, resting majestically on a throne, was the erect penis, anatomically accurate in every detail. After interpreting the dream, Jung was forced to conclude that no 3½-year-old boy could produce such universally symbolic material solely from his own experiences. A collective unconscious, common to the species, was Jung's explanation (Jung, 1961).

Jung believed that hallucinations of psychotic patients also offered evidence for universal archetypes. In 1906, while working as a psychiatric assistant at Burghöltzli, Jung observed a paranoid schizophrenic patient looking through a window at the sun. The patient begged the young psychiatrist to observe too.

> He said I must look at the sun with eyes half shut, and then I could see the sun's phallus. If I moved my head from side to side the sun-phallus would move too, and that was the origin of the wind. (Jung, 1931/1960b, p. 150)

Four years later Jung came across a book by the German philologist Albrecht Dieterich that had been edited in 1910 but was originally published in 1903, still some years after the patient was committed. The book, written in Greek, dealt with a liturgy derived from the so-called Paris magic papyrus, which described an ancient rite of the worshippers of Mithras, the Persian god of light. In this liturgy, the initiate was asked to look at the sun until he could see a tube hanging from it. The tube, swinging toward the east and west, was the origin of the wind. Dieterich's account of the sun-phallus of the Mithraic cult was nearly identical to the hallucination of the mental patient who, almost certainly, had no personal knowledge of the ancient initiation rite. Jung offered many similar examples as proof of the existence of archetypes and the collective unconscious (Jung, 1931/1960b).

As noted in Chapter 2, Freud also believed that people collectively inherit predispositions to action. His concept of *phylogenetic endowment*, however, differs somewhat from Jung's formulation. The first difference is a matter of emphasis. Freud looked first to the personal unconscious, and only when individual explanations failed did he resort to the collective. Jung, on the other hand, placed primary emphasis on the collective unconscious and used personal experiences to round out the total personality. The major distinction between the two, however, was Jung's differentiation of the collective unconscious into autonomous forces called *archetypes*, each with a life and a personality of its own.

Although a great number of archetypes exist as vague images, only a few have evolved to the point where they can be conceptualized. The most notable of these include the persona, shadow, anima, animus, great mother, old wise man, hero, and self.

The Persona

That side of personality one shows to the world is designated as the **persona.** The term is well-chosen because it refers to the mask worn by actors in the early theater. Society dictates a particular role for each of us. A physician is expected to adopt a characteristic "bedside manner," a truck driver tries to look and act like a truck driver, and an actor exhibits the style of life demanded by the public (Jung, 1916/1953).

Although the persona is a necessary side of our personality, we should not confuse our public face with our complete self. If we identify too closely with our persona, we remain unconscious of our individuality and are blocked from attaining *self-realization*. True, we must acknowledge society, but if we over-identify with our persona we lose touch with our inner self and remain dependent on society's expectations of us. To become psychologically healthy, Jung believed, we must strike a balance between the demands of society and what we truly are. To be oblivious of one's persona is to underestimate the importance of society, but to be unaware of one's deep individuality is to be nothing (Jung, 1950/1959).

During Jung's near break with reality from 1913 to 1917, he struggled hard to remain in touch with his persona. He knew that he must maintain a normal life, and his work and family provided that contact. He was frequently forced to tell himself, "I have a medical diploma from a Swiss university, I must help my patients, I have a wife and five children, I live at 228 Seestrasse in Küsnacht" (Jung, 1961, p. 189). Such self-talk kept Jung's feet rooted to the ground and reassured him that he really existed.

The Shadow

The **shadow,** the archetype of darkness and repression, represents those qualities we do not wish to acknowledge but attempt to hide from ourselves and others. The shadow consists of morally objectionable tendencies as well as a number of constructive creative qualities, such as instincts and other archetypes that we, nevertheless, are reluctant to face (Jung, 1951/1959a).

Jung contended that to be whole we must continually strive to know our shadow, and that this quest is our *first test of courage*. It is easier to project the dark side of our personality onto others, to see in them the ugliness and evil that we refuse to see in ourselves. To come to grips with the darkness within ourselves is to achieve the "realization of the shadow." Unfortunately, most of us never realize our shadow but identify only with the bright side of our personality. People who never realize their shadow may, nevertheless, come under its power and lead tragic lives, constantly running into "bad luck" and reaping harvests of defeat and discouragement for themselves (Jung, 1954/1959a).

In *Memories, Dreams, Reflections*, Jung (1961) reported a dream that took place at the time of his break from Freud. In this dream his shadow, a brown-skinned savage, killed the hero, a man named Siegfried who represented the German people. Jung interpreted the dream to mean that he no longer needed Sig Freud (Siegfried); thus his shadow performed the constructive task of eradicating his former hero.

The Anima

Like Freud, Jung believed that all humans are psychologically bisexual and possess both a masculine and a feminine side. The feminine side of men, the **anima,** originates in the collective unconscious as an archetype and remains extremely resistant to consciousness. Few men become well-acquainted with their anima because this task requires great courage and is even more difficult than becoming acquainted with their shadow. To overcome the projections of the anima, men must overcome intellectual barriers, delve into the far recesses of their unconscious, and realize the feminine side of their personality. In Jungian psychology, a man's *second test of courage* is to recognize his anima, a task that can only be achieved after he has realized his shadow (Jung, 1954/1959a, 1954/1959b).

Jung first encountered his own anima during his journey through his unconscious psyche soon after his break with Freud. In *Memories, Dreams, Reflections*, Jung (1961, pp. 185–188) vividly describes this experience. One day while writing down his dreams and visions, he began to ponder, "What am I really doing?" He doubted if his work was science, but was uncertain as to what it was. Suddenly, to his astonishment, he heard a clear, distinct feminine voice from within him say, "It is art." He recognized the voice as that of a gifted female patient who had strong positive feelings for him. He protested to the voice that his work was not art, but no answer was immediately forthcoming. Then, returning to his writing, he again heard the voice say, "That is art." When he tried to argue with the voice, no answer came. He reasoned that the "woman from within" had no speech center so he suggested that she use his. This she did, and a lengthy conversation followed.

Intrigued by this "woman from within," Jung (1961) concluded that

> she must be the "soul," in the primitive sense, and I began to speculate on the reasons why the name "anima" was given to the soul. Why was it thought of as feminine? Later I came to see that this inner feminine figure plays a typical, or archetypal, role in the unconscious of a man, and I called her the "anima." The corresponding figure in the unconscious of woman I called the "animus." (p. 186)

Jung believed that the anima originated from early men's experiences with women—mothers, sisters, and lovers—that combined to form a generalized picture of woman. In time, this global concept became embedded in the collective unconscious of all men as the anima archetype. Since prehistoric days, every man has come into the world with a predetermined concept of womanhood that shapes and molds all his relationships with individual women. A man is especially inclined to project his anima onto his wife and to see her not as she really is, but as his personal and collective unconscious have determined her. This can be the source of much misunderstanding in marriage, but it may also be responsible for the alluring mystique woman has in the psyche of men (Hillman, 1985).

A man may dream about a woman with no definite image and no particular identity. The woman represents no one from his personal experience, but enters his dream from the depths of his collective unconscious. The anima need not appear in dreams as a woman, but can be represented by a feeling or mood (Jung, 1945/1953).

The anima influences the feeling side in man and is the explanation for certain irrational moods and feelings. During these moods a man almost never admits that his feminine side is casting her spell, but instead, he either ignores the irrationality of the feelings or tries to explain them in a very rational masculine manner. In either event he denies that an autonomous archetype, the anima, is responsible for his mood.

The anima's deceptive qualities were elucidated by Jung (1961) in his description of the "woman from within" who spoke to him during his journey into the unconscious and while he was contemplating whether his work was science.

> What the anima said seemed to me full of a deep cunning. If I had taken these fantasies of the unconscious as art, they would have carried no more conviction than visual perceptions, as if I were watching a movie. I would have felt no moral obligation toward them. The anima might then have easily seduced me into believing that I was a misunderstood artist, and that my so-called artistic nature gave me the right to neglect reality. If I had followed her voice, she would in all probability have said to me one day, "Do you imagine the nonsense you're engaged in is really art? Not a bit." Thus the insinuations of the anima, the mouthpiece of the unconscious, can utterly destroy a man. (p. 187)

The Animus

The masculine archetype in women is called the **animus.** Whereas the anima represents irrational moods and feelings, the animus is symbolic of thinking and reasoning. It is capable of influencing the thinking of a woman, yet it does not actually belong to her. It belongs to the collective unconscious and originates from the encounters of prehistoric women with men. In every relationship a woman has with a man, she runs the risk of projecting her distant ancestors' experiences with fathers, brothers, lovers, and sons onto the unsuspecting man. In addition, of course, her personal experiences with men, buried in her personal unconscious, enter into her relationships with men. Couple this with projections from the man's anima and with images from his personal unconscious, and one has the basic ingredients of any male-female relationship.

Jung believed that the animus is responsible for thinking and opinion in women just as the anima produces feelings and moods in men. The animus is also the explanation for the irrational thinking and illogical opinions often attributed to women. Many opinions held by women are objectively valid, but according to Jung, close analysis reveals that they were not thought out, but existed ready-made. If a woman is dominated by her animus, no logical or emotional appeal can shake her from her prefabricated beliefs (Jung, 1951/1959a).

The Great Mother

Two other archetypes, the great mother and the old wise man, are derivatives of the anima and animus. Everyone, man or woman, possesses a **great mother** archetype. This preexisting concept of mother is always associated with both positive and negative feelings. Jung (1954/1959c), for example, spoke of the "loving and terrible mother." The great mother, therefore, represents two opposing forces—fertility and nourishment on the one hand and power and destruction on the other. She is capable of producing and sustaining life (fertility and nourishment), but she may also devour or neglect her offspring (destruction).

The fertility and nourishment dimension of the great mother archetype is symbolized by a tree, garden, plowed field, sea, heaven, home, country, church, and hollow objects such as ovens and cooking utensils. Because the great mother also represents power and destruction, she is sometimes symbolized as a *grand*mother, the Mother of God, Mother Nature, Mother Earth, or a witch.

Fertility and power combine to form the concept of *rebirth*, which may be a separate archetype, but its relation to the great mother is obvious. Rebirth is represented by such processes as reincarnation, baptism, resurrection, and individuation. This concept always remains somewhat unconscious because it derives from an inherited archetypal image (Jung, 1952/1956, 1954/1959c).

The strong fascination mother has for both men and women, often in the absence of a close personal relationship, was taken by Jung as evidence for the great mother archetype. Legends, myths, religious beliefs, art, and literature of all kinds are filled with symbols of the great mother, a person who is both nurturing and destructive.

The Old Wise Man

The archetype of wisdom and meaning, the **old wise man,** symbolizes our preexisting knowledge of the mysteries of life. This archetypal meaning, however, is unconscious and cannot be directly or individually experienced. Politicians and others who speak authoritatively (but not authentically) often sound sensible and wise to others who are all too willing to be misled by their own old wise man archetypes. Similarly, the wizard in Frank Baum's *Wizard of Oz*, modeled after the politician William Jennings Bryan, was an impressive and captivating speaker whose words, however, rang hollow. A man or woman dominated by the old wise man archetype may gather a large following of disciples by using verbiage that sounds profound but really makes little sense because the collective unconscious cannot directly impart its wisdom to an individual. Political, religious, and social prophets who appeal to reason as well as emotion (archetypes are always emotionally tinged) are guided by this unconscious archetype. The danger to society comes when people become swayed by the pseudo knowledge of a powerful prophet and mistake nonsense for real wisdom.

The old wise man archetype is personified in dreams as father, grandfather, teacher, philosopher, guru, doctor, or priest. He appears in fairy tales as the king, the sage, or the magician who comes to the aid of the troubled hero and, through superior wisdom, helps him escape from his current misadventures. The old wise man is also symbolized by life itself. Literature is replete with stories of young people leaving home, venturing out into the world, experiencing the trials and sorrows of life, and in the end acquiring a measure of wisdom (Jung, 1954/1959a).

The Hero

The **hero** archetype is represented in mythology and legends as a powerful man, sometimes part god, who fights against great odds to conquer or vanquish evil in the form of dragons, monsters, serpents, or demons. In the end, however, the hero often is undone by some seemingly insignificant person or event (Jung, 1951/1959b). For example, Achilles, the courageous hero of the Trojan War, was killed by an arrow in his only vulnerable spot—his heel. Similarly, Macbeth was a heroic figure with a single tragic flaw—ambition. This was also the source of his greatness, but it contributed to his fate and his downfall. Heroic deeds can only be performed by someone who is vulnerable, such as Achilles or the comic book character Superman; an immortal person with no weakness cannot be a hero.

The image of the hero touches an archetype within us, as demonstrated by our fascination with the heros of movies, novels, plays, and television programs. When the

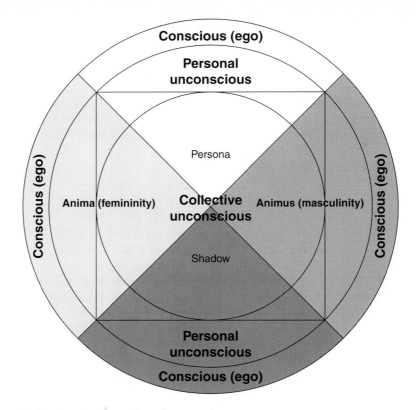

Figure 3.1   Jung's conception of personality.

hero conquers the villain, he frees us from feelings of impotence and misery; at the same time, he serves as our model for the ideal personality (Jung, 1934/1954a).

The origin of the hero motif goes back to earliest human history—to the dawn of consciousness. In conquering the villain, the hero is symbolically overcoming the darkness of prehuman unconsciousness. The achievement of consciousness was one of our ancestors' greatest accomplishments, and the image of the archetypal conquering hero represents victory over the forces of darkness (Jung, 1951/1959b).

The Self
Jung believed that each of us possesses an inherited tendency to move toward growth, perfection, and completion, and he called this innate disposition the **self.** The most comprehensive of all archetypes, the self can be seen as the *archetype of archetypes* because it pulls together the other archetypes and unites them in the process of **self-realization.** Like the other archetypes, it possesses conscious and personal unconscious components, but it is mostly formed by collective unconscious images.

As an archetype, the self is symbolized by our ideas of perfection, completion, and wholeness, but its ultimate symbol is the **mandala,** which is depicted as a circle within a square, a square within a circle, or any other concentric figure. It represents the strivings of the collective unconscious for unity, balance, and wholeness.

The self includes both personal and collective unconscious images and thus should not be confused with the ego, which represents consciousness only. In Figure 3.1, consciousness (the ego) is represented by the outer circle and is only a small part of total personality; the personal unconscious is depicted by the middle circle; the collective unconscious is represented by the inner circle; and totality of all three circles symbolizes the self. Only four archetypes—persona, shadow, animus, and anima—have been drawn in this mandala, and each has been idealistically depicted as being the same size. For most people the persona is more conscious than the shadow, and the shadow may be more accessible to consciousness than either the anima or the animus. As shown in Figure 3.1, each archetype is partly conscious, partly personal unconscious, and partly collective unconscious.

The balance shown in Figure 3.1 between consciousness and the total self is also somewhat idealistic. Many people have an overabundance of consciousness and thus lack the "soul spark" of personality; that is, they fail to realize the richness and vitality of their personal unconscious and especially of their collective unconscious. On the other hand, people who are overpowered by their unconscious are often pathological, with one-sided personalities (Jung, 1951/1959a).

Although the self is almost never perfectly balanced, each person has in the collective unconscious a concept of the perfect, unified self. The mandala represents the perfect self, the archetype of order, unity, and totality. Because self-realization involves completeness and wholeness, it is represented by the same symbol of perfection (the mandala) that sometimes signifies divinity. In the collective unconscious, the self appears as an ideal personality, sometimes taking the form of Jesus Christ, Buddha, or other deified figures.

Jung found evidence for the self archetype in the mandala symbols that appear in dreams and fantasies of contemporary people who have never been conscious of their meaning. Historically, people produced countless mandalas without appearing to have understood their full significance. Jung (1951/1959a) believed that psychotic patients experience an increasing number of mandala motifs in their dreams at the exact time that they are undergoing a period of serious psychic disorder and that this experience is further evidence that people strive for order and balance. It is as if the unconscious symbol of order counterbalances the conscious manifestation of disorder.

In summary, the self includes both the conscious and unconscious mind, and it unites the opposing elements of psyche—male and female, good and evil, light and dark forces. These opposing elements are often represented by the yang and yin (see Figure 3.2), whereas the self is usually symbolized by the mandala. This latter motif stands for unity, totality, and order; that is, *self-realization*. Complete self-realization is seldom if ever achieved, but as an ideal it exists within the collective unconscious of everyone. To actualize or fully experience the self, we must overcome our fear of the unconscious; prevent our persona from dominating our personality; recognize the dark side of ourselves (our shadow); and then muster even greater courage to face our anima or animus.

On one occasion during Jung's midlife crisis, he had a vision in which he confronted a bearded old man who was living with a beautiful blind young girl and a large black snake. The old man explained that he was Elijah and that the young girl was Salome, both biblical figures. Elijah had a certain, sharp intelligence, although Jung did not clearly understand him. Salome gave Jung a feeling of distinct suspiciousness, while the serpent showed a remarkable fondness for Jung. At the time he experienced this vision, Jung was unable to comprehend its meaning, but many years later he came to see the three figures as archetypes. Elijah represented the old wise man, seemingly intelligent, but not making a good deal of sense; the blind Salome was an anima figure, beautiful and seductive, but unable to see the meaning of things; and the snake was the counterpart of the hero, showing an affinity for Jung, the hero of the vision (Jung, 1961). Jung believed that he had to identify these unconscious images in order

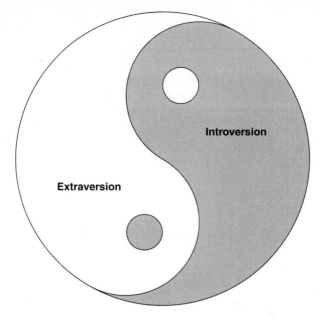

Figure 3.2 The yang and yin.

to maintain his own identity and not lose himself to the powerful forces of the collective unconscious. He later wrote:

> The essential thing is to differentiate oneself from these unconscious contents by personifying them, and at the same time to bring them into relationship with consciousness. That is the technique for stripping them of their power. It is not too difficult to personify them, as they always possess a certain degree of autonomy, a separate identity of their own. Their autonomy is a most uncomfortable thing to reconcile oneself to, and yet the very fact that the unconscious presents itself in that way gives us the best means of handling it. (p. 187)

DYNAMICS OF PERSONALITY

Jung believed that the same principles apply to both physical and psychic energy, and this section looks at his ideas on *equivalence* and *entropy*, *causality* and *teleology*, and *progression* and *regression*.

PRINCIPLES OF EQUIVALENCE AND ENTROPY

From physics, Jung borrowed the principles of equivalence and entropy to explain human motivation. The first law of thermodynamics, the **principle of equivalence,** states that when a given quantity of energy is expended in the performance of an activity, an equal amount of energy will appear elsewhere (Jung, 1928/1960). In other words, energy cannot be destroyed but is merely displaced. Transferred to psychology, this principle holds that for each psychic system a given quantity of energy is available, either actually or potentially. When one psychic function no longer demands a constant expenditure of energy, that same amount of energy is available to perform a second function. The total amount of energy, however, remains the same. For example, we expend some psychic energy whenever we repress an anxiety-provoking image. If the repressed material continually and forcefully threatens to emerge into our consciousness, we must use more energy from other sources to maintain the repression. As a result, we are handicapped in our intellectual functioning, interpersonal relationships, and other activities that demand the free use of psychic energy. Most repressions, fortunately, drain only small amounts of psychic energy, thus freeing the remainder to perform other psychic functions.

The second law of thermodynamics, the **principle of entropy,** states that when objects of different temperatures meet, heat flows from the hotter one into the colder one, bringing about an equalization of temperature. In Jungian psychology, the principle of entropy holds that the greater the differences between two poles, the greater the tension generated by them, and the longer lasting and more satisfying the resulting attitude.

The principle of entropy can also be stated this way: The stronger the conflict within a person, the greater the measure of psychic energy flowing from the conflict. Once resolved, strong conflict situations lead to an equalization of tension, a relatively permanent attitude, and the pleasant experience of overcoming a troublesome obstacle. Thus, we experience more satisfaction in conquering a formidable opponent than in defeating an easy one.

The principle of entropy is responsible for the stability of values in most older people. After the stormy tensions unleashed in youth by the confrontation of opposites, psychic energy gradually achieves a leveling process that solidifies attitudes, opinions, and prejudices. Older people do not necessarily possess less psychic energy than younger ones; they merely transform the oscillating activity of youth into the balanced stability of old age (Jung, 1928/1960).

CAUSALITY AND TELEOLOGY

Does motivation spring from past causes or from teleological goals? Jung insisted that it comes from both. **Causality** holds that present events have their origin in previous experiences. Freud, for example, relied heavily on a causal viewpoint in his explanations of adult behavior in terms of early childhood experiences. Jung criticized Freud for being one-sided in his emphasis on causality and insisted that a causal view could not explain all motivation. Conversely, **teleology** holds that present events are motivated by goals and aspirations for the future that direct our destiny. Adler, for example, held this position, insisting that people are motivated by unconscious perceptions of fictional final goals (see Chapter 4). Jung was less critical of Adler, but he insisted that human behavior is shaped by *both* causal and teleological forces, and that causal explanations must be balanced with teleological ones.

Jung's insistence on balance is seen in his conception of dreams. He agreed with Freud that many dreams have their origins in past events; that is, they are caused by earlier experiences. On the other hand, Jung claimed that some dreams can help a person make decisions about the future, just as dreams of making important discoveries in the natural sciences eventually led to Jung's own career choice.

PROGRESSION AND REGRESSION

To achieve self-realization, people must adapt not only to their outside environment but to their inner world as well. Adaptation to the outside world involves the forward flow of psychic energy and is called **progression,** whereas adaptation to the inner world relies on a backward flow of psychic energy and is called **regression.** Both progression and regression are essential if we are to achieve individual growth or self-realization.

Progression inclines a person to react consistently to a given set of environmental conditions, whereas regression is a necessary backward step in the successful attainment of a goal. Regression activates the unconscious psyche, an essential aid in the solution of most problems. Alone, neither progression nor regression leads to development. Either can bring about too much one-sidedness and failure in adaptation; but the two, working together, can activate the process of healthy personality development (Jung, 1928/1960).

Regression is exemplified in Jung's midlife crisis, during which time his psychic life was turned inward toward the unconscious and away from any significant outward accomplishments. He spent most of his energy becoming acquainted with his unconscious psyche and did little in the way of writing or lecturing. Regression dominated his life while progression nearly ceased. Subsequently, he emerged from this period with a greater balance of the psyche and once again became interested in the extraverted world. However, his regressive experiences with the introverted world had left him permanently and profoundly changed. Jung believed that the regressive step is necessary to create a balanced personality and to grow toward self-realization (Jung, 1961).

TYPOLOGY OF THE PSYCHE

Besides the levels and the dynamics of the psyche, Jung recognized various psychological types, which grow out of a union of two basic *attitudes*—introversion and extraversion—and four separate *functions*—thinking, feeling, sensing, and intuiting.

ATTITUDES

An **attitude** is a predisposition to act or react in a characteristic direction. Jung insisted that each person has both an *introverted* and an *extraverted* attitude. If introversion is conscious, then extraversion is unconscious; if extraversion is conscious, then introversion is unconscious. Like other opposing forces in Analytical Psychology, introversion and extraversion serve in a compensatory relationship to one another and can be illustrated by the yang and yin motif (see Figure 3.2).

Introversion

According to Jung, **introversion** is the turning inward of psychic energy with an orientation toward the subjective. Introverts are tuned in to their inner world with all its biases, fantasies, dreams, and individualized perceptions. These people perceive the external world, of course, but they do so selectively and with their own subjective view (Jung, 1921/1971).

The introverted personality is clearly illustrated by Jung, first through his No. 2 childhood personality and second by his midlife confrontation with his unconscious when he carried on conversations with his anima, experienced bizarre dreams, and induced strange visions that were the "stuff of psychosis" (Jung, 1961, p. 188). During his nearly completely introverted midlife crisis, his fantasies were individualized and subjective. Other people, including even Jung's wife, could not accurately comprehend what he was experiencing. He suspended or discontinued much of his extraverted or objective attitude, no longer actively treated his patients, resigned his position as lecturer at the University of Zürich, stopped his theoretical writing, and for 3 years, found himself "utterly incapable of reading a scientific book" (p. 193). He was in the process of discovering the introverted pole of his existence.

Jung's voyage of discovery, however, was not totally introverted. He knew that unless he retained some objective hold on the outer world, he would risk becoming absolutely possessed by his inner world. Afraid that he might become completely psychotic, he forced himself to continue as much of a normal life as possible with his family and his profession. By this technique, Jung eventually emerged from his inner journey and established a balance between introversion and extraversion.

Extraversion

In contrast to introversion, **extraversion** is the attitude characterized by the turning outward of psychic energy so that a person is oriented toward the objective and away from the subjective. Extraverts are more influenced by their surroundings than by their inner world. They tend to focus on the objective attitude while suppressing the subjective. Like Jung's childhood No. 1 personality, they are pragmatic and well-rooted in the realities of everyday life. At the same time, they are overly suspicious of the subjective attitude, whether their own or that of someone else.

Few people are either completely introverted or completely extraverted. Most have some elements of both attitudes; that is, they are influenced by both the subjective and the objective world. Also, introversion and extraversion should be equally valued. Each tendency has strengths as well as weaknesses, and psychologically healthy people attain a balance of the two attitudes, feeling equally comfortable with their internal and external worlds.

FUNCTIONS

Both introversion and extraversion can combine with any one or more of four functions, forming eight possible orientations, or **types.** The four functions—sensation, thinking, feeling, and intuition—can be briefly defined as follows. Sensation tells us what something is; thinking enables us to recognize its meaning; feeling tells us its value; and intuition allows us to "see around corners" and gain knowledge of it without knowing how we know.

Thinking

Logical intellectual activity that produces a chain of ideas is called **thinking.** The thinking type can be either extraverted or introverted, depending on a person's basic attitude.

Extraverted thinking flows primarily from objective phenomena and is essentially a conscious process. Extraverted thinking people rely heavily on concrete thoughts, but may also use abstract ideas if these ideas have been transmitted to them from without, for example, from parents or teachers. Mathematicians and engineers make frequent use of extraverted thinking in their work. Accountants, too, are extraverted thinking types because they must be objective and not subjective in their approach to numbers. Not all objective thinking, however, is productive. If too little individual interpretation is brought to objective data, the resulting process is merely the presentation of previously known facts, with no originality or creativity (Jung, 1921/1971).

Thinking involves a subject (the thinker) and an object (the ideas thought about). In this sense, it is both subjective and objective, but when the subjective is dominant it is called *introverted thinking*. Introverted thinking people react to external stimuli, but their interpretation of an event is colored more by the internal meaning they bring with them than by the objective facts themselves. Inventors and philosophers are often introverted thinking types because they react to the objective world in a highly subjective and creative manner, interpreting old data in new ways. When carried to an extreme, introverted thinking results in unproductive mystical thoughts that are so individualized that they are useless to any other person (Jung, 1921/1971).

Feeling

The process of valuing an idea or event is called **feeling.** In Analytical Psychology, the term *feeling* is limited to affective *value* responses, such as "I feel sorry for him," or "That is a funny story." It excludes the processes of sensing and intuiting that are sometimes confused with the feeling function. When a person says, "This surface feels smooth," she is using her sensing function, and when she says, "I have a feeling that this will be my lucky day," she is intuiting, not feeling.

The feeling function should be distinguished from emotion. Feeling is the valuation of every conscious activity, even those valued as indifferent. Most of these valuations have no emotional content, but are capable of becoming emotions if their intensity increases to the point of stimulating physiological changes within the person. Emotions, however, are not limited to feelings; any of the four functions can lead to emotion when their strength is increased.

Like the other functions, feeling can be either extraverted or introverted. *Extraverted feeling* people use objective data to make valuations. They are not guided so much by their subjective opinion, but by external values and widely accepted standards of judgment. They are likely to be at ease in social situations, knowing on the spur of the moment what to say and how to say it. They are usually well liked because of their sociability, but in their quest to conform to social standards they may appear artificial, cold, and unreliable. Their value judgments will have an easily detectable false ring. Extraverted feeling people often become businesspeople or politicians because these professions demand and reward the making of value judgments based on objective information (Jung, 1921/1971).

Introverted feeling people base their value judgments primarily on subjective perceptions rather than objective facts. Critics of the various art forms make much use of introverted feeling, making value judgments on the basis of subjective individualized data. These people have an individualized conscience, a taciturn demeanor, and an unfathomable psyche. They ignore traditional opinions and beliefs, and their nearly complete indifference to the objective world (including people) often causes persons around them to feel uncomfortable and to cool their attitude toward them (Jung, 1921/1971).

Sensation

The psychic function that receives physical stimuli and transmits them to perceptual consciousness is called **sensation.** Sensation is not identical to the physical stimulus, but is simply the individual's perception of sensory impulses. These perceptions are not dependent on logical thinking or feeling, but exist as absolute, elementary facts within each person.

Sensations may be perceived with either an extraverted or an introverted attitude. *Extraverted sensing* people perceive external stimuli objectively, in much the same way that these stimuli exist in reality. Their sensations are not greatly influenced by their subjective attitudes. This facility is essential in such occupations as proofreader, house painter, wine taster, or any other job demanding sensory discriminations congruent with those of most people (Jung, 1921/1971).

Introverted sensing people are largely influenced by their subjective sensations of sight, sound, taste, touch, and so forth. They are guided by their interpretation of sense stimuli rather than the stimuli themselves. The introverted sensing attitude can be illustrated by asking several people to describe or reproduce accurately a picture exposed to them for a short length of time. Extraverted sensing people will vary little in their reproductions, whereas introverted sensing people will have widely different interpretations. Portrait artists, especially those whose paintings are extremely personalized, rely on an introverted-sensing attitude. They give a subjective interpretation to objective phenomena, yet are able to communicate meaning to others. When the subjective sensing attitude is carried to its extreme, however, it may result in hallucinations or esoteric and incomprehensible speech (Jung, 1921/1971).

Intuition

Perhaps the most difficult function to understand or describe is **intuition,** which involves perception beyond the workings of consciousness. Intuition, like sensation, is based on the perception of absolute elementary facts, ones that provide the raw material for the thinking and feeling functions. It differs from sensation in that it is more creative, often adding or subtracting elements from conscious sensation.

Intuition, too, can be extraverted or introverted. *Extraverted intuitive people* are oriented toward facts in the external world. Rather than fully sensing them, however, they merely perceive them subliminally. Because strong sensory stimuli interfere with intuition, intuitive people suppress many of their sensations and are guided by hunches and guesses contrary to sensory data. An example of an extraverted intuitive type might be inventors who must inhibit distracting sensory data and concentrate on unconscious solutions to objective problems. They may create things that fill a need few other people realized existed. Often inventors remain unaware of the inner workings of their inventive process (Jung, 1921/1971).

Introverted intuition is unconscious perception of facts that are basically subjective. These internal facts usually have little or no resemblance to external reality but exist in the unconscious as psychological reality. Subjective intuitive perceptions are often remarkably strong and capable of motivating decisions of monumental magnitude. Introverted intuitive people, such as mystics, prophets, surrealistic artists, or religious fanatics, often appear peculiar to people of other types who have little comprehension of their motives. Actually, Jung (1921/1971) believed that intuitive introverted people may not clearly understand their own motivations, yet they are deeply moved by them. The eight Jungian types with some possible examples are seen in Table 3.1.

Table 3.1 *Examples of the Eight Jungian Types*

Functions	Attitudes	
	Introversion	*Extraversion*
Thinking	Philosophers, theoretical scientists, certain inventors	Research scientists, accountants, mathematicians
Feeling	Subjective movie critics, editorial writers	Real estate appraisers, objective movie critics, politicians
Sensation	Artists, classical musicians	Wine tasters, proofreaders, house painters, popular musicians
Intuition	Prophets, mystics, religious fanatics	Certain inventors, religious reformers

The functions usually appear in a hierarchy, with one occupying a *superior* position, another, a *secondary* position, and the other two, *inferior* positions. Jung regarded thinking and feeling as **rational functions** because they require reason and judgment. Both functions rely on raw data gathered through analyzing and synthesizing sensation and intuition, making deductions, and drawing conclusions. In other words, both are involved in the reasoning process; thinking is required in intellectual decisions, feeling in value judgments. The processes of thinking and feeling are always rational, but the decisions and judgments are not necessarily valid or "reasonable."

Sensation and *intuition*, on the other hand, are **irrational functions.** They are not subject to the laws of reason because both involve the immediate perception of data with no judgment or reasoning required. Facts gathered through sensation and intuition have an absolute existence independent of the rational functions.

Most people cultivate only one function so that they characteristically approach a situation relying on the one dominant or superior function. Some people develop two functions, and a few very mature individuals have cultivated three. A person who has theoretically achieved self-realization or individuation would have all four functions highly developed.

The four functions are like the points on a compass, with the self in the center facing a given direction, but using all four points as guides (Jung, 1921/1971) (see Figure 3.3).

DEVELOPMENT OF PERSONALITY

Jung believed that personality develops through a series of stages that culminate in individuation. In contrast to Freud, he emphasized the second half of life, the period after age 35 or 40, when a person has the opportunity to bring together the various aspects of personality and to attain self-realization. However, the opportunity for degeneration and neurotic reactions is also present at that time. The direction that people travel depends on their ability to achieve balance between the poles of the various opposing processes. This ability is proportional to the success achieved in journeying through the previous stages of life.

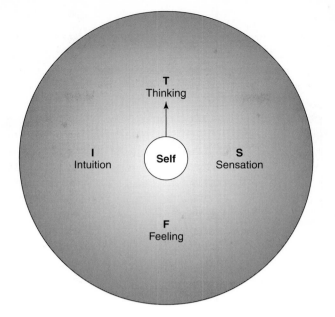

Figure 3.3   The four functions are like points on a compass, with the self facing one direction but using all four points as guides.

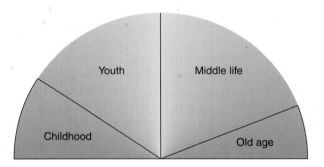

Figure 3.4   Jung compares the stages of life to the sun's journey through the sky, with the brilliance of the sun representing consciousness.

STAGES OF DEVELOPMENT

The stages of life can be grouped into four general periods—*childhood, youth, middle life, and old age.* Jung compared the trip through life to the journey of the sun through the sky, with the brightness of the sun representing consciousness. The early morning sun is childhood, full of potential, but still lacking in brilliance (consciousness); the morning sun is youth, climbing toward the zenith, but unaware of the impending decline; the early afternoon sun is middle life, brilliant like the late morning sun, but obviously headed for the sunset; the evening sun is old age, its once bright consciousness now markedly dimmed (see Figure 3.4). Jung (1931/1960a) argued that values, ideals, and modes of behavior suitable for the morning of life are inappropriate for the second half, and that people must learn to find new meaning in their declining years of life.

Childhood

Jung divided childhood into three substages: (1) the anarchic; (2) the monarchic; and (3) the dualistic. The *anarchic phase* is characterized by chaotic and sporadic consciousness. "Islands of consciousness" may exist, but there is little or no connection between these islands. Experiences of the anarchic phase sometimes enter consciousness as primitive images, incapable of being accurately verbalized.

The *monarchic phase* of childhood is characterized by the development of the ego and by the beginning of logical and verbal thinking. During this time children see themselves objectively and often refer to themselves in the third person. The islands of consciousness become larger, more numerous, and inhabited by a primitive ego. Although the ego is perceived as an object, it is not yet aware of itself as perceiver.

The ego as perceiver arises during the *dualistic phase* of childhood when the ego is divided into the objective and subjective. Children now refer to themselves in the first person and are aware of their existence as separate individuals. During the dualistic period, the islands of consciousness become continuous land, inhabited by an ego-complex that recognizes itself as both object and subject (Jung, 1931/1960a).

Youth

The period from puberty until middle life is called youth. Young people strive to gain psychic and physical independence from their parents, find a mate, raise a family, and make a place in the world. According to Jung (1931/1960a), it is, or should be, a period of increased activity, maturing sexuality, growing consciousness, and recognition that the problem-free era of childhood is gone forever. The major difficulty facing youth is to overcome the natural tendency (found also in middle and later years) to cling to the narrow consciousness of childhood, thus avoiding problems pertinent to the present time of life. This desire to live in the past is called the *conservative principle*.

A person with advancing age who attempts to hold on to youthful values faces a crippled second half of life, handicapped in the capacity to achieve self-realization and impaired in the ability to establish new goals and seek new meaning to life (Jung, 1931/1960a).

Middle Life

Jung believed that middle life begins at approximately age 35 or 40, by which time the sun has passed its zenith and begins its downward descent. Although this decline can present middle-aged people with increasing anxieties, middle life is also a period of tremendous potentiality.

If middle-aged people retain the social and moral values of their early life, they become rigid and fanatical in trying to hold on to their physical attractiveness and agility. Finding their ideals shifting, they may fight desperately to maintain their youthful appearance and lifestyle. Most of us, wrote Jung (1931/1960a) are unprepared to "take the step into the afternoon of life; worse still, we take this step with the false assumption that our truths and ideals will serve us as hitherto. . . . we cannot live in the afternoon of life according to the programme of life's morning; for what was great in the morning will be little at evening, and what in the morning was true will at evening have become a lie" (p. 399).

How can middle life be lived to its fullest? People who have lived youth by neither childish nor middle-aged values are well prepared to advance to middle life and to live fully during that stage. They are capable of giving up the extraverted goals of youth and moving in the introverted direction of expanded consciousness. Their psychological health is not enhanced by success in business, prestige in society, or satisfaction with family life. They must look forward to the future with hope and anticipation, surrender the lifestyle of youth, and discover new meaning in middle life. This often, but not always, involves a mature religious orientation, especially a belief in some sort of life after death (Jung, 1931/1960a).

Old Age

As the evening of life approaches, people experience a diminution of consciousness just as the light and warmth of the sun diminish at dusk. If people fear life during the early years, then they will almost certainly fear death during the later ones. Fear of death is often taken as normal, but Jung believed that death is the goal of life, and that life can only be fulfilling when death is seen in this light. In 1934, during his 60th year, Jung wrote:

> Ordinarily we cling to our past and remain stuck in the illusion of youthfulness. Being old is highly unpopular. Nobody seems to consider that not being able to grow old is just as absurd as not being able to outgrow child's-size shoes. A still infantile man of thirty is surely to be deplored, but a youthful septuagenarian—isn't that delightful? And yet both are perverse, lacking in style, psychological monstrosities. A young man who does not fight and conquer has missed the best part of his youth, and an old man who does not know how to listen to the secrets of the brooks, as they tumble down from the peaks to the valleys, makes no sense; he is a spiritual mummy who is nothing but a rigid relic of the past. (Jung, 1934/1960, p. 407)

Most of Jung's patients were middle-aged or older, and many of them suffered from a backward orientation, clinging desperately to goals and lifestyles of the past and going through the motions of life aimlessly. Jung treated these people by helping them establish new goals and find meaning in living by first finding meaning in death. He accomplished this through dream interpretation, because the dreams of elderly people are often filled with symbols of rebirth, such as long journeys or changes in location. Jung used these and other symbols to determine patients' unconscious attitudes toward death and to help them discover a meaningful philosophy of life (Jung, 1934/1960).

SELF-REALIZATION

Psychological rebirth, also called *self-realization* or **individuation,** was defined by Jung (1939/1959; 1945/1953) as the process of becoming an individual or whole person. Analytical Psychology is essentially a psychology of opposites, and self-realization is the process of integrating the opposite poles into a single homogeneous individual. This process of "coming to selfhood" means that a person has all psychological components functioning in unity, with no psychic process atrophying. A person who has gone through this process has achieved realization of the self; has minimized the persona while actualizing the individual; has become conscious of the anima or animus; has acquired a workable balance between introversion and extraversion; and, perhaps most difficult of all, has elevated all four functions to a superior position.

Self-realization is relatively rare and is achieved only by people who are able to assimilate their unconscious into their total personality. To come to terms with the unconscious is a difficult process that demands courage to face the evil nature of one's shadow and even greater fortitude to accept one's feminine or masculine side. This process is almost never achieved before middle life and then only by men and women who are able to remove the ego as the dominant concern of personality and replace it with the self. The self-realized person must allow the unconscious self to become the core of personality. To merely expand consciousness is to inflate the ego and to produce a one-sided person who lacks the soul spark of personality. The self-realized person is dominated neither by unconscious processes nor by the conscious ego, but achieves a balance between all aspects of personality.

Self-realized people are able to contend with both their external and their internal worlds. Unlike psychotic individuals, they live in the real world and make necessary concessions to it. However, unlike average people, they are neither ignorant nor distrustful of the regressive process that leads to self-discovery. Seeing unconscious images as potential material for new psychic life, self-realized people welcome these images as they appear in dreams and introspective reflections (Jung 1939/1959; 1945/1953).

JUNG'S METHODS OF INVESTIGATION

Jung looked beyond psychology in his search for data to build his conception of humanity. He made no apologies for his ventures into the fields of sociology, history, anthropology, biology, physics, philology, religion, mythology, and philosophy. He strongly believed that the study of personality was not the prerogative of any single discipline, and that the whole person could be understood only by pursuing knowledge wherever it existed. Like Freud, Jung persistently defended himself as a scientific investigator, eschewing the labels of mystic and philosopher. At the same time, however, he asserted that the psyche could not be understood by the intellect alone, but must be grasped by the total person. He once said, "Not everything I bring forth is written out of my head, but much of it comes from the heart also" (Jung, 1943/1953, p. 116).

Jung gathered data for his theories from extensive reading in many disciplines, but primarily, his basic facts came from the observation of people, including himself. Most of these observations were made on patients through the *word association test*, *dream analysis*, *active imagination*, and *psychotherapy*. This information was then combined with readings on medieval alchemy, the other occult sciences, or any other subject in an effort either to confirm or reject the hypotheses of Analytical Psychology.

WORD ASSOCIATION TEST

Jung was not the first to use the word association technique, but he can be credited with helping to develop and refine the test. He originally used the technique as early as 1903 when he was a young psychiatric assistant at Burghöltzli, but he seldom employed it in his later career. In spite of this inattention, the test continues to be closely linked with Jung's name.

His original purpose in using the word association test was to demonstrate the validity of Freud's hypothesis that the unconscious operates as an autonomous process. However, the basic purpose of the test in Jungian psychology today is to uncover feeling-toned complexes. As noted earlier, a complex is an individualized, emotionally toned conglomeration of images grouped around a central core. The word association test is based on the principle that complexes create measurable emotional responses. In administering the test, Jung typically used a list of about 100 stimulus words chosen and arranged to elicit an emotional reaction. He instructed the person to respond to each stimulus word with the first word that came to mind. Jung recorded each verbal response, time taken to make a response, rate of breathing, and galvanic skin response. Usually, he would then repeat the experiment to determine test-retest consistency.

Certain types of reactions indicate that the stimulus word had touched a complex. Critical responses include restricted breathing, changes in the electrical conductivity of the skin, and delayed reactions. Other revealing reactions include multiple responses, that is, those that contain many words; disregard of instructions; inability to reproduce a word, for example, errors in pronunciation not usually made; unusual facial expressions, including blushing; nonverbal sounds such as stammering, laughing, coughing, sighing, clearing the throat, or crying; excessive body movement, especially of the hands or feet; repetition of the stimulus word; silence or failure to give a verbal response; and inconsistency on test-retest. Any one or any combination of these responses might indicate that a complex has been reached (Jung, 1935/1968; Jung & Riklin, 1904/1973).

DREAM ANALYSIS

Jung agreed with Freud that dreams have meaning and that they must be taken seriously. He also agreed with Freud that dreams spring from the depths of the unconscious and that their latent meaning is expressed in symbolic form. However, he objected to Freud's notion that nearly all dreams are wish fulfillments and that most dream symbols represent sexual urges. Jung believed that people used symbols to represent any concepts—not merely sexual ones—to try to comprehend the "innumerable things beyond the range of human understanding" (Jung, 1964, p. 21). Dreams are our unconscious and spontaneous attempt to know the unknowable, to comprehend a reality that can only be expressed symbolically.

The purpose of Jungian dream interpretation is to uncover elements from the personal and collective unconscious and to integrate them into consciousness in order to facilitate the process of self-realization. The Jungian therapist must realize that dreams are often compensatory; that is, feelings and attitudes not expressed during waking life will find an outlet through the dream process. Jung held that the natural condition of humans is to move toward completion or self-realization. Thus, if our conscious life is incomplete in a certain area, our unconscious self will strive to complete that condition through the dream process. For example, if the anima in a man receives no conscious development, she will express herself through dreams filled with self-realization motifs, thus balancing the man's masculine side with his feminine disposition (Jung, 1916/1960).

Correctly interpreting dreams requires knowing the dreamer's conscious attitude because the dream is made up of the unconscious opposite. Jung (1934/1954b) provided an example of how the conscious and unconscious work together in constructing and interpreting dreams. A young man reported the following dream:

> My father is driving away from the house in his new car. He drives very clumsily, and I get very annoyed over his apparent stupidity. He goes this way and that, forward and backwards, and manoeuvres the car into a dangerous position. Finally he runs into a wall and damages the car badly. I shout at him in perfect fury that he ought to behave himself. My father only laughs, and then I see that he is dead drunk. (p. 154)

To interpret this dream, Jung needed to know something about the young man's conscious life and about his relationship with his father. In reality, the young man's father was a very well respected man in his community and would never get drunk, much less drive a car while intoxicated. Also, Jung's patient had an excellent relationship with his father, perhaps too good. He greatly admired his father who was still providing for his welfare, a condition that was blocking the young man's growth toward self-realization. Jung noted that one would make a grave error to interpret this dream to mean that the young man wished to discredit his father. Such an interpretation would take into account only the unconscious wish of the young man. In Jung's interpretation, the purpose of the dream was to contrast the dreamer with the father so that the young man could gain more confidence in himself and to develop a personality uniquely different from that of his father. Such an analysis relied on information about the dreamer's conscious situation and seemed to have hit the mark because the young man immediately saw that the interpretation was correct.

Recall that Jung felt certain dreams offered proof for the existence of the collective unconscious. At least three kinds of dreams are considered as archetypal dreams.

Under the first heading are *big dreams*, those that seem to have special meaning and inexplicable attraction for all people. Jung had such a dream while traveling to the United States with Freud. It was one of several dreams that Jung claimed Freud was unable to accurately interpret, an inability that led Jung to lose some respect for his older mentor. It was also the dream that first led Jung to the idea of a collective unconscious. In this dream Jung was living in the upper floor of a two-story house. This floor had an inhabited atmosphere, although its furnishings were somewhat old. In the dream Jung realized that he did not know what the ground floor was like, so he decided to explore it. After descending the stairs, he noticed that all the furnishings were medieval and dated to the 15th or 16th centuries. While exploring this floor he discovered a stone stairway that led down into a cellar. "Descending again, I found myself in a beautifully vaulted room which looked exceedingly ancient. . . . As soon as I saw this I knew that the walls dated from Roman times" (Jung, 1961, p. 159). As he looked at the floor of this cellar, Jung noticed a ring on one of the stone slabs. When he lifted it, he saw another narrow stairway leading to an ancient cave. There, he discovered broken pottery, scattered animal bones, and two human skulls, half disintegrated and very old.

When Jung finished telling the dream, Freud insisted that he reveal his associations to the two human skulls. Whom did Jung wish were dead? To placate Freud, Jung said his wife and his sister-in-law, two people for whom he had no death wish. Jung's interpretation, of course, was quite different. To him the house and its cellars represented the different levels of the psyche. The top floor was consciousness, while the ground level symbolized the first layer of the unconscious. The cellar was a deeper level of the personal unconscious, and the cave represented the collective unconscious, "the world of the primitive man within myself—a world which can scarcely be reached or illuminated by consciousness" (Jung, 1961, p. 160).

The second kind of collective dreams are the *typical dreams*, those that are common to most people. These include archetypal figures, like mother, father, God, devil, or old wise man; archetypal events, such as birth, death, separation from parents, baptism, marriage, flying, or exploring a cave; and archetypal objects, for example, sun, water, fish, snakes, or predatory animals.

The third category includes *earliest dreams* remembered. These can be traced back to about age 3 or 4 and contain mythological and symbolic images and motifs that could not have reasonably been experienced by the individual child. These early childhood dreams often contain archetypal motifs and symbols such as the hero, the old wise man, the tree, the fish, and the mandala. Jung (1948/1960b, p. 291) wrote of these images and motifs: "Their frequent appearance in individual case material, as well as their universal distribution, prove that the human psyche is unique and subjective or personal only in part, and for the rest is collective and objective." Earlier, we described a dream Jung had during early childhood in which he entered a dark rectangular hole in the ground and encountered several archetypal images beyond the personal experience of a young child. Such a dream, Jung said, suggests the existence of a collective unconscious.

ACTIVE IMAGINATION

A technique Jung used during his own self-analysis as well as with many of his patients was **active imagination.** This method requires a person to begin with any impression—a dream image, vision, picture, or fantasy and to concentrate until the impression begins to "move." The person must follow these images to wherever they lead and then courageously face these autonomous images and freely communicate with them.

The purpose of active imagination is to reveal archetypal images emerging from the unconscious. It can be a useful technique for people who want to become better acquainted with their collective and personal unconscious and who are willing to overcome the resistance that ordinarily blocks open communication with the unconscious. Jung believed that active imagination has an advantage over dream analysis in that its images are produced during a conscious state of mind, thus making them more clear and reproducible. The feeling tone is also quite specific, and ordinarily a person has little difficulty reproducing the vision or remembering the mood (Jung, 1937/1959).

As a variation to active imagination, Jung sometimes asked patients who were so inclined to draw, paint, or express in some other nonverbal manner the progression of their fantasies. Jung relied on this technique during his own self-analysis and many of these reproductions, rich in universal symbolism and often exhibiting the mandala, are scattered throughout his books. *Man and His Symbols* (1964), *Word and Image* (1979), and *Psychology and Alchemy* (1952/1968) are especially prolific sources for these drawings and photographs.

Jung (1961) wrote the following about his experiences with active imagination during his midlife confrontation with the unconscious:

> When I look back upon it all today and consider what happened to me during the period of my work on the fantasies, it seems as though a message had come to me with overwhelming force. There were things in the images which concerned not only myself but many others also. It was then that I ceased to belong to myself alone, ceased to have the right to do so. From then on, my life belonged to the generality. . . . It was then that I dedicated myself to service of the psyche: I loved it and hated it, but it was my greatest wealth. My delivering myself over to it, as it were, was the only way by which I could endure my existence and live it as fully as possible. (p. 192)

PSYCHOTHERAPY

Jung (1931/1954) identified four basic approaches to therapy, representing four developmental stages in the history of psychotherapy. The first is confession of a pathogenic secret. This is the cathartic method practiced by Joseph Breuer and earlier psychiatrists. For patients who merely have a need to share their secrets, catharsis is effective. The second stage involves interpretation, explanation, and elucidation. This approach,

Carl Jung, the old wise man of Küsnacht.

used by Freud, gives the patients insight into the causes of their neuroses, but may still leave them incapable of solving social problems. The third stage, therefore, involves the education of patients as social beings. Unfortunately, says Jung, this often leaves patients merely socially well-adjusted. To go beyond adjustment to the outer world, Jung suggested a fourth stage, **transformation.** By this he meant that the doctor must first be transformed into a healthy human being, preferably by undergoing psychotherapy. Only after transformation and an established philosophy of life is the therapist able to help patients move toward individuation, wholeness, or self-realization. This fourth stage is especially employed with patients who are in the second half of life and who are concerned with realization of the inner self, with moral and religious problems, and with finding a unifying philosophy of life.

Jung was quite eclectic in his theory and practice of psychotherapy. His treatment varied according to the age, the stage of development, and the particular neurosis of the individual patient. About two thirds of Jung's patients were in the second half, and a great many of them suffered from a loss of meaning, general aimlessness, and a fear of death. Jung attempted to help these patients find their own philosophical orientation. He was careful not to prescribe a ready-made philosophy but to encourage them to discover their own individual meaning to life.

The ultimate purpose of Jungian therapy is to help neurotic patients become healthy and to encourage healthy people to work independently toward self-realization. Jung sought to achieve this purpose by using such techniques as dream analysis and active imagination to aid patients in discovering unconscious material and to bring these unconscious images in line with their conscious attitude.

Although Jung encouraged patients to be independent, he admitted to the importance of *transference*, particularly during the first three stages of therapy. He regarded both positive and negative transference as a natural concomitant to patients' revelation of highly personal information. He thought it quite all right that a number of male patients referred to him as "Mother Jung" and quite understandable that others saw him as God or savior. Jung also recognized the process of **countertransference,** a term used to describe a therapist's feelings toward the patient. Like transference, countertransference can be either a help or a hindrance to treatment depending on whether it leads to a better relationship between doctor and patient, something that Jung felt was indispensable to successful psychotherapy.

Because Jungian psychotherapy has many goals and an equal number of techniques, no universal description of a person who has successfully completed analytical treatment is possible. For the mature person, the goal may be to find meaning in life and strive toward achieving balance and wholeness. The self-realized person is able to assimilate much of the unconscious self into consciousness but, at the same time, remains fully aware of the potential dangers hidden in the far recess of the unconscious psyche. Jung once warned against digging too deeply in land not properly surveyed, comparing this practice to a person digging for an artesian well and running the risk of activating a volcano.

RELATED RESEARCH

No area of Jungian psychology has been researched as extensively as the concept of types. The Myers-Briggs Type Indicator (MBTI) (Myers, 1962) and, to a lesser extent, the Jungian Type Survey (JTS) (Wheelwright, Wheelwright, & Buehler, 1964) have stimulated most of these investigations. Of these two type indicators, the JTS is shorter, simpler, and easier to score, but the JTS has only limited validity due primarily to its brevity (Woehlke & Piper, 1980).

The Myers-Briggs Type Indicator employs terminology slightly different from Jung's. It is based on four bipolar personality dimensions that oppose extraversion (E) to introversion (I); sensing (S) to intuition (N); thinking (T) to feeling (F); and judgment (J) to perception (P). This last dimension, (J vs. P), does not reflect basic Jungian typology, but was added by Myers. People who score high on judgment generally prefer ordered, planned, and structured lifestyles, whereas those who score high on perception prefer spontaneous and flexible lifestyles. Although some investigators (McCrae & Costa, 1989) have questioned whether the MBTI adequately measures Jungian typology, others have reported that it is a reliable and valid measure of Jung's basic concept. For example, Carlson (1980) found that the MBTI generally supported Jungian type theory, and McCaulley (1990) cited evidence that the inventory is an accurate representation of Jung's ideas on typology. Also, a study by Steele and Kelley (1976) obtained a very high relationship between the extraversion-introversion scale of the MBTI and the extraversion-introversion scale of the factor analytically developed Eysenck Personality Questionnaire (see Chapter 13 for Eysenck's concept of extraversion/introversion). This relationship is especially impressive because the two instruments are based on quite different theoretical approaches. Myers and McCaulley (1985) reported substantial reliability and validity for the MBTI as a measure of Jungian personality types. In addition, a study by Levy and Ridley (1987) found that over a 10-year period college women changed their scores very little, thus suggesting that the MBTI measures relatively stable personality traits.

The MBTI is so widely used in research on typology that a journal—*The Journal of Psychological Type*—is devoted to just the Myers-Briggs. This journal has published hundreds of empirical studies investigating how Jungian types are related to career choice, major in college, achievement in school and career, learning style, religious belief, brain electrical activity patterns, marital and friendship satisfaction, substance abuse, and theoretical orientation (to name only a few). We summarize a handful of these studies on three selected topics: (1) theoretical orientation, (2) school achievement, and (3) relationship satisfaction.

Recall that in Chapter 1 we argued for the importance of the theorist's personality in the development of a theory of personality. Some research using the MBTI supports our hypothesis that personality characteristics of the theorist influence the type of theory she or he creates. For example, Anita Schacht and Herbert Howe (1989) found that psychologists were more intuitive and less sensing than people who are not psychologists. More specifically, theoretical orientations within psychology tend to attract unique types of psychologists. Behaviorists, for example, are disproportionately thinking (vs. feeling) types, whereas humanistic psychologists are disproportionately feeling (vs. thinking) types. Interestingly, psychoanalysts tend to be evenly distributed between thinking and feeling types.

Empirical research has also demonstrated that different personality types prefer different teaching techniques, choose different majors, drop out of college at different rates, and obtain different grade point averages. John Fourqurean, Charles Meisgeier, and Paul Swank (1990) examined the relationship between Jungian types and learning style among high school students and found two bipolar learning style dimensions: active/passive and structured/unstructured. Active learners tended to be extraverts and preferred learning in groups via simulation and peer teaching. Passive (or reflective) learners tended to be introverts and preferred learning via lecture, auditory, and visual presentation, and learning along. Structured learners were judging types and preferred structured environments, drills and recitation, independent study, and teaching games. Unstructured learners were most likely to be perceiving types who preferred noisy and tactile learning environments. Later research by Terry Schurr and his colleagues (Wittig, Schurr, Ruble, & Ellen, 1994) found that feeling type college students tended to prefer "feminine" sports (such as volleyball), whereas thinking types were more likely to participate in "masculine" sports (such as basketball).

An earlier study by Terry Schurr and Virgil Ruble (1988) investigated the role that personality type had on choice of major, retention, and achievement in college students at a large midwestern university. These researchers found that ENTs (extraverted, intuitive, thinking types) were most likely to choose majors in architecture, engineering, and physical or biological science, whereas ESTs (extraverted, sensing, thinking types) were most likely to choose business, pre-med, or pre-dentistry for a major. Moreover, academic success—defined as remaining in college for at least 2 years and having a high grade point average—was positively related to high scores on judgment but not on perception.

Another area of active research that has used the MBTI is that of relationships and relationship satisfaction. More specifically, some researchers investigated whether similar personality types are more or less likely to result in stable and happy friendships or marriages. The question of how to define similarity of personality, however, is not as straightforward as it first appears. Flavil Yeakly, Jr. (1982), has developed a complex index to measure similarity of personality type and validated it by collecting similarity scores on 90 couples who were going through marriage counseling. According to therapists' reports, relationships for 30 of the couples had gotten worse during the previous 6 months, 30 had no change, and 30 had gotten better. Results of Yeakly's investigation showed that the couples whose relationships had gotten better had personality types that were significantly more similar than were the styles of couples who did not change or who had gotten worse. Other researchers (Carey, Hamilton, & Shankin, 1986) have found similar results on how satisfied college roommates were with their relationships; that is, the researchers found that the most satisfying relationships had more similar personality styles. Finally, Jo Cohen (1992) examined Jung's notion that people unconsciously seek out spouses whose type preference is opposite their own. Cohen found somewhat mixed evidence for this hypothesis—sensing and intuiting people tend to attract one another, as do feeling and thinking types. However, Cohen also found that introverts and extraverts do not tend to marry one another, and neither do judging people and perceiving people.

In addition to research on the MBTI, some investigators have attempted to study Jung's more inaccessible notion of the collective unconscious. To test the relationship between archetypal symbols and the meanings attributed to them, Rosen, Smith, Huston, and Gonzalez (1991) developed the Archetypal Symbol Inventory (ASI), which consists of 40 pictures depicting archetypal symbols and 40 associated words that indicate the symbol's meaning. For example, the numeral 6 should be associated with "harmony," a window with "possibility," an apple with "knowledge," and so forth. Rosen et al. first administered the ASI to a sample of college students to determine if they had conscious knowledge of the symbols' meanings. Participants were briefly exposed to the 40 symbols and asked to write down the one word that best described the figure's symbolic meaning. Because only 1% of the responses were correct, the authors concluded that the students had little or no conscious knowledge of what the symbols meant. Next, the experimenters showed the 40 symbols and 80 descriptive words (40 correct and 40 incorrect) to a second group of college students to see if they could correctly match the word and the symbol. Again, the students showed very little conscious knowledge of the symbols' meanings. Finally, Rosen et al. selected a third sample of students, divided them into two groups, and gave each group 20 matched and 20 mismatched symbol/word pairs. The order of presentation was reversed for the two groups. Both groups viewed each of the 40 symbol/word pairs for 5 seconds and were later asked to recall the word that had previously been paired with the symbol. Participants in both groups recalled more matched words that were archetypically correct than those that were not, suggesting that they had some unconscious knowledge of the symbols' meanings. Although the differences were quite small, they were highly statistically significant. Although Rosen et al. were enthusiastic about these results, the ASI has sparked little additional research and its validity as an inventory of archetypal symbols has yet to be established.

CRITIQUE OF JUNG

Carl Jung and Analytical Psychology continue to fascinate students of humanity. Despite its subjective and philosophical quality, Jungian psychology has attracted a wide audience of both professional and lay people. June Singer (1994) reported that membership in the International Association of Analytical Psychologists grew from fewer than 400 in 1972 to 2,000 by 1992. In addition, each year new books on Jung, his life, and ideas appear (see, for example, Harris, 1996; Homans, 1995; Kerr, 1993; Noll, 1994; Singer, 1994; Walker, 1995).

Nevertheless, Analytical Psychology, like any theory, must be evaluated against the six criteria of a useful theory established in Chapter 1. First, a useful theory must generate *testable hypotheses* and *descriptive research*, and second, it must have the capacity for either verification or *falsification*. Unfortunately, Jung's theory, like Freud's, is nearly impossible to either verify or falsify. The collective unconscious, the core of Jung's theory, remains a difficult concept to test empirically. Although Shelburne (1988), Stevens (1994), and others have argued for the scientific feasibility of the collective unconscious, such arguments do not suggest that Jung's conceptions are valid.

Much of the evidence for the concepts of archetype and the collective unconscious has come from Jung's own inner experiences, which he admittedly found difficult to communicate to others, so that acceptance of these concepts rests more on faith than on empirical evidence. Jung (1961) claimed that "archetypal statements are based upon instinctive preconditions and have nothing to do with reason; they are neither rationally grounded nor can they be banished by rational argument" (p. 353). Such a statement may be acceptable to the artist or the theologian, but it is not likely to win adherents among scientific researchers faced with the problems of designing studies and formulating hypotheses.

On the other hand, that part of Jung's theory concerned with classification and typology, that is, the functions and attitudes, can be studied and tested. Because the Myers-Briggs Type Indicator has yielded a great number of investigations, we give Jung's theory a moderate rating on its ability to generate research.

Third, a useful theory should *organize observations* into a meaningful framework. Analytical Psychology is unique because it adds a new dimension to personality theory, namely, the collective unconscious. Those aspects of human personality dealing with the occult, the mysterious, and the parapsychological are not touched on by most other personality theories. Even though the collective unconscious is not the only possible explanation for these phenomena, and other concepts could be postulated to account for them, Jung is the only modern personality theorist to make a serious attempt to include such a broad scope of human activity within a single theoretical framework.

A fourth criterion of a useful theory is its *practicality*. Does the theory aid therapists, teachers, parents, or others in solving everyday problems? The theory of psychological types or attitudes and the Myers-Briggs Type Indicator are used by many clinicians, but the usefulness of most of Analytical Psychology is limited to those therapists who subscribe to basic Jungian tenets. The concept of a collective unconscious does not easily lend itself to empirical research, but it may have some usefulness in helping people understand cultural myths and adjust to life's traumas.

Is Jung's theory of personality *internally consistent*? Does it possess a set of operationally defined terms? The first question receives a qualified affirmative answer; the second a definite negative one. Jung generally used the same terms consistently, but he often employed several terms to describe the same concept. The words "regression" and "introverted" are so closely related that they can be said to describe the same process. This is also true of "progression" and "extraverted," and the list could be expanded to include several other terms such as "individuation" and "self-realization," which are not clearly differentiated either. Jung's language is often arcane and many of his terms are not adequately defined. As for operational definitions, Jung, like other early personality theorists, did not define terms operationally.

The final criterion of a useful theory is *parsimony*. Jung's psychology is not simple, but neither is human personality. However, his theory is the most complex of all theories and probably more cumbersome than it need be. Jung's proclivity for searching for data from a variety of disciplines and his willingness to explore his own unconscious even beneath the personal level contribute to the great complexities and the broad scope of his theory. The law of parsimony states, "When two theories are equally useful, the simpler one is preferred." In fact, of course, no two are ever equal, and Jung's theory adds a dimension to human personality not greatly dealt with by others.

CONCEPT OF HUMANITY

Jung saw humans as complex beings with many opposing poles. His view of humanity was neither *pessimistic* nor *optimistic*, neither *deterministic* nor *purposive*. To him, people are motivated partly by *conscious* thoughts, partly by images from their personal *unconscious*, and partly by latent memory traces inherited from their ancestral past. Their motivation comes both from *causal* and *teleological* factors.

The complex makeup of humans invalidates any simple or one-sided description. According to Jung, each person is a composition of opposing forces. No one is completely introverted or totally extraverted; all male or all female; solely a thinking, feeling, sensing, or intuitive person; and no one proceeds invariably in the direction of either progression or regression.

The persona is but a fraction of an individual. What one wishes to show others is usually only the socially acceptable side of personality. Every person has a dark side, a shadow, and most try to conceal it from both society and themselves. In addition, each man possesses an anima and every woman an animus.

The various complexes and archetypes cast their spell over us and are responsible for many of our words and actions and most of our dreams and fantasies. Although we are not master in our own house, neither are we completely dominated by forces beyond our control. We have some limited capacity to determine our lives. Through our will, and with great courage, we can explore the hidden recesses of our psyche. We can recognize our shadow as our own, become partially conscious of our feminine or masculine side, and cultivate more than a single function. This process, which Jung called individuation or self-realization, is not easy and demands more fortitude than most of us can muster. Ordinarily, it means we have reached middle life and have lived successfully through the stages of childhood and youth. During middle age, we must be willing to set aside the goals and behaviors of youth and adopt a new style appropriate to our stage of psychic development.

Even after we have achieved individuation, made an acquaintance with our inner world, and brought the various opposing forces into balance, we remain under the influence of an impersonal collective unconscious that controls many of our prejudices, interests, fears, dreams, and creative activities.

On the dimension of *biological vs. social* aspects of personality, Jung's theory is decidedly in the direction of biology. The collective unconscious, responsible for so many of our actions, is part of our biological inheritance. Except for the therapeutic potential of the doctor-patient relationship, Jung had little to say about differential effects of specific social practices. In fact, in his studies of various cultures, he found the differences to be superficial, the similarities profound. Thus, Analytical Psychology can also be rated high on *similarities* among people and low on *individual differences*.

Chapter Summary

Jung's notion of a *collective unconscious* holds that important segments of our unconscious are inherited from our ancient ancestors through the repeated experiences of many generations. Some of the contents of the collective unconscious become highly developed and are identified as *archetypes*. These include the *anima*, or feminine side of men; the *animus*, or masculine disposition in women; the *shadow*, the dark side of our personality; the *old wise man*, the intelligent but deceptive voice of accumulated experience; the *great mother*, the archetype of nourishment and destruction; the *persona*, or mask we show to the outside world; the *hero*, our unconscious image of a person who conquers or vanquishes an evil foe; and the *self*, the archetype of completeness and wholeness.

The layer of the psyche above the collective unconscious is the *personal unconscious*, which is made up of complexes or emotionally toned images revolving around a core concept. Above the personal unconscious is the *conscious*, or those images perceived by the *ego*.

The *principle of equivalence* states that energy is never lost or destroyed but merely transformed to another function. The *principle of entropy* provides the foundation for Jung's psychology of opposites. It states that energy flows from the tension produced by opposing poles such as introversion and extraversion. The concepts of *progression* and *regression* are similar to those of extraversion and introversion and refer to the forward and backward flow of energy necessary to attain eventual balance.

Jung postulated two basic attitudes—*introversion* and *extraversion*. Introverts have a tendency to see the world subjectively, whereas extraverts tend to take an objective view. When these two attitudes combine with the four functions—*thinking, feeling, sensation*, and *intuition*—eight basic types are produced.

Jung emphasized the last half of life, although he suggested that a healthy *middle life* and *old age* depend on proper solutions to the problems of *childhood* and *youth*.

Early in his career Jung developed the *word association test*, which was designed to uncover *complexes*. Later, during his midlife crisis, he used *dream analysis* and *active imagination* to discover the contents of his own collective unconscious. Subsequently, he made use of these techniques in his practice of *psychotherapy*.

Analytical Psychology is the most complex of all personality theories, but it falls short of meeting the standards for a scientific theory, especially in its inability to verify or falsify several of its key concepts and its lack of operationally defined terms. Finally, Jung saw humans as exceedingly complex organisms made up of several opposing forces. He was neither optimistic nor pessimistic, although he believed that people can attain *individuation* or *self-realization* during the second half of life.

Suggested Readings

Jung, C. G. (1961). M*emories, dreams, reflections* (A. Jaffe, Ed.). New York: Random House.
Of all of Jung's works, this is possibly the easiest to read and the most interesting. Written and dictated by Jung as he entered his 9th decade, this book contains an exciting firsthand account of his midlife confrontation with the unconscious.

Jung, C. G. (1979). W*ord and image* (A. Jaffe, Ed.). Princeton, NJ: Princeton University Press.
Mostly biographical and pictorial, this large book includes a chronology and a glossary of technical terms. Anyone interested in Jung will enjoy a leisurely perusal of these pages.

Kerr, J. (1993). A *most dangerous method: The story of Jung, Freud, and Sabina Spielrein.* New York: Knopf.
In this somewhat technical book, John Kerr speculates about the complex story of Jung, Freud, and Sabina Spielrein, who first was a patient of Jung and then his lover. Kerr believes that the feminine voice that spoke to Jung in the form of his anima was that of Spielrein.

Singer, J. (1994). *Boundaries of the soul: The practice of Jung's psychology* (2nd ed.). New York: Doubleday.

Singer's revised and updated book is, perhaps, the best and most complete introduction to the thoughts of Jung. Her account shows that Jung's ideas are as vital and compelling today as ever.

Stevens, A. (1994). *On Jung*. Oxford, England: Oxford University Press.

Anthony Stevens relates Jung's personal and professional development to his theories, especially his ideas on stages of development, dream symbolism, myths, religion, and the collective unconscious.

Walker, S. F. (1995). *Jung and the Jungians on myth: An introduction*. New York: Garland.

This brief book sympathetically presents Jung's views on the archetypes and discusses the psychological meaning of mythology.

Adler

Chapter 4

Adler: Individual Psychology

Biography of Alfred Adler
Introduction to Adlerian Theory
Striving for Success or Superiority
- The Final Goal
- The Striving Force as Compensation
- Striving for Personal Superiority
- Striving for Success

Subjective Perceptions
- Fictionalism
- Organ Inferiorities

Unity of Personality
- Organ Dialect
- Conscious and Unconscious

Social Interest
- Development in a Social Environment
- Necessity of Social Interest
- Criterion of Human Values

Style of Life
Creative Power
Abnormal Development
- General Description
- External Factors in Maladjustment
- Safeguarding Tendencies

Masculine Protest
Applications of Individual Psychology
- Family Constellation
- Early Recollections
- Dreams
- Psychotherapy

Related Research
Critique of Adler
Concept of Humanity
Chapter Summary
Suggested Readings

lfred Adler's **Individual Psychology** holds that people are born small and weak, and that this inadequate physical condition prompts feelings of inferiority. People then attempt to compensate for these feelings of inferiority by striving for superiority or success. An original member of the Vienna Psychoanalytic Society, Adler was the first person to break from Freud and establish an important and opposing theory. In contrast to Freud, Adler was optimistic and idealistic. He emphasized social rather than biological factors; final goals rather than past causes; individual choice and responsibility rather than determinism; and the unity of personality rather than separate and antagonistic regions of the mind.

Adler's differences from Freud cannot be explained in terms of religion or geography. Each came from a middle-class Jewish family and each lived most of his life in Vienna. Adler himself might explain these differences in terms of birth order, social interest, style of life, and subjective perceptions, all important concepts in Individual Psychology.

BIOGRAPHY OF ALFRED ADLER

Alfred Adler was born on February 7, 1870, in Rudolfsheim, a village near Vienna. His father, Leopold, was a middle-class Jewish grain merchant from Hungary and his mother, Pauline, was a hard-working homemaker who kept busy with her seven children. Alfred, a secondborn child, was weak and sickly during the first 5 years of his life— a condition in sharp contrast to the health of his older brother Sigmund. Several of Alfred's earliest memories were concerned with the unhappy comparison between his brother's good health and his own illness. Sigmund Adler, the childhood rival that Adler attempted to surpass, remained a worthy opponent, and in later years he became very successful in business (Bottome, 1939).

The lives of Freud and Adler have several interesting parallels. Although both men came from middle- or lower-middle class Viennese Jewish parents, neither was devoutly religious. However, Freud was much more conscious of his Jewishness than was Adler and often believed himself to be persecuted because of his religion. On the other hand, Adler never claimed to have been mistreated, and in 1904, while still a member of Freud's inner circle, he converted to Protestantism. Despite this conversion he held no deep religious convictions, and, in fact, one of his biographers (Rattner, 1983) regarded him as an agnostic.

Like Freud, Adler had a younger brother who died in infancy. This early experience profoundly affected both men but in vastly different ways. Freud, by his own accounting, had wished unconsciously for the death of his rival and when the infant Julius did, in fact, die, Freud was filled with guilt and self-reproach, conditions that continued into his adulthood. For the 4-year-old Adler, on the other hand, the death of his younger brother Rudoff, along with his own sickly constitution, brought home to him the reality of death. He saw this experience as a challenge and determined then that his goal in life would be to conquer death. Because medicine offered some chance to forestall death, Adler decided at that time to become a physician (Ellenberger, 1970; Hoffman, 1994).

Although Freud was surrounded by a large family, including seven younger brothers and sisters, two grown half-brothers, and a nephew and niece about his age, he was more oriented toward his parents than to these other family members. In contrast, Adler was more interested in social relationships, with siblings and peers playing a pivotal role in his childhood development (Hoffman, 1994). Personality differences between Freud and Adler continued throughout adulthood, with Freud preferring intense one-to-one relationships and Adler feeling more comfortable in group situations. These personality differences were also reflected in their professional organizations. Freud's Vienna Psychoanalytic Society and International Psychoanalytic Association were highly structured in pyramid fashion, with an inner circle of Freud's trusted friends forming a kind of oligarchy at the top. Adler, by comparison, was more democratic. He often met with his group, which included patients as well as colleagues and friends, in Vienna coffee houses. His Individual Psychology Society, in fact, suffered from a loose organization, and Adler had a relaxed attitude toward business details that did not enhance his movement (Ellenberger, 1970).

Adler attended elementary and secondary school with neither difficulty nor distinction. He then entered the Vienna Medical School and again completed work with no special honors, probably because his interest in patient care conflicted with his professors' interest in precise diagnoses (Hoffman, 1994). When he received his medical degree near the end of 1895, he had realized his childhood goal of becoming a physician.

Because his father had been born in Hungary, Adler was a Hungarian citizen and was thus obliged to serve a tour of military duty in the Hungarian army. He fulfilled that obligation immediately after receiving his medical degree and then returned to Vienna for postgraduate study. (Adler became an Austrian citizen in 1911). He began private practice as an eye specialist, but his interest in the whole person led him to give up specialization and turn to general medicine. During these early years as a general practitioner he demonstrated an intense interest in the complete person, regarding illness as a reflection of the total personality and recognizing the essential unity among the physical, psychological, and social aspects of a disease. His concern for the whole person led him to the study of psychiatry, which, of course, did not diminish his interest in general medicine. It did, however, attract the attention of Sigmund Freud.

In the late fall of 1902, Freud invited Adler and three other Viennese physicians to attend a meeting in Freud's home to discuss psychology and neuropathology. This group was soon known as the Wednesday Psychological Society and later became the Vienna Psychoanalytic Society. Although Freud led these discussion groups, Adler never considered Freud to be his mentor and believed somewhat naively that he and others could make contributions to psychoanalysis—contributions that would be acceptable to Freud. Despite the fact that Adler was one of the original members of Freud's inner circle, the two men never shared a warm personal relationship. Neither man was quick to recognize theoretical differences even after Adler's 1907 publication of *Study of Organ Inferiority and Its Psychical Compensation* (1907/1917).

By 1910, Adler was convinced that psychoanalysis should be much broader than Freud's view of infantile sexuality (Hoffman, 1994). The following year, Adler, who was then president of the Vienna Psychoanalytic Society, was asked to present his views before the group. In a series of three papers, he expressed opposition to the strong sexual proclivities of psychoanalysis, and he and Freud finally became convinced that their differences were irreconcilable. Adler resigned his presidency and, along with six other men, left the Freudian circle and formed the Society for Free Psychoanalytic Study, a term that irritated Freud with its implication that his brand of psychoanalysis was opposed to a free expression of ideas. Adler, however, soon changed the name of his organization to the Society for Individual Psychology—a name that clearly indicated he had abandoned psychoanalysis.

In retrospect, we can see that personality differences between Freud and Adler would have made a lasting harmonious relationship extremely unlikely. Freud was personally very ambitious, and he jealously guarded the sacrosanct doctrines of psychoanalysis. Adler, however, was combative and less than respectful to Freud and his fixed ideas. He had developed a fierce boyhood rivalry with his older brother Sigmund that carried over in his dealings with the older Freud, also named Sigmund. Adler was a very vocal member of the Vienna Psychoanalytic Society and often questioned some of the orthodox psychoanalytic views. His quarrelsome attitude was not designed to please Freud, who was quite sensitive to criticism. Adler's competitive nature, it seems, made it necessary for him to become independent of Freud and to establish a psychology that would oppose psychoanalysis.

Unlike Jung, who sunk into a depressed state of inactivity immediately following his break with Freud, Adler became quite active after leaving the Fruedian circle. No longer compelled to defend his views, Adler was busy presiding over his own rapidly growing organization, lecturing, and writing. This activity, however, was stalled in 1916 when, at the age of 46, he was drafted into the service of the Austrian–Hungarian Empire, then engaged in fighting World War I. Like Freud, Adler modified his theoretical views as a result of his experiences with war. While Freud was elevating aggression to the level of sex, Adler was advocating the importance of social interest, a very different concept than aggression. After the war, Adler returned to his lectures in Vienna, established several child guidance clinics, and helped train teachers.

From 1926 until his death he frequently visited the United States. In the late 1920s, he taught individual psychology at the New School for Social Research as well as at Columbia University. By 1932, he was a permanent resident of the United States and held the position of visiting professor for medical psychology at Long Island College of Medicine, now Downstate Medical Center, State University of New York. Unlike Freud, who disliked Americans and their superficial understanding of psychoanalysis, Adler was impressed by Americans and admired their optimism and open-mindedness (Rattner, 1983). His popularity as a speaker in the United States during the mid-1930s had few rivals, and he aimed his last several books toward a receptive American market (Hoffman, 1994).

In December of 1897, Adler married Raissa Epstein, a Russian, whom he met while both were students. Raissa was a fiercely independent woman and much more political than her husband. In later years, while Adler lived in New York, she remained in Vienna and worked to promote Marxist-Leninist views that were quite different from Adler's notion of individual freedom and responsibility. Raissa and Alfred had four children, including Alexandra and Kurt, both of whom became psychiatrists and continued Adler's work in Individual Psychology.

Adler's favorite relaxation was music, but he also maintained an active interest in art and literature. In his work he often borrowed examples from fairy tales, the Bible, Shakespeare, Goethe, and numerous other literary works. He identified himself closely with the common person, and his manner and appearance were consistent with that identification. His patients included a high percentage of people from the lower and middle classes, a rarity among psychiatrists of his time. His personal qualities included an optimistic attitude toward the human condition, an intense competitiveness coupled with friendly congeniality, and a strong belief in the basic equality of the sexes, which combined with a willingness to forcefully advocate women's rights.

On May 28, 1937, Adler died of a heart attack in Aberdeen, Scotland, while on one of his many lecture tours. Freud, who was 14 years older than Adler, had outlived his long-time adversary. On hearing of Adler's death, Freud (as quoted in Jones, 1957) sarcastically remarked "For a Jew boy out of a Viennese suburb a death in Aberdeen is an unheard-of career in itself and a proof of how far he had got on. The world really rewarded him richly for his service in having contradicted psychoanalysis" (p. 208).

INTRODUCTION TO ADLERIAN THEORY

After his death, Adler's popularity and prestige waned for a time, but in more recent years his views have come to acquire greater acceptance in both academic and clinical circles (Hoffman, 1994). His ideas on the importance of interpersonal relationships were further developed by Harry Stack Sullivan, Karen Horney, Julian Rotter, Abraham H. Maslow, Carl Rogers, and others. His emphasis on subjective perception is the basis for Albert Ellis's rational-emotive therapy. In addition, Adler has also influenced Rollo May and other existentialists with his notion of fiction or myth that people create to guide their daily activities (May, 1991).

Yet Adler remains today less well known than either Freud or Jung. At least three reasons account for this. First, he did not establish a tightly run organization to perpetuate his theories. Second, he was not a particularly gifted writer, and most of his books were compiled by a series of editors from Adler's scattered lectures. Third, many of his views were incorporated into the works of later theorists (such as Maslow, Rogers, and Ellis) and thus are no longer associated with Adler's name.

Although his writings revealed great insight into the depth and complexities of human personality, Adler evolved a basically simple and parsimonious theory of personality. To Adler, people are born with weak, inferior bodies—a condition that leads to *feelings* of inferiority and a consequent dependence on other people. Therefore, a feeling of unity with others (social interest) is inherent in people and the ultimate standard for psychological health. More specifically, the main tenets of Adlerian theory can be stated in outline form. The following is adapted from a list that represents the final statement of Individual Psychology (Adler, 1964, pp. 24–25).

1. The one dynamic force behind the person's activity is the *striving for success or superiority*.
2. The *subjective perceptions* of the individual shape behavior and personality.
3. All psychological phenomena are *unified* within the individual in a self-consistent manner.
4. The usefulness of all human activity must be seen from the viewpoint of *social interest*.
5. All human potentialities develop in accordance with the individual's self-consistent *style of life*.
6. The style of life is developed by the individual's *creative power*.

STRIVING FOR SUCCESS OR SUPERIORITY

The one dynamic force behind the person's activity is the striving for success or superiority.

Adler believed that each individual begins life with physical deficiencies that activate feelings of inferiority—feelings that move the person to strive for either superiority or success. Psychologically unhealthy individuals strive for personal superiority whereas psychologically healthy people are motivated to seek success for all humanity. Early in his career, Adler believed *aggression* to be the dynamic power behind all motivation but later changed the name of this force to *masculine protest*, which implied will to power or a domination of others. Still later, he abandoned masculine protest as a universal drive and replaced it with the concept of *striving for superiority*. In his final theory, however, he limited striving for superiority to neurotic people who strive for personal superiority over other people and introduced the term *striving for success*, which described the healthy person's striving for perfection for everyone—a striving motivated by highly developed social interest (Adler, 1956). Regardless of the motivation for striving, each individual is guided by a final goal.

THE FINAL GOAL

According to Adler (1956), we all strive toward a final goal of superiority or success, a fictional goal that has no objective existence. As a subjective ideal, however, this final goal has great significance because it unifies personality and renders all behavior comprehensible.

Each individual has the power to create a personalized fictional goal, one constructed out of the raw materials provided by heredity and environment. However, the goal is neither genetically nor environmentally determined. Rather, it is the product of our *creative power*, that is, our ability to freely shape our behavior and create our own personality. By the time children are 4 or 5 years of age, their creative minds have reached the stage of development that enables them to set a final goal. But even infants have an innate drive toward growth, completion, or success. Because they are small, incomplete, and weak, they feel inferior and powerless and compensate for this deficiency by setting a fictional goal to be big, complete, and strong. This final goal reduces the pain of inferiority feelings and points young children in the direction of superiority or success.

If children are neglected or pampered, their goal remains largely unconscious. Adler hypothesized that children will compensate for feelings of inferiority in devious ways that have no apparent relationship to their fictional goal. The goal of superiority for a pampered girl, for example, may be to make permanent her parasitic relationship with her mother. As an adult, she may appear dependent and self-deprecating. Such behavior may seem to be inconsistent with a goal of superiority, but it is quite consistent with the goal of being a parasite that she set at age 4 or 5, a time when her mother appeared large and powerful, and attachment to her became a natural means of attaining superiority. The fact that the adult behavior of the neglected or pampered person seems inconsistent with a goal of superiority is indicative of an unconscious goal.

Conversely, if children experience love and security, they set goals that are largely conscious and understood. Psychologically secure children strive toward superiority defined in terms of success and social interest. Although their goal never becomes completely conscious, psychologically mature individuals understand and pursue it with a high level of awareness.

In striving for the final goal, many preliminary goals must be created. These subgoals are often conscious, but the connection between them and the final goal usually remains unknown. Furthermore, the relationship among preliminary goals is seldom realized. From the point of view of the final goal, however, they fit together in a self-consistent pattern. Adler (1956) used the analogy of the playwright who builds the characteristics and the subplots of the play according to the final goal of the drama. When the final scene is known, all dialogue and every subplot acquire new meaning. When an individual's final goal is known, all actions make sense and each subgoal takes on new significance.

THE STRIVING FORCE AS COMPENSATION

Every person, whether normal or neurotic, is pulled in the direction of success or superiority. We are all born with the tendency toward completion or perfection. "The striving for perfection is innate in the sense that it is a part of life, a striving, an urge, a something without which life would be unthinkable" (Adler, 1956, p. 104).

Although the striving for success is innate, it must be developed. At birth it exists as potentiality, not actuality, and it remains for each of us to actualize this potential in our own manner. At about age 4 or 5, we begin this process by setting a direction to the striving force and by establishing either a goal of personal superiority or of social success. The goal provides guidelines for motivation, shaping our psychological development and giving it an aim.

People strive for superiority or success as a means of compensation for feelings of inferiority or weakness. Adler (1930, 1964) believed that all humans are "blessed" at birth with small, weak, and inferior bodies. These physical deficiencies ignite feelings of inferiority only because people, by their nature, possess an innate tendency toward completion or wholeness. People are continually pushed by the need to overcome inferiority feelings and pulled by the desire for completion. The minus and plus situations exist simultaneously and cannot be separated because they are two dimensions of a single force. The force itself is innate, but its nature and direction are due both to feelings of inferiority and to the goal of superiority. Without the innate movement toward perfection, children would never feel inferior; but without feelings of inferiority, they would never set a goal of superiority or success. The goal, then, is set as compensation for the deficit feeling, but the deficit feeling would not exist unless a child first possessed a basic tendency toward completion (Adler, 1956).

The goal is not set as a blind reaction to the deficit feeling nor does it need be set in the exact opposite direction. As a creation of the individual, it may take any form. The goal is not necessarily the mirror image of the deficiency, even though it is a compensation for it. For example, a person with a weak body will not necessarily become a robust athlete but instead may become an artist, an actor, or a writer. Success is an individualized concept and all of us formulate our own definition of it. Our creative power is ultimately responsible for that definition, but it is swayed by the forces of heredity and environment. Heredity establishes the potentiality whereas environment contributes to the development of social interest and courage. The forces of nature and nurture can never deprive us of the power to set a unique goal or to choose a unique style of reaching for the goal (Adler, 1956).

Although each of us strives for completion in a unique manner, there are two general avenues of striving. The first is the socially nonproductive attempt to gain personal superiority; the second involves social interest and is aimed at success or perfection for everyone.

STRIVING FOR PERSONAL SUPERIORITY

Some people strive for superiority with little or no concern for others. Their goals are personal ones, and their strivings are motivated largely by exaggerated feelings of personal inferiority. Murderers, thieves, and con artists are obvious examples of people who strive only for personal gain. However, most people, even those with substantial levels of social interest, strive at times for personal superiority. In that sense, the two methods of striving are mutually exclusive.

Also, some people have created clever disguises for their personal striving and may consciously or unconsciously hide their self-centeredness behind the cloak of social concern. A high school teacher, for example, may appear to have a great interest in his students because he establishes a personal relationship with many of them. By conspicuously displaying much sympathy and concern, he encourages vulnerable students to talk to him about their personal problems. This teacher possesses a "private intelligence" that allows him to believe that he is the most accessible and dedicated teacher in his school. To a casual observer, he may appear to be motivated by social interest and success for everyone, but his actions are largely self-serving and motivated by overcompensation for exaggerated feelings of personal superiority.

STRIVING FOR SUCCESS

Psychologically healthy people are able to move beyond striving for personal gain. They are motivated by social interest and are able to strive for the success of all humankind. These healthy individuals are concerned with goals beyond themselves, are capable of helping others without demanding or expecting a personal payoff, and are able to see others not as opponents but as people with whom they can cooperate for social benefit. Their own success is not gained at the expense of others, but is a natural tendency to move toward completion or perfection.

People who strive for success rather than personal superiority maintain a sense of self, of course, but they see daily problems from the view of society's development rather than from a strictly personal vantage point. Their sense of personal worth is tied closely to their contributions to human society. Social progress is more important to them than personal credit (Adler, 1956).

SUBJECTIVE PERCEPTIONS

The subjective perceptions of the individual shape behavior and personality.

People strive for superiority or success to compensate for feelings of inferiority, but the manner in which they strive is shaped, not by reality, but by their subjective perceptions of reality. In other words, personality is not formed by organ inferiorities, early experiences, or basic drives, but by the individual's view of these and other factors. Adler believed that people are motivated more by **fictions,** or expectations of the future, than by experiences of the past. Behavior is consistent with one's perception of the fictional final goal. This goal does not exist in the future but in the person's present perception of the future. It molds contemporary behavior because it is subjectively perceived in the here and now (Adler, 1956).

FICTIONALISM

Adler's ideas on fictionalism originated with Hans Vaihinger's book, *The Philosophy of "As If"* (1911/1925). Vaihinger believed that fictions are ideas that have no real existence, yet they influence people *as if* they really existed. One example of a fiction might be: "Men are superior to women." Although this notion is a fiction, many people, both men and women, act as if it were a reality. Another example would be: "Humans have a free will that enables them to make choices." Again, many people act *as if* they and others have a free will and are thus responsible for their choices. No one can prove that free will exists, yet this fiction guides the lives of most of us. People are motivated not by what is true, but by their subjective perceptions of what is true. Yet another fiction would be a belief in an omnipotent God who rewards the good and punishes evil. Such a belief guides the daily lives of millions of people and helps shape many of their actions and influences many of their other beliefs. Fictions need be neither true nor false to have a powerful influence on people.

Adler's emphasis on fictions is consistent with his strongly held teleological view of motivation. *Teleology*, an explanation of behavior in terms of its final purpose or aim, is opposed to *causality*, which considers behavior as springing from a specific cause. Teleology is usually concerned with future goals or ends, whereas causality ordinarily deals with past experiences that produce some present effect. Freud's view of motivation was basically causal; he believed that people are driven by past events that activate present behavior. Adler, on the other hand, adopted a teleological view, one in which people are motivated by present perceptions of the future. As fictions, these perceptions need not be conscious or understood. Nevertheless, they bestow a purpose on all of one's actions and are responsible for a consistent pattern that runs throughout a person's life.

Our personality is molded, not by reality, but by our subjective beliefs concerning the future. Our most important fiction is the goal of superiority or success, a goal we create early in life, yet one we may only vaguely understand. This subjective, fictional final goal guides our style of life, gives unity to our personality, and, when understood, it confers purpose on all our behavior. Whether that behavior leads to a neurotic or to a healthy style of life depends on the degree of social interest that we develop during the early years of our life.

ORGAN INFERIORITIES

Because we all begin life small, weak, and inferior, we develop a belief system about how to overcome these physical deficiencies and become big, strong, and superior. But even after we attain size, strength, and superiority, we may act *as if* we are still small, weak, and inferior.

As noted earlier, Adler insisted that the whole human race is "blessed" with organ inferiorities. These physical handicaps have little or no importance by themselves but take on meaning when they stimulate subjective feelings of inferiority (Adler, 1929/1969), which serve as an impetus toward perfection or completion. Some people compensate for these feelings of inferiority by moving toward psychological health and a useful style of life, whereas others overcompensate and are motivated to subdue or retreat from other people and to live an essentially useless style of life. History provides many examples of people like Demosthenes or Beethoven overcoming a handicap and making significant contributions to society. Adler himself was weak and sickly as a child, and his illness moved him to become strong, to become a physician, and to conquer death. Other people, however, overcompensate for feelings of inferiority by becoming criminals or deeply neurotic.

Adler (1929/1969) emphasized that physical deficiencies alone do not *cause* a particular style of life; they simply provide present motivation for reaching future goals. Such motivation, like all aspects of personality, is unified and self-consistent.

UNITY OF PERSONALITY

All psychological phenomena are unified within the individual in a self-consistent manner.

In choosing the term "Individual Psychology," Adler wished to stress his belief that each person is unique and indivisible. Thus, Individual Psychology insists on the fundamental unity of personality. A person's thoughts, feelings, and actions are all directed toward a single goal and serve a single purpose. Inconsistent behavior does not exist. If seen in relation to the final goal of superiority or success, all of a person's actions are consistent and meaningful (Adler, 1930).

When we behave erratically or unpredictably, we do so for a single purpose. Such behavior forces other people to be on the defensive, to be watchful so as not to be confused by our capricious actions. Although our behavior may appear inconsistent, when viewed from the perspective of our final goal, it can be seen as an unhealthy attempt to confuse and subordinate other people. By consistently baffling and puzzling other people, we make them incapable of comprehending us, and their incomprehension gives us the upper hand in our relationship with them. The fact that we are successful in our attempt to gain superiority over others does not mean that we set out consciously to do so. We probably remain mostly unaware of our underlying motive and may stubbornly reject any suggestion that we desire superiority over these people.

Adler (1956) recognized several ways in which the entire personality operates with unity and self-consistency. The first of these he called organ jargon, or organ dialect.

ORGAN DIALECT

According to Adler (1956), the whole person strives in a self-consistent fashion toward a single goal and all separate actions and functions can be understood only as parts of that goal. The disturbance of one part of the body cannot be viewed in isolation; it affects the entire person. In fact, the deficient organ expresses the direction of the individual's goal, a condition known as **organ dialect.**

One example of organ dialect, or organ jargon, might be a man suffering from rheumatoid arthritis in his hands. His stiff and deformed joints voice his whole style of life. It is as if they cry out, "See my deformity. See my handicap. You can't expect me to do manual work." Without an audible sound, his hands speak of his desire for sympathy from others.

Adler (1956) presented another example of organ dialect—the case of a young obedient boy who wet the bed at night to send a message that he did not wish to conform to parental wishes. Adler contended that bodily organs "speak a language which is usually more expressive and discloses the individual's opinion more clearly than words are able to do" (p. 223).

CONSCIOUS AND UNCONSCIOUS

A second example of a unified personality is the harmony between conscious and unconscious actions. Adler (1956) defined the unconscious as that part of the goal that is neither clearly formulated nor completely understood by the individual. With this definition Adler avoided a dichotomy between the unconscious and the conscious, which he saw as cooperating parts of the same unified system. Conscious thoughts are those that are understood and regarded by the individual as helpful in striving for success. Whatever a person cannot justify as being helpful is pushed into the unconscious.

> We cannot oppose "consciousness" to "unconsciousness" as if they were antagonistic halves of an individual's existence. The conscious life becomes unconscious as soon as we fail to understand it—and as soon as we understand an unconscious tendency it has already become conscious (Adler, 1929/1964, p. 163).

Consciousness and unconsciousness, rather than being opposing factions, are complementary entities operating under the dominance of a unifying style of life. Whether a thought is conscious or unconscious, it has but one purpose—to realize the goal of superiority or success. Although the goal of personality can motivate both healthy and unhealthy individuals, the goal of success can only be attained by people with high levels of social interest.

SOCIAL INTEREST

The usefulness of all human activity must be seen from the viewpoint of social interest.

Social interest is Adler's somewhat misleading translation of his original German term, **Gemeinschaftsgefühl.** A better translation might be "social feeling" or "community feeling," but *Gemeinschaftsgefühl* actually has a meaning that is not fully expressed by any English word or phrase. Roughly, it means a feeling of oneness with all humanity; it implies membership in the social community of all people. A person with well-developed *Gemeinschaftsgefühl* strives not for personal superiority but for perfection for all people in an ideal community. Social interest can be defined as an attitude of relatedness with humanity in general, as well as an empathy for each member of the human race. It manifests itself as cooperation with others for social advancement rather than for personal gain (Adler, 1964).

Adler (1964) believed that social interest is part of human nature and that some amount of it exists in everyone—the criminal, the psychotic, and the mentally healthy. Social interest is rooted as potentiality in everyone, but it must be developed before it can contribute to a useful style of life.

DEVELOPMENT IN A SOCIAL ENVIRONMENT

According to Adler (1956), other people, especially one's mother, contribute to the development of social interest. Before birth a fetus experiences a oneness with its mother, and then after birth the infant strives to reunite with her through the sucking movement of the lips. Young children depend heavily on their mothers to satisfy both their physiological and their psychological needs.

Because social interest arises from the mother-child relationship, every person who has survived infancy has some amount of it. The mother's task, according to Adler, is to encourage mature social interest in her child. She must develop a bond with her child, thus fostering a sense of cooperation. Ideally, she should have a genuine and deep-rooted love for her child—a love that is centered on the child's well-being, not on her own needs or wants. This healthy love relationship develops from a true caring about people. If the mother has learned to give and receive love from others, she will have little difficulty broadening her child's social interest. On the other hand, if she concentrates affection solely on her child, she will not be able to teach that child to transfer social interest to other people. The mother's love for her husband, for her other children, and for society provides a model for the child. By observing the mother's widespread social interest, a child learns that there are important people other than one's mother and oneself.

Adler (1956) believed that the mother must give equal attention to her three ties—children, husband, and society—if her children are to develop social interest. When a mother favors her children to the neglect of husband and society, the children

Both mother and father can contribute powerfully to the developing social interest of their children.

become pampered and spoiled. Conversely, if she directs her attention exclusively to her husband or to society, her children become neglected and unloved. Either mistake hampers the children's independence and ability to cooperate.

The father is the second important person in a child's social environment. He has a difficult function, one that few fathers are able to successfully fulfill. He must have a good attitude toward the child's mother, his own occupation, and society. In addition, his broad social interest must manifest itself in his relationship with his child. The ideal father cooperates on an equal footing with the child's mother in caring for the child and treating it as a human being. According to Adler's (1956) standards, a successful father avoids the dual errors of emotional detachment and paternal authoritarianism. These errors may represent two attitudes, but they are often found in the same father. Both prevent the growth and spread of social interest in a child. A father's emotional detachment may influence the child to develop a warped sense of social interest, a feeling of neglect, and possibly a neurotic attachment to the mother. A child who experiences paternal detachment creates a goal of personal superiority rather than one based on social interest. The second error, paternal authoritarianism, may also lead to a neurotic style of life. A child who sees the father as tyrannical learns to strive for power and personal superiority.

Adler (1956) believed that the effects of the early social environment are extremely important. The relationship a child has with the mother and father is so powerful that it smothers the effects of heredity. Adler believed that after age 5, the effects of heredity become blurred by the powerful influence of one's social environment. By that time learning has modified or shaped nearly every aspect of a child's personality.

NECESSITY OF SOCIAL INTEREST

Adler (1927) believed that social life is the natural condition of the human species and that social interest is the cement that binds society together. The natural inferiority of individuals necessitates their joining together to form a society. Without protection and nourishment from the father and mother, a baby would perish. Without protection from the family or clan, our ancestors would have been destroyed by animals that were stronger, more ferocious, or endowed with keener senses. Social interest, therefore, is a necessity. It is even responsible for our existence, because if a man and woman did not cooperate in the procreation and subsequent protection of a child, the human race could not survive.

Adler believed that the child naturally looks toward others for love and affection. An infant's inadequacy predisposes it toward a mothering person. People therefore develop an early interest in other people, and most continue to be socially oriented. Adler objected to Freud's belief that people are basically narcissistic. People who appear self-centered simply lack a relationship with their mother that fostered social interest. Narcissism is a form of neurosis, not an inherent characteristic of people. It grows from a neurotic mother-child relationship because an overly indulgent or overly negligent mother teaches her child to be concerned primarily with self-interest (Ansbacher, 1985).

CRITERION OF HUMAN VALUES

Social interest was Adler's yardstick for measuring psychological health and is thus "the sole criterion of human values" (Adler, 1927, p. 167). To the degree that people possess social interest, they are psychologically mature. Immature people lack *Gemeinschaftsgefühl*, are self-centered, and strive for personal power and superiority over others. Healthy individuals are genuinely concerned about people and have a goal of success that encompasses the well-being of all people. Life has no value unless a person contributes to the lives of other people and even to the lives of future generations. Social interest is the only gauge to be used in judging the worth of a person. Adler (1956) referred to it as the *barometer of normality*, that is, the standard to be used in determining the usefulness of a life.

Social interest is not synonymous with charity and unselfishness. Acts of philanthropy and kindness may or may not be motivated by *Gemeinschaftsgefühl*. A wealthy woman may regularly give large sums of money to the poor and needy, not because she feels a oneness with them, but, quite to the contrary, because she wishes to maintain a separateness from them. The gift implies, "You are inferior, I am superior, and this charity is proof of my superiority." Adler believed that the worth of all such acts can only be judged against the criterion of social interest.

In summary, people begin life with a basic striving force that is activated by ever-present physical deficiencies. These organic weaknesses lead inevitably to feelings of inferiority. Thus all people possess feelings of inferiority, and all set a final goal at around age 4 or 5. However, neurotic or pathological individuals develop exaggerated feelings of inferiority and attempt to compensate by setting a goal of personal superiority. They are motivated by personal gain rather than by social interest. On the other hand, healthy people are motivated by normal feelings of incompleteness and high levels of social interest. They strive toward the goal of success, defined in terms of perfection and completion for everyone. Figure 4.1 illustrates how the innate striving force can lead to either a neurotic or a healthy style of life. Notice also that neither physical deficiencies nor their consequent feelings of inferiority lead inexorably to neurotic development. Whether we form a useless style of life or a socially useful one depends on how we view these inevitable feelings of inferiority.

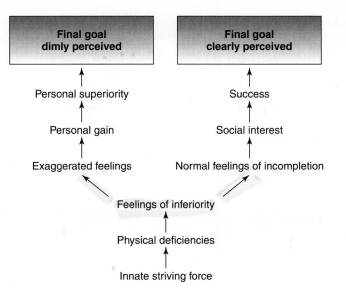

Figure 4.1 Two basic methods of striving toward the final goal.

STYLE OF LIFE

All human potentialities develop in accordance with the individual's self-consistent style of life.

   Style of life is the term Adler used to refer to the flavor of a person's life. It includes not only the person's goal but also self-concept, feelings for others, and attitude toward the world. It is the product of the interaction of heredity, environment, goal of success, social interest, and creative power.

   Style of life is similar to Freud's concept of ego in that it is the governing force of personality. Adler's concept of style of life, however, includes no id or superego waging war against the ego; rather it is the whole organism plus the person's unique manner of self-expression. Adler (1956) used a musical analogy to elucidate style of life. The separate notes of a composition are meaningless without the entire melody, but the melody takes on added significance when we recognize the composer's style or unique manner of expression.

   Our style of life is fairly well established by age 4 or 5. After that time all our actions revolve around our unified style of life. Although the final goal is singular, style of life need not be narrow or rigid. Psychologically unhealthy individuals often lead rather inflexible lives that are marked by an inability to choose new ways of reacting to their environment. In contrast, psychologically healthy people behave in diverse and flexible ways with styles of life that are complex, enriched, and to some extent, subject to change. Healthy people see many ways of striving for success and continually seek to create new options for themselves. Even though their final goal remains constant, the way in which they perceive it continually changes. Thus, they can choose new options at any point in life.

   People with a healthy, socially useful style of life express their social interest through *action*. They actively struggle to solve the three major problems of life—neighborly love, sexual love, and occupation—through cooperation, personal courage, and a willingness to make a contribution to the welfare of another. Adler (1956) believed that people with a socially useful style of life represent the highest form of humanity in the evolutionary process and are likely to populate the world of the future.

CREATIVE POWER

The style of life is developed by the individual's creative power.

Adler believed that each of us is empowered with the freedom to create our own style of life. Ultimately, we are responsible for who we are and how we behave. Our **creative power** places us in control of our own lives, is responsible for our final goal, determines our method of striving for that goal, and contributes to the development of our social interest. In short, our creative power makes each of us a free individual. Creative power is a dynamic concept implying *movement*, and this movement is the most salient characteristic of life. All psychic life involves movement toward a goal, movement with a direction (Adler, 1964).

Adler (1956) acknowledged the importance of heredity and environment in forming personality. Every child is born with a unique genetic makeup and soon comes to have social experiences different from those of any other human. People, however, are much more than a product of heredity and environment. They are creative beings who not only react to their environment but also act on it and cause it to react to them. Adler believed that each of us uses heredity and environment as the bricks and mortar to build personality, but the architectural design reflects our own style. Of primary importance is not what we have been given, but how we put those materials to use. The building materials of personality are secondary. We are our own architect and can build either a useful or a useless life, can choose to remain psychologically healthy or to become neurotic, can construct a gaudy facade or expose the essence of the structure. We are not compelled to grow in the direction of social interest, inasmuch as we have no inner nature that forces us to be good. Conversely, we have no inherently evil nature from which we must escape. We are who we are because of the use we have made of our bricks and mortar.

Adler (1929/1964) used an interesting analogy, which he called "the law of the low doorway," to illustrate the free powers of both the neurotic and the healthy individual. If we are trying to walk through a doorway 4 feet high, we have two basic choices. First, we can use our creative power to bend down as we approach the doorway, thereby successfully solving the problem. This is the manner in which the psychologically healthy individual solves most of life's problems. On the other hand, if we bump our head and fall back, we must still solve the problem correctly or continue bumping our head. Neurotics often choose to bump their head on the realities of life. When approaching the low doorway, we are neither compelled to stoop nor forced to bump our head. We have a creative power that permits us to follow either course.

ABNORMAL DEVELOPMENT

Adler believed that people are what they make of themselves. The creative power endows humans, within certain limits, with the freedom to be either psychologically healthy or unhealthy and to follow either a useful or useless style of life.

Early in his career, Adler's writings were almost exclusively centered around the inadequate personality; later he gave more emphasis to the healthy individual and placed abnormal psychology in a secondary position. Nevertheless, some knowledge of his ideas on maladjustment helps complete an understanding of Individual Psychology.

GENERAL DESCRIPTION

According to Adler (1956), the one factor underlying all types of maladjustment is an *underdeveloped social interest*. Besides lacking social interest, neurotics tend to (1) set their goals too high, (2) have a rigid and dogmatic style of life, and (3) live in their own private world. These three characteristics are inevitable concomitants to lack of social interest. In short, people become failures in life because they are overconcerned with themselves and care little about others.

Maladjusted people set their goals too high as an overcompensation for exaggerated feelings of inferiority. Extravagant goals lead to dogmatic behavior, and the higher the goal, the more rigid the striving. To compensate for deeply rooted feelings of inadequacy and basic insecurity, these individuals narrow their perspective and strive compulsively and rigidly for unrealistic goals.

The exaggerated and unrealistic nature of neurotics' goals set them apart from the community of other people. They live in a private world and endow their goals with private meaning. They approach the problems of friendship, sex, and occupation from a personal angle that precludes successful solutions. Their view of the world is not in focus with that of other individuals and they possess what Adler (1956) called "private meaning" (p. 156).

EXTERNAL FACTORS IN MALADJUSTMENT

Why do some people create maladjustments? Adler (1964) recognized the following three contributing factors, any one of which is sufficient to contribute to abnormality: (1) exaggerated physical deficiencies; (2) a pampered style of life; and (3) a neglected style of life.

Exaggerated Physical Deficiencies

Exaggerated physical deficiencies, whether congenital or the result of injury or disease, are not sufficient to lead to maladjustments. They must be accompanied by accentuated feelings of inferiority. These subjective feelings may be greatly encouraged by a defective body, but they are the progeny of the creative power.

Anyone can develop exaggerated feelings of inferiority, but children born with physical disabilities have an even greater burden and a higher probability of maladjustment than physically healthy children. Physical deficiencies drive children to compensate and often to overcompensate for their inadequacy. As adults, these people tend to be overly concerned with themselves and to develop exaggerated inferiority feelings, which are manifested as an absence of self-confidence, little courage, and no consideration for others. They feel as if they are living in enemy country, fear defeat more than they desire success, and are convinced that life's major problems can only be solved in a selfish manner (Adler, 1927).

Pampered Style of Life

Adler believed that the pampered style of life lies at the heart of most neuroses. Children who are pampered have little social interest and low activity level. They possess strong wishes to be pampered, and their primary desire is to make permanent the pampered, parasitic relationship they originally had with their mother. They expect others to look after them, overprotect them, and satisfy all their selfish needs. They are characterized by extreme discouragement, indecisiveness, oversensitivity, impatience, and exaggerated emotion, especially anxiety. They believe that other people exist for them, and they expect others to pamper them as their mothers once did. They see the world with private vision and believe that they are entitled to be first in everything.

Pampered children have not received too much love; rather, they are unloved. They have been overprotected, hovered over, smothered, and shielded from responsibilities. Their parents have demonstrated a lack of love by doing too much for them and by treating them as if they were incapable of solving their own problems. At least this is their interpretation of the situation, and it is the children's view that matters. If children feel pampered and spoiled, then they are pampered and spoiled (Adler, 1964).

Pampered children also feel neglected. Having been protected by a doting mother, they are fearful in her absence. Whenever they must fend for themselves, they feel left out, mistreated, and neglected. These experiences add to the pampered child's stockpile of inferiority feelings (Adler, 1927).

Neglected Style of Life

The third external factor contributing to maladjustments is neglect. Adler (1927) believed that children who feel unloved and unwanted are likely to borrow heavily from these feelings in creating a neglected style of life. Neglect is a relative concept. No one feels totally neglected or completely unwanted. The fact that a child survived infancy is proof that someone cared for that child and that the seed of social interest has been planted.

Abused and mistreated children develop little social interest and tend to create a neglected style of life. They have little confidence in themselves and tend to overestimate difficulties connected with life's major problems. They expect society to be cold because people have generally treated them coldly. They are spiteful toward others, distrustful of themselves, and unable to cooperate for the common welfare. They see society as enemy country, feel alienated from all other people, and experience a strong sense of envy toward the success of others. Neglected children have many of the characteristics of pampered ones, but generally they are more suspicious and more likely to be dangerous to others (Adler, 1927).

SAFEGUARDING TENDENCIES

According to Adler, all neurotic symptoms are created to safeguard the individual's self-esteem. The symptoms themselves serve as **safeguarding tendencies,** protecting an inflated self-image and maintaining a neurotic style of life.

Adler's concept of safeguarding tendencies can be compared to Freud's concept of defense mechanisms. Basic to both is the idea that symptoms are formed as a protection of the self or ego. However, there are several differences between the two. First, Freud's defense mechanisms protect the ego against anxiety from instinctual sources whereas Adlerian safeguarding tendencies protect the person from outside demands.

Also, Freudian defense mechanisms are common to everyone, but Adler (1956) discussed safeguarding tendencies only with reference to the construction of neurotic symptoms. Nevertheless, probably everyone, the normal as well as the abnormal, relies occasionally on safeguarding tendencies to protect tenuous feelings of self-esteem. Another difference is that defense mechanisms operate solely on an unconscious level whereas safeguarding tendencies may be either conscious or unconscious.

Individual Psychology holds that neurotics fear that their goal of personal superiority will be revealed as erroneous and that they will suffer public disgrace. To compensate for this fiction, they construct safeguarding tendencies that protect themselves against the embarrassing emergence of exaggerated inferiority feelings.

Excuses, aggression, and withdrawal are three commonly used safeguarding tendencies. They are generally unconscious—but occasionally conscious—devices for protecting the neurotic's style of life and for maintaining a fictional, elevated feeling of self-importance (Adler, 1964).

Excuses

The most common safeguarding tendency is **excuses.** The neurotic, as well as the normal individual, typically makes use of the "Yes, but" and the "If only" excuses. In the "Yes, but" excuse, people first state what they claim they would like to do—something that sounds good to others—then they follow with an excuse. A woman might say, "I would like to go to college, *but* my children demand too much of my attention." An executive explains, "I agree with your proposal, *but* company policy will not allow it."

The "If only" statement is the same excuse phrased in a different way. "*If only* my spouse were more supportive, I would have advanced faster in my profession." "*If only* I did not have this physical handicap, I could compete successfully for a job." These excuses protect a weak sense of self-worth and deceive people into believing that they are more superior than they really are (Adler, 1956).

Aggression

Another common safeguarding tendency is **aggression.** Adler (1956) held that neurotics use aggression to safeguard their exaggerated superiority complex, that is, to protect their fragile self-esteem. Safeguarding through aggression may take the form of depreciation, accusation, or self-accusation.

Depreciation is the tendency to undervalue another's achievement and to overvalue one's own. This safeguarding tendency is evident in such aggressive behaviors as sadism, gossip, envy, and intolerance. The intention behind each act of depreciation is to belittle another so that the neurotic, by comparison, will be placed in a favorable light.

Accusation, the second form of neurotic aggression, is the tendency to blame others for one's failures and to seek revenge, thereby safeguarding one's own tenuous self-esteem. Adler (1956) believed that there is an element of aggressive accusation in all neuroses. Neurotics invariably act to cause people around them to suffer more than they do.

The third form of neurotic aggression, **self-accusation,** is marked by self-torture and guilt. Self-torture is evident in masochism, depression, and suicide, and it is a means of safeguarding neurotics' power to hurt those people who are close to them. Adler (1956) believed that guilt is often aggressive, self-accusatory behavior.

Self-accusation is the converse of depreciation, although both are aimed toward personal superiority. In depreciation, neurotics devalue other people to make themselves look good by comparison. In self-accusation, neurotics devalue themselves, with the ultimate purpose of inflicting suffering on others, again to protect their magnified feelings of self-esteem.

Withdrawal

Personality development is sometimes arrested due to neurotics' tendency to run away from difficulties. Adler referred to this tendency as **withdrawal,** or safeguarding through distance. Neurotics unconsciously escape life's problems by setting up a distance between themselves and those problems.

Adler (1956) recognized four modes of safeguarding through withdrawal: moving backward, standing still, hesitating, and constructing obstacles. People are well served by each mode. By making a show of their deficiencies, such as a physical illness, they gain power over others, are relieved from normal obligations, and generally get their own way.

Moving backward is the tendency to safeguard one's fictional goal of superiority by psychologically reverting to a more secure period of life. Moving backward is similar to Freud's concept of regression in that both involve attempts to return to earlier, less anxiety-ridden phases of life. Whereas regression takes place unconsciously and includes the repression of painful experiences, moving backward may sometimes be conscious and is directed at protecting an inflated goal of superiority. It includes suicide, attempts at suicide, most phobias, amnesia, and severe anxiety. People sometimes seek attention from others in order to gain some control over them. For example, attempted suicide usually attracts attention and thus forces other people to worry and fret over the person's well-being. Moving backward is designed to elicit sympathy, the deleterious attitude offered so generously to pampered children.

Psychological distance can also be created by **standing still.** This withdrawal tendency is similar to moving backward but, in general, is not as severe. It is comparable to Freud's concept of fixation in that it blocks normal psychological development. However, standing still differs from fixation in that it may be partly conscious. Also, it safeguards the person's inflated feelings of superiority whereas fixation protects the ego against anxiety. People who stand still simply do not move in any direction; thus they avoid all responsibility by ensuring themselves against any threat of failure. They safeguard their fictional aspirations because they never do anything to prove that they cannot accomplish their goals. A person who never applies to medical school can never be denied entrance; a child who shies away from other children will not be rejected by them. By doing nothing, people safeguard their self-esteem and protect themselves against failure.

Closely related to standing still is **hesitating.** Some people hesitate or vacillate when faced with difficult problems. Their procrastinations eventually give them the excuse, "It's too late now." Most compulsions, Adler believed, are attempts to waste time. Compulsive washing, retracing one's steps, excessive orderliness, destroying work already begun, and leaving work unfinished are examples of hesitation. From a social viewpoint, the hesitating tendency is self-defeating because a person wastes time until it becomes too late to accomplish a task. The tendency, however, is useful from the individual's point of view because it protects the neurotic's inflated sense of self-esteem.

The least severe of the withdrawal safeguarding tendencies is **constructing obstacles.** Some people build a straw house to show that they can knock it down. By overcoming the obstacle, they protect their self-esteem and their prestige. If they fail to hurdle the barrier, they can always resort to an excuse.

Safeguarding tendencies are found in nearly everyone, but when they become overly rigid they lead to neurotic and self-defeating behaviors. Overly sensitive people create safeguarding tendencies to buffer their fear of disgrace, to eliminate their exaggerated inferiority feelings, and to attain self-esteem. However, safeguarding tendencies are self-defeating because their built-in goal of self-interest and personal superiority actually blocks people from securing authentic feelings of self-esteem. Adler believed that neurotics seldom come to realize that their self-esteem would be better safeguarded if they gave up their self-interest and developed genuine interest in others.

MASCULINE PROTEST

Cultural influences cause many men and women to overemphasize the importance of being manly. This condition was Adler's definition of **masculine protest.** In many societies, both men and women place an inferior value on being a woman, an unfortunate and unnatural state of affairs that is the cause of much marital discord and many individual problems of superiority and inferiority complexes. Many boys are taught early that being masculine means being courageous, strong, and dominant. The epitome of success for boys is to win, to be powerful, to be on top. Girls, on the other hand, often learn to be passive and to accept an inferior position in society.

In contrast to Freud, Adler (1930, 1956) believed that the psychic life of women is essentially the same as that of men, and that a male-dominated culture is not a natural state of affairs. Rather, it is the product of historical development. Some women fight against their feminine roles, developing a masculine orientation and becoming assertive and competitive; others revolt by adopting a passive role, becoming exceedingly helpless and obedient; still others become resigned to the belief that they are inferior human beings, acknowledging men's privileged position by shifting responsibilities to them. Each of these modes of adjustment results from cultural influences, not from inherent psychic difference between the sexes.

APPLICATIONS OF INDIVIDUAL PSYCHOLOGY

The practical applications of Individual Psychology can be divided into four areas: family constellation, early recollections, dreams, and psychotherapy.

FAMILY CONSTELLATION

In therapy, Adler almost always asked patients about their family constellation, that is, their birth order, the sex of their siblings, and the age spread between them. Although people's perception of the situation into which they were born is more important than numerical rank, Adler did form some general hypotheses about birth order.

Siblings may feel superior or inferior and adopt different attitudes toward the world depending in part on their order of birth.

Firstborn children, according to Adler (1931), are likely to have intensified feelings of power and superiority, high anxiety, and overprotective tendencies. (Recall that Freud was his mother's firstborn child.) Firstborn children occupy a unique position, being an only child for a time and then experiencing a traumatic dethronement when a younger sibling is born. This event dramatically changes the situation and the child's view of the world. If firstborn children are age 3 or older when a baby brother or sister is born, they incorporate this dethronement into a previously established style of life. They likely will feel hostility and resentment toward the new baby, but if they have already developed a cooperating style, they will eventually adopt this same attitude toward the new sibling. If the firstborn is less than three, hostility and resentment will be largely unconscious, which makes these attitudes more resistant to change in later life.

According to Adler, secondborn children (such as himself) begin life in a better situation for developing cooperation and social interest. To some extent, the personalities of secondborn children are shaped by their perception of the older child's attitude toward them. If this attitude is one of extreme hostility and vengeance, the second child may become highly competitive or overly discouraged. The typical second child, however, does not develop in either of these two directions, but matures toward moderate competitiveness, having a healthy desire to overtake the older rival. If some success is achieved, the child is likely to develop a revolutionary attitude and feel that any authority can be challenged. Again, children's interpretations are more important than their chronological position.

Youngest children, Adler believed, are often the most pampered and, consequently, run a high risk of being problem children. They are likely to have strong feelings of inferiority and to lack a sense of independence. Nevertheless, they possess many advantages. They are often highly motivated to exceed older siblings and to become the fastest runner, the best musician, the most skilled athlete, or the most ambitious student.

Only children are in a unique position of competing, not against brothers and sisters, but against father and mother. They often develop an exaggerated sense of

Table 4.1 Adler's View of Some Possible Traits by Birth Order

Positive Traits	Negative Traits
Oldest Child	
Nurturing and protective of others	Highly anxious
Good organizer	Exaggerated feelings of power
	Unconscious hostility
	Fights for acceptance
	Must always be "right," whereas others are always "wrong"
	Highly critical of others
	Uncooperative
Second Child	
Highly motivated	Highly competitive
Cooperative	Easily discouraged
Moderately competitive	
Youngest Child	
Realistically ambitious	Pampered style of life
	Dependent on others
	Wants to excel in everything
	Unrealistically ambitious
Only Child	
Socially mature	Exaggerated feelings of superiority
	Low feelings of cooperation
	Inflated sense of self
	Pampered style of life

superiority, an inflated self-concept, and a feeling that the world is a dangerous place, especially if their parents were overly concerned with their health. Adler (1931) stated that only children may lack well-developed feelings of cooperation and social interest, possess a parasitic attitude, and expect other people to pamper and protect them. Typical positive and negative traits of oldest, second, youngest, and only children are shown in Table 4.1.

EARLY RECOLLECTIONS

To gain an understanding of patients' personality, Adler would ask them to reveal their **earliest recollections.** Although he believed that the recalled memories yield clues for understanding patients' style of life, he did not consider them to have a causal effect. Whether the recalled experiences correspond with objective reality or are complete fantasies is of no importance. People reconstruct the events so they are consistent with a theme or pattern that runs throughout their lives.

Adler (1929/1969, 1931) insisted that our earliest recollection is always consistent with our present style of life and that our subjective account of this experience yields a clue to understanding both our final goal and our style of life. To illustrate this point, Adler used the example of an outwardly successful man who greatly distrusted women. This man reported the following early memory: "I was going with my mother and little brother to market. Suddenly it began to rain and my mother took me in her arms, and then, remembering that I was the older, she put me down and took up my younger brother" (Adler, 1929/1964, p. 123). Adler saw that this recollection related directly to the man's current distrust of women. Having initially gained a favorite position with his mother, he eventually lost it to his younger brother. Although others may claim to love him, they will soon withdraw their love. Note that Adler did not believe that the early childhood experience *caused* the man's current distrust of women, but rather that his current distrustful style of life shapes and colors his early recollections.

Highly anxious patients will often project their current style of life onto their memory of childhood experiences by recalling fearful and anxiety-producing events, such as being in a motor vehicle crash, losing parents either temporarily or permanently, or being bullied by other children. Socially healthy individuals, on the other hand, tend to recall memories that include pleasant relations with other people. In either case the early experience does not determine the style of life. Adler believed that the opposite was true; that is, our recollections of early experiences are simply shaped by our present style of life. Implicit in this assumption is the notion that early recollections will change as style of life changes. In the section on related research, we discuss evidence dealing with this intriguing hypothesis.

DREAMS

An individual's style of life is also expressed in dreams. Adler rejected Freud's notion that dreams are expressions of infantile wishes; instead, he viewed them as forward-looking and as providing clues for solving future problems. Dreams, however, are not prophetic. Although they cannot foretell the future, they represent the dreamer's attempt to solve a problem that cannot be solved by common sense alone.

Immediately before Adler's first trip to the United States in 1926, he had a vivid and anxious dream that related directly to his desire to spread his Individual Psychology to a new world and to free himself from the constraints of Freud and Vienna. The night before he was to depart for America, Adler dreamed that he was on board the ship when

> suddenly it capsized and sunk. All of Adler's worldly possessions were on it and were destroyed by the raging waves. Hurled into the ocean, Adler was forced to swim for his life. Alone he thrashed and struggled through the choppy water. But through the force of will and determination, he finally reached land in safety. (Hoffman, 1994, p. 151)

Adler interpreted this dream to mean that he had to muster the courage to venture into a new world and to break from old worldly possessions.

Although Adler believed that he could easily interpret this dream, he contended that most dreams are self-deceptions and not easily understood by the dreamer. Dreams are disguised to deceive the dreamer, making self-intrepretation difficult. The more an individual's goal is inconsistent with reality, the more likely that person's dreams will be used for self-deception. For example, a man may have the goal of reaching the top, being above, or becoming president. If he also possesses a dependent style of life, his ambitious goal may be expressed in dreams of being lifted onto another's shoulders or being shot from a cannon. The dream unveils the style of life, but it fools the dreamer by presenting him with an unrealistic, exaggerated sense of power and accomplishment. In contrast, a more courageous and independent man with similar lofty ambitions may dream of unaided flying or reaching a goal without help, much as Adler had done when he dreamed of escaping from a sinking ship.

PSYCHOTHERAPY

Adlerian theory postulates that psychopathology results from lack of courage, exaggerated feelings of inferiority, and underdeveloped social interest. Thus, the chief purpose of Adlerian psychotherapy is to enhance courage, lessen feelings of inferiority, and encourage social interest. This task, however, is not easy because patients struggle to hold on to their existing, comfortable view of themselves. To overcome this resistance to change, Adler would sometimes ask patients, "What would you do if I cured you immediately?" Such a question usually forced patients to examine their goals and to see that responsibility for their current misery rested with them.

Adler often used the motto, "Everybody can accomplish everything." Except for certain limitations set by heredity, he strongly believed this maxim and repeatedly emphasized that what people do with what they have is more important than what they have (Adler, 1925/1968, 1956). Through the use of humor and warmth, Adler tried to increase the patient's courage, self-esteem, and social interest. He believed that a warm, nurturing attitude by the therapist encourages patients to expand their social interest to each of the three problems of life: sexual love, friendship, and occupation.

Although Adler was quite active in setting the goal and direction of psychotherapy, he maintained a friendly and permissive attitude toward the patient. He established himself as a congenial coworker, refrained from moralistic preachings, and placed great value on the human relationship. By cooperating with their therapists, patients establish contact with another person. The therapeutic relationship awakens their social interest in the same manner that children gain social interest from their parents. Once awakened, the patients' social interest must spread to family, friends, and people outside the therapeutic relationship (Adler, 1956).

RELATED RESEARCH

Research interest in Adlerian theory, though still modest, has been slowly increasing. The recent popularity of Frank Sulloway's (1996) book *Born to Rebel* attests to the appeal that birth order has for many people. Although Sulloway's work was not directly inspired by Adler's ideas, its findings that birth order influences personality and that firstborn children are often achievement oriented, conforming, and conventional supports the Adlerian view. However, Sulloway criticized Adler's conception of birth order as being based on anecdotal evidence and nearly impossible to verify or falsify.

The increasing interest in Adler's concepts is evident in a survey conducted by C. Edward Watkins, Jr. (1992c), who compared the frequency of Adlerian research between 1982 and 1990 with research reported between 1970 and 1981. In the areas of birth order, social interest, early recollections, and style of life, more research was reported during the 9-year period from 1982 to 1990 than in the 12-year period from 1970 to 1981. Watkins drew three main conclusions from this simple frequency count: (1) empirical research on Adlerian concepts nearly doubled from the 1970s to the 1980s; (2) research in all areas but style of life was relatively active; and (3) early recollection research showed the largest gain in attention. In addition, Watkins (1992b) has reviewed and evaluated the research on birth order and found general support for Adler's conception of firstborns (see Table 4.1). Watkins (1992a) also reviewed and critiqued the research on early recollections and again found some support for Adler's ideas. Since Watkins's review, Erik Mansager et al. (1995) looked at research on early recollections published in *Individuial Psychology* and found 17 articles in the 4-year period from 1991 to 1994, indicating that researchers continue to be interested in studying Adler's concept of ERs. Later, Watkins (1994) looked at studies that measured social interest and once more found tentative support for Adler's notion of *Gemeinschaftsgefühl*. However, Watkins has called for (1) refinements and revisions of psychometric scales measuring Adler's concepts and (2) the extension of all Adlerian research to minority participants.

Prompting much of this research on early recollections has been the development of several instruments that assess ERs. Guy Manaster and Thomas Perryman have constructed the *Manaster-Perryman Manifest Content Early Recollection Scoring Manual* (Manaster & Perryman, 1974, 1979), which allows judges to score early recollections in seven broad categories: (1) Characters, or people involved in the memory, (2) Themes, or topics of the ER, (3) Concern with Detail—visual, auditory, and motor, (4) Setting, or location of the ER, (5) Active-Passive, that is, the degree to which the person initiated action as opposed to being acted upon, (6) Internal-External Control, or person's acceptance of responsibility for what happened in the early recollection, and (7) Affect, or overall feeling of the memory. Interrater reliability of the Manaster-Perryman is generally quite high (Buchanan, Kern, & Bell-Dumas, 1991).

Using the Manaster-Perryman scoring system, researchers have shown how early recollections relate to a variety of factors, including birth order (Fakouri & Hafner, 1984), depression (Allers, White, & Hornbuckle, 1990; Fakouri, Hartung, & Hafner, 1985), college major (Coram & Shields, 1987), alcoholism in women (Hafner, Fakouri, & Chesney, 1988), alcoholism in men (Chaplin & Orlofsky, 1991), criminal behavior of men (Elliot, Fakouri, & Hafner, 1993), eating disorders in women (Williams & Manaster, 1990), and success in counseling (Statton & Wilborn, 1991).

Two examples of research that used the Manaster-Perryman scoring system were reported by James Hafner and his associates. In one study, Hafner and M. Ebrahim Fakouri (1984) investigated differences in early recollections among graduate students in clinical psychology, dentistry, and law. They found that clinical psychology students, compared with law and dentistry students, reported early memories that contained more expressions of fear and anxiety and less references to interacting with groups of people. In addition, psychology and law students had more early recollections than dentistry students that involved nonfamily members. In a separate study on the early recollections of female alcoholics, Hafner, Fakouri, and Stephen Chesney (1988) found that alcoholic women differed significantly from a control group of nonalcholic women on five of the seven ER themes on the Manaster-Perryman scoring system. Compared with controls, the early memories of alcoholic women (1) mentioned "mother" or other family members less often, (2) had more anxiety- and fear-producing situations, (3) had more hostility or punishment themes, (4) were more passive and dismissive of responsibility, and (5) had more overall negative affect.

Also, A. Rahn Bruhn and his former graduate student Jeffrey Last (Last, 1983; Last & Bruhn, 1983) have developed the *Comprehensive Early Memory Scoring System* (CEMSS) for scoring early recollections. The CEMSS is a multidimensional scoring system that assesses pathological and adaptive early recollection characteristics in eight separate categories: (1) Characters, (2) Settings, (3) Sensory-Motor Aspect, (4) Relation to Reality, (5) Object Relations, (6) Themes, (7) Affect, and (8) Damage Aspect. Although the CEMSS has not produced as many studies as the Manaster-Perryman scoring system has, some recent research has suggested that the CEMSS may be useful in assessing variables that relate to self and others. Using the CEMSS, Candis Nichols and Jess Feist (1994) looked at early recollections of optimistic and pessimistic college students and found that the ERs of optimists, compared with those of pessimists, were more likely to include: (1) other people; (2) scenes in which they were active rather than passive; (3) clear and distinctive events, such as the physical appearance of other people, the location of an event, or their own motivations; (4) sustained interpersonal contact; (5) themes of personal competence and mastery of the environment; and (6) pleasant experiences.

These and other studies tend to lend validity to Adler's notion that there are no chance memories and that people remember things from childhood that match with their adult style of life. However, they do not prove his hypothesis that present style of life shapes one's recall of early childhood experiences. The opposite explanation is possible; that is, early childhood experiences may affect present style of life and habits of thinking. If Adler's hypothesis is correct, then early recollections should change as style of life changes.

Some evidence exists that early recollections change through the course of psychotherapy. For example, Gary Savill and Daniel Eckstein (1987) obtained early recollections and mental status of psychiatric patients both before and after therapy and compared them to ERs and mental status of a matched group of control participants. They found significant changes in both mental status and early recollections for the therapy group but not for the controls. Consistent with Adlerian theory, this finding indicates that when therapy is successful, patients change their early recollections. Similarly, Jane Statton and Bobbie Wilborn (1991) looked at the three earliest recollections of 5- to 12-year-old children after each of 10 weekly counseling sessions and compared them with the early recollections of a control group who did not receive counseling. The researchers found that the counseling group showed greater changes in the theme, character, setting, amount of detail, and the level of affect of their early memories. In addition, they reported one dramatic example of how early recollections can change as present style of life changes. One young child recalled that

> "My uncle and dad took me fishing. They were fishing and my uncle got his line hung on a tree stump in the water. He yanked on the pole and the hook came back and hooked me in the head. . . . I waited for them to pull it out of my head." (p. 341)

After counseling, the child recast this passive early recollection in a more active light.

> "I went fishing when I was about 5 . . . I caught a fish . . . and my uncle threw his line out and he got it hung on a tree stump and he yanked it back and the hook came back and got me in the head. . . . I pulled it out." (p. 344)

Results of these studies (Savill & Eckstein, 1987; Statton & Wilborn, 1991) suggest that ERs are subjective reconstructions of childhood events rather than accurate renderings of those events. If ERs are fictional reconstructions amenable to present shifts in a person's style of life, then we might also expect that created early recollections will also accurately predict general themes in that person's life. Buchanan, Kern, and Bell-Dumas (1991) compared the thematic content of created early recollections with those of actual ERs and found that asking people to make up an early recollection yielded nearly the same manifest content as did actual ERs. These researchers first conducted a pilot study with university students that used only the Theme dimension of the *Manaster-Perryman Manifest Content Early Recollection Scoring Manual* (Manaster & Perryman, 1974). After asking participants for their first three early recollections, Buchanan et al. then requested them to "create ERs which could have happened in someone's life but did not happen in your own" (p. 350). Interestingly, the researchers found that created ERs produced themes that were consistent with those of actual ERs.

They concluded that when people are asked to make up early recollections, "to some degree, their life style may be projected in the created recollections" (p. 352).

In addition to early recollections, Adler's notion of style of life has received some empirical examination. For example, research has looked at style of life themes among unwed pregnant adolescents (Jorgensen & Newlon, 1988), obesity (Laser, 1984), bulimia (Axtell & Newlon, 1993), and childhood trauma (Butler & Newlon, 1992). The most reliable and valid measure of style of life is the 96-item Life Style Personality Inventory (LSPI) developed by Mary Wheeler, Roy Kern, and William Curlette (1982, 1986, 1991). This instrument uses present perceptions of childhood experiences and consists of six bidimensional scales and one single dimensional scale. The six bidimensional scales are: (1) Conforming/Active, (2) Conforming/Passive, (3) Controlling/Active, (4) Controlling/Passive, (5) Exploiting/Active, and (6) Exploiting/Passive. The only single dimensional scale measures feelings of worthlessness and is entitled Displaying Inadequacy. To date, only a few studies have been published on the LSPI. One of these was conducted by K. Klayton Keene and Mary Wheeler (1994) and examined how substance abuse relates to style of life. Previous non-Adlerian research has shown that antisocial personality and passive dependence are two personality traits that consistently relate to substance abuse. Using the Life Style Personality Inventory, Keene and Wheeler found that Theme 6 (Exploiting/Passive) was associated with high-risk drug use. This finding suggests that the LSPI may be a useful instrument for identifying the potential substance abuser, but additional research is clearly needed to establish the clinical validity of the Life Style Personality Inventory.

CRITIQUE OF ADLER

Adler's theory, like those of Freud and Jung, produced many concepts that do not readily lend themselves to verification or *falsification*. For example, the results of previously cited studies on the similarities between early recollections and present style of life do not prove that present style of life shapes one's early memories. An alternative, causal explanation is also possible; that is, one could counter that early experiences determine present style of life. Thus, one of Adler's most important concepts—the notion that present style of life determines early memories rather than vice versa—is difficult to either verify or falsify.

On a more positive note, we have reviewed research on instruments measuring Adler's ideas on early recollections and style of life. In addition, his theory has encouraged researchers to construct several social interest scales, for example, the Social Interest Scale (Crandall, 1975, 1981), the Social Interest Index (Greever, Tseng, & Friedland, 1973), and the Sulliman Scale of Social Interest (Sulliman, 1973). Watkins (1994) has reviewed studies dealing with the psychometric properties of these three instruments and, although he found some problems with the Social Interest Index, he was able to report generally solid reliability and validity for the Social Interest Scale and the Sulliman Scale of Social Interest. In addition, Watkins and Blazina (1994) found the Sulliman scale to possess adequate reliability, and Watkins and St. John (1994) reported acceptable validity for the Sulliman scale. Current research activity on these scales and on birth order, early recollections, and style of life gives Adlerian theory a moderate to high rating on its *ability to generate research*.

How well does Adlerian theory *organize knowledge* into a meaningful framework? In general, Individual Psychology is sufficiently broad to encompass possible explanations for much of what is known about human behavior and development. Even seemingly self-defeating and inconsistent behaviors can be fit into the framework of striving for superiority. Adler's practical view of life's problems allows us to rate his theory high on its ability to make sense out of what we know about human behavior.

As a *guide to action*, Adlerian theory serves the psychotherapist, the teacher, and the parent with guidelines for the solution to practical problems in a variety of settings. Adlerian practitioners gather information through reports on birth order, dreams, early recollections, childhood difficulties, and organ deficiencies. They then use this information to understand a person's style of life and to apply those specific techniques that will both increase that person's individual responsibility and broaden his or her freedom of choice.

Is Individual Psychology *internally consistent*? Does it include a set of operationally defined terms? Although Adlerian theory is a model for self-consistency, it suffers from a lack of *precise operational definitions*. Terms like "goal of superiority" and "creative power" have no scientific definition. Nowhere in Adler's works are they operationally defined, and the potential researcher will look in vain for precise definitions that lend themselves to rigorous study. The term "creative power" is an especially illusory one. Just what is this magical force that takes the raw materials of heredity and environment and molds a unique personality? How does the creative power transform itself into specific actions or operations needed by the scientist to carry out an investigation? Unfortunately, Individual Psychology is somewhat philosophical—even moralistic—and does not provide answers to these questions.

The concept of creative power, of course, is a very appealing one. Probably most of us prefer to believe that we are composed of something more than the interactions of heredity and environment. Intuitively, we feel that we have some agent (soul, ego, self, creative power) within us that allows us to make choices, to be free, and to create our own personality or style of life. As appealing as it is, however, the concept of creative power is simply a fiction and cannot be scientifically studied. Due to lack of operational definitions, therefore, Individual Psychology is rated low on internal consistency.

The final criterion of a useful theory is simplicity or *parsimony*. On this standard we rate Individual Psychology about average. Although Adler's awkward and unorganized writings distract from the theory's rating on parsimony, the work of Heinz Ansbacher and Rowena Ansbacher (Adler, 1956, 1964) improves the simplicity of Individual Psychology.

CONCEPT OF HUMANITY

Adler believed that people are basically self-determined and that they shape their personalities from the meaning they give to their experiences. The building material of personality is provided by heredity and environment, but the creative power shapes this material and puts it to use. Adler frequently emphasized that the use that people make of their abilities and perceptions is the most crucial factor in determining the value of their style of life. In discussing an individual's relationship to the outside world, Adler (1956) wrote:

> It is neither heredity nor environment which determines his relationship to the outside. Heredity only endows him with certain abilities. Environment only gives him certain impressions. These abilities and impressions, and the manner in which he "experiences" them—that is to

say, the interpretation he makes of these experiences—are the bricks which he uses in his own "creative" way in building up his attitude toward life. It is his individual way of using these bricks, or in other words his attitude toward life, which determines this relationship to the outside world. (p. 206)

Adler believed that people's interpretations of experiences are more important than the experiences themselves. Neither the past nor the future determine present behavior. Instead, people are motivated by their present perceptions of the past and their present expectations of the future. These perceptions do not necessarily correspond with reality but are a reflection of the people's individual psychological needs. Adler (1956) stated that "meanings are not determined by situations, but we determine ourselves by the meanings we give to situations" (p. 208).

People are forward-moving, motivated by future goals rather than by innate instincts or causal forces. These future goals are often rigid and unrealistic, but our internal freedom allows us to reshape them and thereby change our lives. We create our personalities and are capable of altering them by learning new attitudes. These attitudes encompass an understanding that change can occur, that no other person or circumstance is responsible for what we are, and that personal goals must be subordinated to social interest.

Although our final goal is fixed during early childhood, we remain free to change our style of life. Because the goal is fictional and unconscious, we can set and pursue temporary goals. These momentary goals are not rigidly circumscribed by the final goal but are created by us merely as partial solutions. Adler (1927) expressed this idea as follows: "We must understand that the reactions of the human soul are not final and absolute: Every response is but a partial response, valid temporarily, but in no way to be considered a final solution of a problem" (p. 24). In other words, even though our final goal is set during childhood, we are capable of change at any point in life. However, Adler maintained that not all our choices are conscious and that style of life is created through both conscious and unconscious choices.

Adler believed that ultimately we are responsible for our own personalities. Our creative power is capable of transforming feelings of inadequacy into either social interest or into the self-centered goal of personal superiority. This means that we remain free to choose between psychological health and neuroticism. Adler regarded self-centeredness as pathological and established social interest as the standard of psychological maturity. Healthy people have a high level of social interest, but throughout their lives, they remain free to accept or reject normality and to become what they will.

On the six dimensions of a concept of humanity listed in Chapter 1, Adler could be rated as follows: high on *free choice*; very high on *optimism*; very low on *causality*; moderate on *unconscious influences*; high on *social factors* underlying personality, and high on *uniqueness* of individuals. In summary, Adler held that we are self-determining social creatures, forward moving and motivated by present fictions to strive toward perfection for ourselves and society.

Chapter Summary

The Individual Psychology of Alfred Adler stands in sharp contrast to Freud's pessimistic view of personality. It suggests that people are self-determined, forward moving, motivated by present perceptions, and capable of putting aside personal needs and of striving for the betterment of all humanity.

Adler believed that each of us begins life with an innate striving force that receives additional impetus from our inevitable physical deficiencies. These organic weaknesses contribute to our feelings of inferiority, and these feelings in turn contribute to our final goal, which we set at around age 4 or 5. Some people develop exaggerated feelings of inferiority and overcompensate by setting a goal of personal superiority. Other people are motivated by normal feelings of incompleteness and high levels of social interest, which they define as perfection and completion for all humankind.

This chapter looked at six major tenets of Adlerian theory: (1) striving for superiority or success, (2) the subjectivity of perceptions, (3) the unity of personality, (4) social interest, (5) style of life, and (6) creative power. In addition, it discussed both abnormal development and the applications of Individual Psychology.

According to Adler, the essential nature of humans dictates that they will *strive for completion* or improvement. Although all people have this innate tendency, not all strive for the welfare of others. Some are motivated more toward personal superiority. However, people with a high level of social interest strive for success, defined as improvement or upward development for everyone.

Human behavior is shaped neither by past events nor by objective reality, but rather by people's *subjective perception* of a situation. Objective realities such as organ deficiencies, order of birth, and early childhood experiences are not as important as our view of them, ourselves, and our environment.

Adler held that all aspects of human personality are *unified* and that all actions are consistent with one's *final goal*, or purpose in life. Seemingly inconsistent behaviors all serve a single purpose.

Social interest, that is, a deep concern for the welfare of other people, is the sole criterion by which human actions should be judged. The three major problems of life—neighborly love, work, and sexual love—can only be solved through social interest. Psychologically unhealthy people lack social interest and try to solve problems with an eye toward personal gain.

All our human potentialities develop in accordance with our self-consistent *style of life*, which includes our final goal, self-concept, feelings toward others, and attitudes toward the world.

The style of life is developed by our *creative power*, that is, our free will. Although we forge our personality from the building materials provided by heredity and environment, our creative power is ultimately responsible for what we make of ourselves.

Adler insisted that neurotics are different from normal individuals to the extent that they lack social interest. People who perceive themselves to have had exaggerated *physical deficiencies*, a *pampered style of life*, or a *neglected style of life* are most likely to become neurotic. All people, but especially neurotics, make use of various *safeguarding tendencies*, such as excuses, aggression, and withdrawal. Each of these represents conscious or unconscious attempts to protect inflated feelings of superiority against public disgrace.

The *masculine protest*, or the belief that men are superior to women, lies at the root of many neuroses, both for men and for women.

Adler used *birth order*, *early recollections*, and *dreams* in his practice of *psychotherapy*. The goal of Adlerian therapy is to foster courage, self-esteem, and social interest through a healthy relationship between the patient and therapist.

As a scientific theory, Individual Psychology is limited by a lack of operationally defined terms, and many of its major tenets elude rigorous empirical investigation. Nevertheless, it provides a useful explanation for much of what is known about human personality and is a helpful model for the practitioner.

Adler's *concept of humanity* is basically optimistic and purposive. People strive toward a final goal of their own creation and have the potential to bring about significant personality change at any time of life. Although social influences are important, ultimately we are all responsible for who we are and what we do with what we have.

Suggested Readings

Adler, A. (1956). *The Individual Psychology of Alfred Adler: A systematic presentation in selections from his writings* (H. L. Ansbacher & R. R. Ansbacher, Eds.). New York: Basic Books.

A systematic presentation of Adler's theory and practice, edited by two advocates of Individual Psychology.

Adler, A. (1979). *Superiority and social interest: A collection of later writings* (3rd ed.) (H. L. Ansbacher & R. R. Ansbacher, Eds.). New York: Norton.

A compilation of Adler's later writings designed to supplement the 1956 volume.

Hoffman, E. (1994). *The drive for self: Alfred Adler and the founding of Individual Psychology.* Reading, MA: Addison-Wesley.

Although several earlier biographies of Adler have appeared, most were fragmentary and incomplete. In this book, Edward Hoffman, who has also penned a biography of Abraham Maslow, presents the first full-length account of Adler, the man and his times.

Klein

I n contrast to Jung and Adler, who eventually repudiated Freud's theories, Melanie Klein sought to validate and extend Freud's ideas within the framework of psychoanalysis. Unlike these three earlier theorists, Klein carefully observed young children and built her **object relations theory** mostly on those observations. In contrast to Freud, who emphasized the first 4 to 6 years of life, Klein stressed the importance of the first 4 to 6 *months* after birth. She insisted that the infant's drives (hunger, sex, and so forth) are directed to an object—a breast, a penis, a vagina, and so on. According to Klein, the child's relation to the breast is fundamental and serves as a prototype for later relations to whole objects, such as mother and father. The very early tendency of infants to relate to partial objects gives their experiences an unrealistic or fantasy-like quality that affects all later interpersonal relations. Thus Klein's ideas tend to shift the focus of psychoanalytic theory from organically based stages of development to the role of early fantasy in the development of interpersonal relationships.

In addition to Klein, other theorists have speculated on the importance of a child's early experiences with its mother. Margaret Mahler believed that children's sense of identity rests on a three-step relationship with their mother. First, infants have basic needs cared for by their mother; next, they develop a safe symbiotic relationship with an all-powerful mother; and finally, they emerge from their mother's protective circle and establish their separate individuality. Otto Kernberg also emphasized the importance of a healthy mother/child relationship, postulating that such a relationship would result in the child developing a stable self-concept and satisfying interpersonal relations. Heinz Kohut theorized that children develop a sense of self during early infancy when parents and others treat them as if they had an individualized sense of identity. John Bowlby investigated infants' attachment to their mother as well as the negative consequences of being separated from their mother.

BIOGRAPHY OF MELANIE KLEIN

Melanie Reizes Klein was born March 30, 1882, in Vienna, Austria, to Dr. Moriz Reizes and his second wife, Libussa Deutsch Reizes. The youngest of four children, Klein believed that her birth was unplanned and, as a consequence, she felt rejected by her parents, especially her father who favored Emilie, the oldest daughter (Sayers, 1991). By the time Melanie was born, her father had long since rebelled against his early Orthodox Jewish training and had ceased to practice any religion. As a consequence, Melanie grew up in a family that was neither proreligious nor antireligious. During her childhood she observed both parents working at jobs they did not enjoy. Her father was a physician who struggled to make a living in medicine and eventually was relegated to working as a dental assistant. Her mother ran a shop selling plants and reptiles, a difficult, humiliating, and fearful job for someone who abhorred snakes (Segal, 1979). Despite her father's meager income as a doctor, Melanie aspired to become a physician.

Klein's early relationships were either unhealthy or ended in tragedy. She felt neglected by her elderly father, whom she saw as cold and distant, and although she loved and idolized her mother, she felt suffocated by her. Melanie had a special fondness for her older sister Sidonie, who was 4 years older and who taught Melanie arithmetic and reading. Unfortunately, when Melanie was 4 years old, Sidonie died. In later years, Klein confessed that she never got over grieving for Sidonie (Segal, 1992). After her sister's death, Melanie became deeply attached to her only brother Emmanuel, who was nearly 5 years older and who became her close confidant. She idolized her brother, and this infatuation may have contributed to her later difficulties in relating to men. Like Sidonie earlier, Emmanuel tutored Melanie, and his excellent instructions helped her pass the entrance examinations of a reputable preparatory school (Petot, 1990).

When Melanie was 18, her father died, but a greater tragedy occurred 2 years later when her beloved brother Emmanuel died. Emmanuel's death left Melanie devastated. While still in mourning over her brother's death, Melanie married Arthur Klein, an engineer who had been Emmanuel's close friend. Melanie believed that her marriage at age 21 prevented her from becoming a physician, and for the rest of her life, she regretted that she had not reached that goal (Grosskurth, 1986).

Unfortunately, Klein did not have a happy marriage; she dreaded sex and abhorred pregnancy (Grosskurth, 1986). Nevertheless, her marriage to Arthur produced three children: Melitta, born in 1904; Hans, born in 1907; and Erich, born in 1914. In 1909, the Kleins moved to Budapest where Arthur had been transferred. There, Melanie met Sandor Ferenczi, a member of Freud's inner circle and the person who introduced her into the world of psychoanalysis. When her mother died in 1914, Klein became depressed and entered analysis with Ferenczi, an experience that served as a turning point in her life. That same year she read Freud's *On Dreams* (1901/1953) "and realized immediately that was what I was aiming at, at least during those years when I was so very keen to find out what would satisfy me intellectually and emotionally" (quoted in Grosskurth, 1986, p. 69). At about the same time she discovered Freud, her youngest child Erich was born. Klein was deeply taken by psychoanalysis and trained her son according to Freudian principles. In addition, she began to psychoanalyze Erich from the time he was very young. She also attempted to analyze Melitta and Hans, both of whom eventually went to other analysts. Melitta, who became a psychoanalyst, was analyzed by Karen Horney as well as by others (Grosskurth, 1986). An interesting parallel between Horney and Klein is the fact that Klein later analyzed Horney's two youngest daughters when they were 12 and 9 years old. (Horney's oldest daughter was 14 and refused to be analyzed.) Unlike Melitta's voluntary analysis by Horney, the two Horney children were compelled to attend analytic sessions, not for treatment of any neurotic disorder but as a preventive measure (Quinn, 1987).

Klein separated from her husband in 1919, but did not obtain a divorce for several years. After the separation, she established a psychoanalytic practice in Berlin and made her first contributions to the psychoanalytic literature with a paper dealing with her analysis of Erich, who was not identified as her son. Not completely satisfied with her own analysis by Ferenczi, she ended the relationship and began an analysis with Karl Abraham, another member of Freud's inner circle. After only 14 months, however, Klein experienced another tragedy when Abraham died. Then, like Freud before her, Klein began a lifelong self-analysis.

Before 1919, psychoanalysts, including Freud, based their theories of child development on their therapeutic work with *adults*. Freud's only case study of a child was Little Hans, a boy whom he saw as a patient only once. Melanie Klein changed that situation by psychoanalyzing children directly. Her work with very young children, including her own, convinced her that children internalize both positive and negative feelings toward their mother and that they develop a superego much earlier than Freud had believed. Her slight divergence from standard psychoanalytic theory brought much criticism from her colleagues in Berlin, causing her to feel increasingly uncomfortable in that city. Then, in 1926, Ernest Jones invited her to London to analyze his children and to deliver a series of lectures on child analysis. These lectures later resulted in her first book, *The Psycho-Analysis of Children* (Klein, 1932). In 1927, she took up permanent residency in England, remaining there until her death on September 22, 1960.

Klein's years in London were marked by division and controversy. Although she continued to regard herself as a Freudian, neither Freud nor his daughter Anna accepted her emphasis on the importance of very early childhood or her analytic technique with children. Her differences with Anna Freud began while the Freuds were still living in Vienna, but they climaxed after Anna moved with her father and mother to London in 1938. Before the arrival of Anna Freud, the English school of psychoanalysis was steadily becoming the "Kleinian School," and Melanie's battles were limited mostly to those with her daughter, Melitta. In 1934, Klein's older son, Hans, was killed in a fall. Melitta, who had recently moved to London with her psychoanalyst husband Walter Schmideberg, maintained that her brother had committed suicide, and she blamed her mother for his death. During that same year, Melitta began an analysis with Edward Glover, one of Klein's rivals in the British Society. Klein and her daughter then became even more personally estranged and professionally antagonistic, and Melitta maintained her animosity even after her mother's death.

Although Melitta Schmideberg was not a supporter of Anna Freud, her persistent antagonism toward Klein increased the difficulties of Klein's struggle with Anna Freud, who never recognized the possibility of analyzing young children (King & Steiner, 1991; Mitchell & Black, 1995). The friction between Klein and Freud never abated, with each side claiming to be more "Freudian" than the other (Hughes, 1989). Finally, in 1946 the British Society accepted three training procedures—the traditional one of Melanie Klein, the one advocated by Anna Freud, and a Middle Group that accepted neither training school but was more eclectic in its approach. By such a division, the British Society remained intact, albeit with an uneasy alliance. Although Klein never reconciled with Anna Freud, the three distinct schools that resulted from their bitter personal and professional differences have continued to the present day. As King (1991) pointed out, the diversity of opinion and the freedom of choice are a source of strength of the British Society.

INTRODUCTION TO OBJECT RELATIONS THEORY

Object relations theory is an offspring of Freud's instinct theory, but it differs from its ancestor in at least three general ways. First, object relations theory places less emphasis on biologically based drives and more importance on consistent patterns of interpersonal relationships. Second, as opposed to Freud's rather paternalistic theory that emphasizes the power and control of the father, object relations theory tends to be more maternal, stressing the intimacy and nurturing of the mother. Third, object relations theorists generally see human contact and relatedness—not sexual pleasure—as the prime motivators of human behavior.

More specifically, however, the concept of object relations has many meanings, just as there are many object relations theorists. This chapter concentrates primarily on Melanie Klein's work, but it also briefly discusses the theories of Margaret S. Mahler, Otto Kernberg, Heinz Kohut, and John Bowlby. In general, Mahler's work was concerned with the infant's struggle to gain autonomy and a sense of self; Kernberg's, with combining drive theory, ego psychology, and object relations; Kohut's, with the formation of the self; and Bowlby's, with the stages of separation anxiety.

If Klein is the mother of object relations theory, then Freud himself is the father. Recall from Chapter 2 that Freud (1915/1957a) believed instincts or drives have an *impetus*, a *source*, an *aim*, and an *object*, with the latter two having greater psychological significance. Although different drives may seem to have separate aims, their underlying aim is always the same—to reduce tension, that is, to achieve pleasure. In Freudian terms, the **object** of the drive is any person, part of a person, or thing through which the aim is satisfied. Klein and other object relations theorists begin with this basic assumption of Freud and then speculate on how the infant's real or fantasized early relations with the mother or the breast become a model for all later interpersonal relationships. Adult relationships, therefore, are not always what they seem. An important portion of any relationship is the internal psychic representations of early significant objects, such as the mother's breast or the father's penis, that have been *introjected* or taken into the infant's psychic structure and then *projected* onto one's partner. These internal pictures are not accurate representations of the other person but are remnants of each person's earlier experiences.

Although Klein continued to regard herself as a Freudian, she extended psychoanalytic theory beyond the boundaries set by Freud. For his part, Freud chose mostly to ignore Klein. When pressed for an opinion on her work, Freud had little to say. For example, in 1925 when Ernest Jones wrote to him concerning Klein's "valuable work" with childhood analysis and play therapy, Freud simply replied that "Melanie Klein's work has aroused considerable doubt and controversy here in Vienna" (Steiner, 1985, p. 30).

PSYCHIC LIFE OF THE INFANT

Whereas Freud emphasized the first 4 or 6 years of life, Klein stressed the importance of the first 4 or 6 *months*. To her, an infant does not begin life with a blank slate but with an inherited predisposition to reduce the anxiety it experiences as a result of the conflict produced by the forces of the life instinct and the power of the death instinct. The infant's innate readiness to act or react presupposes the existence of phylogenetic endowment, a concept that Freud also accepted.

FANTASIES

One of Klein's basic assumptions is that the infant, even at birth, possesses an active fantasy life. These fantasies are psychic representations of unconscious id instincts; they should not be confused with the conscious fantasies of older children and adults. When Klein (1932) wrote of the dynamic fantasy life of infants, she did not suggest that neonates could put thoughts into words. She simply meant that they possess unconscious images of "good" and "bad." For example, a full stomach is "good," an empty one is "bad." Thus, Klein would say that infants who fall asleep while sucking on their fingers are fantasizing about having their mother's "good" breast inside themselves. Similarly, hungry infants who cry and kick their legs are fantasizing that they are kicking or destroying the "bad" breast. This idea of a "good" breast and a "bad" breast is comparable to Sullivan's notion of a "good" mother and a "bad" mother (see Chapter 8 for Sullivan's theory).

As the infant matures, unconscious fantasies connected with the breast continue to exert an impact on psychic life, but newer ones emerge as well. These later unconscious fantasies are shaped by both reality and by inherited predispositions. One of these fantasies involves the Oedipus complex, or the child's wish to destroy one parent and sexually possess the other. (The Oedipus complex is discussed more fully later.) Because these fantasies are unconscious, they can be contradictory. For example, a little boy can fantasize both beating his mother and having babies with her. Such fantasies spring partly from the boy's experiences with his mother and partly from universal predispositions to destroy the "bad" breast and to incorporate the "good" one.

OBJECTS

Klein agreed with Freud that humans have innate drives or instincts, including a *death instinct*. Drives, of course, must have some object. Thus, the hunger drive has the "good" breast as its object, the sex drive has a sexual organ as its object, and so on. Klein (1948) believed that from early infancy, children relate to these external objects, both in fantasy and in reality. The earliest object relations are with the mother's breast, but "very soon interest develops in the face and in the hands which attend to his needs and gratify them" (Klein, 1991, p 757). In their active fantasy, infants *introject*, or take into their psychic structure, these external objects, including their father's penis, their mother's hands and face, and other body parts. Introjected objects are more than internal thoughts about external objects; they are fantasies of internalizing the object in concrete and physical terms. For example, children who have introjected their mother believe that she is constantly inside their own body. Klein's notion of internal objects suggests that these objects have a power of their own, comparable to Freud's concept of a superego, which assumes that the father's or mother's conscience is carried within the child.

POSITIONS

Klein (1946) saw human infants as constantly engaging in a basic conflict between the life instinct and the death instinct, that is, between good and bad, love and hate, creativity and destruction. Because the ego moves toward integration and away from disintegration, infants naturally prefer gratifying sensations over frustrating ones.

In their attempt to deal with this dichotomy of good and bad feelings, infants organize their experiences into **positions,** or ways of dealing with both internal and external objects. Klein chose the term "position" rather than "stage of development" to indicate that positions alternate back and forth; they are not periods of time or phases of development through which a person passes. Although she used psychiatric or pathological labels, Klein intended these positions to represent *normal* social growth and development. The two basic positions are the *paranoid-schizoid position* and the *depressive position*.

PARANOID-SCHIZOID POSITION

During the earliest months of life, an infant comes into contact with both the good breast and the bad breast. These alternating experiences of gratification and frustration threaten the very existence of the infant's vulnerable ego. The infant desires to control the breast by devouring and harboring it. At the same time, the infant's innate destructive urges create fantasies of damaging the breast by biting, tearing, or annihilating it. In order to tolerate both these feelings toward the same object at the same time, the ego splits itself, retaining parts of its life and death instincts while deflecting parts of both instincts onto the breast. Now, rather than fearing its own death instinct, the infant fears the *persecutory breast*. But the infant also has a relationship with the *ideal breast*, which provides love, comfort, and gratification. The infant desires to keep the ideal breast inside itself as a protection against annihilation by persecutors. To control the good breast and to fight off its persecutors, the infant adopts what Klein (1946) called the **paranoid-schizoid position,** a way of organizing experiences that includes both paranoid feelings of being persecuted and a splitting of internal and external objects into the good and the bad.

According to Klein, infants develop the paranoid-schizoid position during the first 3 or 4 months of life, during which time the ego's perception of the external world is subjective and fantastic rather than objective and real. Thus, the persecutory feelings are considered to be paranoid; that is, they are not based on any real or immediate danger from the outside world. The child must keep the good breast and bad breast separate, because to confuse them would be to risk annihilating the good breast and losing it as a safe harbor. In the young child's schizoid world, rage and destructive feelings are directed toward the bad breast, while feelings of love and comfort are associated with the good breast.

The infant, of course, does not use language to identify the good and bad breast. Rather it has a biological predisposition to attach a positive value to nourishment and the life instinct and to assign a negative value to destruction and the death instinct. This preverbal splitting of the world into good and bad serves as a prototype for the subsequent development of ambivalent feelings toward a single person. For example, Klein compared the infantile paranoid-schizoid position to transference feelings that therapy patients often develop toward their therapist.

> Under pressure of ambivalence, conflict and guilt, the patient often splits the figure of the analyst, then the analyst may at certain moments be loved, at other moments hated. Or the analyst may be split in such a way that he remains the good (or bad) figure while someone else becomes the opposite figure. (Klein, 1946, p. 19)

Ambivalent feelings, of course, are not limited to therapy situations. Most people have both positive and negative feelings toward their loved ones. Conscious ambivalence, however, does not capture the essence of the paranoid-schizoid position. When adults adopt the paranoid-schizoid position, they do so in a primitive, unconscious fashion. As Ogden (1990) pointed out, they may experience themselves as a passive object rather than an active subject. They are likely to say "He's dangerous" instead of saying "I am aware that he is dangerous to me." Other people may project their unconscious paranoid feelings onto others as a means of avoiding their own destruction by the malevolent breast. Still others may project their unconscious positive feelings onto another person and see that person as being perfect while viewing themselves as empty or worthless.

DEPRESSIVE POSITION

Beginning at about the 5th or 6th month, an infant begins to view external objects as whole and to see that good and bad can exist in the same person. At that time, the child develops a more realistic picture of the mother and recognizes that she is an independent person who can be both good and bad. Also, the ego is beginning to mature to the point at which it can tolerate some of its own destructive feelings rather than projecting them outward. However, the infant also realizes that the mother might go away and be lost forever. Fearing the possible loss of the mother, the infant desires to protect her and keep her from the dangers of its own destructive forces, those canibalistic impulses that had previously been projected onto her. But the infant's ego is mature enough to realize that it lacks the capacity to protect the mother, and thus the infant experiences guilt for its previous destructive urges toward the mother. The feelings of anxiety over losing a loved object coupled with a sense of guilt for wanting to destroy that object constitute what Klein called the **depressive position.**

Children in the depressive position recognize that the loved object and the hated object are now one and the same. They reproach themselves for their previous destructive urges toward their mother and desire to make *reparation* for these attacks. Because children see their mother as whole and also as being endangered, they are able to feel *empathy* for her, a quality that will be beneficial in their future interpersonal relations.

The depressive position is resolved when children fantasize that they have made reparation for their previous transgressions and when they recognize that their mother will not go away permanently but will return after each departure. When the depressive position is resolved, children close the split between the good and the bad mother. They are able to not only experience love *from* their mother, but they also display their own love *for* her. However, an incomplete resolution of the depressive position can result in lack of trust, morbid mourning at the loss of a loved one, and a variety of other psychic disorders.

PSYCHIC DEFENSE MECHANISMS

Klein (1955) suggested that from very early infancy, children adopt several psychic defense mechanisms to protect their ego against the anxiety that is aroused by their own destructive fantasies. These intense destructive feelings originate with oral-sadistic anxieties concerning the breast—the dreaded, destructive breast on the one hand and the satisfying, helpful breast on the other. To control these anxieties, infants use several psychic defense mechanisms such as *introjection*, *projection*, *splitting*, and *projective identification*.

INTROJECTION

By **introjection,** Klein simply meant that infants fantasize taking into their body those perceptions and experiences that they have had with the external object, originally the mother's breast. Introjection begins with the child's first feeding, when there is an attempt to incorporate the mother's breast into the infant's body. Ordinarily, the infant tries to introject good objects, to take them inside itself as a protection against anxiety. However, sometimes the infant introjects bad objects, such as the bad breast or the bad penis, in order to gain control over them. When dangerous objects are introjected, they become internal persecutors, capable of terrifying the infant and leaving frightening residues that may be expressed in dreams or in an interest in fairy tales, such as "The Big Bad Wolf" or "Snow White and the Seven Dwarfs."

Introjected objects are not accurate representations of the real objects but are colored by children's fantasies. For example, infants will fantasize that their mother is constantly present; that is, they feel that their mother is always inside their body. The real mother, of course, is not perpetually present, but infants nevertheless devour her in fantasy so that she becomes a constant internal object.

PROJECTION

Just as infants use introjection to take in both good and bad objects, they use *projection* to get rid of them. Projection is the fantasy that one's own feelings and impulses actually reside in another person and not within one's body. By projecting unmanageable destructive impulses onto external objects, infants alleviate the unbearable anxiety of being destroyed by dangerous internal forces (Klein, 1935).

Children project both bad and good images onto external objects, especially their parents. An example of projecting a bad impulse is a young boy who desires to castrate his father, but instead he projects these castration fantasies onto his father. By such a projection, the boy can turn his castration wishes around and blame his father for wanting to castrate him. Similarly, a young girl might fantasize devouring her mother, but she projects that fantasy onto her mother, who she fears will retaliate by persecuting her.

People can also project good impulses. For example, infants who feel good about their mother's nurturing breast will attribute their own feelings of "goodness" onto the breast and imagine that the breast is good. Adults sometimes project their own feelings of love onto another person and become convinced that the other person loves them. Projection thus allows people to believe that their own subjective opinions are true.

SPLITTING

Infants can only manage the good and bad aspects of themselves and of external objects by **splitting** them, that is, by keeping apart incompatible impulses. In order to separate bad and good objects, the ego must itself be split. Thus, infants develop a picture of both the "good me" and the "bad me" that enables them to deal with both pleasurable and destructive impulses toward external objects.

Splitting can have either a positive or a negative effect on the child. If it is not extreme and rigid, it can be a positive and useful mechanism not only for infants but also for adults. It enables people to see both positive and negative aspects of themselves, to evaluate their behavior as good or bad, and to differentiate between likable and unlikable acquaintances. On the other hand, excessive and inflexible splitting can lead to pathological repression. For instance, if the ego is too rigid to be split into "good me" and "bad me," then bad experiences cannot be introjected into the good ego. When an infant cannot accept its own "bad" behavior, it must then deal with destructive and terrifying impulses in the only way it can—by repressing them.

PROJECTIVE IDENTIFICATION

A fourth means of reducing anxiety is **projective identification,** a psychic defense mechanism in which infants split off unacceptable parts of themselves, project them onto another object, and introject them back into themselves in a changed or distorted form. By taking the object back into themselves, infants feel that they have become like that object, that is, they identify with that object. For example, infants typically split off parts of their destructive impulse and project them onto the bad, frustrating breast. But then they identify with the breast by introjecting it, a process that permits them to gain control over the dreaded and wonderful breast.

Projective identification exerts a powerful influence in adult interpersonal relations. Unlike simple projection, which can exist wholly in fantasy, projective identification exists only in the world of real interpersonal relationships. For example, a husband with strong but unwanted tendencies to dominate others will project those feelings onto his wife, whom he then sees as domineering. The man subtly tries to get his wife to *become* domineering. He behaves with excessive submissiveness in an attempt to force his wife to display the very tendencies that he has deposited in her.

INTERNALIZATIONS

When object relations theorists speak of **internalizations,** they mean that the person takes in (introjects) aspects of the external world and then organizes those introjections into a psychologically meaningful framework. In Kleinian theory, three important internalizations are the ego, the superego, and the Oedipus complex.

Ego

Klein (1930, 1946) believed that the ego, or one's sense of self, reaches maturity at a much earlier stage than Freud had assumed. Although Freud hypothesized that the ego exists at birth, he did not attribute complex psychic functions to it until about the 3rd or 4th year. To Freud, the young child is dominated by the id. Klein, however, largely ignored the id and based her theory on the ego's early ability to sense both destructive and loving forces and to manage them through splitting, projection, and introjection.

Klein (1959) believed that although the ego is mostly unorganized at birth, it nevertheless is strong enough to feel anxiety, to use defense mechanisms, and to form early object relations in both fantasy and reality. The ego begins to evolve with the infant's first experience with feeding, when the good breast fills the infant not only with milk but with love and security. But the infant also experiences the bad breast—the one that is not present or does not give milk, love, or security. The infant introjects both the good breast and the bad breast, and these images provide a focal point for further expansion of the ego. All experiences, even those not connected with feeding, are evaluated by the ego in terms of how they relate to the good breast and the bad breast. For example, when the ego experiences the good breast, it expects similar good experiences with other objects, such as its own fingers, a pacifier, or the father. Thus, the infant's first object relation (the breast) becomes the prototype not only for the ego's future development but for the individual's later interpersonal relations.

However, before a unified ego can emerge, it must first become split. Klein assumed that infants innately strive for integration, but at the same time, they are forced to deal with the opposing forces of life and death, as reflected in their experience with the good breast and the bad breast. To avoid disintegration, the newly emerging ego must split itself into the "good me" and the "bad me." The "good me" exists when infants are being enriched with milk and love; the "bad me" is experienced when they do not receive milk and love. This dual image of self allows them to manage the good and bad aspects of external objects. As infants mature, their perceptions become more realistic, they no longer see the world in terms of part objects, and their egos become more integrated.

SUPEREGO

Klein's picture of the superego differs from Freud's in at least three important respects. First, it emerges much earlier in life; second, it is *not* an outgrowth of the Oedipus complex; and third, it is much more harsh and cruel. Klein arrived at these differences through her analysis of young children, an experience Freud did not have.

> There could be no doubt that a super-ego had been in full operation for some time in my small patients of between two-and-three-quarters and four years of age, whereas according to the accepted |Freudian| view the super-ego would not begin to be activated until the Oedipus complex had died down—i.e. until about the fifth year of life. Furthermore, my data showed that this early super-ego was immeasurably harsher and more cruel than that of the older child or adult, and that it literally crushed down the feeble ego of the small child. (Klein, 1933, p. 267)

Recall that Freud conceptualized the superego as consisting of two subsystems: an ego-ideal that produces inferiority feelings and a conscience that results in guilt feelings. Klein would concur that the more mature superego produces feelings of inferiority and guilt, but her analysis of young children led her to believe that the *early superego* produces not guilt but *terror*.

To Klein, young children fear being devoured, cut up, and torn into pieces—fears that are greatly out of proportion to any realistic dangers. Why are the children's super-egos so drastically removed from any actual threats by their parents? Klein (1933) suggested that the answer resides with the infant's own destructive instinct, which is experienced as anxiety. To manage this anxiety, the child's ego mobilizes libido (life instinct) against the death instinct. However, the life and death instincts cannot be completely separated, so the ego is forced to defend itself against its own actions. This early ego defense lays the foundation for the development of the superego, whose extreme violence is a reaction to the ego's aggressive self-defense against its own destructive tendencies. Klein (1933) believed that this harsh, cruel superego is responsible for many antisocial and criminal tendencies in adults.

Klein would describe a 5-year-old child's superego in much the same way Freud did. By the 5th or 6th year, the superego arouses little anxiety but a great measure of guilt. It has lost most of its severity while gradually being transformed into a realistic conscience. However, Klein rejected Freud's notion that the superego is a consequence of the Oedipus complex. Instead, she insisted that it grows along with the Oedipus complex and finally emerges as realistic guilt after the Oedipus complex is resolved.

OEDIPUS COMPLEX

Although Klein believed that her view of the Oedipus complex was merely an extension and not a refutation of Freud's ideas, her conception departed from the Freudian one in several ways. First, Klein (1946, 1948, 1952) held that the Oedipus complex begins at a much earlier age than Freud had suggested. Recall that Freud believed that the Oedipus complex took place during the phallic stage, when children are about 4 or 5 years old and after they have experienced an oral and anal stage. In contrast, Klein held that the Oedipus complex begins during the earliest months of life, overlaps with the oral and anal stages, and reaches its climax during the **genital stage,** at around age 3 or 4. (Klein preferred the term "genital" stage rather than "phallic," because the latter suggests a masculine psychology.) Second, Klein believed that a significant part of the Oedipus complex is children's fear of retaliation from their parent for their fantasy of emptying the parent's body. Third, she stressed the importance of children retaining positive feelings toward *both* parents during the Oedipal years. Fourth, she hypothesized that during its early stages, the Oedipus complex serves the same need for both sexes, that is, to establish a positive attitude with the good or gratifying object (breast or penis) and to avoid the bad or terrifying object (breast or penis). In this position, children of either sex can direct their love either alternately or simultaneously toward each parent. Thus, children are capable of both homosexual and heterosexual relations with both parents. Like Freud, Klein assumed that boys and girls eventually come to experience the Oedipus complex differently.

Male Oedipal Development

Klein (1945) believed that during the early months of Oedipal development, the boy shifts some of his oral desires from his mother's breast to his father's penis. At this time the little boy is in his *feminine position*; that is, he adopts a passive homosexual attitude toward his father. Next, he moves to a heterosexual relationship with his mother, but because of his previous homosexual feeling for his father, he has no fear that his father will castrate him. Klein believed that this passive homosexual position is a prerequisite for the boy's development of a healthy heterosexual relationship with his mother. More simply, the boy must have a good feeling about his father's penis before he can value his own.

As the boy matures, however, he develops oral-sadistic impulses toward his father and wants to bite off his penis and to murder him. These feelings arouse castration anxiety and the fear that his father will retaliate against him by biting off his penis. This fear convinces the little boy that sexual intercourse with his mother would be extremely dangerous to him.

The boy's Oedipus complex is resolved only partially by his castration anxiety. A more important factor is his ability to establish positive relationships with both parents at the same time. At that point the boy sees his parents as whole objects, a condition that enables him to work through his depressive position.

Female Oedipal Development

Like the young boy, a little girl first sees her mother's breast as both "good" and "bad." Then around six months of age, she begins to view the breast as more positive than negative. Later, she sees her whole mother as full of good things, and this attitude leads her to imagine how babies are made. She fantasizes that her father's penis feeds her mother with riches, including babies. Because the little girl sees her father's penis as the giver of children, she develops a positive relationship to it and fantasizes that her father will fill her body with babies. If the female Oedipal stage proceeds smoothly, the little girl adopts a "feminine" position and has a positive relationship with both parents.

However, under less ideal circumstances, the little girl will see her mother as a rival and will fantasize robbing her mother of her father's penis and stealing her mother's babies. Just as the boy's hostility toward his father leads to fear of retaliation, the little girl's wish to rob her mother produces a paranoid fear that her mother will retaliate against her by injuring her or taking away her babies. The little girl's principal

Margaret Mahler

anxiety comes from a fear that the inside of her body has been injured by her mother, an anxiety that can only be alleviated when she later gives birth to a healthy baby. According to Klein (1945), penis envy stems from the little girl's wish to internalize her father's penis and to receive a baby from him. This fantasy precedes any desire for an external penis. Contrary to Freud's view, Klein could find no evidence that the little girl blames her mother for bringing her into the world without a penis. Instead, Klein contended that the girl retains a strong attachment to her mother throughout the Oedipal period.

For both girls and boys, a healthy resolution of the Oedipus complex depends on their ability to allow their mother and father to come together and to have sexual intercourse with each other. No remnant of rivalry remains. Children's positive feelings toward both parents later serve to enhance their adult sexual relations.

In summary, Klein believed that we are born with two strong drives—the life instinct and the death instinct. As infants, we develop a passionate caring for the good breast and an intense hatred for the bad breast, and throughout our lifetime we struggle to reconcile these unconscious psychic images of good and bad, pleasure and pain. The most crucial stage of life is the first few months, a time when our relationships with mother and other significant objects form a model for our later interpersonal relations. Our adult ability to love or to hate originates with these early object relations.

LATER VIEWS ON OBJECT RELATIONS

Since Melanie Klein's bold and insightful descriptions, a number of other theorists have expanded and modified object relations theory. Among the more prominent of these later theorists are Margaret Mahler, Otto Kernberg, Heinz Kohut, and John Bowlby.

MARGARET MAHLER'S VIEW

Margaret Schoenberger Mahler (1897–1985) was born in Sopron, Hungary, and received a medical degree from the University of Vienna in 1923. In 1938, she moved to New York where she was a consultant to the Children's Service of the New York State Psychiatric Institute. She later established her own observational studies at the Masters Children's Center in New York. From 1955 to 1974, she was clinical professor of psychiatry at Albert Einstein College of Medicine.

Mahler was primarily concerned with the psychological birth of the individual that takes place during the first 3 years of life, a time when the child gradually surrenders security for autonomy. Originally, Mahler's ideas came from her observation of the behaviors of disturbed children interacting with their mothers. Later, she observed normal babies as they bonded with their mothers during the first 36 months of life (Mahler, 1952).

To Mahler, an individual's psychological birth begins during the first weeks of postnatal life and continues for the next 3 years or so. By *psychological birth*, Mahler meant that the child becomes an *individual* separate from his or her primary caregiver, an accomplishment that leads ultimately to a *sense of identity*.

To achieve psychological birth and individuation, a child proceeds through a series of three major developmental stages and four substages (Mahler, 1967, 1972; Mahler, Pine, & Bergman, 1975). The first major developmental stage is **normal autism,** which spans the period from birth until about age 3 or 4 weeks. To describe the normal autism stage, Mahler (1967) borrowed Freud's (1911/1958) analogy that compared psychological birth with an unhatched bird egg. The bird is able to satisfy its nutritional needs autistically (without regard to external reality) because its food supply is enclosed in its shell. Similarly, the newborn infant satisfies various needs within the all-powerful protective orbit of the mother's care. The neonate has a sense of omnipotence, because, like the unhatched bird, its needs are cared for automatically and without it having to expend any effort. Unlike Klein, who conceptualized the newborn infant as being terrified, Mahler pointed to the relatively long periods of sleep and general lack of tension in the neonate. She believed that this is a period of absolute primary narcissism in which the infant is unaware of any other person. Thus, she referred to normal autism as an "objectless" stage, a time when an infant naturally searches for the mother's breast. She disagreed with Klein's notion that the infant incorporates good breast and other objects into its ego.

As infants gradually realize that they cannot satisfy their own needs, they begin to recognize their primary caregiver and to seek a symbiotic relationship with her, a condition that leads to **normal symbiosis,** the second developmental stage in Mahler's theory. Normal symbiosis begins around the 4th or 5th week of age but reaches its zenith during the 4th or 5th month. During this time, "the infant behaves and functions as though he and his mother were an omnipotent system—a dual unity within one common boundary" (Mahler, 1967, p. 741). In the analogy of the bird egg, the shell is now beginning to crack, but a psychological membrane in the form of a symbiotic relationship still protects the newborn. Mahler recognized that this is not a true symbiosis because, although the infant's life is dependent on the mother, the mother does not absolutely need the infant. The symbiosis is characterized by a mutual cuing of infant and mother. The infant sends cues to the mother of hunger, pain, pleasure, and so forth, and the mother responds with her own cues, such as feeding, holding, or smiling. By this age, the infant can recognize the mother's face and can perceive her pleasure or distress. However, object relations have not yet begun—mother and others are still "preobjects." Older children and even adults sometimes regress to this stage, seeking the strength and safety of their mother's care.

The third major developmental stage, **separation-individuation,** spans the period from about the 4th or 5th month of age until about the 30th or 36th month. During this time, children become psychologically separated from their mothers, achieve a sense of individuation, and begin to develop feelings of personal identity. Because children no longer experience a dual unity with their mother, they must surrender their delusion of omnipotence and face their vulnerability to external threats. Thus, young children in the separation-individuation stage experience the external world as being more dangerous than it was during the first two stages.

Mahler divided the separation-individuation stage into four overlapping substages. The first is *differentiation*, which lasts from about the 5th to the 7th–10th month of age and is marked by a bodily breaking away from the mother/infant symbiotic orbit. For this reason, the differentiation substage is analogous to the hatching of an egg. At this age, Mahler observed, infants smile in response to their own mother, indicating a bond with a specific other person. Psychologically healthy infants who expand their world beyond the mother will be curious about strangers and will inspect them; unhealthy infants will fear strangers and recoil from them.

As infants physically begin to move away from their mothers by crawling and walking, they enter the *practicing* substage of separation-individuation, a period from about the 7th–10th month of age to about the 15th or 16th month. During this subphase, children easily distinguish their body from their mother's, establish a specific bond with their mother, and begin to develop an autonomous ego. Yet, during the early stages of this period, they do not like to lose sight of their mother; they follow her with their eyes and show distress when she is away. Later, they begin to walk and to take in the outside world, which they experience as fascinating and exciting.

From about 16 to 25 months of age, children experience a *rapprochement* with their mother; that is, they desire to bring their mother and themselves back together, both physically and psychologically. Mahler noticed that children of this age want to share with their mother every new acquisition of skill and every new experience. Now that they can walk with ease, children are more physically separate from the mother, but paradoxically, they are more likely to show separation anxiety during the rapprochement stage than during the previous period. Their increased cognitive skills make them more aware of their separateness, causing them to try various ploys to regain the dual unity they once had with their mother. Because these attempts are never completely successful, children of this age often fight dramatically with their mother, a condition called the *rapprochement crisis*.

The final subphase of the separation-individuation process is *libidinal object constancy*, which approximates the 3rd year of life. During this time, children must develop a constant inner representation of their mother so that they can tolerate being physically separate from her. If this libidinal object constancy is not developed, children will continue to depend on their mother's physical presence for their own security. Besides gaining some degree of object constancy, children must consolidate their individuality; that is, they must learn to function without their mother and to develop other object relationships (Mahler et al., 1975).

The strength of Mahler's theory is its elegant description of psychological birth based on empirical observations that she and her colleagues made on child-mother interactions. Although many of her tenets rely on inferences gleaned from reactions of preverbal infants, her ideas can easily be extended to adults. Any errors made during the first 3 years—the time of psychological birth—may result in later regressions to a stage when a person had not yet achieved separation from the mother and thus a sense of personal identity.

Otto Kernberg

OTTO KERNBERG'S VIEW

Otto F. Kernberg (1928–) was born in Vienna, received a medical degree from the University of Chile in 1953, but has lived in the United States since joining the staff at the Menninger Clinic in Topeka in 1957. Presently, Kernberg is a training and supervising analyst at the Columbia University Center for Psychoanalytic Training and Research as well as professor of psychiatry at Cornell University Medical College and director of the Institute for Personality Disorders at New York Hospital—Cornell Medical Center in New York.

Unlike Klein and Mahler, who worked almost exclusively with young children, Kernberg observed mostly older patients. His work with seriously disturbed adults has led him to formulate a model of how the healthy infant develops and how mature adult relationships evolve from childhood experiences. Like Klein, he regards his work as an extension of Freudian psychoanalysis rather than an alternate approach.

Kernberg (1975, 1976, 1984, 1986, 1993, 1995) believes that the key to understanding personality organization—from the extremely disturbed to the normal—is the mother-child relationship. Healthy early object relations result in an integrated ego, a punishing superego, a stable self-concept, and fulfilling interpersonal relations. Inadequate early mother-child relations lead to contradictory ego states and various levels of adult psychopathology.

In all levels of personality organization, Kernberg found the same structural units, or **internalized object relationships,** namely, a self-image, an object-image, and a certain affect that colors the self-image and the object-image. For example, in relating to the mother, an infant might sometimes have the image of a "good me," a "good mother," and a strong positive feeling, while at other times the infant experiences the "bad me," the "bad mother," and strong negative affect. In this example, the infant is able to separate contradictory aspects of self by *splitting* its ego. In an adult, continual splitting would represent a defect in the ego, but in infants and sometimes in adults, splitting is a helpful defense against anxiety.

Kernberg (1986) linked split-off ego states to the defense mechanisms of *introjection* and *identification*. The earliest and most primitive level of internalized object relationships is introjection, or the "swallowing whole" of an object-image, a self-image, and the affect generated by the interaction of the object and the self. At this early stage of development, introjected images are undifferentiated and kept apart by the splitting process, enabling the infant to keep separate images of, for example, the "good mother" *and* the "bad mother." The affective portion of each introjection is important, because it helps the child synthesize images with similar feeling tones. For example, oral gratification, nurturance, and mother-child contact may all fuse to become the "good internal object."

Identification, a higher form of introjection, is the second level of internalized object relations. As infants mature cognitively, they acquire the capacity to see themselves and their mother as having specific social *roles*. "Role implies the presence of a socially recognized function that is being carried out by the object or by both participants in the interaction" (Kernberg, 1976, p. 30). For example, when a mother helps dress a child, she is interacting in a specific way with that child as well as fulfilling the socially acceptable role of a mother. Again, the child has a specific self-image (subject) as a dependent person who needs help getting dressed, an image of the mother (object) as a helper in getting dressed, and a specific affect related to the interaction with mother during the dressing situation. The various roles played by the child eventually lead to consistent patterns of behavior, which in turn facilitate *ego identity*.

Kernberg's concept of ego identity closely follows that of Erik Erikson (Chapter 9). "Ego identity refers to the overall organization of identifications and introjections under the guiding principle of the synthetic function of the ego" (Kernberg, 1976, p. 32). Ego identity gives the person a sense of continuity of the self. An established self-identity organizes other self-images, allows the person to see object-images more consistently, and facilitates stable interpersonal relations. Ego identity is the highest level of organization of the self, and it leads to integrated ego development and a mature, functioning superego. Lack of stable ego identity results in a continuation of the split-off ego, disintegration, and an assortment of psychological disorders.

Kernberg's attempt to synthesize Freudian drive theory, object relations theory, and developmental theory has been accepted more by clinicians—both psychologists and psychiatrists—than by academic psychologists. The theory departs from Freud in that it sees people as being shaped by social experiences rather than by instinctual drives, and it departs from Klein and Mahler in that it is not based on observations of the mother-child interaction and is therefore less specific or detailed.

HEINZ KOHUT'S VIEW

Heinz Kohut (1913–1981) was also born in Vienna, and, like Kernberg, he spent most of his professional life in the United States, where he was a professional lecturer in the Department of Psychiatry at the University of Chicago, a member of the faculty at the Chicago Institute for Psychoanalysis, and visiting professor of psychoanalysis at the University of Cincinnati. A neurologist and a psychoanalyst, Kohut upset many psychoanalysts in 1971 with his publication of *The Analysis of the Self*, which replaced the ego with the concept of self. In addition to this book, aspects of his self psychology are found in *The Restoration of the Self* (1977) and *The Kohut Seminars* (1987), the latter of which was edited by Miriam Elson after Kohut's death.

More than the other object relations theorists, Kohut emphasized the process by which the *self* evolves from a vague and undifferentiated image to a clear and precise sense of individual identity. As did the other object relations theorists, he focused on the early mother-child relationship as the key to understanding later development.

Heinz Kohut

Kohut believed that human relatedness, not innate instinctual drives, are at the core of human personality.

According to Kohut, infants require adult caregivers not only to gratify physical needs but also to satisfy basic psychological needs. In caring for both physical and psychological needs, adults, or **selfobjects,** treat infants as if they had a sense of self. For example, parents will act with warmth, coldness, or indifference depending in part on their infant's behavior. Through the process of empathic interaction, the infant takes in the selfobject's responses as pride, guilt, shame, or envy, all attitudes that eventually form the building blocks of the self. Kohut (1977) defined the self as "the center of the individual's psychological universe" (p. 311). The self gives unity and consistency to one's experiences, remains relatively stable over time, and is "the center of initiative and a recipient of impressions" (p. 99). The self is also the child's focus of interpersonal relations, shaping how he or she will relate to parents and other selfobjects.

Kohut (1971, 1977) believed that infants are naturally narcissistic. They are self-centered, looking out exclusively for their own welfare and wishing to be admired for who they are and what they do. The early self becomes crystallized around two basic *narcissistic needs*: (1) the need to exhibit the grandiose self and (2) the need to acquire an idealized image of one or both parents. The *grandiose-exhibitionistic self* is established when the infant relates to a "mirroring" selfobject who reflects approval of its behavior. The infant thus forms a rudimentary self-image from messages such as: "If others see me as perfect, then I am perfect." The *idealized parent image* is opposed to the grandiose self because it implies that someone else is perfect. Nevertheless, it too satisfies a narcissistic need because the infant adopts the attitude, "You are perfect, but I am part of you."

Both narcissistic self-images are necessary for healthy personality development. Both, however, must change as the child grows older. If they remain unaltered, they result in a pathologically narcissistic adult personality. Grandiosity must change into a realistic view of self, and the idealized parent image must grow into a realistic picture of the parents. The two self-images should not entirely disappear; the healthy adult continues to have positive attitudes toward self and continues to see good qualities in parents or parent substitutes. However, a narcissistic adult does not transcend these infantile needs and continues to be self-centered and to see the rest of the world

John Bowlby

as an admiring audience. Freud believed that such a narcissistic person was a poor candidate for psychoanalysis, but Kohut held that psychotherapy could be effective with these patients.

JOHN BOWLBY'S ATTACHMENT THEORY

John Bowlby (1907–1990) was born in London, where his father was a well-known surgeon. From an early age, Bowlby was interested in natural science, medicine, and psychology—subjects he studied at Cambridge University. After receiving a medical degree, he started his practice in psychiatry and psychoanalysis in 1933. At about the same time, he began his training in child psychiatry under Melanie Klein. During World War II, Bowlby served as an army psychiatrist, and in 1946 he was appointed director of the Department for Children and Parents of the Tavistock Clinic. During the late 1950s, Bowlby spent some time at Stanford's Center for the Advanced Study in the Behavioral Sciences but returned to London where he remained until his death in 1990.

In the 1950s, Bowlby became more and more dissatisfied with the object relations perspective, primarily for its inadequate theory of motivation and its lack of empiricism. With his knowledge of **ethology** and evolutionary theory (especially Konrad Lorenz's idea of early bonding to a mother-figure), he realized that object relations theory could be integrated with an evolutionary perspective. By forming such an integration, he felt he could correct the empirical shortcomings of the theory and extend it in a new direction. Bowlby's *attachment theory* also departed from psychoanalytic thinking by taking childhood as its starting point and then extrapolating forward to adulthood (Bowlby, 1969/1982). Bowlby firmly believed that the attachments formed during childhood have an important impact on adulthood. Because childhood attachments are so crucial to later development, Bowlby argued that one should study childhood directly and not rely on distorted retrospective accounts from adults.

The origins of attachment theory came from Bowlby's observations that both human and primate infants go through a clear sequence of reactions when separated from their primary caregivers. Bowlby observed three stages of this **separation anxiety.** When their caregiver is first out of sight, infants will cry, resist soothing by other people, and search for their caregiver. This stage is called the *protest* stage. As separation continues, infants become quiet, sad, passive, listless, and apathetic. This second stage is called *despair*. The last stage is the only one unique to humans and is called *detachment*. During this stage, infants become emotionally detached from other people, including their caregiver. If their caregiver (mother) returns, infants will disregard and avoid her. Children who become detached are no longer upset when their mother leaves them. As they become older, they play and interact with others with little emotion but appear to be sociable. However, their interpersonal relations are superficial and lack warmth.

From such observations, Bowlby developed his attachment theory, which he published in a trilogy entitled *Attachment and Loss* (Bowlby, 1969/1982, 1973, 1980). Bowlby's theory rests on a few fundamental assumptions, the first of which is that a responsive and accessible caregiver (usually the mother) creates a secure base for the child. The infant needs to know that the caregiver is accessible and dependable. If this dependability is present, the child is better able to develop confidence and security in exploring the world. This bonding relationship serves the critical function of attaching the caregiver to the infant, thereby making survival of the infant, and ultimately the species, more likely.

A second assumption of attachment theory is that a bonding relationship (or lack thereof) becomes internalized and serves as a mental working model on which future friendships and love relationships are built. The first bonding attachment is therefore the most critical of all relationships. However, for bonding to take place, the infant must be more than a mere passive receptor to the caregiver's behavior, even if that behavior radiates accessibility and dependability. Attachment style is a *relationship* between two people and not a trait given to the infant by the caregiver. It is a two-way street—the infant and the caregiver must be responsive to each other and each must influence the other's behavior.

Influenced by Bowlby's theory, Mary Ainsworth and her associates (Ainsworth, Blehar, Waters, & Wall, 1978) developed a technique for measuring the type of attachment style that exists between caregiver and infant, known as the *strange situation*. This procedure consists of a 20-minute laboratory session in which a mother and infant are initially alone in a playroom. Then a stranger comes into the room, and after a few minutes the stranger begins a brief interaction with the infant. The mother then goes away for two separate 2-minute periods. During the first period, the infant is left alone with the stranger; during the second period, the infant is left completely alone. The critical behavior is how the infant reacts when the mother returns, and it is this behavior that is the basis of the attachment style rating. Ainsworth et al. found three attachment style ratings: secure, anxious-resistant, and avoidant.

In a *secure attachment*, when their mother returns, infants are happy and enthusiastic and initiate contact; for example, they will go over to their mother and want to be held. All securely attached infants are confident in the accessibility and responsiveness of their caregiver, and this security and dependability provides the foundation for play and exploration. In an *anxious-resistant attachment* style, infants are ambivalent. When their mother leaves the room, they become unusually upset, and when their mother returns, they seek contact with her but reject attempts at being soothed. With the anxious-resistant attachment style, infants give very conflicted messages. On the one hand, they seek contact with their mother, while on the other hand, they squirm to be put down and may throw away toys that their mother has offered them. The third attachment style is *anxious-avoidant*. With this style, infants stay calm when their mother leaves; they accept the stranger, and when their mother returns, they ignore and avoid her. In both kinds of insecure attachment (anxious-resistant and anxious-avoidant), infants lack the ability to engage in effective play and exploration.

PSYCHOTHERAPY

Klein, Mahler, Kernberg, Kohut, and Bowlby were all psychoanalysts trained in ortho-dox Freudian practices. However, each modified psychoanalytic treatment to fit her or his own theoretical orientation. Because these theorists varied among themselves on therapeutic procedures, we will limit our discussion of therapy to the approach used by Melanie Klein.

Klein's pioneering use of psychoanalysis with children was not well accepted by other analysts during the 1920s and 1930s. Anna Freud was especially resistive to the notion of childhood psychoanalysis, contending that young children who were still attached to their parents could not develop a transference to the therapist because they have no unconscious fantasies or images. Therefore, she claimed, young children could not profit from psychoanalytic therapy. In contrast, Klein believed that both dis-turbed and healthy children should be psychoanalyzed; disturbed children would receive the benefit of therapeutic treatment, whereas healthy children would profit from a prophylactic analysis. Consistent with this belief, she insisted that her own children be analyzed. She also insisted that negative transference was an essential step toward successful treatment, a view not shared by Anna Freud and many other psychoanalysts.

To foster negative transference and aggressive fantasies, Klein provided each child with a variety of small toys, pencil and paper, paint, crayons, and so forth. She substituted *play therapy* for Freudian dream analysis and free association, believing that young children express their conscious and unconscious wishes through play. In addi-tion to expressing negative transference feelings through play, Klein's young patients often attacked her verbally, which gave her an opportunity to interpret the unconscious motives behind these attacks (Klein, 1943).

The aim of Kleinian therapy is to reduce depressive anxieties and persecutory fears and to mitigate the harshness of internalized objects. To accomplish this, Klein encouraged her patients to reexperience early emotions and fantasies, but this time with the therapist pointing out the differences between reality and fantasy, between conscious and unconscious. She also allowed patients to express both positive and negative transference, a situation that is essential for patients' understanding of how unconscious fantasies connect with present everyday situations. Once this connection is made, patients feel less persecuted by internalized objects, experience reduced depressive anxiety, and are able to project previously frightening internal objects onto the outer world.

RELATED RESEARCH

Object relations theory has a long history of generating debate and discussion among clinicians but only a relatively recent history of generating empirical research. Both object relations theory and attachment theory posit the importance of early bonding relationships and the cognitive models that become internalized from these relation-ships. Internal cognitive models not only become the foundation for all future rela-tionships, but they also play a large role in basic mental health. For instance, both object relations and attachment theory predict that insecure attachments are likely to lead to mental illnesses such as borderline personality disorder, eating disorder, and depression. Attachment theory has also been useful in predicting satisfaction and sta-bility in love relationships and friendships.

In one study, Drew Westen and his associates (Westen, Lohr, Silk, Gold, & Kerber, 1990) administered the Thematic Apperception Test (TAT) to three groups: (1) those diagnosed with borderline personalities, (2) those suffering from major depression, and (3) a control group of "normal" personalities. The researchers found that the TAT identified four separate categories of object relations: (1) Complexity of Representations of People, or the extent to which participants differentiated self and others as stable personalities with complex motives and subjective experiences; (2) Affect-Tone of Relationship Paradigms, or the extent to which people expect other people to be malevolent (malicious and hurtful) or benevolent (benign and helpful); (3) Capacity for Emotional Investment in Relationships, or the extent to which people see others as ends rather than means to need gratification; and (4) Understanding of Social Causality, or the extent to which people make logical attributions of others' actions, thoughts, or feelings. Westen et al. found that people with borderline personality scored lower on all four scales than did normals, especially on malevolent affect tone. Furthermore, using the picture arrangement subtest of the Wechsler Adult Intelligence Scale-R (WAIS-R) as a projective test, Westen and his colleagues replicated the main findings from the TAT: borderlines have more malevolent object relations compared with depressives and normals (Segal, Westen, Lohr, Silk, & Cohen, 1992). Finally, Westen and his associates (Westen, Ludolph, Block, Wixom, & Wiss, 1990; Westen, Ludolph, Misle, Ruffins, & Block, 1990) found very similar results in studies of physically and sexually abused adolescent girls. This latter study found that the pre-Oedipal experience that these girls had with their mothers contributed to subsequent expectations of malevolent relationships.

Westen and his colleagues have also used objective personality tests to obtain ratings of parents and then examine the relationship between "object representation" and borderline personality disorder (Baker, Silk, Westen, Nigg, & Lohr, 1992). These researchers obtained parental descriptions from three groups: borderline patients, major depressive disorder patients, and nonpatient controls. They hypothesized that: (1) borderline patients would have more negative views of their parents than either of the other two groups; and (2) that borderline patients would be more likely to "split" parents into extremes of good and bad. Participants then rated both parents' personalities using the Adjective Check List (ACL). Results supported the first hypothesis but not the second; that is, borderline patients did in fact have a more negative view of each of their parents than depressed or control participants, but they did not "split" their parents into extremes of good and bad.

Another measure of object relations is the Bell Object Relations Inventory (BORI) (Bell, Billington, & Becker, 1986). The BORI is a self-report questionnaire that asks participants to respond either "true" or "false" to 90 descriptive statements based on their most recent experience. Using a factor analytic approach, Bell et al. identified four main factors that constitute object relations. Factor I: Alienation (ALn) is the broadest dimension of object relations. People who score high on ALn lack basic trust, are unable to attain closeness, despair over ever achieving interpersonal intimacy, are suspicious and guarded, and believe that others will fail them. The second factor, Insecure Attachment (IA), measures painfulness of interpersonal relations. High scorers on the IA dimension are sensitive to rejection, overconcerned about being liked or accepted, and jealous of other people. Factor III, Egocentricity (EGC), indicates self-centeredness and a mistrust of others. People who score high on EGC have a narcissistic view of other people, believing that people exist simply to satisfy their needs and that people may be manipulated for their own self-centered aims. Factor IV, Social Incompetence

(SI), describes people who have difficulty making friends, especially those of the opposite sex. They are shy, nervous, socially insecure, and find social relations bewildering and unpredictable.

Studies using the BORI have also examined whether object relations distinguish borderline patients from other clinical groups. For instance, Morris Bell, Randall Billington, Dominic Cicchetti, and Judith Gibbons (1988) have shown that borderline patients are higher on all four dimensions of the BORI than patients with schizophrenia or depression. Alienation most clearly distinguished the borderline patients from the others, which indicates that borderline patients have a lack of intimacy and no longer value interpersonal relationships. Insecure attachment scores also revealed borderline patients to be painfully insecure and overly dependent in the relationships they do have.

OBJECT RELATIONS AND EATING DISORDERS

Roberta Heesacker and Greg Neimeyer (1990) have used the BORI to assess eating disorders. They studied undergraduate women and found that disturbed eating patterns, as measured by the Eating Disorder Inventory (Garner, Olmstead, & Polivy, 1983), were linked to disturbances in early object relations. More specifically, college women with a strong "drive for thinness" scored high on the Insecure Attachment (IA) and Social Incompetence (SI) scales of the BORI.

Later research by Howard Steiger and his colleagues (Steiger & Houle, 1991; Steiger, Leung, & Thibaudeau, 1993) showed that college women with eating disorders have more object relations problems and relied more on maladaptive defenses than did other college women. Moreover, Steiger and Houle suggested that difficulties in interpersonal relations *preceded* eating disturbances and were not a consequence of eating problems. Steiger and his colleagues have also found that, of the college women who received treatment for bulimia (binging and purging), those with object relations problems prior to therapy were more likely to have eating problems after therapy. These studies suggest that women with insecure attachment and other interpersonal difficulties are at risk for eating disorders.

OBJECT RELATIONS AND DEPRESSION

In another measure of mental representation of object relations, Donald Quinlan, Sidney Blatt, and their colleagues (Quinlan, Blatt, Chevron, & Wein, 1992) developed an open-ended self-report measure by having participants spontaneously describe each of their parents. These researchers gave blank sheets of paper to participants and asked them to "describe your mother" and "describe your father." They then instructed independent judges to code these written responses on ratings such as "evaluative," "affectionate," "punitive," and "benevolent." These ratings formed three scales: Benevolent, Punitive, and Ambitious. How people described their parents on these dimensions was related to their level of depression. Quinlan et al. found that participants who described their parents as benevolent and ambitious were less depressed, whereas those who described their parents as punitive tended to be more depressed. Furthermore, Blatt and Erika Homann (1992) have demonstrated how attachment style is a clear and significant predictor of adult depression. Parental inaccessibility, authority, and criticism lead to insecure attachment, which in turn makes adult depression more likely.

ATTACHMENT THEORY AND STABILITY OF RELATIONSHIPS

Some research from an attachment perspective has investigated the impact of early bonding relationships on the formation of later love relationships and friendships. In particular, Cindy Hazan and Phil Shaver (Hazan & Shaver, 1987; Kobak & Hazan, 1991) have been key figures in demonstrating the importance of early attachment in love relationships, whereas L. Alan Sroufe and his colleagues (Sroufe, Carlson, & Shulman, 1993) have studied how attachment longitudinally influences friendship patterns during childhood and adolescence.

In a now classic piece of research, Hazan and Shaver (1987) applied Bowlby and Ainsworth's attachment types to adult romantic relationships. They predicted that different types of attachment styles would distinguish the kind, duration, and stability of adult love relationships that people develop. More specifically, they expected that people who had secure attachments with their caregivers would experience more trust, closeness, and positive emotions in their adult love relationships than people in either of the two insecure groups. Likewise, they predicted that avoidant adults would fear closeness and lack trust, whereas anxious/ambivalent adults would be preoccupied and obsessed by their relationships. In two different samples, one with more than 600 adults and one with more than 100 college students, they found support for each of these predictions. Securely attached adults did experience more trust and closeness in their love relationships than avoidant or anxious/ambivalent adults. Moreover, based on Bowlby's idea that different attachment styles should lead to different internal cognitive models, Hazan and Shaver predicted that the three groups would vary on their views of what love relationships ideally should be. Consistent with attachment theory, they found that securely attached adults were more likely than adults in either of the two insecure groups to believe that romantic love can be long lasting. In addition, they were less cynical about love in general. Finally, securely attached adults had longer lasting relationships and were less likely to divorce than either avoidant or anxious/ambivalent adults.

Roger Kobak and Cindy Hazan (1991) examined how one's internal working models of object relations influence marital satisfaction as well as coping skills in resolving marital conflict. In a sample of 40 married couples, Kobak and Hazan tested hypotheses that secure marital relationships would foster constructive communication during problem solving and that agreement of internal models would promote relationship adjustment. They found that the most secure marriages did have effective communication styles. During a problem solving session, secure wives and husbands were less rejecting and more supportive of one another than were less secure spouses.

L. Alan Sroufe and his colleagues (Sroufe, Carlson, & Shulman, 1993) recruited women in their third trimester of pregnancy for a longitudinal study on attachment. These women and their children were assessed extensively throughout the child's first 15 years of life. For instance, they were studied seven times in the 1st year of the child's life, twice in each of the next 3 years, and then yearly up through Grade 7. A subset of these participants were studied at a summer camp at ages 10 and 15. At each of these time periods, personality and behavioral ratings were made by parents, teachers, camp counselors, and the children themselves. Sroufe and his colleagues reported that people with the three different attachment styles developed different personality traits and related to people differently. Up until the preschool period, securely attached children, compared with children in the two anxiously attached groups, were more self-reliant, were able to flexibly manage their impulses, participated more actively in peer groups, and were popular. Insecurely attached children, on the other hand, were rated by teachers as being more dependent and likely to cling to the teachers. Moreover, the teachers behaved more overly nurturant or more controlling with these insecurely attached children than with securely attached ones. By middle childhood, the securely attached children were still more self-reliant, socially skilled, and resilient, but different friendship patterns also began to emerge. Securely attached children formed friendship groups that were semipermeable and allowed for outsiders to join in selectively, whereas insecurely attached children had friendship patterns that were either totally permeable and open or totally impermeable and closed.

CRITIQUE OF OBJECT RELATIONS THEORY

Currently, object relations theory continues to be more popular in Britain than it is in the United States, although it is beginning to become more firmly established in America (Solomon, 1995). The "British School," which included not only Melanie Klein but also W. R. D. Fairbairn and D. W. Winnicott, has exerted a strong influence on psychoanalysts and psychiatrists in England. In the United States, however, the influence of object relations theorists, while growing, has been less direct. Writing about Klein's theory, Robert Caper (1988) observed that:

> Despite their opposition to Klein's ideas when presented in direct or undiluted form, many American psychoanalysts have recognized that, in a practical sense, an adequate understanding of their day-to-day clinical experience with patients requires them to employ something like her discoveries. As a consequence, while her ideas as a whole have encountered strong *official* opposition from most American psychoanalysts, many of her fundamental theses are accepted under an alias . . . by those who claim to oppose them. (p. 129)

Object relations theory grew out of orthodox psychoanalytic theory and thus suffers from some of the same limitations that confront Freud's theory. Most of its tenets are based on what is happening inside the nescient infant's psyche, and thus these assumptions cannot be falsified. The theory does not lend itself to *falsifications* because it generates very few testable hypotheses.

Perhaps the most useful feature of object relations theory is its *ability to organize* information about the behavior of infants. More than almost any other personality theorists, object relations theorists have speculated on how humans gradually come to acquire a sense of identity. Klein, and especially Mahler and Bowlby, built their theories on careful observations of the mother-child relationship. They watched the interactions between infant and mother and drew inferences based on what they saw. However, beyond the early childhood years, object relations theory lacks usefulness as an organizer of knowledge.

As a *guide to the practitioner*, the theory fares somewhat better than it does in organizing data or suggesting testable hypotheses. Parents of young infants can learn of the importance of a warm, accepting, and nurturing caregiver. Psychotherapists may find object relations theory useful, not only in understanding the early development of their clients, but also in understanding and working with the transference relationship that clients form with the therapist, whom they view as a substitute parent.

On the criterion of consistency, each of the theories discussed in this chapter has a high level of *internal consistency*, but the different theorists disagree among themselves on a number of points. Even though they all place primary importance on human relationships, the differences among them far exceed the similarities. In addition, we rate object relations theory about average on the criterion of *parsimony*.

CONCEPT OF HUMANITY

Object relations theorists generally see human personality as a product of the early mother-child relationship. The interaction between mother and infant lays the foundation for future personality development because that early interpersonal experience serves as a prototype for subsequent interpersonal relations. Klein saw the human psyche as "unstable, fluid, constantly fending off psychotic anxieties" (Mitchell & Black, 1995, p. 87). Moreover, "each of us struggles with the deep terrors of annihilation . . . and utter abandonment" (p. 88).

Because they emphasize the mother-child relationship and view these experiences as crucial to later development, object relations theorists rate high on *determinism* and low on free choice. For the same reason, these theorists can be seen as either *pessimistic* or *optimistic*, depending on the quality of the early mother-infant relationship. If that relationship is healthy, then a person will grow into a psychologically healthy adult; if it is not, the person will acquire a pathological, self-absorbed personality.

On the dimension of *causality vs. teleology*, object relations theory tends to be more causal. Early experiences are the primary shapers of personality. Expectations of the future play a very minor role in object relations theory. As an extension of Freudian psychoanalysis, object relations theory is rated rather high on *unconscious determinants of behavior*. Most of the theorists believed that the prime determinants of behavior can be traced back to very early infancy, a time before verbal language. Thus, people acquire many personal traits and attitudes on a preverbal level and remain unaware of the complete nature of these traits and attitudes. In addition, Klein's acceptance of an innately acquired phylogenetic endowment places her theory even further in the direction of unconscious determinants.

The emphasis that Klein placed on the death instinct and phylogenetic endowment would seem to suggest that she saw biology as more important than environment in shaping personality. However, Klein shifted the emphasis from Freud's biologically based infantile stages to an interpersonal one (Cashdan, 1988; Mitchell & Black, 1995). Because the intimacy and nurturing that infants receive from their mother are environmental experiences, Klein and other object relations theorists lean more toward *social determinants* of personality.

On the dimension of *uniqueness vs. similarities*, object relations theorists tend more toward similarities. As clinicians dealing mostly with disturbed patients, Klein, Mahler, Kernberg, Kohut, and Bowlby limited their discussions to the distinction between healthy personalities and pathological ones and were little concerned with differences among psychologically healthy personalities.

Chapter Summary

Melanie Klein's object relations theory assumes that the first 4 or 5 months of life are the most critical time. Her theory differs from Freud's paternalistic theory in that she strongly emphasized the importance of the mother-child relationship. As a consequence, object relations theory concentrates more on interpersonal relations and less on instinctual drives than does Freudian psychoanalysis. Klein and other object relations theorists built theories either on observation of the mother-child relationship or on speculation concerning the infant's real or fantasized early relations with the mother or the breast. They believed that the quality of adult relationships can be traced back to the very early mother-infant interaction. An important portion of any relationship is the internal psychic representations of early significant objects, such as the mother's breast or the father's penis, that have been introjected or taken into the infant's psychic structure and then projected onto an external object, that is, another person. These internal pictures are not accurate representations of the other person but are remnants of earlier interpersonal experiences.

In order to deal with both the nurturing breast and the frustrating breast, infants split these objects into "good" and "bad," and, at the same time, they split their ego so that they have a dual image of self. In older children the ego becomes unified, but separate aspects of the ego may continue to exist. Klein believed that the ego exists at birth and that it can sense both destructive and loving forces. It can experience anxiety and even establish defense mechanisms from the first few weeks. Klein also held that the superego comes into existence much earlier than Freud had speculated and that it grows along with the Oedipus complex rather than being a product of it.

Like Freud, Klein believed that girls and boys experience the Oedipus complex somewhat differently. But unlike Freud, whose theory held that the father is the parent responsible for penis envy in girls and castration anxiety in boys, Klein suggested that the child's relationship with the mother plays a central role in the Oedipal process. During the early Oedipal years, the little boy adopts a "feminine" position and has no fear of being castrated as punishment for his sexual feelings for his mother. Later, he projects his destructive drive onto his father, who he fears will bite or castrate him. The male Oedipus complex is resolved when the boy establishes good relations with both parents and feels comfortable about his parents having sexual intercourse with one another. Like the boy, the little girl adopts a "feminine" position toward both parents early in the Oedipal experience. She has a positive feeling both for her mother's breasts and for her father's penis, which she believes will feed her with babies. Sometimes the little girl develops hostility toward her mother, who she fears will retaliate against her and rob her of her babies. However, in many cases the female Oedipus complex is resolved without any antagonism and the little girl experiences no jealousy toward her mother.

Object relations theory is currently one of the leading personality theories among therapists in Great Britain, but it does not occupy the same status in the United States. As a scientific theory, it suffers from most of the same problems as other psychodynamic theories; namely, it is very difficult to either verify or falsify. It has some ability to organize information about infant behavior and is useful to some therapists as a guide to action. In contrast, attachment theory has attracted much attention in the United States, and currently many researchers are studying hypotheses drawn from it.

Human personality is shaped largely by the child's early relationship with its mother. This emphasis on mother-infant interaction, which serves as a model for later personality development, places object relations theorists high on determinism, causality, and social influences. In addition, these theorists rate high on unconscious determinants of behavior and about average on the issue of optimism versus pessimism.

Suggested Readings

Hinshelwood, R. D. (1994). *Clinical Klein: From theory to practice.* New York: Basic Books.
   Klein's theoretical ideas and clinical procedures are not easy to comprehend, but in this book, Hinshelwood makes her complex views as accessible as possible.

Klein, M. (1991). The emotional life and ego-development of the infant with special reference to the depressive position. In P. King & R. Steiner (Eds.), *The Freud-Klein controversies* 1941–45 (pp. 752–797). London: Tavistock/Routledge.
   Although all of Klein's writings are difficult, this chapter is perhaps the most accessible. In it, Klein presents a brief summary of her object relations theory.

Segal, J. (1992). *Melanie Klein.* London: Sage.
   This brief paperback is easier to read and less technical than Grosskurth's (1986) book. Segal includes a summary of Klein's life and work, as well as a chapter on criticisms of her theory and rebuttals to the criticisms.

Solomon, I. (1995). *A primer of Kleinian therapy.* Northvale, NJ: Aronson.
   This introduction to Klein's ideas defines and illustrates her most basic concepts while demonstrating the application of object relations to psychotherapy.

St. Clair, M. (1986). *Object relations and self psychology: An introduction.* Monterey, CA: Brooks/Cole.
   St. Clair's introduction to object relations theory and self psychology looks at how the different theorists, including Klein, Mahler, Kernberg, Kohut, and others, compare with each other and how their theories compare to Freudian theory.

Horney

6

Horney:
Psychoanalytic Social Theory

The **psychoanalytic social theory** of Karen Horney is built on the assumption that social and cultural conditions, especially childhood experiences, are largely responsible for shaping personality. People who do not have their needs for love and affection satisfied during childhood develop *basic hostility* toward their parents and, as a consequence, suffer from *basic anxiety*. Horney theorized that people combat basic anxiety by adopting one of three fundamental styles of relating to others: (1) moving toward people; (2) moving against people; or (3) moving away from people. Normal individuals may use any of these modes of relating to other people, but neurotics are compelled to rigidly employ only one. Their compulsive behavior generates a basic *intrapsychic conflict* that may take the form of either an idealized self-image or self-hatred. The idealized self-image is expressed as: (1) neurotic search for glory, (2) neurotic claims, or (3) neurotic pride. Self-hatred is expressed as either self-contempt or alienation from self.

Although Horney's writings are concerned mostly with the neurotic personality, many of her ideas can also be applied to normal individuals. This chapter looks at Horney's basic theory of neurosis, compares her ideas to those of Freud, examines her views on feminine psychology, and briefly discusses her ideas on psychotherapy.

As with other personality theorists, Horney's views on personality are a reflection of her life experiences. Bernard Paris (1994) wrote that "Horney's insights were derived from her efforts to relieve her own pain, as well as that of her patients. If her suffering had been less intense, her insights would have been less profound" (p. xxv). We look now at the life of this often troubled woman.

BIOGRAPHY OF KAREN HORNEY

The biography of Karen Horney has several parallels with the life of Melanie Klein (see Chapter 5). Each was born during the 1880s, the youngest child of a 50-year-old father and his second wife. Each had older siblings who were favored by the parents, and each felt unwanted and unloved. Also, each had wanted to become a physician, but only Horney fulfilled that ambition. Finally, both Horney and Klein engaged in an extended self-analysis—Horney's, beginning with her diaries from age 13 to 26, continuing with her analysis by Karl Abraham, and culminating with her book *Self-Analysis* (1942).

Karen Danielsen Horney was born in Eilbek, a small town near Hamburg, Germany, September 15, 1885 (Quinn, 1987). Karen was the only daughter of Berndt (Wackels) Danielsen, a sea captain, and Clothilda van Ronzelen Danielsen, a woman nearly 18 years younger than her husband. The only other child of this marriage was a son, about 4 years older than Karen. However, the old sea captain had been married earlier and had four other children, most of whom were adults by the time Karen was born. The Danielsen family was an unhappy one, in part because Karen's older half-siblings turned their father against his second wife. Karen felt great hostility toward her stern, devoutly religious father and regarded him as a religious hypocrite. However, she idolized her mother, who both supported and protected her against the stern old sea captain. Nevertheless, Karen was not a happy child. She resented the favored treatment given to her older brother, and in addition, she worried about the bitterness and discord between her parents.

When she was 13, Karen decided to become a physician, but at that time no university in Germany admitted women (Paris, 1994). By the time she was 16, this situation had changed. So Karen, over the objections of her father who wanted her to stay home and take care of the household, entered the gymnasium, a school that would lead to a university and then to medical school. On her own for the first time, Karen was to remain independent for the rest of her life. According to Paris, however, Horney's independence was mostly superficial; on a deeper level, she retained a compulsive need to merge with a great man. This morbid dependency, which typically included idealization and fear of inciting angry rejection, haunted Horney during her relationships with a series of men.

In 1906 she entered the University of Freiburg, becoming one of the first women in Germany to study medicine. There she met Oskar Horney, a political science student. The relationship began as a friendship, but it eventually became a romantic one. After their marriage in 1909, the couple settled in Berlin where Oskar, now with a Ph.D., worked for a coal company and Karen, not yet with an M.D., specialized in psychiatry.

By this time, Freudian psychoanalysis was becoming well established, and Karen Horney became familiar with Freud's writings. Early in 1910, she began an analysis with Karl Abraham, one of Freud's close associates and a man who later analyzed Melanie Klein. After Horney's analysis was terminated, she attended Abraham's evening seminars where she became acquainted with other psychoanalysts. By 1917 she had written her first paper on psychoanalysis, "The Technique of Psychoanalytic Therapy" (Horney, 1917/1968), which reflected the orthodox Freudian view and gave little indication of Horney's subsequent independent thinking.

The early years of her marriage were filled with many notable personal experiences for Horney. Her father and mother, who were now separated, died within less than a year of each other; she gave birth to three daughters in 5 years; she received her M.D. degree in 1915 after 5 years of psychoanalysis; and, in her quest for the right man, she had several love affairs (Paris, 1994; Quinn, 1987).

After World War I, the Horneys lived a prosperous, suburban lifestyle, with several servants and a chauffeur. Oskar did well financially while Karen enjoyed a thriving psychiatric practice. This idyllic scene, however, soon ended. The inflation and economic disorder of 1923 cost Oskar his job, and the family was forced to move back to an apartment in Berlin. In 1926, Karen and Oskar separated but did not officially divorce until 1938 (Paris, 1994).

The early years following her separation from Oskar were the most productive of Horney's life. In addition to seeing patients and caring for her three daughters, she became more involved with writing, teaching, traveling, and lecturing. Her papers now showed important differences with Freudian theory. She believed that culture, not anatomy, was responsible for psychic differences between men and women. When Freud reacted negatively to Horney's position, she became even more outspoken in her opposition.

In 1932, Horney left Germany for a position as associate director of the newly established Chicago Psychoanalytic Institute. Several factors contributed to her decision to immigrate—the anti-Jewish political climate in Germany (although Horney was not Jewish); increasing opposition to her unorthodox views; and an opportunity to extend her influence beyond Berlin. During the 2 years she spent in Chicago, she met Margaret Mead, Harry Stack Scullion, John Dollard, and many of the same scholars who had influenced Sullivan (see Chapter 8). In addition, she renewed acquaintances with Erich Fromm and his wife, Frieda Fromm-Reichmann, whom she had known in Berlin. During the next 10 years, Horney and Fromm were close friends, greatly influencing one another and eventually becoming lovers (Quinn, 1987).

After 2 years in Chicago, Horney moved to New York, where she taught at the New School for Social Research. While in New York, she became a member of the Zodiac group that included Fromm, Fromm-Reichmann, Sullivan, and others (see Chapter 8). Although Horney was a member of the New York Psychoanalytic Institute, she seldom agreed with the established members. Moreover, her book, *New Ways in Psychoanalysis* (1939), made her the leader of an opposition group. In this book, she called for abandoning the instinct theory and placing more emphasis on ego and social influences. In 1941, she resigned from the Institute over issues of dogma and orthodoxy and helped form a rival organization—the Association for the Advancement of Psychoanalysis (AAP). This new group, however, also quickly suffered from internal strife. In 1943, Fromm (whose intimate relationship with Horney had recently ended) and several others resigned from the AAP, leaving that organization without its strongest members. Despite the rift, the association continued, but under a new name—the Karen Horney Psychoanalytic Institute. In 1952, the Karen Horney Clinic was founded, and both organizations have continued to the present time.

In 1950, Horney published her most important work, *Neurosis and Human Growth*. This book sets forth theories that were no longer merely a reaction to Freud, but rather an expression of her own creative and independent thinking.

After a short illness, Horney died of cancer on December 4, 1952.

INTRODUCTION TO PSYCHOANALYTIC SOCIAL THEORY

The early writings of Karen Horney, like those of Adler, Jung, and Klein, have a distinctive Freudian flavor. Like Adler and Jung, she eventually became disenchanted with orthodox psychoanalysis and constructed a revisionist theory that reflected her own personal experiences—clinical and otherwise.

Although Horney wrote nearly exclusively about neuroses and neurotic personalities, her works suggest much that is appropriate to normal healthy development. Culture, especially early childhood experiences, plays a leading role in shaping human personality, either neurotic or healthy. Horney, then, agreed with Freud that early childhood traumas are important, but she differed from him in her insistence that social rather than biological forces are paramount in personality development.

HORNEY AND FREUD COMPARED

Horney criticized Freud's theories on several accounts. First, she cautioned that strict adherence to orthodox psychoanalysis would lead to stagnation in both theoretical thought and therapeutic practice (Horney, 1937). Second, Horney (1937, 1939) objected to Freud's ideas on feminine psychology, a subject we return to later. Third, she stressed the view that psychoanalysis should move beyond instinct theory and emphasize the importance of cultural influences in shaping personality. "Man is ruled not by the pleasure principle alone but by two guiding principles: safety and satisfaction" (1939, p. 73). Similarly, she claimed that neuroses are not the result of instincts but rather of the person's "attempt to find paths through a wilderness full of unknown dangers" (p. 10). This wilderness is created by society and not by instincts or anatomy.

Despite becoming increasingly critical of Freud, Horney continued to recognize his perceptive insights. Her main quarrel with Freud was not so much the accuracy of his observations but the validity of his interpretations. In general terms, she held that Freud's explanations result in a pessimistic concept of humanity based on innate instincts and the stagnation of personality. In contrast, her view of humanity is an optimistic one and is centered on cultural forces that are amenable to change (Horney, 1950).

The Impact of Culture

Although Horney did not overlook the importance of genetic factors, she repeatedly emphasized cultural influences as the primary bases for both neurotic and normal personality development. Modern culture, she contended, is based on *competition* among individuals. "Everyone is a real or potential competitor of everyone else" (Horney, 1937, p. 284). Competitiveness and the *basic hostility* it spawns result in feelings of *isolation*. These feelings of being alone in a potentially hostile world lead to intensified *needs for affection*, which, in turn, cause people to overvalue love. As a result, many people in our culture see love and affection as the solution for all their problems. Genuine love, of course, can be a healthy, growth-producing experience, but the desperate need for love (such as that shown by Horney herself) provides a fertile ground for the development of neuroses. Rather than benefitting from the need for love, neurotics strive in pathological ways to find it. Their self-defeating attempts result in low self-esteem, increased hostility, basic anxiety, more competitiveness, and a continual excessive need for love and affection.

According to Horney, our society contributes to this vicious circle in several respects. First, we are imbued with the cultural teachings of brotherly love and humility. These teachings, however, run contrary to another prevailing attitude, namely aggressiveness and the drive to win or be superior. Second, society's demands for success and achievement are nearly endless, so that even when we achieve our material ambitions, additional goals are continually being placed before us. Third, our society tells us that we are free, that we can accomplish anything through hard work and perseverance. In reality, however, the freedom of most people is greatly restricted by genetics, social position, and the competitiveness of others.

These contradictions—all stemming from cultural influences rather than biological ones—provide intrapsychic conflicts that threaten the psychological health of normal people and provide nearly insurmountable obstructions for neurotics.

The Importance of Childhood Experiences

Horney believed that neurotic conflict can stem from almost any developmental stage, but childhood is the age from which the vast majority of problems arise. A variety of traumatic events, such as sexual abuse, beatings, open rejection, or pervasive neglect, may leave their impressions on future development, but Horney (1937) insisted that these debilitating experiences can almost invariably be traced to lack of genuine warmth and affection. Horney's own lack of love from her father and her close relationship with her mother must have had a powerful effect on her personal development as well as on her theoretical ideas.

Horney (1939) hypothesized that a difficult childhood is primarily responsible for neurotic needs. These needs become powerful because they are the child's only means of gaining feelings of safety. Nevertheless, no single early experience is responsible for later personality. Horney cautioned that "the sum total of childhood experiences brings about a certain character structure, or rather, starts its development" (p. 152). In other words, the totality of early relationships molds personality development. "Later attitudes to others, then, are not repetitions of infantile ones but emanate from the character structure, the basis of which is laid in childhood" (p. 87).

Although later experiences can have an important effect, especially in normal individuals, childhood experiences are primarily responsible for personality development. People who rigidly repeat patterns of behavior do so because they interpret new experiences in a manner consistent with those established patterns.

BASIC HOSTILITY AND BASIC ANXIETY

Horney (1950) believed that each of us begins life with the potential for healthy development, but, like other living organisms, we need favorable conditions for growth. These conditions must include a warm and loving environment, yet one that is not overly permissive. As children, we need to experience both genuine love and healthy discipline. Such conditions provide us with feelings of *safety* and *satisfaction* and permit us to grow in accordance with our real self.

Unfortunately, a multitude of adverse influences may interfere with these favorable conditions. Primary among these is the parents' inability or unwillingness to love their child. Because of their own neurotic needs, parents often dominate, neglect, overprotect, reject, or overindulge. If parents do not satisfy the child's needs for safety and satisfaction, the child develops feelings of **basic hostility** toward the parents. However, children seldom overtly express rage toward their parents; instead, they repress their hostility and have no awareness of it. Repressed hostility then leads to profound feelings of insecurity and a vague sense of apprehension. This condition is called **basic anxiety,** which Horney (1950) defined as "a feeling of being isolated and helpless in a world conceived as potentially hostile" (p. 18). Earlier, she gave a more graphic description, calling basic anxiety "a feeling of being small, insignificant, helpless, deserted, endangered, in a world that is out to abuse, cheat, attack, humiliate, betray, envy" (Horney, 1937, p. 92).

Horney (1937, p. 75) believed that basic hostility and basic anxiety are "inextricably interwoven." Hostile impulses are the principal source of basic anxiety, but basic anxiety can also contribute to feelings of hostility. As an example of how basic hostility can lead to anxiety, Horney wrote about a young man with repressed hostility who went on a hiking trip in the mountains with a young woman with whom he was deeply in love. His repressed hostility, however, also led him to become jealous of the woman. While walking on a dangerous mountain pass, the young man suddenly suffered a severe "anxiety attack" in the form of rapid heart rate and heavy breathing. The anxiety resulted from a seemingly inappropriate but conscious impulse to push the young woman over the edge of the mountain pass.

In this case, basic hostility led to severe anxiety, but anxiety and fear can also lead to strong feelings of hostility. Children who feel threatened by their parents develop a reactive hostility in defense of that threat. This reactive hostility, in turn, may create additional anxiety, thus completing the interactive circle between hostility and anxiety. Horney (1937) contended that "it does not matter whether anxiety or hostility has been the primary factor" (p. 74). The important point is that their reciprocal influence may intensify a neurosis without a person experiencing any additional outside conflict.

Basic anxiety itself is not a neurosis, but "it is the nutritive soil out of which a definite neurosis may develop at any time" (Horney, 1937, p. 89). Basic anxiety is constant and unrelenting, needing no particular stimulus such as taking a test in school or giving a speech. It permeates all relationships with others and leads to unhealthy ways of trying to cope with people.

Although she later amended her list of defenses against basic anxiety, Horney (1937) originally identified four general ways that people in our culture protect themselves against this feeling of being alone in a potentially hostile world. The first was *affection*, a strategy that does not always lead to authentic love. In their search for affection, some people may try to purchase love with self-effacing compliance, material goods, or sexual favors. The second protective device was *submissiveness*. Neurotics may submit themselves either to people or to institutions such as an organization or a religion. Neurotics who submit to another person often do so in order to gain affection.

Neurotics may also try to protect themselves by striving for *power, prestige,* or *possession*. Power is a defense against the real or imagined hostility of others and takes the form of a tendency to dominate others; prestige is a protection against humiliation and is expressed as a tendency to humiliate others; possession acts as a buffer against destitution and poverty and manifests itself as a tendency to deprive others. The fourth protective mechanism was *withdrawal*. Neurotics frequently protect themselves against basic anxiety either by developing an independence from others or by becoming emotionally detached from them. By psychologically withdrawing, neurotics feel that they cannot be hurt by other people.

These protective devices did not necessarily indicate a neurosis, and Horney believed that all people use them to some extent. They become unhealthy when people feel compelled to rely on them and are thus unable to employ a variety of interpersonal strategies. Compulsion, then, is the salient characteristic of all neurotic drives.

COMPULSIVE DRIVES

Neurotic individuals have the same problems that affect normal people, except neurotics experience them to a greater degree. Everyone uses the various protective devices to guard against the rejection, hostility, and competitiveness of others. But, whereas normal individuals are able to use a variety of defensive maneuvers in a somewhat useful way, neurotics compulsively repeat the same strategy in an essentially unproductive manner.

Horney (1942) insisted that neurotics do not enjoy misery and suffering. They cannot change their behavior by free will but must continually and compulsively protect themselves against basic anxiety. This defensive strategy traps them in a vicious circle in which their compulsive needs to reduce basic anxiety lead to behaviors that perpetuate low self-esteem, generalized hostility, inappropriate striving for power, inflated feelings of superiority, and persistent apprehension, all of which result in more basic anxiety.

NEUROTIC NEEDS

In 1942, Horney tentatively identified 10 categories of **neurotic needs** that characterize neurotics in their attempts to combat basic anxiety. These needs were more specific than the four protective devices discussed earlier, but they describe the same basic defensive strategies. The 10 categories of neurotic needs overlapped one another, and a single person might employ more than one. Each of the following neurotic needs relates in some way or another to other people.

1. *The neurotic need for affection and approval.* In their quest for affection and approval, neurotics attempt indiscriminately to please others. They try to live up to the expectations of others, tend to dread self-assertion, and are quite uncomfortable with the hostility of others as well as the hostile feelings within themselves.

2. *The neurotic need for a partner.* Lacking self-confidence, neurotics try to attach themselves to a powerful partner. This need includes an overvaluation of love and a dread of being alone or deserted. Horney's own life story reveals a strong need to relate to a great man, and she had a series of such relationships during her adult life.

3. *The neurotic need to restrict one's life within narrow borders.* Neurotics frequently strive to remain inconspicuous, to take second place, and to be content with very little. They downgrade their own abilities and dread making demands on others.

4. *The neurotic need for power.* Power and affection are perhaps the two greatest neurotic needs. The need for power is usually combined with the needs for prestige and possession and manifests itself as the need to control others and to avoid feelings of weakness or stupidity.

5. *The neurotic need to exploit others.* Neurotics frequently evaluate others on the basis of how they can be used or exploited, but at the same time, they fear being exploited by others.

6. *The neurotic need for social recognition or prestige.* Some people combat basic anxiety by trying to be first, to be important, or to attract attention to themselves.

7. *The neurotic need for personal admiration.* Neurotics have a need to be admired for what they are rather than for what they possess. Their inflated self-esteem must be continually fed by the admiration and approval of others.

8. *The neurotic need for ambition and personal achievement.* Neurotics often have a strong drive to be the best—the best salesperson, the best bowler, the best lover. They must defeat other people in order to confirm their superiority.

9. *The neurotic need for self-sufficiency and independence.* Many neurotics have a strong need to move away from people, thereby proving that they can get along without others. The "playboy" who cannot be tied down by any woman exemplifies this neurotic need.

10. *The neurotic need for perfection and unassailability.* By striving relentlessly for perfection, neurotics receive "proof" of their self-esteem and personal superiority. They dread making mistakes and having personal flaws and desperately attempt to hide their weaknesses from others.

NEUROTIC TRENDS

As her theory evolved, Horney began to see that the list of 10 neurotic needs could be grouped into three general categories, each relating to a person's basic attitude toward self and others. In 1945, she identified the three basic attitudes, or **neurotic trends,** as (1) *moving toward people,* (2) *moving against people,* and (3) *moving away from people.*

Although these neurotic trends constitute Horney's theory of neurosis, they also apply to normal individuals. There are, of course, important differences between normal and neurotic attitudes. Whereas normal people are mostly or completely conscious of their strategies toward other people, neurotics are unaware of their basic attitude; although normals are free to choose their actions, neurotics are forced to act; whereas normals experience mild conflict, neurotics experience severe and insoluble conflict; and whereas normals can choose from a variety of strategies, neurotics are limited to a single trend. Figure 6.1 shows Horney's conception of the mutual influence of basic hostility and basic anxiety and both normal and neurotic defenses against anxiety.

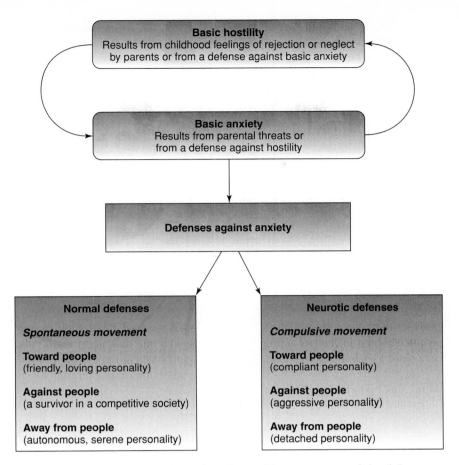

Figure 6.1   The interaction of basic hostility and basic anxiety and the defenses against anxiety.

People can use each of the neurotic trends to solve basic conflict, but unfortunately, these solutions are essentially nonproductive or neurotic. Horney (1950) used the term **basic conflict** because very young children are driven in all three directions—toward, against, and away from people. In healthy children, these three drives are not necessarily incompatible. But the feelings of isolation and helplessness that Horney described as *basic anxiety* drive some children to act compulsively, thereby limiting their repertoire to a single neurotic trend. Experiencing basically contradictory attitudes toward others, these children attempt to solve this basic conflict by making one of the three neurotic trends consistently dominant. In moving *toward* people, some children behave in a *compliant* manner as a protection against feelings of *helplessness*; in moving *against* people, other children act with *aggression* to circumvent the *hostility* of others; and in moving *away from* people, still other children adopt a *detached* manner as a means of alleviating feelings of *isolation* (Horney, 1945).

Moving Toward People

Horney's concept of **moving toward people** does *not* mean moving toward them in the spirit of genuine love. Rather, it refers to a neurotic need to protect oneself against feelings of helplessness.

In their attempts to protect themselves against feelings of *helplessness*, compliant people employ either or both of the first two neurotic needs; that is, they desperately strive for affection and approval of others, or they seek a powerful partner who will take responsibility for their lives. Horney (1937) referred to these needs as "morbid dependency," a concept that anticipated the term "codependency."

The neurotic trend of moving toward people involves a complex of strategies. It is "a whole way of thinking, feeling, acting—a whole way of life" (Horney, 1945, p. 55). Horney also called it a philosophy of life. Neurotics who adopt this philosophy are likely to see themselves as loving, generous, unselfish, humble, and sensitive to other people's feelings. They are willing to subordinate themselves to others, to see others as more intelligent or attractive, and to rate themselves according to what others think of them.

Moving Against People

Just as compliant people assume that everyone is nice, aggressive people take for granted that everyone is *hostile*. As a result, they adopt the strategy of **moving against people.** Neurotically aggressive people are just as compulsive as compliant people, and their behavior is just as much prompted by basic anxiety. Rather than moving toward people in a posture of submissiveness and dependence, these people move against others by appearing tough or ruthless. They are motivated by a strong need to exploit others and to use them for their own benefit. They seldom admit their mistakes and are compulsively driven to appear perfect, powerful, and superior.

Five of the 10 neurotic needs are incorporated in the neurotic trend of moving against people. They include the need to be powerful, to exploit others, to receive recognition and prestige, to be admired, and to achieve. Aggressive people play to win rather than for the enjoyment of the contest. They may appear to be hard working and resourceful on the job, but they take little pleasure in the work itself. Their basic motivation is for power, prestige, and personal ambition.

In American society, the striving for these goals is usually viewed with admiration. Compulsively aggressive people, in fact, frequently come out on top in many endeavors valued by our society. They may acquire desirable sex partners, high-paying jobs, and the personal admiration of many people. Horney (1945) said that it is not to the credit of our civilization that such characteristics are rewarded while love, affection, and the capacity for true friendship—the very qualities that aggressive people lack— are valued less highly.

Moving toward others and moving against others are, in many ways, polar opposites. The compliant person is compelled to have affection for everyone, whereas the aggressive person sees everyone as a potential enemy. For both types, however, "the center of gravity lies outside the person" (Horney, 1945, p. 65). Both need other people. Compliant people need others to satisfy their feelings of helplessness; aggressive people use others as a protection against real or imagined hostility. With the third neurotic trend, in contrast, other people are of lesser importance.

Moving Away from People

In order to solve the basic conflict of *isolation*, some people behave in a detached manner and adopt a neurotic trend of **moving away from people.** This strategy is an expression of needs for privacy, independence, and self-sufficiency. Again, each of these needs can lead to positive behaviors and, indeed, they are often pursued in a healthy fashion.

Moving away from people is a neurotic trend that many people use in an attempt to solve the basic conflict of isolation.

However, they become neurotic when people try to satisfy them by compulsively putting emotional distance between themselves and other people.

Many neurotics find associating with others an intolerable strain. As a consequence, they are compulsively driven to move away from people, to attain autonomy and separateness. They frequently build a world of their own and refuse to allow anyone to get close to them. They value freedom and self-sufficiency and often appear to be aloof and unapproachable. If married, they maintain their detachment even from their spouse. They shun social commitments, but their greatest fear is to need other people.

Although all neurotics possess a need to feel superior, detached personalities have an intensified need to be strong and powerful. Their basic feelings of isolation can be tolerated only by the self-deceptive belief that they are perfect and therefore beyond criticism. They dread competition, fearing a blow to their illusory feelings of superiority. Instead, they prefer that their hidden greatness be recognized without any effort on their part (Horney, 1945).

Although Horney did not explicitly group the 10 neurotic needs within the three neurotic trends, most fit easily into one of these categories. Also, each of the three neurotic trends has an analogous set of characteristics that describe normal individuals. Table 6.1 summarizes the three *neurotic trends*, the *basic conflicts* that give rise to them, the *outstanding characteristics* of each, the 10 *neurotic needs* that compose them, and the three *analogous* traits that characterize normal people.

INTRAPSYCHIC CONFLICTS

The neurotic trends flow from basic anxiety, which, in turn, stems from a child's relationships with other people. To this point, our emphasis has been on culture and interpersonal conflict. However, Horney did not neglect the impact of intrapsychic factors in the development of personality. As her theory evolved, she began to place greater emphasis on the inner conflicts that both normal and neurotic individuals experience. Intrapsychic processes originate from interpersonal experiences, but as they become

Table 6.1 Summary of Horney's Neurotic Trends

	Neurotic Trends		
	Toward People *The compliant personality*	**Against People** *The aggressive personality*	**Away from People** *The detached personality*
Basic conflict or source of neurotic trend	Feelings of helplessness	Protection against hostility of others	Feelings of isolation
Neurotic needs	1. Affection and approval 2. Powerful partner 3. Narrow limits to life	4. Power 5. Exploitation 6. Recognition and prestige 7. Personal admiration 8. Personal achievement	9. Self-sufficiency and independence 10. Perfection and unassailability
Normal analogue	Friendly, loving	Ability to survive in a competitive society	Autonomous, serene

part of our belief system, they develop a life of their own—an existence separate from the interpersonal conflicts that gave them life.

This section looks at two important intrapsychic conflicts; *the idealized self-image* and **self-hatred.** Briefly, the idealized self-image is an attempt to solve conflicts by painting a godlike picture of oneself. Self-hatred is an interrelated yet equally irrational and powerful tendency to despise one's real self. As people build an idealized image of their self, their real self lags farther and farther behind. This creates a growing alienation between the real self and the idealized self and leads neurotics to hate and despise their actual self because it falls so short in matching the glorified self-image (Horney, 1950).

THE IDEALIZED SELF-IMAGE

Horney believed that human beings, if given an environment of discipline and warmth, will develop feelings of security and self-confidence and a tendency to move toward *self-realization*. Unfortunately, early negative influences often impede one's natural tendency toward self-realization, a situation that leaves a person with feelings of isolation and inferiority. Added to this failure is a growing sense of alienation from self.

Feeling alienated from self, the person needs desperately to acquire a stable *sense of identity*. This dilemma can only be solved by creating an **idealized self-image,** an extravagantly positive view of self that exists only in the person's mind. The person "endows himself with unlimited powers and exalted faculties; he becomes a hero, a genius, a supreme lover, a saint, a god" (Horney, 1950, p. 22). The idealized self-image is not a global construction. Neurotics glorify and worship themselves in different ways. Compliant people see themselves as good and saintly; aggressive people build an idealized image of themselves as strong, heroic, and omnipotent; and detached neurotics paint their self-portraits as wise, self-sufficient, and independent.

As the idealized self-image becomes solidified, neurotics begin to believe in the reality of that image. They lose touch with their real self and use the idealized self as the standard for self-evaluation. Rather than growing toward self-realization, they move toward actualizing the idealized self.

Horney (1950) recognized three aspects of the idealized image: (1) the neurotic search for glory; (2) neurotic claims; and (3) neurotic pride.

The Neurotic Search for Glory

As neurotics come to believe in the reality of their idealized self, they begin to incorporate it into all aspects of their lives—their goals, their self-concept, and their relations with others. Horney (1950) referred to this comprehensive drive toward actualizing the ideal self as the **neurotic search for glory.** In addition to *self-idealization*, the neurotic search for glory includes three other elements: the need for perfection, neurotic ambition, and the drive toward a vindictive triumph.

The *need for perfection* refers to the drive to mold the whole personality into the idealized self. Neurotics are not content to merely make a few alterations; nothing short of complete perfection is acceptable. They try to achieve perfection by erecting a complex set of "shoulds" and "should nots." Horney (1950) referred to this as the **tyranny of the should.** Striving toward an imaginary picture of perfection, a neurotic "unconsciously tells himself: 'Forget about the disgraceful creature you actually *are*; this is how you *should be*' " (p. 64).

A second key element in the neurotic search for glory is *neurotic ambition*, that is, the compulsive drive toward superiority. Although neurotics have an exaggerated need to excel in everything, they ordinarily channel their energies into those activities that are most likely to bring success. This drive, therefore, may take several different forms during a person's lifetime (Horney, 1950). For example, while still in school, a girl may direct her neurotic ambition toward being the best student in school. Later, she may be driven to excel in business or to raise the very best show dogs. Neurotic ambition may also take a less materialistic form, such as being the most saintly or most charitable person in the community.

The third aspect of the neurotic search for glory is the *drive toward a vindictive triumph*, the most destructive element of all. The need for a vindictive triumph may be disguised as a drive for achievement or success, but "its chief aim is to put others to shame or defeat them through one's very success; or to attain the power . . . to inflict suffering on them—mostly of a humiliating kind" (Horney, 1950, p. 27). The drive for a vindictive triumph grows out of the childhood desire to take revenge for real or imagined humiliations. No matter how successful neurotics are in vindictively triumphing over others, they never lose their drive for a vindictive triumph—instead, they increase it with each victory. Every success raises their fear of defeat and increases their feelings of grandeur, thus solidifying their need for further vindictive triumphs.

Neurotic Claims

A second aspect of the idealized image is **neurotic claims.** In their search for glory, neurotics build a fantasy world—a world that is out of sync with the real world. Believing that something is wrong with the outside world, they proclaim that they are special and therefore entitled to be treated in accordance with their idealized view of themselves. Because these demands are very much in accord with their idealized self-image, they fail to see that their claims of special privilege are unreasonable.

Neurotic claims grow out of normal needs and wishes, but they are quite different. When normal wishes are not fulfilled, people become understandably frustrated, but when neurotic claims are not met, neurotics become indignant, bewildered, and unable to comprehend why others have not granted their claims. The difference between normal desires and neurotic claims might be illustrated by a situation in which many people are waiting in line for tickets for a popular movie. Most people near the end of the line might wish to be up front, and some of them may even try some ploy to get a better position. Nevertheless, these people know that they don't really deserve to cut ahead of others. Neurotic people, on the other hand, truly believe that they are entitled to be near the front of line, and they feel no guilt or remorse in moving ahead of others.

Neurotic Pride

The third aspect of an idealized image is **neurotic pride,** a false pride based, not on a realistic view of the true self, but on a spurious image of the idealized self. Neurotic pride is qualitatively different from healthy pride or realistic self-esteem. Genuine self-esteem is based on realistic attributes and accomplishments and is generally expressed with quiet dignity. Neurotic pride, on the other hand, is based on an idealized image of self and is usually loudly proclaimed in order to protect and support a glorified view of one's self (Horney, 1950).

Neurotics imagine themselves to be glorious, wonderful, and perfect, so when others fail to treat them with special consideration, their neurotic pride is hurt. To prevent the hurt, they avoid people who refuse to yield to their neurotic claims; instead, they try to become associated with socially prominent and prestigious institutions and acquisitions.

Self-Hatred

People with a neurotic search for glory can never be happy with themselves because when they realize that their real self does not match the insatiable demands of their idealized self, they will begin to hate and despise themselves:

> The glorified self becomes not only a *phantom* to be pursued; it also becomes a measuring rod with which to measure his actual being. And this actual being is such an embarrassing sight when viewed from the perspective of a godlike perfection that he cannot but despise it. (Horney, 1950, p. 110)

Horney (1950) recognized six major ways in which people express self-hatred. First, self-hatred may result in *relentless demands on the self*, which are exemplified by the tyranny of the should. Some people, for example, will make demands on themselves that never stop. Even when they achieve a measure of success, they continue to push themselves toward perfection.

The second mode of expressing self-hatred is *merciless self-accusation*. Neurotics constantly berate themselves. "If people only knew me, they would realize that I'm pretending to be knowledgeable, competent, and sincere. I'm really a fraud, but no one knows it." Self-accusation may take a variety of forms—from obviously grandiose expressions, such as taking responsibility for natural disasters, to scrupulously questioning the virtue of their own motivations.

Third, self-hatred may take the form of *self-contempt*, which might be expressed as belittling, disparaging, doubting, discrediting, and ridiculing oneself. Self-contempt prevents us from striving for improvement or achievement. A young man may say to himself, "You conceited idiot! What makes you think you can get a date with the best-looking woman in town?" A woman may attribute her successful career to "luck." Although these people may be aware of their behavior, they have no perception of the self-hatred that motivates it.

Self-hatred is sometimes expressed through abuse of alcohol.

A fourth expression of self-hatred is *self-frustration*. Horney (1950) distinguished between healthy self-discipline and neurotic self-frustration. The former involves postponing or forgoing pleasurable activities in order to achieve reasonable goals. Self-frustration stems from self-hatred and is designed to actualize an inflated self-image. Neurotics are frequently shackled by taboos against enjoyment. "I don't deserve a new ar." "I must not wear nice clothes because many people around the world are in rags." "I must not strive for a better job because I'm not good enough for it."

Fifth, self-hatred may be manifested as *self-torment*, or self-torture. Although self-torment can exist in each of the other forms of self-hatred, it becomes a separate category when people's main intention is to inflict harm or suffering on themselves. Some people attain masochistic satisfaction by anguishing over a decision, exaggerating the pain of a headache, cutting themselves with a knife, starting a fight that they are sure to lose, or inviting physical abuse.

The sixth and final form of self-hatred is *self-destructive actions and impulses*, which may be either physical or psychological, conscious or unconscious, acute or chronic, carried out in action or enacted only in the imagination. Overeating, abusing alcohol and other drugs, working too hard, driving recklessly, and suicide are common expressions of physical self-destruction. Neurotics may also attack themselves psychologically, for example, quitting a job just when it begins to be fulfilling, breaking off a healthy relationship in favor of a neurotic one, or engaging in promiscuous sexual activities.

Horney (1950) summarized the neurotic search for glory and its attendant self-hatred with these descriptive words:

> Surveying self-hate and its ravaging force, we cannot help but see in it a great tragedy, perhaps the greatest tragedy of the human mind. Man in reaching out for the Infinite and Absolute also starts destroying himself. When he makes a pact with the devil, who promises him glory, he has to go to hell—to the hell within himself. (p. 154)

FEMININE PSYCHOLOGY

As a woman trained in the promasculine psychology of Freud, Horney gradually realized that the traditional psychoanalytic view of women was skewed. She then set forth her own theory of feminine psychology, one that rejected several of Freud's basic ideas.

For Horney, psychic differences between men and women are not the result of anatomy, but rather of cultural and social expectations. Men who subdue and rule women and women who degrade or envy men do so because of the neurotic competitiveness that is rampant in many societies. Horney (1937) insisted that basic anxiety is at the core of men's need to subjugate women and women's wish to humiliate men.

Although Horney (1939) recognized the existence of the *Oedipus complex*, she insisted that it was due to certain environmental conditions and not to biology. If it were the result of anatomy, as Freud contended, it would be universal (as Freud indeed believed). However, Horney (1967) saw no evidence for a universal Oedipus complex. Instead, she held that it is found only in some people and is an expression of the neurotic need for love. We have seen that the neurotic need for affection and the neurotic need for aggression usually begin in childhood and are two of the three basic neurotic trends. A child may passionately cling to one parent and express jealousy toward the other, but these behaviors are means of alleviating basic anxiety and not manifestations of an anatomically based Oedipus complex. Even when there is a sexual aspect to these behaviors, the child's main goal is security, not sexual intercourse.

Horney (1939) found the concept of *penis envy* even less tenable. Although the concept rests on a biological basis, Horney contended that it is contradictory to biological thinking. There is no more anatomical reason why girls should be envious of the penis than boys should desire a breast or a womb. In fact, boys sometimes do express a desire to have a baby, but this is not the result of a universal male "womb envy."

Horney agreed with Adler that many women possess a *masculine protest*; that is, they have a pathological belief that men are superior to women. This perception easily leads to the neurotic desire to be a man. The desire, however, is not an expression of penis envy but rather "a wish for all those qualities or privileges which in our culture are regarded as masculine" (Horney, 1939, p. 108). (This view is nearly identical to that expressed by Erikson and discussed in Chapter 9.)

In 1994, Bernard J. Paris published a talk that Horney had delivered in 1935 to a professional and business women's club in which she summarized her ideas on feminine psychology. By that time Horney was less interested in differences between men and women than in a general psychology of both sexes. Because culture and society are responsible for psychological differences between women and men, Horney felt that "it was not so important to try to find the answer to the question about differences as to understand and analyze the real significance of this keen interest in feminine 'nature' " (Horney, 1994, p. 233). Horney concluded her speech by saying that:

> Once and for all we should stop bothering about what is feminine and what is not. Such concerns only undermine our energies. Standards of masculinity and femininity are artificial standards. All that we definitely know at present about sex differences is that we do not know what they are. Scientific differences between the two sexes certainly exist, but we shall never be able to discover what they are until we have first developed our potentialities as human beings. Paradoxical as it may sound, we shall find out about these differences only if we forget about them. (p. 238)

PSYCHOTHERAPY

Horney believed that neuroses grow out of basic conflict that usually begins in childhood. As people attempt to solve this conflict, they are likely to adopt one of the three neurotic trends, namely, moving toward, against, or away from others. Each of these tactics can produce temporary relief, but eventually they drive the person farther and farther from actualizing the real self and deeper and deeper into a neurotic spiral (Horney, 1950).

The general goal of Horneyian therapy is to help patients gradually grow in the direction of self-realization. More specifically, the aim is to have patients give up their idealized self-image, relinquish their neurotic search for glory, and change self-hatred to acceptance of the real self. Unfortunately, patients are usually convinced that their neurotic solutions are correct, so they are reluctant to surrender their neurotic trends. Even though patients have a strong investment in maintaining the status quo, they do not wish to remain ill. They find little pleasure in their sufferings and would like to be free of them. Unfortunately, they tend to resist change and cling to those behaviors that perpetuate their illness. As we have seen, the three neurotic trends can be cast in favorable terms such as "love," "mastery," or "freedom." Because patients usually see their behaviors in these positive terms, their actions appear to them to be healthy, right, and desirable (Horney, 1942, 1950).

The therapist's task is to convince patients that their present solutions are perpetuating rather than alleviating the core neurosis, a task that takes much time and hard work. Patients may look for quick cures or solutions, but only the long, laborious process of self-understanding can effect positive change. Self-understanding must go beyond information; it must be accompanied by an emotional experience. Patients must understand their pride system, their idealized image, their neurotic search for glory, their self-hatred, their shoulds, their alienation from self, and their conflicts. Moreover, they must see how all these are interrelated and operate to preserve their basic neurosis.

Although a therapist can help encourage patients toward self-understanding, ultimately successful therapy is built on self-analysis (Horney, 1942, 1950). Patients must understand the difference between their idealized self-image and their real self. Fortunately, people possess an inherent curative force that allows them to move inevitably in the direction of self-realization once self-understanding and self-analysis are achieved.

As to techniques, Horneyian therapists use many of the same ones employed by Freudian therapists, especially dream interpretation and free association. Horney saw dreams as attempts to solve conflicts, but the solutions can be either neurotic or healthy. When therapists provide a correct interpretation, patients are helped toward a better understanding of their real self. "From dreams . . . the patient can catch a glimpse, even in the initial phase of analysis, of a world operating within him which is peculiarly his own and which is more true of his feelings than the world of his illusions" (Horney, 1950, p. 349).

In the second major technique, free association, patients are asked to say everything that comes to mind regardless of how trivial or embarrassing it may seem (Horney, 1987). They are also encouraged to express whatever feelings may arise from the associations. As with dream interpretation, free association eventually reveals patients' idealized self-image and persistent but unsuccessful attempts at accomplishing it.

When therapy is successful, patients gradually develop confidence in their ability to assume responsibility for their psychological development. They move toward self-realization and all those processes that accompany it; they have a deeper and clearer understanding of their feelings, beliefs, and wishes; they relate to others with genuine feelings instead of using people to solve basic conflicts; at work, they take a greater interest in the job itself rather than seeing it as a means to perpetuate a neurotic search for glory.

RELATED RESEARCH

Horney's theory has been one of the least productive with regard to generating research. Nevertheless, her ideas have stimulated some recent research in the areas of morbid dependency and hostile movement against others. The concept of morbid dependency was investigated by Deborah Lyon and Jeff Greenberg (1991), who studied this type of codependency in women with an alcoholic parent. These authors theorized that women learn to receive approval and to build self-esteem by conforming to the demands of an exploitative person. They further suggested that women of alcoholic parents continue to seek opportunities to help people who are exploiting them.

More specifically, Lyon and Greenberg hypothesized that women with an alcoholic parent would offer more help to a person perceived as exploitative than to a person seen as nurturing. They compared 24 undergraduate women with one alcoholic parent to 24 undergraduate women with no alcoholic parent on their willingness to offer assistance. The methodology called for three participants and one confederate to meet with the male experimenter who was administering a battery of tests. The confederate and the experimenter spoke briefly to each other, demonstrating to the participants that they were acquainted. Then, with the experimenter out of the room, the confederate interrupted the other women on the pretense of breaking her pencil. After asking if anyone could lend her a new pencil, she uttered one of two comments regarding the experimenter. In the *nurturant condition*, she said that the experimenter had dated her friend, and she further commented that the experimenter had helped her friend with laundry and other tasks. In the *exploitative condition*, the confederate went through the same routine except that she stated that the experimenter had exploited her friend, getting her to do his laundry and other jobs. Then the experimenter came back into the room and asked the participants to volunteer their time—anywhere from 0 to 3 hours—to help with a worthwhile project.

As expected, women with an alcoholic parent volunteered more than twice as much time to the experimenter perceived as exploitative than to the same person portrayed as nurturing. Moreover, the codependent women liked the exploitative experimenter better than the nurturing one, and they also saw him as needing to be nurtured. These findings support Horney's concept that people with neurotic needs to move toward others will do nearly anything to win the approval of other people.

During the past decade, Richard Ryckman and his colleagues have researched the concept of hypercompetitiveness—a concept based on Horney's notion of moving against others, and which includes the personality traits of competitiveness, callousness, aggressiveness, and hostility. First, Ryckman and his colleagues constructed a 26-item self-report called the Hypercompetitive Attitude Scale (HCA) and validated it against an established neuroticism scale (Ryckman, Hammer, Kaczor, & Gold, 1990).

From her observation of patients, Horney concluded that highly aggressive and competitive individuals tend to not only have low self-esteem and to feel powerless, but they compensate for these feelings of inferiority by fantasizing about their tremendous power and success. That is, they often develop a narcissistic personality style. Horney further theorized that hypercompetitive people would be narcissistic in order to cover feelings of low self-worth. Ryckman and his colleagues (Ryckman et al., 1990; Ryckman, Thornton, & Butler, 1994) have found that the HCA consistently relates to low self-esteem and to narcissism. In fact, Ryckman et al. (1994) found that narcissism was a better predictor of hypercompetitiveness than any of the other personality characteristics they examined.

To further validate Horney's theory, Ryckman and colleagues have demonstrated that hypercompetitive individuals also tend to dislike other people and to be deceitful and manipulative toward them (Ryckman et al., 1994), and that hypercompetitive men, as expected, had more hostile attitudes toward rape victims (Kaczor, Ryckman, Thornton, & Kuehnel, 1991). Although Horney did not specifically predict attitudes toward rape victims, she did observe that overly competitive men had very hostile and calloused attitudes toward women.

Finally, Horney (1945) often commented on the extremely competitive nature of Western culture in general and U.S. culture in particular. She pointed out that this competitive ambition is directly opposed to strivings toward closeness and affiliation with others. She further argued that the conflict between these two inherently opposing needs (competitiveness and affiliation) is at the foundation of almost all neurosis and that U.S. culture places greater value on competition than do other cultures. In support of Horney's beliefs, Ryckman, H. W. Van den Borne, and Jef Syroit (1992) collected hypercompetitive attitude data from two samples of U.S. students and two samples of Dutch students. In both comparisons, the U.S. students scored higher on hypercompetitiveness than did the Dutch students. Although this study was limited to two cultures, it did tend to support Horney's views about the highly competitive nature of U.S. culture.

Horney believed that because needs for affiliation and competition are diametrically opposed, the more competitive a culture the higher the incidence of neurosis. To date, no researchers have directly tested this assumption, and the study by Ryckman et al. (1992) stands alone in attempting to address this hypothesis.

CRITIQUE OF HORNEY

Karen Horney was regarded as an important contributor to psychoanalytic theory during her lifetime, but after her death in 1952, interest in her work began to diminish. However, since the publication of *Feminine Psychology* in 1967, a growing number of theorists, therapists, and social thinkers have been drawn to her ideas (Paris, 1994).

Horney's social psychoanalytic theory provides interesting perspectives on the nature of humanity, but it suffers from lack of current research that might support her suppositions. The strength of Horney's theory is her lucid portrayal of the neurotic personality. No other personality theorist has written so well (or so much) about neuroses. Her comprehensive descriptions of neurotic personalities provide an excellent framework for understanding unhealthy people. However, her nearly exclusive concern with neurotics is a serious limitation to her theory. Her references to the nonneurotic personality are general and not well-explicated. She says that people by their very nature will strive toward self-realization, but she paints no clear picture of what self-realization would be.

Horney's theory falls short on its power both to *generate research* and to submit to the criterion of *falsifiability*. Speculations from the theory do not easily yield testable hypotheses and therefore lack both verifiability and falsifiability. Horney's theory was based largely on clinical experiences that put her in contact mostly with neurotic individuals. To her credit, she was reluctant to make specific assumptions about psychologically healthy individuals. Because her theory deals mostly with neurotics, it is rated high on its ability to *organize knowledge* of neurotics but very low on its capacity to explain what is known about people in general.

As a *guide to action*, Horney's theory fares somewhat better. Teachers, therapists, and especially parents can use her assumptions concerning the development of neurotic trends to provide a warm, safe, and accepting environment for their students, patients, or children. Beyond this, however, the theory is not specific enough to give the practitioner a clear and detailed course of action. On this criterion, the theory receives a low rating.

Is Horney's theory *internally consistent*, with clearly defined terms used uniformly? In Horney's book, *Neurosis and Human Growth* (1950), her concepts and formulations are precise, consistent, and unambiguous. However, when all her works are examined, a different picture emerges. Through the years, she used terms such as "neurotic needs" and "neurotic trends" sometimes separately and sometimes interchangeably. Also, the terms "basic anxiety" and "basic conflict" were not always clearly differentiated. These inconsistencies render her entire work somewhat inconsistent, but again, her final theory (1950) is a model of lucidity and consistency.

Another criterion of a useful theory is *parsimony*, and Horney's final theory, as expressed in the last chapter of *Neurosis and Human Growth* (Horney, 1950, chap. 15), would receive a high mark on this standard. This chapter, which provides a useful and concise introduction to Horney's theory of neurotic development, is relatively simple, straightforward, and clearly written.

CONCEPT OF HUMANITY

Horney's concept of humanity was based almost entirely on her clinical experiences with neurotic patients; therefore, her view of human personality is strongly colored by her concept of neurosis. According to Horney, the prime difference between a healthy person and a neurotic individual is the degree of compulsivity with which each moves toward, against, or away from people.

The compulsive nature of neurotic trends suggests that Horney's concept of humanity is deterministic. However, a healthy person would have a large element of free choice. Even a neurotic individual, through psychotherapy and hard work, can wrest some control over those intrapsychic conflicts. For this reason, Horney's psychoanalytic social theory is rated slightly higher on *free will* than on determinism.

On the same basis, Horney's theory is somewhat more *optimistic* than pessimistic. Horney believed that people possess inherent curative powers that lead them toward self-realization. If basic anxiety (the feeling of being alone and helpless in a potentially hostile world) can be avoided, people will feel safe and secure in their interpersonal relations and consequently will develop healthy personalities.

> My own belief is that man has the capacity as well as the desire to develop his potentialities and become a decent human being, and that these deteriorate if his relationship to others and hence to himself is, and continues to be, disturbed. I believe that man can change and go on changing as long as he lives. (Horney, 1945, p. 19)

On the dimension of *causality vs. teleology*, Horney tended to slightly favor teleology, believing that the natural goal for people is self-realization. Childhood experiences, however, can block that movement. "The past in some way or other is always contained in the present" (Horney, 1939, p. 153). Included in our past experiences, however, is the formation of a philosophy of life and a set of values that give both our present and our future some direction.

Although Horney adopted a middle stance regarding *conscious vs. unconscious motivation*, she believed that most people have only limited awareness of their motives. Neurotics, especially, have little understanding of themselves and do not see that their behaviors guarantee the continuation of their neuroses. They mislabel their personal characteristics, couching them in socially acceptable terms, and remain largely unaware of their basic conflict, their self-hate, their neurotic pride and neurotic claims, and their need for a vindictive triumph.

Horney's concept of personality strongly emphasized *social influences* more than biological ones. Psychological differences between men and women, for example, are due more to cultural and societal expectations than to anatomy. To Horney, the Oedipus complex and penis envy are not inevitable consequences of biology, but rather are shaped by social forces. Horney did not neglect biological factors completely, but her main emphasis was on social influences.

Because Horney's theory looks almost exclusively at neuroses, it tends to highlight *similarities among people* more than uniqueness. Not all neurotics are alike, of course, and Horney described three basic types—the helpless, the hostile, and the detached. However, she placed little emphasis on individual differences within each of these categories.

Chapter Summary

The psychoanalytic social theory of Karen Horney goes beyond extending psychoanalysis to cultural and sociological issues. Though trained in orthodox Freudian theory, Horney soon objected to the rigidity of Freud's views, especially those regarding women. She insisted that social and cultural influences were more important than biological ones. To her, people's experiences in childhood with warm and accepting parents or with cold and rejecting ones lay the foundation upon which they erect either a healthy or a neurotic personality. When children lack warmth and affection, their needs for safety and satisfaction are unfilled, and they develop feelings of isolation and helplessness in a potentially hostile world. These feelings of *basic anxiety* prevent them from moving spontaneously toward, against, or away from other people.

The inability to employ different tactics in their relationships with others generates basic conflict, which results in people being compulsively driven to solve their problems by (1) attaching themselves to a powerful partner in a posture of compliance and submissiveness; (2) striking out against people in an effort to exploit, embarrass, or master them; or (3) adopting a detached attitude, manifested by independence and separation from people.

These three *neurotic trends* (moving toward, against, and away from people) are a combination of 10 *neurotic needs* that Horney had earlier identified and are reactions to *interpersonal conflicts*. In her later writings, she identified two major *intrapsychic conflicts*—the idealized self-image and self-hatred. The *idealized self-image* represents neurotics' attempts to solve conflicts by constructing a godlike picture of themselves. *Self-hatred* is the tendency for neurotics to hate and despise their real self.

Horney believed that psychological differences between men and women are not due to anatomy but to cultural and social expectations. Many men wish to subjugate women, and many women desire to humiliate men, but these needs are neurotic and result from basic anxiety.

The Horneyian approach to *psychotherapy* is to bring about growth toward actualization of the real self. To accomplish this, patients must understand that their idealized self-image is a false picture of their true self and they must work toward relinquishing their neurotic search for glory and change self-hatred into acceptance of the real self.

Horney's *concept of humanity* is somewhat positive and optimistic. People possess an inherent drive toward self-realization and, in the absence of basic anxiety, will ultimately achieve it. Social influences, especially those of early childhood, sometimes block the road to self-realization, but through therapy and hard work, people can overcome those obstacles.

Although Horney's formulation of neurotic development was well-conceived, her general theory of personality rates low on its ability to generate research and to organize knowledge. It is moderately useful as a guide to action and is somewhat parsimonious and internally consistent.

Suggested Readings

Horney, K. (1950). Theoretical considerations. In *Neurosis and human growth: The struggle toward self-realization* (pp. 366–378). New York: Norton.

A concise summary of Horney's theoretical position, this book is more difficult than *Our Inner Conflicts* (1945), but the two sources together provide a comprehensive view of psychoanalytic social theory.

Horney, K. (1967). The flight from womanhood: The masculinity-complex in women as viewed by men and women. In H. Kelman (Ed.), *Feminine psychology* (pp. 54–70). New York: Norton.

Originally published in 1926, this article is important because it represents the first significant opposition to Freud's views on penis envy and the female Oedipus complex written from a woman's perspective.

O'Connell, A. N. (1990). Karen Horney (1885–1952). In A. N. O'Connell & N. F. Russo (Eds.), *Women in psychology: A bio-bibliographic sourcebook* (pp. 185–196). New York: Greenwood Press.

This chapter presents a brief account of Horney's career, her major contributions, and her influence on later personal theorists such as Abraham H. Maslow and Carl Rogers.

Paris, B. J. (1994). *Karen Horney: A psychoanalyst's search for self-understanding*. New Haven, CT: Yale University Press.

This book supplements Susan Quinn's (1987) biography by providing more information on Horney's inner struggles, her search for self-understanding, and her views on feminine psychology during her later years.

Quinn, S. (1987). *A mind of her own: The life of Karen Horney*. New York: Summit Books.

An excellent biography of Horney.

Quinn, S. (1994). Awakened to life: Sources of independence in the girlhood of Karen Horney. In M. M. Berger (Ed.), *Women beyond Freud: New concepts of feminine psychology* (pp. 1–14). New York: Brunner/Mazel.

A very brief and readable summary of Horney's early life and later theories, by the author of a full-length biography on Horney.

Fromm

Chapter

Fromm:
Humanistic Psychoanalysis

7

Trained in Freudian psychoanalysis and influenced by Karl Marx, Karen Horney, and other socially oriented theorists, Erich Fromm developed a theory of personality that emphasizes the influence of sociobiological factors, history, economics, and class structure. His **humanistic psychoanalysis** assumes that *basic anxiety*, or feelings of loneliness and isolation, results from humanity's separation from the natural world.

Fromm was more than a personality theorist. He was a social critic, psychotherapist, philosopher, biblical scholar, cultural anthropologist, and psychobiographer. His humanistic psychoanalysis looks at people from a historical and cultural perspective rather than a strictly psychological one. It is less concerned with the individual and more concerned with those characteristics common to a culture.

Fromm takes an evolutionary view of humanity. When humans emerged as a separate species in animal evolution, they lost most of their animal instincts but gained "an increase in brain development that permitted self-awareness, imagination, planning, and doubt" (Fromm, 1992, p. 5). This combination of weak instincts and a highly developed brain makes humans distinct from all other animals.

A more recent event in human history has been the rise of capitalism, which on one hand has contributed to the growth of leisure time and personal freedom, but on the other, has resulted in feelings of anxiety, isolation, and powerlessness. The cost of freedom, Fromm maintained, has exceeded its benefits. The isolation wrought by capitalism has been unbearable, leaving people with two alternatives: (1) to escape from freedom into interpersonal dependencies, or (2) to move to self-realization through productive love and work.

BIOGRAPHY OF ERICH FROMM

Like all personality theorists, Erich Fromm's view of human nature was shaped by childhood experiences. With Fromm, a Jewish family life, the suicide of a young woman, and the extreme nationalism of the German people contributed to his conception of humanity.

Fromm was born on March 23, 1900, in Frankfurt, Germany, the only child of middle-class Orthodox Jewish parents. His father, Naphtali, was the son of a rabbi and the grandson of two rabbis. His mother, Rosa, was the niece of Ludwig Krause, a well-known Talmudic scholar. As a boy, Erich studied the Old Testament with several prominent scholars, including Rabbi Krause. All of these men were "humanists of extraordinary tolerance and with a complete absence of authoritarianism" (Landis & Tauber, 1971, p. xi). Fromm was especially moved by the compassionate and redemptive tone of the prophets Isaiah, Hosea, and Amos. His humanistic psychology can be traced to the reading of these prophets, "with their vision of universal peace and harmony, and their teachings that there are ethical aspects to history—that nations can do right and wrong, and that history has its moral laws" (p. x). Although Fromm later abandoned organized religion, these early experiences with the Bible and with the Talmudic scholars contributed to his humanistic views.

Erich's early childhood was less than ideal. He recalled that he had "very neurotic parents," and that he was "probably a rather unbearably neurotic child" (Evans, 1966, p. 56). He saw his father as being moody and his mother as prone to depression. Moreover, he grew up in two very distinct worlds, one the traditional Orthodox Jewish world, the other the modern capitalist world. This split existence created tensions that were nearly unbearable, but it generated a lifelong tendency to see events from more than one perspective (Fromm, 1986; Hausdorff, 1972).

When Erich was 12, he was both shocked and puzzled by the suicide of an attractive young woman who had been an acquaintance of the Fromm family. The woman was intelligent, artistic, and beautiful; yet she killed herself so that she could be buried with her widowed father who had just died. How could such an action be explained? In the eyes of young Erich, the father was quite uninteresting and unattractive whereas the daughter seemingly had much to live for. "How is it possible that a beautiful young woman should be so in love with her father that she prefer to be buried with him to being alive to the pleasures of life and painting?" (Fromm, 1962, p. 4)

How was it possible? This question haunted Fromm for the next 10 years and eventually led to an interest in Sigmund Freud and psychoanalysis. As Fromm read Freud, he began to learn about the Oedipus complex and to understand how such an event might be possible. Later, Fromm would interpret the young woman's irrational dependence on her father as a nonproductive symbiotic relationship, but in those early years he was content with the Freudian explanation.

Fromm was 14 when World War I began, too young to fight but not too young to be impressed by the irrationality of the German nationalism that he had observed firsthand. He was sure that the British and French were equally irrational, and once again he was struck by a troubling question. How could normally rational and peaceful people become so driven by national ideologies, so intent on killing, so ready to die? "When the war ended in 1918, I was a deeply troubled young man who was obsessed by the question of how war was possible, by the wish to understand the irrationality of human mass behavior, by a passionate desire for peace and international understanding" (Fromm, 1962, p. 9).

During adolescence Fromm was deeply moved by the writings of Freud and Karl Marx, but he was also stimulated by differences between the two. As he studied more, he began to question the validity of both systems. "My main interest was clearly mapped out. I wanted to understand the laws that govern the life of the individual man, and the laws of society" (Fromm, 1962, p. 9).

After the war, Fromm became a socialist, although at that time, he refused to join the Socialist Party. Instead, he concentrated on his studies in psychology, philosophy, and sociology at the University of Heidelberg, where he received his Ph.D. in sociology at the age of 22. Still not confident that his training could answer such troubling questions as the suicide of the young woman or the insanity of war, Fromm turned to psychoanalysis, believing that it promised answers to questions of human motivation not offered in other fields. From 1925 until 1930 he studied psychoanalysis, first in Munich, then in Frankfurt, and finally at the Berlin Psychoanalytic Institute, where he was analyzed by Hanns Sachs, a student of Freud. Although Fromm never met Freud, most of his teachers during those years were strict adherents of Freudian theory (Knapp, 1989).

In 1926, the same year that he repudiated Orthodox Judaism, Fromm married Frieda Reichmann, a psychoanalyst who was more than 10 years his senior, and who later would obtain an international reputation for her work with schizophrenic patients. Knapp (1989) claimed that Reichmann was clearly a mother figure to Fromm and that she even resembled his mother. The marriage, however, was not a happy one. They separated in 1930 but were not divorced until much later, after both had emigrated to the United States.

In 1930, Fromm and several others founded the South German Institute for Psychoanalysis in Frankfurt, but with the Nazi threat becoming more intense, he soon moved to Switzerland where he joined the newly founded International Institute of

Social Research in Geneva. In 1933, he accepted an invitation to deliver a series of lectures at the Chicago Psychoanalytic Institute. The following year he emigrated to the United States and opened a private practice in New York City.

In both Chicago and New York, Fromm renewed his acquaintance with Karen Horney, whom he had known casually at the Berlin Psychoanalytic Institute. Horney, who was 15 years older than Fromm, eventually became a strong mother figure and mentor to him (Knapp, 1989). Fromm joined Horney's newly formed Association for the Advancement of Psychoanalysis (AAP) in 1941. Although he and Horney had been lovers, by 1943 dissension within the association had made them rivals. When students requested that Fromm, who did not hold an M.D. degree, teach a clinical course, the organization split over his qualifications. With Horney siding against him, Fromm, along with Harry Stack Sullivan, Clara Thompson, and several other members, quit the association and immediately made plans to begin an alternative organization (Quinn, 1987). In 1946, this group established the William Alanson White Institute of Psychiatry, Psychoanalysis, and Psychology, with Fromm chairing both the faculty and the training committee.

In 1944, Fromm married Henny Gurland, a woman whose interest in religion and mystical thought furthered Fromm's own inclinations toward Zen Buddhism. In 1951, the couple moved to Mexico for a more favorable climate for Henny, who suffered from rheumatoid arthritis. Fromm joined the faculty at the National Autonomous University in Mexico City, where he established a psychoanalytic department at the medical school. After his wife died in 1952, he continued to live in Mexico and commuted between his home in Cuernavaca and the United States, where he held various academic positions, including professor of psychology at Michigan State University from 1957 to 1961 and adjunct professor at New York University from 1962 to 1970. While in Mexico he met Annis Freeman, whom he married in 1953. In 1968, Fromm suffered a serious heart attack and was forced to slow down his busy schedule. Still ill, he and his wife moved to Muralto, Switzerland, in 1974. There he died on March 18, 1980, a few days short of his 80th birthday.

Fromm began his professional career as a psychotherapist using orthodox psychoanalytic technique, but after 10 years he became "bored" with the Freudian approach and developed his own more active and confrontational methods (Fromm, 1986, 1992; Sobel, 1980). Over the years his cultural, social, economic, and psychological ideas have attained a wide audience. Among his best known books are *Escape from Freedom* (1941), *Man for Himself* (1947), *Psychoanalysis and Religion* (1950), *The Sane Society* (1955), *The Art of Loving* (1956), *Marx's Concept of Man* (1961), *The Heart of Man* (1964), *The Anatomy of Human Destructiveness* (1973), *To Have or Be* (1976), and *For the Love of Life* (1986).

Fromm's theory of personality borrows from myriad sources and is, perhaps, the most broadly based of any theory in this book. Landis and Tauber (1971) listed five important influences on Fromm's thinking: (1) the teachings of the humanistic rabbis; (2) the revolutionary spirit of Karl Marx; (3) the equally revolutionary ideas of Sigmund Freud; (4) the rationality of Zen Buddhism as espoused by D. T. Suzuki; and (5) the writings of Johann J. Bachofen (1815–1887) on matriarchal societies.

FROMM'S BASIC ASSUMPTIONS

Fromm's most basic assumption is that individual personality can be understood only in the light of human history. "The discussion of the human situation must precede that of personality, [and] psychology must be based on an anthropologico-philosophical concept of human existence" (Fromm, 1947, p. 45).

Fromm (1947) believed that humans, unlike other animals, have been "torn away" from their prehistoric union with nature. They have no powerful instincts to adapt to a changing world; instead, they have acquired the facility to reason—a condition Fromm called the *human dilemma*. We experience this basic dilemma because we have become separate from nature and yet have the capacity to be aware of ourselves as isolated beings. Our ability to reason, however, is both a blessing and a curse. On one hand, it permits us to survive, but on the other, it forces us to attempt to solve basic insoluble dichotomies. Fromm referred to these as "existential dichotomies" because they are rooted in our very existence. We cannot do away with these existential dichotomies; we can only react to them relative to our culture and our individual personalities.

The first and most fundamental dichotomy is that between life and death. Self-awareness and reason tell us that we will die, but we try to negate this dichotomy by postulating life after death, an attempt that does not alter the fact that our lives end with death.

A second existential dichotomy is that we are capable of conceptualizing complete self-realization, but because life is short, we can never reach it. "Only if the life span of the individual were identical with that of mankind could he participate in the human development which occurs in the historical process" (Fromm, 1947, p. 42). Some people try to solve this dichotomy by assuming that their own historical period is the crowning achievement of humanity, while others postulate a continuation of development after death.

The third existential dichotomy is that we are ultimately alone, yet we cannot tolerate isolation. We are aware of ourselves as separate individuals, and at the same time, we are aware that our happiness depends on uniting with our fellow human beings. Although we cannot completely solve the problem of aloneness vs. union, we must make an attempt or else run the risk of insanity.

HUMAN NEEDS

As animals, we are motivated by such physiological needs as hunger, sex, and safety, but we can never resolve our human dilemma by satisfying these animal needs. Only the distinctive *human needs* can move us toward a reunification with the natural world. These **existential needs** have emerged during the evolution of human culture, growing out of our attempts to find an answer to our existence and to avoid becoming insane. Indeed, Fromm (1955) contended that one important difference between mentally healthy individuals and neurotic or insane ones is that healthy people find answers to their existence—answers that more completely correspond to their total human needs. In other words, healthy individuals are better able to find ways of reuniting to the world by productively solving the human needs of *relatedness, transcendence, rootedness, a sense of identity,* and *a frame of orientation.*

RELATEDNESS

The first human, or existential, need is **relatedness,** the drive for union with another person or persons. Fromm postulated three basic ways in which a person may relate to the world: (1) submission, (2) power, and (3) love. A person can submit to another, to a group, or to an institution in order to become one with the world. "In this way he transcends the separateness of his individual existence by becoming part of somebody or

Relatedness can take the form of submission, power, or love.

something bigger than himself and experiences his identity in connection with the power to which he has submitted" (Fromm, 1981, p. 2).

Whereas submissive people search for a relationship with domineering people, power-seekers welcome submissive partners. When a submissive person and a domineering person find each other, they frequently establish a *symbiotic relationship*, one that is satisfying to both partners. Although such symbiosis may be gratifying, it blocks growth toward integrity and psychological health. The two partners "live on each other and from each other, satisfying their craving for closeness, yet suffering from the lack of inner strength and self-reliance which would require freedom and independence" (Fromm, 1981, p. 2).

People in symbiotic relationships are drawn to one another, not by love, but by a desperate need for relatedness, a need that can never be completely satisfied by such a partnership. Underlying the union are unconscious feelings of hostility. People in symbiotic relationships blame their partners for not being able to completely satisfy their needs. They find themselves seeking additional submission or power, and as a result, they become more and more dependent on their partners and less and less of an individual.

Fromm believed that **love** is the only route by which a person can become united with the world and, at the same time, achieve individuality and integrity. He defined love as a "union with somebody, or something outside oneself *under the condition of retaining the separateness and integrity of one's own self*" (Fromm, 1981, p. 3). Love involves sharing and communion with another, yet it allows a person the freedom to be unique and separate. It enables a person to satisfy the need for relatedness without surrendering integrity and independence. In love, two people become one, yet remain two.

In *The Art of Loving*, Fromm (1956) identified care, responsibility, respect, and knowledge as four basic elements common to all forms of genuine love. To love another we must *care* for that person and be willing to take care of him or her. Love also means *responsibility*, that is, a willingness and ability to respond. When we love others, we respond to their physical and psychological needs, respect them for who they are, and avoid the temptation of trying to change them. But we can respect others only if we have *knowledge* of them. To know others means to see them from their own point of view. Thus, care, responsibility, respect, and knowledge are all entwined in a love relationship.

TRANSCENDENCE

Like other animals, humans are thrown into the world without their consent or will and then removed from it—again without their consent or will. But unlike other animals, human beings are driven by the need for **transcendence,** defined as the urge to rise above a passive and accidental existence and into "the realm of purposefulness and freedom" (Fromm, 1981, p. 4). Just as relatedness can be pursued through either productive or nonproductive methods, transcendence can be sought through either positive or negative approaches. We can transcend our passive nature by either creating life or by destroying it. Although other animals can create life through reproduction, only humans are aware of themselves as creators. Also, humans can be creative in other ways. They can create art, religions, ideas, laws, material production, and love.

To create means to be active and to care about that which we create. But we can also transcend life by destroying it and thus rising above our slain victims. In *The Anatomy of Human Destructiveness* (1973), Fromm argued that humans are the only species to use **malignant aggression;** that is, to kill for reasons other than survival. Although malignant aggression is a dominant and powerful passion in some individuals and cultures, it is not common to all humans. It apparently was unknown to many prehistoric societies, as well as some contemporary "primitive" societies.

ROOTEDNESS

A third existential need is for **rootedness,** or the need to establish roots or to feel at home again in the world. When humans evolved as a separate species, they lost their home in the natural world. At the same time, their capacity for thought enabled them to realize that they were without a home, without roots. The consequent feelings of isolation and helplessness became unbearable.

Rootedness, too, can be sought in either productive or nonproductive strategies. With the productive strategy, people are weaned from the orbit of their mother and become fully born; that is, they actively and creatively relate to the world and become whole or integrated. This new tie to the natural world confers security and reestablishes a sense of belongingness and rootedness. However, people may also seek rootedness through the nonproductive strategy of **fixation**—a tenacious reluctance to move beyond the protective security provided by one's mother. People who strive for rootedness through fixation are "afraid to take the next step of birth, to be weaned from the mother's breast. [They] . . . have a deep craving to be mothered, nursed, protected by a motherly figure; they are the externally dependent ones, who are frightened and insecure when motherly protection is withdrawn" (Fromm, 1955, p. 40).

Rootedness can also be seen phylogenetically in the evolution of the human species. Fromm agreed with Freud that incestuous desires are universal, but he disagreed with Freud's belief that they are essentially sexual. According to Fromm (1955, pp. 40–41), incestuous feelings are based in "the deep-seated craving to remain in, or to return to the all-enveloping womb, or to the all-nourishing breasts." Fromm was influenced by J. J. Bachofen's (1861/1967) ideas on early matriarchal societies. Unlike Freud, who believed that early societies were patriarchal, Bachofen held that the mother was the central figure in these ancient social groups. It was she who provided roots for her children and motivated them to either develop their individuality and reason or become fixated and incapable of psychological growth.

SENSE OF IDENTITY

The fourth human need is for a **sense of identity,** or the capacity to be aware of ourselves as a separate entity. Because we have been torn away from nature, we need to form a concept of our self, to be able to say, "I am I," or "I am the subject of my actions." Fromm (1981) believed that primitive people identified more closely with their clan and did not see themselves as individuals existing apart from their group. Even during medieval times, people were identified largely by their social role in the feudal hierarchy. In agreement with Marx, Fromm believed that the rise of capitalism has given people more economic and political freedom. However, this freedom has given only a minority of people a true sense of "I." The identity of most people still resides in their attachment to others or to institutions such as nation, religion, occupation, or social group.

> Instead of the pre-individualistic clan identity, a new herd identity develops in which the sense of identity rests on the sense of an unquestionable belonging to the crowd. That this uniformity and conformity are often not recognized as such, and are covered by the illusion of individuality, does not alter the facts. (Fromm, 1981, p. 9)

Without a sense of identity, we could not retain our sanity, and this threat provides a powerful motivation for us to do almost anything to acquire a sense of identity. Neurotics try to attach themselves to powerful people or to social or political institutions. Healthy people, however, have less need to conform to the herd, less need to give up their sense of self. They do not have to surrender their freedom and individuality in order to fit into society because they possess an authentic sense of identity.

FRAME OF ORIENTATION

A final human need is for a **frame of orientation.** Being split off from nature, we need a road map, a frame of orientation, to make our way through the world. Without such a map we would be "confused and unable to act purposefully and consistently" (Fromm, 1973, p. 230). A frame of orientation enables us to organize the various stimuli that impinge on us. "Man finds himself surrounded by many puzzling phenomena and, having reason, he has to make sense of them, has to put them in some context which he can understand" (Fromm, 1955, p. 63).

Every person has a philosophy, a consistent way of looking at things. Many people take this philosophy or frame of reference for granted so that anything at odds with their view is judged as "crazy" or "unreasonable." Anything consistent with it is seen simply as "common sense." People will do nearly anything to acquire and retain a frame of orientation, even to the extreme of following irrational or bizarre philosophies such as those espoused by Adolf Hitler or other fanatical leaders.

A road map without a *goal* or destination is worthless. As humans, we have the mental capacity to imagine many alternative paths to follow. To keep from going insane, however, we need a final goal or "object of devotion." According to Fromm

Table 7.1 Summary of Fromm's Human Needs

	Negative Components	Positive Components
Relatedness	Submission or domination	Love
Transcendence	Destructiveness	Creativeness
Rootedness	Fixation	Wholeness
Sense of identity	Adjustment to a group	Individuality
Frame of orientation	Irrational goals	Rational goals

(1973), this goal or object of devotion focuses our energies in a single direction, enables us to transcend our isolated existence, and confers meaning to our lives.

SUMMARY OF HUMAN NEEDS

In addition to physiological or animal needs, people are motivated by five distinctively human needs—relatedness, transcendence, rootedness, a sense of identity, and a frame of orientation. These needs have evolved from our existence as a separate species and are aimed at moving us toward a reunification with the natural world. Fromm believed that lack of satisfaction of any of these needs is unbearable and results in insanity. Thus, we are strongly driven to fulfill them in some way or another, either positively or negatively.

Table 7.1 shows that relatedness can be satisfied through submission, domination, or love, but only love produces authentic fulfillment; transcendence can be satisfied by either destructiveness or creativeness, but only the latter permits joy; rootedness can be satisfied by either fixation to the mother or by moving forward into full birth and wholeness; the sense of identity can be based on adjustment to the group, or it can be satisfied through creative movement toward individuality; and a frame of orientation may be either irrational or rational, but only a rational philosophy can serve as a basis for the growth of total personality (Fromm, 1981).

THE BURDEN OF FREEDOM

The central thesis of Fromm's writings is that humans have been torn from nature, yet they remain part of the natural world, subject to the same physical limitations as other animals. As the only animal possessing self-awareness, imagination, and reason, humans are "the freak[s] of the universe" (Fromm, 1955, p. 23). Reason is both a curse and a blessing. It is responsible for feelings of isolation and loneliness, but it is also the process that enables humans to become reunited with the world.

Historically, as people gained more and more economic and political freedom, they came to feel increasingly more isolated. For example, during the Middle Ages people had relatively little personal freedom. They were anchored to prescribed roles in society, roles that provided security, dependability, and certainty. Then, as they acquired more *freedom to* move both socially and geographically, they found that they were *free from* the security of a fixed position in the world. They were no longer tied to one geographic region, one social order, or one occupation. They became separated from their roots and isolated from one another.

A parallel experience exists on a personal level. As children become more independent of their mothers, they gain more *freedom to* express their individuality, to move around unsupervised, to choose their friends and clothes, and so on. At the same time, they experience the burden of freedom; that is, they are *free from* the security of being one with the mother. On both a social and an individual level, this burden of freedom results in **basic anxiety,** the feeling of being alone in the world.

Mechanisms of Escape

Because basic anxiety produces a frightening sense of isolation and aloneness, people attempt to flee from freedom through a variety of escape mechanisms. In *Escape from Freedom*, Fromm (1941) identified three primary mechanisms of escape—authoritarianism, destructiveness, and conformity. Unlike Horney's *neurotic* trends (see Chapter 6), Fromm's mechanisms of escape are the driving forces in normal people, both individually and collectively.

Authoritarianism

Fromm (1941) defined **authoritarianism** as the "tendency to give up the independence of one's own individual self and to fuse one's self with somebody or something outside oneself, in order to acquire the strength which the individual is lacking" (p. 141). This need to unite with a powerful partner can take one of two forms—masochism and sadism. *Masochism* results from basic feelings of powerlessness, weakness, and inferiority and is aimed at joining the self to a more powerful person or institution. Masochistic strivings often are disguised as love or loyalty, but unlike love and loyalty, they can never contribute positively to independence and authenticity.

Compared with masochism, *sadism* is more neurotic and more socially harmful. Like masochism, sadism is aimed at reducing basic anxiety through achieving unity with another person or persons. Fromm (1941) identified three kinds of sadistic tendencies, all more or less clustered together. The first is manifested as the need to make others dependent on oneself and to gain power over those who are weak. The second is the need to exploit others, to take advantage of them, and to use them for one's benefit or pleasure. A third sadistic tendency is the desire to see others suffer, either physically or psychologically.

Destructiveness

Like authoritarianism, **destructiveness** is rooted in the feelings of aloneness, isolation, and powerlessness. Unlike sadism and masochism, however, destructiveness does not depend on a continuous relationship with another person; rather, it seeks to eliminate other people.

Both individuals and nations can employ destructiveness as a mechanism of escape. By destroying people and objects, a person or a nation attempts to restore lost feelings of power. Serial killers are typically lonely people, searching for union with another person. Their contact with their victims, however, is usually short and ends with the destruction of a human who might have provided intimacy and unity. Obviously, destructiveness is self-defeating, for in destroying, one can no longer unite. Destructive people, however, are attracted to a kind of perverted isolation that would be achieved only if they could eliminate the outside world.

Conformity

The most common means of escape in American society, Fromm believed, is **conformity.** People who conform try to escape from a sense of aloneness and isolation by giving up their individuality and becoming whatever other people desire them to be. Thus, they become robots, reacting predictably and mechanically to the whims of others. They seldom express their own opinion, cling to expected standards of behavior, and often appear still and mechanical.

People in the modern world are free from many external bonds and are free to act according to their own will, but at the same time, they do not know what they want, think, or feel. They conform like automatons to some anonymous authority and adopt a self that is not authentic. The more they conform, the more powerless they feel; the more powerless they feel, the more they must conform. People can break this cycle of conformity and powerlessness only by achieving self-realization or positive freedom (Fromm, 1941).

POSITIVE FREEDOM

The emergence of political and economic freedom does not lead inevitably to the bondage of isolation and powerlessness. A person "can be free and not alone, critical and yet not filled with doubts, independent and yet an integral part of mankind" (Fromm, 1941, p. 257). People can attain this kind of freedom, called **positive freedom,** by a spontaneous and full expression of both their rational and their emotional potentialities. Spontaneous activity is frequently seen in small children and artists who have little or no tendency to conform to whatever others want them to be. They act according to their basic natures and not according to conventional rules.

Positive freedom represents a successful solution to the human dilemma of being part of the natural world and yet separate from it. Through positive freedom and spontaneous activity, we overcome the terror of aloneness, achieve a union of our self with the world, and maintain our individuality. Fromm (1941) held that love and work are the twin components of positive freedom. Through active love and work, we unite with others and with the world without sacrificing our integrity. We affirm our uniqueness as individuals and achieve full realization of our potentialities.

CHARACTER ORIENTATIONS

In Fromm's theory, personality is reflected in one's **character orientation,** that is, a person's relatively permanent way of relating to people and things. Fromm (1947) defined personality as "the totality of inherited and acquired psychic qualities which are characteristic of one individual and which make the individual unique" (p. 50). The most important of the acquired qualities of personality is **character,** defined as *"the relatively permanent system of all noninstinctual strivings through which man relates himself to the human and natural world"* (Fromm, 1973, p. 226). Fromm (1992) believed that character is a substitute for our lack of instincts. Instead of acting according to our instincts, we act according to our character. If we had to stop and think about the consequences of our behavior, our actions would be very inefficient and inconsistent. By acting according to our character traits, we can behave both efficiently and consistently.

People relate to the world in two ways—by acquiring and using things (*assimilation*) and by relating to self and others (*socialization*). In general terms, people can relate to things and to people either nonproductively or productively.

NONPRODUCTIVE ORIENTATIONS

The nonproductive orientation includes *receptive, exploitative, hoarding,* and *marketing* characters. Fromm used the term "nonproductive" to suggest strategies that fail to move people closer to positive freedom and self-realization. Nonproductive orientations are, however, not entirely negative; each has both a negative and a positive aspect. Personality is always a blend or combination of several orientations, although one orientation is usually dominant.

Receptive

Receptive characters feel that the source of all good lies outside themselves and that the only way they can relate to the world is to receive things, including love, knowledge, and material possessions. They are more concerned with receiving than with giving, and they want others to shower them with love, ideas, and gifts.

The positive qualities of receptive people include loyalty, acceptance, and trust; their negative traits include passivity, submissiveness, servility, and lack of self-confidence.

Exploitative

Like receptive people, **exploitative characters** believe that the source of all good is outside themselves. Unlike receptive people, however, they aggressively take what they desire rather than passively receive it. In their social relationships, they are likely to use cunning or force to take someone else's friend. An exploitative man may "fall in love" with a married woman, not so much because he is truly fond of her, but because he wishes to exploit her husband. In the realm of ideas, exploitative people prefer to steal or plagiarize rather than create. Unlike receptive characters, they are willing to express an opinion, but it is usually an opinion that has been pilfered.

On the negative side, exploitative characters are egocentric, conceited, arrogant, and seducing; their positive qualities include impulsiveness, pride, and self-confidence. They are active, captivating, and able to take initiative.

Hoarding

Rather than valuing things outside themselves, **hoarding characters** seek to save that which they have already obtained. They hold everything in and do not let go of anything. They keep their money, their feelings, and their thoughts for themselves. In a love relationship, they try to possess the loved one and to preserve the relationship rather than allowing it to change and grow. They tend to live in the past and are repelled by anything new. They are similar to Freud's anal characters in that they are excessively orderly, stubborn, and miserly. Fromm (1964), however, believed that hoarding characters' anal traits are not the result of sexual drives, but rather are part of their general interest in all that is not alive, including the feces.

Positive traits of the hoarding personality are orderliness, cleanliness, and punctuality; negative characteristics include rigidity, sterility, obstinacy, compulsivity, and lack of creativity.

Marketing

The **marketing character** is an outgrowth of modern commerce where trade is no longer personal but carried out by large, faceless corporations. Consistent with the demands of modern commerce, marketing characters see themselves as commodities, with their personal value dependent on their exchange value, that is, their ability to sell themselves.

Marketing personalities must see themselves as being in constant demand; they must make others believe that they are skillful and salable. Their personal security rests on shaky ground because they must adjust their personality to that which is currently in fashion. They play many roles and are guided by the motto, "'I am as you desire me'" (Fromm, 1947, p. 73).

Marketing characters are aimless, opportunistic, inconsistent, and wasteful. They are without a past or a future and have no permanent principles or values. They have fewer positive traits than the other orientations because they are basically empty, waiting to be filled with whatever characteristic is most marketable. Some of the positive qualities Fromm (1947) used to describe the marketing personality include changeability, open-mindedness, undogmatic, adaptable, and generous.

THE PRODUCTIVE ORIENTATION

Fromm's single productive orientation has three dimensions—working, loving, and reasoning. Because productive people work toward positive freedom and a continuing realization of their potential, they are the most healthy of all character types. Only through productive activity can people solve the basic human dilemma, which is to unite with the world and with others while retaining uniqueness and individuality. This can be accomplished only through productive work, love, and thought.

Healthy people value *work*, not as an end in itself, but as a means of creative self-expression. They do not work to exploit others, to market themselves, to withdraw from others, or to accumulate needless material possessions. They are neither lazy nor compulsively active, but use work as a means of producing life's necessities.

Productive *love* is characterized by the four qualities of love discussed earlier—care, responsibility, respect, and knowledge. Healthy people possess **biophilia,** meaning that they have a passionate love of life and all that is alive. They desire to further all life—the life of people, animals, plants, ideas, and cultures. They are concerned with the growth and development of themselves as well as others. Biophilic individuals want to influence people through love, reason, and example—not by force. Fromm believed that love of others and self-love are inseparable, but that self-love must come first. All people have the capacity for productive love, but most do not achieve it because they cannot first love themselves.

Productive *thinking*, which cannot be separated from productive work and love, is motivated by a concerned interest in another person or object. A healthy individual see others as they are and not as the individual would wish them to be. Similarly, healthy people know themselves for who they are and have no need for self-delusion.

Fromm (1947) believed that healthy people rely on some combination of all five character orientations. Their survival as healthy individuals depends on their ability to *receive* things from other people, to *take* things when appropriate, to *preserve* things, to *exchange* things, and to *work*, *love*, and *think* productively.

PERSONALITY DISORDERS

If healthy people are able to work, love, and think productively, then unhealthy personalities are characterized by a failure to use their full potential, especially their power to love. In our discussion of the nonproductive orientations—receptive, exploitative, hoarding, and marketing—the emphasis was mostly on modes of *assimilation*, that is, one's method of acquiring and using objects or things. Serious psychopathology, however, has roots in modes of *socialization*, that is, one's pattern of relating to other people. Fromm (1981) held that psychologically disturbed people are incapable of love and have failed to establish union with others.

Fromm recognized three severe personality disorders—*necrophilia, malignant narcissism*, and *incestuous symbiosis*.

NECROPHILIA

The term "necrophilia" means love of death and usually refers to a sexual perversion in which a person desires sexual contact with a corpse. However, Fromm (1964, 1973) used **necrophilia** in a more generalized sense to denote any attraction to death. Necrophilia is an alternative character orientation to *biophilia*. People naturally love life, but when social conditions stunt biophilia, they may adopt a necrophilous orientation.

Necrophilous personalities hate humanity; they are racists, warmongers, and bullies; they love bloodshed, destruction, terror, and torture; and they delight in destroying life. They are strong advocates of law and order; love to talk about sickness, death, and burials; and are fascinated by dirt, decay, corpses, and feces. They prefer night to day and love to operate in darkness and shadow.

Necrophilous people do not simply *behave* in a destructive manner; rather, their destructive behavior is a reflection of their basic *character*. All of us behave aggressively and destructively at times, but the entire lifestyle of the necrophilous person revolves around death, destruction, disease, and decay.

MALIGNANT NARCISSISM

If all of us display some necrophilous behavior, so too are all of us narcissistic. In its benign form, **narcissism** is manifested as a greater interest in our own body and concerns than in those of others. In its malignant form, narcissism impedes our perception of reality so that everything belonging to our self is highly valued and everything belonging to another is devalued. Narcissistic people are preoccupied with themselves, but this concern is not limited to admiring themselves in a mirror. Preoccupation with one's body often leads to **hypochondriasis,** or an obsessive attention to one's health. Fromm (1964) also recognized **moral hypochondriasis,** which is a preoccupation with *guilt* about previous transgressions. People who are fixated on themselves are likely to internalize experiences and to dwell on both physical and moral aspects of their being.

"The narcissism underlying physical or moral hypochondriasis is the same as the narcissism of the vain person" (p. 69). Each stems from an intense interest in oneself.

Narcissistic people possess what Horney (see Chapter 6) called "neurotic claims." They achieve security by holding on to the distorted belief that their extraordinary personal qualities give them superiority over everyone else. Because what they *have*—looks, physique, wealth—is so wonderful, they believe that they need not *do* anything to prove their value. Their sense of worth depends on their narcissistic self-image and not on their achievements. When their efforts are criticized by others, they react with anger and rage, frequently striking out against their critics, trying to destroy them. If the criticism is overwhelming, they may be unable to destroy it, and so they turn their rage inward. The result is *depression*, a feeling of worthlessness that marks unconscious narcissism. Although depression, intense guilt, and hypochondriasis may appear to be anything but self-glorification, Fromm believed that each of these could be symptomatic of deep underlying narcissism.

INCESTUOUS SYMBIOSIS

A third pathological orientation is **incestuous symbiosis,** or an extreme dependence on the mother or mother surrogate. Incestuous symbiosis is an exaggerated form of the more common and more benign *mother fixation*. Men with a mother fixation need a woman to care for them, comfort them, and admire them; they feel somewhat anxious and depressed when their needs are not fulfilled. This condition is relatively normal and does not greatly interfere with their daily life.

With incestuous symbiosis, however, people are inseparable from the *host* person; their personalities are blended with the other person and their individual identities are lost. Incestuous symbiosis originates in infancy as a natural attachment to the mothering one. The attachment is more crucial and fundamental than any sexual interest that may develop during the Oedipal period. Fromm agreed more with Harry Stack Sullivan (see Chapter 8) than with Freud in suggesting that attachment to the mother rests on the need for security and not for sex. "Sexual strivings are not the cause of the fixation to mother, but the *result*" (Fromm, 1964, p. 99).

People living in incestuous symbiotic relationships feel extremely anxious and frightened if that relationship is threatened. They believe that they cannot live without their mother substitute. (The host need not be another human—it can be a family, clan, church, or country.) The incestuous orientation distorts reasoning powers, destroys the capacity for authentic love, and prevents people from achieving independence and integrity.

In summary, Fromm (1964) wrote:

> The tendency to remain bound to the mothering person and her equivalents—to blood, family, tribe—is inherent in all men and women. It is constantly in conflict with the opposite tendency—to be born, to progress, to grow. In the case of normal development, the tendency for growth wins. In the other case a severe pathology, the regressive tendency for symbiotic union, wins, and it results in the person's more or less total incapacitation. (p. 107)

In some severely pathological personalities, such as Adolf Hitler, necrophilia, malignant narcissism, and incestuous symbiosis are combined into what Fromm (1964) termed the *syndrome of decay*. Such people are attracted to death, take pleasure in destroying those who are regarded as inferiors, and act in the name of the homeland,

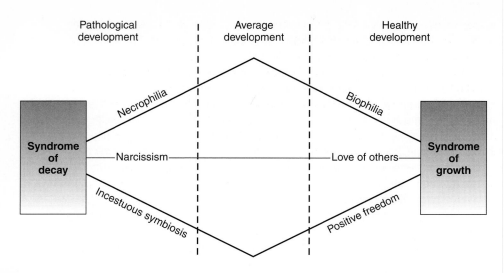

Figure 7.1 Three pathological orientations converge in the syndrome of decay, and three healthy orientations converge in the syndrome of growth.

the clan, or the party. Fromm contrasted the syndrome of decay with the *syndrome of growth*: the former is a convergence of necrophilia, malignant narcissism, and incestuous symbiosis; the syndrome of growth is made up of the opposite qualities; namely, biophilia, love, and positive freedom. As shown in Figure 7.1, both the syndrome of decay and the syndrome of growth are extreme forms of development; most people are probably in the average range.

PSYCHOTHERAPY

Fromm was trained as an orthodox Freudian analyst but became bored with standard analytic techniques. "With time I came to see that my boredom stemmed from the fact that I was not in touch with the life of my patients" (Fromm, 1986, p. 106). He then evolved his own system of therapy, which he called *humanistic psychoanalysis*. Compared with Freud, Fromm was much more concerned with the interpersonal aspects of a therapeutic encounter. He believed that the aim of therapy is for patients to come to know themselves. Without knowledge of ourselves, we cannot know any other person or thing.

> How is one to live and react properly if the very instrument which is to act, which is to decide, is not known to ourselves? We are the guide, the leader of this "I" which manages in some way to live in the world, to make decisions, to have priorities, to have values. If this "I," this main subject which decides and acts, is not properly known to us, it must follow that all our actions, all our decisions are done half blindly or in a half-awakened state. (Fromm, 1994a, p. 45)

Fromm also believed that patients come to therapy seeking satisfaction of their basic human needs—relatedness, transcendence, rootedness, a sense of identity, and a frame of orientation. Therefore, therapy should be built on a personal relationship between therapist and patient. Because accurate communication is essential to therapeutic growth, the therapist must relate "as one human being to another with utter concentration and utter sincerity" (Fromm, 1963, p. 184). In this spirit of relatedness the patient will once again feel at one with another person. Although *transference* and even *countertransference* may exist within this relationship, the important point is that two real human beings are involved with one another.

As part of his attempt to achieve shared communication, Fromm asked patients to reveal their dreams. He believed that dreams, as well as fairy tales and myths, are expressed in symbolic language—the only universal language humans have developed (Fromm, 1951). Because dreams have meaning beyond the individual dreamer, Fromm would ask for the patient's associations to the dream material. Not all dream symbols, however, are universal; some are accidental and depend on the dreamer's mood before going to sleep; others are regional or national and depend on climate, geography, and dialect. Many symbols have several meanings because of the variety of experiences that are connected with them. For example, fire may symbolize warmth and home to some people but death and destruction to others. Similarly, the sun may represent a threat to desert people, but growth and life to people in cold climates.

Fromm (1963) believed that the therapist should not try to be too scientific in understanding the patient. Only with the attitude of relatedness can another person be truly understood. The patient should not be viewed as an illness or a thing, but as a person, with all of the same human needs as the therapist.

FROMM'S METHODS OF INVESTIGATION

Fromm gathered data on human personality from many sources, including psychotherapy, cultural anthropology, and psychohistory. In this section we look briefly at his anthropological study of life in a Mexican village and his psychobiographical analysis of Adolf Hitler.

SOCIAL CHARACTER IN A MEXICAN VILLAGE

During the late 1950s and extending into the mid-1960s, Fromm and a group of psychologists, psychoanalysts, anthropologists, physicians, and statisticians studied social character in Chiconcuac, a Mexican village about 50 miles south of Mexico City. The team interviewed every adult and half the children in this isolated farming village of 162 households and about 800 inhabitants. The people of the village were mostly farmers, earning a living from small plots of fertile land. As Fromm and Michael Maccoby (1970) described them:

> They are selfish, suspicious of each others' motives, pessimistic about the future, and fatalistic. Many appear submissive and self-deprecatory, although they have the potential for rebelliousness and revolution. They feel inferior to city people, more stupid, and less cultured. There is an overwhelming feeling of powerlessness to influence either nature or the industrial machine that bears down on them. (p. 37)

Could one expect to find Fromm's character orientations in such a society? After living among the villagers and gaining their acceptance, the research team employed an assortment of techniques designed to answer this and other questions. Included among the research tools were extensive interviews, dream reports, detailed questionnaires, and two projective techniques—the Rorschach Inkblot Test and the Thematic Apperception Test.

Recall that Fromm believed that the *marketing character* was a product of modern commerce, and that it is most likely to exist in societies where trade is no longer personal and where people regard themselves as commodities. Not surprisingly, the research team found that the marketing orientation did not exist among these peasant villagers.

However, the researchers did find evidence for several other character types, the most common of which was the *nonproductive-receptive* type. People of this orientation tended to look up to others and devoted much energy in trying to please those whom they regarded as superiors. On paydays, working men who belonged to this type would accept their pay in servile fashion, as if they somehow had not earned it.

The second most frequently found personality type was the *productive-hoarding* character. People of this type were hard working, productive, and independent. They usually farmed their own plot of land and relied on saving part of each crop for seed and for food in the event of a future crop failure. Hoarding, rather than consuming, was essential to their lives.

The *nonproductive-exploitative* personality was identified as a third character orientation. Men of this type were most likely to get into knife or pistol fights, whereas the women tended to be malicious gossipmongers (Fromm & Maccoby, 1970). Only about 10% of the population were dominantly exploitative, a surprisingly small percentage considering the extreme poverty of the village.

An even smaller number of inhabitants were described as *productive-exploitative*—no more than 15 individuals in the whole village. Among them were the richest and most powerful men in the village—men who had taken advantage of new agricultural technology and the recent increase in tourism to accumulate capital. They had also taken advantage of the nonproductive-receptive villagers by keeping them economically dependent.

In general, Fromm and Maccoby (1970) reported a remarkable similarity between character orientations in this Mexican village and the theoretical orientations Fromm had suggested some years earlier. This anthropological study, of course, cannot be considered a confirmation of Fromm's theory. As one of the study's principal investigators, Fromm may simply have found what he had expected to find.

A PSYCHOHISTORICAL STUDY OF HITLER

Following Freud (see Chapter 2), Fromm examined historical documents in order to sketch a psychological portrait of a prominent person, a technique called *psychohistory* or *psychobiography*. The subject of Fromm's most complete psychobiographical study was Freud (Fromm, 1959), but Fromm (1941, 1973, 1986) also wrote at length on the life of Adolf Hitler.

Fromm regarded Hitler as the world's most conspicuous example of a person with the *syndrome of decay*, possessing a combination of necrophilia, malignant narcissism, and incestuous symbiosis. Hitler displayed all three pathological disorders. He was attracted to death and destruction; he was narrowly focused on self-interests, greatly delighting in self-aggrandizement; and he was driven by an incestuous devotion to the Germanic "race," being fanatically dedicated to preventing its blood from being polluted by Jews and other "non-Aryans."

Unlike some psychoanalysts who look only to early childhood for clues to adult personality, Fromm believed that each stage of development is important and that nothing in Hitler's early life bent him inevitably toward the syndrome of decay. As a child, Hitler was somewhat spoiled by his mother, but her indulgence did not cause his

Adolf Hitler personified for Fromm the syndrome of decay.

later pathology. It did, however, foster narcissistic feelings of self-importance. "Hitler's mother never became to him a person to whom he was lovingly or tenderly attached. She was a symbol of the protecting and admiring goddesses, but also of the goddess of death and chaos" (Fromm, 1973, p. 378).

Hitler was an above-average student in elementary school, but a failure in high school. During adolescence he experienced some conflict with his father, who wanted him to be more responsible and to take a reliable civil service job. Hitler, on the other hand, somewhat unrealistically desired to be an artist. Also during this time he began to lose himself more and more in fantasy. His narcissism ignited a burning passion for greatness as an artist or architect, but reality brought him failure after failure in this area. "Each failure caused a graver wound to his narcissism and a deeper humiliation than the previous one; in the same degree as his failures, grew also his indulgence in fantasy, his resentment, his wish for revenge, and his necrophilia" (Fromm, 1973, p. 395).

The terrible realization of his failure as an artist was blunted by the outbreak of World War I. His fierce ambition could now be channeled into being a great war hero fighting for his homeland. Although he was no great hero, he was a responsible, disciplined, and dutiful soldier. After the war, however, he experienced more failure. Not only had his beloved nation lost, but revolutionaries within Germany had "attacked everything that was sacred to Hitler's reactionary nationalism, and they won . . . The victory of the revolutionaries gave Hitler's destructiveness its final and ineradicable form" (Fromm, 1973, p. 394).

We saw earlier that *necrophilia* does not simply refer to behavior; it pervades a person's entire character. And so it was with Hitler. After he came to power, he demanded that his enemies not merely surrender, but that they be annihilated as well. His necrophilia was expressed in his mania for destroying buildings and cities, his orders to kill "defective" people, his boredom, and his slaughter of millions of Jews.

Another trait Hitler manifested was *malignant narcissism*. He was interested only in himself, his plans, and his ideology. His conviction that he could build a "Thousand-Year Reich" shows an inflated sense of self-importance. He had no interest in anyone unless that person was of service to him. His relations to women lacked love and tenderness; he seemed to have used them solely for perverted personal pleasure, especially for voyeuristic satisfaction.

According to Fromm's analysis, Hitler also possessed an *incestuous symbiosis*, manifested by his passionate devotion, not to his real mother, but to the Germanic "race." Consistent with this trait, he also was sadomasochistic, withdrawn, and lacking in feelings of genuine love or compassion. All these characteristics, Fromm contended, did not make Hitler psychotic. They did however, make him a sick and dangerous man.

Insisting that Hitler not be seen as inhuman, Fromm (1973) concluded his psychohistory with these words: "Any analysis that would distort Hitler's picture by depriving him of his humanity would only intensify the tendency to be blind to the potential Hitlers unless they wear horns" (p. 433).

RELATED RESEARCH

In his theoretical ideas, with topics ranging from love to sadism, Erich Fromm was an eloquent and thought-provoking writer who helped people understand the human condition. Throughout his life, Fromm was motivated to improve the lives of his fellow human beings. Yet, as stimulating and insightful as his ideas may be, they have produced almost no empirical research. The few empirical studies that directly test Fromm's theoretical assumptions have examined four different components of his theory: (1) personality orientation (Pendse, 1978); (2) existential needs (Lonky, Kaus, & Roodin, 1984); (3) biophilia (Maccoby, 1972; Ray & Lovejoy, 1982, 1984); and (4) love (Critelli, 1977).

First, Fromm's theory predicts four nonproductive orientations: receptive, exploitative, hoarding, and marketing. By using the statistical technique known as *factor analysis*, Shripad Pendse (1978) tested the hypothesis that adjectives will cluster together in these four orientations. Simply put, factor analysis puts responses together in a cluster, or factor, based on how similar they are to one another. The more similar the responses, the more coherent the factor. So if Fromm's theory has validity, the adjectives should cluster into the four predicted orientations. Pendse administered a set of adjectives to college students and found strong support for the marketing and exploitative orientations but only moderate support for the receptive and hoarding orientations. Although these findings yield at least partial support for Fromm's theory, this line of research has not been followed up by further studies.

A different approach to investigating Fromm's ideas has been the work of Edward Lonky, Cheryl Kaus, and Paul Roodin (1984), who developed an Existential Coping Interview (ECI) to measure the five existential needs—relatedness, transcendence, rootedness, identity, and frame of orientation. The ECI is a semistructured interview consisting of 35 questions that probe participants' affirmative (positive) or abortive (negative) modes of coping with personal loss. Responses are ranged on a 4-point scale from "strongly affirmative" to "strongly abortive." For the relatedness need, for example, the interviewer asks participants whether they sought other people or joined groups following a personal loss. Responses indicating that participants appropriately sought out others were rated as "strongly affirmative," whereas those participants who reflected an overreliance on others were seen as "strongly abortive." From a sample of adult women who had taken the Defining Issues Test (Rest, 1979), Lonky et al. selected a group of principled reasoning women and another group whose members manifested conventional reasoning. After administering the Existential Coping Interview to these women, Lonky et al. found that conventional moral reasoners dealt with personal loss in an abortive or nonproductive manner, whereas principled reasoners coped with loss by using affirmative or productive strategies. They also found that existential coping was positively related to openness to experience and to problem-focused coping strategies. Although this study suggests that the Existential Coping Interview has both reliability and validity in measuring Fromm's existential needs, no additional research has been generated by ECI.

A third area of research on Fromm's assumptions revolves around the concept of biophilia. If biophilia is the passionate love for life and all that is alive, then environmentalists should score higher on biophilia than nonenvironmentalists. This idea has received weak support from a study of students, unemployed youths, and members of conservative political parties. In this study, John Ray and F. H. Lovejoy (1984) administered measures of biophilia and environmentalism to the participants and found a modest correlation of .27 between the two measures. In 1972, Michael Maccoby, who developed the original assessment of biophilia, found that people high in biophilia were: (a) in favor of ending the Vietnam war; (b) against capital punishment; (c) likely to value life over property; and (d) more liberal and radical in their political views. In summary, Fromm's ideas have generated little empirical investigation, and currently no personality researchers are actively engaged in testing hypotheses suggested by his writings.

CRITIQUE OF FROMM

Erich Fromm was perhaps the most brilliant essayist of all personality theorists. He wrote beautiful essays on international politics (Fromm, 1961), on the relevance of biblical prophets for people today (Fromm, 1986), on the psychological problems of the aging (Fromm, 1981), on Marx, Hitler, Freud, and Christ, and on myriad other topics. Regardless of the topic, at the core of all Fromm's writings was an unfolding of the essence of human nature.

Like other psychodynamic theorists, Fromm tended to take a global approach to theory construction, erecting a grand, highly abstract model that was more philosophical than scientific. His insights into human nature strike a responsive chord, as evidenced by the popularity of his books. Unfortunately, his essays and arguments are not as popularly known today as they were 40 years ago. Paul Roazen (1996) stated that during the mid-1950s no one could be considered educated without having read Fromm's eloquently written *Escape from Freedom*. Today, however, Fromm's books are seldom required reading on college campuses.

Eloquence, of course, does not equal science. From a scientific perspective, we must ask how Fromm's ideas rate on the six criteria of a useful theory. First, Fromm's imprecise and vague terms have rendered his ideas nearly sterile as a *generator of empirical research*. Indeed, our search of the last 30 years of psychology literature (using PsycINFO) yielded only six empirical studies that directly tested Fromm's theoretical assumptions. This paucity of scientific investigations places him among the least empirically validated of all 23 theorists covered in this book. Second, Fromm's theory is too philosophical to be either *falsifiable* or verifiable. Nearly any empirical findings generated by Fromm's theory (if they existed) could be explained by alternative theories.

Third, the breadth of Fromm's theory enables it to *organize and explain* much of what is known about human personality. Fromm's social, political, and historical perspective provides both breadth and depth to our understanding of the human condition, but his theory's lack of precision makes prediction difficult and falsification impossible.

Fourth, as a *guide to action*, the chief value of Fromm's writings is to stimulate readers to think productively. Unfortunately, however, neither the researcher nor the therapist receive much practical information from Fromm's essays.

Fifth, Fromm's views are *internally consistent* in the sense that a single theme runs throughout his writings. However, the theory lacks a structured taxonomy, a set of operationally defined terms, and a clear limitation of scope. Therefore, it rates low on internal consistency.

Finally, because Fromm was reluctant to abandon earlier concepts or to relate them precisely to his later ideas, his theory lacks simplicity and unity; that is, it must be rated low on the criterion of *parsimony*.

CONCEPT OF HUMANITY

More than any other personality theorist, Erich Fromm emphasized the differences between humans and the other animals. The essential nature of humans rests on their unique experience of *"being in nature* and subject to all its laws, and simultaneously *transcending nature"* (Fromm, 1992, p. 24). He believed that only humans are aware of themselves and their existence.

More specifically, Fromm's view of humanity is summed up in his definition of the species: *"The human species can be defined as the primate who emerged at that point of evolution where instinctive determinism had reached a minimum and the development of the brain a maximum"* (Fromm, 1976, p. 137). Human beings, then, are freaks of nature, the only species ever to have evolved this combination of minimal instinctive powers and maximal brain development. "Lacking the capacity to act by the command of instincts while possessing the capacity for self-awareness, reason, and imagination . . . the human species needed a frame of orientation and an object of devotion in order to survive" (Fromm, 1976, p. 137).

Human survival, however, has been paid for by the price of basic anxiety, loneliness, and powerlessness. In every age and culture, people have been faced with the same fundamental problem: How to escape from feelings of isolation and find unity with nature and with other people?

In general, Fromm was moderately *pessimistic*, believing that most people do not accomplish a reunion with nature or other people. Thus, few of us achieve positive freedom. Although Fromm believed that most people remain isolated and lost, he was hopeful enough to believe that some of us will achieve reunion and will therefore realize our human potential. Fromm had a rather negative attitude toward modern capitalism, which he insisted results in most people feeling isolated and alone while clinging desperately to the illusion of independence and freedom. Yet he believed that a sense of identity, positive freedom, and growing individuality were possible in a capitalistic society. In *Man for Himself* (1947), he wrote: "I have become increasingly impressed by . . . the strength of the strivings for happiness and health, which are part of the natural equipment of man" (p. x).

On the dimension of *free choice vs. determinism*, Fromm took a middle position, insisting that this issue cannot be applied to the entire species. Instead, he believed that individuals have degrees of inclinations toward freely chosen action, even though they are seldom aware of all the possible alternatives. Nevertheless, their ability to reason enables them to take an active part in their own fate (Fromm, 1964).

On the dimension of *causality vs. teleology*, Fromm tended to slightly favor teleology. Fromm believed that people constantly strive for a frame of orientation, a road map, by which to plan their lives into the future.

Fromm took a middle stance regarding *conscious vs. unconscious motivation*, placing slightly more emphasis on conscious motivation and contending that one of the uniquely human traits is *self-awareness*. Humans are the only animal who can reason, visualize the future, and consciously strive toward self-erected goals. Fromm insisted, however, that self-awareness is a mixed blessing, and that many people repress their basic character to avoid mounting anxiety. On the issue of *social influences* vs. *biological ones*, Fromm stressed the impact of history, culture, and society. Although he insisted that human personalities are historically and culturally determined, he did not overlook biological factors.

Finally, Fromm placed moderate emphasis on *similarities among people*, but he allowed room for some individuality. He believed that, although history and culture impinge heavily on personality, we can retain some degree of uniqueness. We are one species sharing many of the same human needs, but interpersonal experiences throughout our life give us some measure of uniqueness.

Chapter Summary

Fromm's basic thesis is that modern-day people have been torn away from their prehistoric union with nature and also with one another, yet they have the power of reasoning, foresight, and imagination. This combination of lack of animal instincts and presence of rational thought makes humans the freaks of the universe. Self-awareness contributes to feelings of loneliness, isolation, and homelessness. To escape from these feelings, people strive to become reunited with others and with nature.

Only the uniquely *human needs* can move people toward reunification. These needs include *relatedness*, the need to unify with another person through submission, power, or love; *transcendence*, the need to rise above a passive existence and create or destroy life; *rootedness*, the need to establish roots; a *sense of identity*, a feeling of "I" or "me"; and a *frame or orientation*, or the need to develop a consistent way of looking at the world.

Fromm believed that during our history as a species we have gained a degree of economic and political freedom, but this achievement has brought about ever greater feelings of isolation and separation from the world. This *burden of freedom* has produced *basic anxiety*, or a sense of being alone in the world. To relieve basic anxiety, we employ various *mechanisms of escape*, especially authoritarianism, destructiveness, and conformity. Some people succeed in becoming one with the world and acquire *positive freedom*, or the spontaneous activity of a whole, integrated personality.

Fromm identified one productive and four nonproductive *character orientations*. The *productive orientation* has three dimensions: loving, working, and thinking. Healthy people are characterized by all three and also by *biophilia*, or a passionate love of life and all that is living. The *nonproductive types*, which have both positive and negative traits, include *receiving*, *exploiting*, *hoarding*, and *marketing*.

The opposite of biophilia is *necrophilia*, or the love of death, destruction, and decay. Necrophilia is one of three traits making up the *syndrome of decay*, the other two being *malignant narcissism*, or infatuation with self, and *incestuous symbiosis*, or the tendency to remain bound to the mothering person or her equivalents.

The goal of Fromm's *psychotherapy* is to establish union with patients so that they can become reunited with the world. In his *concept of humanity*, Fromm takes a middle road position on free will vs. determinism, optimism vs. pessimism, conscious vs. unconscious forces, and uniqueness vs. similarities. His theory is rated high on teleology and very high on social influences.

As a scientific theory, unfortunately, Fromm's psychoanalytic social theory cannot be rated high. It has above average ability to organize knowledge, but it has generated very little empirical research. It is also rated low on being a practical guide to action, on internal consistency, and on parsimony.

Suggested Readings

Fromm, E. (1941). *Escape from freedom*. New York: Holt, Rinehart & Winston.
    Fromm's first important work, this book was once required reading for anybody who wished to be considered educated.
Fromm, E. (1956). *The art of loving*. New York: Harper & Brothers.
    Perhaps the most widely read of all Fromm's works, this book boldly suggests that love is the answer to the problems of human existence.
Fromm, E. (1992). *The revision of psychoanalysis*. Boulder, CO: Westview Press.
    Published a dozen years after Fromm's death, this book clearly discusses areas in which Fromm agreed and disagreed with Freud.
Fromm, E. (1994b). *On being human*. New York: Continuum.
    Complied from lectures and other sources several years after his death, this book demonstrates Fromm's humanistic view of science, socialism, industrial society, religion, management, psychoanalysis, and ethics.
Knapp, G. P. (1989). *The art of living: Erich Fromm's life and works*. New York: Peter Lang.
    This book presents a critical appraisal of the life and work of Fromm, a man the author calls "one of this century's most influential thinkers." Knapp's book is more accessible than Daniel Burston's (1991) *The Legacy of Erich Fromm*.

Sullivan

Chapter

8

Sullivan: Interpersonal Theory

H arry Stack Sullivan, the first American to construct a comprehensive personality theory, believed that we develop our personality within a social context. Without other people, Sullivan contended, we would have no personality. "A personality can never be isolated from the complex of interpersonal relations in which the person lives and has his being" (Sullivan, 1953a, p. 10). Sullivan insisted that knowledge of human personality can be gained only through the scientific study of interpersonal relations. His **interpersonal theory** emphasizes the importance of various developmental stages—infancy, childhood, the juvenile era, preadolescence, early adolescence, late adolescence, and adulthood. Healthy human development rests on a person's ability to establish intimacy with another person, but unfortunately, anxiety can interfere with satisfying interpersonal relations at any age. Perhaps the most crucial stage of development is preadolescence—a period when children first possess the capacity for intimacy but have not yet reached an age at which their intimate relationships are complicated by lustful interests. Sullivan believed that people achieve healthy development when they are able to experience both intimacy and lust toward the same other person.

Ironically, Sullivan's own relationships with other people were seldom satisfying. As a child, he was lonely and physically isolated; as an adolescent, he suffered at least one schizophrenic episode; and as an adult, his interpersonal relationships remained superficial and ambivalent. Despite, or perhaps because of, these interpersonal difficulties, Sullivan contributed much to our understanding of human personality. In Leston Haven's (1987) language, "he made his contributions walking on one leg . . . he never gained the spontaneity, receptiveness, and capacity for intimacy his own interpersonal school worked to achieve for others" (p. 184).

BIOGRAPHY OF HARRY STACK SULLIVAN

Harry Stack Sullivan was born in the small farming town of Norwich, New York, on February 21, 1892, the sole surviving child of poor Irish Catholic parents. His mother, Ella Stack Sullivan, was 32 when she married Timothy Sullivan and 39 when Harry was born. She had given birth to two other sons, neither of whom lived past the first year. As a consequence, she pampered and protected her only child, whose survival she knew was her last chance for motherhood. Harry's father, Timothy Sullivan, was a shy, withdrawn, and taciturn man who never developed a close relationship with his son until after his wife had died and Harry had become a prominent physician. Timothy Sullivan had been a farm laborer and a factory worker who moved to his wife's family farm outside the village of Smyrna, some 10 miles from Norwich, before Harry's third birthday. At about this same time, Ella Stack Sullivan was mysteriously absent from the home, and Harry was cared for by his maternal grandmother, whose Gaelic accent was not easily understood by the young boy. After more than a year's separation, Ella Stack Sullivan—who likely had been in a mental hospital—returned home. In effect, Harry then had two women to mother him—his mother and his grandmother. Even after his grandmother died in 1903, he continued to have two mothers because a maiden aunt then came to share in the child rearing duties.

Although both parents were of Irish Catholic descent, his mother regarded the Stack family as socially superior to the Sullivans. Harry accepted the social supremacy of the Stacks over the Sullivans until he was a prominent psychiatrist developing an interpersonal theory that emphasized similarities among people rather than differences. He then realized the folly of his mother's claims.

As a preschool child, Harry had neither friends nor acquaintances of his age, although he did invent several imaginary playmates before the age of five. After beginning school he still felt like an outsider, being an Irish Catholic boy in an Anglo-Saxon Protestant community. His Irish brogue and his sharp mind made him unpopular with his classmates throughout his years of schooling in Smyrna.

When Harry was 8½ years old, he formed a close friendship with a 13-year-old boy from a neighboring farm. This chum was Clarence Bellinger, who lived a mile beyond Harry in another school district, but who was now beginning high school in Smyrna. Although the two boys were not peers chronologically, they had much in common socially and intellectually. Both were retarded socially but advanced intellectually; both later became psychiatrists and neither ever married. Chapman (1976) believes that this was probably a gay male relationship, although Perry (1982) doubts that any overt sexual activity ever took place between the two. In either case the relationship had a transforming effect on Sullivan's life. It awakened in him the power of intimacy, that is, the ability to love another who was more or less like himself. In Sullivan's mature theory of personality, he placed heavy emphasis on the therapeutic, almost magical power of an intimate relationship during the preadolescent years. This belief, along with many other Sullivanian hypotheses, seems to have grown out of his own childhood experiences.

Sullivan was interested in books and science, not in farming. Although he was an only child growing up on a farm that required much hard work, Harry was able to escape many of the chores by absentmindedly "forgetting" to do them. This ruse was successful because his indulgent mother completed them for him and allowed Harry to receive credit.

A bright student, Sullivan graduated from high school as valedictorian at age 16. He then entered Cornell University intending to become a physicist, although he and Clarence also shared an interest in psychiatry. His academic performance at Cornell was a disaster, however, and he was suspended after one year. The suspension may not have been solely for academic deficiencies. He got into trouble with the law at Cornell, possibly for mail fraud. He was probably a dupe of older, more mature students who used him to pick up some chemicals illegally ordered through the mail. In any event, for the next 2 years Sullivan mysteriously disappeared from the scene. Perry (1982) reported he may have suffered a schizophrenic breakdown at this time and was confined to a mental hospital. Alexander (1990), however, surmised that Sullivan spent this time under the guidance of an older male model who helped him overcome his sexual panic and who intensified his interest in psychiatry. Whatever the answer to Sullivan's mysterious disappearance from 1909 to 1911, his experiences seemed to have matured him academically and possibly sexually.

In 1911, with only one very unsuccessful year of undergraduate work, Sullivan enrolled in the Chicago College of Medicine and Surgery, where his grades, though only mediocre, were a great improvement over those he earned at Cornell. He finished his medical studies in 1915, but did not receive his degree until 1917. Sullivan claimed that the delay was because he had not yet paid his tuition in full, but Perry (1982) found evidence that he had not completed all his academic requirements by 1915 and needed, among other requirements, an internship. How was Sullivan able to obtain a medical degree if he lacked all the requirements? None of Sullivan's biographers has a satisfactory answer to this question. Alexander (1990) hypothesized that Sullivan, who had accumulated nearly a year of medically related employment, used his considerable persuasive abilities to convince authorities at Chicago College of Medicine and Surgery to accept that experience in lieu of an internship. Any other deficiency may have been waived if Sullivan agreed to enlist in the military. (The United States had recently entered World War I and was in need of medical officers.)

After the war Sullivan continued to serve as a military officer, first for the Federal Board for Vocational Education and then for the Public Health Service. However, this period in his life was still confusing and unstable, and he showed little promise of the brilliant career that lay just ahead (Perry, 1982).

In 1921, with no formal training in psychiatry, he went to St. Elizabeth Hospital in Washington, D.C., where he became closely acquainted with William Alanson White, one of America's best known neuropsychiatrists. At St. Elizabeth, Sullivan had his first opportunity to work with large numbers of schizophrenic patients. While in Washington, he began an association with the Medical School of the University of Maryland and with the Sheppard and Enoch Pratt Hospital in Towson, Maryland. During this "Baltimore period" of his life, he conducted intensive studies of schizophrenia, which led to his first hunches about the importance of interpersonal relationships. In trying to make sense out of the speech of schizophrenic patients, Sullivan realized that their illness was a means of coping with the anxiety generated from social and interpersonal environments. His experiences as a practicing clinician gradually transformed themselves into the beginnings of an interpersonal theory of psychiatry.

Sullivan spent much of his time and energy at Sheppard selecting and training hospital attendants. Although he did little therapy himself, he developed a system in which nonprofessional but sympathetic attendants treated schizophrenic patients with human respect and care. This innovative program gained him a reputation as a clinical wizard. However, he became disenchanted with the political climate at Sheppard when he was passed over for a position as head of the new reception center that he had advocated. In March of 1930 he resigned from Sheppard.

Later that year he moved to New York City and opened a private practice, hoping to enlarge his understanding of interpersonal relations by investigating nonschizophrenic disorders, especially those of an obsessive nature (Perry, 1982). Times were hard, however, and his expected wealthy clientele did not come in the numbers he needed to maintain his expenses.

On a more positive note, his residence in New York brought him into contact with several psychiatrists and social scientists with a European background. Among these were Karen Horney, Erich Fromm, and Frieda Fromm-Reichmann who, along with Sullivan, Clara Thompson, and others, formed the Zodiac group, an informal organization that met regularly over drinks to discuss old and new ideas in psychiatry and the related social sciences. Sullivan, who had met Thompson earlier, persuaded her to travel to Europe to take a training analysis under Sandor Ferenczi, a disciple of Freud. Sullivan learned from all members of the Zodiac group, and through Thompson, his therapeutic technique was indirectly influenced by Freud. Sullivan also credited two other outstanding practitioners, Adolf Meyer and William Alanson White, as having had an impact on his practice of therapy. Despite some Freudian influence on his therapeutic technique, Sullivan's theory of interpersonal psychiatry is neither psychoanalytic nor neo-Freudian.

During his residence in New York, Sullivan also came under the influence of several noted social scientists from the University of Chicago, which was the center of American sociological study during the 1920s and 1930s. Included among them were social psychologist George Herbert Mead, sociologists Robert Ezra Park and W. I. Thomas, anthropologist Edward Sapir, and political scientist Harold Lasswell. Sullivan, Sapir, and Lasswell were primarily responsible for establishing the William Alanson White Psychiatric Foundation in Washington, D.C., for the purpose of joining psychiatry to the other social sciences. Sullivan served as the first president of the foundation and also as editor of the foundation's journal, *Psychiatry*. Under Sullivan's guidance, the foundation began a training institution known as the Washington School of Psychiatry.

Because of these activities, Sullivan gave up his New York practice, which was not very lucrative anyway, and moved back to Washington, D.C., where he remained closely associated with the school and the journal.

In January 1949, Sullivan attended a meeting of the World Federation for Mental Health in Amsterdam. While on his way home, January 14, 1949, he died of a cerebral hemorrhage in a Paris hotel room, a few weeks short of his 57th birthday. Not uncharacteristically, he was alone at the time.

On the personal side, Sullivan was not comfortable with his sexuality and had ambivalent feelings toward marriage (Perry, 1982). As an adult, he brought into his home a 15-year-old boy who was probably a former patient (Alexander, 1990). This young man—James Inscoe—remained with Sullivan, looking after his financial affairs, typing manuscripts, and generally running the household. Although Sullivan never officially adopted Jimmie, he regarded him as a son and even had his legal name changed to James I. Sullivan.

Sullivan also had ambivalent attitudes toward his religion. Born to Catholic parents who attended church only irregularly, he abandoned Catholicism early on. In later life, his friends and acquaintances regarded him as nonreligious or even anti-Catholic, but to their surprise, Sullivan had written into his will a request to receive a Catholic burial. Incidentally, this request was granted despite the fact that Sullivan's body had been cremated in Paris. His ashes were returned to the United States where they were placed inside a coffin and received a full Catholic burial, complete with a requiem mass.

Sullivan's chief contribution to personality theory is his conception of developmental stages. Before turning to Sullivan's ideas on the stages of development, we need to understand some of his unique terminology.

TENSIONS

Like Freud and Jung, Sullivan saw personality as an energy system. Energy can exist as *tension* (potentiality for action) or as actions themselves (*energy transformations*). Sullivan (1953b) defined **tension** as potentiality for action that may or may not be experienced in awareness. Thus, not all tensions are consciously felt. Many tensions, such as anxiety, premonitions, drowsiness, hunger, and sexual excitement, are felt but not always on a conscious level. In fact, probably all felt tensions are at least partial distortions of reality.

Tensions are divided into those of *needs* and those of *anxiety*. Tensions of needs represent potentiality for productive actions, whereas tensions of anxiety bring about nonproductive or disintegrative behaviors.

NEEDS

Needs are tensions brought on by a biological imbalance between the person and the physiochemical environment, both inside and outside the organism. Needs are episodic—once we satisfy them they temporarily lose their power, but after a time, they are likely to recur. Needs differ from tensions of anxiety in that they are integrative or conjunctive, whereas anxiety is disjunctive in nature (Sullivan, 1953b).

Although needs originally have a biological component, many of them stem from the interpersonal situation. The most basic *interpersonal need* is that of **tenderness.**

An infant develops a need to receive tenderness from its primary caretaker (called by Sullivan "the mothering one"). Unlike some needs, tenderness requires actions from at least two people. For example, an infant's need *to receive* tenderness may be expressed as a cry, smile, or coo, whereas the mother's need *to give* tenderness may be transformed into touching, fondling, or holding. In this example, the infant uses its *mouth* while the mother uses her *hands* to satisfy the need for tenderness.

Tenderness is a *general need* because it is concerned with the overall well-being of the person. General needs, which also include oxygen, food, and water, are opposed to *zonal needs*, which arise from a particular area of the body. Several areas of the body are instrumental in satisfying both general and zonal needs. For example, the mouth satisfies general needs by taking in food and oxygen, but it also satisfies the zonal need for oral activity. Also, the hands may be used to help satisfy the general need of tenderness, but they can likewise be used to satisfy the zonal need for manual activity. Similarly, other body zones, such as the anus and the genitals, can be used to satisfy both kinds of needs.

Very early in life, the various zones of the body gain importance beyond the satisfaction of general needs and begin to play a significant and lasting role in interpersonal relations. While satisfying general needs for food, water, and so forth, an infant expends more energy than necessary, and the excess energy is transformed into consistent characteristic modes of behavior, which Sullivan called *dynamisms*.

ANXIETY

A second type of tension, *anxiety*, differs from tensions of needs in that it is disjunctive, is more diffuse and vague, and calls forth no consistent actions for its relief. If an infant lacks food (a need), its course of action is clear, but if it is anxious, it can do little to escape. In this sense anxiety is distinguished from all other needs (Sullivan, 1953b).

How does anxiety originate? Sullivan postulated that it is transferred from the parent to the infant through the process of **empathy.** Anxiety in the mothering one inevitably induces anxiety in the infant. Because all mothers have some amount of anxiety while caring for their babies, all infants will become anxious to some degree.

Just as the infant does not have the capacity to reduce anxiety, the parent has no effective means of dealing with the baby's anxiety. Any signs of anxiety or insecurity by the infant are likely to lead to attempts by the parent to satisfy the infant's *needs*. For example, a mother may feed her anxious, crying baby because she mistakes anxiety for hunger. If the baby hesitates in accepting the milk, the mother may become more anxious herself, which generates additional anxiety within the infant. Finally, the baby's anxiety reaches a level at which it interferes with sucking and swallowing. Anxiety, then, operates in opposition to tensions of needs and prevents them from being satisfied.

Anxiety has a deleterious effect on adults too. It is the *chief disruptive force blocking our development of good interpersonal relations.* Sullivan (1953b) likened severe anxiety to a blow on the head. It makes us incapable of learning, impairs memory, narrows perception, and may result in complete amnesia. It is unique among the tensions in that it maintains the status quo even to our overall detriment. Whereas other tensions result in actions directed specifically toward their relief, anxiety produces behaviors that (1) prevent us from learning from our mistakes; (2) keep us pursuing the childish wish for security; and (3) generally ensure that we will not learn from our experiences.

Sullivan held that anxiety and loneliness are unique among all experiences in that they are totally unwanted and undesirable. Because anxiety is painful, we have a natural tendency to avoid it, inherently preferring the state of *euphoria*, or complete lack of tension. Sullivan (1954) summarized this concept by stating simply that *"the presence of anxiety is much worse than its absence"* (p. 100).

Sullivan distinguished anxiety from fear in several important ways. First, anxiety usually stems from complex interpersonal situations and is only vaguely represented in awareness; fear is more clearly discerned and its origins more easily pinpointed. Second, anxiety has no positive value. Only when transformed into another tension, anger or fear for example, can anxiety lead to profitable actions. Third, anxiety blocks the satisfaction of needs, whereas fear sometimes helps us satisfy certain needs. This opposition to the satisfaction of needs is expressed in words that can be considered Sullivan's definition of anxiety: "Anxiety is a tension in opposition to the tensions of needs and to action appropriate to their relief" (Sullivan, 1953b, p. 44).

ENERGY TRANSFORMATIONS

Tensions that are transformed into actions, either overt or covert, are called **energy transformations.** This somewhat awkward term simply refers to our behaviors that are aimed at satisfying needs and reducing anxiety—the two great tensions. Not all energy transformations are obvious, overt actions; many take the form of emotions, thoughts, or covert behaviors that can be hidden from other people.

In summary, Sullivan identified two kinds of experience—tensions and energy transformations. Tensions, or potentiality for action, include tensions of needs and tensions of anxiety. Whereas needs are helpful or conjunctive when satisfied, anxiety is always disjunctive. Energy transformations literally involve the transformation of potential energy into actual energy or behavior for the purpose of satisfying needs or reducing anxiety.

DYNAMISMS

Energy transformations become organized as typical behavior patterns that characterize a person throughout a lifetime. Sullivan (1953b) called these behavior patterns **dynamisms,** a term that means about the same as traits or habit patterns. Dynamisms are of two major classes: first, those related to specific zones of the body, including the mouth, anus, and genitals; and second, those related to tensions. This second class is composed of three categories—the disjunctive, the isolating, and the conjunctive. Disjunctive dynamisms include all those destructive patterns of behavior that are related to the concept of *malevolence*; the isolating dynamisms include those such as *lust*, which are unrelated to interpersonal relations; and the conjunctive dynamisms are beneficial behavior patterns, such as *intimacy* and the *self-system*.

MALEVOLENCE

Malevolence is the disjunctive dynamism of evil and hatred, which is characterized by the feeling that one is living among one's enemies (Sullivan, 1953b). It originates around ages 2 or 3, when children's actions that earlier had brought about maternal tenderness, are rebuffed, ignored, or met with anxiety and pain. Many parents attempt

Significant intimate relationships prior to puberty are usually boy-boy or girl-girl friendships, according to Sullivan.

to control their children's behavior by inflicting punishments, usually in the form of physical pain or reproving remarks. Consequently, some children learn to withhold any expression of the need for tenderness and to protect themselves by adopting the malevolent attitude. Parents and peers then find it more and more difficult to react with tenderness, and this, in turn, solidifies the child's negative attitude toward the world. Malevolent actions often take the form of timidity, mischievousness, cruelty, or other kinds of asocial or antisocial behavior. Sullivan (1953b) expressed the malevolent attitude with this colorful statement: "Once upon a time everything was lovely, but that was before I had to deal with people" (p. 216).

INTIMACY

Intimacy grows out of the earlier need for tenderness but is more specific and involves a close interpersonal relationship between two people who are more or less of equal status. Both tenderness and intimacy are related to the popular term "love." Tenderness refers to an increase in euphoria brought on by anyone—mother, father, siblings, friends, or pet animals. Intimacy, however, is restricted to the tender feelings one person has for an equal.

Intimacy involves a close relationship between two persons who must react to each other in the give and take of close collaboration. Each is seen by the other as a person of equal value, not merely as an object of gratification. Intimacy must not be confused with sexual interest. In fact, it develops prior to puberty, ideally during preadolescence when it usually exists between two children of the same gender. Ordinarily, intimate relationships with a person of the opposite sex do not develop until late adolescence or even later. Because intimacy is a dynamism that requires an equal partnership, it does not usually exist in parent-child relationships unless both are adults and see one another as equals.

Intimacy is an integrating dynamism that tends to draw out loving reactions from the other person, thereby decreasing anxiety and loneliness, two extremely painful experiences. Because intimacy helps us avoid anxiety and loneliness, it is a rewarding experience that most healthy people desire (Sullivan, 1953b).

Lust

On the other hand, **lust** is an isolating tendency, requiring no other person for its satisfaction. It manifests itself as autoerotic behavior even when another person is the object of one's lust. Lust is an especially powerful dynamism during adolescence, at which time it often leads to a reduction in self-esteem. Attempts at lustful activity are often rebuffed by others, which increases anxiety and decreases feeling of self-worth. In addition, lust often hinders an intimate relationship, especially during early adolescence when it is easily confused with sexual attraction. (We discuss this possible confusion in the section on early adolescence.)

Self-System

The most complex and inclusive of all the dynamisms is the **self-system,** a consistent pattern of behaviors that maintains our interpersonal security by protecting us from anxiety. Like intimacy, the self-system is a conjunctive dynamism that arises out of the interpersonal situation. However, it develops earlier than intimacy, at about 12 to 18 months of age when a child begins to learn which behaviors are related to an increase or decrease in anxiety. Prior to this time, fear and pain were the principal forms of unpleasant experience, and their arrival seemed independent of the infant's behavior. Now, however, the mothering one begins the process of training by rewarding some behaviors and punishing others. The punishments and disapprovals result in a third unpleasant condition—anxiety.

Intelligence and foresight enable people to detect slight increases and decreases in anxiety, and this ability provides the self-system with a built-in warning device. This is a mixed blessing, however. On one hand, the warning serves as a signal, alerting people to increasing anxiety and giving them an opportunity to protect themselves. On the other hand, this same characteristic makes the self-system resistant to change and prevents people from profiting from anxiety-filled experiences. Because the primary task of the self-system is to protect people against anxiety, it is "the principal stumbling block to favorable changes in personality" (Sullivan, 1953b, p. 169). Personality is not static, however, being especially subject to change at the beginning of the various stages of development when newly maturing needs begin to emerge (Sullivan, 1964).

As the self-system develops, people begin to form a consistent image of themselves. Thereafter, any interpersonal experiences that they perceive as contrary to their self-regard threatens their security. As a consequence, people attempt to defend themselves against interpersonal tensions by means of **security operations,** the purpose of which is to reduce feelings of insecurity or anxiety that result from endangered self-esteem. People tend to deny or distort interpersonal experiences that conflict with their self-regard. For example, when people who think highly of themselves are called incompetent, they may choose to believe that the name-caller is stupid or, perhaps, merely joking. Sullivan (1953b) called security operations "a powerful brake on personal and human progress" (p. 374).

Sullivan (1953a) distinguished between the pursuit of security and the pursuit of *satisfactions*. Whereas security operations are connected with interpersonal experiences, satisfactions are end states connected with such physiological conditions as food, drink, sleep, lust, and loneliness. The needs for satisfaction and the needs for security sometimes collide, as when a person on a diet feels hungry but believes that an attractive physique is essential to maintain self-regard.

Two important security operations are *dissociation* and *selective inattention*. **Dissociation** includes those impulses, desires, and needs that a person refuses to allow into awareness. Some infantile experiences become dissociated when a baby is neither rewarded nor punished for its behavior, so those experiences simply do not become part of the self-system. Adult experiences that are too foreign to one's standards of conduct can also become dissociated. These experiences do not cease to exist but continue to influence personality on an unconscious level. Dissociated images manifest themselves in dreams, daydreams, and other unintentional activities outside of awareness and are directed toward maintaining interpersonal security (Sullivan, 1953b).

The control of focal awareness, called **selective inattention,** is a refusal to see those things that we do not wish to see. It differs from dissociation in both degree and origin. Selectively inattended experiences are more accessible to awareness and more limited in scope. They originate after we establish a self-system and are triggered by our attempts to block out experiences that are not consistent with our existing self-system. For example, people who regard themselves as scrupulously law-abiding drivers may "forget" about the many occasions when they exceeded the speed limit or the times when they failed to stop completely at a stop sign. Like dissociated experiences, selectively inattended perceptions remain active even though they are not fully conscious. They are crucial in determining which elements of an experience will be attended and which will be ignored or denied (Sullivan, 1953b).

PERSONIFICATIONS

Beginning in infancy and continuing throughout the various developmental stages, we acquire certain images of ourselves and others. These images, called **personifications,** may be relatively accurate, or because they are colored by our needs and anxieties, they may be grossly distorted. Sullivan (1953b) described three basic personifications that develop during infancy—the bad-mother, the good-mother, and the me. In addition, some children acquire an eidetic personification (imaginary playmate) during childhood.

Bad-Mother, Good-Mother

Sullivan's notion of the bad-mother and good-mother is similar to Klein's concept of the bad breast and good breast. The *bad-mother personification*, in fact, grows out of the infant's experiences with the bad-nipple; that is, the nipple that does not satisfy hunger needs. Whether the nipple belongs to the mother or to a bottle held by the mother, the father, a nurse, or anyone else is not important. The bad-mother personification is almost completely undifferentiated, inasmuch as it includes everyone involved in the nursing situation. It is not an accurate image of the "real" mother but merely the infant's vague representation of not being properly fed.

After the bad-mother personification is formed, an infant will acquire a *good-mother personification* based on the tender and cooperative behaviors of the mothering one. These two personifications, one based on the infant's perception of an anxious malevolent mother and the other based on a calm, tender mother, combine to form a complex personification composed of contrasting qualities projected onto the same person. Until the infant develops language, however, these two opposing images of mother can easily coexist (Sullivan, 1953b).

ME PERSONIFICATIONS

During midinfancy a child acquires the three me personifications (bad-me, good-me, and not-me), which form the building blocks of the self personification. Each is related to the evolving conception of me or my body. The *bad-me personification* is fashioned from experiences of punishment and disapproval that an infant receives from the mothering one. The resulting anxiety is strong enough to teach an infant that it is bad, but it is not so severe as to cause the experience to be dissociated or selectively inattended. Like all personifications, the bad-me is shaped out of the interpersonal situation; that is, an infant can learn that it is bad only from someone else, ordinarily from the bad-mother.

The *good-me personification* results from an infant's experiences with reward and approval. The infant feels good about itself when it perceives its mother's expressions of tenderness. Such experiences diminish anxiety and foster the good-me personification. Sudden severe anxiety, however, may cause an infant to form the *not-me personification* and to either dissociate or selectively inattend experiences related to that anxiety. The infant denies these experiences to the me image, so that they become part of the not-me personification. These shadowy not-me personifications are also encountered by adults and are expressed in dreams, schizophrenic episodes, and other dissociated reactions. Sullivan believed that these nightmarish experiences are always preceded by a warning. When adults are struck by sudden severe anxiety, they are overcome by *uncanny emotion*. Although this experience incapacitates people in their interpersonal relationships, it serves as a valuable signal for approaching schizophrenic reactions. Uncanny emotion may be experienced in dreams or may take the form of awe, horror, loathing, or a "chilly crawling" sensation (Sullivan, 1953b).

EIDETIC PERSONIFICATIONS

Not all interpersonal relations are with real people. Children often have *imaginary playmates*, which are a form of **eidetic personification,** that is, unrealistic traits or people children invent in order to protect their self-esteem. Sullivan (1964) believed that these imaginary friends may be as significant to a child's development as real playmates.

Eidetic personifications, however, are not limited to children; most adults see fictitious characteristics in other people. Eidetic personifications can create conflict in interpersonal relations when people project onto others imaginary traits that are remnants from previous relationships. They also hinder communication and prevent people from functioning on the same level of cognition.

LEVELS OF COGNITION

Sullivan recognized three levels or modes of cognition: *prototaxic, parataxic,* and *syntaxic.* Levels of cognition refer to ways of perceiving, imagining, and conceiving. Experiences on the prototaxic level are impossible to communicate; parataxic experiences are personal, prelogical, and communicated only in distorted form; and syntaxic cognition is meaningful interpersonal communication.

PROTOTAXIC LEVEL

The earliest and most primitive experiences of an infant take place on a **prototaxic** level. Because these experiences cannot be communicated to others, they are difficult to describe or define. We can try to understand the term by attempting to imagine the earliest subjective experiences of a newborn baby. These experiences must, in some way, relate to different zones of the body. A neonate feels hunger and pain, and these prototaxic experiences result in observable action, for example, sucking or crying. The infant does not know the reason for the actions and sees no relationship between its actions and being fed. During early infancy, hunger and pain are prototaxic because they cannot be differentiated from one another nor from any other stimuli. As undifferentiated experiences, prototaxic events are beyond conscious recall.

In adults, prototaxic experiences take the form of momentary sensations, images, feelings, moods, and impressions. These primitive images of dream and waking life are dimly perceived or completely unconscious. Although they are incapable of being communicated to others, we can sometimes tell another person that we have just had a strange sensation, one that we cannot put into words.

PARATAXIC LEVEL

Parataxic experiences are prelogical and usually result when a person assumes a cause and effect relationship between two events that occur coincidentally. Parataxic cognitions are more clearly differentiated than prototaxic experiences but their meaning remains private. Therefore, they can be communicated to others only in a distorted fashion.

The parataxic level of cognition begins very early in infancy and continues to be an important mode of experience throughout a person's lifetime. For example, the infant sucking the nipple at first sees no relationship between sucking and receiving nourishment, but very soon it makes a connection between its behavior and that of its mother. Because sucking and feeding occurred coincidentally, the infant believes that its sucking behavior *caused* the mother's feeding behavior. This process of seeing a cause and effect relationship between two events in close temporal proximity is called a **parataxic distortion.**

An example of parataxic thinking is the conditioning experiences of humans and animals. If children are conditioned to say "please" in order to receive candy, they may eventually reach the illogical conclusion that their supplications caused the candy's appearance. This is a parataxic distortion because uttering the word "please" does not, by itself, cause the candy to appear. A dispensing person must be present who hears the word and is able and willing to honor the request. When no such person is present, a child may ask God or imaginary people to grant favors. A good bit of adult behavior comes from similar parataxic thinking.

SYNTAXIC LEVEL

Experiences that are consensually validated and that can be symbolically communicated take place on a **syntaxic** level. Consensually validated experiences are those upon whose meaning two or more persons agree. Words, for example, are consensually validated because different people more or less agree on their meaning. The most common symbols used by one person to communicate with another are those of language, including words and gestures.

Experience takes place on three levels: prototaxic, parataxic, and syntaxic. In addition, there are two kinds of experience—tensions and energy transformations

  I. *Tensions* (potential for action)
    A. Needs (conjunctive; they help integrate personality)
      1. General needs (facilitate the overall well-being of a person)
        a. Interpersonal (tenderness, intimacy, and love)
        b. Physiological (food, oxygen, water, and so forth)
      2. Zonal needs (may also satisfy general needs)
        a. Oral
        b. Genital
        c. Manual
    B. Anxiety (disjunctive; it interferes with the satisfaction of needs)
  II. *Energy Transformations* (overt or covert actions designed to satisfy needs or to reduce anxiety. Some energy transformations become relatively consistent patterns of behavior called dynamisms)
  III. *Dynamisms* (traits or behavioral patterns)
    A. Malevolence (a feeling of living in enemy country)
    B. Intimacy (an integrating experience marked by a close personal relationship with another person who is more or less of equal status)
    C. Lust (an isolating dynamism characterized by an impersonal sexual interest in another person)

Sullivan hypothesized that the first instance of syntaxic cognition appears about 12 to 18 months after birth, when a sound or gesture begins to have the same meaning for parents as it does for a child. The syntaxic level of cognition becomes more prevalent as the child begins to develop formal language, but it never completely supplants prototaxic and parataxic cognition. Adult experience takes place on all three levels.

In summary, Sullivan held that experience takes place on three levels or modes of cognition: *prototaxic, parataxic,* and *syntaxic*. In addition, experience is of two kinds: *tensions* (potential for action) and *energy transformations* (actions themselves). Some actions form consistent patterns of behavior called *dynamisms*. Sullivan also recognized two categories of tension: *needs*, which are conjunctive or helpful to development; and *anxiety*, which is the chief disjunctive force in interpersonal relations and which interferes with the satisfaction of needs. Table 8.1 summarizes Sullivan's concept of experience.

STAGES OF DEVELOPMENT

Sullivan (1953b) postulated seven epoches or stages of development, each crucial to the formation of human personality. The thread of interpersonal relations runs throughout the stages; other people are indispensable to a person's development from infancy to mature adulthood.

Personality change can take place at any time, but it is most likely to occur during the transition from one stage to the next. In fact, these threshold periods are more crucial than the stages themselves. Experiences previously dissociated or selectively inattended may enter into the self-system during one of the transitional periods. Sullivan (1953b) hypothesized that, "as one passes over one of these more-or-less determinable thresholds of a developmental era, everything that has gone before becomes reasonably open to influence" (p. 227). His seven stages are infancy, childhood, the juvenile era, preadolescence, early adolescence, late adolescence, and adulthood.

INFANCY

Infancy begins at birth and continues until a child develops articulate or syntaxic speech, usually at about 18 to 24 months. Sullivan believed that an infant becomes human through tenderness received from the mothering one. The satisfaction of nearly every human need demands the cooperation of another person. Infants cannot survive without a mothering one to provide food, shelter, moderate temperature, physical contact, and the cleansing of waste materials.

The emphatic linkage between mother and infant leads inexorably to the development of anxiety for the baby. Being human, the mother enters the relationship with some degree of previously learned anxiety. Her anxiety may spring from any one of a variety of experiences, but the infant's first anxiety is always associated with the nursing situation and the oral zone. Unlike its mother, the infant's repertory of behaviors is not adequate to handle anxiety. So, whenever it feels anxious (a condition originally transmitted to it by the mother), the infant tries whatever means it has to reduce anxiety. These attempts typically include rejecting the nipple, but this neither reduces anxiety nor satisfies the need for food. The infant's rejection of the nipple, of course, is not responsible for the mother's original anxiety but now adds to it. Eventually the infant discriminates between the good-nipple and the bad-nipple; the former being associated with relative euphoria in the feeding process, the latter with enduring anxiety (Sullivan, 1953b).

An infant expresses both anxiety and hunger through crying. We have seen that the mothering one may mistake anxiety for hunger and force the nipple onto an anxious (but not hungry) infant. The opposite situation may also take place. After the mothering one learns that the cry does not always signify hunger, she may believe that her crying baby is merely anxious and neglect to feed it. When its needs are not satisfied, the baby will experience rage, which increases the mother's anxiety and interferes with her ability to cooperate with her baby. With mounting tension the infant loses its capacity to receive satisfaction, but its need for food, of course, continues to increase. Finally, as tension approaches terror, the infant experiences difficulty with breathing. It may even stop breathing and turn a bluish color, but the built-in protections of **apathy** and **somnolent detachment** keep it from death. Apathy and somnolent detachment allow the infant to fall asleep despite its hunger; they do not completely abolish the need for food but lessen it, thus allowing the infant to return to a relative state of euphoria (Sullivan, 1953b).

During the feeding process, the infant not only receives food but also has some of its needs for *tenderness* satisfied. The tenderness received by the infant at this time demands the cooperation of the mothering one and introduces the infant to the various strategies required by the interpersonal situation. The mother/infant relationship, however, is like a two-sided coin. The infant develops a dual personification of mother, who is seen as both good-mother and bad-mother; she is "good" when she satisfies the baby's needs and "bad" when she stimulates anxiety.

Around midinfancy, infants begin to learn how to communicate through language. In the beginning their language is not consensually validated but takes place on an individualized or parataxic level. This period of infancy is characterized by **autistic**

language, defined as "a primary unsocialized, unacculturated state of symbol activity" (Sullivan, 1953a, p. 17). Early communication takes place in the form of facial expressions and the sounding of various phonemes. Both are learned through imitation, and eventually gestures and speech sounds have the same meaning for the infant as they do for other people. This marks the beginning of syntaxic language and the end of infancy.

CHILDHOOD

The era of childhood begins with the advent of syntaxic language and continues until the appearance of the need for playmates of an equal status. The age of childhood varies from culture to culture and from individual to individual, but in Western society it covers the period from about 18 to 24 months until about 5 or 6 years.

During this stage, the mother remains the most significant other person, but her role is different from what it was in infancy. The dual personifications of mother are now fused into one, and the child's perception of the mother is more congruent with the "real" mother. Nevertheless, the good-mother and bad-mother personifications are usually retained on a parataxic level. In addition to combining the mother personifications, the child differentiates the various persons who previously formed the concept of the mothering one, separating mother and father and seeing each as having a distinct role.

At about the same time, children are fusing the me-personifications into a single self-dynamism. Once they establish syntaxic language, they can no longer consciously deal with the bad-me and good-me at the same time; now they label behaviors as good or bad in imitation of their parents. However, these labels differ from the old personifications of infancy because they are on a syntaxic level and originate from children's behavior rather than from decreases or increases in their anxiety. Also, good and bad now imply social or moral value and no longer refer to the absence or presence of that painful tension called anxiety.

During childhood, emotions become reciprocal; a child is able to give tenderness as well as receive it. The relationship between mother and child becomes more personal and less one-sided. Rather than seeing the mother as good or bad based on how she satisfied hunger needs, the child evaluates the mother syntaxically according to whether she shows reciprocal tender feelings, develops a relationship based on the mutual satisfaction of needs, or exhibits a rejecting attitude.

Besides their parents, preschool-aged children often have one other significant relationship—an *imaginary playmate*. This eidetic friend enables children to have a safe, secure relationship that produces little anxiety. Parents sometimes observe their preschool-aged children talking to an imaginary friend, calling the friend by name and possibly even insisting that an extra place be set at the table or space be made available in the car or the bed for this playmate. Also, many adults can recall their own childhood experiences with imaginary playmates. Sullivan insisted that having an imaginary playmate is not a sign of instability or pathology but a positive event that helps children become ready for intimacy with real friends during the preadolescence stage. These playmates offer children an opportunity to interact with another "person" who is safe and who will not increase their level of anxiety. This comfortable, nonthreatening relationship with an imaginary playmate permits children to be more independent of parents and to make friends in later years.

Sullivan (1953b) referred to childhood as a period of rapid acculturation. Besides acquiring language, children learn cultural patterns of cleanliness, toilet training, eating habits, and sex-role expectancies. They also learn two other important

During the juvenile stage, children need to learn competition, cooperation, and compromise.

processes: *dramatizations* and *preoccupations*. Dramatizations are attempts to act like or sound like significant authority figures, especially mother and father. Preoccupations are strategies for avoiding anxiety and fear-provoking situations by remaining occupied with an activity that has earlier proved useful or rewarding.

The malevolent attitude reaches a peak during the preschool years, giving some children an intense feeling of living in hostile or enemy country. At the same time, children learn that society has placed certain restraints on their freedom. From these restrictions and from experiences with approval and disapprobation, children evolve their self-dynamism, which helps them handle anxiety and stabilize their personality. In fact, the self-system introduces so much stability that it makes future changes exceedingly difficult.

JUVENILE ERA

The juvenile era begins with the appearance of the need for peers or playmates of equal status and ends when one finds a single chum to satisfy the need for intimacy. In American society, the juvenile stage is roughly parallel to the first 3 years of school, beginning around ages 5 or 6 and ending at about age 8½. (It is interesting that Sullivan was so specific with the age at which this period ends and the preadolescent stage begins. Remember that Sullivan was age 8½ when he began an intimate relationship with a 13-year-old boy from a nearby farm.)

During the juvenile stage, Sullivan believed, a child should learn to compete, compromise, and cooperate. The degree of *competition* found among children of this age varies with the society, but Sullivan believed that people in the United States have generally overemphasized competition. Parents and teachers conspire to teach youngsters to be competitive and successful, and when success does not come, the child is liable to be ridiculed by authorities and peers alike. *Compromise*, too, can be overdone. A 7-year-old child who learns to continually give in to others is handicapped in the socialization process, and this yielding trait may continue to characterize the person in later life. *Cooperation* involves more than simply combining competition and compromise; it includes all those processes necessary to get along with others. The juvenile must learn to cooperate with others in the real world of interpersonal relationships. This is a critical step in becoming socialized and is the most important task confronting a person during the juvenile era.

During the juvenile stage, children associate with other children who are of equal standing. One-to-one relationships are rare, but if they exist, they are more likely to be based on convenience than on genuine intimacy. Boys and girls play with one another with little regard for the gender of the other person. Although permanent dyadic (two-person) relationships are still in the future, children of this age are beginning to make discriminations among themselves and to distinguish among adults. They see one teacher as kinder than another, one parent as more indulgent. The real world is coming more into focus, allowing them to operate increasingly on the syntaxic level.

The world begins to appear more complex and complicated to a primary school child. If the complexity is too anxiety-provoking, the juvenile may attempt to maintain security by blocking it from awareness. This selective inattention safeguards the child from having to deal with things that make no sense to the self-system, but this process of ignoring or distorting experiences that are inconsistent with the self-system may lead to some loss of the ability to communicate syntaxically and to problems in interpersonal relationships. These interpersonal difficulties are the price one pays for maintaining security.

By the end of the juvenile stage, a child should have developed an orientation toward living that makes it easier to consistently handle anxiety, satisfy zonal and tenderness needs, and set goals based on memory and foresight. This *orientation toward living* readies a person for the deeper interpersonal relationships to follow (Sullivan, 1953b).

PREADOLESCENCE

The period from the appearance of the need for intimacy until puberty is called preadolescence. This stage, which begins around age 8 or 9 and ends with adolescence, is a time for interest in one particular person, usually a person of the same gender. All preceding stages have been egocentric, with friendships being formed on the basis of self-interest. A preadolescent, for the first time, takes a genuine interest in the other person. Sullivan (1953a) called this process of becoming a social being the "quiet miracle of preadolescence" (p. 41), a likely reference to the personality transformation he experienced during his own preadolescence.

The outstanding characteristic of preadolescence is the genesis of the capacity to love. Previously, all interpersonal relationships were based on personal need satisfaction, but during preadolescence, intimacy and love become the essence of friendships. Intimacy involves a relationship in which the two partners consensually validate one another's personal worth. Love exists "when the satisfaction or the security of another person becomes as significant to one as is one's own satisfaction or security" (Sullivan, 1953a, pp. 42–43).

A preadolescent's intimate relationship ordinarily involves another person of the same gender and of approximately the same age or social status. Infatuations with teachers or movie stars are not intimate relationships because they are not consensually validated. The significant relationships of this age are typically boy-boy or girl-girl chumships. To be liked by one's peers is more important to the preadolescent than to be liked by teachers or parents. Chums are able to freely express opinions and emotions to one another without fear of humiliation or embarrassment. This free exchange of personal thoughts and feelings initiates the preadolescent into the world of intimacy. Each

The early adolescent's search for intimacy can increase anxiety and threaten security.

chum becomes more fully human, acquires an expanded personality, and develops a wider interest in the humanity of all people.

Sullivan believed that in American society preadolescence is the most untroubled and carefree time of life. Parents are still significant, even though they have been reappraised in a more realistic light. Preadolescents can experience unselfish love that has not yet been complicated by lust. The cooperation they acquired during the juvenile era evolves into collaboration or the capacity to work with another, not for self-prestige, but for the well-being of that other.

Preadolescence is critical for the future development of personality. If intimate collaboration is not learned at this time, a person is likely to be seriously stunted in later personality growth. During preadolescence, a person may show symptoms of maladjustment that can be traced to unsatisfactory interpersonal relationships in earlier stages. Earlier negative influences, however, can be extenuated by the positive effects of an intimate relationship. Even the malevolent attitude can be reversed, and many other juvenile problems, such as loneliness and self-centeredness, are diminished by the achievement of intimacy. This relatively brief and uncomplicated period of life is shattered by the onset of puberty.

EARLY ADOLESCENCE

Early adolescence begins with puberty and ends with the need for sexual love with one person. It is characterized by the eruption of genital interest and the advent of lustful relationships. In the United States, early adolescence is generally parallel with the junior high school years. As with most other stages, however, Sullivan placed no great emphasis on chronological age.

The need for intimacy achieved during the preceding stage continues during early adolescence, now accompanied by a parallel but separate need—lust. In addition, security, or the need to be free from anxiety, remains active during early adolescence. Thus, intimacy, lust, and security often collide with one another, bringing stress and conflict to the young adolescent. First, lust interferes with security operations because genital activity in American culture is frequently ingrained with guilt, embarrassment, and anxiety. Second, intimacy can also threaten security. For example, after puberty, a person ordinarily seeks intimate friendships with other gender adolescents. These attempts are fraught with self-doubt, uncertainty, and ridicule from others, usually leading to loss of self-esteem and an increase in anxiety. Thus, intimacy, or at least the attempt to shift intimacy to a person of the other gender, can diminish one's sense of security. Finally, intimacy and lust are frequently in conflict during early adolescence. For at least four reasons, adolescents have difficulty combining lust with intimacy and directing both toward the same person. First, some adolescents sublimate their genital need, thereby preventing a union of lust and intimacy. Second, intimacy is inclined toward other people, whereas lust is isolating. The powerful genital tensions seek outlet without regard for the intimacy need. Because lust can be satisfied autoerotically or in nonintimate relationships, the early adolescent has no compelling reason to combine it with intimacy. Third, society divides sexual objects into "good" and "bad," whereas chums are always seen as "good." A fourth reason for the chasm between lust and intimacy is also culturally induced. Parents, teachers, and other authority figures actively dissuade early adolescent boys and girls from becoming intimate. They sanction same-sex friendships, but from fear of sexually transmitted diseases, pregnancy, and early marriage, they often discourage opposite-sex chumships.

Because the lust dynamism is biological, it bursts forth at puberty regardless of the individual's interpersonal readiness for it. A boy with no previous experience with intimacy may become a Don Juan, sexually conquering girls but with no real interest in them; a girl may become a "teaser," exploiting the lust dynamism but unable to relate to a boy on an intimate level.

Sullivan (1953b) believed that early adolescence is a turning point in personality development. The person either emerges from this stage in command of the intimacy and lust dynamisms or faces serious interpersonal difficulties during future stages. Although sexual adjustment is important to personality development, Sullivan felt that the real issue lies in getting along with other people.

LATE ADOLESCENCE

Late adolescence begins when young people are able to feel both lust and intimacy toward the same person, and it ends in adulthood when they establish a lasting love relationship. Late adolescence embraces that period of self-discovery when adolescents are determining their preferences in genital behavior, usually during the senior high school years or about ages 15 to 17 or 18. As with other stages of development, however, its attainment is individual—many reach it several years later, others never attain it.

The outstanding feature of late adolescence is the fusion of intimacy and lust. The troubled attempts at self-exploration of early adolescence evolve into a stable pattern of sexual activity in which the loved one is also the object of lustful interest. People of the other gender are no longer desired solely as sexual objects but as people who are capable of being loved nonselfishly. Unlike the previous stage that was ushered in by biological changes, late adolescence is completely determined by interpersonal relations.

Successful late adolescence is characterized by growth of the syntaxic mode. At college or in the workplace, late adolescents begin exchanging ideas with others and having their opinions and beliefs either validated or repudiated. They learn from others how to live in the adult world, but a successful journey through the earlier stages facilitates this adjustment. If previous developmental epochs were unsuccessful, young people come to late adolescence with no intimate interpersonal relations, inconsistent patterns of sexual activity, and a great need to maintain security operations. They rely heavily on the parataxic mode to avoid anxiety and strive to preserve

Table 8.2 *Summary of Sullivan's Stages of Development*

Stage	Age	Significant Others	Interpersonal Process	Important Learnings
Infancy	0–2	Mothering one	Tenderness	Good mother/bad mother; good me/bad me
Childhood	2–6	Parents	Protect security through imaginary playmates	Syntaxic language
Juvenile era	6–8½	Playmates of equal status	Orientation toward living in the world of peers	Competition, compromise, cooperation
Preadolescence	8½–13	Single chum	Intimacy	Affection and respect from peers
Early adolescence	13–15	Several chums	Intimacy and lust toward different persons	Balance of lust, intimacy, and security operations
Late adolescence	15 →	Lover	Fusion of intimacy and lust	Discovery of self and the "real" world

self-esteem through selective inattention, dissociation, and neurotic symptoms. They face serious problems in bridging the gulf between society's expectations and their own inability to form intimate relations with persons of the other sex. Believing that love is a universal condition of young people, they are often pressured into "falling in love." However, only the mature person has the capacity to love; others merely go through the motions of being "in love" in order to maintain security (Sullivan, 1953b).

ADULTHOOD

The successful completion of late adolescence culminates in adulthood, a stage characterized by the establishment of a love relationship with at least one significant other person. Writing of this love relationship, Sullivan (1953b) stated that "this really highly developed intimacy with another is not the principal business of life, but is, perhaps, the principal source of satisfaction in life" (p. 34).

Sullivan had little to say about adulthood because he believed that maturity was beyond the scope of interpersonal psychiatry; people who have achieved the capacity to love are not in need of psychiatric counsel. His sketch of the mature person, therefore, was not founded on clinical experience but was an extrapolation from the preceding stages.

Mature adults are perceptive of other people's anxiety and security, sensitive to their needs, and genuinely understand their problems. They have a low level of anxiety, operate predominantly on the syntaxic level, and find life interesting and exciting (Sullivan, 1953b).

Table 8.2 summarizes the six Sullivanian stages of development and shows the importance of interpersonal relationships at each stage.

MENTAL DISORDERS

Sullivan believed that all mental disorders have an interpersonal origin and can be understood only with reference to the person's social environment. He also held that the deficiencies found in psychiatric patients are found in every person, but to a lesser degree. There is nothing unique about mental difficulties; they are derived from the same kind of interpersonal troubles faced by all people. Sullivan (1953a) insisted "that everyone is much more simply human than unique, and that no matter what ails the patient, he is *mostly* a person like the psychiatrist" (p. 96).

Most of Sullivan's early therapeutic work was with schizophrenic patients, and many of his subsequent lectures and writings dealt with schizophrenia. Sullivan (1962) distinguished two broad classes of schizophrenia. The first includes all those symptoms that originate from organic causes and are therefore beyond the study of interpersonal psychiatry. The second class includes all schizophrenic disorders grounded in situational factors. These were the only ones of concern to Sullivan because they are the only ones amenable to change through interpersonal psychiatry.

Dissociated reactions, which often precede schizophrenia, are characterized by loneliness, low self-esteem, the uncanny emotion, unsatisfactory relations with others, and ever-increasing anxiety (Sullivan, 1953b). People with a dissociated personality, in common with all people, attempt to minimize anxiety by building an elaborate self-system that blocks out those experiences that threaten their security. Whereas normal individuals feel relatively secure in their interpersonal relations and do not need to constantly rely on dissociation as a means of protecting self-esteem, mentally disordered individuals dissociate many of their experiences from their self-system. If this strategy becomes persistent, these people will begin to operate more and more in their own private worlds, with increasing parataxic distortions and decreasing consensually validated experiences (Sullivan, 1956).

PSYCHOTHERAPY

Because he believed that mental disorders grow out of interpersonal difficulties, Sullivan based his therapeutic procedures on an effort to improve a patient's relationship with others. To facilitate this process, the therapist serves as a *participant observer*, becoming part of an interpersonal, face-to-face relationship with the patient and providing the patient an opportunity to establish syntaxic communication with another human being.

While at St. Elizabeth Hospital, Sullivan devised a then radical means of treating seriously disturbed patients. His supervisors agreed to grant him a ward for his own patients and to allow him to select and train nurses who could treat the patients as fellow human beings. At that time, most schizophrenic and other psychotic patients were warehoused and regarded as subhuman. But Sullivan's experiment worked. A high rate of his patients got better. Erich Fromm (1994a) regarded Sullivan's near miraculous results as evidence that a psychosis is not merely a physical disorder, and that the personal relationship of one human being to another is the essence of psychological growth.

In general terms, the Sullivanian therapist is primarily concerned with uncovering patients' difficulties in relating to others and strives to replace disjunctive motivations with conjunctive ones. Conjunctive motivations integrate personality and allow patients to satisfy their needs and enhance their feelings of security. To accomplish this, patients must give up some security in dealing with other people and realize that they can achieve mental health only through consensually validated personal relations. The therapeutic ingredient in this process is the face-to-face relationship between psychiatrist and patients, which permits patients to reduce anxiety and to communicate with others on the syntaxic level.

Although they are participants in the interview, Sullivanian therapists avoid getting personally involved. They do not place themselves on the same level with the patient, but on the contrary, they try to convince the patient of their expert abilities. In other words, friendship is not a condition of psychotherapy—therapists must be trained as experts in the difficult business of making discerning observations of the patient's interpersonal relations (Sullivan, 1954).

Sullivan was primarily concerned with understanding patients and helping them to improve foresight, discover difficulties in interpersonal relations, and restore their ability to participate in consensually validated experiences. To accomplish these goals, he concentrated his efforts on answering three continuing questions: Precisely what is the patient saying to me? How can I best put into words what I wish to say to the patient? What is the general pattern of communication between us?

Sullivan divided the interview into four stages: formal inception, reconnaissance, detailed inquiry, and termination. The first stage, *formal inception*, involves the therapist's introduction to the patient, including an inquiry into the reason for therapy and the source of referral. The initial contact is extremely important because it is the first instance of communication between therapist and patient. At this time, the therapist promotes confidence in the patient by demonstrating interpersonal skill, permits the patient to express the reasons for seeking therapy, formulates tentative hypotheses, and decides on a possible course of action (Sullivan, 1954).

During the *reconnaissance stage*, the therapist obtains a general personal and social history, makes observations concerning patients' interpersonal identity, and tries to discover why they came to develop a particular personality. During this period, the therapist will ask open-ended questions that allow patients to respond at random until their thought patterns circle around to something relevant. The reconnaissance stage typically lasts from 7 to 15 hours, but it may be as brief as 20 minutes if therapy is to consist of a single interview. At the end of this phase, the therapist summarizes the important data, after which the patient amends or adds any details. This ensures that therapy can proceed on a consensually valid basis (Sullivan, 1954).

The third stage, *detailed inquiry*, varies with the purpose of the interview, but in general, it is a time for testing hypotheses formulated during the two preceding stages. The therapist tries to improve understanding by asking a series of detailed questions concerning patients' personal history and their current attitude toward themselves and significant others. In the search for durable characteristics of patients, a skillful therapist listens carefully to all possible meanings behind the answers to these questions and strives to verify impressions formulated during earlier stages (Sullivan, 1954).

The fourth and final stage of the interview is *termination* or, in some cases, *interruption*. Termination means that the therapist would not expect to see the patient again; interruption suggests that an interview session is finished, although it may be resumed the following day, week, or some other designated time. After each interruption, the psychiatrist gives the patient "homework," something to do or some memory to recall. With either interruption or termination, the therapist consolidates whatever progress the patient has made by revealing what has been learned about the patient, by prescribing a course of action, by giving the patient a final assessment of prognosis, and finally, by taking formal leave. The formal leave-taking must proceed smoothly or else therapeutic benefits so carefully accumulated may be destroyed (Sullivan, 1954).

RELATED RESEARCH

Although Sullivan's interpersonal theory has not been the object of intense empirical investigation, directly and indirectly it has stimulated research on interpersonal relationships. These relationships can be divided into two categories: (1) therapeutic relationships and (2) friendships, which can be further divided into imaginary friends and intimacy with real friends.

At the foundation of Sullivan's view of therapy is the idea that all mental illness results from interpersonal conflicts and difficulties. More specifically, in important early relationships, children often internalize a parent's negative perceptions of them and thereby develop some form of mental disturbance as an adult. In short, people learn to treat themselves the way they have been treated by others (Sullivan, 1953a). Sullivan reasoned that if interpersonal relationships can be the cause of mental disturbance, then they can also be the cure. One form of interpersonal relationship that is critical in mental health is the one between therapist and patient. In particular, Sullivan and his followers have argued that what the therapist says and does may play an important role in the patient's well-being and progress and that the purpose of therapy is to create a new relationship in which the patient internalizes positive rather than negative aspects of the therapist-patient relationship.

Research suggests that just as negative comments and behaviors by the therapist can lead to negative outcomes, so too can positive actions by the therapist lead to positive outcomes in the patient. For instance, William Henry, Thomas Schacht, and Hans Strupp (1990) used the Structural Analysis of Social Behavior (SASB) (Benjamin, 1974) to see how interpersonal dynamics between patient and therapist effects the success of therapy. They hypothesized that patients would develop views of themselves that are consistent with how the therapist viewed them.

In general, Henry et al. found that patients developed relatively stable behaviors that were consistent with the way their therapist treated them. More specifically, these researchers found that therapists' hostile and controlling statements were highly correlated with patients' self-derogatory statements. Also, patients of therapists who belittled, blamed, ignored, or neglected them tended to blame themselves and to show poor therapeutic outcome.

In a later study, Steven Harrist, Stephen Quintana, Hans Strupp, and William Henry (1994) used the SASB to demonstrate the positive effect of therapists' behavior on patient's self-perceptions and on the therapeutic outcome. When therapists in this study used affirming, helping, and nurturing techniques, patients tended to be more disclosing, expressive, and trusting as well as more self-accepting and self-nourishing. Further, by internalizing the more positive aspects of the relationship, patients showed less depression and anxiety and greater overall improvement in psychosocial functioning.

In addition to the importance of therapeutic relationships, the topic of friendships was central to Sullivan's views on psychological well-being. Sullivan was one of the first to acknowledge the importance of imaginary friends, although not all psychologists who discuss imaginary friends do so from a Sullivanian perspective. The topic of imaginary friends or playmates has received a modest amount of theoretical and empirical attention. In past years, many people believed that children who developed imaginary friends were either maladjusted or socially inept, or they were compensating for lack of real relationships (Bender & Vogel, 1941; Benson & Pryor, 1973). More recently this view has changed. Evidence now exists that children who develop imaginary friends, compared with those who do not, are more creative (Fern, 1991; Schaefer, 1969; Somers & Yawkey, 1984), more intelligent (Fern; Pines, 1978), more friendly and sociable and less aggressive (Pines), and do not use imaginary friends in place of real relationships (Seiffge-Krenke, 1993). For example, Charles Schaefer studied 800 high school students and divided them into four creative groups and four control groups of 100 each. Creativity was based on teacher evaluations and scores on standardized creativity tests. Schaefer then matched participants with a control group on such factors as school, year, class, and grade point average. Results showed that 31% of the artistically creative boys had had imaginary friends as children compared with only 12% of the controls. In addition, 26% of the girls with creative writing ability had had imaginary friends compared with only 10% of the control group.

A later study by Tami Fern (1991) looked at gifted-child humorists in grades 3 to 6 and found that they were more likely to have imaginary friends, show more imaginative thinking, and have higher IQ scores than a comparison group of children. Finally, Inge Seiffge-Krenke (1993) explored the question of whether imaginary companions serve as substitutes for a deficit in one's relations with family and friends. However, after analyzing the diary content of adolescent students, she could find no support for this so-called deficit hypothesis. Adolescents who write about imaginary friends had the same levels and kinds of intimate friendships as adolescents who did not write about imaginary friends. Students with imaginary friends did not ignore or fail to develop real friendships, nor were they trying to compensate for poor friendships.

Research does not always paint such a positive picture of people who have or had imaginary friends. For example, Martin Manosevitz, Sheila Fling, and Norman Prentice (1977) found no relationship between having imaginary friends and being intelligent or creative. However, they sampled preschool children whose reliability and validity on measures of intelligence and creativity is usually quite low. At least one study (Harter & Chao, 1992) found that children who make use of imaginary friends are rated by their teachers as less competent and by their peers as less popular than children who do not use imaginary friends. Furthermore, some studies have found a possible relationship between having imaginary friends and psychopathology. For instance, Colin Ross, Sharon Heber, G. Ron Norton, and Geri Anderson (1989) found that people with multiple personalities, compared to those with schizophrenia, panic disorder, or eating disorder, were more likely to have had an imaginary playmate during childhood. In summary, these studies suggest that people who invent and spend time with an imaginary friend are different in several ways from those who do not. However, no cause and effect relationship has yet been established between having an imaginary playmate and such personality factors as creativity, intelligence, sociability, humor, or multiple personality disorder.

Sullivan (1953a) also suggested that we all have a need for warm, close, and intimate relationships with real—not just imaginary—people. Sullivan argued that intimate exchanges between friends can and do begin before puberty. However, in a review of the empirical literature on the development of self-disclosure and intimacy, Thomas Berndt and Nancy Hanna (1995) concluded that intimate exchanges are very rare before age 12. They also concluded, in agreement with Sullivan, that adolescents who self-disclose and develop intimate friendships are psychologically more adjusted than those who do not; that is, they have higher self-esteem and are less anxious and depressed. Furthermore, Berndt and Hanna reported on a laboratory study in which third and seventh graders talked to both a close friend and a random classmate. These conversations were videotaped and coded on number of self-disclosures, gossips, agreements, disagreements, verbal aggressions, questions, and whispers. Surprisingly, Berndt and Hanna found that close friends did not self-disclose more than classmates. However, as predicted, seventh graders (13-year-olds) did disclose and gossip more than third graders (9-year-olds); girls disclosed more than boys; and friends were more than twice as likely to disagree with one another than were classmates. Other researchers (Fischer, 1981; Moore & Boldero, 1991) have also found gender differences in young adults as well as in adolescents, with young women and girls developing deeper, more intimate relationships with same-sex peers than young men and boys. Finally, Dan McAdams (1980) examined personality differences of people who were high on a need for intimacy compared with those who were low on this need. He found that people high on the need for intimacy were described by their friends and acquaintances as more warm, sincere, natural, and loving and less dominant, outspoken, and self-centered than those who were low on the need for intimacy.

In summary, much empirical work on the development of intimate, close relationships has corroborated some of Sullivan's basic assumptions of interpersonal relationships. Most people seem to have a need for intimate, close relationships, and the development of these relationships tends to bode well for their overall psychological well-being. However, not all of Sullivan's theoretical ideas have been supported. For example, intimacy does not seem to develop as early as Sullivan suggested. Also, Sullivan had little to say about the consistent gender differences in intimacy.

CRITIQUE OF SULLIVAN

Although Sullivan's theory of personality is quite comprehensive, it is not as popular among academic psychologists as the theories of Freud, Adler, Jung, or Erik Erikson (see Chapter 9). However, the ultimate value of any theory does not rest on its popularity but on the six criteria enumerated in Chapter 1.

The first criterion of a useful theory is its ability to *generate research*. Although much research is currently being conducted on interpersonal theory in general, only a few researchers are actively investigating hypotheses specifically drawn from Sullivan's theory. One possible explanation for this deficiency is Sullivan's lack of popularity among those most apt to conduct research—the academicians. This might be accounted for by Sullivan's close association with psychiatry, his isolation from any university setting, and the relative lack of organization in his writings and speeches.

Second, a useful theory must be *falsifiable*; that is, it must be specific enough to suggest research that may either support or fail to support its major assumptions. On this criterion Sullivan's theory, like those of Freud, Jung, Klein, Horney, and Fromm, must receive a very low mark. As we have seen, Sullivan's notion of the importance of interpersonal relations for psychological health has received a moderate amount of indirect support. However, alternative explanations are possible for most of these findings.

Third, how well does Sullivanian theory provide an organization for all that is known about human personality? Despite its many elaborate postulates, the theory can receive only a moderate rating on its ability to *organize knowledge*. Moreover, the theory's extreme emphasis on interpersonal relations subtracts from its ability to organize knowledge, because much of what is presently known about human behavior has a biological basis and does not easily fit into a theory restricted to interpersonal relations.

The relative lack of testing of Sullivan's theory diminishes its usefulness as a *practical guide* for parents, teachers, psychotherapists, and others concerned with the care of children and adolescents. However, if one accepts the theory without supporting evidence, then many practical problems can be managed by resorting to Sullivanian theory. As a guide to action, then, the theory receives a fair to moderate rating.

Is the theory *internally consistent*? Sullivan's ideas suffer from his inability to write well, but the theory itself is logically conceptualized and holds together as a unified entity. Although Sullivan used some unusual terms, he did so in a consistent fashion throughout his writings and speeches. Overall, his theory is consistent, but it lacks the organization that might have been achieved had he committed more of his ideas to the printed page.

Finally, is the theory *parsimonious* or simple? Here Sullivan must receive a low rating. His penchant for creating his own terms and the awkwardness of his writing add needless bulk to a theory that, if streamlined, would be far more useful.

CONCEPT OF HUMANITY

Sullivan's basic conception of humanity is summed up in his *one-genus hypothesis*, which states that *"everyone is much more simply human than otherwise"* (1953b, p. 32). This was his way of saying that similarities among people are much more important than differences. People are more like people than anything else.

> In other words, the differences between any two instances of human personality—from the lowest grade imbecile to the highest-grade genius—are much less striking than the difference between the least-gifted human being and a member of the nearest other biological genus. (Sullivan, 1953b, p. 33)

Sullivan's ability to successfully treat schizophrenic patients undoubtedly was greatly enhanced by his deeply held belief that they shared a common humanity with the therapist. Having experienced at least one schizophrenic episode himself, Sullivan was able to form an empathic bond with these patients through his role as a participant observer.

The one influence separating humans from all other creatures is interpersonal relations. We are born biological organisms—animals with no human qualities except the potential for participation in interpersonal relations. Soon after birth we begin to realize this potential when interpersonal experiences transform us into human beings. Sullivan believed that the mind contains nothing except what was put there through interpersonal experiences. Unlike Freud and Jung, he contended that there are no human instincts. We are motivated only by environmental influences—interpersonal relationships.

Sullivan insisted that humans have no existence outside the interpersonal situation. As isolated entities we are nothing, but through our relationships with other humans we develop our personality. Each of us begins life with a somewhat one-sided relationship with a mothering one who both cares for our needs and imparts anxiety to us. Later we are able to reciprocate feelings for our parents, and these relationships serve as a foundation upon which subsequent interpersonal relations are built. At about the time we first go to school, we should learn to compete, cooperate, and compromise with children our own age, and if we do, we then have the tools necessary for the intimacy and love that come later. Through our intimate and love relationships, we become healthy personalities. However, an absence of these relationships leads to stunted psychological growth.

Personal individuality is an illusion; we exist only in relation to other people and have as many personalities as we have interpersonal relations. Thus the concepts of *uniqueness* and *individuality* do not concern interpersonal psychiatry. The subject matter of Sullivan's theory is the interaction between the observer and the observed, with the observer being a participant in the relationship. This interaction is the essence of personality.

Anxiety and interpersonal relations are tied together in a cyclic manner, which makes significant personality changes difficult. Anxiety interferes with interpersonal relations, and unsatisfactory interpersonal relations lead to the use of rigid behaviors that may temporarily buffer anxiety. But because these inflexible behaviors do not solve the basic problem, they eventually lead to increases in anxiety, which lead to further deterioration in interpersonal relations. The increasing levels of anxiety must then be held in check by an ever-rigid self-system. For this reason, Sullivan would have to be rated as being *neither optimistic nor pessimistic* concerning the potential for growth and change within human beings. Interpersonal relations can transform us into healthy personalities, but they can also be restrictive by creating anxiety and its resultant rigid self-structure.

Because personality is built solely on interpersonal relations, Sullivan is rated *very high on social influence.* Interpersonal relations are responsible for both positive and negative characteristics in people. If an infant has its needs satisfied by the mothering one, is not disturbed by the mothering one's anxiety, and receives genuine feelings of tenderness, it can avoid being a malevolent personality during childhood and will develop tender feelings toward others. On the other hand, unsatisfactory interpersonal relations may trigger malevolence and leave some children with the feeling that people cannot be trusted and that they are essentially alone among their enemies.

Chapter Summary

Harry Stack Sullivan was the first American to develop a comprehensive theory of personality. Like many other theorists, his ideas on personality were a reflection of his own life experiences, and his early loneliness and isolation led to a theory that emphasized the importance of personal relationships. Although his isolation also led to a rather esoteric language, his insights as a psychotherapist resulted in an eloquent description of anxiety, interpersonal relations, and the stages of psychological development.

Anxiety is the chief descriptive force in interpersonal relations and is the cause of much pain and suffering. *Interpersonal relations* can either create additional anxiety or lead to healthy psychological growth and development, which reduce anxiety.

The first *developmental stage* in Sullivan's theory is *infancy*—a period lasting from birth to the development of syntaxic language. During this stage, an infant's primary interpersonal relationship is with the mothering one, and its principal source of anxiety is the feeding situation.

Childhood begins with the development of syntaxic language and continues until 5 or 6 years of age. The most important interpersonal relationship for children of this age is ordinarily with the mother, although children of this age often create a relationship with an imaginary playmate, which can have positive and lasting effects on later development.

The third Sullivanian stage is the *juvenile era,* a period roughly encompassing the first 3 years of school in Western culture. At this time, children should learn competition, compromise, and cooperation—skills that will enable them to move successfully through later stages of development.

The most crucial stage of development is *preadolescence*, because mistakes made during this phase are exceedingly difficult to overcome later. During preadolescence, a child should learn intimacy, ordinarily with a person of the same age and gender. This close interpersonal relationship is free from the complications of a sexual encounter and is the positive force that allows a person to subsequently relate to members of the opposite sex in an intimate rather than a strictly sexual manner.

As young people reach *early adolescence*, their sexual interest is stimulated by biological changes. If they learned intimacy during preadolescence, then they will be able to maintain these same-sex intimate relationships and at the same time develop lustful encounters with adolescents of the opposite sex.

People attain *late adolescence* when they are able to direct their intimacy and lust toward one other person. Unfortunately, not everyone achieves this stage, and many people are never able to develop feelings of genuine love toward the person for whom they have the strongest sexual desire. The successful completion of late adolescence culminates in *adulthood*, a stage marked by a stable love relationship.

Suggested Readings

Chapman, A. H. (1976). *Harry Stack Sullivan: His life and his work*. New York: Putnam's.
   A very readable account of Sullivan's life combined with a discussion of the principal principles of interpersonal theory.
Perry, H. S. (1982). *Psychiatrist of America: The life of Harry Stack Sullivan*. Cambridge, MA: Belknap Press.
   Written by the former managing editor of Sullivan's journal, *Psychiatry*, this biography is the result of 20 years of careful research. Sullivan's personality emerges more fully than in any other biography.
Sullivan, H. S. (1953b). *The interpersonal theory of psychiatry*. New York: Norton.
   As the first book prepared from Sullivan's unpublished lectures, this work contains the most complete account of interpersonal theory, including the six developmental epoches.

Erikson

Erikson:
Post-Freudian Theory

Biography of Erik Erikson
Ego Psychology
    Society's Influence
    Epigenetic Principle
Stages of Psychosocial Development
    Infancy
    Early Childhood
    Play Age
    School Age
    Adolescence
    Young Adulthood
    Adulthood
    Old Age
    Summary of the Life Cycle
Erikson's Methods of Investigation
    Anthropological Studies
    Psychohistory
    Play Construction
Related Research
    Identity in Adolescence and Early
        Adulthood
    Generativity in Adulthood and Old Age
Critique of Erikson
Concept of Humanity
Chapter Summary
Suggested Readings

Erik Erikson, unlike Jung, Adler, Horney, Fromm, and Sullivan, intended his theory of personality to be an extension rather than a repudiation or revision of Freud's psychoanalysis. His **post-Freudian theory** extended Freud's stages of development into adolescence, adulthood, and old age. Erikson suggested that at each stage a specific psychosocial struggle contributes to the formation of personality. From adolescence on, that struggle takes the form of an identity crisis—an experience that may either strengthen or weaken the personality.

Erikson took psychoanalysis for granted and used Freudian theory as the foundation for his life-cycle approach to personality theory. In general, he differed from Freud in placing more emphasis on the ego, on social and historical influences, and on his extension of developmental stages into adulthood and old age. Because Erikson's theoretical model is an extension of psychoanalysis and not merely a refinement, he preferred the term *post-Freudian* rather than *revisionist* or *neo-Freudian*. He regarded his conceptions of personality as something Freud might have done in time. Nevertheless, his notion that the ego and a sense of identity develops over the life span represents a marked departure from Freud's child-oriented theory.

Erikson was not a physician; in fact, he had no college degree of any kind. Yet, he became one of the world's foremost psychoanalysts, even though his professional credentials were limited to a training analysis by Freud's daughter Anna. Erikson's post-Freudian theory, like those of other personality theorists, is a reflection of his background, a background that included art and extensive travels and experiences with a variety of cultures.

BIOGRAPHY OF ERIK ERIKSON

The life of Erik Homburger Erikson was marked by several "identity crises," a term Erikson began to popularize more than 50 years ago. Erikson's early identity crises were due in part to his own clouded origins. He was born June 15, 1902, near Frankfurt, Germany, the son of Karla Abrahamsen and a father of unknown identity. During his first 3 years, he lived alone with his mother, who then married Dr. Theodor Homburger, Erik's pediatrician (Coles, 1970). Erikson grew up in Karlsruhe, a town in southern Germany, believing he was Homburger's son. In his autobiography, Erikson (1975) claimed that his parents "kept from me the fact that my mother had been married previously, and that I was the son of a Dane who had abandoned her before my birth" (p. 27). However, Paul Roazen (1976) cited a speech Erikson had given 20 years earlier in which he reported that his father had died around the time of his birth. Roazen further suggested that Erikson may have been born to unmarried parents and that his unknown paternal lineage contributed to an image of himself as a perpetual stepson. This image is seen in Erikson's persistent loyalty to Freud who, in many ways, became Erikson's mythical stepfather.

Erikson's real stepfather, Theodor Homburger, was from a small Jewish bourgeois family. He was a kindly man who expected his stepson to become a doctor like himself. Erikson's mother, a native of Copenhagen, Denmark, had both Jewish and Lutheran heritage. When Erik attended temple, his blond hair and blue eyes made him appear to be an outsider. At school, on the other hand, his Aryan classmates referred to him as a Jew, so Erik felt out of place in both arenas.

At 18, Erikson completed school at the Gymnasium—the last academic graduation of his life. Feeling "alienated from everything my bourgeois family stood for," he set out in quest of a different style of life (Erikson, 1975, p. 28). Gifted at sketching, he divided his time between art school and wandering throughout southern Germany and northern Italy, hiking and carrying a knapsack with books of his favorite authors. His identity as an artist meant a kind of rebellious way of life rather than a specific occupation, and that way of life was antiestablishment. These were years of discontent, rebellion, and confusion.

At age 25, he returned to Karlsruhe to teach art. However, a letter from his friend Peter Blos was to have a permanent effect on the direction of his life. Erikson had known Blos from their youth in Karlsruhe, and the two were friends in Italy. Both were artists and both later became well-known psychoanalysts. Erikson (1975) considered Blos's letter to have rescued him from the life of a wandering artist. The letter asked Erikson to join with Blos in teaching in a newly established school for children in Vienna. The school was run by Dorothy Tiffany Burlingham, a wealthy American and lifetime friend of Anna Freud. During the 6 years Erikson spent in Vienna, he studied psychoanalytic psychology and Montessori education. In addition, he completed a personal analysis with Anna Freud, only 7 years older than Erikson. Anna shared a waiting room with her father, then in his seventies, so Erikson became personally acquainted with Sigmund Freud. However, he rarely addressed the older Freud, not only out of shyness and deference, but also because Freud's cancer of the jaw made speech quite painful. Even though Erikson's personal relationship with Freud was minimal, he remained a lifelong ardent admirer of the father of psychoanalysis.

While in Vienna, Erikson met and married Joan Serson, a Canadian-born dancer, artist, and teacher who had also undergone psychoanalysis. With her psychoanalytic background and her facility with the English language, she became a valuable editor and occasional coauthor of Erikson's books. The Eriksons had three children, a daughter and two sons. The older son, Kai Erikson, became a professor of sociology and occasionally collaborated with his father on professional writings.

In 1933, Erikson (still known as Homburger) completed studies at the Vienna Psychoanalytic Institute. Then, with fascism on the rise, the Eriksons left Vienna for Denmark, the land of Erik's biological parents. After one summer in Copenhagen, they immigrated to the United States, settling first in the Boston area.

With neither medical credentials nor college degree of any kind, Erikson received an offer to teach at the Harvard Medical School and to work at the Harvard Psychological Clinic. While at Harvard, he enrolled in the Ph.D. program in psychology but soon dropped out. During his years at Harvard, he met Margaret Mead, Ruth Benedict, Henry Murray, Kurt Lewin, and others who had also influenced Harry Stack Sullivan (Chapter 8) and Karen Horney (Chapter 6).

In 1936, Erikson went to Yale where he was associated with the famous Institute of Human Relations and where he also taught at the Medical School. Three years later, he moved to the University of California at Berkeley, but not before living among and studying the people of the Sioux nation in South Dakota. (He later lived with people of the Yurok nation in northern California and these experiences in cultural anthropology added to the richness and completeness of his theory of personality.)

At about the same time that Erikson moved to the West Coast, he became a United States citizen and changed his name. Erikson was not his biological father's name, and his choice of that name is not adequately explained in his autobiography (Erikson, 1975). Perhaps his newly acquired American identity allowed him to identify with Leif Ericsson, the first European explorer to land in North America. Or perhaps Erik's sons wanted to be known as Erikson.

During his California period, Erikson gradually evolved a theory of personality, separate from but not incompatible with Freud's. In 1950, Erikson published *Childhood and Society,* a book that became a classic and made for him an international reputation as an imaginative thinker.

Erikson remained at Berkeley until 1950 when faculty members were asked to sign a loyalty oath. As a matter of principle, Erikson refused to sign and left California for Stockbridge, Massachusetts, where he worked at Austen Riggs, a treatment center for psychoanalytic training and research. He returned to Harvard in 1960 as professor of human development and remained there until his retirement in 1970. After retirement, he continued an active career—writing, lecturing, seeing a few patients, and doing research with his wife, Joan, on aging (see J. M. Erikson, 1988; Erikson, Erikson, & Kivnick, 1986). During the early years of his retirement, he lived in Marin County, California, but moved back to Cambridge, Massachusetts, in 1987 when the Erik Erikson Center was founded there. He died on May 12, 1994, at age 91.

Erikson's best known works include *Childhood and Society* (1950, 1963); *Young Man Luther* (1958); *Identity, Youth, and Crisis* (1968); *Gandhi's Truth* (1969), a book that won both the Pulitzer Prize and the National Book Award; *Dimensions of a New Identity* (1974); *Life History and the Historical Moment* (1975); *Identity and the Life Cycle* (1980); and *The Life Cycle Completed* (1982). Many of his papers have been compiled in *A Way of Looking at Things* (Schlein, 1987).

Erikson made three important additions to Freudian theory. First, to Freud's early psychosexual stages (oral, anal, phallic, and latency), he added four later stages, thus extending the life cycle throughout adulthood and into old age. Second, he moved beyond the consulting room and gathered data from historical and cultural sources, thereby elevating social factors above biological explanations. Third, he emphasized the ego over the id as the key to personality development.

EGO PSYCHOLOGY

In Chapter 2, we saw that Freud used the analogy of a rider on horseback to describe the relationship between the ego and the id. The rider (ego) is ultimately at the mercy of the stronger horse (id). The ego has no strength of its own but must borrow its energy from the id. Moreover, the ego is constantly attempting to balance blind demands of the superego against the relentless forces of the id and the realistic opportunities of the external world. Freud believed that, for mature people, the ego may be sufficiently developed to rein in the id, even though its control is still tenuous and id impulses might erupt and overwhelm the ego at any time.

In contrast, Erikson held that the ego is more than a mediator between the irrational forces of the id and the unrelenting demands of the superego. To him, the ego was a positive force, one that establishes self-identity and also adapts to the various conflicts and crises of life. The adaptation is not always constructive. At times, the ego struggles to defend itself, and on occasion, it may even succumb to the forces of society. In any event, it is the ego (the sense of "I" or self-identity) that is the center of personality.

During childhood, the ego is weak, pliable, and fragile, but by adolescence, it should begin to take form and gain strength. Throughout an individual's life, it unifies personality and guards indivisibility. Erikson (1963) defined the ego as a person's "capacity to unify his experiences and his actions in an adaptive manner" (p. 16).

Erikson (1968) saw the ego as a partially unconscious organizing agency that synthesizes present experiences with past selves and also with anticipated selves. He also identified three interrelated aspects of ego: (1) the *body ego*, which refers to experiences with one's body; (2) the *ego ideal*, which represents the image we have of ourselves in comparison with an established ideal; and (3) *ego identity*, the image we have of ourselves in a variety of social roles. Although adolescence is ordinarily the time when these three components are changing most rapidly, alterations in body ego, ego ideal, and ego identity can and do take place at any stage of life.

SOCIETY'S INFLUENCE

Although inborn capacities are important in personality development, the ego emerges from and is largely shaped by society. Erikson's emphasis on social and historical factors was in contrast with Freud's mostly biological viewpoint. To Erikson, the ego exists as potential at birth, but it must emerge from within a cultural environment. Different societies, with their variations in child-rearing practices, tend to shape personalities that fit the needs and values of their culture. For example, Erikson (1963) found that prolonged and permissive nursing of infants of the Sioux nation (sometimes for as long as 4 or 5 years) resulted in what Freud would call "oral" personalities. The Sioux place great value on generosity, and Erikson believed that the reassurance resulting from unlimited breast feeding lays the foundation for the virtue of generosity. However, Sioux parents quickly suppress biting, a practice that may contribute to the child's fortitude and ferocity. On the other hand, people of the Yurok nation set strict regulations concerning elimination of urine and feces, practices that tend to develop "anality." In European American societies, orality and anality are often considered undesirable traits or neurotic symptoms. Erikson (1963), however, argued that orality among the Sioux hunters and anality among the Yurok fishermen are adaptive characteristics that help both the individual and the culture. The fact that European American culture views orality and anality as deviant traits merely displays its own ethnocentric view of other societies. Erikson (1968, 1974) argued that historically all tribes or nations, including the United States, have developed what he called a **pseudospecies,** that is, an illusion perpetrated and perpetuated by a particular society that it is somehow chosen to be *the* human species. In past centuries, this belief has aided the survival of the tribe, but with modern means of world annihilation, such a prejudiced perception (as demonstrated by Nazi Germany) threatens the survival of every nation.

One of Erikson's principal contributions to personality theory was his extension of the Freudian early stages of development to include school age, youth, adulthood, and old age. Before looking more closely at Erikson's theory of ego development, we discuss his view of how personality develops from one stage to the next.

EPIGENETIC PRINCIPLE

Erikson believed that the ego develops throughout the various stages of life according to an **epigenetic principle,** a term he borrowed from embryology. Epigenetic development implies a step-by-step growth of fetal organs. The embryo does not begin as a completely formed little person, waiting to merely expand its structure and form. Rather, it develops, or should develop, according to a predetermined rate and in a fixed sequence. If the eyes, liver, or other organs do not develop during that critical period for their development, then they will never attain proper maturity.

In similar fashion, the ego follows the path of epigenetic development, with each stage developing at its proper time. One stage emerges from and is built on a previous stage, but it does not replace that earlier stage. This is analogous to the

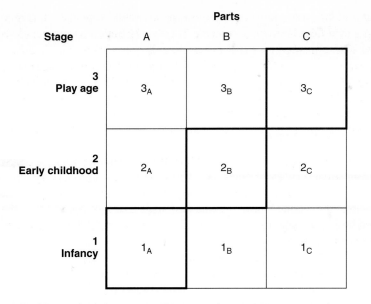

Parts

	A	B	C
3 **Play age**	3_A	3_B	3_C
2 **Early childhood**	2_A	2_B	2_C
1 **Infancy**	1_A	1_B	1_C

Stage

Figure **9.1**   Three Eriksonian stages, depicting the epigenetic principle.
Reprinted from *The Life Cycle Completed, a review* by Erik H. Erikson, by permission
of W. W. Norton & Company, Inc. Copyright © 1982 by Rikan Enterprises, Ltd.

physical development of children, who crawl before they walk, walk before they run,
and run before they jump. When children are still crawling, they are developing the
potential to walk, run, and jump, and after they are mature enough to jump, they still
retain their ability to run, walk, and crawl. Erikson (1968) described the epigenetic
principle, saying that "anything that grows has a ground plan, and that out of this
ground plan the parts arise, each part having its time of special ascendancy, until all
parts have arisen to form a functioning whole" (p. 92). More succinctly, "epigenesis
means that one characteristic develops on top of another in space and time" (Evans,
1967, pp. 21–22).

The epigenetic principle is illustrated in Figure 9.1, which depicts the first three
Eriksonian stages. The sequence of stages (1, 2, 3) and the development of their component parts (A, B, C) are shown in the heavily lined boxes along the diagonal. Figure
9.1 shows that each part exists before its critical time (at least as biological potential),
emerges at its proper time, and finally, continues to develop during subsequent stages.
For example, component part B of Stage 2 (early childhood) exists during Stage 1
(infancy) as shown in Box 1_B. Part B reaches its full ascendance during Stage 2 (Box 2_B),
but continues into Stage 3 (Box 3_B). Similarly, all components of Stage 3 exist during
Stages 1 and 2, reach full development during Stage 3, and continue throughout all
later stages (Erikson, 1982).

STAGES OF PSYCHOSOCIAL DEVELOPMENT

To appreciate Erikson's eight stages of psychosocial development, several points must
be understood. First, growth takes place according to the *epigenetic principle.* That is, one
component part arises out of another, has its own time of ascendancy, but it does not
entirely replace earlier components.

Second, in every stage of life there is an *interaction of opposites*, that is, a conflict between a **syntonic** (harmonious) element and a **dystonic** (disruptive) element. For example, during infancy, *basic trust* (a syntonic tendency) is opposed to *basic mistrust* (a dystonic tendency). Both trust and mistrust, however, are necessary for proper adaptation. An infant who learns only to trust becomes gullible and is ill-prepared for the realities encountered in later development. Of course, an infant who learns only to mistrust becomes overly suspicious and cynical. Similarly, during each of the other seven stages, people must have both harmonious (syntonic) and disruptive (dystonic) experiences.

Third, at each stage the conflict between the dystonic and syntonic elements produces an ego quality or ego strength, which Erikson referred to as a **basic strength.** For instance, from the antithesis between trust and mistrust emerges "hope," an ego quality that allows the infant to move into the next stage. Likewise, each of the other stages is marked by a basic ego strength that emerges from the clash between the harmonious and the disruptive elements of that stage.

Fourth, although Erikson referred to these periods as *psychosocial stages*, he never lost sight of the *somatic* (biological) aspect of human development.

Fifth, events in earlier stages do not cause later personality development. Ego identity is shaped by a *multiplicity of conflicts and events*—past, present, and anticipated.

Sixth, during each stage, but especially from adolescence forward, personality development is characterized by an **identity crisis,** which Erikson (1968) called "a turning point, a crucial period of increased vulnerability and heightened potential" (p. 96). Thus, during each crisis, a person is especially susceptible to major modifications in identity, either positive or negative. Contrary to popular usage, an identity crisis is not a catastrophic event but rather an opportunity for either adaptive or maladaptive adjustment.

Erikson's eight stages of psychosocial development are shown in Figure 9.2. The boldfaced capitalized words are the ego qualities or basic strengths that emerge from the conflicts or psychosocial crises that typify each period. The "vs." separating syntonic and dystonic elements signifies not only an antithetical relationship but also a complementary one. Only the boxes along the diagonal are filled in; that is, Figure 9.2 highlights only the basic strengths and psychosocial crises that are *most* characteristic of each stage of development. However, the epigenetic principle suggests that all the other boxes would be filled (as in Figure 9.1), though with other items less characteristic of their stage of psychosocial development. Each item in the ensemble is vital to personality development, and each is related to all the others. Although one may wish to start at old age and work backward (as Erikson does in *The Life Cycle Completed*), we begin our discussion of the developmental stages with infancy.

INFANCY

The first psychosocial stage is **infancy,** a period encompassing approximately the first year of life and paralleling Freud's oral phase of development. However, Erikson's model adopts a broader focus than Freud's oral stage, which was concerned almost exclusively with the mouth. To Erikson (1963, 1989), infancy is a time of *incorporation*, with infants "taking in" not only through their mouth but through their various sense organs as well. Through their eyes, for example, infants take in visual stimuli. As they take in food and sensory information, infants learn to either trust or mistrust the outside world, a situation that gives them realistic hope. Infancy, then, is marked by the

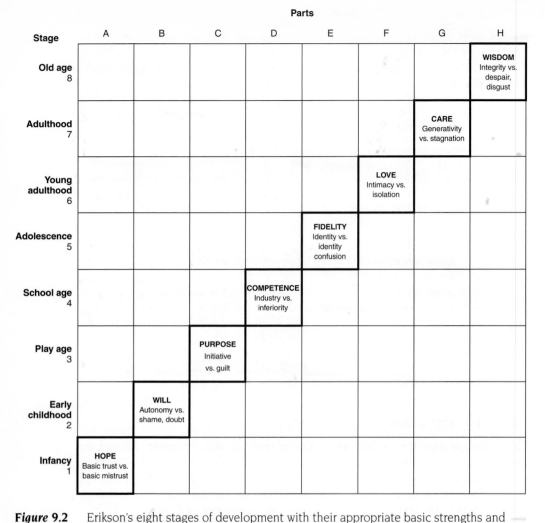

Parts

Stage	A	B	C	D	E	F	G	H
Old age 8								**WISDOM** Integrity vs. despair, disgust
Adulthood 7							**CARE** Generativity vs. stagnation	
Young adulthood 6						**LOVE** Intimacy vs. isolation		
Adolescence 5					**FIDELITY** Identity vs. identity confusion			
School age 4				**COMPETENCE** Industry vs. inferiority				
Play age 3			**PURPOSE** Initiative vs. guilt					
Early childhood 2		**WILL** Autonomy vs. shame, doubt						
Infancy 1	**HOPE** Basic trust vs. basic mistrust							

Figure 9.2   Erikson's eight stages of development with their appropriate basic strengths and psychosocial crises.

Reprinted from *The Life Cycle Completed, a review* by Erik H. Erikson, by permission of W. W. Norton & Company, Inc. Copyright © 1982 by Rikan Enterprises, Ltd.

oral-sensory psychosexual mode, the psychosocial crisis of *basic trust vs. basic mistrust*, and the basic strength of *hope*.

Oral-Sensory Mode

Erikson's expanded view of infancy is expressed in the term **oral-sensory,** a phrase he uses to describe infants' principal *psychosexual* mode of adapting.

The oral-sensory stage is characterized by two modes of incorporation—receiving and accepting what is given. Infants can receive even in the absence of other people; that is, they can take in air through the lungs and can receive sensory data without having to manipulate others. The second mode of incorporation, however, implies a social context. Infants not only must *get*, but they also must get someone else to *give*. This early training in interpersonal relations helps them learn to eventually become givers. In getting other people to give, they learn to trust or mistrust other people, thus setting up the basic *psychosocial crisis* of infancy, namely, basic trust vs. basic mistrust.

Basic Trust vs. Basic Mistrust

Infants' most significant interpersonal relations are with their primary caregiver, ordinarily their mother. If they realize that their mother will provide food regularly, then they begin to learn *basic trust*; if they consistently hear the pleasant, rhythmic voice of their mother, then they develop more basic trust; if they can rely on an exciting visual environment, then they solidify basic trust even more. In other words, if infants' pattern of accepting things corresponds with culture's way of giving them, infants will learn basic trust. On the other hand, if they find no correspondence between their oral-sensory needs and their environment, they will learn *basic mistrust*.

Basic trust is ordinarily syntonic and basic mistrust, dystonic. Nevertheless, infants must develop both attitudes. As noted earlier, too much trust makes them gullible and vulnerable to the vagaries of the world, whereas too little trust leads to frustration, anger, hostility, cynicism, or depression.

Both trust and mistrust are inevitable experiences of infants. All babies who have survived have been fed and otherwise cared for, and therefore have some reason to trust. In addition, all have been frustrated by pain, hunger, or discomfort, and thus have a reason to mistrust. Erikson believed that some ratio of trust and mistrust is critical to our ability to adapt. He told Richard Evans (1967) that "when we enter a situation, we must be able to differentiate how much we can trust and how much we must mistrust, and I use mistrust in the sense of a readiness for danger and an anticipation of discomfort" (p. 15).

The inevitable conflict between basic trust and basic mistrust results in our first psychosocial crisis, which in turn leads to our first basic strength—*hope*.

Hope: The Basic Strength of Infancy

Hope emerges from the conflict between basic trust and basic mistrust. Without the antithetical relationship between trust and mistrust, people cannot develop hope. Infants must experience hunger, pain, and discomfort as well as the alleviation of these unpleasant conditions. By having both painful and pleasurable experiences, infants learn to expect that future distresses will meet with satisfactory outcomes.

The antithesis of hope is *withdrawal*, which Erikson called the **core pathology** of infancy. With little to hope for, infants will retreat from the outside world and begin the journey toward serious psychological disturbance.

EARLY CHILDHOOD

The second psychosocial stage is **early childhood,** a period paralleling Freud's anal stage and encompassing approximately the 2nd and 3rd years of life. Again, some differences exist between the views of Freud and Erikson. In Chapter 2, we saw that Freud regarded the anus as the primary erogenous zone during this period and that during the early sadistic-anal phase, children receive pleasure in destroying or losing objects, while later they take satisfaction in defecating. Once again, Erikson took a broader view. To him, young children receive pleasure not only from mastering the sphincter muscle but also from mastering other body functions such as urinating, walking, throwing, holding, and so on. In addition, children develop a sense of control over their interpersonal environment, as well as a measure of self-control. However, early childhood is also a time of experiencing doubt and shame as children learn that many of their attempts at autonomy are unsuccessful.

Anal-Urethral-Muscular Mode

During the 2nd year, children's primary psychosexual adjustment is the **anal-urethral-muscular** mode. At this time children learn to control their body, especially in relation to cleanliness and mobility. Early childhood is more than a time of toilet training; it is also a time of learning to walk, run, hug parents, and hold on to toys and other objects. With each of these activities, young children are likely to display some stubborn tendencies. They may retain their feces or eliminate them at will; snuggle up to their mother or suddenly push her away; delight in hoarding objects or ruthlessly discard them.

Early childhood is a time of contradiction, a time of stubborn rebellion and meek compliance, a time of *impulsive* self-expression and *compulsive* deviance, a time of loving cooperation and hateful resistance (Erikson, 1968). This obstinate insistence on conflicting impulses triggers the major psychosocial crisis of childhood: autonomy vs. shame and doubt.

Autonomy vs. Shame and Doubt

If early childhood is a time for self-expression and *autonomy*, then it is also a time for *shame and doubt*. As children stubbornly express their anal-urethral-muscular mode, they are likely to find a culture that attempts to inhibit some of their self-expression. Parents may shame their children for soiling their pants or for making a mess with their food. They may also instill doubt by questioning their children's ability to meet their standards. The conflict between autonomy and shame and doubt becomes the major psychosocial crisis of early childhood.

Ideally, children should develop a proper ratio between autonomy and shame and doubt, and the ratio should be in favor of autonomy, the syntonic quality. If children develop too little autonomy, then they will have difficulties in subsequent stages. They will lack the initiative required during the play age and will continue to be handicapped in their later development. According to Erikson's epigenetic diagrams (see Figures 9.1 and 9.2), autonomy grows out of basic trust, and if basic trust has been established in infancy, then children learn to have faith in themselves, and their world remains intact while they experience a mild psychosocial crisis. Conversely, if children do not develop basic trust during infancy, then their attempts to gain control of their anal, urethral, and muscular organs during childhood will be met with a strong sense of shame and doubt, setting up a serious psychosocial crisis. *Shame* is a feeling of self-consciousness, of being looked at and exposed. *Doubt*, on the other hand, is the feeling of not being certain, the feeling that something remains hidden and cannot be seen. Both shame and doubt are dystonic qualities, and both grow out of the basic mistrust that was established in infancy.

Will: The Basic Strength of Childhood

The basic strength of *will* or willfulness evolves from the resolution of the crisis of autonomy vs. shame and doubt. This is the beginning of free will and will power—but only a beginning. Mature will power and a significant measure of free will are reserved for later stages of development, but they originate in the rudimentary will that emerges during early childhood. Anyone who has spent much time around 2-year-olds knows how willful they can be. Toilet training often epitomizes the conflict of wills between adult and child, but willful expression is not limited to this area. The basic conflict during this stage is between the child's striving for autonomy and the parent's attempts to control the child through the use of shame and doubt.

Rudimentary will can emerge only if children are permitted some self-expression in the control of their sphincters and other muscles. If culture instills too much shame and doubt and inhibits autonomy, children will not adequately develop this second important basic strength. Inadequate will is expressed as *compulsion*, the core pathology of early childhood. Too little will and too much compulsivity carry forward into the play age as lack of purpose and into the school age as lack of confidence.

PLAY AGE

Erikson's third stage of development is the **play age,** a period covering the same time as Freud's phallic phase—roughly ages 3 to 5 years. Again, we find differences between the views of Freud and Erikson. Whereas the Oedipus complex is a central theme in Freudian theory, Erikson believed that it is but one of several important developments during the play age. Erikson (1968) contended that, in addition to identifying with their parents, preschool-age children are developing locomotion, language skills, curiosity, imagination, and the ability to set goals. During this psychosexual period of *genital and locomotor* development, young children experience the crisis of *initiative vs. guilt* and develop a realistic sense of *purpose*.

Genital-Locomotor Mode

The primary psychosexual mode during the play age is **genital-locomotor.** Erikson (1982) saw the Oedipal situation as a prototype "of the lifelong power of human playfulness" (p. 77). In other words, the Oedipus complex is a drama played out in the child's imagination and includes the budding understanding of such basic concepts as reproduction, growth, future, and death. The Oedipus and castration complexes, therefore, are not always to be taken literally. A child may play at being a mother, a father, a wife, or a husband, but such play is an expression not only of the genital mode but also of the child's rapidly developing locomotor abilities. A little girl may envy boys, not because boys possess a penis, but rather because society grants more prerogatives to children with a penis. A little boy may have anxiety about losing something, but this refers not only to the penis but to other body parts as well. The Oedipus complex, then, is both more than and less than what Freud believed, and infantile sexuality is "a mere promise of things to come" (Erikson, 1963, p. 86). Unless sexual interest is provoked by cultural sex play or by adult sexual abuse, the Oedipus complex produces no harmful effects on later personality development.

The interest that play-age children have in genital activity is accompanied by their increasing facility at locomotion. They can now move with ease, running, jumping, and climbing with no conscious effort, and their play shows both initiative and imagination. Their rudimentary will, developed during the preceding stage, is now evolving into activity with a *purpose*. Children's cognitive abilities enable them to manufacture elaborate fantasies including Oedipal fantasies but also including imagining what it is like to be grown-up, to be omnipotent, or to be a ferocious animal. These fantasies, however, also produce guilt and thus contribute to the psychosocial crisis of the play age, namely, initiative vs. guilt.

Initiative vs. Guilt

As children begin to move around more easily and vigorously and as their genital interest awakens, they adopt an intrusive head-on mode of approaching the world. Although they begin to adopt *initiative* in their selection and pursuit of goals, many goals, such as marrying their mother or father or leaving home, must either be repressed or delayed. The consequence of these taboos and inhibited goals is *guilt*. The conflict between initiative and guilt becomes the dominant psychosocial crisis of the play age.

Again, the ratio between these two should favor the syntonic quality—initiative. Unbridled initiative, however, may lead to chaos and a lack of moral principles. On the other hand, if guilt is the dominant element, children may become compulsively moralistic or overly inhibited. *Inhibition*, which is the antipathy of purpose, constitutes the core pathology of the play age.

Purpose: The Basic Strength of the Play Age

The conflict of initiative vs. guilt produces the basic strength of *purpose*. Children now play with a purpose, competing at games in order to win or to be on top. Their genital interests have a direction, with mother or father being the object of their sexual desires. They set goals and pursue them with purpose. Play age is also the stage in which children are developing a conscience and beginning to attach labels such as right and wrong to their behavior. This youthful conscience becomes the "cornerstone of morality" (Erikson, 1968, p. 119).

Erikson (1968) summed up the play age with these words:

> We may now see what induced Freud to place the Oedipus complex at the core of man's conflicted existence, and this not only according to psychiatric evidence but also to the testimony of great fiction, drama, and history. For the fact that man began as a playing child leaves a residue of play-acting and role playing even in what he considers his highest purposes. (p. 121)

School Age

Erikson's concept of **school age** covers development from about age 6 to approximately age 12 or 13—covering the elementary school years in U.S. society and matching the latency years of Freud's theory. At this age, the social world of children is expanding beyond family to include peers, teachers, and other adult models. For school-age children, the wish to know becomes strong and is tied to their basic striving for competence. In normal development, children strive industriously to read and write, to hunt and fish, or to learn the skills required by their culture. School age does not necessarily mean formalized schools. In contemporary literate cultures, schools and professional teachers play a major part in children's education, whereas in preliterate societies, adults use less formalized but equally effective methods to instruct children in the ways of society.

Latency

Erikson agreed with Freud that school age is a period of psychosexual **latency.** Sexual latency is important because it allows children to divert their energies to learning the technology of their culture and the strategies of their social interactions. As children work and play hard to acquire these essentials, they begin to form a picture of themselves as competent or incompetent. These self images are the origin of *ego identity*—that feeling of "I" or "me-ness" that evolves more fully during adolescence.

Industry vs. Inferiority

If school age is a period of little *sexual* development, then it is a time of tremendous *social* growth. The psychosocial crisis of this stage is industry vs. inferiority. *Industry*, a syntonic quality, means industriousness, a willingness to remain busy with something and to finish a job. School age children learn to work and play at activities directed both toward acquiring job skills and toward learning the rules of cooperation.

As children learn to make and do things well, they develop a sense of industry, but if their work is insufficient to accomplish their goals, they acquire a sense of *inferiority*—the dystonic quality of the school age. Earlier inadequacies can also contribute to children's feelings of inferiority. For example, if children acquire too much guilt and too little purpose during the play age, they will likely feel inferior and incompetent during the school age. However, failure is not inevitable. Erikson was optimistic in suggesting that people can successfully handle the crisis of any given stage even though they were not completely successful in previous stages.

The ratio between industry and inferiority should, of course, favor industry, but inferiority, like the other dystonic qualities, should not be avoided. As Alfred Adler (Chapter 4) pointed out, inferiority can serve as an impetus to do one's best. Conversely, an oversupply of inferiority can block productive activity and stunt one's feelings of competence.

Competence: The Basic Strength of the School Age

From the conflict of industry vs. inferiority, school-age children develop the basic strength of *competence*. Erikson (1968) defined competence as "the free exercise of dexterity and intelligence in the completion of serious tasks unimpaired by an infantile sense of inferiority" (p. 126). Competence lays the foundation for "co-operative participation in productive adult life" (p. 126).

If the struggle between industry and inferiority favors either inferiority or an over-abundance of industry, children are likely to give up and regress to an earlier stage of development. They may become preoccupied with infantile genital and Oedipal fantasies and spend most of their time in nonproductive play. This regression is called *inertia*, which is the antipathy of competence and represents the core pathology of the school age.

ADOLESCENCE

Adolescence, the period from puberty to young adulthood, is one of the most crucial developmental stages because, by the end of this period, a person must gain a firm sense of *ego identity*. Although ego identity neither begins nor ends during adolescence, the crisis between *identity* and *identity confusion* reaches its ascendance during this stage. From this crisis of identity vs. identity confusion emerges *fidelity*, the basic strength of adolescence.

Erikson (1982) saw adolescence as a period of *social* latency, just as he saw school age as a time of *sexual* latency. Although adolescents are developing sexually and cognitively, they are allowed to postpone lasting commitment to an occupation, a sex

The late adolescent's search for identity includes a discovery of sexual identity.

partner, or an adaptive philosophy of life. They are permitted to experiment in a variety of ways and to try out new roles and beliefs while seeking to establish a sense of ego identity. Adolescence, then, is an adaptive phase of personality development, a period of trial and error.

Puberty

The principal psychosexual mode of the adolescent stage is *puberty*, defined by Erikson (1968) as genital maturation. Actually, puberty itself plays a relatively minor role in Erikson's concept of adolescence. For most young people, genital maturation presents no major sexual crisis. Nevertheless, puberty is important psychologically because it triggers expectations of adult roles yet ahead—roles that are essentially social and can be filled only through a struggle to attain a sense of ego identity.

In Freudian theory, puberty ushers in the genital period, but Freud was not specific in describing the psychosocial conflicts of this, the final stage of his developmental theory. Erikson, on the other hand, devoted much attention to youths' quest for identity and their establishment of a stable system of beliefs.

Identity vs. Identity Confusion

The search for ego *identity* reaches a climax during adolescence as young people strive to find out who they are and who they are not. With the advent of puberty, adolescents look for new roles to help them discover their sexual, ideological, and occupational identities. In this search, young people draw from a variety of earlier self-images that have been accepted or rejected. Thus, the seeds of identity begin to sprout during infancy and continue to grow through childhood, the play age, and the school age. But during adolescence, identity strengthens into a crisis as young people learn to cope with the psychosocial conflict of identity vs. identity confusion.

The word "crisis" should not suggest a threat or catastrophe but rather "a turning point, a crucial period of increased vulnerability and heightened potential" (Erikson,

1968, p. 96). An identity crisis may last for many years and can result in either greater or lesser ego strength.

According to Erikson (1982), identity emerges from two sources: (1) adolescents' affirmation or repudiation of childhood identifications and (2) their historical and social contexts, which encourage conformity to certain standards. Young people frequently reject the standards of their elders, preferring instead the values of a peer group or gang. In any event, the society in which they live plays a substantial role in shaping their identity.

Identity is defined both positively and negatively, as adolescents are deciding what they want to become and what they believe. But they are also finding out what they *do not* wish to be and what they *do not* believe. Often they must either repudiate the values of parents or reject those of the peer group, a dilemma that may intensify their *identity confusion*.

Identity confusion is a syndrome of problems that includes a divided self-image, an inability to establish intimacy, a sense of time urgency, a lack of concentration on required tasks, and a rejection of family or community standards (Erikson, 1968, 1980). As with the other dystonic tendencies, some amount of identity confusion is both normal and necessary. Young people must experience some doubt and confusion about who they are before they can evolve a stable identity. They may leave home (as Erikson did) to wander alone in search of self; experiment with drugs and sex; identify with a street gang; join a religious order; or rail against the existing society, with no alternative answers. Or they may simply and quietly consider where they fit into the world and what values they hold dear.

Although identity confusion is a necessary part of one's search for identity, too much confusion can lead to pathological adjustment in the form of regression to earlier stages of development. The responsibilities of adulthood are thus postponed for years as a person drifts aimlessly from one job to another, from one sex partner to another, or from one ideology to another. Conversely, the proper ratio of identity to identity confusion results in (1) a *faith* in some sort of ideological principle, (2) the ability to freely decide how one should behave, (3) a trust in peers and adults who give advice regarding goals and aspirations, and (4) an eventual choice of occupation.

Fidelity: The Basic Strength of Adolescence

The basic strength emerging from the identity crises of adolescence is *fidelity*, that is, faith in some ideological view or vision of the future (Erikson, 1975). With the establishment of internal standards of conduct, adolescents are no longer in need of parental guidance, and they can now have confidence that their religious, political, and social ideologies will provide a consistent standard of conduct.

The trust learned in infancy is basic for fidelity in adolescence. Young people must learn to trust others before they can have faith in their own view of the future. They must have developed hope during infancy, and they must follow hope with the other basic strengths—will, purpose, and competence. Each is a prerequisite for fidelity, just as fidelity is required for the acquisition of subsequent ego strengths.

The pathological counterpart of fidelity is **role repudiation,** or the inability to synthesize various self-images and values into a workable identity. Role repudiation can take the form of either diffidence or defiance (Erikson, 1982). D*iffidence* is an extreme lack of self-trust or self-confidence and is expressed as shyness or hesitancy to express oneself. D*efiance,* on the other hand, is the open act of rebelling against authority. Defiant adolescents stubbornly hold to socially unacceptable beliefs and practices simply because these beliefs and practices are unacceptable. Some amount of role repudiation, Erikson believed, is necessary, not only for the formation of personal identity, but also for the injection of new ideas and new vitality into the social structure.

YOUNG ADULTHOOD

The search for identity that adolescents experience is indispensable to **young adulthood,** a time from about age 19 to 30 for most people. During adolescence, people must acquire a solid sense of who they are in order to be able to fuse their identity with the identity of another person, a necessary condition for young adulthood.

The period of young adulthood is circumscribed not so much by time as by the acquisition of *intimacy* at the beginning of the stage and the development of *generativity* at the end. For some people, this is a relatively short time, lasting perhaps only a few years. For others, young adulthood may continue for several decades. Young adults should develop mature *genitality*, experience the conflict between *intimacy* and *isolation*, and acquire the basic strength of *love*.

Genitality

Much of the sexual activity during adolescence is an expression of one's search for identity and is basically self-serving. True **genitality** can develop only during young adulthood when it is characterized by mutual trust and a more or less permanent sharing of sexual satisfactions with a loved person. It represents the chief psychosexual accomplishment of young adulthood and can be found only in an intimate relationship in which the two partners neither compulsively obey nor sadistically dominate one another (Erikson, 1963).

Intimacy vs. Isolation

Young adulthood is marked by the psychosocial crisis of intimacy vs. isolation. **Intimacy** is the ability to fuse one's identity with that of another person without fear of losing it. Because intimacy can only be achieved after people have formed a stable ego, the infatuations that often characterize young adolescence are not true intimacy. People who are unsure of their identity may either shy away from psychosocial intimacy or desperately seek intimacy through meaningless sexual encounters.

In contrast, mature intimacy means an ability and willingness to share a mutual trust. It involves sacrifice, compromise, and commitment within a relationship of two equals. It should be a requirement for marriage, but many marriages lack intimacy because some young people marry as part of their search for the identity that they failed to establish during adolescence.

The psychosocial counterpart to intimacy is **isolation,** which Erikson (1968) defined as "the incapacity to take chances with one's identity by sharing true intimacy" (p. 137). Some people become financially or socially successful, yet retain a deep sense of isolation because they are unable to accept the adult responsibilities of productive work, procreation, and mature love.

Again, some degree of isolation is essential before one can acquire mature love. Too much togetherness can diminish one's sense of ego identity, which leads a person to a psychosocial regression and an inability to face the next developmental stage. The greater danger, of course, is too much isolation, too little intimacy, and a deficiency in the basic strength of love.

Love: The Basic Strength of Young Adulthood

Love, the basic strength of young adulthood, emerges from the crisis of intimacy vs. isolation. Erikson (1968, 1982) defined love as mature devotion that overcomes basic differences between males and females. Although love includes intimacy, it also contains some degree of isolation, because each partner is permitted to retain a separate identity. Mature love means commitment, sexual passion, cooperation, competition, and friendship. It is the basic strength of young adulthood, enabling a person to cope productively with the final two stages of development.

The antipathy of love is *exclusivity*, the core pathology of young adulthood. Some exclusivity, however, is necessary for intimacy; that is, a person must be able to exclude certain people, activities, and ideas in order to develop a strong sense of identity. Exclusivity becomes pathological when it blocks one's ability to cooperate, compete, or compromise, all prerequisite ingredients for intimacy and love.

ADULTHOOD

The seventh stage of development is **adulthood,** that time when people begin to take their place in society and assume responsibility for whatever society produces. For most people, this is perhaps the longest stage of development, spanning the years from about age 31 to 60. Adulthood is characterized by the psychosexual mode of **procreativity,** the psychosocial crisis of *generativity vs. stagnation*, and the basic strength of *care*.

Procreativity

Erikson's psychosexual theory assumes an instinctual drive to perpetuate the species. This drive is the counterpart of an adult animal's instinct toward procreation and is an extension of the genitality that marks young adulthood (Erikson, 1982). However, **procreativity** refers to more than genital contact with an intimate partner. It includes assuming responsibility for the care of offspring that result from that sexual contact. Ideally, procreation should follow from the mature intimacy and love established during the preceding stage. Obviously, people are physically capable of producing offspring before they are psychologically ready to care for the welfare of these children. Intimacy alone is not sufficient for mature adulthood. Two people can be intimate yet, as a pair, remain isolated from society at large.

Mature adulthood demands more than procreating offspring; it includes caring for one's children as well as other people's children. In addition, it encompasses working productively to transmit culture from one generation to the next.

Generativity vs. Stagnation

The syntonic quality of adulthood is *generativity*, defined as "the generation of new beings as well as new products and new ideas" (Erikson, 1982, p. 67). Generativity, which is concerned with establishing and guiding the next generation, includes the procreation of children, the production of work, and the creation of new things and ideas that contribute to the building of a better world.

People have a need not only to learn but also to teach and to instruct. This need extends beyond one's own children to an altruistic concern for other young people. Generativity grows out of earlier syntonic qualities such as intimacy and identity. As we have seen, intimacy calls for the ability to fuse one's ego to that of another person without fear of losing it. This unity of ego identities leads to a gradual expansion of interests. One-to-one intimacy is no longer enough. Other people, especially children, become part of one's concern. Instructing others in the ways of culture is a drive found in all societies. For the mature adult, this is not merely an obligation or a selfish need, but an evolutionary drive to make a contribution to succeeding generations and to ensure the continuity of human society as well.

The antithesis of generativity is *self-absorption and stagnation*. The generational cycle of productivity and creativity is crippled when people become too absorbed in themselves, too self-indulgent. Such an attitude fosters a pervading sense of stagnation. Some elements of stagnation and self-absorption, however, are necessary. Creative people must, at times, remain in a dormant stage and be absorbed with themselves in order to eventually generate new growth. The interaction of generativity and stagnation produces care, the basic strength of adulthood.

Care: The Basic Strength of Adulthood

Erikson (1982) defined **care** as "a widening commitment to *take care of* the persons, the products, and the ideas one has learned to *care for*" (p. 67). As the basic strength of adulthood, care arises from each earlier basic ego strengths. One must have hope, will, purpose, competence, fidelity, and love in order to take care of that which one cares for. Care is not a duty or obligation but a natural desire emerging from the conflict between generativity and stagnation or self-absorption.

The antipathy of care is *rejectivity*, the core pathology of adulthood. Rejectivity is the unwillingness to take care of certain persons or groups (Erikson, 1982). It is manifested as self-centeredness, provincialism, or *pseudospeciation*; that is, the belief that other groups of people are, by nature, an inferior species from one's own. It is responsible for much of human hatred, destruction, atrocities, and wars. According to Erikson, rejectivity "has far-reaching implications for the survival of the species as well as for every individual's psychosocial development" (p. 70).

OLD AGE

The eighth and final stage of development is **old age,** that period from about age 60 to the end of life. Old age need not mean that people are no longer generative. Procreation, in the narrow sense of producing children, may be absent, yet old people can remain productive and creative in other ways. They can be caring grandparents, not only to their own grandchildren, but also to other younger members of society. Erikson, in an interview with Elizabeth Hall, said, "I'm convinced that old people and children need one another and that there's an affinity between old age and childhood that, in fact, rounds out the life cycle" (Hall, 1983, p. 24). Old age can be a time of playfulness, joy, and wonder, but it also can be a time of senility, depression, and despair. The psychosexual mode of old age is *generalized sensuality*; the psychosocial crisis is *integrity vs. despair*, and the basic strength is *wisdom*.

Generalized Sensuality

The final psychosexual stage is *generalized sensuality*. Erikson had little to say about this mode of psychosexual life, but one may infer that it means to take pleasure in a variety

Erikson's stages of development extend into old age.

of different physical sensations—sights, sounds, tastes, odors, embraces, and perhaps genital stimulation. Generalized sensuality may also include a greater appreciation for the traditional lifestyle of the opposite sex. Men become more nurturant and more acceptant of the pleasures of nonsexual relationships, including those with their grand-children and great-grandchildren. Women become more interested and involved in pol-itics, finance, and world affairs (Erikson, Erikson, & Kivnick, 1986). A generalized sen-sual attitude, however, is dependent on one's ability to hold things together, that is, to maintain integrity in the face of despair.

Integrity vs. Despair

A person's final identity crisis is *integrity vs. despair.* At the end of life, the dystonic qual-ity of despair may prevail, but for people with a strong ego identity who have learned intimacy and who have taken care of both people and things, the syntonic quality of integrity will predominate. Integrity means a feeling of wholeness and coherence, an ability to hold together one's sense of "I-ness" despite diminishing physical and intel-lectual powers.

Ego integrity is sometimes difficult to maintain when people see that they are losing familiar aspects of their existence, for example, spouse, friends, physical health, body strength, mental alertness, independence, and social usefulness. Under such pressure, people often feel a pervading sense of despair, which they may express as dis-gust, depression, contempt for others, or any other attitude that reveals a nonaccep-tance of the finite boundaries of life.

Despair literally means to be without hope. A reexamination of Figure 9.2 reveals that despair, the last dystonic quality of the life cycle, is in the opposite corner from hope, a person's first basic strength. From infancy to old age, there is always hope. Once hope is lost, despair follows and life ceases to have meaning.

Wisdom: The Basic Strength of Old Age

Some amount of despair is natural and necessary for psychological maturity. The inevitable struggle between integrity and despair produces *wisdom*, the basic strength of old age. Erikson (1982) defined wisdom as "informed and detached concern with life itself in the face of death itself" (p. 61). People with detached concern do not lack concern; rather, they exhibit an active but dispassionate interest. With mature wisdom, they maintain their integrity in spite of declining physical and mental abilities. Wisdom draws from and contributes to the traditional knowledge passed from generation to generation. In old age, people are concerned with ultimate issues, including nonexistence (Erikson, Erikson, & Kivnick, 1986).

The antithesis of wisdom and the core pathology of old age is *disdain*, which Erikson (1982, p. 61) defined as "a reaction to feeling (and seeing others) in an increasing state of being finished, confused, helpless." Disdain is a continuation of rejectivity, the core pathology of adulthood. It means to reject with aloof contempt and is a natural reaction to human depravity, deceit, and weakness.

SUMMARY OF THE LIFE CYCLE

Erikson's cycle of life is summarized in Table 9.1. Each of the eight stages is characterized by a psychosexual mode as well as a psychosocial crisis. The psychosocial crisis is stimulated by a conflict between the predominating syntonic element and its antithetical dystonic element. From this conflict emerges a basic strength, or ego quality. Each basic strength has an underlying antipathy that becomes the core pathology of that stage. Humans have an ever-increasing radius of significant relations, beginning with the maternal person in infancy and ending with an identification with all humanity during old age.

Personality always develops during a particular historical period and within a given society. Nevertheless, the eight developmental stages transcend chronology and geography and are appropriate to nearly all cultures, past or present.

ERIKSON'S METHODS OF INVESTIGATION

Erikson insisted that personality is a product of history, culture, and biology, and his diverse methods of investigation reflect this belief. He employed anthropological, historical, sociological, and clinical methods to learn about children, adolescents, mature adults, and elderly people. He studied middle-class Americans, European children, the Sioux and Yurok nations of North America, and even sailors on a submarine. He wrote biographical portraits of Adolf Hitler, Maxim Gorky, Martin Luther, and Mohandas K. Gandhi, among others. In this section, we look at three approaches Erikson used to explain and describe human personality—anthropological studies, psychohistory, and play construction.

ANTHROPOLOGICAL STUDIES

In 1937, Erikson made a field trip to the Pine Ridge Indian Reservation in South Dakota to investigate the causes of apathy among Sioux children. Erikson (1963) reported on early Sioux training in terms of his newly evolving theories of psychosexual and psychosocial development. He found that apathy was an expression of an extreme dependency the Sioux had developed as a result of their reliance on various federal programs. At one time, they had been courageous buffalo hunters, but by 1937, the Sioux had lost

Table 9.1 Erikson's Eight Stages of the Life Cycle

Stages	A Psychosexual Stages and Modes	B Psychosocial Crises	C Radius of Significant Relations	D Basic Strengths	E Core Pathology, Basic Antipathies	F Related Principles of Social Order	G Binding Ritualizations	H Ritualism
I Infancy	Oral-respiratory, sensory-kinesthetic (incorporative modes)	Basic trust vs. basic mistrust	Maternal person	Hope	Withdrawal	Cosmic order	Numinous	Idolism
II Early childhood	Anal-urethral-muscular (retentive-eliminative)	Autonomy vs. shame, doubt	Parental persons	Will	Compulsion	"Law and order"	Judicious	Legalism
III Play age	Infantile genital-locomotor (intrusive, inclusive)	Initiative vs. guilt	Basic family	Purpose	Inhibition	Ideal prototypes	Dramatic	Moralism
IV School age	"Latency"	Industry vs. inferiority	"Neighborhood," school	Competence	Inertia	Technological order	Formal (technical)	Formalism
V Adolescence	Puberty	Identity vs. identity confusion	Peer groups and outgroups: models of leadership	Fidelity	Repudiation	Ideological worldview	Ideological	Totalism
VI Young adulthood	Genitality	Intimacy vs. isolation	Partners in friendship, sex, competition, and cooperation	Love	Exclusivity	Patterns of cooperation and competition	Affiliative	Elitism
VII Adulthood	Procreativity	Generativity vs. stagnation	Divided labor and shared household	Care	Rejectivity	Currents of education and tradition	Generational	Authoritism
VIII Old age	(Generalization of sensual modes)	Integrity vs. despair	"Mankind," "My kind"	Wisdom	Disdain	Wisdom	Philosophical	Dogmatism

From *The Life Cycle Completed: A Review* by Erik H. Erikson. Copyright © 1982 by Rikan Enterprises, Ltd. Reprinted by permission of W. W. Norton & Company, Inc.

their group identity as hunters and were trying half-heartedly to scrape out a living as farmers. Child-rearing practices, which in the past had trained young boys to be hunters and young girls to be helpers and mothers of future hunters, were no longer appropriate for an agrarian society. As a consequence, the Sioux children of 1937 had great difficulty achieving a sense of ego identity, especially after they reached adolescence.

Two years later, Erikson made a similar field trip to northern California to study people of the Yurok nation, who lived mostly on salmon fishing. Although the Sioux and Yurok had vastly divergent cultures, each tribe had a tradition of training its youth in the virtues of its society. Yurok people were trained to catch fish, and therefore they possessed no strong national feeling and had little taste for war. Obtaining and retaining provisions and possessions were highly valued among people of the Yurok nation.

According to Erikson, Mahatma Gandhi developed basic strengths from his several identity crises.

Erikson (1963) was able to show that early childhood training was consistent with this strong cultural value and that history and society helped shape personality.

PSYCHOHISTORY

During this century, a relatively new discipline called psychohistory has evolved that combines psychoanalytic concepts with historical methods. Freud (1910/1957) originated psychohistory with an investigation of Leonardo da Vinci and later collaborated with American Ambassador William Bullitt to write a book-length psychological study of President Woodrow Wilson (Freud & Bullitt, 1967). Although Erikson (1975) deplored this latter work, he took up the methods of psychohistory and refined them, especially in his study of Martin Luther (Erikson, 1958, 1975) and Mahatma Gandhi (Erikson, 1969, 1975).

Erikson (1974) defined psychohistory as "the study of individual and collective life with the combined methods of psychoanalysis and history" (p. 13). He used psychohistory to demonstrate his fundamental belief that each person is a product of his or her historical time. Psychohistory differs from a case history in that it is more likely to deal with a person who is able to maintain ego identity and integrity in the face of neurotic conflict. In contrast, case histories often depict neurotic individuals who are unable to maintain integrity.

As an author of psychohistory, Erikson believed that he should be emotionally involved in his subject. For example, he developed a strong emotional attachment to Gandhi, which he attributed to his own lifelong search for the father he had never seen

(Erikson, 1975). In *Gandhi's Truth*, Erikson (1969) revealed strong positive feelings for Gandhi as he attempted to answer the question of how healthy individuals such as Gandhi work through conflict and crisis when other people are debilitated by lesser strife. In searching for an answer, Erikson examined Gandhi's entire life cycle but concentrated on one particular crisis, which climaxed when a middle-aged Gandhi first used self-imposed fasting as a political weapon.

As a child, Gandhi was close to his mother but experienced conflict with his father. Rather than viewing this situation as an Oedipal conflict, Erikson saw it as Gandhi's opportunity to work out conflict with authority figures—an opportunity Gandhi was to have many times during his life.

Gandhi was born October 2, 1869, in Porbandar, India. As a young man, he studied law in London and was inconspicuous in manner and appearance. Then, dressed like a proper British subject, he returned to India to practice law. After 2 years of unsuccessful practice, he went to South Africa, another British colony. He intended to remain for a year, but his first serious identity crisis kept him there for more than 20 years.

A week after a judge excluded him from a courtroom, Gandhi was thrown off a train when he refused to give up his seat to a "white" man. These two experiences with racial prejudice changed Gandhi's life. By the time he resolved this identity crisis, his appearance had changed dramatically. No longer attired in silk hat and black coat, he dressed in the cotton loincloth and shawl that were to become familiar to millions of people throughout the world. During those years in South Africa, he evolved the technique of passive resistance known as *Satyagraha* and used it to solve his conflicts with authorities.

After returning to India, Gandhi experienced another identity crisis when, in 1918, at age 49, he became the central figure in a workers' strike against the mill owners at Ahmedabad. Erikson referred to the events surrounding the strike as "The Event," and devoted the core of *Gandhi's Truth* to this crisis. Although this strike was only a minor event in the history of India and received only scant attention in Gandhi's autobiography, Erikson (1969) saw it as having a great impact on Gandhi's identity as a practitioner of militant nonviolence.

The mill workers had pledged to strike if their demands for a 35% pay increase were not met. But the owners, who had agreed among themselves to offer no more than a 20% increase, locked out the workers and tried to break their solidarity by offering the 20% increase to those who would come back to work. Gandhi, the workers' spokesman, agonized over this impasse. Then, somewhat impetuously, he pledged to eat no more food until the workers' demands were met. This, the first of his 17 "fasts to the death," was not undertaken as a threat to the mill owners, but to demonstrate to the workers that a pledge must be kept. In fact, Gandhi feared that the mill owners might surrender out of sympathy for him rather than from recognition of the worker's desperate plight. Indeed, on the third day, the workers and owners reached a compromise that allowed both to save face—the workers would work one day for a 35% increase, one day for a 20% increase, and then for whatever amount an arbitrator decided. The next day Gandhi ended his hunger strike, but his passive resistance had helped shape his identity and had given him a new tool for peaceful political and social change.

Unlike neurotic individuals whose identity crises result in core pathologies, Gandhi had developed strength from this and other crises. Erikson (1969) described the difference between conflicts in great people, such as Gandhi, and psychologically disturbed people: "This, then, is the difference between a case history and a life-history: patients, great or small, are increasingly debilitated by their inner conflicts, but in historical actuality inner conflict only adds an indispensable momentum to all superhuman effort" (p. 363).

PLAY CONSTRUCTION

From his clinical experiences with children, Erikson developed a projective technique called **play construction.** Although he employed this approach with play-age children (see Erikson, 1977), his most famous and controversial use of play construction involved somewhat older children.

Three times over a 2-year period, Erikson asked 10- to 12-year-old boys and girls to imagine that they were movie directors and to construct an exciting scene from a movie, using a random selection of available toys. The toys included people, animals, furniture, cars, blocks, and other assorted objects. Interestingly, very few participants actually recreated an exact movie scene or named their dolls after real movie stars. Erikson (1963) believed that the stories the children told about the scenes, as well as the scenes themselves, were an unconscious expression of their life history.

Erikson looked for both common and unique elements in play construction. To test for reliability and objectivity, he asked two independent observers to make judgments based on photographs of the completed scenes. The most significant and controversial common element noted was a difference between girls and boys in the way they arranged their scenes. The two sexes used space differently, with girls tending to construct interior scenes and boys, exterior ones. Girls used more furniture, people, and domesticated animals to construct peaceful scenes, whereas boys more often selected blocks, cars, and wild animals to build scenes dominated by height, downfall, and motion. The arrangements of girls were simple, static, and low; those of boys were complex, action-oriented, and tall or elongated. Girls frequently constructed circular enclosures with low doors and gates that might be either open or closed. In contrast, boys usually built tall towers and included action themes such as rising and falling.

Erikson (1963, 1968) suggested that these differences were at least partially due to anatomical differences between the sexes. He pointed out that play constructions "closely parallel the morphology of the sex organs; in the male, *external* organs, *erectable* and *intrusive* in character, *conducting* highly *mobile* sperm cells; *internal* organs in the female, with a vestibular *access* leading to *statically expectant* ova" (Erikson, 1963, p. 106).

Such an interpretation has not gone uncriticized. Some critics (see Janeway, 1971) have accused Erikson of sexism, pointing out that socialization practices might easily explain these differences. Erikson (1975) accepted the argument that social influences might account for some of the differences, but he insisted that anatomy is the principal source of gender differences in play constructions. Does this mean that Erikson agreed with Freud that anatomy is destiny? Erikson's answer was yes, anatomy is destiny, but he quickly qualified that dictum to read: "Anatomy, history, and personality are our combined destiny" (Erikson, 1968, p. 285). In other words, anatomy alone does not determine destiny, but it combines with past events, including socialization practices and various personality dimensions such as temperament and intelligence, to determine who a person will become. "Destiny, for both men and women, depends on what you can make of the fact that you have a specific kind of body in a particular historical setting " (Erikson, 1974, p. 116).

RELATED RESEARCH

In recent years, Erikson's psychosocial stage theory has sparked more empirical interest than any of the other psychoanalytically oriented theories. In particular, Erikson's ideas concerning identity in adolescence and generativity in adulthood have received much attention from researchers. One of Erikson's major contributions was to extend the idea of development into adulthood. By expanding Freud's notion of development all the way into old age, Erikson challenged the idea that psychological development stops with adolescence.

IDENTITY IN ADOLESCENCE AND EARLY ADULTHOOD

One boost to research on Erikson's theory has been the development of reliable and valid measures of psychosocial development. Perhaps the best known researcher on ego identity status has been James Marcia (1966, 1976, 1980, 1987, 1994). Marcia's identity status interview is typically used with adolescents and young adults and measures both commitment and crisis in the areas of (1) occupation, (2) religion, and (3) politics. Since Marcia's early work, Doreen Rosenthal and her colleagues (Rosenthal, Gurney, & Moore, 1981) created the Erikson Psychosocial Stage Inventory (EPSI), a 72-item self-report inventory that measures how completely people have resolved each of their first six psychosocial conflicts. That is, the EPSI assesses a person's level of trust, autonomy, initiative, industry, identity, and intimacy. Resolution of each of these six stages is measured by 12 items rated on a 1- to 5-point scale from "hardly ever true" to "almost always true."

The EPSI has been used to investigate hypotheses suggested by several of Erikson's developmental stages, including how identity relates to intimacy in friendships, and how it develops in males and females, in delinquents, and in young adults who, while infants, received varying amounts of child care away from their mothers.

Susan Moore and Jenifer Boldero (1991) looked at how identity relates to intimacy in adolescence and found that those with a relatively resolved sense of identity tended to have deeper, richer, and more satisfying relationships than adolescents with unresolved identities. Similarly, Steven Mellor (1989) reported that junior high and high school students who had a relatively solid sense of identity were more likely to describe their relationships as "connected" rather than "separate." Recall that Erikson believed that identity versus identity confusion was the central conflict of adolescents and that the outcome of this conflict had repercussions for other psychosocial tasks. If this assumption is valid, argued D. M. Arehart and P. Hull Smith (1990), then troubled adolescents should have less consolidated identities than a comparison group of adolescents. Using the EPSI, Arehart and Smith collected identity data on young delinquents in detention centers and on a comparison group of high school juniors. As predicted, delinquent youths had lower scores on the identity scale than nondelinquent youths. Furthermore, in a second sample, Arehart and Smith found that students with less developed identity scores also tended to have lower self-esteem and that college freshmen had more identity confusion than did high school seniors. This latter finding is not surprising, because going to college is the first time many young people have lived on their own and have been away from their parents. By comparison, high school is much more closely connected to the stability of one's childhood and adolescence.

Another way of looking at identity is to consider the effects of early childhood experience, namely child care. Given the current pervasiveness of child care and the increased time that infants are spending away from their parents, the question arises: Do infants and toddlers who spend the most time away from their parents and in child care have the most difficulty forming identities in late adolescence and early adulthood? Johnetta Morrison, Jean Ispa, and Kathy Thornburg (1994) examined this question in a sample of nearly 300 African American college students. The researchers asked the participants to report who took care of them when they were 2 and 4 years old. Full-time child care was defined as care by a nonparent more than 20 hours per week, whereas part-time care was defined as 1 to 20 hours per week. Each participant also completed the EPSI. Results showed that college students who reported either full-time child care or no child care had significantly higher scores on the identity scale of the EPSI than those who reported part-time child care. Moreover, participants who had full-time child care were more self-confident than those who had no or part-time child care. These results seem to indicate that full-time child care does not retard later identity development and self-confidence and may even enhance them.

GENERATIVITY IN ADULTHOOD AND OLD AGE

Erikson originally defined generativity as "the concern in establishing and guiding the next generation" (1963, p. 267) but later as "the generation of new beings as well as new products and new ideas" (1982, p. 67). This second definition makes clear that generativity does not have to be expressed solely in terms of having children or teaching, but also can be exhibited through the creation of products and ideas. Both these aspects of generativity have been investigated and tested empirically.

Dan McAdams and Ed de St. Aubin (1992) developed the Loyola Generativity Scale (LGS) to tap into different aspects of generativity, the syntonic element of adulthood. The LGS includes such items as "I have important skills that I try to teach others" and "I do not volunteer to work for a charity." The scale measures several aspects of generativity, including *concern* for the next generation; generative *action* in creating, maintaining, and offering up; and personal *narration*, or the subjective story or theme that an adult creates about providing for the next generation. Using adults 15 to 74 years of age, McAdams and de St. Aubin found that *concern* was related to both *action* and *narration*, suggesting that people who are concerned for the next generation tend to transform that concern into action and to have a dominant and recurrent theme of generativity that runs throughout their lives.

To examine Erikson's idea that generativity should peak in middle adulthood, McAdams, de St. Aubin, and Regina Logan (1993) collected generativity data on three different age groups from the Chicago area: young adult (ages 22–27), midlife adult (ages 37–42), and older adult (67–72). They found partial support for Erikson's idea that generativity should have a **curvilinear relationship** to age. That is, as age increases, generativity increases, but only to old age, when generativity then begins to decrease. McAdams et al. found that this curvilinear relationship appeared only when generativity was measured by narration and not by concern or action. They also found that concern (but not action or narration) was related to overall life satisfaction. Being concerned about the next generation goes together with being happy about one's life.

Bill Peterson and Abigal Stewart (1993) investigated whether generativity was related to a person's need to achieve, to have power, and to affiliate and be intimate with others. Peterson and Stewart had a broader measure of generativity than McAdams et al., because it included not only "number of children," "parenting involvement," and "societal concern," but "personal productivity" as well. Personal productivity was measured by items such as having a sense of accomplishment, doing something important, being really good at something, achieving something on one's own, and feeling successful. Peterson and Stewart looked at young adults and found differences between men and women. For women, being childless and having a high need to achieve predicted high scores on personal productivity, whereas for men, being driven by power and having children predicted high scores on personal productivity. For women, having a strong need to affiliate with others and being driven by power predicted parenting involvement, whereas for men, parenting involvement is related to strong needs for affiliation and achievement. Finally, other researchers have reported that generativity is positively related to having a sense of humor and using humor to cope with stressful situations (Hampes, 1993), and for men, generativity is related positively to self-esteem but not to caregiving (Bailey, 1992).

In summary, research on Erikson's developmental stages suggests that identity development plays an important role in friendship intimacy, delinquency, self-esteem, and self-confidence. Furthermore, being raised by one's own parent and another caregiver appears to have positive rather than negative effects on identity. Specifically, college students who experienced full-time child care had a stronger sense of identity and were more self-confident in late adolescence and early adulthood. As Erikson predicted, generativity appears to peak in middle age and decline thereafter. However, Erikson failed to predict that generativity would have a positive relation with life satisfaction, self-esteem, humor, and needs for power and achievement, or that gender differences would moderate some of these relationships.

CRITIQUE OF ERIKSON

Erikson's work is widely recognized in both professional and popular circles, and the eight stages of human development are frequently cited in the scientific literature as well as in the popular press. His popularity, in part, is due to his decision to extend Freud's theories rather than to attack them. Many observers have seen Erikson's work as a continuation of what Freud might have done had he lived another 50 years.

Erikson built his theory largely on ethical principles and not necessarily on scientific data. He came to psychology from art and acknowledged that he saw the world more through the eyes of an artist than through those of a scientist. In *Childhood and Society* (1950), he wrote that he had nothing to offer except "a way of looking at things." His books are admittedly subjective and personal, which undoubtedly adds to their appeal. Nevertheless, Erikson's theory must be judged by the standards of science, not ethics or art.

The first criterion of a useful theory is its ability to *generate research*, and by this standard Erikson's theory is rated somewhat higher than average. For example, Marcia (1994) reported that the topic of ego identity alone has generated more than 300 studies. In addition, several other aspects of Erikson's developmental stages, such as intimacy and isolation (Gold & Rogers, 1995) and generativity (Peterson & Stewart, 1993) as well as the entire life cycle (Whitbourne, Zuschlag, Elliot, & Waterman, 1992) are currently being investigated. Despite this active research, Erikson's theory can be rated only average on the criterion of *falsifiability*.

In its ability to *organize knowledge*, Erikson's theory is limited mostly to developmental stages. It does not adequately address such issues as personal traits or motivation, a limitation that subtracts from the theory's ability to shed meaning on much of what is currently known about human personality. The eight stages of development remain an eloquent statement of what the life cycle should be, and research findings in these areas usually can be fit into an Eriksonian framework. However, the theory lacks sufficient scope to be rated high on this criterion.

As a *guide to action*, Erikson's theory provides many general guidelines, but offers little specific advice. Compared to other theories discussed in this book, it ranks near the top in suggesting approaches to dealing with middle-aged and older adults. Erikson's views on aging have been helpful to people in the field of gerontology, and his ideas on ego identity are nearly always cited in adolescent psychology textbooks. In addition, his concepts of intimacy vs. isolation and generativity vs. stagnation have much to offer to marriage counselors and others concerned with intimate relationships among young adults.

Erikson's theory is rated high on *internal consistency*, mostly because the terms used to label the different psychosocial crises, basic strengths, and core pathologies are very carefully chosen. English was not Erikson's first language, and his extensive use of a dictionary while writing increased the precision of his terminology. Yet concepts like hope, will, purpose, love, care, and so on are not operationally defined. They have little scientific usefulness, although they rank high in both literary and emotional value. On the other hand, Erikson's epigenetic principle and the eloquence of his description of the eight stages of development mark his theory with conspicuous internal consistency.

On the criterion of simplicity, or *parsimony*, the theory has only a moderate rating. The precision of its terms is a strength, but the descriptions of psychosexual stages and psychosocial crises, especially in the later stages, are not always clearly differentiated. In addition, Erikson used different terms and even different concepts to fill out the 64 boxes (see Figure 9.2) that constitute his developmental theory. Such inconsistency subtracts from the theory's simplicity.

CONCEPT OF HUMANITY

How did Erikson conceptualize humanity in terms of the six dimensions we introduced in Chapter 1? First, is the life cycle determined by *external forces* or do people have some *choice* in molding their personalities and shaping their lives? Erikson was not as deterministic as Freud, but neither did he believe strongly in free choice. His position was somewhere in the middle. Although our destiny lies with anatomy, history, and personality, we retain some limited control over both history and personality, giving us some measure of choice. We can search for our own identities and are not completely constrained by history or society. Individuals, in fact, can change history and alter their environment. The two subjects of Erikson's most extensive psychohistories, Luther and Gandhi, each had a profound effect on world history and on his own immediate surroundings. Similarly, each of us has the power to determine our own life cycles, even though our global impact may be on a lesser scale.

On the dimension of *pessimism vs. optimism*, Erikson tended to be somewhat optimistic. If core pathologies predominate our early stages of development, we are not inevitably doomed to continue a pathological existence in later stages. Although weaknesses in early life make it more difficult for us to acquire basic strengths later on, we remain capable of changing at any stage of life. Each psychosocial conflict consists of a syntonic and a dystonic quality. Each crisis can be resolved in favor of the harmonious element, regardless of past resolutions.

Erikson did not specifically address the issue of *causality vs. teleology*, but his view of humanity suggests that we are influenced more by biological and social forces than by our view of the future. We are a product of a particular historical moment and a specific social setting. Although we can set goals and actively strive to achieve these goals, we cannot completely escape the powerful causal forces of anatomy, history, and sociology. For this reason, Erikson rates high on causality.

On the fourth dimension, *conscious vs. unconscious determinants*, Erikson's position is mixed. Prior to adolescence, our personality is largely shaped by unconscious motivation. Psychosexual and psychosocial conflicts during the first four developmental stages occur before we have firmly established our identity. We seldom are clearly aware of these crises and the ways in which they mold our personalities. From adolescence forward, however, we ordinarily are aware of our actions and most of the reasons underlying them.

Erikson's theory, of course, is more *social* than biological, although it does not overlook anatomy and other physiological factors in personality development. Each psychosexual mode has a clear biological component. However, as we advance through the eight stages, social influences become increasingly more powerful. Also, the radius of social relations expands from the single maternal person to a global identification with all humanity. Erikson's emphasis on social forces is in sharp contrast to Freud's biological theory. Indeed, Erikson's model is sometimes identified as a social psychoanalytic theory.

The sixth dimension for a concept of humanity is *uniqueness vs. similarities*. Erikson tended to place more emphasis on individual differences than on universal characteristics. Although people in different cultures advance through the eight developmental stages in the same order, myriad differences are found in the pace of that journey. Each of us resolves our psychosocial crises in a unique manner, and each uses the basic strengths in a way that is peculiarly ours.

Chapter Summary

The work of Erik Erikson provides a logical extension of Freud's psychoanalysis. An artist by early training, Erikson offered a "way of looking at things" rather than a theory based on scientifically gathered data. Although he took for granted most of Freud's work, he (1) placed more emphasis on the ego and less on the id, (2) extended the stages of development into adulthood and old age, and (3) elevated social influences over the biologically based instincts.

The eight stages of development rest on an *epigenetic principle*, meaning that each component proceeds in a step-by-step fashion with later growth building on earlier development. In every stage, people face an interaction of opposing attitudes, which leads to a conflict, or *psychosocial crisis*. Resolution of the crisis produces an appropriate *basic strength* and enables a person to move on to the next stage. In addition, *biological components* lay a ground plan for each individual, but a multiplicity of historical, social, and physiological events shape ego identity.

The first stage of development is *infancy*, characterized by the oral-sensory mode of incorporation, the psychosocial crisis of basic trust vs. mistrust, the basic strength of hope, and the core pathology of withdrawal. Infancy covers the first year of life, a time equivalent to Freud's oral stage.

The second stage is called *early childhood* and parallels Freud's anal stage. During early childhood, the anal, urethral, and muscular psychosexual modes are in ascendance and the psychosocial conflict of autonomy vs. shame and doubt produces the basic strength called will or its antipathy, called compulsion.

From about 3 to 5 years of age, a child goes through the *play age*, a time corresponding to Freud's phallic or Oedipal period. A play-age child experiences genital-locomotor psychosexual development and undergoes a psychosocial crisis of initiative vs. guilt. Either the basic strength of purpose or the core pathology of inhibition may emerge from the play age.

Erikson's fourth stage, *school age*, covers the period from about 6 to 11 years of age, and corresponds to Freud's latency stage. A school-age child experiences the psychosocial crisis of industry vs. inferiority, from which arises the basic strength of competence or the core pathology of inertia. The school-age child's radius of significant relations expands beyond the family to include peers and teachers, who serve as models.

Adolescence is a crucial stage in Erikson's theory because one's clear and consistent image of self—ego identity—should emerge from this period. However, identity confusion may dominate the psychosocial crisis, thereby postponing identity. Fidelity is the basic strength of adolescence; role repudiation its core pathology.

Young adulthood, the time from about age 18 to 30, is characterized by genitality, a psychosexual mode that can exist in the absence of intimacy. Ideally, however, intimacy should win out in its conflict with isolation and produce the basic strength of love. If the psychosocial crisis is not completely resolved, the core pathology of exclusivity results.

The seventh and often longest stage is *adulthood*, a time not only of procreation but also of productive work and social commitment. The dominant psychosocial crisis is generativity vs. stagnation, while care is the basic strength and rejectivity a possible core pathology.

The final stage, *old age*, is marked by a generalized sensuality and the crisis of integrity vs. despair. Wisdom, the basic strength of old age, is opposed by disdain, the core pathology.

Erikson's *concept of humanity* is generally optimistic and idealistic. People can overcome early pathologies, but crisis, anxiety, and conflict are a normal and necessary part of living. People cannot be abstracted from society or from the historical period in which they live. Although we are one species, history, culture, and biology lead to individual differences among us.

Erikson's theory has been well received both popularly and professionally. Although not built on an abundance of scientific data, it has sparked a great deal of research and discussion. The theory has an eloquent logic and consistency, but it is only moderately successful in organizing knowledge and providing guidelines to practitioners.

Suggested Readings

Erik Erikson, 91, psychoanalyst who reshaped views of human growth, dies. (1994, May 13). *The New York Times*, p. B9.
> The *New York Times* obituary of Erikson contains highlights of his life, as well as an excellent summary of his life's work.

Erikson, E. H. (1950, 1963, 1985). *Childhood and society*. New York: Norton.
> This is Erikson's first important work, the one that laid the foundation to his post-Freudian theory. It is one of the most popular and frequently recommended psychology books in the United States. Erikson added some afterthoughts in 1985, the 35th anniversary edition.

Erikson, E. H. (1989). Elements of a psychoanalytic theory of psychosocial development. In S. I. Greenspan & G. H. Pollock (Eds.), *The course of life*: Vol. 1. *Infancy* (pp. 15–83). Madison, CT: International Universities Press.
> In this chapter, Erikson presents a summary of his theory of psychosocial development.

Hall, E. (1983, June). A conversation with Erik Erikson. *Psychology Today*, pp. 20–30.
> In this article, Elizabeth Hall, former managing editor of *Psychology Today*, interviewed Erikson at age 81. Erikson talked of the human life cycle, with emphasis on old age.

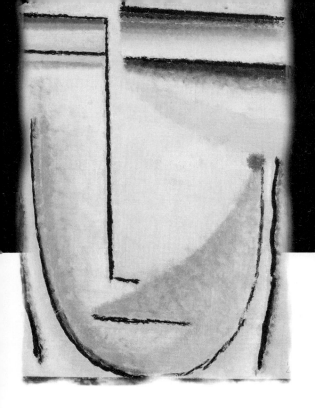

3

Learning Theories

Behavioral Analysis   260

11   *Bandura*
Social Cognitive Theory   296

12   *Rotter and Mischel*
Cognitive Social Learning Theory   327

Skinner

During the early years of the 20th century, while Freud, Jung, Adler, and other psychodynamic theorists were relying on clinical practice to speculate on the nature of human personality, a new approach called **behaviorism** emerged from laboratory studies of animals and humans. As both psychoanalysis and behaviorism gained ascendency during the 1940s and 1950s, some theorists attempted to merge these two popular forces in psychology (see Zuriff, 1995). The most successful of these attempts was that of John Dollard and Neal E. Miller (Dollard & Miller, 1950; Miller & Dollard, 1941). Both Dollard, a sociologist, and Miller, an experimental psychologist, had studied psychoanalysis in Europe before they became colleagues at Yale's Institute of Human Relations during the mid-1930s. Their collaboration resulted in a learning theory explanation of psychodynamic concepts such as aggression, frustration, repression, and the unconscious. Human personality, they believed, was mostly learned, and all learning begins with a drive that stimulates action and cues that guide it. Responses that reduce the drive are reinforced and tend to be learned; those that do not reduce the drive tend to drop out and allow others to appear (Dollard & Miller, 1950).

B. F. Skinner, however, believed that concepts such as drive reduction, cues, frustration, aggressive tendencies, and unconscious motives are nonobservable hypothetical constructs that have no place in a scientific analysis of behavior. Skinner's **behavioral analysis** is a clear departure from the highly speculative psychodynamic theories discussed in previous chapters, as well as from the speculative learning theory of Dollard and Miller. Skinner minimized speculation and focused almost entirely on observable behavior. Although he argued that psychology, as a natural science, must focus on observable phenomena, he did not claim that observable behavior is limited to external events. Instead, he included within the scope of observable behavior such private events as thinking, remembering, and anticipating. Skinner's strict adherence to observable behavior earned his approach the label **radical behaviorism.**

Radical behaviorism insists that the scientific study of human behavior must avoid all hypothetical constructs (such as id, ego, superego, style of life, social interest, archetypes, drives, needs, and so forth) often used by other theorists to explain human personality. To Skinner, behaviors, not fictional constructs, are the basic data of psychological science.

In addition to being a radical behaviorist, Skinner can rightfully be regarded as a determinist and an environmentalist. As a *determinist*, he rejected the notion of volition or free will. Human behavior does not stem from an act of the will, but like any observable phenomenon, it is lawfully determined and can be studied scientifically.

As an *environmentalist*, Skinner held that psychology must not explain behavior on the basis of the physiological or constitutional components of the organism but rather on the basis of environmental stimuli. He recognized that genetic factors are important, but he insisted that, because they are fixed at conception, they are of no help in the control of behavior. The *history* of the individual, rather than anatomy, provides the most useful data for predicting and controlling behavior.

BIOGRAPHY OF B. F. SKINNER

Burrhus Frederic Skinner was born on March 20, 1904, in Susquehanna, Pennsylvania, the first child of William and Grace Madge Burrhus Skinner. His father was a lawyer and an aspiring politician who never quite became successful in politics, but who, nevertheless, earned a comfortable living as an attorney and who had a more successful career than Skinner portrayed in his autobiography (Skinner, 1976, 1979, 1983). Both parents had lived in Susquehanna as children and both had attended high school there. All four grandparents lived in the same town, and young Fred (he was almost never called Burrhus or B. F.) often visited with them after school and on weekends. The family's roots were deeply embedded in Susquehanna, and Skinner grew up in a comfortable, happy, upper-middle-class home where his parents practiced the values of temperance, service, honesty, and hard work. The Skinners were Presbyterian, but Fred began to lose his faith during high school and thereafter never practiced any religion.

When Fred was 2½ years old, a second son, Edward, was born. Fred and Ebbie (as he was known) got along well considering that they did not share many interests and that Fred felt Ebbie was treated more leniently and loved more by both parents. However, Fred did not feel unloved. He was simply more independent and less emotionally attached to his mother and father. But after Ebbie died suddenly of a massive cerebral hemorrhage during Fred's first year at college, the parents became less and less willing to let the older son go. They wanted him to become "the family boy," and indeed succeeded in keeping him financially obligated even after B. F. Skinner became a well-known name in American psychology (Skinner, 1976, 1979). For example, his parents bought him an automobile when he was 28 and 2 years past graduate school, and his father purchased a house for him and his wife when Skinner was 42 and head of the psychology department at Indiana University (Bjork, 1993).

As a child, Skinner was inclined toward music and literature. From an early age, he was interested in writing and wanted to become a professional writer. In addition to artistic interests, he liked to invent and build a variety of gadgets. His ability to build things served him well in his career as a behavior psychologist, enabling him to design and construct much of the equipment used in his experiments.

Skinner attended public school in Susquehanna, where all 12 grades were in the same building, and where his favorite teacher moved with him throughout most of his elementary and high school years. After he finished high school, Skinner and his family moved about 30 miles to Scranton, Pennsylvania. Almost immediately, however, he entered Hamilton College, an all-male liberal arts school in Clinton, New York.

After taking his bachelor's degree in English, Skinner set about to realize his ambition of being a creative writer. When he wrote his father informing him of his wish to spend a year at home working at nothing except writing, his request was met with lukewarm acceptance. Warning his son of the necessity of making a living, William Skinner reluctantly agreed to support him for 1 year on condition that he would get a job if his writing career was not successful. This unenthusiastic reply was followed by a more encouraging letter from Robert Frost, who had read some of Skinner's writings.

Skinner returned to Scranton, built a study in the attic and every morning went to work at writing. But nothing happened. His efforts were unproductive because he had nothing to say and no firm position on any current issue. In his autobiography, Skinner (1976) referred to this period as his "Dark Year." However, Elms (1981, 1994) saw this time as Skinner's first, but not last, major identity crisis.

At the end of this unsuccessful year (actually 18 months), Skinner was faced with the task of looking for a new career. Science beckoned. After reading some of the works of John B. Watson and Ivan Pavlov, Skinner became determined at that early date to be a behaviorist. He never wavered from that determination and threw himself wholeheartedly behind radical behaviorism. Elms (1994) suggested that Skinner's adoption of radical behaviorism helped lift him from the depths of a severe identity crisis. By embracing an extreme ideology, Elms argued, Skinner was able to emerge from his "Dark Year" with a clearly defined identity—that of a radical behaviorist.

Although Skinner had never taken an undergraduate course in psychology, Harvard accepted him as a graduate student in psychology for the fall 1928 term, 2 years after he received his bachelor's degree. At Harvard he quickly became a leader of a small group of graduate students dedicated to behaviorism, and thus solidified his identity as a leading advocate of behaviorism. His zealous identification with radical behaviorism is apparent in a letter he wrote his parents informing them of a colloquium he was to present.

> I am looked upon as the leader of a certain school of psychological theories and this will be a broadside, as it were, into the camp of the enemy in announcing our position for the year. There are two or three "camps" among the faculty and the graduate students, according to the special system of the science which each follows. The behaviorists, whom I represent, have acquired a good deal of strength this year. (Skinner, 1979, p. 48)

When he completed his Ph.D. in 1931, Skinner received a fellowship from the National Research Council to continue his laboratory research at Harvard. Now confident of his identity as a behaviorist, he drew up a plan for himself outlining his goals for the years 1930–1960. The plan also reminded him to adhere closely to behavioristic methodology and not to "surrender to the physiology of the central nervous system" (Skinner, 1979, p. 115). By 1960 Skinner had reached the most important phases of the plan, although he fell short in some specifics.

When his fellowship ended in 1933, he was faced for the first time with the chore of hunting for a permanent job. Positions were scarce during this depression year and prospects looked dim. But soon his worries were alleviated. In the spring of 1933, Harvard created the Society of Fellows, a program designed to promote creative thinking among young intellectually gifted men at the university. Skinner was selected as a Junior Fellow and spent the next 3 years doing more laboratory research.

At the end of his 3-year term as a Junior Fellow, he was again in the position of having to look for a job. Curiously, he knew almost nothing of traditional academic psychology and was not interested in learning about it. He had a Ph.D. in psychology, 5½ years of additional laboratory research, but he was ill-prepared to teach within the mainstream of psychology, having "never even read a text in psychology as a whole" (Skinner, 1979, p. 179).

In 1936, Skinner began a teaching and research position at the University of Minnesota, where he remained for 9 years. Soon after moving to Minneapolis, he married Yvonne Blue following a short and erratic courtship. Skinner and his wife had two daughters—Julie, born in 1938, and Deborah (Debbie), born in 1944. During his Minnesota years, he published his first book, *The Behavior of Organisms* (1938), but beyond that, he was involved with two of his most interesting ventures—the pigeon-guided missile and the baby-tender.

The first adventure occurred during World War II, when Skinner trained pigeons to pilot bombs into enemy ships. Using the principles of positive reinforcement, he taught pigeons to peck at keys that controlled a bomb they were riding. Although these Kamikaze pigeons and their guided missiles never saw battle, Skinner demonstrated in simulated tests that this unique weapon of war could have been successful. Unfortunately, Skinner spent 4 years on this project, 2 of which were full time, before being notified that Project Pigeon was to be scuttled. In his autobiography, Skinner (1979) called this outcome discouraging, but he also claimed that all the preliminary work lifted his experimental analysis to the level of a technology and taught him the practical applications of his earlier work.

Immediately after discarding Project Pigeon, Skinner began work on a second adventure—an enclosed baby crib for his baby daughter Debbie. He constructed a physically and psychologically safe and healthy environment for Debbie, one that would also free his wife and him from unnecessary tedious labor. The crib, or baby tender, had a large sliding window and a heating unit that supplied the baby with fresh warm air. The Skinners frequently removed Debbie from her crib for play, but for most of the day she was alone in her baby-tender.

After *Ladies' Home Journal* published an article in October of 1945 on the baby-tender, Skinner was both condemned and praised for his invention. Interest from other parents persuaded him to market the device, but unfortunately, he experienced many difficulties in securing the necessary patent. Moreover, his association with a business partner who, according to Skinner (1979), was both incompetent and unscrupulous led him to eventually abandon the commercial venture. When Debbie outgrew the baby-tender at age 2½, the crib unceremoniously became a home for some of Skinner's pigeons.

The disappointments and frustrations with the baby-tender and especially the missile project led to what Elms (1981, 1994) has referred to as Skinner's midlife crisis. Furthermore, when he left Minnesota in 1945 to become chairman of the psychology department at Indiana University, the move was not without added frustrations. His wife had ambivalent feelings about leaving friends, his administrative duties proved irksome, and he still felt out of the mainstream of scientific psychology. However, his personal crisis was soon to end, and his professional career would take another turn.

In the summer of 1945, while on vacation, Skinner wrote *Walden Two*, a utopian novel that portrayed a society in which problems were solved through behavioral engineering. Although not published until 1948, the book provided its author with immediate therapy in the form of an emotional catharsis. At last Skinner had done what he failed to accomplish during his Dark Year nearly 20 years earlier, and according to Elms (1981, 1994), his midlife crisis came to an end with the writing of *Walden Two*. Skinner (1967) admitted that the book's two main characters, Farazier and Burris, represented his attempt to reconcile two separate aspects of his own personality. *Walden Two* was also a benchmark in Skinner's professional career. No longer would he be confined to the laboratory study of rats and pigeons, but thereafter he would be involved with the application of behavioristic findings to the technology of shaping human behavior. His concern with the human condition was elaborated in *Science and Human Behavior* (1953) and reached philosophical expression in *Beyond Freedom and Dignity* (1971).

In 1948, Skinner returned to Harvard, where he was Professor of Psychology until his retirement in 1974 and then continued as Professor Emeritus. While at Harvard, Skinner gained recognition as one of America's best known psychologists, and his books on human behavior, *About Behaviorism* (1974), *Reflections on Behaviorism and Society* (1978), and *Upon Further Reflection* (1987a) became widely read. In addition, he wrote a three-volume autobiography, *Particulars of My Life* (1976), *The Shaping of a Behaviorist* (1979), and *A Matter of Consequences* (1983).

On August 18, 1990, Skinner died of leukemia. One week before his death, he delivered an emotional address to the American Psychological Association (APA) convention in which he continued his advocacy of radical behaviorism. At this convention, he received an unprecedented Citation for Outstanding Lifetime Contribution to Psychology, the only person to receive such an award in the 100-year history of APA. During his career, Skinner received other honors and awards, including serving as William James Lecturer at Harvard, being granted the APA Distinguished Scientific Award, and winning the President's Medal of Science.

E. L. Thorndike

Like other personality theorists, Skinner had a characteristic way of looking at the world that was reflected in both his work and his subjective view of himself. Skinner's autobiography reveals a lengthy struggle to break away from the control of authority figures, including his father, and to eventually gain freedom. After attaining some amount of freedom during his college days, Skinner returned home for 18 months, then left again to pursue his Ph.D., but he remained financially dependent on his father for a number of years. Such a step-by-step pattern of becoming free can be found in both Skinner's earliest scientific work and his autobiography. Amy Demorest and Paul Siegel (1996) investigated the hypothesis that an analysis of Skinner's first research design and the first paragraph of his autobiography would yield many similarities. In his presidential address to the Eastern Psychological Association, Skinner (1956) talked about his Ph.D. thesis, in which he released a rat from the far end of a tunnel and then observed its cautious advances and retreats through the tunnel. Similarly, in the first paragraph of his autobiography, Skinner (1976) described the behavior of the Susquehanna River as it retreats and advances from New York State, through Pennsylvania, into Maryland, and finally into the Atlantic Ocean. Participants in Demorest and Siegel's empirical study found themes of leaving one's origins, returning, and finally leaving again not only in both these writings, but in the remainder of Skinner's autobiography as well. Thus Skinner, like other scientists, had a typical way of observing things, and this pattern seemed to extend to both his life and his work.

PRECURSORS TO SKINNER'S SCIENTIFIC BEHAVIORISM

For centuries, observers of human behavior have known that people generally do those things that have pleasurable consequences and avoid doing those things that have punitive consequences. However, the first psychologist to systematically study the consequences of behavior was Edward L. Thorndike, who worked originally with animals (Thorndike, 1898, 1913) and then later with humans (Thorndike, 1931). Thorndike observed that learning takes place mostly because of the effects that follow a response, and he called this observation the **law of effect.** As originally conceived by Thorndike, the law of effect had two parts. The first stated that responses to stimuli that are followed immediately by a *satisfier* tend to be "stamped in"; the second held that responses

John B. Watson

to stimuli that are followed immediately by an *annoyer* tend to be "stamped out." Thorndike later amended the law of effect by minimizing the importance of annoyers. Whereas rewards (satisfiers) strengthen the connection between a stimulus and a response, punishments (annoyers) do not usually weaken stimulus/response connections. Skinner (1954) acknowledged that the law of effect was crucial to the control of behavior and saw his job as making sure that the effects *do* occur and that they occur under conditions optimal for learning. He also agreed with Thorndike that the effects of rewards are more predictable than the effects of punishments in shaping behavior.

A second and more direct influence on Skinner was the work of John B. Watson (Watson, 1913, 1925; Watson & Rayner, 1920). Watson had studied both animals and humans and became convinced that the concepts of consciousness and introspection must play no role in the scientific study of human behavior. In *Psychology as the Behaviorist Views It*, Watson (1913) argued that human behavior, like the behavior of animals and machines, can be studied objectively. He attacked not only consciousness and introspection, but also the notions of instinct, sensation, perception, motivation, mental states, mind, and imagery. Each of these concepts, he insisted, is beyond the realm of scientific psychology. Watson further argued that the goal of psychology is the prediction and control of behavior and that that goal could best be reached by limiting psychology to an objective study of habits formed through stimulus/response connections. As we have seen, Skinner was influenced by Watson even before he entered graduate school, and he and Watson are largely responsible for making behaviorism a dominant influence on present-day psychology.

SCIENTIFIC BEHAVIORISM

Like Thorndike and Watson before him, Skinner insisted that human behavior should be studied scientifically. His scientific behaviorism holds that behavior can best be studied without reference to needs, instincts, or motives. Attributing motivation to human behavior would be like attributing free will to natural phenomena. The wind does not blow because it wants to turn windmills; rocks do not roll downhill because they possess a sense of gravity; and birds do not migrate because they like the climate better in other regions. Scientists can easily accept the idea that the behavior of the wind, rocks, and even birds can be studied without reference to an internal motive, but most personality theorists assume that people are motivated by internal drives and that an understanding of the drives is essential.

Skinner disagreed. Why postulate an inner mental function that is outside the scope of scientific analysis? People do not eat because they are hungry. Hunger is an inner condition not directly observable. If psychologists wish to increase the probability that a person will eat, then they must first observe the variables related to eating. If deprivation of food increases the likelihood of eating, then they can deprive a person of food in order to better predict and control subsequent eating behavior. Both deprivation and eating are physical events that are clearly observable and therefore within the province of science. To say that a person eats because of hunger is to assume an unnecessary and unobservable mental condition between the physical fact of deprivation and the physical fact of eating. This assumption clouds the issue and relegates much of psychology to that realm of philosophy known as **cosmology,** or the concern with causation. To be scientific, Skinner (1953, 1987a) insisted, psychology must avoid internal mental factors and confine itself to observable physical events.

Although Skinner believed that internal states are outside the domain of science, he did not deny their existence. Such conditions as hunger, emotions, values, self-confidence, aggressive needs, religious beliefs, and spitefulness exist, but they are not explanations for behavior. To use them as explanations not only is fruitless but also limits the advancement of scientific behaviorism. Other sciences have made greater advances because they have long since abandoned the practice of attributing motives, needs, or will power to the motion (behavior) of living organisms and inanimate objects. Skinner's scientific behaviorism follows their lead (Skinner, 1945).

PHILOSOPHY OF SCIENCE

Scientific behaviorism allows for an *interpretation* of behavior but not an *explanation* of its causes. Interpretation permits generalization from the simple learning condition to the more complex. For example, Skinner generalized from animal studies to children and then to adults. Any science, including that of human behavior, begins with the simple and eventually evolves generalized principles that permit an interpretation of the more complex. Skinner (1978) used principles derived from laboratory studies to interpret the behavior of human beings but insisted that interpretation should not be confused with an explanation of why people behave.

CHARACTERISTICS OF SCIENCE

According to Skinner (1953), science has three main characteristics: First, science is *cumulative*; second, it is *an attitude that values empirical observation*; and third, science is *a search for order and lawful relationships*.

Science, in contrast to art, philosophy, and literature, advances in a *cumulative* manner. The amount and nature of scientific knowledge that today's high school students have of physics or chemistry is vastly more sophisticated than that of even the most educated Greeks 2,500 years ago. The same cannot be said for the humanities. The wisdom and genius of Plato, Michelangelo, and Shakespeare is clearly not inferior to any modern philosopher, artist, or writer. However, cumulative knowledge is not to be confused with technological progress. Science is unique, not because of technology, but rather because of its attitude.

The second and most critical characteristic of science is *an attitude that places value on empirical observation* above all else. In Skinner's words: "It is a disposition to deal with facts rather than with what someone has said about them" (1953, p. 12). In particular, there are three components to the scientific attitude: First, it *rejects authority*—even its own authority. Just because some well-respected person, such as Einstein, says something, that in itself does not make the statement true. It must stand the test of empirical observation. Recall from Chapter 1 our discussion of Aristotle's belief that bodies of different masses fall at different rates. That was accepted as fact for roughly 1,000 years simply because Aristotle said it. Galileo, however, tested that idea scientifically and discovered that it was not true. A second attitude of science is that it *demands intellectual honesty* and requires scientists to accept facts even when those facts are opposed to their wishes and desires. This does not mean that scientists are inherently more honest than other people. They are not. Scientists have been known to fabricate data and misrepresent their findings. However, as a discipline, science puts a high premium on intellectual honesty simply because the right answer ultimately will be discovered. Scientists have no choice but to report results that go against their expectations and hopes, because if they don't, someone else will, and the new results will show that the scientists who misrepresented data were wrong. "Where right and wrong are not so easily or so quickly established, there is no similar pressure" (Skinner, 1953, p. 13). Finally, science *suspends judgment* until clear trends emerge. Nothing is more damaging to a scientist's reputation than to rush into print findings that are insufficiently verified and tested. If reported findings do not hold up to replication, the scientist appears foolish at best and dishonest at worst. A healthy skepticism and willingness to suspend judgment are therefore essential to being a scientist.

A third characteristic of science is *a search for order and lawful relationships*. All science begins with observation of single events and then attempts to infer general principles and laws from those events. In short, the scientific method consists of prediction, control, and description. A scientist makes observations guided by theoretical assumptions, develops hypotheses (makes predictions), tests these hypotheses through controlled experimentation, describes honestly and accurately the results, and finally modifies the theory to match the actual empirical results. This is the circular relationship between theory and research that we discussed in Chapter 1.

Skinner (1953) believed that prediction, control, and description are possible in scientific behaviorism because behavior is both determined and lawful. Human behavior, like that of physical and biological entities, is neither whimsical nor the outcome of free will. It is determined by certain identifiable variables and follows definite lawful principles, which hypothetically can be known. Behavior that appears to be capricious or individually determined is simply beyond our present capacity to predict or control. But, hypothetically, the conditions under which it occurs can be discovered, thus permitting both prediction and control as well as description. Skinner devoted much of his time to trying to discover these conditions, using a procedure he called operant conditioning.

OPERANT CONDITIONING

Skinner (1953) recognized two kinds of conditioning, respondent and operant. In **respondent conditioning** (also called classical or Pavlovian), a response is drawn out of the organism by a specific, identifiable stimulus. The simplest examples include reflexive behavior. Light shined in the eye stimulates the pupil to contract; food placed on the tongue brings about salivation; and pepper in the nostrils results in the sneezing reflex. With reflexive behavior, responses are unlearned, involuntary, and common not only to the species but across species as well. Respondent conditioning, however, is not limited to simple reflexes. It can also be responsible for more complex human learning like phobias, fears, and anxiety.

An early example of respondent conditioning with humans was described by John Watson and Rosalie Rayner in 1920 and involved a young boy—Albert B., usually referred to as Little Albert. Albert was a normal, healthy child who, at 9 months of age, showed no fear of such objects as a white rat, a rabbit, a dog, a monkey with masks, and so forth. When Albert was 11 months old, the experimenters presented him with a white rat. Just as Albert was beginning to touch the rat, one of the experimenters struck a bar behind Albert's head. The little boy immediately showed signs of fear, although he did not cry. Then, just as he touched the rat with his other hand, the bar was struck again. Once again, Albert showed fear and began to whimper. A week later, Watson and Rayner repeated the procedure several times and finally presented the white rat without the loud, sudden sound. By this time, Albert had learned to fear the rat by itself and quickly began to crawl away from it. A few days later, the experimenters presented Albert with some blocks. He showed no fear. Next, they showed him the rat by itself. Albert showed fear. Then, they offered him the blocks again. No fear. They followed this with a rabbit by itself. Albert immediately began to cry and crawl away from the rabbit. Watson and Rayner followed the rabbit with blocks again, then a dog, then blocks again, then a fur coat, then a package of wool. For all objects except the blocks, Albert showed some fear. Finally, in fun Watson, whose hair by then was turning white, put his head down to see if Albert would play with his hair. The little boy showed no inclination to do so, although he did play with the hair of other observers. Watson then brought in a Santa Claus mask, to which Albert showed signs of fear. This experiment, which was never completed because Albert's mother intervened, demonstrated at least four points. First, infants have few, if any, innate fears of animals; second, they can learn to fear an animal if it is presented in association with an aversive stimulus; third, infants can *discriminate* between a furry white rat and a hard wooden block, so that fear of a rat does not generalize to fear of a block; and fourth, fear of a furry white rat can *generalize* to other animals as well as to other white hairy or furry objects.

Although respondent conditioning is responsible for the learning of some of our behaviors, Skinner believed that most human behaviors are learned through **operant conditioning.** The key to operant conditioning is the immediate reinforcement of a response. The organism first *does* something and then is reinforced by the environment. Reinforcement, in turn, increases the probability that the same behavior will occur again. This is called operant conditioning because the organism operates on the environment to produce a specific effect. Operant conditioning changes the frequency of a response or the probability that a response will occur. The reinforcement does not cause the behavior, but it increases the likelihood that it will be repeated.

One distinction between respondent and operant conditioning is that, in respondent conditioning, behavior is *elicited* from the organism, whereas in operant conditioning, behavior is *emitted*. Skinner made a distinction between elicited and emitted behavior. An elicited response is drawn from the organism, whereas an emitted response is one that simply appears. Because responses do not exist inside the organism and thus cannot be drawn out, Skinner preferred the term "emitted." Emitted responses do not previously exist inside the organism; they simply appear because of the organism's individual history of reinforcement or the species' evolutionary history.

Let's look at an example of operant conditioning. A father who wishes to increase the frequency of his daughter's smiles watches the child constantly and gives her candy every time she smiles. In this example, as in all instances of operant conditioning, three conditions are present: the *antecedent* (A), the *behavior* (B), and the *consequence* (C). The antecedent (A) refers to the environment or setting in which the behavior takes place. In our example, this would include the home, school, playground, or any other place the child might be.

The second essential condition in the operant conditioning paradigm is the response or behavior (B). In our example, the behavior is smiling, a relatively simple response that would undoubtedly occur without any previous training. More complex behavior must be gradually "shaped" through the use of "successive approximations," terms explained later. The response must be within the organism's repertoire and must not be interfered with by competing or antagonistic behaviors.

The third factor in operant conditioning is the consequence (C). If no consistent consequence follows an operant behavior during the history of the organism, no learning will occur; that is, there will be no change in the frequency of the behavior. But if some consequence does follow the response (and some sort of consequence always does), then the probability of future similar responses will be either increased or decreased, depending on whether the consequence is rewarding or not. In the above example, candy is a reward and it acts to reinforce the behavior of smiling and to increase its frequency. However, if the father gave his daughter candy every time she smiled, the child would eventually reach her fill. To ensure that an organism remained at a certain level of deprivation, Skinner carefully rationed the amount of food given to his experimental animals prior to training, using body weight as a measure of deprivation. He also employed various *intermittent schedules* of reinforcement, so that the organism was not reinforced for every desired response and would thus remain in a state of partial deprivation. This sort of rigorous control is usually not available with the conditioning of humans.

Shaping

In our experiment, the child was reinforced whenever she smiled. In most cases, the desired behavior is more complex than a smile and will be emitted only through the process of **shaping,** a procedure in which the experimenter first rewards gross approximations of the behavior, then closer approximations, and finally, the desired behavior itself. Through this process of reinforcing **successive approximations,** the experimenter gradually shapes the final complex set of behaviors (Skinner, 1953).

Shaping can be illustrated by the example of training a severely mentally retarded boy to dress himself. The ultimate behavior is to have the child put on all his own clothes. If the parent withheld reinforcement until this target behavior occurred, the child would never successfully complete the chore. To train the boy, the parent must break down the complex behavior of dressing into simple segments. First, the parent gives the child a reward, say, candy, whenever he approximates the behavior of positioning his left hand near the inside of the left sleeve of his shirt. Once that behavior is sufficiently reinforced, the parent withholds reward until the child places his hand into the proper sleeve. Then the parent rewards the child only for putting his left arm entirely through the sleeve. Following this, the same procedures are used with the right sleeve, the buttons, trousers, socks, and shoes. After the child learns to dress himself completely, reinforcement need not follow every successful trial. By this time, in fact, the ability to put on all his clothes will probably become a reward in itself. Quite apparently, the child can only reach the final target behavior if the parent breaks up the complex behavior into its component parts and then reinforces successive approximations to each response. Shaping allows conditioning to take place quite quickly. In only 2 or

Even complex behavior, such as learning to work a computer, is acquired through shaping and successive approximation.

3 minutes, Skinner conditioned pigeons to raise their heads to heights never before reached. Chickens have been trained to play a facsimile of baseball and dogs have been conditioned to jump through hoops in a very short time.

If reinforcement increases the probability that a given response will recur, how can behavior be shaped from the relatively undifferentiated into the highly complex? In other words, why doesn't the organism simply repeat the old reinforced response? Why does it emit new responses that have never been reinforced, but that gradually move it toward the target behavior? The answer is that behavior is not discrete but continuous; that is, the organism usually moves slightly beyond the previously reinforced response. If behavior were discrete, shaping could not occur because the organism would become locked into simply emitting previously reinforced responses. Because behavior is continuous, the organism moves slightly beyond the previously reinforced response, and this slightly exceptional value can then be used as the new minimum standard for reinforcement. (The organism may also move slightly backward or slightly sideways, but only movements toward the desired target are reinforced.) Skinner (1953) compared shaping behavior to a sculptor molding a statue from a large lump of clay. In both cases, the final product seems to be different from the original form, but the history of the transformation reveals continuous behavior and not a set of discrete steps.

Operant behavior always takes place in some environment, and the environment has a selective role in shaping and maintaining behavior. The organism, throughout its history, will have been reinforced by reacting to some elements in the environment but not to others. This history of differential reinforcement results in **operant discrimination.** Skinner claimed that discrimination is not an ability that people possess but a consequence of a person's reinforcement history. We do not come to the dinner table because we discern that the food is ready; we come because our previous experiences of reacting in a similar way have been mostly reinforced. This distinction may seem to be splitting hairs, but Skinner felt that it had important theoretical and practical implications. The first explanation sees discrimination as a cognitive function, existing within the person; the second accounts for it by environmental differences and by individual history. The first is beyond the scope of empirical observation; the second can be scientifically studied.

A response to a similar environment in the absence of previous reinforcement is called **stimulus generalization.** Buying a ticket to a movie we have never seen because we were reinforced by viewing the director's earlier movies is an example of stimulus generalization. Technically, we do not generalize from one situation to another, but react to the new situation in the same manner that we reacted to the first because the two situations possess identical elements. Skinner (1953) put it this way: "The reinforcement of a response increases the probability of all responses containing the same elements" (p. 94).

Reinforcement

We have seen that reinforcement increases the probability that an operant response will be emitted, and we have described the role of reinforcement in shaping behavior. Now let's examine this powerful force more closely.

Reinforcement is anything within the environment that strengthens a behavior. Actually, Skinner (1987a) said that reinforcement has two effects: it *strengthens the behavior* and it *rewards the person.* Reinforcement and reward, therefore, are not synonymous. Not every behavior that is reinforced is rewarding or pleasing to the person. For example, people are reinforced for working, but many find their jobs boring, uninteresting, and unrewarding. Reinforcers exist in the environment and are not something felt by the person. Food is not reinforcing because it tastes good; rather, it tastes good because it is reinforcing (Skinner, 1971).

Any behavior that increases the probability that the species or the individual will survive tends to be strengthened. Food, sex, and parental care are necessary for the survival of the species and any behavior that produces these conditions is reinforced; injury, disease, and extremes in climate are detrimental to survival and any behavior that tends to reduce or avoid these conditions is likewise reinforced. Reinforcement, therefore, can be divided into that which produces a beneficial environmental condition and that which reduces or avoids a detrimental one. The first is called *positive reinforcement* and the second, *negative reinforcement.*

Positive Reinforcement
Any stimulus that, when added to a situation, increases the probability that a given behavior will occur is termed a **positive reinforcer** (Skinner, 1953). Food, water, sex, money, social approval, and physical comfort are examples. When made contingent on behavior, each has the capacity to increase the frequency of a response. For example, if clear water appears whenever a person turns on the kitchen faucet, then that behavior is strengthened because a beneficial environmental stimulus has been added. Much human and animal behavior is acquired through positive reinforcement. With humans, reinforcement is often haphazard and therefore learning is inefficient. Under controlled conditions, however, Skinner was able to train animals to perform a multitude of relatively complex tasks.

Negative Reinforcement
The removal of an aversive stimulus from a situation also increases the probability that the preceding behavior will occur. This removal results in **negative reinforcement** (Skinner, 1953). The reduction or avoidance of loud noises, shocks, and hunger pangs would be negatively reinforcing because they strengthen the behavior immediately preceding them. Negative reinforcement differs from positive reinforcement in that it requires the removal of an aversive condition, whereas positive reinforcement involves

the presentation of a beneficial stimulus. The effect of negative reinforcement, however, is identical to that of positive reinforcement; both strengthen behavior. Some people eat because they like a particular food; others eat to diminish hunger pangs. For the first group, food is a positive reinforcer; for the second, removal of hunger is a negative reinforcer. In both instances, the behavior of eating is strengthened because the consequences are rewarding.

There is an almost unlimited number of aversive stimuli, the removal of which may be negatively reinforcing. Anxiety, for example, is an aversive stimulus, and any behavior that reduces it (repression, making excuses, and the like) is reinforcing. Other examples include guilt, illness, pain, scoldings, threats of imprisonment, and fear of damnation. Behavior that reduces or avoids any of these conditions tends to be strengthened. On the other hand, the presence of any of these aversive stimuli is called *punishment*.

Punishment

Negative reinforcement should not be confused with punishment. Negative reinforcers remove, reduce, or avoid aversive stimuli, whereas **punishment** is the presentation of an aversive stimulus, such as an electric shock, or the removal of a positive one, such as disconnecting an adolescent's telephone. A negative reinforcer strengthens a response; punishment does not. Although punishment does not strengthen a response, neither does it inevitably weaken it. Skinner (1953) agreed with Thorndike that the effects of punishment are less predictable than those of reward.

Effects of Punishment

The control of human and animal behavior is better served by positive and negative reinforcement than by punishment. The effects of punishment are not opposite those of reinforcement. When the contingencies of reinforcement are strictly controlled, behavior can be precisely shaped and accurately predicted. With punishment, however, no such exactitude is possible. The reason for this is simple. Punishment ordinarily is imposed to prevent people from acting in a particular way. When it is successful, people will stop behaving in that manner, but they still must do something. What they do cannot be accurately predicted because punishment does not tell them what they should do; it merely suppresses the tendency to behave in the undesirable fashion. Consequently, one effect of punishment is to *suppress behavior*. For example, if a boy teases his younger sister, his parents can make him stop by spanking him, but unfortunately, this punishment will not improve his disposition toward his sister. It merely suppresses teasing temporarily or while in the presence of his parents.

Another effect of punishment is the *conditioning of a negative feeling* by associating a strong aversive stimulus with the behavior being punished. In the above illustration, if the pain of the spanking is strong enough, it will instigate a response (crying, withdrawal, attack) that is incompatible with the behavior of teasing a younger sibling. In the future, when the boy thinks about mistreating his younger sister, that thought may elicit, through classical conditioning, the conditioned response of fear, anxiety, guilt, or shame. This negative emotion then serves to prevent the undesirable behavior from recurring. Lamentably, it offers no positive instruction to the child.

A third outcome of punishment is the *spread of its effects*. Any stimulus associated with the punishment may be suppressed or avoided. In our example, this might include the younger sister, the parent, the paddle, or the place where the spanking occurred. The boy may deny the feelings of hostility toward his parents, or he may avoid almost all contact with his sister. As a result, his behavior toward them becomes maladaptive. Yet this inappropriate behavior serves the purpose of preventing future punishment. Skinner recognized the classical Freudian *defense mechanisms* as effective means of avoiding pain and its attendant anxiety. The punished person may fantasize, project feelings onto others, rationalize aggressive behaviors, or displace them toward other people or animals.

Punishment and Reinforcement Compared

Punishment has several characteristics in common with reinforcement. Just as there are two kinds of reinforcements (positive and negative), there are two types of punishment. The first requires the presentation of an aversive stimulus, the second involves the removal of a positive reinforcer. An example of the former would be pain encountered from falling as the result of walking too fast on an icy sidewalk. An example of the latter is a heavy fine levied against a motorist for driving too fast. This first example (falling) results from a natural condition; the second (being fined) follows from human intervention. This is a second characteristic common to punishment and reinforcement: both can derive from either natural consequences or from human imposition. A third common ingredient is that both punishment and reinforcement are means of controlling behavior, whether the control is by design or by accident. Skinner obviously favored planned control, and his book *Walden Two* (Skinner, 1948) presents many of his ideas on the control of human behavior.

Conditioned and Generalized Reinforcers

Food is a reinforcement for humans and animals because it removes a condition of deprivation. But how can money, which cannot directly remove a condition of deprivation, be reinforcing? The answer is that money is a **conditioned reinforcer.** Conditioned reinforcers are those things that are not by nature satisfying but become so because they are associated with such unlearned or *primary reinforcers* as food, water, sex, or physical comfort. Money is a conditioned reinforcer because it can be exchanged for a great variety of primary reinforcers; because it is associated with more than one primary reinforcer, it is also considered a **generalized reinforcer.**

Skinner (1953) recognized five important generalized reinforcers that sustain much of our behavior: attention, approval, affection, submission of others, and tokens (money). Each can be used as reinforcers in a variety of situations. Attention, for example, is a conditioned generalized reinforcer because it is associated with such primary reinforcers as food and physical contact. When children are being fed or held, they are also receiving attention. After food and attention are paired a number of times, attention itself becomes reinforcing through the process of respondent (classical) conditioning. Children, and adults too, will work for attention with no expectation of receiving food or physical contact. In much the same way, approval, affection, submission of others, and money acquire generalized reinforcement value. Behavior can be shaped and responses learned with generalized conditioned reinforcers supplying the sole reinforcement.

Schedules of Reinforcement

We have seen that any behavior followed immediately by the presentation of a positive reinforcer or the removal of an aversive stimulus tends thereafter to occur more frequently. The frequency of that behavior, however, is subject to the conditions under which training occurred, more specifically, to the various schedules of reinforcement (Ferster & Skinner, 1957).

Reinforcement can follow behavior on either a continuous schedule or an intermittent one. **Continuous schedules** call for reinforcing the organism for every trial, a procedure that leads to an increase in frequency of the response, but is inefficient in its use of reinforcement. Skinner preferred **intermittent schedules** that make more efficient use of reinforcement because the organism is not reinforced for every response. Interestingly, Skinner first began using intermittent schedules because he was running low on food pellets (Bjork, 1993). Intermittent schedules are based either on the behavior of the organism or on elapsed time; they can be set either at a fixed rate or can vary according to a randomized program. Ferster and Skinner (1957) recognized a large number of reinforcement schedules, but the four basic intermittent schedules are: *fixed-ratio*, *variable-ratio*, *fixed-interval*, and *variable-interval*.

Fixed-Ratio

With a **fixed-ratio schedule,** the organism is reinforced intermittently according to the number of responses it makes. Ratio refers to the ratio of responses to reinforcers. An experimenter may decide to reward a pigeon with a pellet of grain for every fifth peck it makes at a disc. The pigeon is then conditioned at a fixed-ratio schedule of 5 to 1, that is, FR 5.

Nearly all intermittent schedules begin by reinforcing the organism for every desired response, that is, on a continuous basis. But soon, continuous reward can be ended and reinforcement can proceed intermittently. In the same way, extremely high fixed-ratio schedules, like 200 to 1, must begin at a low rate of responses and gradually build to a higher one. A pigeon can be conditioned to work long and rapidly in exchange for one food pellet provided it has been previously reinforced at lower rates.

Technically, almost no pay scale for humans follows a fixed-ratio or any other schedule because workers ordinarily do not begin with a continuous schedule of immediate reinforcement. An approximation of a fixed-ratio schedule would be the pay to bricklayers who receive a fixed amount of money for each brick they lay. However, bricklayers are not paid immediately after laying 1 brick or even 100 bricks, so their payment does not technically follow a fixed-ratio schedule.

Variable-Ratio

With a fixed-ratio schedule, the organism is reinforced after every *n*th response. With the **variable-ratio schedule,** it is reinforced after the *n*th response *on the average*. Again, training must start with continuous reinforcement, proceed to a low response number, and then increase to a higher rate of response. A pigeon rewarded every third response on the average can build to a VR 6 schedule, then VR 10, and so on, but the mean number of responses must be increased gradually to prevent *extinction*. After a high mean is reached, say, VR 500, responses become extremely resistant to extinction. (More on rate of extinction later.)

For humans, playing slot machines is an example of a variable-ratio schedule. The machine is set to pay off at a certain rate, but the ratio must be flexible, that is, variable, to prevent players from predicting payoffs.

Because slot machines pay off on a variable-ratio schedule, some people become compulsive gamblers.

Fixed-Interval

With the **fixed-interval schedule,** the organism is reinforced for the first response following a designated period of time. For example, FI 5 indicates that the organism is rewarded for its first response after every 5-minute interval. Employees working for salary or wages approximate a fixed-interval schedule. They are paid every week, every 2 weeks, or every month, but this is not strictly a fixed-interval schedule. Why do workers distribute their efforts fairly evenly over time rather than loafing most of the time and then showing an end-of-the-period spurt characteristic of the fixed-interval schedule? It is because their rate of work is controlled by many other factors, such as watchful supervisors, threats of dismissal, promises of promotion, or self-generated reinforcers.

Variable-Interval

A **variable-interval schedule** is one in which the organism is reinforced after the lapse of random or varied periods of time. For example, VI 5 means that the organism is reinforced following random-length intervals that average 5 minutes. Such schedules result in more responses per interval than do fixed-interval schedules. For humans, reinforcement results more often from one's effort rather than the passage of time. For this reason, ratio schedules are more common than interval schedules, and the variable-interval schedule is probably the least common of all. An example of a variable-interval schedule would be television addicts who watch their favorite program every week, hoping it will be enjoyable. Sometimes it is, often it is not.

Extinction

Once learned, responses can be lost for at least four reasons. First, they can simply be forgotten during the passage of time. Second, and more likely, they can be lost because preceding or subsequent learnings interfere. Third, they can disappear due to punishment, repression being included in this category. A fourth cause of lost learnings is **extinction,** defined as the tendency of a previously acquired response to become progressively weakened upon nonreinforcement.

Operant extinction is the systematic withholding of reinforcement previously contingent upon a response until the probability of the response diminishes to zero. Rate of operant extinction depends largely on the schedule of reinforcement under which learning occurred. However, the extinction curve may be complicated by emotion, as when anger brings about more violent responses.

Compared with a continuous schedule, behavior trained on an intermittent schedule is much more resistant to extinction. Skinner (1953) observed as many as 10,000 nonreinforced responses with intermittent schedules. Such behavior appears to be self-perpetuating and is practically indistinguishable from *functionally autonomous* behavior, a concept suggested by Gordon Allport and discussed in Chapter 14. In general, the higher the rate of responses per reinforcement, the slower the rate of extinction; the fewer responses an organism must make or the shorter the time between reinforcers, the more quickly extinction will occur. This suggests that praise and other reinforcers should be used sparingly in training children.

Extinction is seldom systematically applied to human behavior outside therapy or behavior modification. Most of us live in relatively uncontrolled environments and almost never experience the methodical withholding of reinforcement. Thus many of our behaviors persist over a long period of time because they are being intermittently reinforced, even though the nature of that reinforcement may be obscure to us.

THE HUMAN ORGANISM

Our discussion of Skinnerian theory to this point has dealt primarily with the technology of behavior, a technology based exclusively on the study of animals. But do the principles of behavior gleaned from rats and pigeons apply to the human organism? Skinner's (1974, 1987a) view was that an understanding of the behavior of laboratory animals can generalize to human behavior, just as physics can be used to interpret what is observed in outer space and an understanding of basic genetics can help in interpreting complex evolutionary concepts.

Skinner (1953, 1990a) agreed with Watson (1913) that psychology must be confined to a scientific study of observable phenomena, namely behavior. Science must begin with the simple and move to the more complex. This sequence might proceed from the behavior of animals to that of psychotics, to that of retardates, then to that of children, and finally to the complex behavior of adults. Skinner (1974, 1987a), therefore, made no apology for beginning with the study of animals.

According to Skinner (1987a, 1990a), human behavior (and human personality) is shaped by three forces. The first is natural selection or the evolutionary history of the species; the second is the evolution of social environments or cultures; and the third is the individual's personal history of reinforcement, which we have discussed.

NATURAL SELECTION

The human organism is the product of a long evolutionary history. As individuals, our behavior is determined by genetic composition and especially by our personal histories of reinforcement. As a species, however, we are shaped by the contingencies of survival. Natural selection plays an important part in human behavior (Skinner, 1974, 1987a, 1990a).

Individual behavior that is reinforcing tends to be repeated; that which is not, tends to drop out. Similarly, those behaviors that, throughout history, were beneficial to the species tended to survive, whereas those that were only idiosyncratically reinforcing tended to drop out. For example, natural selection has favored those individuals whose pupils dilated and contracted with changes in lighting. Their superior ability to see during both daylight and nighttime enabled them to avoid life-threatening dangers and to survive to the age of reproduction. Similarly, infants whose heads turned in the direction of a gentle stroke on the cheek were able to suckle, thereby increasing their chances of survival and the likelihood that this rooting characteristic would be passed on to their offspring. These are but two examples of several reflexes that characterize the human infant today. Some, such as the pupillary reflex, continue to have survival value whereas others, like the rooting reflex, are of diminishing benefit.

The contingencies of reinforcement and the contingencies of survival interact, and some behaviors that are individually reinforcing also contribute to the survival of the species. For example, sexual behavior is generally reinforcing to an individual, but it also has natural selection value because those individuals who are more strongly aroused by sexual stimulation were also the ones who were most likely to produce offspring capable of similar patterns of behavior.

Not every remnant of natural selection continues to have survival value. In our early history, overeating was adaptive because it allowed people to survive during those times when food was less plentiful. Now, in societies where food is continuously available, obesity has become a health problem to many, and overeating has lost its survival value.

Although natural selection helped shape some human behavior, it is probably responsible for only a small number of our actions. Skinner (1989a) claimed that the contingencies of reinforcement, especially those that have shaped our culture, account for most of our behavior.

> We can trace a small part of human behavior . . . to natural selection and the evolution of the species, but the greater part of human behavior must be traced to contingencies of reinforcement, especially to the very complex social contingencies we call cultures. Only when we take those histories into account can we explain why people behave as they do. (p. 18)

CULTURAL EVOLUTION

In his later years, Skinner (1987a, 1989a) elaborated more fully on the importance of culture in shaping human behavior. *Selection* is responsible for those cultural practices that have survived, just as selection plays a key role in our evolutionary history and also with the contingencies of reinforcement. "People do not observe particular practices in order that the group will be more likely to survive; they observe them because groups that induced their members to do so survived and transmitted them" (Skinner, 1987a, p. 57). In other words, humans do not make a cooperative decision to do what is best for the society; but those societies whose members behaved cooperatively tended to survive.

Cultural practices such as tool making and verbal behavior begin when an individual is reinforced for using a tool or uttering a distinctive sound. Eventually, a cultural practice evolves that is reinforcing to the group, although not necessarily to the individual. Both tool making and verbal behavior have survival value for a group, but few of us now make tools and some people (for example, monks who have taken a vow of silence) do not emit verbal behavior.

The remnants of culture, like those of natural selection, are not all adaptive. For example, the division of labor that evolved from the Industrial Revolution has helped society produce more goods, but it has led to work that is no longer directly reinforcing. Another example is warfare, which in the preindustrialized world benefited certain societies, but which now has evolved as a threat to human existence. In summary, Skinner (1987a) wrote that

> human behavior is the joint product of (1) the contingencies of survival responsible for the natural selection of the species and (2) the contingencies of reinforcement responsible for the repertoires acquired by its members, including (3) the special contingencies maintained by an evolved social environment. (Ultimately, of course, it is all a matter of natural selection, since operant conditioning is an evolved process, of which cultural practices are special applications.) (p. 55)

INNER STATES

Although he rejected explanations of behavior founded on nonobservable hypothetical constructs, Skinner (1989b) did not deny the existence of internal states, such as feelings of love, anxiety, or fear. Internal or private events can be studied just as any other behavior, but their observation is, of course, limited. In a personal communication of June 13, 1983, Skinner wrote, "I believe it is possible to talk about private events and, in particular, to establish the limits with which we do so accurately. I think this brings so-called 'nonobservables' within reach." What, then, is the role of such inner states as self-awareness, drives, emotions, and purpose or intention?

Self-Awareness

Skinner (1974) believed that humans not only have consciousness, but they are also aware of their consciousness; they are not only aware of their environment, but they are also aware of themselves as part of their environment; they not only observe external stimuli, but they are also aware of themselves observing that stimuli.

Behavior is a function of the environment, and part of that environment is within one's skin. This portion of the universe is peculiarly one's own and is therefore private. Each of us is subjectively aware of our own thoughts, feelings, recollections, and intentions. These private events are real; they have physical properties and thus are potentially subject to the same scientific analysis as any other physical phenomena (Skinner, 1974).

Self-awareness and private events can be illustrated by the following example. A worker reports to a friend, "I was so frustrated today that I almost quit my job." What can we make of such a statement? First, the report itself is verbal behavior and, as such, can be studied in the same way as any other behavior. Second, the statement that she was on the verge of quitting her job refers to a nonbehavior. Responses never emitted are not responses and, of course, have no meaning to science. Third, a private event transpired "within the skin" of the worker. This private event, along with her verbal report to the friend, can be scientifically analyzed. At the time the worker felt like quitting, she might have observed the following covert behavior: "I am observing within myself increasing degrees of frustration, which are raising the probability that I will inform my boss that I am quitting." This is more accurate than saying "I almost quit my job," and it refers to behavior that, although private, is within the boundaries of scientific analysis.

Emotions are subjectively real and may have observable concomitants, but they are not directly observable themselves.

Drives

From the viewpoint of radical behaviorism, drives are not causes of behavior but merely explanatory fictions. To Skinner (1953), drives simply refer to the effects of deprivation and satiation and to the corresponding probability that the organism will respond. To deprive a person of food increases the likelihood of eating; to satiate a person decreases that likelihood. However, deprivation and satiation are not the only correlates of eating. Other factors that increase or decrease the probability of eating are internally observed hunger pangs, availability of food, and previous experiences with food reinforcers.

If we knew enough about the three essentials of behavior (antecedent, behavior, and consequences), then we would know why a person behaves, that is, what drives are related to specific behaviors. Only then would drives have a legitimate role in the scientific study of human behavior. For the present, however, explanations based on fictionalized constructs like drives or needs are merely untestable hypotheses.

Emotions

Skinner (1974), of course, recognized the subjective existence of emotions, but he insisted that behavior must not be attributed to them. He accounted for emotions by the contingencies of survival and the contingencies of reinforcement. Throughout the millennia, individuals most strongly disposed toward fear or anger were those who escaped from or triumphed over danger and thus were able to pass on those characteristics to their offspring. On an individual level, behaviors followed by delight, joy, pleasure, and other pleasant emotions tend to be reinforced, thereby increasing the probability that these behaviors would recur in the life of that individual.

Purpose and Intention

Skinner (1974) also recognized the concepts of purpose and intention, but again, he cautioned against attributing behavior to them. Purpose and intention exist within the skin, but they are not subject to direct outside scrutiny. A felt, ongoing purpose may itself be reinforcing. For example, if I believe that my purpose for jogging is to feel better and live longer, then this thought per se acts as a reinforcing stimulus, especially while undergoing the drudgery of jogging or when trying to explain my motivation to a nonrunner.

A person may "intend" to see a movie Friday evening because viewing similar films has been reinforcing. At the time the person intends to go to the movie, she feels a physical condition within the body and labels it an "intention." What are called intentions or purposes, therefore, are physically felt stimuli within the organism and not mentalistic events responsible for behavior. "The consequences of operant behavior are not what the behavior is now for; they are merely similar to the consequences that have shaped and maintained it" (Skinner, 1987a, p. 57).

COMPLEX BEHAVIOR

Human behavior can be exceedingly complex, yet Skinner believed that even the most abstract and complex behavior is shaped by natural selection, cultural evolution, or the individual's history of reinforcement. Once again, Skinner did not deny "higher mental processes" such as cognition, reason, and recall; nor did he ignore complex human endeavors like creativity, unconscious behavior, dreams, and social behavior. He did, of course, insist that they are subject to behavioral analysis.

Higher Mental Processes

Skinner (1974) admitted that human thought is the most difficult of all behaviors to analyze; but potentially, at least, it can be understood as long as one does not resort to a hypothetical fiction such as "mind." Thinking, problem solving, and reminiscing are covert behaviors that take place within the skin but not inside the mind. As behavior, they are amenable to the same contingencies of reinforcement as overt behavior. For example, when a woman has misplaced her car keys, she searches for them because similar searching behavior has been previously reinforced. In like manner, when she is unable to recall the name of an acquaintance, she searches for that name covertly because this type of behavior has earlier been reinforced. However, the acquaintance's name did not exist in her mind any more than did the car keys. Skinner (1974) summed up this procedure, saying that "techniques of recall are not concerned with searching a storehouse of memory but with increasing the probability of responses" (pp. 109–110).

Problem solving also involves covert behavior and often requires the person to covertly manipulate the relevant variables until the correct solution is found. Ultimately these variables are environmental and do not spring magically from the person's mind. A chess player seems to be hopelessly trapped, surveys the board, and suddenly makes a move that allows his marker to escape. What brought about this unexpected burst of "insight"? He did not solve the problem in his mind. He manipulated the various markers (not by touching them but in covert fashion), rejected moves not accompanied by reinforcement, and finally selected the one that was followed by internal reinforcement. Although the solution may have been facilitated by his previous experiences of reading a book on chess, listening to expert advice, or playing the game, it was initiated by environmental contingencies and not manufactured by mental machinations.

Creativity

How does the radical behaviorist account for creativity? Logically, if behavior were nothing other than a predictable response to a stimulus, novel or creative behavior could not exist because only previously reinforced behavior would be emitted. Skinner (1974) answered this problem by comparing creative behavior with natural selection in evolutionary theory. "As accidental traits, arising from mutations, are selected by their contribution to survival, so accidental variations in behavior are selected by their reinforcing consequences" (p. 114). Just as natural selection explains differentiation among the species without resorting to an omnipotent creative mind, so behaviorism accounts for novel behavior without recourse to a personal creative mind.

The concept of mutation is crucial to both natural selection and creative behavior. In both cases, random or accidental conditions are produced that have some possibility of survival. Creative writers change their environment, thus producing responses that have some chance of being reinforced. When their "creativity dries up," they may move to a different location, travel, read, talk to others, put words on paper with little expectancy that they will be the finished product, or try out various words, sentences, and ideas covertly. To Skinner, then, creativity is simply the result of *random* or *accidental* behaviors (overt or covert) that happen to be rewarded. The fact that some people are more creative than others is due both to differences in genetic endowment and to experiences that have shaped their creative behavior.

Unconscious Behavior

As a radical behaviorist, Skinner could not accept the notion of a storehouse of unconscious ideas or emotions. He did, however, accept the idea of unconscious *behavior*. In fact, because we rarely observe the relationship between genetic and environmental variables and our own behavior, nearly all our behavior is unconsciously motivated (Skinner, 1987a). In a more limited sense, behavior is labeled unconscious when we no longer think about it because it has been suppressed through punishment. Behavior that has aversive consequences has a tendency to be ignored or not thought about. A child repeatedly and severely punished for sexual play may both *suppress* the sexual behavior and *repress* any thoughts or memories of such activity. Eventually the child may deny that the sexual activity took place. Such *denial* avoids the aversive aspects connected with thoughts of punishment and is thus a negative reinforcer. In other words, the child is rewarded for *not thinking* about certain sexual behaviors.

Repression also takes place when a person avoids certain thoughts or actions by engaging in opposite or competing forms of behavior. For example, a man troubled by problems at home may enmesh himself in work, thereby not only physically avoiding home life but also blocking out any thoughts of it.

A more severe example of not thinking about aversive stimuli is a child who behaves in hateful ways toward her mother. In doing so, she will also exhibit some less antagonistic behaviors. If the loathsome behavior is punished, it will become suppressed and replaced by the more positive behaviors. Eventually the child will be rewarded for gestures of love, which will then increase in frequency. After a time, her behavior becomes more and more positive, and it may even resemble what Freud (1926/1959a) called "reactive love." The child no longer has any thoughts of hatred toward her mother and behaves in an exceedingly loving and subservient manner. Skinner (1953) accounted for this "reaction formation" as an effect of the contingencies of reinforcement. No unconscious feelings of hatred can be observed, only slightly stilted signs of love.

Dreams

Skinner (1953) saw dreams as covert and symbolic forms of behavior that are subject to the same contingencies of reinforcement as any other behavior. He agreed with Freud that dreams may serve a wish-fulfillment purpose. Dream behavior is reinforcing when repressed sexual or aggressive stimuli are allowed expression. To act out sexual fantasies or to actually inflict damage on an enemy are two behaviors likely to be associated with punishment. To even covertly think about these behaviors may have punitive effects, but in dreams these behaviors may be expressed symbolically and without any accompanying punishment.

Social Behavior

Groups do not behave—only individuals do. Individuals establish groups because they have been rewarded for doing so. For example, individuals form clans so that they might be protected against animals, natural disasters, or enemy tribes. Individuals also form governments, establish churches, or become part of an unruly crowd because they are reinforced for that behavior.

The social environment, however, is not always reinforcing. People are sometimes ridiculed, insulted, or physically abused within the context of a group, yet, for at least three reasons, they continue to remain part of that group. First, because the group consists of several people, the abused person may be receiving positive reinforcement from one or more persons while incurring the punishment from some others. For example, a child abused by the father may be reinforced by family life because his mother shows him loving care. This suggests a second possibility for remaining in a group even while suffering abuse: The person (in this case, a child) may not possess sufficient means of countercontrol, and therefore, he can neither change the behavior of other members nor physically flee from the group. Third, reinforcement may occur on an intermittent schedule so that the abuse suffered by the individual is intermingled with occasional reward. If the positive reinforcement is strong enough and occurs on a variable-ratio or variable-interval schedule, then its effects will be more powerful than those of punishment.

CONTROL OF HUMAN BEHAVIOR

Ultimately, an individual's behavior is controlled by environmental contingencies. Those contingencies may have been erected by society, by another individual, or by oneself, but the environment, not free will, is responsible for behavior.

Social Control

Individuals act to form social groups because such behavior tends to be reinforcing. Groups, in turn, exercise control over their members by formulating written or unwritten laws, rules, and customs that have physical existence beyond the lives of individuals. The laws of a nation, the rules of an organization, and the customs of a culture transcend any one individual's means of countercontrol and serve as powerful controlling variables in the lives of individual members. In addition, social control includes the influence that one individual exercises over another in a one-to-one relationship (Skinner, 1974).

Social forces control our behavior in a nearly infinite variety of ways, but all these techniques can be grouped under the following headings: (1) operant conditioning, (2) describing contingencies, (3) deprivation and satiation, and (4) physical restraint (Skinner, 1953).

Operant Conditioning

Society exercises control over its members through the four principal methods of operant conditioning: positive reinforcement, negative reinforcement, and the two techniques of punishment (adding an aversive stimulus and removing a positive one). Each of these methods can be illustrated by observing the controlling techniques available to a fourth-grade teacher.

The teacher shapes the behavior of her students through the use of positive reinforcement when she gives high grades for excellent work, compliments socially desirable behaviors, or awards prizes for perfect attendance. She can also reinforce acceptable behavior through negative reinforcement, such as shortening the time of detention if the punished student remains silent and gives the appearance of working hard, or ceasing to scold a child when he apologizes for unacceptable behavior. On the other hand, she can also rely on two methods of punishment. She can add an aversive condition, such as extra work for disobedient behavior, or she can remove positive reinforcers, such as moving a very talkative child away from friends.

In all these examples, the teacher makes reward or punishment contingent on the behavior of the child. The effectiveness of each technique depends on the consistency with which it is used, the individual student's genetic makeup and personal history of reinforcement, and the existence of any other conflicting modes of behavioral control.

Describing Contingencies

A second technique of social control is to describe to a person the contingencies of reinforcement. Describing contingencies involves language, usually verbal, to inform people of the consequences of their not-yet-emitted behavior.

Many examples of describing contingencies are available. Highway signs warn motorists to watch out for ice on the next bridge. Threats are also a means of describing contingencies: "If you don't buy me a gift for my birthday, I will divorce you." Advertising is another method of control through describing contingencies: "Use our brand of toothpaste and you will improve your love life." In none of these examples will the attempt at control be perfectly successful, yet each of them increases the likelihood that the desired response will be emitted. Also, none of these attempts is designed to change a person's "mind," but rather to alter the environment.

Deprivation and Satiation

Behavior can also be controlled either by depriving people or by satiating them with reinforcers. Again, even though deprivation and satiation are internal states, the control originates with the environment. Deprived individuals are more likely to respond in ways designed to alleviate deprivation. When children habitually have no appetite at mealtime, parents can increase the chances of them eating dinner by depriving them of snacks between meals.

Satiating a person is also a means of control. A satiated person is less likely to respond with behavior that is undesirable to the controlling person. A parent can diminish, at least temporarily, the likelihood that children will nag by giving them many interesting toys. A government can decrease the chances that its citizens will revolt by establishing generous social welfare programs. In the long run, social control through

Physical restraint is one means of social control.

satiation has the obvious disadvantage of costs to the controller and therefore is likely to be used only by those who can afford those costs.

Physical Restraint

Another example of social control involves physically restraining individuals so that they cannot behave in a particular manner. We erect fences to keep others from trespassing on our property; society builds prisons to restrain criminals; and we hold back a child who plays near a deep ravine. Physical restraint acts to counter the effects of conditioning, and it results in behavior contrary to that which would have been emitted had the person not been restrained.

Some people might say that physical restraint is a means of denying an individual's freedom. However, Skinner (1971) held that behavior has nothing to do with personal freedom but is shaped by the contingencies of survival, the effects of reinforcement, and the contingencies of the social environment. Therefore, the act of physically restraining a person does no more to negate freedom than any other technique of control, including self-control.

Self-Control

If personal freedom is a fiction, then how can a person exercise self-control? Skinner would say that, just as we can alter the variables in another person's environment, so we can manipulate the variables within our own environment and thus exercise some measure of self-control. The contingencies of self-control, however, do not reside within the individual and cannot be freely chosen. When we control our own behavior, we do so by manipulating the same variables that we would use in controlling someone else's behavior, and ultimately these variables lie outside ourselves.

How can we exercise self-control without resorting to free choice? Skinner (1953) and Skinner and Vaughan (1983) pointed to several techniques, some of which are also used in social control. For example, *physical restraint* is not limited to social control but can also be used for self-control. Although we cannot physically hold ourselves back, we can arrange environmental contingencies so that they will restrict our behavior. For example, an angry person can clench his teeth to prevent himself from speaking inappropriately.

Self-control can also be produced through the use of *physical aids* such as tools, machines, and financial resources. A carpenter speeds work by using power equipment; a shopper increases the likelihood of spontaneous purchases by bringing enough money.

Another means of self-control is *changing the stimulus*, thereby increasing the probability of the desired behavior. Students wishing to concentrate on their studies can turn off a distracting television set. A woman desiring to quit smoking can stop carrying cigarettes. A man who wishes to call a friend more frequently can tape the telephone number someplace where he will see it more frequently. All these techniques involve the manipulation of environmental variables, thereby increasing the probability that one's own behavior will be changed.

Another technique of self-control is to arrange the environment so that we can *escape from aversive stimulation* only by producing the proper response. Skinner (1953) used the illustration of setting an alarm clock so that the aversive sound can be stopped only by getting up to shut off the alarm.

Skinner (1953) also listed *drugs*, especially alcohol, as a means of self-control. A disgruntled employee takes several drinks, knowing that this behavior will increase his chances of telling off his boss. A drug addict injects heroin to prevent withdrawal discomfort. A person takes tranquilizers to make her behavior more placid. Examples of self-control through the use of drugs can be expanded almost endlessly.

The technique of *doing something else* is used solely with self-control and cannot be applied to social control. We do something else in order to avoid behaving undesirably. This procedure is effective only if the substitute behavior is more powerful than the unwanted behavior. An obsessive neurotic counts repetitious patterns in wallpaper to avoid thinking about previous experiences that would create guilt. A person tempted to overeat goes jogging instead. In these examples, the substitute behaviors are negatively reinforcing because they allow a person to avoid unpleasant thoughts.

THE UNHEALTHY PERSONALITY

Unfortunately the techniques of social control and self-control sometimes produce detrimental effects, which result in inappropriate behavior and unhealthy personality development.

COUNTERACTING STRATEGIES

When social control is excessive, people can use three basic strategies for counteracting it—they can escape, revolt, or use passive resistance (Skinner, 1953). With the defensive strategy of *escape*, people withdraw from the controlling agent either physically or psychologically. Because the original controlling agent is ordinarily the parents, and very young children have little means of running away from home, a frequent mode of escape is to psychologically withdraw from parents, a strategy that may later lead to seclusion from society. People whose behavior is characterized by escape find it difficult to become involved in intimate personal relationships, tend to be mistrustful of people, and prefer to live lonely lives of noninvolvement.

People who *revolt* against society's controls behave more actively, counterattacking the controlling agent. Children who revolt oppose their parent's control by openly defying their authority or, more indirectly, by writing on the walls and mistreating furniture. Older people rebel through vandalizing public property, tormenting teachers, verbally abusing others, pilfering equipment from employers, provoking the police, or overthrowing established organizations such as religions or governments.

People who counteract control through *passive resistance* are more subtle than those who rebel and more irritating to the controllers than those who rely on escape. Skinner (1953) believed that passive resistance is most likely to be used where escape and revolt have failed. The conspicuous feature of this strategy is stubbornness. A child with homework to do finds a dozen excuses why it cannot be finished; the employee slows down progress by undermining the work of others; and the husband allows important chores to pile up by staying busy with trifles.

INAPPROPRIATE BEHAVIORS

Inappropriate behaviors follow from self-defeating techniques of counteracting social control or from unsuccessful attempts at self-control, especially when either of these failures is accompanied by strong emotion. Like most behaviors, inappropriate or unhealthy responses are learned. They are shaped by positive and negative reinforcement and especially by the effects of punishment.

Inappropriate behavior takes many forms, and Skinner (1953) listed several of the more common patterns along with their reinforcement contingencies. The first of these is taking *drugs*. The effects of alcohol and other drugs are reinforcing because they enable a person to avoid aversive stimuli, but their long-term consequences may be detrimental, leading to dependence or to a chronic mode of escape from the problems of everyday life.

Another inappropriate pattern is *excessively vigorous behavior*, which makes no sense in terms of the contemporary situation, but might be reasonable in terms of past history. Excessively vigorous behavior may stem from repression or reaction formation and is likely to manifest itself as extreme restlessness, preservation, or a compulsive tendency to repeat a response. An opposite pattern is *excessively restrained behavior*, a pattern that develops from a history of punishment. People learn responses that allow them to avoid the aversive stimuli associated with punishment, and these responses frequently take passive forms like shyness, stubbornness, inhibition, or hysterical paralysis.

Another type of inappropriate behavior is simply *blocking out reality*. This is similar to Sullivan's concept of selective inattention (see Chapter 8) in which a person pays no attention to aversive stimuli like a nagging spouse or the punitive thoughts associated with an earlier guilt-producing experience.

A fifth form of undesirable behavior results from *defective self-knowledge* and is manifested in such self-deluding responses as boasting, rationalizing, or believing oneself to be Jesus Christ or Julius Caesar. This pattern is usually an unsuccessful attempt at self-control and continues to be reinforcing because the person avoids the aversive stimulation associated with thoughts of inadequacy.

A final detrimental effect of control on behavior is *aversive self-stimulation*, exemplified by self-punishment or the arrangement of environmental variables so that one is punished by others. How can this "masochistic" behavior be rewarding? Several possibilities might explain it. First, aversive self-stimulation may permit a person to avoid even more painful stimuli, as when a soldier shoots himself in the foot in order to escape battle. Also, masochistic behavior is negatively reinforcing when it avoids the aversive conditions of guilt or sin by inflicting "deserved" punishment on the person. Finally, self-punishment can be learned through respondent conditioning. For example, when an aversive stimulus (pain) is paired with a strong reward (sex), the pleasure may override the pain so that the entire event (sexual pleasure coupled with pain) becomes reinforcing, and in some cases, the aversive stimulus (pain) may become, by itself, a reward. As a result, a person gains enjoyment from pain inflicted by self or others.

Most of these inappropriate patterns are behavioral descriptions of several Freudian defense mechanisms (repression, regression, reaction formation) and Adlerian safeguarding tendencies (excuses, aggression, withdrawal) as well as Sullivan's notion of selective inattention. The psychodynamic theorists viewed these behaviors as totally or partially motivated by unconscious urges within the person, but Skinner saw them simply as overt behaviors shaped by the environmental contingencies of reinforcement and punishment. Whereas the psychodynamic theorists saw these mechanisms as expressing some hidden motive, Skinner attributed no special purpose to them other than the avoidance of aversive stimulation and the attainment of positive reinforcement.

PSYCHOTHERAPY

Skinner (1987b) believed that psychotherapy is one of the chief obstacles blocking psychology's attempt to become scientific. Nevertheless, his ideas on the shaping of behavior (both appropriate and inappropriate) have had a significant impact on the current behavior therapy movement. However, his notions on treatment are not limited to the approach called behavior therapy, but extend to a description of how all therapy works.

The therapist, whether psychoanalytic, client-centered, or behavioral, is a controlling agent. Not all controlling agents, however, are harmful, and the patient must learn to discriminate between punitive authority figures (both past and present) and a permissive therapist who dispenses positive reinforcers. Whereas a parent may have been cold and rejecting, the therapist is warm and accepting; although the parent was critical and judgmental, the therapist is supportive and empathic.

The shaping of any behavior takes time, and therapeutic behavior is no exception. A therapist molds desirable behavior by reinforcing slightly improved changes in behavior. The nonbehavioral therapist may do this accidentally or unknowingly, whereas the behavioral therapist attends specifically to this technique (Skinner, 1953).

Traditional therapists generally explain behaviors by resorting to a variety of fictional constructs such as the Oedipus complex, striving for superiority, collective unconscious, and self-actualization needs. Skinner, however, believed that psychotherapists should work on the assumption that fantasies, slips of the tongue, defensive mechanisms, safeguarding tendencies, and so on are behaviors that can be accounted for by learning principles. No explanatory fictions or inner causes are needed to explain "neurotic" or inappropriate behavior, and no therapeutic purpose is enhanced by postulating them. Skinner reasoned that if behavior is shaped by inner causes, then some force must be responsible for the inner cause. Traditional theories must ultimately account for this cause, but behavior therapy merely skips it and deals directly with the history of the organism; and it is this history that, in the final analysis, is responsible for any hypothetical inner cause.

Behavior therapists have developed a variety of techniques over the years, most based on operant conditioning (Skinner, 1988), although some are built around the principles of respondent conditioning. In general, these therapists play an active role in the treatment process, pointing out the positive consequences of certain behaviors and the aversive effects of others and also suggesting behaviors that, over the long haul, will result in positive reinforcement.

RELATED RESEARCH

Skinner's theory is the most prolific of all theories of personality, having generated thousands of research studies on human participants. In its early history, operant conditioning was used mostly in studies with animals, then it was applied to simple human responses, but more recently, Skinner's ideas have been used in a multitude of studies dealing with complex human behaviors. Some of these studies have been concerned with the relationship between long-term behavior patterns (that is, personality) and contingencies of reinforcement. These studies are generally of two kinds; either they have asked how conditioning affects personality or how personality affects conditioning.

HOW CONDITIONING EFFECTS PERSONALITY

Evidence that shaping and conditioning can change personality is most clearly demonstrated in the clinical domain through behavior modification techniques. For example, in a study of cocaine abusers, Stephen Higgins et al. (1991) compared the effectiveness of a contingency management program with a traditional counseling approach. All participants were outpatients who met criteria for active cocaine dependence as defined by the DSM-III-R (American Psychiatric Association, 1987). All submitted to regular urine tests, which the experimenters used to detect cocaine use.

Participants in the contingency management group were awarded voucher points worth 15 cents each for remaining drug free. Although money was not exchanged, the vouchers could be used to purchase retail items such as cameras and bicycles. The first cocaine-free specimen was worth 10 points, or $1.50. The value of each subsequent consecutive drug-free specimen increased by 5 points, so that the second negative report was worth 15 points, the third, 20 points, and so forth. In addition, patients could receive a $10.00 voucher for each of four consecutive negative specimens. Submission of a positive specimen or failure to submit a urine specimen would reset the schedule back to $1.50, from which patients could begin again to earn points according to the original schedule. Once earned, points could not be lost. In addition to the vouchers, participants in the behavioral management group attended counseling sessions that focused on four issues. First, participants identified a nonabusing spouse, friend, or relative who gave them positive reinforcement whenever they submitted a negative specimen. Second, therapists taught participants to use drug-refusal skills and to recognize the antecedents and consequences of their cocaine use. Third, unemployed participants and others who were interested in job information received employment counseling. Fourth, participants were encouraged to develop new hobbies and recreational activities.

Participants in the traditional counseling group followed the 12-step program of Narcotics Anonymous, which is patterned after the Alcoholics Anonymous program.

They submitted specimens on the same schedule as the contingency management group, except that they were not informed of urinalysis results. They also participated in both group and individual therapy sessions, attended lectures on cocaine dependence, AIDS, the disease model of addiction, self-help, and relapse prevention. In addition, they identified a sponsor from a local self-help group who would supply aid and comfort as needed.

Results of the study easily favored the behavioral management approach. More than 80% of the patients in the behavioral group remained in treatment for the full 12 weeks, whereas only about 40% of the counseling group remained in treatment. Also, compared with patients in the counseling group, more patients in the behavioral treatment group remained cocaine free after 4 weeks, 8 weeks, and 12 weeks. Higgins et al. (1995) conducted a 1-year follow-up of these patients and found that all members of both treatment groups were using less cocaine than at intake and that patients who received vouchers continued to have lower rates of cocaine use than did control patients.

Although these results suggest the superiority of a behavioral treatment approach over traditional drug treatment, the monetary cost of this intervention was not inconsequential. Patients who remained drug free could receive more than $1,000 over the course of the original 12-week program. This amount is small, however, compared with the costs of cocaine addiction.

In addition, behavior modification techniques have been shown to be effective in changing so-called Type A behaviors, which are characterized by hostility, impatience, and time urgency, and which were once thought to be associated with increased risk for coronary heart disease (Haynes, Feinleib, & Kannel, 1980). For example, Keiko Nakano (1990) used an operant-self-control procedure to reduce Type A behaviors such as eating quickly, not relaxing, putting words into a speaker's mouth, and not listening to a speaker. Participants had to monitor and evaluate their own behaviors and then reinforce themselves when they increased non-Type A behaviors such as taking more time to eat or spending more time relaxing. The results showed that such operant self-control techniques produced a significant decrease in Type A behaviors. Furthermore, these results could not be attributed to passage of time or merely to self-monitoring. In short, operant conditioning techniques have been quite effective at getting people to change long-term behavior patterns or even "personality."

How Personality Effects Conditioning

Skinnerian theory and research has effectively shown that consequences of behavior can be powerful tools for shaping animal behavior. Yet, a question still remains of whether the same reinforcement strategies will have the same effect on different people. Research findings from various sources suggest that different personalities may react differently to the same environmental stimuli. For example, results from studies with infants as young as 2 to 3 months suggest that temperamental differences play a role in how effectively infants respond to conditioning tasks. In a study by Carl Dunst and Barbara Lingerfelt (1985), infants who were rated by their parents as most consistent in daily feeding and sleep patterns and who had longer attention spans were most responsive to operant conditioning tasks. Moreover, a series of studies on adults has demonstrated that extraverts are more sensitive to and learn more quickly with reinforcers, whereas introverts are more sensitive to and learn more quickly with punishment (Gupta, 1984; Gupta & Gupta, 1984; Gupta & Shukla, 1989).

Finally, Edelgard Wulfert and colleagues (Wulfert, Greenway, Farkas, Hayes, & Dougher, 1994) have demonstrated the role that rigidity of personality plays in conditioning and extinction of learned behaviors. These researchers began with the notion that in many studies of operant conditioning a conflict exists between what participants are told to do and what they are reinforced for doing. Operant conditioning assumes that under normal conditions people modify those behaviors that are reinforced; that is, they change their behavior to maximize reinforcements. However, in some studies, verbal instructions lead participants to behave one way, whereas the behavioral contingencies reinforce contradictory behaviors. Wulfert and colleagues asked, Will participants do as they are told or do as they are reinforced? They predicted that some people would be more likely to do as they are told (rigid people) and some would do as they are reinforced (flexible people). They administered the Scale for Personality Rigidity (Rehfish, 1958) to college students in order to compare the 12 most rigid students with the 12 most flexible ones. In general, they found that the rigid participants were more likely to be insensitive to behavioral contingencies and to persist in what they were told to do. Wulfert et al. recognized that rigid people's behavior is not completely insensitive to contingencies of reinforcement, but they insisted that it is also controlled by other contingencies.

CRITIQUE OF SKINNER

One of Skinner's major goals was to provide a scientific foundation for the study of human behavior and to make psychology as scientific as biology, chemistry, and physics. To what extent he achieved his goal may be a matter of debate, but what is not debatable is the fact that Skinner's ideas have generated a multitude of research. Our search of PsychINFO from 1967 to 1996 revealed that the topics of operant conditioning, schedules of reinforcement, shaping, and behavior modification have been the focus of about 3,000 studies, ranking Skinner's theory as the most prolific of all personality theorists during this time period.

Although Skinner was opposed to hypothetico-deductive systems and the testing of fabricated hypotheses, the quantity of descriptive research generated by Skinner's ideas obviously rates behavioral analysis very high on the first criterion of a useful theory—the *generation of research*. Similarly, most of Skinner's ideas can be either falsified or verified, so we have rated his theory high on the second criterion of a useful theory, that is, its *falsifiability*.

Third, how well does Skinner's theory *organize all that is known about human personality*? On this criterion the theory must receive only a moderate rating. Skinner's approach was to describe behavior and the environmental contingencies under which it takes place. His purpose was to bring together these descriptive facts and to generalize from them. Many personality traits can be accounted for by the principles of operant conditioning, and Skinner even offered explanations for such human characteristics as defense mechanisms, neurotic reactions, altruistic behaviors, and dreams. However, other concepts such as insight, creativity, motivation, inspiration, and self-efficacy do not fit easily into an operant conditioning framework.

The abundance of descriptive research turned out by Skinner and his followers has made operant conditioning an extremely practical procedure. For example, Skinnerian techniques have been used to train mentally retarded children to speak and dress themselves, condition phobic patients to overcome their fears, enhance compliance to medical recommendations, help people overcome tobacco and drug addictions, improve healthy eating habits, and increase assertiveness. In fact, Skinnerian theory can be applied to almost all areas of training, teaching, and psychotherapy. As a *guide to action*, therefore, the theory must be evaluated very highly.

The fifth criterion of a useful theory is *internal consistency*, and judged by this standard, Skinnerian theory again would be rated very high. Skinner defined his terms precisely and operationally, a process greatly aided by the avoidance of fictionalized mentalistic concepts.

Is the theory *parsimonious*? On this final criterion, Skinner's theory is difficult to rate. On one hand, the theory is free from cumbersome hypothetical constructs, but on the other hand, it demands a novel expression of everyday phrases. For example, instead of saying, "I got so mad at my husband, I threw a dish at him, but missed," one would need to say, "The contingencies of reinforcement within my environment were arranged in such a manner that I observed my organism throwing a dish against the kitchen wall."

CONCEPT OF HUMANITY

Without doubt, B. F. Skinner held a *deterministic view* of human nature, and concepts like free will and individual choice had no place in his behavioral analysis. People are not free but are controlled by environmental forces. They may seem to be motivated by inner causes, but in reality those causes can be traced to sources outside the individual. Self-control depends ultimately on environmental variables and not on some inner strength. When people control their own lives, they do so by manipulating their environment, which in turn shapes their behavior. This environmental approach negates hypothetical constructs such as will power or responsibility. Human behavior can be perfectly predicted if all genetic and environmental factors are known. At the present stage of the science of human behavior, of course, these factors are not completely known. Human behavior is extremely complex, but people behave under many of the same laws as do machines and animals.

The notion that human behavior is completely determined is an extremely problematic one for many people who believe that they observe daily many examples of free choice in both themselves and others. What accounts for this illusion of freedom? Skinner (1971) held that freedom and dignity are reinforcing concepts because people find satisfaction in the belief that they are free to choose and also in their faith in the basic dignity of human beings. Because these fictional concepts are reinforcing in many modern societies, people tend to behave in ways that increase the probability that these constructs will be perpetuated. Once freedom and dignity lose their reinforcement value, people will stop behaving *as if* they existed.

In the days preceding Louis Pasteur, many people believed that maggots spontaneously generated on the bodies of dead animals. Skinner (1974) used this observation to paint an analogy with human behavior, pointing out that the spontaneous generation of behavior is no more of a reality than the spontaneous generation of maggots. Behavior that is haphazard or random may appear to be freely chosen, but it is actually the product of haphazard or random environmental and genetic conditions. People are not autonomous, but the illusion of autonomy persists because of our ignorance of the individual's history. We attribute free will to humanity simply because we do not take the time to understand behavior. Every action we fail to understand, we assign to some internal concept such as beliefs, intentions, values, or motives. Skinner did not deny that people are capable of reflecting upon their own nature, but he insisted that this reflective behavior can be observed and studied just like any other.

Is Skinner's concept of humanity optimistic or pessimistic? At first thought, it may appear that a deterministic stance is necessarily pessimistic. However, Skinner's view of human nature tends, if anything, to be somewhat *optimistic*. Because human behavior is shaped by the principles of reinforcement, the species is quite adaptable. Of all behaviors, the most satisfying ones tend to increase in frequency of occurrence. People, therefore, learn to live quite harmoniously with their environment. The evolution of the species is in the direction of greater control over environmental variables, and this results in an increasing repertoire of behaviors beyond those essential for mere survival. However, Skinner (1987a) was also concerned that modern cultural practices have not yet evolved to the point at which nuclear war, overpopulation, and depletion of natural resources can be stopped. In this sense, he was more of a realist than an optimist.

Nevertheless, Skinner provided a blueprint for a utopian society (see *Walden Two*, Skinner, 1948). If his recommendations were followed, then people could be taught how to arrange the variables in their environments so that the probability of correct or satisfying solutions would be increased. Skinner was interested in improving humanity, and his efforts with the baby-tender and with teaching machines are but two examples of this interest.

Is humanity basically good or evil? Skinner hoped for an idealistic society in which people behave in ways that are loving, sensible, democratic, independent, and good, but people are not by nature this way. But neither are they essentially evil. Within limits set by heredity, people are flexible in their adaptation to the environment, but no evaluation of good or evil should be placed on an individual's behavior. If a person typically behaves altruistically for the good of others, it is because this behavior, either in the species' evolutionary history or in the individual's personal history, has been previously reinforced. If one behaves cowardly, it is because the rewards for cowardice outweigh the aversive variables (Skinner, 1978).

On the dimension of causality vs. teleology, Skinner's theory of personality is very high on *causality*. Behavior is caused by the person's history of reinforcement as well as by the species' contingencies for survival and by the evolution of cultures. Although people behave covertly (within the skin) when thinking about the future, all those thoughts are determined by past experiences (Skinner, 1990b).

The complex of environmental contingencies responsible for these thoughts, as well as for all other behaviors, are beyond our awareness. We rarely have knowledge of the relationship between all genetic and environmental variables and our own behavior. For this reason, Skinner would be placed very high on the *unconscious dimension of personality*.

The history of a person determines behavior, and because each of us has our own history of reinforcement contingencies, our behavior and personality are relatively unique. Genetic differences also account for *uniqueness among people*. Biological and historical differences make us unique individuals, and Skinner emphasized those differences more than he did our similarities.

Although he believed that genetics plays an important role in personality development, Skinner held that human personality is largely shaped by the environment. Because an important part of that environment is other people, Skinner's concept of humanity inclines more toward social than toward biological determinants of behavior. As a species, humans have developed to their present form because of particular environmental factors that they have encountered. Climate, geography, and physical strength relative to other animals have all helped shape the human species. But *social environment*, including family structure, early experiences with parents, educational systems, governmental organization, and so forth, has played an even more important role in the development of personality.

Skinner hoped that people might be trustworthy, understanding, warm, and empathic, characteristics that his friendly adversary Carl Rogers (see Chapter 16) believed to be at the core of the psychologically healthy personality. In contrast to Rogers, who believed that these positive behaviors are at least partially the result of our capacity to be self-directed, Skinner held that they are completely under the control of environmental variables. We are not by nature good, but we can become so if we are exposed to the proper contingencies of reinforcement. Although his view of the ideal person would be similar to those of Rogers and Abraham H. Maslow (see Chapter 17), Skinner believed that the means of becoming autonomous, loving, and self-actualizing must not be left to chance, but should be specifically designed into the society.

Chapter Summary

As a radical behaviorist, B. F. Skinner avoided all hypothetical concepts such as "mind" or "personality" and based his concept of humanity solely on observable behavior. Although most of his observations were made on rats and pigeons, Skinner believed that these observations could be generalized to human behavior. Rather than testing hypotheses, he simply observed behavior for the purpose of describing, predicting, and controlling it. His philosophy of science permitted an interpretation of behavior, but not an explanation of its causes.

Skinner recognized the existence of inner states such as thinking and feeling, but he insisted that these events are beyond the realm of behavioral analysis. Thoughts and feelings can be observed by the individual, but only overt behavior can be studied by the scientist.

Skinner believed that human behavior is shaped by three forces: (1) the individual's personal history of *reinforcement*, (2) *natural selection*, and (3) the *evolution of cultural practices*. His views on natural selection and cultural evolution were based largely on speculation, but his ideas on reinforcement were founded on his laboratory work on *operant conditioning*, a process in which reinforcement (or punishment) is contingent upon the occurrence of a particular behavior.

Skinner recognized two types of reinforcement—positive and negative. A *positive reinforcer* is any event that, when added to a situation, increases the probability that a given behavior will occur. A *negative reinforcer* is any aversive stimulus that, when removed, also increases the probability of a given behavior. Similarly, Skinner identified two types of *punishment*; the first is the presentation of an aversive stimulus and the second involves the removal of a positive stimulus. The effects of punishment are far less predictable than those of reinforcement.

Reinforcement can be either *continuous* or *intermittent*, but intermittent schedules are more efficient. The four principal intermittent schedules of reinforcement are the *fixed-ratio*, in which the organism is reinforced after a predetermined number of responses; the *variable-ratio*, in which reinforcement occurs after every *n*th response on the average; the *fixed-interval*, in which reinforcement occurs according to a designated period of time; and the *variable-interval*, in which reinforcement occurs after a lapse of random or variable periods of time.

Skinner offered several means by which human behavior is controlled. The first is *social control*, in which another person, a group, a society, or a nation shapes an individual's behavior. This is accomplished through (1) operant conditioning, (2) describing the contingencies of reinforcement, (3) depriving or satiating a person, or (4) physically restraining the individual. People can also control their own behavior through *self-control*, but all control ultimately rests with the environment. Self-control, therefore, is not a function of free will.

Unhealthy behaviors are learned in the same way as any other behaviors, that is, mostly through operant conditioning. In order to change unhealthy behaviors, many behavior therapists have employed a multitude of techniques based on the principles of operant conditioning.

Skinner's behavioral analysis has generated volumes of research, most of it descriptive rather than hypothesis testing. The theory receives high marks for being internally consistent and for guiding the practitioner. However, it is only moderately successful in organizing all that we currently know about human behavior.

In his concept of humanity, Skinner was both a *determinist* and an *environmentalist*. As a determinist, he rejected the notion of free choice and insisted that all behavior is lawfully determined and, potentially at least, can be perfectly predicted and controlled. As an environmentalist, he de-emphasized anatomy and stressed the environment, including natural selection, as the final shaper of human behavior.

Suggested Readings

Bjork, D. W. (1993). B. F. *Skinner: A life*. New York: Basic Books.
>   Bjork used a variety of resources, including interviews with Skinner during the last months of his life, to write this scholarly biography, which is both more interesting and more concise than Skinner's three-volume autobiography.

Skinner, B. F. (1953). *Science and human behavior*. New York: Macmillan.
>   Skinner's first and most complete work on the science of *human* rather than animal behavior, this book provides a comprehensive foundation for the scientific analysis of behavior.

Skinner, B. F. (1971). *Beyond freedom and dignity*. New York: Knopf.
>   In this, his most controversial book, Skinner argued that the concepts of freedom and dignity are detrimental to the building of an effective society. *Beyond Freedom and Dignity* was on nearly every best-seller list in 1971.

Skinner, B. F. (1974). *About behaviorism*. New York: Knopf.
>   In this book, Skinner defined, analyzed, and defended behaviorism and also presented 20 commonly held beliefs about behaviorism, all of which, he believed, were wrong.

Skinner, B. F. (1987a). *Upon further reflection*. Englewood Cliffs, NJ: Prentice-Hall.
>   A collection of Skinner's later works, this brief book challenges the reader in such areas as survival of the world, the importance of cultural evolution, and cognitive science. Also included is a chapter updating *Walden Two*.

Bandura

Bandura:
Social Cognitive Theory

Albert Bandura's **social cognitive theory** holds that personality is molded by an interaction of behavior, personal factors (especially cognition), and the environment. In this way it differs from Skinner's behavioral analysis that emphasizes the ultimate importance of the environment. Bandura's theory also differs from Skinner's in other fundamental ways. Unlike Skinner, Bandura believes that responses need not occur in order to be learned. According to Bandura, we can learn by observing another person's performance. For example, we might watch a magician do a particular trick, see how it was done, and go home and perform the trick ourselves. Learning obviously occurred prior to our performance. Bandura's theory further differs from Skinner's in that it gives more consideration to the cognitive capacities of the individual and less to environmental factors. Also, Bandura stresses the idea that reinforcement can be vicarious; that is, we can be reinforced by observing another person receive a reward. This indirect reinforcement accounts for a good bit of human learning. Bandura also differs from Skinner on the relationship between reinforcement and cognition. Whereas Skinner held that learning does not occur without reinforcement, Bandura asserts that reinforcement does not occur without prior cognition. In order for an event to be reinforcing, Bandura says, we must be cognizant of the connection between actions and their outcomes. Conditioning, then, is cognitively mediated and not an inevitable consequence of the environment alone.

BIOGRAPHY OF ALBERT BANDURA

Albert Bandura is a native of Canada but has spent his professional career in the United States. He was born on December 4, 1925, in Mundare, a small town in northern Alberta, where he attended elementary and secondary grades at the only school in town. After graduating from high school, Bandura spent a summer in Alaska working on the Alaska highway, built during World War II to connect the United States with the territory of Alaska. Bandura's experience brought him into contact with a wide variety of fellow workers, many of whom manifested various degrees of psychopathology. Although his observations of these workers kindled in him an interest in clinical psychology, he did not decide to become a psychologist until after he had enrolled in the University of British Columbia in Vancouver.

Bandura told Richard Evans (Evans, 1989) that his decision to become a psychologist was quite accidental, that is, it was a fortuitous event. As an undergraduate student, Bandura commuted to school with pre-med and engineering students who were early risers. Rather than do nothing during this early hour, Bandura decided to enroll in a psychology class that happened to be offered at that time period. He found the class fascinating and eventually decided to take a psychology major. Later we will see that Bandura considers fortuitous events (such as his riding to school with students who were enrolled in early classes) to be important influences in people's lives.

After graduating from British Columbia in just 3 years, Bandura looked for a graduate program in clinical psychology that had a strong learning theory base. His advisor recommended the University of Iowa, so Bandura left Canada for the United States. He completed a master's degree in 1951 and a Ph.D. in clinical psychology the following year. Then he spent a year in Wichita completing a postdoctoral internship at the Wichita Guidance Center. In 1953, he joined the faculty at Stanford University where, except for 1 year, he has remained until the present time.

While still a graduate student, Bandura had a chance encounter that altered the course of his life. Chance encounters, like fortuitous events, have largely been ignored by other personality theorists, even though most of us recognize that we have had unplanned experiences that have greatly changed our lives. In Bandura's case, an uninteresting reading assignment eventually led to a chance meeting with his future wife. Bored with schoolwork, Bandura and a friend decided to play golf. By chance, this male twosome found themselves playing behind two women golfers. During the course of the round, two twosomes became one foursome. Thus, by chance, Albert Bandura met Virginia (Ginny) Varns. The couple now have two daughters, Mary and Carol, who like most of us, owe their existence to a chance encounter.

Most of Bandura's early publications were in clinical psychology, dealing primarily with psychotherapy and the Rorschach test. Then, in 1958, he collaborated with the late Richard H. Walters, his first doctoral student, to publish a paper on aggressive delinquents. The following year, their book *Adolescent Aggression* (1959) appeared. Since then, Bandura has continued to publish on a wide variety of subjects, often in collaboration with his graduate students. His most monumental work, *Social Foundations of Thought and Action*, was published in 1986.

Bandura has received many honors and awards, including the Guggenheim Fellowship in 1972 and the Distinguished Scientific Contribution Award from Division 12 (Clinical) of the American Psychological Association (APA) in the same year. In 1974 he was elected president of the APA; in 1977 he received the James McKeen Cattell Award; in 1980 he was elected fellow, American Academy of Arts and Sciences; and also in 1980 he won the Distinguished Contribution Award from the International Society for Research on Aggression, as well as the prestigious Award for Distinguished Scientific Contribution from the APA. Bandura is currently David Starr Jordan Professor of Social Science in Psychology at Stanford University.

INTRODUCTION TO SOCIAL COGNITIVE THEORY

Bandura's social cognitive theory of personality rests on several basic assumptions. First, although biology plays some role in personality formation, humans are largely a product of *learning*. An outstanding characteristic of humans is their plasticity—their ability to learn a variety of behaviors. We can and do learn through direct experience, but much of our behavior is shaped through the observation of others. Bandura (1986) stated that "virtually all learning phenomena, resulting from direct experience, can occur vicariously by observing other people's behavior and its consequences for them" (p. 19).

Second, humans have a tremendous capacity for symbolization that serves as "a powerful tool for comprehending their environment and for creating and regulating environmental events that touch virtually every aspect of their lives" (Bandura, 1994b, p. 62). Our use of symbols, especially language, enables us to "transform transient experiences into internal models that serve as guides for future action" (Bandura, 1986, p. 18). These transformations give some consistency and structure to the *self system*. Without this capacity, people would merely react to sensory experiences and would lack the capacity to anticipate events, create new ideas, or use internal standards to evaluate present experiences. People have the capacity for reflective self-consciousness; they not only can think but can think about thinking. "People form beliefs about what they can do, they anticipate the likely consequences of prospective actions, they set goals for themselves, and they otherwise plan courses of action that are likely to produce desired outcomes" (Bandura, 1991b, p. 248).

Finally, although our symbolic and cognitive capacities can account for much of our behavior, they are not solely responsible for our actions. Human functioning is molded by the reciprocal interaction of personal factors (including cognition), environmental events, and our own behavior. Bandura calls this triadic model **reciprocal determinism.**

RECIPROCAL DETERMINISM

In Chapter 10 we saw that Skinner believed that behavior is a function of the environment; that is, behavior ultimately can be traced to forces outside the person. As environmental contingencies change, behavior changes. But what impetus changes the environment? Skinner acknowledged that human behavior can exercise some measure of countercontrol over the environment, but he insisted that, in the final analysis, behavior is environmentally determined.

Bandura adopts quite a different stance. In his theory, a reciprocal interaction among three variables—the environment, the behavior, and the person—is responsible for human action. In this scheme, behavior is partially a function of the environment, but conversely, the environment is partially a function of behavior. However, Bandura also adds a crucial third factor—the person. By "person" he means largely, but not exclusively, internal factors such as cognition. Because people possess cognitive capacities of memory and anticipation, they are able to influence both their environment and their own behavior. Cognition determines, at least partially, which environmental events people will attend, what value they will place on these events, and how they will organize these events for future use. Cognition, however, is not an autonomous entity, independent of behavior and environment. Bandura (1986) criticized those theorists who attribute the source of human behavior to internal forces such as instincts, drives, needs, or intentions. Cognition itself is determined, being formed by both behavior and environment. But behavior and environment are also partially determined by cognition. Therefore, Bandura sees personal conduct in terms of *reciprocal determinism*, a term that suggests a three-way interaction of environment, behavior, and person (Bandura, 1977, 1982a, 1986).

Reciprocal determinism is represented schematically in Figure 11.1, where B signifies behavior; E is the external environment; and P represents the person, including biological characteristics such as gender, social position, size, and physical attractiveness, but especially the internal state of cognition, including thought, memory, judgment, foresight, and so on.

Consider this example of reciprocal determinism. A child begging her father for a cookie is, from the father's viewpoint, an environmental event. If the father automatically (without thought) were to give the child a cookie, then the two would be conditioning one another's behavior in the Skinnerian sense. The behavior of the father would be controlled by the environment, but his behavior, in turn, would have a countercontrolling effect on the environment, namely the child. In Bandura's theory, however, the father is capable of thinking about the consequences of rewarding or ignoring the child's behavior. He may think, "If I give her a cookie, she will stop crying temporarily, but in future cases, she will be more likely to persist until I give in to her. Therefore, I will not allow her to have a cookie." Hence the father has an effect on both his environment (the child) and his own behavior (rejecting his daughter's request). The child's subsequent behavior (father's environment) helps shape the cognition and the behavior of the father. If the child stops begging, the father may then have other thoughts. For example, he may evaluate his behavior by thinking, "I'm a good father because I did the right thing." The change in environment also allows the father to

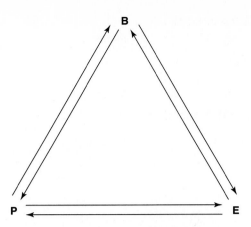

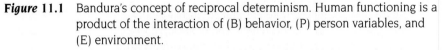

Figure 11.1   Bandura's concept of reciprocal determinism. Human functioning is a product of the interaction of (B) behavior, (P) person variables, and (E) environment.
Source: From Albert Bandura, 1994b. Social cognitive theory and mass communication. In J. Bryant & D. Zillmann (Eds.), *Media effects: Advances in theory and research* (p. 62). Hillsdale, NJ: Erlbaum. Reproduced by permission.

pursue different behaviors. Thus, his subsequent behavior is partially determined by the reciprocal interaction of his environment, cognition, and behavior.

This example illustrates the reciprocal interaction of behavioral, environmental, and personal factors from the father's point of view. First, the child's pleas affected the father's behavior (E → B); they also partially determined the father's cognition (E → P); the father's behavior helped shape the child's behavior, that is, his own environment (B → E); his behavior also impinged on his own thoughts (B → P); and his cognition partially determined his behavior (P → B). To complete the cycle, P (person) must influence E (environment). How can the father's cognition directly shape the environment, without first being transformed into behavior? It cannot. However, P does not signify cognition alone; it stands for person. Bandura (1978b) hypothesized that "people activate different environmental reactions, apart from their behavior, by their physical characteristics (e.g., size, physiognomy, race, sex, attractiveness) and socially conferred attributes, roles, and status" (p. 346). The father then, by virtue of his role and status as a father and perhaps in conjunction with his size and strength, has a decided effect on the child. Thus the final determination is completed (P → E).

DIFFERENTIAL CONTRIBUTIONS

Bandura uses the term "reciprocal" to indicate a mutual interaction of forces, not a similar or opposite counteraction. The three reciprocal factors need neither to be of equal strength nor to make an equal contribution. The relative potency of the three varies with the individual and with the situation.

At times, behavior might be the most powerful, as when a person plays the piano for her own enjoyment. Other times, the environment exerts the greatest influence, as when a boat overturns and every survivor begins thinking and behaving in a very similar fashion. At still other times, cognition (person) may gain ascendancy, as when a person believes that there are sinister plans being plotted to destroy her.

The relative influence of behavior, environment, and person depends on which of the triadic factors is strongest at a particular moment (Bandura, 1982a).

MEANING OF DETERMINISM

Determinism does not mean that behavior is completely determined by forces outside the individual. Bandura (1988a) sees no incompatibility between human agency and determinism. He is not an absolute determinist who believes that all behavior is caused by external events, but neither does he accept the concept of complete free will. Although human personality and behavior are influenced by external events, they are not inevitably determined by them. They are also molded by cognition, an internal state that at least partially determines which environmental events will be perceived, evaluated, and acted upon. In other words, the environment itself does not determine our actions, but our perception of the environment is one factor that contributes to our behavior. Within limits, then, people can choose to behave in a manner that increases the probability that the environment will interact with them in a somewhat predictable way. Behavior, therefore, is not only a dependent variable, but also an independent variable, exerting an influence on both the environment and the person.

CHANCE ENCOUNTERS AND FORTUITOUS EVENTS

Bandura believes that people are remarkably flexible and resilient. They "must develop their basic capabilities over an extended period, and they must continue to master new competencies to fulfill changing demands throughout their life span" (Bandura, 1986, p. 20). Resilience is possible because any of the three triadic factors—environment, behavior, or person—may be altered at any time. Two important potential changes are **chance encounters** and **fortuitous events.**

Bandura (1986) defined a chance encounter as "an unintended meeting of persons unfamiliar to each other" (p. 32). A fortuitous event is an environmental experience that is unexpected and unintended. The everyday lives of people are affected to a greater or lesser extent by the people they chance to meet. One's marital partner, occupation, place of residence, and the like may largely be the result of a fortuitous meeting that was unplanned and unexpected.

Just as fortuity has influenced the lives of all of us, it has shaped the lives and careers of famous personality theorists. Two such examples are Abraham H. Maslow (Chapter 17) and Hans J. Eysenck (Chapter 13). As a young man, Maslow was exceedingly shy, especially with women. At the same time, he was passionately in love with his cousin Bertha Goodman, but he was too bashful to express his love. One day while he was visiting his cousin's home, Bertha's older sister pushed him toward his beloved cousin, saying: "For the love of Pete, kiss her, will ya!" (Hoffman, 1988, p. 29). Maslow did, and to his surprise, Bertha did not fight back. She kissed him, and from that moment, Maslow's previous aimless life became transformed. He and Bertha were quickly married, and his marriage changed him from a mediocre college student to a brilliant scholar who eventually shaped the course of humanistic psychology in the United States.

Also, Hans Eysenck, the noted British psychologist, came to psychology completely by chance. He had intended to study physics at the University of London, but first he had to pass an entrance examination. After waiting a year to take the exam, he was told that he had taken the wrong test, and that he would have to wait another year to take the right one. Rather than delaying his education further, he asked whether there might be any scientific subject that he could pursue. When told that he could enroll in a psychology program, Eysenck asked, "What on earth is psychology?" (Eysenck, 1982, p. 290). Eysenck, of course, went on to major in psychology and to become one of the world's most famous psychologists.

Fortuity adds a separate dimension in any scheme used to predict human behavior, and it makes accurate predictions practically impossible. However, chance encounters influence people only by entering the reciprocal determinism paradigm at point E (environment) and adding to the mutual interaction of person, behavior, and environment. In this sense, they influence us in the same manner as do planned events. Once a chance encounter occurs, people behave toward their new acquaintance on the basis of their prior history of reinforcements, their expectations for this new relationship, and the other person's reaction to them.

SELF SYSTEM

Bandura deviates from Skinner's radical behaviorism in postulating the existence of a **self system,** which acts upon both the environment and behavior. If behavior were completely a function of the environment, Bandura reasons, then our behavior would be more variable and less consistent because we would constantly be reacting to the great diversity of environmental stimuli. "If actions were determined solely by external rewards and punishments, people would behave like weathervanes" (Bandura, 1986, p. 335). But "people do not behave like weathervanes, constantly shifting to whatever social influence happened to impinge upon them at the moment" (Bandura, 1995b, p. 350). Although personality is largely learned and can be quite complex and variegated within any one person, some consistencies of speech, self-expression, and behavioral traits are difficult to account for on the bases of environmental contingencies alone. Cognitive factors such as memory and foresight bring some unity and consistency to personality.

However, Bandura does not go to the other extreme and suggest that we have an autonomous agent within us that shapes our behavior to conform to a preexisting self-concept. In fact, Bandura believes that behavior is generally more varied than it appears and that different behaviors should not be attributed to single or dual motives like striving for success (Adler) or sex and aggression (Freud). If behavior were regulated by a single motive, people would be more consistent. For example, a person who is usually moral would never behave immorally, but we know that this frequently happens. In Chapter 14 we will see that Gordon Allport argued that people possess personal dispositions or traits that have the power to render divergent stimuli functionally equivalent. Bandura would not countenance such an argument. An aggressive person, for example, is not always aggressive because the environment does not always reinforce aggressive behavior. Differential experiences with reward and punishment, to a large degree, shape one's behavior.

Bandura (1994b) sees the self system as a set of cognitive structures that include perception, evaluation, and regulation of behavior. Our self system allows us to observe and symbolize our own behavior and to evaluate it on the basis of memories of past reinforced or nonreinforced behavior as well as anticipated future consequences. Then, using these cognitive processes as a reference point, we are able to exercise some measure of self-direction or self-regulation.

Self-Regulation

Although people have no independent self with the capacity to manipulate the environment at will, they are capable of some degree of self-regulation. By using reflective thought, they can manipulate their environments and produce consequences of their actions. These consequences feed back into the reciprocal determinism paradigm and enable people to partially regulate their own behavior.

Bandura (1994b) believes that people use both reactive and proactive strategies for self-regulation. That is, they *reactively* attempt to reduce the discrepancies between their accomplishments and their goal; but after they close those discrepancies, they *proactively* set newer and higher goals for themselves. "People motivate and guide their actions through proactive control by setting themselves valued goals that create a state of disequilibrium and then mobilizing their abilities and effort based on anticipatory estimation of what is required to reach the goals" (p. 63). The notion that people seek a state of disequilibrium is similar to Gordon Allport's belief that people are motivated at least as much to create tension as to reduce it (see Chapter 14).

We have seen that Bandura believes that behavior is regulated by the reciprocal interaction of person, environment, and prior behavior and that people have some limited capacity to regulate their own behavior. What processes contribute to this self-regulation? First, we humans possess some capacity to manipulate the external factors that feed into the reciprocal interactive paradigm. Second, we are capable of monitoring our own behavior and evaluating it in terms of both proximate and distant goals. Behavior, then, stems from a reciprocal influence of both external and internal factors (Bandura, 1986).

External Factors in Self-Regulation

External factors affect self-regulation in at least two ways. First, they provide us with a standard for evaluating our own behavior. Standards do not stem solely from internal forces. Environmental factors, interacting with personal influences, shape individual standards for evaluation. By precept we learn from parents and teachers the value of honest and friendly behavior; by direct experience, we learn to place more value on being warm and dry than on being cold and wet; and through observing others, we evolve a multitude of standards for evaluating self-performance. In each of these examples, personal factors affect which standards we will learn, but environmental forces also play a role.

Second, external factors aid self-regulation by providing the means for reinforcement. Intrinsic rewards are not always sufficient; we also need incentives that emanate from external factors. An artist, for example, may require more reinforcement than self-satisfaction to complete a large mural. Environmental support in the form of a monetary retainer or praise and encouragement from others may also be necessary.

The incentives to complete a lengthy project usually come from the environment and often take the form of small rewards contingent upon the completion of subgoals. The artist may enjoy a cup of coffee after having completed the hand of one of the subjects or break for lunch after finishing another small section of the mural. However, self-reward for inadequate performance is likely to result in environmental sanctions. Friends may criticize or mock the artist's work, patrons may withdraw financial support, or the artist may be self-critical. When performance does not meet self-standards, we tend to withhold rewards from ourselves.

Internal Factors in Self-Regulation

External factors interact with internal or personal factors in self-regulation. Bandura (1986, 1991b) recognizes three internal requirements in the ongoing exercise of self-influence.

Self-Observation

The first internal factor in self-regulation is *self-observation* of performance. We must be able to monitor our own performance, even though the attention we give to it need not be complete or even accurate. We attend selectively to some aspects of our behavior and ignore others altogether. What we observe depends on interests and other preexisting self-conceptions. In achievement situations, such as painting pictures, playing games, or taking examinations, we pay attention to the quality, quantity, speed, or originality of our work; in interpersonal situations, such as meeting new acquaintances or reporting on events, we monitor the sociability or morality of our conduct.

Judgmental Process

Self-observation alone does not provide a sufficient basis for regulating our own behavior. We must also evaluate our performance. This second or *judgmental process* helps us regulate our behavior through the process of cognitive mediation. We are capable not only of reflective self-awareness but also of judging the worth of our actions on the basis of goals we have set for ourselves. More specifically, the judgmental process depends on personal standards, referential performances, valuation of activity, and performance attribution.

Personal standards allow us to evaluate our performances without comparing them to the conduct of others. To a profoundly retarded 10-year-old child, the act of tying his shoelaces may be highly prized. He need not devalue his accomplishment simply because other children can perform this same act at a younger age.

Personal standards, however, are a limited source of evaluation. For most of our activities, we evaluate our performances by comparing them to a *standard of reference*. Students compare their test scores to those of their classmates, and tennis players judge their personal skills against those of other players. In addition, we use our own previous levels of accomplishment as a reference for evaluating present performance. "Am I as good a salesperson as I was 5 years ago?" "Has my singing voice improved over the years?" "Is my teaching ability better now than ever?" Also, we may judge our performance by comparing it to that of a single individual—a brother, sister, parent, or even a hated rival—or we can compare it to a standard norm such as par in golf or a perfect score in bowling.

Besides personal and reference standards, the judgmental process is also dependent on the overall *value* we place on an activity. If we place minor value on our ability to wash dishes or dust furniture, then we will spend little time or effort in trying to improve these abilities. On the other hand, if we place high value on getting ahead in the business world or attaining a professional or graduate degree, then we will expend much effort to achieve success in these areas.

Finally, self-regulation also depends on how we judge the causes of our behavior, that is, *performance attribution*. If we believe that our success is due to our own efforts, we will take pride in our accomplishments and tend to work harder to attain our goals. However, if we attribute our performance to external factors, we will not derive as much self-satisfaction and will probably not put forth strenuous effort to attain our goals. Conversely, if we believe that we are responsible for our own failures or inadequate performance, we will work more readily toward self-regulation than if we are convinced that our shortcomings and our fears are due to factors beyond our control (Bandura, 1986, 1991b).

Affective Self-Reaction

The third and final internal factor in self-regulation is *active self-reaction*. We respond with positive or negative affect to our behavior depending on how it measures up to our personal standards. That is, we create incentives for our own actions through self-reinforcement or self-punishment. For example, a diligent student may reward herself for completing a reading assignment by watching her favorite television program.

Self-reinforcement does not rest on the fact that it immediately follows a response; rather, it relies in large part on the use of our cognitive ability to mediate the consequences of our behavior. We set standards for performance that, when met, tend to regulate behavior by such self-produced rewards as pride and self-satisfaction. When we fail to meet our standards, our behavior is followed by self-dissatisfaction or self-criticism.

This concept of self-mediated consequences is a sharp contrast to Skinner's notion that the consequences of behavior are environmentally determined. Bandura hypothesizes that we work to attain rewards and to avoid punishments according to self-erected standards. Even when rewards are tangible, they are often accompanied by self-mediated intangible incentives such as a sense of accomplishment. The Nobel Prize, for example, carries a substantial cash award, but its greater value to most recipients must be the feeling of pride or self-satisfaction in performing the tasks that led to the award.

SELECTIVE ACTIVATION AND DISENGAGEMENT OF INTERNAL CONTROL

After people have adopted social and moral standards of conduct, they regulate their behavior by two major sources of sanctions: (1) social sanctions and (2) internalized self-sanctions (Bandura, 1994b). Social sanctions discourage people from transgressing their standards of conduct because they fear social censure or other adverse consequences. Internalized self-sanctions prevent people from violating personal standards either through *selective activation* or *disengagement of internal control.*

Bandura (1994b) stated that "people do not ordinarily engage in reprehensible conduct until they have justified to themselves the morality of their actions" (p. 72). Yet people have no automatic internal controlling agent such as a conscience or superego. Self-regulatory influences are not automatic but operate only if they are activated, a concept Bandura (1986) calls **selective activation.** What people see as proper conduct in one situation, they may view as improper in another. How and when people activate their self-regulatory function is influenced both by self-evaluation and by environmental conditions. When people clearly understand that a particular course of action is inconsistent with their self-evaluation and that it will result in injury to another person, they will choose a different behavior. In another situation, people may evaluate the same course of action as proper and unharmful and will act accordingly. Thus, people selectively activate behavior according to their interpretation of the situation. Bandura's concept of selective activation is somewhat analogous to Sullivan's idea of selective inattention (see Chapter 8). Recall that Sullivan used the term "selective inattention" to refer to people's refusal to see things that they do not wish to see.

Bandura refers to the second self-reactive control of conduct as **disengagement of internal control.** When faced with an ambiguous situation—one that is neither clearly in violation of personal standards nor clearly consistent with them—we may disengage our behavior from its negative consequences. Disengagement of internal control, like selective activation, allows us to engage in socially and morally diverse behaviors while retaining our moral standards. These behaviors are beneficial to us but are harmful to others.

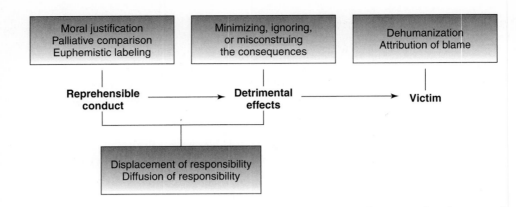

Figure 11.2 Mechanisms through which internal control is selectively activated or disengaged from reprehensible conduct at different points in the regulatory process.
From *Social Foundations of Thought and Action: A Social Cognitive Theory*, by Bandura, Albert, © 1986. Adapted by permission of Prentice-Hall, Inc., Upper Saddle River, NJ.

Figure 11.2 illustrates the various mechanisms through which self-control is disengaged or selectively activated. First, we can *redefine the nature of the behavior* itself by such techniques as morally justifying it or euphemistically labeling our actions. Second, we can *displace or diffuse responsibility* for our behavior by obscuring the relationship between our actions and the effects of our actions. Third, we can *distort, minimize, or ignore the detrimental consequences of our behavior.* Fourth, we can *blame or dehumanize the victim.*

Redefine the Behavior

With *redefinition of behavior*, we justify otherwise reprehensible actions by a cognitive restructuring that allows us to minimize or escape responsibility. We can relieve ourselves of responsibility for our behavior by at least three techniques (see upper-left box in Figure 11.2).

The first is *moral justification*, in which otherwise culpable behavior is made to seem defensible or even noble. Bandura (1991a) cited the example of World War I hero Sergeant Alvin York who, as a conscientious objector, believed that killing was morally wrong. After his battalion commander quoted from the Bible the conditions under which it was morally justified to kill, and after a long prayer vigil, York became convinced that killing enemy soldiers was morally defensible. After redefining killing, York became one of the greatest war heroes in American history, killing and capturing more than 100 German soldiers.

A second method of reducing responsibility through redefining wrongful behavior is to make advantageous or *palliative comparisons* between that behavior and the even greater atrocities committed by others. The child who vandalizes a school building uses the excuse that others broke even more windows. Politicians accuse their opponents of having accepted more campaign money from tobacco companies than they have.

A third technique in redefining behavior is the use of *euphemistic labels*. Politicians who have pledged not to raise taxes speak of "revenue enhancement" rather than taxes; some Nazis leaders called the murder of millions of Jews the "purification of Europe" or "the final solution," and professional killers speak of "fulfilling a contract."

Displace or Diffuse Responsibility

The second method of dissociating our actions from their consequences is to *displace or diffuse responsibility* (see lower box in Figure 11.2). With *displacement*, we minimize the consequences of our actions by placing responsibility on an outside source. An employee claims that her boss is responsible for her inefficiency; Nazi prison officers protested that they were carrying out orders from higher officers.

A related procedure is to *diffuse responsibility*—to spread it so thin that no one person is responsible. A civil servant may diffuse responsibility for her actions throughout the entire bureaucracy with such comments as "That's the way things are done around here" or "That's just policy."

Disregard or Distort the Consequences of Behavior

A third method of avoiding responsibility involves *distorting or obscuring the relationship between the behavior and its detrimental consequences* (see upper-center box of Figure 11.2). Bandura (1986, 1991b) recognized at least three techniques of distorting or obscuring the detrimental consequences of one's actions. First, we can *minimize the consequences of our behavior.* For example, a driver runs a red light and strikes a pedestrian. As the injured party lies bleeding and unconscious on the pavement, the driver says, "She's not really hurt badly. She's going to be okay."

Second, we can *disregard or ignore the consequences of our actions*, as when we do not see firsthand the harmful effects of our behavior. In wartime, heads of state and army generals seldom view the total destruction and death resulting from their decisions.

Finally, we can *distort or misconstrue the consequences* of our actions, as when a parent beats a child badly enough to cause serious bruises but explains that the child needs discipline in order to mature properly.

Blame the Victims

Fourth, we can obscure responsibility for our actions by either *dehumanizing our victims or attributing blame to them* (see upper-right box in Figure 11.2). In time of war, people often see the enemy as subhuman so they need not feel guilty for killing enemy soldiers. At various times in U.S. history, Jews, African Americans, Native Americans, Asian Americans, homosexuals, beggars, and elderly people have become *dehumanized victims.* Otherwise kind, considerate, and gentle people have perpetrated acts of violence, insult, or other forms of mistreatment against these groups in order to avoid responsibility for their own behavior.

When victims are not dehumanized, they are sometimes *blamed* for the perpetrator's culpable conduct. A rapist may blame his victim for his crime, citing her provocative dress or behavior. A business may overcharge customers and then blame them for being gullible.

DISENGAGEMENT VS. DEFENSE MECHANISMS

Although Bandura's concept of disengagement may appear similar to Freud's idea of defense mechanisms or Adler's notion of safeguarding tendencies, the similarities are more superficial than substantive. With all three, a person is protected from conditions of discomfort, but aside from this, differences outweigh similarities. Freudian defense mechanisms operate unconsciously and automatically to protect the ego from anxiety. Adlerian safeguarding tendencies are erected for the purpose of protecting a person against external threats to fictionalized feelings of personal superiority. They also operate automatically, can be conscious as well as unconscious, and are directed toward gaining superiority over other people.

On the other hand, disengagement procedures are neither unconscious nor automatic; rather, they are cognitively mediated. They protect a person from neither instinctual demands nor external threats, but instead, they permit us to minimize or avoid responsibility in an ambiguous situation by justifying behavior that ordinarily would be foreign to our self-evaluation. Unlike safeguarding tendencies, they are not specifically directed toward other people, but are used to justify to ourselves behavior that we would otherwise devalue or condemn.

SELF-EFFICACY

How we will act in a particular situation depends on the reciprocity of environmental and cognitive conditions, especially those cognitive factors that relate to our beliefs that we can or cannot execute the behavior necessary to effect a successful change in that situation. Bandura (1986) calls these expectations **self-efficacy.** According to Bandura (1994b) "people's beliefs in their personal efficacy influence what courses of action they choose to pursue, how much effort they will invest in activities, how long they will persevere in the face of obstacles and failure experiences, and their resiliency following setbacks" (p. 65). Although self-efficacy has a powerful causal influence on our actions, it is not their sole determinant. Rather, self-efficacy combines with environment, prior behavior, and other personal variables, especially outcome expectations, to produce behavior.

In the triadic reciprocal determinism model, which postulates that the environment, behavior, and person have an interactive influence on one another, self-efficacy refers to the P (person) factor.

SELF-EFFICACY DEFINED

Bandura (1989) defined self-efficacy as "people's beliefs about their capabilities to exercise control over events that affect their lives" (p. 1175). People with high self-efficacy believe that they can do something to alter environmental events; those with low self-efficacy regard themselves as essentially incapable of executing consequential behavior.

Self-efficacy is not the expectation of our action's outcomes or effects. Bandura (1986, 1995b) distinguished between efficacy expectations and *outcome expectations*. Efficacy refers to people's confidence that they have the ability to perform certain behaviors, whereas an outcome expectancy refers to one's prediction of the likely *consequences* of that behavior. Outcome should not be confused with successful accomplishment of an act; it refers to the consequences of behavior, not the completion of the act itself. For example, a job applicant may have confidence that she will perform well during an interview, have the ability to answer any possible question, remain relaxed and controlled, and exhibit an appropriate level of friendly behavior. Therefore, she has high self-efficacy in regard to the employment interview. However, despite these high efficacy expectations, she may have low outcome expectations. A low outcome expectancy would exist if she believes that she has little chance of being offered

The most influential source of self-efficacy is performance.

a position. This judgment might be due to unpromising environmental conditions, such as high unemployment, depressed economy, or superior competition. In addition, other personal factors such as age, gender, height, weight, or physical health may negatively affect outcome expectancies.

Besides being different from outcome expectancies, self-efficacy must be distinguished from several other concepts. First, efficacy does not refer to the ability to execute basic motor skills such as walking, reaching, or grasping. Also, efficacy does not imply that we can perform designated behaviors without anxiety, stress, or fear; it is merely our judgment, accurate or faulty, as to whether or not we can execute the required actions. Finally, judgments of efficacy are not the same as levels of aspiration. Heroin addicts, for example, often aspire to be drug-free but may have little confidence in their ability to successfully break the habit (Bandura, 1982c).

SOURCES OF SELF-EFFICACY

Personal efficacy is acquired, enhanced, or decreased through any one or combination of four sources: (1) mastery experiences; (2) vicarious experiences; (3) social persuasion; and (4) physiological and emotional states (Bandura, 1995a). With each method, information about oneself and the environment is cognitively processed and, together with recollections of previous experiences, alters perceived self-efficacy. Besides these four sources, efficacy is affected by one's internal standards of conduct.

Mastery Experiences

The most influential sources of self-efficacy are *mastery experiences*, that is, past performances (Bandura, 1986, 1995a). In general, successful performance raises efficacy expectancies, whereas failure tends to lower them. This general statement has six corollaries.

First, successful performance raises self-efficacy in proportion to the difficulty of the task. Highly skilled tennis players gain little self-efficacy by defeating clearly inferior opponents, but they gain much by performing well against superior opponents.

Verbal persuasion can raise or lower self-efficacy.

Second, tasks successfully accomplished by oneself are more efficacious than those completed with the help of others. In sports, team accomplishments do not increase personal efficacy as much as do individual achievements. Third, failure is most likely to decrease efficacy when we know that we put forth our best effort. To fail when only half-trying is not as inefficacious as to fall short in spite of our best efforts. Fourth, failure under conditions of high emotional arousal or distress are not as self-debilitating as failure under maximal conditions. Fifth, failure after a sense of efficacy is firmly established is less detrimental to feelings of personal efficacy than early failure. A sixth and related corollary is that occasional failure has little effect on efficacy, especially for people with a generally high expectancy of success.

Vicarious Experiences

A second source of efficacy is **vicarious experiences** provided by social models. Our self-efficacy is raised when we observe others succeed (Bandura, Adams, Hardy, & Howells, 1980), but it is lowered when we see another person of equal competence fail (Brown & Inouye, 1978). When the model we observe is dissimilar to us, then vicarious experience has little effect on our self-efficacy. An old, sedentary coward watching a young, active, brave circus performer successfully walk a high wire will undoubtedly have little enhancement of efficacy expectations for duplicating the feat.

In general, the effects of modeling are not as strong as those of personal performance in raising levels of efficacy, but they can have powerful effects where inefficacy is concerned. Watching a swimmer of equal ability fail to negotiate a choppy river will likely dissuade the observer from attempting the same task. The effects of this vicarious experience may even last a lifetime.

Social Persuasion

Self-efficacy can also be acquired or weakened through social persuasion (Bandura, 1995a). The effects of this source are limited, but under proper conditions, persuasion from others can raise or lower self-efficacy (Chambliss & Murray, 1979). The first condition is that we must believe the persuader. Exhortations or criticisms from a credible source have more efficacious power than those from an uncredible person. The second condition for boosting self-efficacy through social persuasion is that the activity one is being exhorted to attempt must realistically be within one's repertoire of behavior. No amount of verbal persuasion can alter someone's efficacy judgment on the ability to limbo dance under a stick 12 inches from the floor.

Bandura (1986) hypothesized that the efficacious power of suggestion is directly related to the perceived status and authority of the persuader. Status and authority, of course, are not identical. For example, a psychotherapist's suggestion to phobic patients that they can ride in a crowded elevator is more likely to increase self-efficacy than will encouragement from one's spouse or children. But if that same psychotherapist tells patients that they have the ability to change a faulty light switch, these patients will probably not enhance their self-efficacy for this activity. Also, social persuasion is most effective when combined with successful performance. Persuasion may convince someone to attempt an activity, and if performance is successful, both the accomplishment and the subsequent verbal rewards will increase future efficacy.

Physiological and Emotional States

The final source of efficacy are people's physiological and emotional states (Bandura, 1995a). Strong emotion ordinarily lowers performance; when people experience intense fear, acute anxiety, or high levels of stress, they are likely to have lower efficacy expectancies. An actor in a school play knows his lines during rehearsal but realizes that the fear he feels on opening night may block his recall. Incidentally, for some situations emotional arousal, if not too intense, is associated with *increased* performance, so that moderate anxiety felt by our actor on opening night may raise his efficacy expectancies. Most of us, when not afraid, have the ability to successfully handle snakes. We merely have to grasp the snake firmly behind the head; but for many of us, the fear that accompanies snake handling is debilitating and greatly lowers our performance expectancy.

Psychotherapists have long recognized that a reduction in anxiety or an increase in physical relaxation can facilitate performance. Arousal information is related to several variables. First, of course, is the level of arousal—ordinarily, the higher the arousal, the lower the self-efficacy. The second variable is the perceived realism of the arousal. If one knows that the fear is realistic, as when driving on an icy mountain road, personal efficacy may be raised. However, when one is cognizant of the absurdity of the phobia, for example, fear of the outdoors, then the emotional arousal tends to lower efficacy. Finally, the nature of the task is an added variable. Emotional arousal may facilitate the successful completion of simple tasks, but it is likely to interfere with performance of complex activities.

SELF-EFFICACY AS A PREDICTOR OF BEHAVIOR

Self-efficacy is one of several self-influences that affect our behavior. For Bandura, the source of control does not reside in the environment, but in the reciprocation of environment, behavior, and person. An important person variable is self-efficacy, and when combined with specific goals and knowledge of performance, it can serve as an important contributor to future behavior (Bandura, 1988b, 1994a).

Bandura (1981) has been critical of self-theories, such as the one developed by Carl Rogers (Chapter 16), that center on a composite self-concept rather than many specific self-precepts. Self-efficacy is not a global concept. It varies from situation to situation depending on the competencies required for different activities; the presence or absence of other people; the perceived competence of these other people, especially if they are competitors; the person's predisposition to attend to failure of performance rather than to success; and the accompanying physiological states, particularly the presence of fatigue, anxiety, apathy, or despondency.

High and low efficacy combine with responsive and unresponsive environments to produce four possible predictive variables (Bandura, 1982c). When efficacy is high and the environment is responsive, outcomes are most likely to be successful. When low efficacy is combined with a responsive environment, people may become depressed when they observe that others are successful at tasks that seem too difficult for them. When people with high efficacy encounter unresponsive environmental situations, they usually intensify their efforts to change the environment. They may use protest, social activism, or even force to instigate change, but if all efforts fail, Bandura hypothesized, they will either give up that course and take on a new one or they will seek a more responsive environment. Finally, when low self-efficacy combines with an unresponsive environment, people are likely to feel apathy, resignation, and helplessness. For example, a junior executive with low self-efficacy who realizes the difficulties of becoming company president will develop feelings of discouragement, give up, and fail to transfer productive efforts toward a similar but lesser goal.

COLLECTIVE EFFICACY

Like Freud, Adler, Skinner, Rogers, and most other personality theorists, Bandura has become more concerned with national and global affairs as his theory has matured. Part of that concern is exemplified in his concept of collective efficacy. **Collective efficacy** refers to the confidence people have that their combined efforts will produce social change. It does not spring from a collective "mind," but rather from the personal efficacy of many individuals working together.

Bandura believes that people exercise control over their lives not only through individual self-efficacy but also through collective efficacy. In the matter of health, for example, people may have high self-efficacy that they can quit smoking or change their diet, but they may have low collective efficacy that they can reduce environmental pollution, hazardous working conditions, or infectious disease. However, personal and collective efficacy are not antithetical. Rather, they complement one another to change people's lifestyles.

Bandura (1995a) listed several factors that can undermine collective efficacy. First, we live in a transnational world; what happens in one part of the globe can affect people in other countries, giving them a sense of helplessness. Destruction of the Amazon rain forests, international trade policies, or depletion of the ozone, for example, can affect the lives of everyone and undermine their confidence to shape a better world for themselves.

Second, recent technology that we neither understand nor believe that we can control may lower our sense of collective efficacy. In past years many motorists, for example, had confidence in their ability to keep their car in running condition. With the advent of computerized controls in modern automobiles, many moderately skilled mechanics not only have lost personal efficacy for repairing their vehicle but have low collective efficacy for reversing the trend toward more and more complicated automobiles.

A third condition undermining collective efficacy is the complex social machinery, with layers of bureaucracy that prevent social change. People who attempt to change bureaucratic structures are often discouraged by failure or by the long lapse of time between their actions and any noticeable change. Having become discouraged, many people, "rather than developing the means for shaping their own future, . . . grudgingly relinquish control to technical specialists and to public officials" (Bandura, 1995a, p. 37).

Fourth, the tremendous scope and magnitude of human problems can undermine our collective efficacy. Wars, famine, overpopulation, crime, and natural disasters are but a few of the global problems that can leave us with a sense of powerlessness. Despite these huge transnational problems, Bandura believes that positive changes are possible if people will persevere with their collective efforts and not become discouraged. "The times call for social initiatives that build people's sense of collective efficacy to influence conditions that shape their lives and that of future generations" (Bandura, 1995a, p. 38).

LEARNING

In the previous section we saw that one source of self-efficacy was vicarious experience. Bandura believes that much of what we learn is acquired through observing others. "If knowledge could be acquired only through the effects of one's own actions, the process of cognitive and social development would be greatly retarded, not to mention exceedingly tedious" (Bandura, 1986, p. 47).

Not all learning, however, comes through observing others. We also learn by experience. We enact or perform behaviors that have consequences and thereby learn from the effects of our actions. Bandura (1986) discusses two major kinds of learning—observational and enactive.

OBSERVATIONAL LEARNING

Bandura believes that *observation* allows us to learn without performing any behavior. We observe natural phenomena, plants, animals, waterfalls, the motion of the moon and stars, and so forth; but especially important to social cognitive theory is the assumption that we learn through observing the behavior of other people. In this respect, Bandura differs from Skinner, who held that enactive behavior is the basic datum of psychological science. He also departs from Skinner in his belief that reinforcement is not essential to learning. Although reinforcement facilitates learning, Bandura says that it is not a necessary condition for it. We can learn, for example, by observing models being reinforced.

Bandura (1986) believes that observational learning is much more efficient than learning through direct experience. By observing others we are spared countless responses that might be followed by punishment or by no reinforcement. Children observe characters on television, for example, and repeat what they hear or see; they need not enact random behaviors, hoping that some of them will be rewarded.

The core of observational learning is modeling.

Modeling

The core of observational learning is **modeling.** Learning through modeling involves adding and subtracting from the observed behavior and generalizing from one observation to another. In other words, modeling involves cognitive processes and is not simply mimicry or imitation. It is more than matching the actions of another and involves symbolically representing information and storing it for use at a future time (Bandura, 1986, 1994b).

Several factors determine whether we will learn from a model in any particular situation. First, the characteristics of the model are important. We are more likely to model high-status people rather than those of low status, competent individuals rather than unskilled or incompetent ones, and powerful people rather than impotent ones.

Second, the characteristics of the observer affect the likelihood of modeling. People who lack status, skill, or power are most likely to model. Children model more than older people, and novices are more likely to model than experts.

Third, the consequences of the behavior being modeled may have an effect on the observer. The greater the value that the observer places on the behavior, the more likely that that behavior will be learned. Also, learning may be facilitated when the observer views a model receiving severe punishment; for example, seeing another person receive a severe shock from touching an electric wire teaches us a valuable lesson.

Processes Governing Observational Learning

Bandura (1986) recognized four processes that govern observational learning: attention, representation, behavioral production, and motivation.

Attention

Before we can model another person, we must attend to that person. What factors regulate attention? First, because we have more opportunities to observe individuals with whom we frequently associate, we are most likely to attend to these people. Second, attractive models are more likely to be observed than unattractive ones—popular figures on television, in sports, or in movies are often closely attended. Also, the nature of the behavior being modeled affects our attention—we observe behavior that we think is important to us and from which we believe we can profit.

Representation

In order for observation to lead to new response patterns, those patterns must be symbolically represented in memory. Symbolic representation need not be verbal, because some observations are retained in imagery and can be summoned in the absence of the physical model. This process is especially important in infancy when verbal skills are not yet developed.

Verbal coding, however, greatly speeds the process of observational learning. With language, we can verbally evaluate those behaviors we are observing and decide which ones we wish to discard and which ones we desire to try. Verbal coding also helps us to rehearse the behavior symbolically, that is, to tell ourselves over and over again how we will perform the behavior once given the chance. Rehearsal can also entail the actual performance of the modeled response, and this rehearsal aids the retention process.

Behavioral Production

After attending to a model and retaining what we have observed, we then produce the behavior. In converting cognitive representations into appropriate actions, we must ask ourselves several questions about the behavior to be modeled. First we ask, "How can I do this?" After symbolically rehearsing the relevant responses, we try out our new behavior. While performing, we monitor ourselves with the question, "What am I doing?" Finally, we evaluate our performance by asking, "Am I doing this right?" This last question is not always easy to answer, especially if it pertains to a motor skill, such as ballet dancing or platform diving, in which we cannot actually see ourselves. Carroll and Bandura (1982, 1985), however, found that self-monitoring by use of a video recorder facilitates the learning of some motor skills.

Motivation

Observational learning is most effective when learners are motivated to perform the modeled behavior. Attention and representation can lead to the acquisition of learning, but performance is facilitated by motivation to enact that particular behavior. Even though observation of others may teach us *how* to do something, we may have no desire to perform the necessary action. One person can watch another use a power saw or run a vacuum cleaner and not be motivated to try either activity. Most sidewalk superintendents have no wish to emulate the observed construction worker.

Observing a model being punished for performance will diminish one's likelihood of enacting the same behavior. For example, if you notice a classmate receiving an embarrassing admonition from a professor after asking a question, you will probably learn not to ask questions in that class. In summary, then, modeling is facilitated by observing appropriate activities, properly coding the events for representation in memory, actually performing the behavior, and being sufficiently motivated.

ENACTIVE LEARNING

Every response a person makes is followed by some consequence. Some of these consequences are satisfying, some are dissatisfying, and others are simply not cognitively attended and hence have little effect.

Reinforcers can be either positive or negative, but Bandura believes that their effects do not follow automatically from the consequences of a response. Complex human behavior involves the cognitive mediation of the individual in order for the consequences of a response to have an effect. Verbal reinforcement, for example, must be attended and comprehended before it can have meaning. The meaning for the receiver, however, may be different from that intended by the sender. For example, a dance instructor compliments her pupils for performing a particularly difficult maneuver, hoping to encourage them and to improve their skill level. However, her words may have an opposite effect or no effect on the dancers, who may reason that if they really possessed the potential to be great performers, their teacher would not need to compliment them for such a simple move.

The consequences of a response serve at least three functions. They (1) impart information, (2) motivate future behavior, and (3) reinforce present behavior (Bandura, 1977). First, response consequences inform us of the effects of our actions. We can retain this information and use it as a guide for future actions.

A second function of response consequences is to motivate anticipatory behavior. People are capable of symbolically representing future outcomes and acting accordingly. They not only possess insight but are also capable of foresight. We do not have to suffer the discomfort of cold temperatures before deciding to wear a coat when going outside in freezing weather. Instead, we anticipate the effects of cold wet weather and dress accordingly. The symbolic representation of discomfort serves as a stimulus for our thinking about wearing a coat, and it also increases the likelihood that we will actually wear one.

Third, the consequences of responses serve to reinforce behavior, a function that has been firmly documented by Skinner (Chapter 10) and other reinforcement theorists. Bandura (1986), however, contended that, although reinforcement may at times be unconscious and automatic, complex behavioral patterns are greatly facilitated by cognitive intervention. Bandura maintained that learning occurs much more efficiently when the learner is cognitively involved in the learning situation and understands what behaviors precede successful responses.

DYSFUNCTIONAL BEHAVIOR

Bandura's concept of reciprocal determinism assumes that behavior is learned as a result of the interaction of person, behavior, and environment. Dysfunctional behavior is no exception, being determined by a mutual interaction of the person, including cognition and neurophysiological processes; the environment, including interpersonal relations and socioeconomic conditions; and behavioral factors, especially previous experiences with reinforcement. Bandura's concept of dysfunctional behavior lends itself most readily to depressive reactions, phobias, and aggressive behaviors.

DEPRESSIVE REACTIONS

High personal standards and goals can lead to achievement and self-satisfaction. However, when people set their goals too high, they are likely to fail. Failure frequently leads to depression, and depressed people often undervalue their own accomplishments. The result is chronic misery, feelings of worthlessness, lack of purposefulness, and pervasive depression. Bandura (1986) believes that dysfunctional depression can occur in any of the three self-regulatory subfunctions: (1) self-observation, (2) judgmental processes, and (3) self-reactions.

First, during self-observation, people can misjudge their own performance or distort their memory of past accomplishments. Depressed people are more likely to underestimate their successes and overestimate their failures. More frequently, however, depression relates to distorted recollections. Depressed people tend to exaggerate their past mistakes and minimize their prior accomplishments (Bandura, 1991b).

Second, depressed people are likely to make faulty judgments. They set their standards unrealistically high so that any performance attainment will be judged as a failure. Even when they achieve success in the eyes of others, they continue to berate their own accomplishments. Depression is especially likely when goals and personal standards are much higher than one's perceived efficacy to attain them. "People who judge themselves unfavorably are not inclined to treat themselves positively. . . . Compared to nondepressed persons, those who are prone to depression react less self-rewardingly for similar successes but more self-critically for similar failures" (Bandura, 1991b, pp. 274–275).

Finally, the self-reactions of depressed individuals are quite different from those of nondepressed persons. Depressed people not only judge themselves harshly, but they are also inclined to treat themselves badly for their shortcomings. Bandura (1986) suggested that depressed people "generally evaluate themselves less favorably and reward themselves less than the nondepressed, who are more inclined to savor their successes. The depressed are also inclined to punish themselves more severely for poor performances" (p. 361).

PHOBIAS

Phobias are fears that are strong enough and pervasive enough to have severe debilitating effects on one's daily life. For example, snake phobias prevent people from holding a variety of jobs and from enjoying many kinds of recreational activities. Phobias and fears are learned by direct contact, inappropriate generalization, and especially by observational experiences (Bandura, 1986). They are difficult to extinguish because the phobic person simply avoids the threatening object. Unless the fearsome object is somehow encountered, the phobia will endure indefinitely.

Bandura (1986) credited television and other news media for generating many of our fears. Well-publicized rapes, armed robberies, or murders can terrorize a community, causing people to live more confined lives behind locked doors. Most people have never been raped, robbed, or intentionally injured, yet many live in fear of being criminally assaulted. Violent criminal acts that seem random and unpredictable are most likely to instigate phobic reactions.

Once established, phobias are maintained by consequent determinants, that is, the negative reinforcement the phobic person receives for avoiding the fear-producing situation. For example, if people expect to receive aversive experiences (being mugged) while walking through the city park, they will reduce their feeling of threat by not entering the park or even going near it. In this example, dysfunctional (avoidance) behavior is produced by the mutual interaction of people's expectancies (belief that they will be mugged), the external environment (the city park), and behavioral factors (their prior experiences with fear).

AGGRESSIVE BEHAVIORS

Aggressive behaviors, when carried to extremes, can also be dysfunctional. Bandura (1986) contended that aggressive behavior is acquired through observation of others, direct experiences with positive and negative reinforcements, training, or instruction, and bizarre beliefs.

Once established, people continue to aggress for at least five different reasons: (1) they enjoy inflicting injury on the victim (positive reinforcement); (2) they avoid or counter the aversive consequences of aggression by others (negative reinforcement); (3) they receive injury or harm for not behaving aggressively (punishment); (4) they live up to their personal standards of conduct by their aggressive behavior (self-reinforcement); and (5) they observe others receiving rewards for aggressive acts or punishment for nonaggressive behavior (Evans, 1976).

Bandura believes that aggressive actions ordinarily lead to further aggression. This belief is based on the now classic study of Bandura, Ross, and Ross (1963), which found that children who observed others behaving aggressively displayed more aggression than a control group of children who did not view aggressive acts. In this study, Stanford University nursery school boys and girls were divided into three matched experimental groups and one control group.

Children in the first experimental group observed a live model behaving with both verbal and physical aggression toward a number of toys, including a large inflated Bobo doll; the second experimental group observed a film showing the same model behaving in an identical manner; the third experimental group saw a fantasy film in which a model, dressed as a black cat, behaved equally aggressively against the Bobo doll. Children in the control group were matched with those in the experimental groups on previous ratings of aggression, but they were not subjected to an aggressive model.

After children in the three experimental groups observed a model scolding, kicking, punching, and hitting the Bobo doll with a mallet, they proceeded into another room where they were mildly frustrated. Immediately following this frustration, each child went into the experimental room, which contained some toys (such as a smaller version of the Bobo doll) that could be played with aggressively. In addition, some nonaggressive toys (such as a tea set and coloring materials) were present. Observers watched the children's aggressive or nonaggressive response to the toys through a one-way mirror.

As hypothesized, children exposed to an aggressive model displayed more aggressive responses than those who had not been exposed. But contrary to expectations, the researchers found no differences in the amount of total aggression shown by children in the three experimental groups. Children who had observed the cartoon character were at least as aggressive as those exposed to a live model or to a filmed model. In general, children in each experimental group exhibited about twice as much aggressive behavior as did those in the control group. In addition, the particular kind of aggressive response was remarkably similar to that displayed by the adult models. Children scolded, kicked, punched, and hit the doll with a mallet in close imitation to the behavior that had been modeled.

THERAPY

According to Bandura, deviant behaviors are not caused by weaknesses of character, a single master motive, or unhappy childhood experiences. They are initiated on the basis of social cognitive learning principles, and they are maintained because, in some ways, they continue to serve a purpose. Therapeutic change, therefore, is difficult because it involves eliminating behaviors that are satisfying to the person. Smoking, overeating, and drinking alcoholic beverages, for example, generally have positive effects initially and their long-range aversive consequences are usually not sufficient to produce avoidance behavior.

The ultimate goal of social cognitive therapy is self-regulation. To achieve this end, the therapist introduces strategies designed not only to induce behavioral change but to maintain that change. Bandura (1978a) visualized three levels of treatment, the first level being the *induction of change*. If therapy is to be effective, it must at least instigate some change in behavior. For example, if a therapist is able to extinguish fear of height in a previously acrophobic person, then change has been induced and that person will have no fear of climbing a 20-foot ladder.

The second level of treatment accomplishment is *generalization*. The acrophobic person not only will be able to ascend a ladder but also will generalize that behavior to other situations. This is a more effective level than simple induction of change, and it allows the person to ride in airplanes or look out windows of tall buildings.

Some therapies induce change and facilitate generalization, but in time, the therapeutic effects are lost and the person reacquires the dysfunctional behavior. This is particularly true with extinguishing maladaptive habits such as smoking and overeating. The most effective therapy reaches the third level of accomplishment, which is *maintenance* of newly acquired functional behaviors.

Because dysfunctional behavior is produced by reciprocal determinism, "the likelihood that a given behavior will be performed can vary markedly in different environmental settings toward different people, and at different times" (Bandura, 1978a, p. 96). This broad conceptualization of both maladaptive behavior and treatment permits a variety of therapeutic techniques and strategies. The first criterion of any approach is that it bring about behavioral change. Beyond that, generalization and maintenance become important goals.

Bandura suggests several basic treatment approaches, including *overt or vicarious modeling*. People who observe live or filmed models performing threatening activities often feel less fear and anxiety and are then able to perform those same activities (Rosenthal & Bandura, 1978).

In a second treatment mode, *covert or cognitive modeling*, the therapist trains patients to visualize models performing fearsome behaviors (Bandura et al., 1980). Overt and covert modeling strategies are most effective, however, when combined with performance-oriented approaches (Bandura, 1977).

A third procedure, called *enactive mastery*, requires patients to perform those behaviors that previously produced incapacitating fears. Enactment, however, is not ordinarily the first step in treatment. Patients typically begin by observing models or by having their emotional arousal lessened through **systematic desensitization** (Wolpe, 1973), which involves the extinction of anxiety or fear through self-induced or therapist-induced relaxation. With systematic desensitization, the therapist and patient work together to place fearsome situations on a hierarchy from least to most threatening. Patients, while relaxed, enact the least threatening behavior and then gradually move through the hierarchy until they can perform the most threatening activity, all the while remaining at a low state of emotional arousal (Bandura, Blanchard, & Ritter, 1969).

Bandura has demonstrated that each of these strategies can be effective and that they are most powerful when used in combination with one another (Bandura et al., 1980). Bandura believes that the reason for their effectiveness can be traced to a common mechanism found in each of these approaches, namely, *cognitive mediation*. When people use cognition to increase self-efficacy, that is, when they become convinced that they can perform difficult tasks, then in fact, they become able to cope with previously intimidating situations (Bandura, 1989).

RELATED RESEARCH

The social cognitive theory of Albert Bandura has generated more testable hypotheses and research than almost any other theory. In fact, only Skinner and Eysenck have built up more of an empirical foundation than Bandura. Several hundred studies have tested Bandura's basic assumptions, but the two most widely investigated topics have been self-efficacy and modeling of violence.

Self-efficacy has been applied to a wide variety of performance domains, for example, education, work, psychotherapy, and physical health. With regard to academic performance, the overriding question is: How do perceptions about scholastic abilities (scholastic self-efficacy) influence how one performs in school (GPA)? In one study, Barry Zimmerman, Albert Bandura, and Manuel Martinez-Pons (1992) examined the impact of self-efficacy beliefs and personal goals on class performance of high school students. These researchers predicted that final grades are directly influenced by three variables: (1) prior grades, (2) student grade goals, and (3) self-efficacy for academic achievement. They defined student grade goals as the grade students hoped to receive and the lowest grade with which they would be satisfied. Next, they measured self-efficacy for academic achievement with a nine-item questionnaire that asked about perceptions of aptitudes in various academic domains (for example, mathematics, science, reading, English). In addition, the authors predicted that self-efficacy for self-regulated learning and parental grade goals would indirectly influence final grade attainment. They assessed self-efficacy for self-motivated learning with an 11-item questionnaire that asked questions such as "How well can you finish homework assignments by deadlines?" or "How well can you arrange a place to study without distractions?" To measure parental grade goals, Zimmerman et al. asked parents what grade they expected their child to receive and the lowest grade they would find satisfying.

Zimmerman et al. found that self-efficacy for academic achievement and student grade goals predicted the obtained grade (in a social studies class), but that prior grades, parental grade goals, and self-efficacy for self-regulated learning did not. However, self-efficacy for self-regulated learning directly influenced self-efficacy for academic achievement, which in turn directly influenced final grade. Furthermore, parental grade goals had a direct impact on student grade goals, which in turn had a direct impact on final grade. In summary, the self-efficacy for self-regulated learning and parental grade goals indirectly influenced a student's final grade, whereas self-efficacy and student grade goals directly influenced final grades. Students who did well in courses were those who had faith in their ability to do well and who set a goal to do well.

Zimmerman and Bandura (1994) continued this line of investigation with a second study on self-efficacy, self-regulation, and academic performance (in writing). The main difference between this and the former study was that the participants were college students at a selective university, and the grade outcome concerned a writing rather than a social studies class. Writing is important in a self-regulation model because, more than most other scholarly activities, it involves self-scheduling, self-discipline, and solitary activity over a long period of time. Zimmerman and Bandura predicted that grade goals ("What grade are you striving for in this course?") and self-efficacy for academic achievement would directly influence final grade. Moreover, they predicted that verbal aptitude and self-evaluative standards would directly influence the final grade. Verbal aptitude was measured by Scholastic Aptitude Test (SAT) scores, and self-evaluative standards were obtained by asking students to rate how satisfied they would be with each grade (A through F). Results showed that the only two direct influences of final grade were grade goals and self-efficacy for academic achievement. Verbal aptitude as measured by the SAT and self-evaluative standards had no direct influence on final grade. Efficacy concerning one's ability to self-regulate directly influenced self-efficacy for academic achievement, but not final grade. These results replicate the earlier study with high school students in that they demonstrate that having faith in one's ability and expecting to do well are the strongest and most direct predictors of academic success.

Perhaps the most influential application of Bandura's notion of modeling has been studies that examine the effect of television and film violence on aggressive behavior in real life. As discussed earlier, Bandura himself conducted the best known of these studies using the Bobo doll (Bandura, Ross, & Ross, 1963), and there have been a number of replications of this basic finding (Huesmann & Miller, 1994; Slife & Rychlak, 1982). Indeed, hundreds of other studies have looked at the general effect of watching TV violence on real violence, especially in children. The overall findings from hundreds of such studies have been quantitatively summarized using **meta-analysis,** a technique that collects results from multiple studies and quantifies the magnitude of the effect. A meta-analysis allows the investigator to draw conclusions on the basis of a multiplicity of studies instead of only one study (Cooper & Hedges, 1994).

Are people influenced enough by the violence they see on TV and movies to imitate it in real life? A meta-analysis by Haejung Paik and George Comstock (1994) on the effects of TV violence on antisocial behavior found that some people are likely to behave more aggressively than they would if they had not seen the filmed violence. Paik and Comstock drew this conclusion after performing a meta-analysis of more than 200 studies (including Bandura's classic Bobo doll studies) conducted between 1957 and 1990. The average effect size was medium to small, which may seem unimpressive. However, even with a small effect size, 10 viewers out of 100 would be affected by the violence they see on TV or film. Projected to the entire population, this relatively small percentage would yield a very large number of people affected by media violence. Another review of the literature by Lynette Friedrich-Cofer and Aletha Huston (1986) looked at a possible bidirectional causal relationship between viewing TV violence and aggressive behaviors. (A bidirectional relationship would suggest that an aggressive disposition influences a preference for watching violent TV shows, and TV violence influences aggressive behavior.) This review found evidence to support such a bidirectional causal relationship, although some later studies (Strasburger, 1995; Wiegman, Kuttschreuter, & Baarda, 1992) have suggested that the unidirectional relationship between watching TV violence and subsequent aggressive behaviors tends to disappear when starting levels of aggression are controlled.

Recall that Bandura argued that people imitate not just any behavior, but rather rewarded behavior. Most research on TV violence and actual violence does not measure whether the violent TV behavior was rewarded. Perhaps one could argue that children in particular believe that the violent behavior is rewarded by the very fact that it is on TV. However, most of the research does not explicitly distinguish between rewarded and unrewarded observed violent behavior, so therefore, much of the research does not test Bandura's theory directly but rather indirectly. Nevertheless, the bulk of the studies are consistent with Bandura's theory of observational learning and the modeling of violent or aggressive behavior.

CRITIQUE OF BANDURA

Bandura has evolved his social cognitive theory by a careful balance of the two principal components of theory building—innovative speculation and accurate observation. His theoretical speculations have seldom outdistanced his data but have been carefully advanced, only one step in front of observations. This scientifically sound procedure has increased the likelihood that his hypotheses would yield positive results and that his theory would generate additional testable hypotheses.

As with other theories, the usefulness of Bandura's personality theory rests on its ability to generate research, to offer itself to falsification, and to organize knowledge. In addition, it must serve as a practical guide to action, be internally consistent, and parsimonious. How does Bandura's theory rate on these six criteria?

Bandura's theory receives a very high rating on its capacity to *generate research*. Our check of PsychLIT from 1990 to June 1996 revealed that the concept of self-efficacy alone is a key term in nearly 1,400 journal articles. Indeed, the term self-efficacy is quite often used without reference to Bandura, indicating that it is now part of the general psychology lexicon and no longer specifically associated with Bandura's name. In addition to self-efficacy, Bandura's ideas on modeling, moral development, and the control of behavior have generated hundreds of research articles.

On the standard of *falsifiability*, Bandura's theory is difficult to rate. For example, self-efficacy theory suggests that "people's beliefs in their personal efficacy influence what courses of action they choose to pursue, how much effort they will invest in activities, how long they will persevere in the face of obstacles and failure experiences, and their resiliency following setbacks" (Bandura, 1994b, p. 65). Although this statement lends itself to falsification, it adds little to earlier learning theories, such as Julian Rotter's (1954) expectancy for success theory (see Chapter 12). Irving Kirsch (1982, 1985, 1986, 1995), a long-time critic of Bandura and colleague of Rotter, believes that the concept of self-efficacy is an imprecise construct and probably an unnecessary one. He contends that differences between expectancy theory and self-efficacy theory are largely semantic, that both have been investigated by theorists and researchers for 60 years, and that "self efficacy has a short history, but a long past" (Kirsch, 1995, p. 331). Thus, although self-efficacy is capable of producing specific and testable hypotheses, results from these tests will have implications not only for self-efficacy theory but for a variety of expectancy theories.

On its ability to *organize knowledge*, Bandura's theory receives a high rating. Many findings from psychology research can be organized by social cognitive theory. Reciprocal determinism is a comprehensive concept that offers a viable explanation for the acquisition of most observable behaviors. The inclusion of three variables in this paradigm gives Bandura's theory more flexibility to organize and explain behavior than does Skinner's radical behaviorism, which relies nearly exclusively on environmental variables.

How *practical* is Bandura's social cognitive theory? To the therapist, teacher, parent, or anyone interested in the acquisition and maintenance of new behaviors, self-efficacy theory provides useful and specific guidelines. In addition to presenting techniques for enhancing personal and collective efficacy, Bandura's theory suggests ways in which observational learning and modeling can be used to acquire behaviors.

Is the theory *internally consistent*? Bandura chooses words carefully, so that no single term carries more than one definition. The theory itself, because it is not highly speculative, has outstanding internal consistency. Bandura is not afraid to speculate, but he never ventures far beyond the empirical data available to him. The result is a carefully couched, rigorously written, and internally consistent theory.

The final criterion of a useful theory is *parsimony*. Again, Bandura's social cognitive theory meets high standards. The theory is simple, straightforward, and unencumbered by hypothetical or fanciful explanations.

CONCEPT OF HUMANITY

Bandura sees humans as having the capacity to become many things. "Human nature is characterized by a vast potentiality that can be fashioned by direct and observational experience into a variety of forms within biological limits" (Bandura, 1986, p. 21). Bandura's belief that people are quite plastic and flexible in their personality does not mean that they have no basic nature. Bandura (1995b) believes that plasticity and flexibility *is* our basic nature. Because humans have evolved neurophysiological mechanisms for symbolizing their experiences, their nature is marked by a large degree of plasticity or flexibility. People have the capacity to store past experiences and to use this information to chart future actions.

Our capacity to use symbols provides us with a powerful tool for understanding and controlling our environment. It enables us to solve problems without resorting to inefficient trial-and-error behavior, to imagine the consequences of our actions, and to set goals for ourselves (Bandura, 1988a).

As humans, we are *goal-directed*, purposive animals who can view the future and bestow it with meaning by being aware of the possible consequences of future behavior. We anticipate the future and behave accordingly in the present. The future does not determine behavior, but its cognitive representation can have a powerful effect on present actions. "By being represented cognitively in the present, conceived futures can have causal impact on current behavior. Through the exercise of forethought, people motivate themselves and guide their actions anticipatorily" (Bandura, 1994b, p. 64).

Although we are basically goal-oriented, Bandura believes that we have specific rather than general intentions and purposes. We are not motivated by a single master goal such as striving for superiority or self-actualization but by a multiplicity of goals, some distant and some proximate. These individual intentions, however, are not ordinarily anarchical; they possess some stability and order. Cognition gives us the capacity to evaluate probable consequences and to eliminate behaviors that do not meet our standards of conduct. Personal standards, therefore, tend to give human behavior a degree of consistency, even though that behavior lacks a master motive to guide it.

Bandura's concept of humanity is more *optimistic* than pessimistic, because it holds that people are capable of learning new behaviors throughout their lives. However, dysfunctional behaviors may persist because of low self-efficacy or because they are perceived as being reinforced. Nevertheless, these unhealthy behaviors need not continue, because most people have the capacity to change by imitating the productive behaviors of others and by using cognitive abilities to solve problems.

Bandura's social cognitive theory, of course, emphasizes *social factors* more than biological ones. However, it recognizes that genetics contributes to the person (P) variable in the reciprocal determinism paradigm. But even within this variable, cognition ordinarily gains ascendance, so that biological factors become less important. Moreover, social factors are clearly more crucial to the other two variables—environment (E) and behavior (B).

Are humans free to control their own actions? Bandura's answer is qualified. Reciprocal determinism postulates a mutual interlocking system in which person, behavior, and environment all influence one another. Thus, neither outside forces nor personal factors are solely responsible for human behavior. People have some capacity to control their behavior. Although they are affected by both the environment and their experiences with reinforcement, people in turn have some power to mold these two external conditions. To some extent, people can manage those environmental conditions that will shape their future behavior, and they can choose to ignore or augment their previous experiences. People can "serve as a causal contributor to their own life course by selecting, influencing, and constructing their own circumstances" (Bandura, 1986, p. 38).

This concept of self-regulation goes beyond Skinner's notion of counter control. Skinner held that ultimately the environment is the force behind the organism's behavior, whereas Bandura believes that people are *partially free* to create those environments that later impinge upon them. Personal freedom, then, is limited; it is restricted by physical constraints such as laws, prejudices, regulations, and the rights of other people. In addition, personal factors such as perceived inefficacy and lack of confidence restrict individual freedom. Some people have more freedom than others. "Given the same environmental conditions, persons who have the capabilities for exercising many options and are adept at regulating their own behavior will have greater freedom than will those who have limited means of personal agency" (Bandura, 1986, p. 39). Bandura defined freedom as "the number of options available to people and their right to exercise them" (p. 42).

Bandura seems to straddle the fence on the issue of *freedom and determinism*, because he says that behavior is determined by an interaction of self-regulation and external sources of influence. He believes that neither freedom nor responsibility should be considered antithetical to determinism. To him, outside influences operate deterministically on human behavior, but the person retains some measure of self-influence, which also operates deterministically on behavior. Because a degree of self-regulation is always possible, personal responsibility cannot be abdicated. As people recognize the possibility of alternative actions, they must assume partial responsibility for their actions (Bandura, 1982a, 1986).

On the issue of *causality or teleology*, Bandura's position would be described as moderate. Human functioning is a product of environmental factors interacting with behavior and personal variables, especially cognitive activity. We move with a purpose toward goals that we have set, but motivation exists neither in the past nor the future. It is contemporary. Although future events cannot motivate us, our conception of them is "converted into current motivators and regulators of behavior" (Bandura, 1988b, p. 37).

Social cognitive theory emphasizes *conscious thought* over unconscious determinants of behavior. Self-regulation of actions relies on self-monitoring, judgment, and self-reaction, all of which are ordinarily conscious during the learning situation. "People do not become thoughtless during the learning process. They make conscious judgments about how their actions affect the environment" (Bandura, 1986, p. 116). After learnings are well established, especially motor learning, they may become unconscious. We do not have to be aware of all our actions while walking or driving a car.

Bandura recognizes the limitations that biological forces place on us, while at the same time, he believes that we have a remarkable plasticity. Our social environments allow us a wide range of behaviors, including using other people as models. All of us live in a number of social networks and are thus influenced by a variety of people. Modern technology in the form of computers and the media facilitate the spread of social influences (Bandura, 1994b).

Because we have a remarkable plasticity and capacity for learning, vast individual differences exist among us. Bandura's emphasis on *uniqueness*, however, is moderated by biological and social influences, both of which contribute to some similarities among people.

Chapter Summary

Bandura's social cognitive theory holds that human functioning is a product of the mutual interaction of environmental events, behavior, and personal factors, especially cognitive activity. This triadic model is called *reciprocal determinism*. The three reciprocal factors do not necessarily make an equal contribution to thought and action. At different times and under different conditions, any one of the three may be the most powerful. However, none of the factors is ever solely responsible for behavior. All three constantly operate in mutual interaction.

Two important environmental factors, often overlooked by other theorists, are *chance encounters* and *fortuitous events*. Bandura believes that many of the crucial influences in our life originate from these unplanned and unexpected events. Once they occur, however, they enter into the triadic model in the same manner as do planned events.

As cognitive animals, we have the capacity to use symbols, especially language, to transform contemporary experiences into relatively consistent patterns of behavior. This gives the *self system* some stability. The self system refers to cognitive structures that enable us to perceive, evaluate, and regulate our behavior.

Within limits, we have the capacity for self-regulation and can use both external and internal factors to do so. External factors provide us with *standards for evaluating our behavior* as well as *external reinforcement* in the form of rewards received from others. Internal factors in self-regulation include (1) self-observation, (2) judgmental processes, and (3) self-reaction.

Self-regulatory processes, however, are specific and operate only when activated. Through *selective activation* and *disengagement of internal control*, we can separate ourselves from the injurious consequences of our actions. Four principal techniques of selective activation and disengagement of internal control are: (1) redefining our behavior, (2) displacing or diffusing our responsibility, (3) disregarding or distorting the consequences of our behavior, and (4) blaming our victims for their injuries.

Performance is generally enhanced when we have high *self-efficacy*, that is, high expectations that we can perform those behaviors that will produce desired outcomes in a particular situation. Self-efficacy is enhanced or reduced by (1) mastery experience, that is, successful performance, (2) vicarious experiences, (3) social persuasion, and (4) physiological and emotional states. *Collective efficacy* refers to the confidence that groups of people have that their combined efforts will produce social change.

Bandura believes that people can learn without performing any behavior. He refers to this as *observational learning* and distinguishes it from *enactive learning*. To learn through observation, we must: (1) attend to our model, (2) organize and retain our observations, (3) try out our new actions, and (4) be motivated to perform the modeled behavior. Enactive learning takes place when our responses produce consequences. Response consequences can impart information, motivate future behavior, or reinforce present behavior.

Like all human behavior, *dysfunctional behavior* is acquired through the reciprocal interaction of environment, personal factors, and behavior. Bandura has most intensely investigated depressive reactions, fears and phobias, and aggressive behaviors.

Social cognitive theory has influenced a number of behaviorally oriented therapies, but Bandura's chief emphasis is on cognitive mediation, especially perceived self-efficacy.

Bandura conceives humans as having a unique potential to learn a variety of responses through their ability to symbolize experiences. We can recall the past and set goals for the future—but we live in the present. We have some limited capacity for personal freedom, although our behavior is also constricted by social and biological influences.

Overall, Bandura's social cognitive theory receives very high marks for its usefulness. We rated it high or very high on five of the six criteria for a useful theory—generates research, organizes knowledge, guides the practitioner, is internally consistent, and has parsimonious expression. On the criterion of falsifiability, we gave the theory only a moderate rating.

Suggested Readings

Bandura, A. (1982b). The psychology of chance encounters and life paths. *American Psychologist*, 37, 747–755.

Chance encounters and fortuitous events cannot be predicted by the science of psychology, yet they frequently exert a major influence on a person's life. Here Bandura argues that chance encounters have their own causal determinants, and having once occurred, they enter the reciprocal determinism paradigm and can be analyzed in the same manner as other environmental events.

Bandura, A. (1986). *Social foundations of thought and action: A social cognitive theory.* Englewood Cliffs, NJ: Prentice-Hall.

As the most complete expression of social cognitive theory, this book is "must" reading for any serious student of Bandura. However, the esoteric language and lack of organization make for difficult reading.

Bandura, A. (1995a). Exercise of personal and collective efficacy in changing societies. In A. Bandura (Ed.), *Self-efficacy in changing societies* (pp. 1–45). Cambridge, England: Cambridge University Press.

In this chapter, Bandura provides his most recent views on self-efficacy, including its application to the changing structure of family systems, intellectual development, career pursuits, and health-promotion behaviors. He also discusses the concept of collective efficacy.

Evans, R. I. (1989). *Albert Bandura: The man and his ideas—A dialogue.* New York: Praeger.

In April of 1988, Richard Evans interviewed Bandura for several hours. This transcript of the filmed dialogue offers some glimpses into the personal side of Bandura as well as Bandura's views on aggression and violence, moral development, moral disengagement, and self-efficacy.

Rotter

Mischel

Chapter

12

Rotter and Mischel:
Cognitive Social Learning Theory

he cognitive social learning theories of Julian Rotter and Walter Mischel each rest on the assumption that *cognitive* factors help shape how people will react to environmental forces. Both theorists object to Skinner's explanation that behavior is shaped by immediate reinforcement and suggest that one's *expectations* of future events are prime determinants of performance.

Rotter contends that our cognitions, past histories, and expectations of the future are keys to predicting behavior. He holds that human behavior is best predicted from an understanding of the *interaction* of people with their meaningful environments. As an **interactionist,** he believes that neither the environment itself nor the individual is completely responsible for behavior. In this respect he differs from Skinner, who believes that reinforcement ultimately stems from the environment.

Mischel's cognitive social theory has much in common with Bandura's social cognitive theory and Rotter's social learning theory. Like Bandura and Rotter, Mischel believes that cognitive factors, such as expectancies, subjective perceptions, values, goals, and personal standards, play important roles in shaping personality. His unique contributions are his research on **delay of gratification** and his subsequent theory regarding the consistency or inconsistency of personality.

BIOGRAPHY OF JULIAN ROTTER

Julian B. Rotter was born in Brooklyn, New York, on October 22, 1916, the third and last son of Jewish immigrant parents. Rotter (1993) recalled that he fit Adler's description of a highly competitive, "fighting" youngest child. Although his parents observed the Jewish religion and customs, they were not very religious. Rotter (1993) described his family's socioeconomic condition as "comfortably middle class until the Great Depression when my father lost his wholesale stationery business and we became part of the masses of unemployed for two years" (pp. 273–274). The depression sparked in Rotter a lifelong concern for social injustice and taught him the importance of situational conditions affecting human behavior.

As an elementary school and high school student he was an avid reader and by his junior year had read nearly every book of fiction in the local public library. That being the case, he turned one day to the psychology shelves where he found Adler's *Understanding Human Nature* (1927), Freud's *Psychopathology of Everyday Life* (1901/1960), and Karl Menninger's *The Human Mind* (1920). He was particularly impressed by Adler and Freud and soon returned for more (Rotter, 1982, 1993).

When he entered Brooklyn College, he was already seriously interested in psychology, but he chose to major in chemistry because it seemed to be a more employable degree during the depression of the 1930s. As a junior at Brooklyn College, he learned that Adler was, at that time, a professor of medical psychology at Long Island College of Medicine. He attended Adler's medical lectures and several of his clinical demonstrations. Eventually, he came to personally know Adler, who invited him to attend meetings of the Society for Individual Psychology (Rotter, 1993).

When Rotter graduated from Brooklyn College in 1937, he had more credits in psychology than in chemistry. He then entered graduate school in psychology at the University of Iowa, from which he received a master's degree in 1938. He completed an internship in clinical psychology at Worcester State Hospital in Massachusetts, where he met his future wife, Clara Barnes. Next, Rotter entered Indiana University and received his Ph.D. degree in clinical psychology in 1941, the same year he was married.

In 1941, Rotter accepted a position as clinical psychologist at Norwich State Hospital in Connecticut, where his duties included training interns and assistants from the University of Connecticut and Wesleyan University. In 1942, he was drafted into the army and spent more than three years as an army psychologist.

After the war, Rotter returned briefly to Norwich, but he soon took a job at Ohio State University, where he attracted a number of outstanding graduate students, including Walter Mischel. Carl Rogers (see Chapter 16) had recently left Ohio State, leaving Rotter and George Kelly (see Chapter 15) as the two most dominant members of the psychology department. However, Rotter was unhappy with the political effects of McCarthyism in Ohio, and in 1963, he took a position at the University of Connecticut as Director of the Clinical Training Program. He continued in that position until his retirement at age 70. Since 1987, he has been Professor Emeritus at the University of Connecticut and has continued an active teaching schedule. Rotter and his wife, Clara (who died in 1986), had two children, a daughter, Jean, and a son, Richard, who died in 1995.

Among Rotter's most important publications are *Social Learning and Clinical Psychology* (1954); *Clinical Psychology* (1964); *Applications of a Social Learning Theory of Personality*, with J. E. Chance and E. J. Phares (1972); *Personality*, with D. J. Hochreich (1975); *The Development and Application of Social Learning Theory: Selected Papers* (1982); the Rotter Incomplete Sentences Blank (Rotter, 1966); and the Interpersonal Trust Scale (Rotter, 1967). Rotter has been active in professional organizations, serving as president of the Eastern Psychological Association and of the divisions of Social and Personality Psychology and Clinical Psychology of the American Psychological Association (APA). He has also served two terms on the APA Education and Training Board. In 1988, he received the prestigious APA Distinguished Scientific Contribution Award. The following year he earned the Distinguished Contribution to Clinical Training Award from the Council of University Directors of Clinical Psychology.

INTRODUCTION TO ROTTER'S SOCIAL LEARNING THEORY

Rotter's social learning theory rests on five basic assumptions. First, he assumes that *humans interact with their meaningful environments* (Rotter, 1982). People's reaction to environmental stimuli depends on the meaning or importance that they attach to an event. Reinforcements are not dependent on external stimuli alone but are given meaning by the individual's cognitive capacity. Likewise, personal characteristics such as needs or traits cannot, by themselves, cause behavior. Rather, Rotter believes that human behavior stems from the interaction of environmental and personal factors.

A second assumption of Rotter's theory is that *human personality is learned* (Rotter, 1982). Thus, it follows that personality is not set or determined at any particular age of development; instead, it can be changed or modified as long as people are capable of learning. Although our accumulation of earlier experiences gives our personalities some stability, we are always amenable to change through new experiences. We learn from past experiences, but those experiences are not absolutely constant; they are colored by intervening experiences that then affect present perceptions.

Rotter's third assumption is that *personality has a basic unity*, which means that our personalities possess relative stability (Rotter, 1982). As we become more experienced, we learn to evaluate new experiences on the basis of previous reinforcement. This relatively consistent evaluation leads to greater stability and unity of personality.

Rotter's fourth basic assumption is that *motivation is goal directed* (Rotter, 1982). He rejects the notion that people are primarily motivated to reduce tension or seek pleasure, insisting that the best explanation for human behavior lies in people's expectations that their behaviors are advancing them toward goals. For example, most college students have a goal of graduation and are willing to endure stress, tension, and hard work in order to reach that goal. Rather than reducing tension, the prospect of several difficult years of college classes promises to increase it.

Other things being equal, people are most strongly reinforced by behaviors that move them in the direction of anticipated goals. This refers to Rotter's **empirical law of effect,** which "defines reinforcement as any action, condition, or event which affects the individual's movement toward a goal" (Rotter & Hochreich, 1975, p. 95).

Rotter's fifth assumption is that *people are capable of anticipating events.* Moreover, they use their perceived movement in the direction of the anticipated event as a criterion for evaluating reinforcers. Beginning with these five general assumptions, Rotter has built a personality theory that attempts to predict human behavior.

VARIABLES OF PREDICTION

Because Rotter's primary concern is the prediction of human behavior, he suggested four variables that must be analyzed in order to make accurate predictions in any specific situation. These are behavior potential, expectancy, reinforcement value, and the psychological situation. *Behavior potential* refers to the likelihood that a given behavior will occur in a particular situation; *expectancy* is a person's expectation of being reinforced; *reinforcement value* is the person's preference for a particular reinforcement; and the *psychological situation* refers to a complex pattern of cues that the person perceives during a specific time period.

BEHAVIOR POTENTIAL

Broadly considered, **behavior potential** (BP) refers to the possibility that a particular response will occur at a given time and place. Rotter and Hochreich (1975) defined it as "the potential for any given behavior to occur in a particular situation or set of situations as calculated in relation to any single reinforcement or set of reinforcements" (p. 95). Several behavior potentials of varying strength exist in any psychological situation. For example, as Megan walks toward a restaurant, she has several behavioral potentials. She might pass by without noticing the restaurant; actively ignore it; stop to eat; think about stopping to eat, but go on; examine the building and contents with a consideration to purchase it; or stop, go inside, and rob the cashier. For Megan in this situation, the potential for some of these behaviors would approach zero, some would be very likely, and others would be in between these extremes. How can we predict which behaviors are most or least likely to occur?

The behavior potential in any situation is a function of both expectancy and reinforcement value. If we wish to know the likelihood that Megan will rob the cashier rather than purchase the restaurant or stop to eat, for example, we could hold expectancy constant and vary reinforcement value. If each of these behavior potentials carried a 70% expectancy of being reinforced, then we could make a prediction as to their relative probability of occurrence based solely on the reinforcement value of each. If holding up the cashier carries positive reinforcement value greater than ordering food or buying the restaurant, then that behavior has the greatest occurrence potential.

The second approach to prediction is to hold reinforcement value constant and vary expectancy. If total reinforcements from each possible behavior are of equal value, then the one with the greatest expectation of reinforcement is most likely to occur. More specifically, if reinforcement from robbing the cashier, buying the business, and ordering a dinner are all valued equally, then the response that is most likely to produce a reinforcement has the highest behavior potential.

Rotter employs a broad definition of behavior, which refers to any response, implicit or explicit, that can be observed or measured, directly or indirectly. This comprehensive concept allows Rotter to include as behavior such hypothetical constructs as generalizing, problem solving, thinking, analyzing, and so forth.

EXPECTANCY

Rotter and Hochreich (1975) defined **expectancy** (E) as "the probability held by the individual that a particular reinforcement will occur as a function of a specific behavior on his part in a specific situation or situations" (p. 96). The probability is not determined by the individual's history of reinforcements, as Skinner contended, but is subjectively held by the person. History, of course, is a contributing factor, but so too are unrealistic thinking, expectations based on lack of information, and fantasies, so long as the person sincerely believes that a given reinforcement or group of reinforcements is contingent on a particular response.

Expectancies can be general or specific. Generalized expectancies (GEs) are learned through previous experiences with a particular response or similar responses and are based on the belief that certain behaviors will be followed by positive reinforcement. For example, college students whose previous hard work has been reinforced by high grades will have a generalized expectancy of future reward and will work hard in a variety of academic situations.

Specific expectancies are designated as E' (E *prime*). In any situation the expectancy for a particular reinforcement is determined by a combination of a specific expectancy (E') and the generalized expectancy (GE). For example, a student may have general expectancy that a given level of academic work will be rewarded by good grades but may believe that an equal amount of hard work in a French class will go unrewarded.

Total expectancy of success is a function of both one's generalized expectancy and one's specific expectancy. Total expectancy partially determines the amount of effort people will expend in pursuit of their goals. A person with low total expectancy for success in obtaining a prestigious job is not likely to apply for the position, whereas a person with high expectancy for success will exert much effort and persist in the face of setbacks to achieve goals that appear possible.

REINFORCEMENT VALUE

Another variable in the prediction formula is **reinforcement value** (RV), which is defined as "the degree of preference for any reinforcement to occur if the possibilities of their occurring were all equal" (Rotter & Hochreich, 1975, p. 97). Reinforcement value can be illustrated by a vending machine with several possible selections, each costing the same. A woman approaches the machine able and willing to pay 75 cents in order to receive a snack. The vending machine is in perfect working condition, so there is a 100% probability that her response will be followed by some sort of reinforcement. Her expectancy of reinforcement, therefore, for the candy bar, corn chips, potato chips, popcorn, tortilla chips, and Danish pastry are all equal. Her response, that is, which button she presses, is determined by the reinforcement value of each snack.

When expectancies and situational variables are held constant, behavior is shaped by one's preference for the possible reinforcements, that is, reinforcement value. In most situations, of course, expectancies are seldom equal, and prediction is difficult because both expectancy and reinforcement value can vary.

In determining reinforcement value, one must consider both positive and negative aspects of reinforcement. Rotter agrees with Skinner that positive reinforcement is any event or condition that increases the probability that a particular behavior will occur again under the same or similar circumstances. However, his definition of negative reinforcement is different. Whereas Skinner defined negative reinforcement as the removal of an aversive stimulus that consequently increases the probability that a particular behavior will occur, Rotter uses the term to refer to any negatively valued event. To Rotter, therefore, negative reinforcement is the same as punishment, and it decreases the likelihood that a particular behavior will occur again (Rotter, Chance, & Phares, 1972).

What determines the reinforcement value for any event, condition, or action? First, the individual's perception contributes to the positive or negative value of an event. Rotter calls this **internal reinforcement** and distinguishes it from **external reinforcement,** which refers to events, conditions, or actions that one's society or culture values. Internal and external reinforcements may be either in harmony or at a variance with one another. For example, if you like popular movies, that is, the same ones that most other people like, then your internal and external reinforcement for attending these are in agreement. However, if your taste in movies runs contrary to that of your friends, then your internal and external reinforcements are discrepant.

Another contributor to reinforcement value is one's needs. Generally, a specific reinforcement tends to increase in value as the need it satisfies becomes stronger. A starving child places a higher value on a bowl of soup than does a moderately hungry one. (Needs are more fully discussed later in this chapter.)

Reinforcements are also valued according to their expected consequences for future reinforcements. Rotter believes that people are capable of using cognition to anticipate a sequence of events leading to some future goal, and that the ultimate goal contributes to the reinforcement value of each event in the sequence. Reinforcements seldom occur independently of future related reinforcements but are likely to appear in **reinforcement-reinforcement sequences,** which Rotter (1982) refers to as clusters of reinforcement.

Humans are goal-oriented; they anticipate achieving a goal if they behave in a particular way. Other things being equal, goals with the highest reinforcement value are most desirable. Desire alone, however, is not sufficient to predict behavior. The potential for any behavior is a function of both expectancy and reinforcement value, as well as the psychological situation.

Psychological Situation

The **psychological situation** (s), the fourth variable in the prediction formula, refers to that part of the external and internal world to which the person is responding. It is not synonymous with external stimuli, although physical events are usually important to the psychological situation.

People do not behave in a vacuum but respond to cues in their perceived environment.

Behavior is a function neither of environmental events nor of central traits or characteristics within the person; rather, it stems from the interaction of the person with his or her meaningful environment. If physical stimuli alone determined behavior, then two individuals would respond in exactly the same way to identical stimuli. If personal traits were responsible for behavior, then a person would always respond in a consistent and characteristic fashion, even to different events. Because neither of these conditions is valid, something other than the environment or personal traits must shape behavior. Rotter's social learning theory hypothesizes that the *interaction* between person and environment is a crucial factor in shaping behavior.

The psychological situation is "a complex set of interacting cues acting upon an individual for any specific time period" (Rotter, 1982, p. 318). People do not behave in a vacuum; instead, they respond to cues within their perceived environment. These cues serve to determine for them certain expectancies for behavior-reinforcement sequences as well as for reinforcement-reinforcement sequences. The time period for the cues may vary from momentary to lengthy; thus, the psychological situation is not limited by time. One's marital situation, for example, may be relatively constant over a long period of time, whereas the psychological situation faced by a driver spinning out of control on an icy road may be extremely short. The psychological situation must be considered along with expectancies and reinforcement value in determining the probability of a given response.

BASIC PREDICTION FORMULA

As a hypothetical means of predicting behavior, Rotter proposed a basic formula that includes all four variables of prediction. The formula represents an idealistic rather than a practical means of prediction, and no precise values can be plugged into it. Consider the case of La Juan, an academically gifted college student who is listening to a dull and lengthy lecture by one of her professors. To the internal cues of boredom and the external cues of seeing slumbering classmates, what is the likelihood that La Juan will respond by resting her head on the desk in an attempt to sleep? The psychological situation alone is not responsible for her behavior, but it interacts with her expectancy for reinforcement plus the reinforcement value of sleep in that particular situation. La Juan's behavior potential can be estimated by Rotter's basic formula for the prediction of goal-directed behavior:

$$BP_{x,s_1,R_a} = f(E_{x,R_a,s_1} \, \& \, RV_{a,s_1})$$

This formula is read: The potential for Behavior x to occur in Situation 1 in relation to Reinforcement a is a function of the expectancy that Behavior x will be followed by Reinforcement a in Situation 1 and the value of Reinforcement a in Situation 1 (Rotter & Hochreich, 1975).

Applied to our example, the formula suggests that the likelihood (behavior potential or BP) that La Juan will rest her head on her desk (behavior x) in a dull and boring class with other students slumbering (the psychological situation or s_1) with the goal of sleep (reinforcement or R_a) is a function of her expectation that such behavior (E_x) will be followed by sleep (R_a) in this particular classroom situation (s_1) plus a measure of how highly she desires to sleep (reinforcement value or RV_a) in this specific situation (s_1).

Consider a second example. David, who has worked for 18 years in Hoffman's Hardware Store, has just been informed that because of a business decline, Mr. Hoffman must cut his workforce, and that David may lose his job. How can we predict David's subsequent behavior? Will he beg Mr. Hoffman to let him remain with the company? Will he strike out in violence against the store or Mr. Hoffman? Will he displace his anger and act aggressively toward his wife or children? Will he begin drinking heavily and become apathetic toward searching for a new job? Will he immediately and constructively begin looking for another position?

GENERALIZED EXPECTANCIES

Because most of these possible behaviors are new to David, how can we predict what he will do? At this point, the concepts of **generalization** and **generalized expectancy** enter into Rotter's personality theory. If, in the past, David has generally been rewarded for behaviors that have increased his social status, then only a slight probability exists that he will beg Mr. Hoffman for a job, because such actions are contrary to increased social status. On the other hand, if his previous attempts at responsible and independent behaviors have generally been reinforced, and if he has the *freedom of movement*, that is, the opportunity to apply for another job, then, assuming he needs work, a high probability exists that he will apply for another job or otherwise behave independently. This prediction, though not as specific as the one predicting the college student's likelihood of sleep in a boring classroom, is nevertheless more useful in situations where rigorous control of pertinent variables is not possible. Predicting David's reaction to the probable loss of a job is a matter of knowing how he views the options available to him and also the status of his present *needs*.

NEEDS

Unlike Skinner, Rotter is willing to hypothesize the existence of inner states such as needs, goals, and expectancies. He assumes that people are goal-oriented, and that needs can be defined as any behavior or set of behaviors that people see as moving them in the direction of that goal. Rotter does not see needs as states of deprivation or arousal but as indicators of the direction of behavior. The difference between needs and goals is semantic only. When focus is on the environment, Rotter (1982) speaks of goals; when it is on the person, he talks of needs.

The concept of needs allows for more generalized predictions than that permitted by the four specific variables that comprise the basic prediction formula. Ordinarily, personality theory deals with broad predictions of human behavior. We know, for example, that a person with strong needs for dominance will usually try to gain the power position in most interpersonal relationships as well as in a variety of other situations. In specific situations, however, a dominant person may frequently behave in a non-dominant or even submissive fashion. The basic prediction formula permits specific predictions, assuming, of course, that all relevant information is at hand. It is the more appropriate formula for controlled laboratory experiments but is inadequate in predicting everyday behaviors. For this reason, Rotter introduced the concept of needs and their accompanying *general prediction formula*, which will be cited later.

CATEGORIES OF NEEDS

Rotter and Hochreich (1975) listed six broad categories of needs, with each category representing a group of functionally related behaviors, that is, behaviors that lead to the same or similar reinforcements. For example, people can have their recognition needs met in a variety of situations and by many different people. Therefore, they can receive reinforcement for a group of functionally related behaviors, all of which satisfy their need for recognition. The following list is not exhaustive, but it represents most of the important human needs.

Recognition-Status

The need to be recognized by others and to achieve status in their eyes is a powerful need for most people. Recognition-status includes the need to excel in those things that a person regards as important, for example, school, sports, occupation, hobbies, and physical appearance. It also includes the need for socioeconomic status and personal prestige. Playing a good game of bridge would be an example of the need for recognition-status.

Dominance

Dominance, or the need to control the behavior of others, includes any set of behaviors directed at gaining power over the lives of friends, family, colleagues, superiors, and subordinates. Talking colleagues into accepting your ideas is a specific example of dominance.

Independence

Independence is the need to be free of the domination of others. It includes those behaviors aimed at gaining the freedom to make your own decisions, to rely on yourself, and to attain your goals without the help of others. Declining help in repairing a bicycle could demonstrate the need for independence.

Protection-Dependency

A set of needs nearly opposite independence are those of protection and dependency. This category includes the needs to have others take care of us, keep us from experiencing frustration and harm, and help us satisfy the other need categories. A specific example of protection-dependency would be asking your spouse to stay home from work and take care of you when you are ill.

Love and Affection

Most of us have strong needs for love and affection, that is, needs for acceptance by others that go beyond recognition and status to include some indications that other people have warm positive feelings for us. The needs for love and affection include those behaviors aimed toward securing friendly regard, interest, and devotion from others. Doing favors for others in anticipation of receiving verbal expressions of positive regard and gratitude might be an example of this need.

Physical Comfort

Physical comfort is perhaps the most basic need because other needs are learned in relation to it. This need includes those behaviors aimed at securing food, good health, and physical security. Other needs are learned as an outgrowth of our needs for pleasure, physical contact, and well-being. Turning on the air conditioner or hugging another person could be examples of the need for physical comfort.

Need Components

A need complex has three essential components—*need potential, freedom of movement*, and *need value*—which are analogous to the more specific concepts of behavior potential, expectancy, and reinforcement value (Rotter, Chance, & Phares, 1972).

Need Potential

Need potential (NP) refers to the possible occurrence of a set of functionally related behaviors directed toward the satisfaction of the same or similar goals. Need potential is analogous to the more specific concept of behavior potential. The difference between the two is that need potential refers to a *group* of functionally related behaviors, whereas behavior potential is the likelihood that a *particular* behavior will occur in a given situation in relation to a specific reinforcement.

Need potential cannot be measured solely through observation of behavior. If we see different people behaving in apparently the same manner—for example, eating in a fancy restaurant—we should not conclude that they are all satisfying the same need potential. One person may be satisfying the need for physical comfort, that is, food; another may be more interested in love and affection; and the third person may be trying primarily to satisfy the need for recognition-status. Probably any of the six broad needs could be satisfied by eating in this restaurant. Whether one's need potential is realized, however, depends not only on the value or preference one has for that reinforcement but also on one's freedom of movement in making responses leading to that reinforcement.

Freedom of Movement

We have seen that our behavior is partly determined by our expectancies, that is, our best guess that a particular reinforcement will follow a specific response. In the general prediction formula (discussed later), **freedom of movement** (FM) is analogous to expectancy and is defined as the "mean expectancy of obtaining positive satisfactions as a result of a set of related behaviors directed toward obtaining a group of functionally related reinforcements" (Rotter, Chance, & Phares, 1972, p. 34). In other words, freedom of movement is one's overall expectation of being reinforced for performing those behaviors that are directed toward satisfying some general need. To illustrate, a person with a strong need for dominance could behave in a variety of ways to satisfy that need. She might select the clothes her husband will wear, decide what college curriculum her son will pursue, direct actors in a play, organize a professional conference involving dozens of colleagues, or perform any one of a hundred other behaviors aimed at securing reinforcement for her dominance need. The average or mean level of expectancies that these behaviors will lead to the desired satisfaction is a measure of her freedom of movement in the area of dominance.

Freedom of movement can be determined by holding need value constant and observing one's need potential. For example, if a person places exactly the same value on dominance, independence, love and affection, and each of the other needs, then that person will perform those behaviors judged to have the greatest expectancy of being reinforced. If the person performs behaviors leading to physical comfort, for example, then there will be more freedom of movement in that need complex than in any of the other need complexes. Ordinarily, of course, need value is not constant, because most people prefer the satisfaction of one need over others.

Need Value

A person's **need value** (NV) is the degree to which she or he prefers one set of reinforcements to another. Rotter, Chance, and Phares (1972) defined need value as the "mean preference value of a set of functionally related reinforcements" (p. 33). In the general prediction formula, need value is the analogue of reinforcement value. When freedom of movement is held constant, people will perform those behavior sequences that lead to satisfaction of the most preferred need. If people have equal expectancies of obtaining positive reinforcement for behaviors aimed at the satisfaction of any need, then the value they place on a particular need complex will be the principal determinant of their behavior. If they prefer independence to any other need complex, and if they have an equal expectation of being reinforced in the pursuit of any of the needs, then their behavior will be directed toward achieving independence.

GENERAL PREDICTION FORMULA

The basic prediction formula cited earlier is limited to highly controlled situations where expectancies, reinforcement value, and the psychological situation are all relatively simple and discrete. In most situations, however, prediction of behavior is much more complex because behaviors and reinforcements usually occur in functionally related sequences. Consider again the case of La Juan, the gifted student who was having difficulty staying awake in a dull and boring class. The basic prediction formula

Basic prediction formula

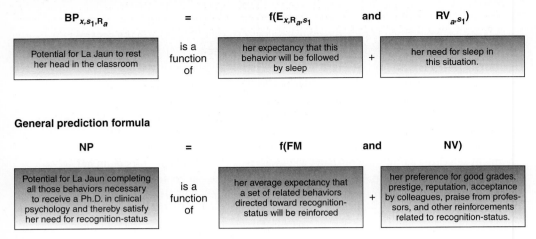

General prediction formula

Figure 12.1 Comparison of the basic prediction formula and the general prediction formula.

gives us some indication of the likelihood that in the specific situation of a boring lecture, La Juan will rest her head on her desk. However, a more generalized prediction formula is needed to predict her need potential for gaining the recognition-status that comes from graduating with highest honors. La Juan's likelihood of satisfying this need depends on a complex of behaviors. To make generalized predictions regarding a set of behaviors designed to satisfy needs, Rotter introduces the following general prediction formula:

$$NP = f \, (FM \, \& \, NV)$$

This equation means that need potential (NP) is a function of freedom of movement (FM) and need value (NV). The formula is analogous to the basic prediction formula, and each factor is parallel to the corresponding factors of that basic formula (Rotter & Hochreich, 1975). To illustrate the general prediction formula, we can look at La Juan's situation with regard to her future academic work. To predict her *need potential* for working toward graduation with highest honors, we would have to measure her *freedom of movement*, that is, her mean expectancy of being reinforced for a series of behaviors necessary to reach her goal, plus her *need value* of all those reinforcements, that is, the value she places on recognition-status or any other need she associates with receiving academic honors. The value La Juan places on recognition-status (need value), plus her average expectancy of being reinforced for performing the required series of behaviors (freedom of movement), equals her potential for pursuing the set of required behaviors (need potential). A comparison of the basic (specific) prediction formula and the generalized prediction formula is shown in Figure 12.1.

Rotter's general prediction formula allows for the fact that people use similar experiences from the past to anticipate present reinforcement. That is, they have a *generalized expectancy* for success. Rotter's two most popular scales for measuring generalized expectancies are the Internal-External Control Scale and the Interpersonal Trust Scale.

Table 12.1 Sample Items from Rotter's Internal-External Control Scale

1. a. Many of the unhappy things in people's lives are partly due to bad luck.
   b. People's misfortunes result from the mistakes they make.
2. a. One of the major reasons we have wars is that people don't take enough interest in politics.
   b. There will always be wars, no matter how hard people try to prevent them.
3. a. In the long run people get the respect they deserve in this world.
   b. Unfortunately, an individual's worth often passes unrecognized no matter how hard he or she tries.
4. a. The average citizen can have an influence in government decisions.
   b. The world is run by the few people in power and there isn't much the little guy can do about it.
5. a. The idea that teachers are unfair to students is nonsense.
   b. Most students don't realize the extent to which their grades are influenced by accidental happenings.
6. a. No matter how hard you try some people just don't like you.
   b. People who can't get others to like them don't understand how to get along with others.

SOURCE: From J. B. Rotter, "Generalized Expectancies for Internal Versus External Control of Reinforcement" *Psychological Monographs*, 80, (Whole No. 608), 1966. Copyright © 1966 by the American Psychological Association. Reprinted with permission.

INTERNAL AND EXTERNAL CONTROL OF REINFORCEMENT

At the core of Rotter's social learning theory is the notion that reinforcement does not automatically stamp in behaviors, but that people have the ability to see a causal connection between their own behavior and the occurrence of the reinforcer (Rotter, 1954; Rotter & Hochreich, 1975). People strive to reach their goals because they have a *generalized expectancy* that such strivings will be successful. People who generally believe that they can control their own fate will behave differently in many (but not all) situations from people who typically believe that their destiny is controlled by luck, chance, or powerful others.

During the 1950s and early 1960s, Rotter became intrigued by the observation that many people did not increase their feelings of personal control after experiencing success and that others did not lower their expectancies after repeated failure (Rotter, 1990, 1993; Zuroff & Rotter, 1985). In other words, some people tended to explain away successful outcomes as luck or chance, whereas others retained a high sense of personal control even after several nonreinforced behaviors. This seemed to be especially true in situations that people regarded as ambiguous or novel (Rotter, 1992), or when they were not clear whether the outcome of their behavior was due to their skill or to chance. Rotter (1990) has suggested that both the situation and the person contribute to feelings of personal control. Thus, a person with a generalized expectancy for success in one situation may have low feelings of personal control in another situation.

To assess internal and external control of reinforcement, or **locus of control,** Rotter (1966) developed the Internal-External Control Scale, basing it on the doctoral dissertations of two of his students, E. Jerry Phares (1955) and William H. James (1957). The I-E Scale consists of 29 forced-choice items; 23 pairs that are scored for either internal or external control and 6 filler statements designed to disguise the purpose of the scale. The scale is scored in the direction of external control so that 23 is the highest possible external score and 0 is the highest possible internal score. Table 12.1 shows several sample items from the I-E Scale. People must select either alternative *a* or alternative *b* from each pair of items. Although the internal or external direction of these items may seem obvious, Rotter (1990) reported that scores have only a modest correlation with a social desirability scale.

The I-E Scale attempts to measure the degree to which people perceive a causal relationship between their own efforts and environmental consequences. People who score high on internal control generally believe that the source of control resides within themselves and that they exercise a high level of personal control in most situations. People who score high on external control generally believe that their life is largely controlled by forces outside themselves, such as chance, destiny, or the behavior of other people.

Rotter's Internal-External Control Scale has become one of the most thoroughly investigated topics in psychology as well as in other social sciences, having been cited in more than 7,000 publications since its inception. Despite this popularity, the concepts of internal and external control are not always clearly understood. Although Rotter (1975) pointed out several common misconceptions concerning internal and external control of reinforcement (he seldom refers to it as "locus of control"), people continue to misuse and misinterpret the instrument. One misconception that Rotter mentioned is that scores on the scale are determinants of behavior. They should not be seen as causes of behavior but as indicators of *generalized expectancies* (GEs). As such, they must be considered along with *reinforcement value* (RV) when predicting behavior potential. A second misconception is that locus of control is specific and can predict achievement in a specific situation. Again, the concept refers to *generalized* expectancies of reinforcement and indicates the degree to which people generally believe that they are in control of their lives. A third common misconception is that the scale divides people into two distinct types—internals and externals. Rotter (1975, 1990) has always insisted that generalized expectancies imply a *gradient* of generalization and that, in certain specific situations, a person with generally high feelings of internal control may believe that the outcome of his or her behavior is due mostly to chance or to the behavior of powerful others. Fourth, many people seem to believe that high internal scores signify socially desirable traits and that high external scores indicate socially undesirable characteristics. Actually, extreme scores in either direction would be undesirable. Very high external scores might be related to apathy and despair, with people believing that they have no control over their environments; whereas extremely high internal scores would mean that people accept responsibility for everything that happens to them—accidents, business failure, delinquent children, and so forth. Scores somewhere in between these extremes, but inclined in the direction of internal control, would probably be most healthy or desirable.

INTERPERSONAL TRUST SCALE

Another example of a generalized expectancy (GE) that has provoked considerable interest and research is the concept of **interpersonal trust.** Rotter (1980) defined interpersonal trust as "a generalized expectancy held by an individual that the word, promise, oral or written statement of another individual or group can be relied on" (p. 1). Interpersonal trust does not refer to the belief that people are naturally good or that we live in the best of all possible worlds. Neither should it be equated with gullibility. Rotter saw interpersonal trust as a belief in the communications of others when there is no evidence for disbelieving, whereas gullibility is foolishly or naively believing the words of other people.

Pair skating demands a high level of interpersonal trust.

Rotter's social learning theory hypothesizes that, because many of our reinforcements come from other people, we develop generalized expectancies that positive or negative reinforcers will follow from verbal promises or threats made by others. Sometimes these promises and threats are kept; other times they are broken. In this way, each of us learns to trust or distrust the words of others. Because we have differential experiences with the words of others, it follows that individual differences will exist among people with regard to interpersonal trust.

To measure differences in interpersonal trust, Rotter (1967) developed an Interpersonal Trust Scale, which asked people to respond to 25 items such as "In dealing with strangers one is better off to be cautious until they have provided evidence that they are trustworthy" and "Most elected public officials are really sincere in their campaign promises" (p. 654). Scores for each of the 25 items are added so that high scores indicate the presence of interpersonal trust and low scores mean a generalized expectancy of distrust.

Is it more desirable to score high or low on the scale, to be trustful or distrustful? When trust is defined independently of gullibility, as Rotter (1980) contended, then high trust is not only desirable but essential for the survival of civilization. We trust that the food we buy is not poisoned; that the gasoline in our cars will not explode on ignition; that airline pilots know how to fly the plane in which we travel; and even that the postal service will deliver our mail without tampering with it. Societies can function smoothly only when people have at least a moderate amount of trust in each other.

Rotter (1980) has summarized results of studies that indicate that people who score high in interpersonal trust, as opposed to those who score low, are (1) less likely to lie; (2) probably less likely to cheat or steal; (3) more likely to give others a second chance; (4) more likely to respect the rights of others; (5) less likely to be unhappy, conflicted, or maladjusted; (6) somewhat more likable and popular; (7) more trustworthy; (8) neither more nor less gullible; and (9) neither more nor less intelligent. In other words, high trusters are not gullible or naive, and rather than being harmed by their trustful attitude, they seem to possess many of the characteristics that other people regard as positive and desirable.

MALADAPTIVE BEHAVIOR

Maladaptive behavior in Rotter's social learning theory is any persistent behavior that fails to move a person closer to a desired goal. It frequently, but not inevitably, arises from the combination of high need value and low freedom of movement, that is, from goals that are unrealistically high in relation to one's ability to achieve them (Rotter, 1964).

For example, the need for love and affection is realistic, but some people unrealistically set a goal to be loved by everyone. Hence, their need value will exceed their freedom of movement, resulting in behavior that is likely to be defensive or maladaptive. When people set their goals too high, they cannot learn productive behaviors because their goals are beyond reach. Instead, they learn how to avoid failure or how to defend themselves against the pain that accompanies failure. For example, a woman whose goal is to be loved by everyone inevitably will be ignored or rejected by someone. To obtain love, she may become socially aggressive (a nonproductive, self-defeating strategy), or she may withdraw from people, which prevents her from being hurt by them, but which is also nonproductive.

Setting goals too high is only one of several possible contributors to maladaptive behavior. Another frequent cause is low freedom of movement. People may have low expectancies of success because they lack information or the ability to perform those behaviors that will be followed by positive reinforcement. A person who values love, for example, may lack the interpersonal skills necessary to obtain it.

People may also have low freedom of movement because they make a faulty evaluation of the present situation. For example, people sometimes underestimate their intellectual abilities because, in the past, they have been told that they were stupid. Even though their need values are not unrealistically high, they have low expectations of success because they wrongly believe that they are incapable, for example, of performing well in school or competing successfully for a higher level job.

People may also have low freedom of movement because they generalize from one situation in which, perhaps, they are realistically inadequate to other situations in which they could have sufficient ability to be successful. For example, a physically weak adolescent who lacks the skills to be an accomplished athlete may erroneously see himself as unable to compete for a role in the school play or to be a leader in a social club. He inappropriately generalizes his inadequacies in sports to lack of ability in unrelated areas.

In summary, maladjusted individuals are characterized by unrealistic goals, inappropriate behaviors, inadequate skills, or unreasonably low expectancies of being able to execute the behaviors necessary for positive reinforcement. Although they have learned inadequate ways of solving problems within a social context, they can unlearn these behaviors and also learn more appropriate ones within the controlled social environment provided by psychotherapy.

PSYCHOTHERAPY

To Rotter (1964), "the problems of psychotherapy are problems of how to effect changes in behavior through the interaction of one person with another. That is, they are problems in human learning in a social situation" (p. 82). Although Rotter adopts a problem-solving approach to psychotherapy, he does not limit his concern to quick solutions to immediate problems. His interest is more long range, involving a change in the patient's orientation toward life.

In general, the goal of Rotter's therapy is to bring freedom of movement and need value into harmony, thus reducing defensive and avoidance behaviors. The therapist assumes an active role as a teacher and attempts to accomplish the therapeutic goal in two basic ways: (1) changing the importance of goals and (2) eliminating unrealistically low expectancies for success (Rotter, 1964, 1970, 1978; Rotter & Hochreich, 1975).

CHANGING GOALS

Many patients are unable to solve life's problems because they are pursuing skewed or distorted goals. The role of the therapist is to help these patients understand the faulty nature of their goals and to teach them constructive means of striving toward realistic goals. Rotter and Hochreich (1975) listed three sources of problems that follow from inappropriate goals.

First, two or more important goals may be in conflict. For example, adolescents frequently value both independence and protection-dependency. On the one hand, they wish to be free from their parents' domination and control, but on the other, they retain their need for a nurturing person to care for them and protect them from painful experiences. Their ambivalent behaviors are often confusing both to themselves and to their parents. In this situation, the therapist may try to help adolescents see how specific behaviors are related to each of these needs and proceed to work with them in changing the value of one or both needs. By gradually altering need value, patients begin to behave more consistently and to experience greater freedom of movement in obtaining their goals.

A second source of problems is a destructive goal. Some patients persistently pursue self-destructive goals that inevitably result in failure and punishment. The job of the therapist is to point out the detrimental nature of this pursuit and the likelihood that it will be followed by negative reinforcement (punishment). One possible technique used by a therapist in these cases is to positively reinforce movements away from destructive goals. Rotter, however, is both pragmatic and eclectic and is not bound to a specific set of techniques for each conceivable problem. To him, the appropriate procedure is the one that works with a given patient.

Many people find themselves in trouble because they set their goals too high and are continually frustrated when they cannot reach or exceed them. This is the third area of inappropriate goals and perhaps the most common one. High goals lead to failure and pain, so instead of learning constructive means of obtaining a goal, people learn nonproductive ways of avoiding pain. For example, a person may learn to avoid painful experiences by physically running away or by psychologically repressing the experience. Because these techniques are successful, the person learns to use flight and repression in a variety of situations. Therapy in this case would consist of getting the patient to realistically reevaluate and lower exaggerated goals by reducing the reinforcement value of those goals. Because high reinforcement value is often learned through generalization, the therapist would work toward teaching patients to discriminate between past legitimate values and present spurious ones. For example, a patient may have been previously rewarded with food or affection for associating with his mother, who may have praised him for his cleanliness behaviors. As a consequence, the son learned to place an unrealistically high value on compulsive neatness, and as an adult, he is never quite comfortable amid clutter and disarray. The therapist must teach this patient that nourishment and love are independent from compulsively neat and orderly behavior. Rotter, however, does not stop with giving patients insight and eliminating their maladjustive behaviors. He also attempts to teach them new behaviors that will lead to the reinforcements they seek.

ELIMINATING LOW EXPECTANCIES

Rotter's second general approach is to attack low expectancies of success and its analogue, low freedom of movement. As noted in the section on maladjustment, people may have low freedom of movement for at least three reasons.

First, they may lack the skills or information needed to successfully strive toward their goals (Rotter, 1970). With such patients, a therapist becomes a teacher, warmly and emphatically instructing them in more effective techniques for solving problems and satisfying needs. If a patient, for example, has difficulties in interpersonal relationships, the therapist has an arsenal of techniques, including extinguishing inappropriate behaviors by simply ignoring them; using the therapist/patient relationship as a model for an effective interpersonal encounter that may then generalize beyond the therapeutic situation; and advising the patient of specific behaviors to try out in the presence of those other people who are most likely to be receptive.

A second source of low freedom of movement is faulty evaluation of the present situation. For example, an adult may lack assertiveness with her colleagues because, during childhood, she was punished for competing with her siblings. This patient must learn to differentiate between past and present as well as between siblings and colleagues. The therapist's task is to help her make these distinctions and to teach her assertiveness techniques in a variety of appropriate situations.

Finally, low freedom of movement can spring from inadequate generalization. Patients often use failure in one situation as proof that they cannot be successful in other areas. Earlier we saw the example of the physically feeble adolescent who, because he was unsuccessful in sports, generalized his failure to nonathletic areas. His present problems come from faulty generalization, and the therapist must reinforce even small successes in social relationships, academic achievements, and other situations. The patient will eventually learn to discriminate between realistic shortcomings in one area and successful behaviors in other situations.

Although Rotter recognizes that therapists should be flexible in their techniques and should utilize different approaches with different patients, he does suggest several interesting techniques that he has found to be effective. The first is to teach patients to look for alternative courses of action (Rotter, 1978). Patients frequently complain that their spouse, parent, child, or employer does not understand them, treats them unjustly, and is the source of their problems. In this situation, Rotter would simply teach the patient to change the other person's behavior. This can be accomplished by examining those behaviors of the patient that typically lead to negative reactions by spouse, parent, child, or employer. If the patient can find an alternative method of behaving toward important others, then those others will probably change their behavior toward the patient. Thereafter, the patient will be rewarded for behaving in a more appropriate fashion.

Rotter (1978) suggested a related approach designed to help patients develop a more accurate understanding of other people's motives. Many patients have a suspicious or distrustful attitude toward others. They believe that their spouse, teacher, or boss is intentionally and spitefully trying to harm them. Rotter would attempt to teach these patients to look at ways in which they may be contributing to the other people's defensive or negative behavior and to help them realize that these other people are frequently frightened or threatened by the patient and that they are not simply nasty or spiteful.

Rotter (1978) also suggested that a therapist can help a patient look at the long-range consequences of behavior and to understand that many maladaptive behaviors produce secondary gains that outweigh the patient's present frustration. For example, a woman may adopt the role of a helpless child in order to gain control over her husband. She complains to her therapist that she is dissatisfied with her helplessness and would like to become more independent, both for her sake and for the benefit of her husband. What she may not realize, however, is that her current helpless behavior is satisfying her basic need for dominance. The more helpless she acts, the more control she exercises over her husband, who must respond to her helplessness. The positive reinforcement she receives from her husband's recognition is stronger than the accompanying negative reinforcement. In addition, she may not clearly see the long-range positive consequences of self-confidence and independence. The task of the therapist is to train the patient to postpone minor contemporary satisfactions for more important future ones.

Another novel technique suggested by Rotter (1978) is to have patients enter into a previously painful social situation, but rather than speaking as much as usual, they are asked to remain as quiet as possible and largely to observe. By observing others, patients have a better chance of learning their motives. They can use that information in the future to alter their own behavior, thereby changing the reactions of others and reducing the painful effects of future encounters with those other persons.

In summary, Rotter believes that a therapist should be an active participant in a social interaction with the patient. An effective therapist possesses the characteristics of warmth and acceptance, not only because these attitudes encourage the patient to verbalize problems, but also because reinforcement from a warm, accepting therapist is more effective than reinforcement from a cold, rejecting one (Rotter, Chance, & Phares, 1972). The therapist attempts to minimize the discrepancy between need value and freedom of movement by helping patients alter their goals or by teaching effective means of obtaining those goals. Even though the therapist is an active problem solver, Rotter (1978) believes that eventually patients must learn to solve their own problems.

INTRODUCTION TO MISCHEL'S COGNITIVE SOCIAL THEORY

Personality theorists from Freud (Chapter 2) to Raymond Cattell and Hans Eysenck (Chapter 13) have frequently seen people as being motivated by a limited number of drives or personal traits that tend to render a person's behavior somewhat consistent. For example, Freud would say that a person with the anal triad of compulsive neatness, stubbornness, and stinginess is driven to be neat, obstinate, and miserly. Such a person would exhibit these behaviors in a variety of settings or situations. Similarly, Cattell would say that a person with a strong dominance trait will generally (but not always) behave assertively, aggressively, or competitively, and Eysenck would say that an extraverted person will usually behave in an extraverted manner. Walter Mischel objects to this trait theory explanation of behavior. While recognizing the existence of personal dispositions, Mischel proposes that psychologists should shift their emphasis from global traits inferred from behavior to cognitive activities and to specific situations in which behavior occurs. "The focus shifts from attempting to compare and generalize about what different individuals 'are like' to an assessment of what they do—behaviorally and cognitively—in relation to the psychological conditions in which they do it" (Mischel, 1973, p. 265).

Mischel does not suggest that people are empty vessels with no personal traits that endure over time. Rather, he holds that many basic dispositions can be stable over a long period of time. His objection to the use of traits as predictors of behaviors rests not with their temporal instability but with their inconsistency from one *situation* to another. For example, a student may have a history of being conscientious with regard to academic work but fail to be conscientious in cleaning his apartment or maintaining his car in working condition. His lack of conscientiousness in cleaning his apartment may be due to disinterest, and his neglect of his car may be the result of insufficient knowledge. Thus, the specific situation interacts with the person's competencies, interests, goals, expectancies, and so forth to predict behavior. Mischel's cognitive social learning theory holds that the person and the situation are interdependent—people's behavior partially shapes the situations in their lives, just as situations help shape people's behavior.

BIOGRAPHY OF WALTER MISCHEL

Walter Mischel, the second son of upper-middle-class parents, was born on February 22, 1930, in Vienna. He and his brother Theodore, who later became a philosopher of science, grew up in a pleasant environment only a short distance from Freud's home. The tranquility of childhood, however, was shattered when the Nazis invaded Austria in 1938. That same year, which also marked Freud's departure from Vienna, the Mischel family fled Austria and moved to the United States. After living in various parts of the country, they settled in Brooklyn in 1940, where Walter attended primary and secondary schools. Before he could accept a college scholarship, his father suddenly became ill, and Walter was forced to take a series of odd jobs. Eventually he was able to attend New York University, where he became passionately interested in art (painting and sculpture) and divided his time among art, psychology, and life in Greenwich Village.

In college, Mischel was appalled by the rat-centered introductory psychology classes that seemed to him far removed from the everyday lives of humans. His humanistic inclinations were solidified by reading Freud, the existential thinkers, and the great poets. After graduation, he entered the M.A. program in clinical psychology at City College of New York. While working on his degree, he was employed as a social worker in the Lower East Side slums, work that led him to doubt the usefulness of psychoanalytic theory and to see the necessity of using empirical evidence to evaluate all claims of psychology.

Mischel's development as a cognitive social psychologist was further enhanced by his doctoral studies at Ohio State University from 1953 to 1956. At that time the psychology department at Ohio State was informally divided into the supporters of its two most influential faculty members—Julian Rotter and George Kelly. Unlike most students who strongly supported one or the other position, Mischel admired both Rotter and Kelly and learned from each of them. As a consequence, Mischel's cognitive social theory shows the influence of Rotter's social learning theory as well as Kelly's cognitively based theory of personal constructs (see Chapter 15). Rotter taught Mischel the importance of research design for improving assessment techniques and for measuring the effectiveness of therapeutic treatment; Kelly taught him that participants in psychology experiments are like the psychologists who study them in that they are thinking, feeling human beings.

From 1956 to 1958, Mischel lived much of the time in the Caribbean, studying religious cults that practiced spirit possession and investigating delay of gratification in a cross-cultural setting. He became determined to learn more about why people prefer future, valuable rewards over immediate, less valuable ones. Much of his later research has revolved around this issue.

Next, Mischel taught for 2 years at the University of Colorado. He then joined the Department of Social Relations at Harvard, where his interest in personality theory and assessment was further stimulated by discussions with Gordon Allport (see Chapter 14), Henry Murray, David McClelland, and others. In 1962, Mischel moved to Stanford and became a colleague of Albert Bandura (see Chapter 11). After more than 20 years at Stanford, Mischel returned to New York, joining the faculty at Columbia University, where he remains as an active researcher and continues to hone his cognitive social learning theory.

While at Harvard, Mischel met and married Harriet Nerlove, another graduate student in cognitive psychology. Before their divorce, the Mischels collaborated to produce three daughters and several scientific projects (H. N. Mischel & W. Mischel, 1973; W. Mischel & H. N. Mischel, 1976, 1983). Mischel's most important early work was *Personality and Assessment* (1968), an outgrowth of his efforts to identify successful Peace Corps volunteers. His experiences as consultant to the Peace Corps taught him that under the right conditions, people are at least as capable as standardized tests at predicting their own behavior. In *Personality and Assessment*, Mischel argued that traits are weak predictors of performance in a variety of situations and that the situation is more important than traits in influencing behavior. This book upset many clinical psychologists, who argued that the inability of personal dispositions to predict behavior across situations was due to the unreliability and imprecision of the instruments that measure traits. Some believed that Mischel was trying to undo the concept of stable personality traits and even deny the existence of personality. Later, Mischel (1979) answered his critics, saying that he was not opposed to traits as such, but only to generalized traits that negate the individuality and uniqueness of each person.

Much of Mischel's research has been a cooperative effort with a number of his graduate students. In recent years, many of his publications have been collaborations with Yuichi Shoda, who received his Ph.D from Columbia in 1990. Mischel's most popular book, *Introduction to Personality* (1971), was revised in 1976, 1981, 1986, and 1993. Mischel has won several awards, including the Distinguished Scientist award from the clinical division of the American Psychological Association (APA) in 1978 and the APA's award for Distinguished Scientific Contribution in 1982.

A CONDITIONAL VIEW OF PERSONAL DISPOSITIONS

In the next chapter, we will see that Raymond Cattell and Hans Eysenck view traits or factors as important determinants of human behavior. In Chapter 14, we will see that Gordon Allport used the term "personal dispositions" to refer to those personality structures that are capable of initiating and guiding an individual's behavior. To Mischel, these views of traits or personal dispositions overlook the importance of the specific situation in which people function. However, Mischel does not believe that the situation alone determines behavior; he insists that personal qualities are also important. Therefore, he has proposed a *conditional model* for understanding the influence of traits or personal dispositions (Mischel, 1990; Wright & Mischel, 1987). This view suggests that behavior is not caused by global personal traits but by people's perceptions of themselves in a particular situation. For example, a person who typically is socially shy may, under certain conditions, behave in an outgoing, extraverted manner.

The conditional view of dispositions emphasizes the importance of *goals* in predicting behavior. Whereas trait theory would suggest that global dispositions predict behavior, the conditional theory holds that behavior is shaped more by a person's specific goals. For example, traditional trait theory suggests that people with the trait of conscientiousness will usually be led to behave in a conscientious manner. However, Mischel's goal-based conditional theory holds that, in a variety of situations, a conscientious person may use conscientiousness along with other cognitive-affective processes to accomplish a specific outcome, that is, to achieve a goal.

In an exploratory study to test this model, Wright and Mischel (1988) interviewed 8- and 12-year-old children as well as adults and asked them to report everything they knew about "target" groups of children. Both adults and children recognized the variability of other people's behavior, but adults were more certain about the conditions under which particular behaviors would occur. Whereas children would hedge their descriptions in such terms as "Carlo sometimes hits other kids," adults would be more specific, for example, "Carlo hits when provoked." These findings suggest that people readily recognize the interrelationship between situations and behavior and that they intuitively follow a conditional view of dispositions.

THE CONSISTENCY PARADOX

Mischel has long been interested in what he terms the **consistency paradox,** that is, the observation that both laypersons and professional psychologists seem to intuitively believe that people's behavior is relatively consistent, yet empirical evidence suggests much variability in behavior. To many people, it seems self-evident that personal dispositions such as aggressiveness, honesty, miserliness, punctuality, and so forth are global traits and that they account for much of our behavior. We elect people to political office because they have honesty, trustworthiness, decisiveness, and integrity; employers and personnel managers select workers who are punctual, loyal, cooperative, hardworking, organized, and sociable. Many people assume that such traits will be manifested over a period of time and also from one situation to another. Mischel (1990) suggested that, at best, these people are only half right. He contended that some basic traits do persist over time, but he has found little evidence that they generalize from one situation to another.

For many years, research has failed to support the consistency of personal traits across situations. Hartshorne and May, in their classic 1928 study, found that schoolchildren who were honest in one situation were deceitful in another. For example, some children would cheat on tests but not steal party favors; others would break rules in an athletic contest but not cheat on a test. Some psychologists, such as Seymour Epstein (1979, 1980), have argued that studies such as Hartshorne and May's used behaviors that are too specific. Epstein contended that, rather than relying on single behaviors, researchers must aggregate measures of behavior; that is, they must obtain a sum of many behaviors. In other words, Epstein would say that even though people do not *always* display a strong personal trait, for example, conscientiousness, the sum total of their individual behaviors will reflect a generally conscientious core.

However, Mischel (1965) had earlier found that a three-person assessment committee, which used aggregated information from a variety of scores, could not reliably predict performance of Peace Corps teachers. The correlation between the committee's judgment and the performance of the teachers was a nonsignificant 0.20. Moreover, Mischel (1968) contended that correlations of about 0.30 between different measures of the same trait as well as between trait scores and subsequent behaviors represented the outer limits of trait consistency. Thus, these relatively low correlations between traits and behavior are not due to the unreliability of the assessment instrument but to the inconsistencies in behavior. Even with perfectly reliable measures, Mischel argued, specific behaviors will not accurately predict personal traits.

Mischel acknowledges that most people have some consistency in their behavior. One person is generally friendly and gregarious, whereas another is usually unfriendly and taciturn. Psychologists as well as laypeople have long summarized people's behavior by using such descriptive trait names. However, Mischel strongly objects to attempts to attribute behavior to these global traits (Mischel & Shoda, 1994; Shoda & Mischel, 1993). To classify individuals as friendly, extraverted, or conscientious is one way of defining personality, but it is a sterile taxonomy that fails to explain behavior.

A COGNITIVE-AFFECTIVE PERSONALITY SYSTEM

To solve the classical consistency paradox, Mischel and Shoda (1995) proposed a **cognitive-affective personality system** that accounts for variability across situations as well as stability of behavior within the person. Apparent inconsistencies in a person's behavior are due neither to random error nor solely to the situation. Rather, they are potentially predictable behaviors that reflect stable *patterns of variation* within a person. Cognitive-affective theory predicts that a person's behavior will change from situation to situation but in a meaningful manner.

Mischel and Shoda believe that variations in behavior can be conceptualized in this framework: *If* A, *then* X; *but if* B, *then* Y. For example, if Mark is provoked by his wife, then he will react with aggression. However, when the "if" changes, so does the "then." If Mark is provoked by his boss, then he will react with submission. Mark's behavior may seem inconsistent because he apparently reacts differently to the same stimulus. Mischel and Shoda, however, would argue that being provoked by two different people does not constitute the same stimulus. Mark's behavior is not inconsistent and may well reflect a stable lifetime pattern of reacting. Such an interpretation, Mischel and Shoda believe, solves the consistency paradox by taking into account both the long history of observed variability in behavior and the intuitive conviction of both psychologists and laypeople that personality is relatively stable. The frequently observed variability in behavior is simply an essential part of a unifying stability of personality.

This theory does *not* suggest that behaviors are an outgrowth of stable, global personality traits. If behaviors were a result of global traits, then there would be little intraindividual variation in behavior. In other words, Mark would react in much the same manner to provocation, regardless of the specific situation. However, Mark's longstanding pattern of variability attests to the inadequacy of both the situation theory and the trait theory. His pattern of variability is his **personality signature;** that is, his consistent manner of varying his behavior in particular situations. His personality has a signature that remains stable across situations even as his behavior changes.

PREDICTING BEHAVIOR

Mischel believes that behavior can be predicted from knowledge of the interaction between situation variables and such personal qualities as competencies, goals and values, expectancies, encoding strategies, and affective responses. Although behavior may at times seem to be inconsistent, an understanding of situation variables and personal qualities will reveal a pattern of variation within a relatively stable personality.

SITUATION VARIABLES

Situation variables, which include all those stimulus inputs that people attend to in a particular situation, *interact* with personal qualities to produce behavior. Mischel (1973) stated that situations "affect behavior insofar as they influence such person variables as the individual's encoding, his expectancies, the subjective value of stimuli, or the ability to generate response patterns" (p. 276).

We can determine the relative influence of situation variables and personal qualities by observing the uniformity or diversity of people's responses in a given situation. When different people are behaving in a very similar manner—for example, while watching an emotional scene in an engrossing movie—we know that situation variables are more powerful than personal characteristics. On the other hand, events that appear the same may produce widely different reactions because personal qualities override situational ones. For example, several workers may all be laid off from their jobs, but individual differences will lead to diverse behaviors, depending on the workers' perceived need to work, confidence in their level of skill, and perceived ability to find another job.

Early in his career, Mischel conducted studies demonstrating that the interaction between the situation and various personal qualities was an important determinant of behavior. In one study, for example, Mischel and Staub (1965) looked at conditions that influenced a person's choice of a reward and found that both the situation and an individual's expectancy for success were important. These investigators first asked eighth-grade boys to rate their expectancies for success on verbal reasoning and general information tasks. Later, after the students worked on a series of problems, some were told that they had succeeded on those problems; some were informed that they had failed; and the third group received no information. The boys were then asked to choose between an immediate, less valuable, noncontingent reward and a delayed, more valuable, contingent reward. Consistent with Mischel's interaction theory, students who had been told that they had succeeded on the earlier similar task were more likely to wait for the more valued reward that was contingent on their performance; those who were informed that they had previously failed tended to choose an immediate, less valuable reward; and those who had received no earlier feedback made choices based on their original expectancies for success; that is, students in the no-information group who originally had high expectancies for success made choices similar to those who believed that they were successful, whereas those who originally had low expectancies for success made choices similar to those who believed that they had failed. Figure 12.2 shows how situational feedback interacts with expectancy for success to influence choice of rewards.

Mischel and his associates have also shown that children can use their cognitive processes to change a difficult situation into an easier one. For example, Mischel and Ebbesen (1970) found that some children were able to use their cognitive ability to change an unpleasant wait for a treat into a more pleasant situation. In this delay of gratification study, nursery school children were told that they would receive a small reward after a short period of time, but a larger treat if they could wait longer. Children who thought about the treat had difficulty waiting, whereas children who were able to wait the longest used a variety of self-distractions to avoid thinking about the reward.

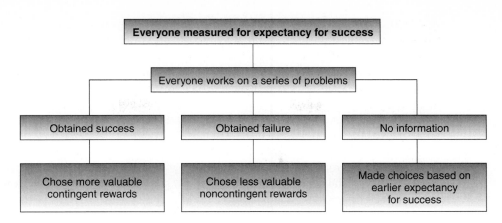

Figure 12.2 Model used by Mischel and Staub (1965).

They looked away from the treat, closed their eyes, or sang songs in order to change the aversive waiting situation into a more pleasant one.

This finding led Mischel and Moore (1973) to use symbolic representations of rewards to see what effect they would have on waiting time. They taught children to imagine that the real rewards were pictures and that the pictures of treats were real. They found that cognitive representations (that is, what children imagine in their heads) are more important than actual rewards in determining how long children can delay gratification. Children who faced real rewards but imagined that they were pictures were able to wait for a long time, whereas children who faced pictures but imagined that they were real were not able to wait as long. These and other research results led Mischel to conclude that both the situation and various cognitive-affective components of personality play a role in determining behavior.

COGNITIVE-AFFECTIVE UNITS

In 1973, Mischel proposed a set of five overlapping person variables that interact with the situation to determine behavior. These person variables shifted the emphasis from what a person *has* (that is, global traits) to what a person *does* in a particular situation. What a person does includes more than actions; it includes cognitive and affective qualities such as thinking, planning, feeling, and evaluating.

More recently, however, Mischel and Shoda (1995) have presented a broader conception of person variables, which they call *cognitive-affective units*, a term more consistent with their cognitive-affective personality theory. Cognitive-affective units include all those psychological, social, and physiological aspects of people that cause them to interact with their environment with a relatively stable pattern of variation. These units include people's (1) competencies and self-regulatory strategies, (2) encoding strategies, (3) expectancies and beliefs, (4) goals and values, and (5) affective responses.

Competencies and Self-Regulatory Strategies

How we behave depends in part on the potential behaviors available to us, our beliefs of what we can do, our plans and strategies for enacting behaviors, and our expectancies for success. Our beliefs in what we can do relate to our **competencies.** Mischel (1973, 1990) used the term "competencies" to refer to that vast array of information we acquire about the world and our relationship to it. By observing our own behaviors and those of others, we learn what we can do in a particular situation as well as what we cannot do. Mischel agreed with Bandura that we do not attend to all stimuli in our environment; rather, we selectively *construct* or generate our own version of the real world. Thus, we acquire a set of beliefs about our performance capabilities, often in the absence of actual performance. For example, an outstanding student may believe that she has the competence to do well on the Graduate Record Exam (GRE) even though she has never taken that test.

Cognitive competencies, such as doing well on the GRE, are generally more stable temporally and cross-situationally than other cognitive-affective units. That is, people's scores on mental ability tests do not ordinarily show large fluctuations from one time to the next or from one situation to another. In fact, Mischel (1990) has argued that one of the reasons for the apparent consistency of traits is the relative stability of "intelligence," a basic trait that underlies many personal dispositions. He contended that cognitive competencies, as measured by traditional mental ability tests, have proven to be some of the best predictors of social and interpersonal adjustment and thus give social and interpersonal traits some appearance of stability. Moreover, Mischel suggested that when intelligence is assessed by nontraditional measures that include a person's potential for seeing alternate solutions to problems, it accounts for even larger portions of the consistency found in other traits.

In Chapter 11, we discussed Bandura's concept of self-regulation, by which people control their own behavior through self-observation, self-judgment, and such self-reactions as self-reinforcement and self-punishment. Similarly, Mischel believes that people use **self-regulatory strategies** to control their own behavior through self-imposed goals and self-produced consequences. We do not require external rewards and punishments to shape our behavior; we can set goals for ourselves and then reward or criticize ourselves contingent upon whether our behavior moves us in the direction of those goals.

Our self-regulatory system enables us to plan, initiate, and maintain behaviors even when environmental support is weak or nonexistent. People such as Abraham Lincoln and Mohandas Gandhi were able to regulate their own behavior in the face of a nonsupportive and hostile environment, but each of us can persist without environmental encouragement if we have powerful self-produced goals and values. However, inappropriate goals and ineffective strategies increase anxiety and lead to failure. For example, people with inflexible, exaggerated goals may persist in trying to realize those goals, but their lack of competence and environmental support prevent them from achieving those goals.

Encoding Strategies

Another important cognitive-affective unit that ultimately affects behavior is people's personal constructs and **encoding strategies,** that is, people's ways of categorizing information received from external stimuli. People use cognitive processes to transform these stimuli into personal constructs, including their self-concept, their view of other people, and their way of looking at the world. Different people encode the same events in different ways, which accounts for individual differences in personal constructs. For example, one person may react angrily when insulted, whereas another may choose to ignore the same insult. In addition, the same person may encode the same event differently in different situations. For example, a man who ordinarily construes a telephone call from his best friend as a pleasant experience may in one situation perceive it as a nuisance.

Again, stimulus inputs are substantially altered by what people selectively attend, how they interpret their experience, and the way in which they categorize those inputs. Mischel and former Ph.D. student Bert Moore (1973) found that children can transform environmental events by focusing on selected aspects of stimulus inputs. In this delay-of-gratification study, children exposed to pictures of rewards (snacks or pennies) were able to wait longer for the rewards than children who were encouraged to cognitively construct (imagine) real rewards while viewing the pictures. A previous study (Mischel, Ebbesen, & Zeiss, 1972) had demonstrated that children exposed to real rewards during a wait period had more difficulty waiting than those exposed to no reward. These two studies suggest that, in at least some situations, cognitive transformations of stimuli can have about the same effect as actual stimuli.

Expectancies and Beliefs

Any situation presents an enormous number of behavioral potentials, but how people behave depends on their specific *expectancies and beliefs* about the consequences of each of the different behavioral possibilities. Knowledge of people's hypotheses or beliefs concerning the outcome of any situation is a better predictor of behavior than knowledge of their ability to perform.

From previous experience and by observing others, people learn to enact those behaviors that they expect will result in the most subjectively valued outcome. When people have no information about what they can expect from a behavior, they will enact those behaviors that received the greatest reinforcement in past similar situations. For example, a college student who has never taken the GRE nevertheless has had experience preparing for other tests. What that student does in getting ready for the GRE is partially influenced by what previous test preparation behaviors resulted in the most valuable outcome. A student who has previously been rewarded for using self-relaxation techniques to prepare for tests will expect that the same techniques will help in doing well on the GRE. Mischel (1973, 1990) referred to this type of expectancy as a *behavior-outcome expectancy*. People often construe behavior-outcome expectancies in an "if . . . , then . . ." framework. "If I use self-relaxation procedures, then I can expect to do well on the GRE." "If I tell my boss what I really think of her, then I might lose my job."

Mischel also identified a second type of expectancy—*stimulus-outcome expectancies*, which refers to the "multitude of stimulus conditions that moderate the probable consequences of any pattern of behavior" (Mischel, 1973, p. 271). Stimulus-outcome expectancies help us predict what events are likely to occur following certain stimuli. Perhaps the most obvious example would be an expectancy of loud, unpleasant thunder following the observance of lightning (the stimulus). Mischel believes that stimulus-outcome expectancies are important units for understanding classical conditioning. For example, a child who has been conditioned to associate pain with a particular setting begins to cry and show fear upon seeing a nurse with a hypodermic syringe.

Mischel (1990) believes that one reason for the inconsistency of our behavior is our inability to predict other people's behavior. We have little hesitancy in attributing personal traits to others, but when we notice that their behavior is inconsistent with those traits, we become less certain about how to react to them. Our behavior will be cross-situationally consistent to the extent that our expectancies are unchanging. But our expectancies are not constant; they change because we can discriminate and evaluate the multitude of potential reinforcers in any given situation.

One reason for the inconsistency of our own behavior is our inability to predict the behavior of others.

Goals and Values

People do not react passively to situations but are active and goal-directed. They formulate goals, devise plans for attaining their goals, and in part create their own situations. Our subjective goals, values, and preferences represent a fourth cognitive-affective unit. "Even if individuals have similar expectancies, they may select to perform different behaviors because of differences in the *subjective values* of the outcomes which they expect" (Mischel, 1973, p. 272). For example, two college students may have equal academic ability and also equal expectancy for success in graduate school. The first, however, places more value on entering the job market than on going to graduate school, while the second chooses to go to graduate school rather than to pursue an immediate career. The two may have had many similar experiences during college, but because they have different goals, they have made very different decisions.

Values, goals, and interests, along with competencies, are among the most stable cognitive-affective units. One reason for this consistency is the emotion-eliciting properties of these units. For instance, a person may place a negative value to a certain food because he associates it with the nausea he once experienced while eating that food. Without counterconditioning, this aversion is likely to persist because of the strong negative emotion elicited by the food. Similarly, patriotic values may last a lifetime because they are associated with positive emotions such as security, attachment to one's home, and love of one's mother.

Affective Responses

During the early 1970s, Mischel's theory was mostly a cognitive theory. It was based on the assumption that people's thoughts and other cognitive processes interact with a particular situation to determine behavior. More recently, however, Mischel and Shoda

(1995) have added affective responses to the list of important cognitive-affective units. Affective responses include emotions, feelings, and physiological reactions. Mischel and Shoda see affective responses as inseparable from cognitions and regard the interlocking cognitive-affective units as more basic than the other cognitive-affective units.

Affective responses, then, do not exist in isolation. Not only are they inseparable from cognitive processes, but they influence each of the other cognitive-affective units. For example, the encoding of our view of self includes certain positive and negative *feelings.* "I see myself as a competent psychology student and that pleases me." "I'm not very good at mathematics and I don't like that." Similarly, our competencies and coping strategies, our beliefs and expectancies, and our goals and values are all colored by our affective responses.

Mischel and Shoda (1995) stated that:

> Cognitive-affective representations are not unconnected discrete units that are simply elicited as "responses" in isolation: These cognitive representations and affective states interact dynamically and influence each other reciprocally, and it is the organization of the relationships among them that forms the core of the personality structure and that guides and constrains their impact. (p. 253)

In summary, interrelated cognitive-affective units contribute to behavior as they interact with a receptive environment. The most important of these variables include (1) *competencies and self-regulating strategies,* that is, what people can do and their strategies and plans to accomplish a desired behavior; (2) *encoding strategies,* or how people construe or categorize an event; (3) behavior-outcome and stimulus-outcome *expectancies and beliefs* regarding a particular situation; (4) subjective *goals, values, and preferences* that partially determine selective attention to events; and (5) *affective responses,* including feelings and emotions as well as the affects that accompany physiological reactions.

RELATED RESEARCH

The cognitive social learning theories of Rotter and Mischel both have generated a large amount of research. For example, our literature search for the words "locus of control" and "Rotter" on PsychLIT resulted in more than 2,000 references for the years 1967 to 1996. Mischel's notion of delay of gratification has also been widely researched.

As mentioned earlier, Rotter developed the Internal-External (I-E) Control Scale to measure the extent to which people believe that chance, luck, or powerful others control their lives. This scale (usually called the locus of control scale) has been applied to a multitude of domains, including addictive behaviors. Of the many varieties of addiction, smoking cigarettes and drinking alcohol are among the most common and have also been the most widely studied. Therefore, we examine the evidence for a relationship between locus of control and smoking and drinking.

In a study on smoking, J. M. Bunch and H. G. Schneider (1991) administered Rotter's I-E Scale and a more focused measure for smoking locus of control to a group of nonsmokers and a group of smokers. The smoking-focused scale assesses how much control people believe they have over their smoking behavior and consists of items such as: "It is not difficult for smokers to have control over their smoking" or "If someone offers a smoker a cigarette, they can easily refuse it." Results showed that Rotter's general I-E Scale did not predict addiction to cigarettes, but the more specific smoking-focused scale did.

Paul Norman (1995) studied the relationship between health locus of control (that is, how much control people believe they have over their own health) and smoking behaviors. For smokers in general, Norman found no significant relationship between health locus of control and amount of smoking. However, when he looked at people who valued being healthy, he found that health locus of control predicted smoking. That is, people who valued being healthy and who believed they had control over their health were less likely to smoke than were people who did not value being healthy but who believed they had control over their health.

Control over alcohol is another frequently investigated topic. For example, Chwan-Shyang Jih, Vivian Sirgo, and James Thomure (1995) studied locus of control and drinking behavior in college and high school students. The measure of locus of control was Rotter's I-E Scale, while drinking behavior was measured using a 21-item Alcohol Consumption Questionnaire (ACQ). The ACQ assesses both hypothetical and actual drinking behavior after pleasant, unpleasant, and neutral events. An example of a hypothetical pleasant event was: "You just received a promotion or reward." An example of a hypothetical negative event was: "You just experienced the loss of a loved one." Actual events also consisted of positive (e.g., "at last year's Halloween party") and negative ("after a funeral") events. Results showed that externally focused students tended to drink more in all four situations: hypothetical and actual, pleasant and unpleasant events.

In a study using a drinking-focused control scale, Lisa Clements, Reginald York, and Glenn Rohrer (1995) examined how Drinking Related Internal-External (DRIE) scores relate to alcoholism and parental alcoholism. Participants were classified into one of four groups: (1) neither they nor a parent were alcoholic (Neither group); (2) only a parent was alcoholic (adult children of alcoholics; ACOA group); (3) they were alcoholic but neither parent was (Alcoholic group); and (4) both they and a parent were alcoholic (Both group). Clements et al. found a strong and linear relationship between external scores on the DRIE and degree of self and/or parental alcoholism. Being alcoholic oneself and having an alcoholic parent each contributed to high external scores on the DRIE. Furthermore, the Alcoholic group was more external than the ACOA group. In another study using the DRIE, Anja Koski-Jannes (1994) found that internal scores on the DRIE predicted abstinence from drinking for alcoholics who attended 6- and 12-month treatment programs.

Despite the very widespread use of Rotter's I-E Scale, some researchers (Brosschot, Gebhardt, & Godaert, 1994; Duttweiler, 1984; Levenson, 1973, 1974; Palenzuela, 1988) have argued that the I-E Scale measures only the external dimension. Furthermore, critics recognize that Rotter's scale measures *generalized* expectancies and is thus too broad to assess people's specific locus of control beliefs. These critics argue, for example, that a person may believe she has no control over her smoking, but much control over her career. A key figure in this line of argument has been Hanna Levenson (1973, 1974, 1981), who has developed a new scale that measures three distinct locus of control dimensions: Internal (I), Powerful Others (P), and Chance (C). Using the IPC scales of Levenson as well as Rotter's I-E Scale, Jos Brosschot, Winifred Gebhardt, and Guido Godaert (1994) found that the specific IPC Scales were better and more differentiated predictors of personality, coping, stress, and health behavior than was the general I-E Scale. For example, the I Scale correlated positively with the personality dimensions of dominance, self-esteem, achievement motivation, and expression of anger, and the P and C Scales correlated positively with neuroticism, social inadequacy, hostility, and avoidance strategies. Nevertheless, both the IPC Scales and the I-E Scale suggest that internal locus of control tends to be associated with greater psychological and physical health than does external locus of control. Not only is internal locus related to self-esteem, achievement, and dominance, but an external locus is related to abuse of both alcohol and cigarettes.

Although Walter Mischel's cognitive social learning theory has not produced the volume of research that Rotter's theories have, his *delay of gratification* concept has interested researchers for nearly 40 years. Beginning when he was still at the University of Colorado and continuing when he went to Harvard, Mischel (1958, 1961a, 1961b) reported on a series of experiments he had conducted when he lived in the Caribbean. He found that the citizens of Trinidad who preferred larger, delayed rewards over smaller, immediate ones had higher needs for achievement and showed more social responsibility. Later, at Stanford University, Mischel teamed with his colleague Albert Bandura (Bandura & Mischel, 1965) as well as with a number of graduate students to more fully pursue issues related to delay of gratification.

The delay of gratification concept avoids such global terms as "willpower" and "ego strength," which do not explain why people who can exhibit self-control in one situation are not able to do so in others. Mischel has found that delay of gratification, or self-control, is specific and that cognitive factors influence how long people will be able to wait for a reward.

Mischel and his colleagues investigated the correlates of delay of gratification in 4- and 5-year-old children attending the Bing Nursery School at Stanford (Mischel & Ebbesen, 1970; Mischel, Ebbesen, & Zeiss, 1972). The design of their studies generally called for an experimenter to show a child some interesting toys that the child could play with later. Then the experimenter would show the child a pair of treats with slightly different values, for example, two cookies vs. five pretzels or one marshmallow vs. two marshmallows. Next, the experimenter indicated that she must leave the room, but gave the child a choice between eating the less preferred treat at any time or waiting until the experimenter returned and then eating the preferred treat. The child could bring the experimenter back prematurely by ringing a bell, but this impatience, of course, would result in the child receiving the lesser of the two treats. Thus, the experimenter returned to the room when the child rang the bell, began eating a treat, or was able to wait for the entire predetermined length of time, usually 15 to 30 minutes.

In early studies, Mischel and Metzner (1962) found, as expected, that ability to delay gratification increases with age, intelligence, and shorter time intervals that the child is required to wait. Also, Mischel and Ebbesen (1970) found that children could use self-distraction to ease their impatience, and Mischel and Moore (1973) found that children were able to wait longer if they could cognitively transform real treats into pictures of treats. These results suggest that self-control does not depend so much on exercising "willpower" as it does on cognitively changing a difficult task into an easy one or a boring unpleasant job into an interesting, pleasant one.

In another early study, Mischel and Baker (1975) examined *arousal* as a condition in children's ability to delay reinforcement. Using the typical delay of gratification design, these researchers gave half the children a choice between one marshmallow or two marshmallows, while the other half chose between one pretzel and two pretzels. All children waited with the relevant rewards facing them, either one or two marshmallows or one or two pretzels. The experimenters instructed children waiting for pretzels to focus their thoughts on the arousing qualities of the pretzels, such as their crunchy, salty taste, and they instructed children waiting for marshmallows to think about the sweet, soft, and chewy taste of the marshmallows. These children constituted the *consume-relevant* group. In this arousal situation, the focus was on the motivating, or "hot," qualities of the snack.

The experiment also called for a *consume-irrelevant* condition in which children were given the same instructions, except that those waiting for marshmallows were told to think about the crunchy, salty taste of pretzels, whereas those waiting for pretzels were instructed to think about the soft, sweet, chewy taste of marshmallows.

Mischel and Baker also introduced two transformation conditions. In the *transform-relevant* condition, they gave children instructions designed to distract attention from the consummatory aspects of the snacks. For example, they instructed children waiting for pretzels to think of pretzels as long, thin, brown logs and children waiting for marshmallows to think of them as white, puffy clouds or cotton balls. In the *transform-irrelevant* condition, children were given the same set of instructions, except they were switched, so that children facing pretzels were told to think of marshmallows as white puffy clouds or cotton balls and vice versa. Mischel and Baker also used a *control group* that received no instructions.

Results showed that children waiting for one snack while thinking about the "cool" or nonconsummatory aspects of the other were able to delay gratification the longest, almost 17 minutes. The second longest mean delay time (about 13 minutes) was achieved by the transform-relevant group, that is, those children who could cognitively transform pretzels into logs or marshmallows into clouds. However, those who had the same type of thoughts directed at the snack that was not their reward could wait less than 5 minutes. Children in the consume-relevant group (those focusing on the salty aspect of their pretzels or the sweet taste of their marshmallows) waited only about 5½ minutes. The control group that received no information had a mean delay time of about 9 minutes, or somewhat less than that of students who cognitively transformed the snacks, but somewhat more than those who focused on the arousing qualities of the reward object. These results suggest that attention to the rewards may either facilitate or interfere with delay of gratification, depending on whether the focus is arousing or abstract.

Mischel, Shoda, and Rodriquez (1989) summarized much of this earlier research as well as later follow-up studies that investigated characteristics of adolescents who had been participants in the nursery school experiments. Mischel, Shoda, and Peake (1988) and Shoda, Mischel, and Peake (1990) found that participants who waited longer at age 4 were described by their parents 10 years later as being more academically and socially competent than their peers. They were also better able to cope with frustration and stress, more capable of resisting temptation, more verbally fluent, more able to express ideas, more self-assured, and better able to concentrate, plan, and think ahead than their classmates. Moreover, seconds of delay time at age 4 predicted Scholastic Aptitude Test (SAT) scores when applying for college; that is, the longer children could wait for a reward at age 4, the higher they scored on the SAT more than 10 years later.

Mischel's research on delay of gratification suggests that self-control is not dependent on willpower, but on people's ability to distract themselves from an unpleasant task. It also demonstrates that one's ability to delay gratification is positively related to later social and academic competence and to the ability to cope with frustration and stress.

More recently, Mischel and his colleagues have examined behavior patterns in the *if* A, *then she* X; *but if* B, *then she* Y framework. For example, Shoda, Mischel, and Wright (1993) looked at the reactions of 6- to 13-year-old "problem" children at a summer camp when presented with five different interpersonal situations. A large number of adult counselors observed the social interaction of these children 5 hours a day, 6 days a week, during the entire 6-week program. After the children were divided into "aggressive," "withdrawn," or "friendly," the observers recorded each child's social interaction (1) when teased, provoked, or threatened by peers; (2) when a peer approached in a positive, prosocial manner; (3) when praised by an adult; (4) when warned by an adult, and (5) when punished by an adult. In general, Shoda et al. found that both personality and context related to behavior. For example, although children judged to be aggressive tended to react aggressively when provoked by a peer or warned or punished by an adult, they did not react aggressively when approached prosocially by a peer. Similarly, withdrawn children reacted with compliance only when teased, provoked, or threatened by peers or when they were approached positively by other children, and friendly children reacted with prosocial talk only when teased or provoked by peers, when punished by adults, and when approached positively by peers.

These results show that, although people do not behave the same way in different situations, they do exhibit a potentially predictable pattern of variation in their behavior. After reporting on the above study, Shoda, Mischel, and Wright (1994) concluded that "individuals in the present sample were characterized by distinctive and predictable patterns of behavior variation across the particular psychological situations" (pp. 682–683). It is this predictable pattern of variation that has occupied much of the interest of Mischel and his colleagues in recent years.

CRITIQUE OF COGNITIVE SOCIAL LEARNING THEORY

Cognitive social learning theory is attractive to those who value the rigors of learning theory and the speculative assumption that people are forward-looking, cognitive beings. Rotter and Mischel have evolved learning theories for thinking, valuing, goal-directed humans rather than for laboratory animals. Like other theories, cognitive social learning theory's value rests on how it rates on the six criteria for a useful theory.

The first criterion of a useful theory is its ability to *generate significant research*. We have seen that the theories of both Rotter and Mischel have generated large amounts of research. For example, Rotter's concept of locus of control has been, and continues to be, one of the most widely researched topics in psychological literature. Locus of control, however, is not the core of Rotter's personality theory, and the theory itself has not generated a comparable level of research. On the other hand, Mischel's theory has generated somewhat less research, but that research is more relevant to his core ideas, namely the consistency paradox and delay of gratification.

Second, is cognitive social learning theory *falsifiable*? The empirical nature of both Rotter and Mischel's work exposes these theories to possible falsification and verification. Nevertheless, neither theory can be easily falsified. Rotter's basic prediction formula and general prediction formula are completely hypothetical and cannot be accurately tested. Also, Mischel's delay of gratification and children's summer camp investigations have narrow methodological approaches, and other investigators using normal adults (for example, Moskowitz, 1994) have not always confirmed his results.

On the criterion of *organizing knowledge*, cognitive social theory rates about average, with Rotter's theory faring somewhat better than Mischel's. Theoretically at least, Rotter's general prediction formula and its components of need potential, freedom of movement, and need value can provide a useful framework for understanding much of human behavior. When behavior is seen as a function of these variables, it takes on a different hue. By comparison, Mischel's theory is narrower and thus does not lend itself to global explanations of behavior.

Does cognitive social learning theory serve as a useful *guide to action*? On this criterion, we rate the theory only moderately high. Rotter's ideas on psychotherapy are quite explicit and are a helpful guide to the therapist, but his theory of personality is not as practical. The mathematical formulas serve as a useful framework for organizing knowledge, but they do not suggest any specific course of action for the practitioner because the value of each factor within the formula cannot be known with mathematical certainty. Likewise, Mischel's theory is only moderately useful to the therapist, teacher, or parent. It suggests to practitioners that they should expect people to behave differently in different situations and even from one time to another, but it provides them with few specific guidelines for action.

Are the theories of Rotter and Mischel *internally consistent*? Rotter is careful in defining terms so that the same term does not have two or more meanings. In addition, separate components of the theory are logically compatible. The basic prediction formula, with its four specific factors, is logically consistent with the three broader variables of the general prediction formula. Mischel, like Bandura (see Chapter 11), has evolved a theory from solid empirical research, a procedure that greatly facilitates consistency.

Finally, is cognitive social learning theory *parsimonious*? In general, it is relatively simple and does not purport to offer explanations for all human personality. Again, the emphasis on research rather than philosophical speculation has contributed to the parsimony of the cognitive social learning theories of both Rotter and Mischel.

CONCEPT OF HUMANITY

Rotter and Mischel both see people as cognitive animals whose perceptions of events are more important than the events themselves. People are capable of construing events in a variety of ways, and these cognitive perceptions are generally more influential than the environment in determining the value of the reinforcer. Cognition enables different people to see the same situation differently and to place different values on reinforcement that follows their behavior.

Both Rotter and Mischel see humans as goal-directed animals who do not merely react to their environments but who interact with their psychologically meaningful environments. Hence, cognitive social learning theory is more *teleological* or future-oriented than it is causal. People place positive value on those events that they perceive as moving them closer to their goals, and they place negative value on those events that prevent them from reaching their goals. Goals, then, serve as criteria for evaluating events. People are motivated less by past experiences with reinforcement than by their expectations of future events.

Cognitive social learning theory holds that people move in the direction of goals they have established for themselves. These goals, however, change as people's expectancies for reinforcement and their preference for one reinforcement over another change. Because people are continually in the process of setting goals, they have some choice in directing their lives. *Free choice* is not unlimited, however, because past experiences and limits to personal competencies partially determine behavior.

Because both Rotter and Mischel are realistic and pragmatic, they are difficult to rate on the *optimism* vs. *pessimism* dimension. They believe that people can be taught constructive strategies for problem solving and that they are capable of learning new behaviors at any point in life. However, they do not hold that people have within themselves an inherent force that moves them inevitably in the direction of psychological growth.

On the issue of *conscious vs. unconscious motives*, cognitive social learning theory generally leans in the direction of conscious forces. People can consciously set goals for themselves and consciously strive to solve old and new problems. However, people are

*I*n the last chapter, we saw that Walter Mischel rejects the notion of global traits as determinants of behavior. In this chapter, we will see that Raymond Cattell and Hans Eysenck believe that traits, or relatively permanent personal dispositions, are important variables in understanding behavior, and in Chapter 14, we will see that Gordon Allport developed a personality theory that utilized the concept of personal dispositions. Allport, however, relied more on intuition and deductive reasoning than on mathematical procedures. In contrast, both Cattell and Eysenck have applied a more systematic method to the problems of identifying traits. The approach they use is *factor analysis*, a technique that will be briefly described later. Because they employed different factor analytic procedures, Cattell and Eysenck arrived at different traits. Cattell identified a comparatively large number of traits, whereas Eysenck remains convinced that only a few basic factors underlie human personality.

Cattell has spent his professional life mapping the entire sphere of human personality. He found a number of both normal and abnormal temperament or structural traits and then turned his attention to measuring the dynamics of personality. To that end he discovered a variety of motivational traits. Cattell believes that if we know both the structure and the dynamics of personality, we can predict human behavior.

On the other hand, Eysenck has used factor analysis to extract only three general factors or types—extraversion/introversion, neuroticism/stability, and psychoticism/superego. Much of Eysenck's later work has revolved around applying these three personality types to a variety of human behaviors and socially relevant conditions.

BIOGRAPHY OF RAYMOND B. CATTELL

Raymond Bernard Cattell was born in Staffordshire, England, on March 20, 1905, of proper Victorian middle-class parents. The second of three sons, he was protected by his mother from a domineering father who centered his scrutiny on the oldest child. This relative freedom allowed young Raymond to roam the beach of Devonshire, where his family had moved when he was six, and to explore the coast in boats he had learned to sail at an early age (Cattell, 1974a). Although three years younger, he nearly caught up to his older brother in school, but the rivalry between the two was lessened when the older boy was moved to a different school.

His relatively carefree childhood was dampened by World War I. Cattell was too young to be a soldier, but he had viewed the devastation of war and had watched the trainloads of bloodstained wounded. Suddenly the tranquility of childhood had vanished: "Silently there came an abiding sense of seriousness into my life, compounded of a feeling that one could not be less dedicated than these [wounded soldiers], and of a new sense, for a boy, of the brevity of life and the need to accomplish while one might" (Cattell, 1974a, p. 63).

At age 16, he entered King's College of the University of London and at age 19, graduated with highest honors with a degree in chemistry and physics. As an undergraduate, his interests were wide ranging and included a concern for social problems. By his final year, he had realized that his life would be devoted to psychology, so against the advice of his physical science classmates, he pursued an advanced degree and a career in psychology. In 1929, he received a Ph.D. from the University of London and later was awarded an honorary D.Sc. from the same school. As a graduate student, he worked in the laboratory of Charles Spearman, the noted British quantitative psychologist, who was then at work on his monumental studies of human abilities. After finishing his Ph.D., Cattell found that his friends from undergraduate days were right—there were no jobs available in academic psychology (Cattell, 1974a, 1993).

Consequently, he took a position as an "educationist" at Exeter University, where he remained until 1932 when he moved to Leicester, a city that was beginning a child guidance clinic. His 5 years as director of the Child Guidance Clinic at Leicester were spent mostly in administration and clinical work, but he was able to conduct some research on intelligence testing and to publish several articles and a book during this time. By 1937, Cattell realized that his research plans could only be realized in a university setting. However, only six psychology professorships existed in all of England, and the same "hale and hearty" professors who had occupied those positions 10 years earlier were still entrenched (Cattell, 1974a).

As a consequence, he decided to accept E. L. Thorndike's unexpected offer to journey to the United States and become a research assistant at Columbia University in New York. Thus, Cattell followed in the steps of Abraham H. Maslow (Chapter 17), who had been Thorndike's assistant 2 years earlier. Cattell was reluctant to leave his beloved England and intended to remain in the United States for only a year. After leaving Columbia, however, he accepted what later became known as the G. Stanley Hall professorship at Clark University in Worcester, Massachusetts. That position, unfortunately, did not allow him a relaxed atmosphere for psychological research and he soon moved to neighboring Harvard as a lecturer.

During World War II, he worked with the Adjutant General's Office developing personality tests to use in the selection of officers. His work there taught him the advantages of the team approach, which was generally lacking in most universities. After the war, he finally found the academic position that allowed him the opportunity to conduct research in the manner he had long desired. This position was with the University of Illinois, where he was to spend 30 years as director of the Laboratory of Personality and Group Analysis. Most of Cattell's productive years were spent at Illinois where he was eventually honored as Distinguished Research Professor. In 1949, he helped found the Institute for Personality and Ability Testing (IPAT), an organization that has served as an outlet for the many tests developed by Cattell and his colleagues.

In 1973, Cattell retired from the University of Illinois and moved to Boulder, Colorado, where he established the Institute for Research on Morality and Adjustment. After a short time in Colorado, Cattell joined the Department of Psychology at the University of Hawaii. Currently, he is with the Forest Institute of Professional Psychology in Honolulu, Hawaii.

Early in his career, while still in England and even before he completed his Ph.D., Cattell set a plan for his life's work, much as Skinner (Chapter 10) had outlined his goals for the years 1930–1960. Cattell's strategy, which took only a year to design but nearly a lifetime to execute, was to measure and describe personality structure objectively from three media of observation—ratings of life behavior, questionnaires, and objective test data—as well as to explore motivational traits (Cattell, 1974b). By 1993, Cattell was able to comment that the measurement of personality and motivational traits "completes the round of structured research that we began long ago" (Cattell, 1993, p. 108).

Cattell's early professional life was not always easy. His long hours of work, poor pay, and residence in a damp basement flat had adverse effects on both his health and his marriage (Cattell, 1974a). He developed, as a result of his work schedule and eating habits, a functional stomach disorder from which he never completely recovered. Also, his wife of 2 years, Monica Rogers, not being accustomed to such a spartan life, left him. Cattell had one son by his first marriage and three daughters and another son by his second marriage to Alberta Schuettler, a mathematician whom he married in

1946. One daughter, Heather E. P. Cattell, has carried on Cattell's work with the Institute for Personality and Ability Testing (IPAT) at the University of Illinois.

Cattell has been a prolific writer, having published some 40 books and more than 400 articles. He has also won many awards, including the Darwin Fellowship, the Wenner Gren Prize of the New York Academy of Sciences, presidency of the Society of Multivariate Experimental Psychology, a distinguished foreign honorary membership in the British Psychological Society, and the American Psychological Association Award for Distinguished Service to Measurement. Now in the tenth decade of his life, Cattell continues a diminished yet active and productive work schedule. He admits that his personality theory still has gaps, but he adds that "filling them is a matter of whether psychologists are ready, by training, to attack the complex questions involved." He adds that he has "no doubts about the firmness of theory so far built up by the pursuit of measurement of structures and processes" (Cattell, 1993, p. 110).

BASICS OF FACTOR ANALYSIS

Both Cattell and Eysenck use **factor analysis** to identify traits. A comprehensive knowledge of the mathematical operations involved in factor analysis is not essential to our understanding of trait and factor theories of personality. Nevertheless, a general description of factor analysis should be helpful. To use factor analysis, we begin by making specific observations on many individuals. These observations are then quantified in some manner; for example, height is measured in inches, weight in pounds, aptitude in test scores, job performance by rating scales, and so on. Let us assume that we have 1,000 such measures on 5,000 people. Our next step is to determine which of these variables (scores) are related to which other variables and to what extent. To do this, we calculate the **correlation coefficient** between each variable and each of the other 999 scores. (A correlation coefficient is a mathematical procedure for expressing the degree of correspondence between two sets of scores.) To correlate 1,000 variables with the other 999 scores involves 499,500 individual correlations (1,000 multiplied by 999 divided by 2). Results of these calculations require a table of intercorrelations or a *matrix* with 1,000 rows and 1,000 columns. Some of these correlations would be high and positive, some near zero, and some would be negative. For example, we might observe a high positive correlation between leg length and height, because one is partially a measure of the other. We may also find a positive correlation between a measure of leadership ability and ratings on social poise. This relationship might be due to the fact that they are each part of a more basic underlying trait—self-confidence.

With 1,000 separate variables, our table of intercorrelations is too cumbersome. At this point, we turn to *factor analysis*, which can account for a large number of variables with a smaller number of more basic dimensions. For our purposes, these more basic dimensions can be called *traits*, that is, factors that represent a cluster of closely related variables. For example, we may find high positive intercorrelations among test scores in algebra, geometry, trigonometry, and calculus. We have now identified a cluster of scores that we might call Factor M, which represents mathematical ability. In similar fashion, we can identify a number of other **factors,** or units of personality derived through factor analysis. The number of factors, of course, will be smaller than the original number of observations.

Our next step is to determine the extent to which each individual score contributes to the various factors. Correlations of scores with factors are called **factor loadings.** For example, if scores for algebra, geometry, trigonometry, and calculus

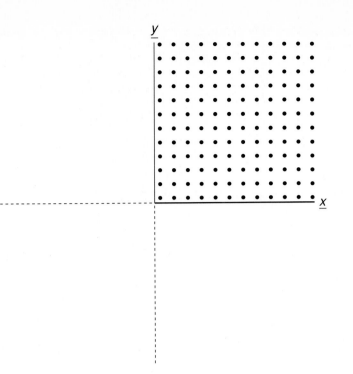

Figure 13.1   Orthogonal axes.

contribute highly to Factor M, but not to other factors, they will have high factor loadings on M. Factor loadings give us an indication of the purity of the various factors and enable us to interpret their meanings.

Traits generated through factor analysis may be either unipolar or bipolar. **Unipolar traits** are scaled from zero to some large amount. Height, weight, and intellectual ability are examples of unipolar traits. **Bipolar traits,** on the other hand, extend from one pole to an opposite pole, with zero representing a midpoint. Introversion vs. extraversion, liberalism vs. conservatism, and social ascendancy vs. timidity are examples of bipolar traits.

In order for mathematically derived factors to have psychological meaning, the axes on which the scores are plotted are usually turned or *rotated* into a specific mathematical relationship with each other. This rotation can be either orthogonal or oblique, but most factor analysts favor the **orthogonal rotation.** Cattell, however, has pioneered the **oblique rotation** method.

Mathematically, orthogonally rotated axes are at right angles to each other, which means that the intercorrelation between the factors is zero; that is, they are independent of one another. The oblique method assumes some positive or negative correlation and refers to an angle of less than or more than 90°. Figure 13.1 shows a scattergram of scores for two variables (*x* and *y*) that are totally uncorrelated (*r* = .00). As scores on the *x* variable increase, scores on the *y* axis may have any value; that is, they are completely unrelated to or independent of scores on the *x* axis.

Figure 13.2 depicts a scattergram of scores in which *x* and *y* are positively correlated with one another; that is, as scores on the *x* variable increase, scores on the *y* axis have a tendency also to increase. (Note that the correlation is not perfect; some people may score high on the *x* variable but relatively low on *y* and vice versa.) A perfect correlation (*r* = 1.00) would result in *x* and *y* occupying the same line. In the factor

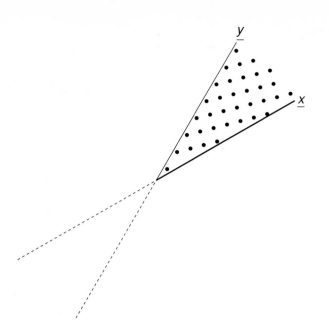

Figure 13.2. Oblique axes.

analytical technique of Eysenck and others, the orthogonal axes are maintained throughout rotation, whereas Cattell keeps the axes in the oblique position.

Psychologically, orthogonal rotation usually results in only a few meaningful traits, whereas oblique methods ordinarily produce a larger number. This partially explains why Cattell has extracted more traits than Eysenck, but the psychological meanings of his traits are not directly comparable to those produced through orthogonal methods. Because traits identified by Cattell are themselves intercorrelated (oblique), it becomes possible to factor analyze the results of the original factor analysis. In this way, *high-order factors* are produced. Cattell has utilized this possibility to extract second, third, and even fourth stratum factors, which are increasingly smaller in number but broader in scope.

CATTELL'S TRAIT THEORY

Cattell (1993) has opposed the clinical methods of earlier personality theorists as being unscientific and based more on unsupported speculation than on hard data. In his scientific analysis of personality, he uses an **inductive method** as opposed to a *hypothetical-deductive method*. In the latter approach, the investigator has some hypothesis or theory in mind *before* gathering data. In other words, the nature of the scores that enter the correlation matrix is determined by some previous ideas as to what traits are to be measured. With Cattell's inductive approach, the investigator, with no preexisting hypotheses, collects a large body of data, runs a factor analysis on these data, and only after these results are available, draws hypotheses that can be tested later.

An understanding of Cattell's scientific analysis of personality is enhanced by an acquaintance with his methods of investigation and with the rationale underlying them. Therefore, we must briefly discuss P technique and the three media of observation.

P TECHNIQUE

When Cattell was a lecturer at Harvard during the early 1940s, he often lunched with Gordon Allport (Chapter 14), and the relationship between the two proved to be productive. Allport was a strong advocate of individual or *unique traits*, and he chided factor analysts in general and Cattell in particular for limiting investigations to *common traits*; that is, traits extracted from the study of many people. At that time, the correlational method typically used was the so-called R technique, which involves many persons taking two or more tests on one occasion. Results of factor analytical studies using the R technique can only identify traits that are common to a large number of people. Allport's criticisms stimulated Cattell to begin thinking of ways by which the single case could be extensively and objectively studied. The result was the **P technique,** a correlational method that involves one person taking two or more tests on many occasions. Actually, as used by Cattell, the P technique employs 30 or more variables obtained from one person on more than 100 occasions. In the beginning, that one person was Cattell's second wife, who understandably grew tired after 9 weeks of daily testing with "electric shocks and other indignities of the experiment" (Cattell, 1974b, p. 106). Cattell, of course, later found other volunteers as he continued to use the P technique.

As a companion to the P technique, Cattell devised the **differential R (dR) technique,** which correlates the scores of a large number of people on many variables obtained at two different occasions. The P and dR techniques should complement one another in determining common state or mood patterns. The P technique alone is susceptible to sampling errors with regard to persons, whereas the dR technique is open to error in the sampling of occasions. In other words, although the P technique satisfies Allport's call for methods of studying the single case, factors derived from it cannot be generalized to other people. On the other hand, although the dR technique allows for generalization to other people, it samples only two points in time, either one of which might be affected by some unusual event. By combining the P technique with the dR technique, one is able to obtain information about moods or states that are shared by many people.

Cattell distinguishes between mood states and traits. The concept of **state** refers to temporary changes in behavior as the result of immediate environmental changes. Examples of psychological mood states include joy, anger, fear, and arousal. Physiological states include heart rate, body temperature, and blood pressure. Fluctuations in these behavioral and physiological states are most reliably calculated by the P and dR techniques. A **trait,** on the other hand, is a relatively permanent property or disposition, defined by Cattell (1979–1980) as "that which defines what a person will do when faced with a defined situation" (Vol. 1, p. 14). Traits are revealed by the traditional R technique.

MEDIA OF OBSERVATION

From the beginning of his professional career, Cattell concentrated his psychometric procedures on three different media of observation, that is, three sources of data that enter the correlation matrix (Cattell, 1983). The first is one's life record, or **L data,** which comes from observations made by other people. It includes both objective information, called L(T) data, and more subjective information based on ratings, called L(R) data. An example of L(T) data might be number of residences in a 20-year period, and an example of L(R) data would be an evaluation of a worker by a supervisor.

The second source of information is the person's self-reports, or **Q data,** which are based on questionnaires that call for a person to respond to questions or statements on the basis of self-observation and introspection. Most personality inventories, for example, yield Q data. Because Q data rely on self-observations, they are subject to deliberate faking and self-delusion. Therefore, they should be corroborated by correlations with behavioral data. Unverified self-reports are regarded as Q' data, whereas only those that have been corroborated by objective behavioral scales can truly be called Q data (Cattell & Kline, 1977).

The third medium of observation is **T data,** or information obtained from objective tests, that is, tests for which the true purpose is hidden from the subject or for which answers cannot be faked. These data include such observations as cognitive abilities, reaction time, response to humor, ability to follow directions, and many other such activities that measure objective performance rather than evaluation of performance (Krug, 1994). Cattell's use of L, Q, and T data gives his investigations a false appearance of being unrelated, but viewed from the perspective of his entire career, one can see that all his studies have been attempts to measure the global concept of personality.

SOURCE TRAITS

Cattell (1950) defined personality as "that which permits a prediction of what a person will do in a given situation" (p. 2). How can these predictions most accurately be made? Cattell's answer is to measure and describe the *source traits* that underlie behavior. Source traits must be distinguished from *surface traits*. In Cattell's system, surface traits are not very important except as starting points and as indicators of source traits. Allport and Odbert (1936) identified nearly 18,000 trait-names in an unabridged dictionary, then reduced the list to more than 4,500, most of which could be considered surface traits. Cattell used this list as a starting point for factor analyzing personality traits. Many of these 4,500 traits are interrelated; that is, they tend to cluster together. If several surface traits are highly interrelated, some underlying source must be holding the traits together.

The underlying factor responsible for the intercorrelation among surface traits is called a *source trait.* Source traits are smaller in number than surface traits, but they are better predictors of behavior. Figure 13. 3 shows a hypothetical example of three surface traits—humor, gregariousness, and unselfishness—that cluster together with considerable overlap or intercorrelation among them. What holds these surface traits together; that is, what do these three traits have in common? If surface traits consistently cluster together, then some common trait, represented by the shaded area in Figure 13.3, must be the unifying source. In this case, that source trait might be called *friendliness.*

Source traits can be identified through each of the three media of observation. Ideally, if measurement techniques in L, Q, and T data were perfectly reliable and valid, then information from any one of the three would yield exactly the same factors or source traits as data from the other two. Practically, of course, this state of infallibility has not yet been reached, but Cattell (1957, 1979–1980) has discovered some significant overlap among the various media of observation, with especially good matches in factors obtained from L and Q data.

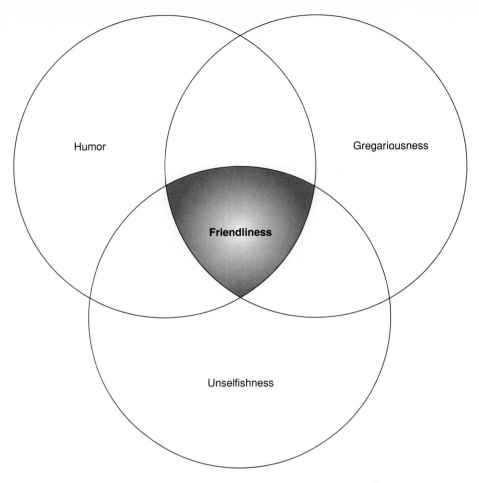

Figure 13.3 Three surface traits held together by the source trait of friendliness.

TEMPERAMENT TRAITS

We have seen that traits can be divided into *common traits* (shared by many) and *unique traits* (peculiar to one individual). Also, *source traits* can be distinguished from trait indicators, or *surface traits*. A third dimension for dividing traits is by classifying them into *temperament, motivation* (dynamic), and *ability*. Traits of temperament are concerned with *how* a person behaves, motivation deals with *why* one behaves, and ability refers to *how far* or *how fast* one can perform. (A discussion of abilities need not detain us here, but the interested reader is referred to Cattell [1971] for a lengthy discussion on the structure of abilities.)

Over the years, Cattell and his associates have identified some 35 **primary traits,** or first-order traits, measuring personality. Of these factors, 23 characterize the normal population and 12 measure the pathological dimension. Temperament traits have been isolated using L and Q data obtained from both adult and child samples (Cattell, 1983).

Normal Traits

The largest and most frequently studied of the normal traits are the 16 personality factors found on Cattell's (1949) Sixteen Personality Factor Questionnaire (16 PF Scale), now in its fifth edition (Cattell & Cattell, 1995). Because the 16 PF is a personality inventory in a questionnaire format, each of the 16 traits, of course, is obtained through Q media. The 7 additional factors that make up the total of 23 normal traits were originally identified only through L data, although some of them, particularly J (zeppia) and K (social unconcern), show up in the more sophisticated measures of Q data (Cattell, 1979–1980). Table 13.1 depicts the 23 primary source traits found in normal personality of both adults and children. Cattell made up unusual trait names because he wanted people to see each of these traits without a predisposition to attach conventional meanings to them. He began his career with no bias regarding the number or name of traits and types, and he wished that others would also see traits from an unbiased point of view. In his words, he "forsook the 'mainstream' of existing concepts about personality types and traits, and started by factoring afresh the 'personality sphere' of total human behavior" (Cattell, 1990, p. 101).

As seen in Table 13.1, normal primary source traits in L and Q data are lettered from A through Q_7. (Traits identified through T media are numbered according to the Cattell's Universal Index system, for example, U.I.1, U.I.2, U.I.3, etc.). Traits are lettered in descending order of magnitude. In other words, Factor A (sizia/affectia) is the largest factor, meaning that it emerges the most clearly from factor analyzes and accounts for the largest amount of variance. The size of this factor agrees with clinical practice and with everyday observation, which suggests that an obvious dimension of personality is flatness of affect (sizia) vs. proneness to affect (affectia). Likewise, Factor B (intelligence) is a substantial factor easily noted in the measurement of personality. Incidentally, Factor B represents the ability dimension of personality, whereas the other primary source traits are basically temperament traits. Because each succeeding factor becomes "fuzzier" or more difficult to extract, Factors N through Q_7 are termed traits of lesser variance (Cattell, 1979–1980). These latter factors are successively weaker and more difficult for the factor analyst to identify with certainty.

The 23 traits reveal a complete picture of normal personality, at least in terms of temperament traits. All measures of normal temperament, whether from Cattell's laboratory or from some other source, whether obtained from adult samples or from children, should match with one or more of these 23 primary traits. In other words, probably all the important personality traits have now been identified by Cattell and his associates. Cattell, in fact, stated some time ago that "the pioneer years of hewing out the major human personality structures are essentially over" (Cattell, 1974a, p. 86). Subsequent work has been aimed at identifying traits across the three media sources within each of the various age groups and across cultures, and at refining the precise psychological meaning of these 23 traits (Cattell, 1993).

Abnormal Traits

Cattell believes that pathological individuals possess the same traits as normal people, but in addition, they exhibit certain abnormal traits. However, normal and abnormal traits overlap to some extent. For example, factors such as low ego strength and guilt proneness are strongly characteristic of neurotic and psychotic individuals, although they appear among the 23 normal factors (Cattell, 1979–1980).

Cattell (1973) hypothesized two forms of pathology. The first is an *imbalance of normal function*. For example, affectia (Factor A) carried to extreme would result in a manic-depressive disorder. The second form of abnormality is a separate and distinct disease process, characterized by traits not found among the 23 normal factors. The abnormal

Table 13.1 Cattell's 23 Normal Primary Source Traits

Factor	Low Score Description	High Score Description
A	**Sizia** Reserved, detached, critical, aloof	**Affectia** Warmhearted, outgoing, easygoing, participating
B	**Low Intelligence**[1] Low mental capacity, dull, quitting	**High Intelligence** High mental capacity, bright, persevering
C	**Low Ego Strength** Affected by feelings, easily upset, changeable	**High Ego Strength** Emotionally stable, faces reality, calm
D	**Phlegmatic Temperament**[2] Undemonstrative, deliberate, inactive, stodgy	**Excitability** Excitable, impatient, demanding, overactive, unrestrained
E	**Submissive** Obedient, mild, easily led, docile, accommodating	**Dominance** Assertive, aggressive, competitive, stubborn
F	**Desurgency** Sober, taciturn, serious	**Surgency** Enthusiastic, heedless, happy-go-lucky
G	**Low Superego Strength** Disregards rules and group moral standards, expedient	**High Superego Strength** Conscientious, persistent, moralistic, staid
H	**Threctia** Shy, timid, restrained, threat-sensitive	**Parmia** Adventurous, "thick-skinned," socially bold
I	**Harria** Tough-minded, rejects illusions	**Permsia** Tender-minded, sensitive, dependent, overprotected
J	**Zeppia**[2] Zestful, liking group action	**Coasthenia** Circumspect individualism, reflective, internally restrained
K	**Social Unconcern**[2] Socially untutored, unconcerned, boorish	**Social-Role Concern** Socially mature, alert, self-disciplined
L	**Alaxia** Trusting, accepting conditions	**Protension** Suspecting, jealous, dogmatic
M	**Praxernia** Practical, has "down to earth" concerns	**Autia** Imaginative, bohemian, absent-minded
N	**Naivete** Forthright, unpretentious	**Shrewdness** Astute, worldly, polished, socially aware
O	**Untroubled Adequacy** Self-assured, placid, secure, complacent	**Guilt Proneness** Apprehensive, self-reproaching, insecure, troubled
P	**Cautious Inactivity**[2] Melancholy, cautious, takes no risks	**Sanguine Casualness** Sanguine, speculative, independent
Q_1	**Conservatism** Disinclined to change, respects traditional values	**Radicalism** Experimenting, analytic, free-thinking

Table 13.1 (Continued)

Factor	Low Score Description	High Score Description
Q_2	**Group Dependency** A "joiner," sound follower	**Self-Sufficiency** Self-sufficient, resourceful, prefers own decisions
Q_3	**Low Self-Sentiment** Uncontrolled, lax, follows own urges	**High Self-Sentiment** Controlled, exacting will power, socially precise, compulsive, follows self-image
Q_4	**Low Ergic Tension** Relaxed, tranquil, unfrustrated, composed	**High Ergic Tension** Tense, frustrated, driven, overwrought, fretful
Q_5	**Lack of Social Concern**[2] Does not volunteer for social service, experiences no obligation, self-sufficient	**Group Dedication with Sensed Inadequacy** Concerned with social good works, not doing enough, joins in social endeavors
Q_6	**Self-Effacement**[2] Quiet, self-effacing	**Social Panache** Feels unfairly treated by society, self-expressive, makes abrupt antisocial remarks
Q_7	**Lacks Explicit Self-Expression**[2] Is not garrulous in conversation	**Explicit Self-Expression** Enjoys verbal-social expression, likes dramatic entertainment, follows fashionable ideas

[1]Factor B (INTELLIGENCE) is an ability trait rather than a temperament trait.
[2]One of the "seven missing factors," so termed because they were not identified by the original 16 PF.
SOURCE: From R.B. Cattell, *Personality and Learning Theory*, Vol. 1, 1979. Copyright © 1979 Springer Publishing Company, Inc., New York, NY 10012. Used by permission.

traits listed in Table 13.2 represent the second category, that is, *pathological traits as separate factors*. The first seven, symbolized by the letter D, represent depressive traits. The last five (Pa, Pp, Sc, As, Ps) are not only more serious clinically, but as factors, they are also more readily identified than the depressive traits.

Cattell isolated these 12 factors using primarily Q data obtained from items on the Minnesota Multiphasic Personality Inventory (MMPI) (Hathaway & McKinley, 1951). In addition, he has used textbook descriptions of abnormal behavior, and he and his associates have written new items as their work continued. Both normal and abnormal populations were included in the test sample. Interestingly, when used with normal people, factor analysis of these "abnormal" items revealed the same normal traits found with nonpathological items. Alongside these 23 traits, though, were the 12 pathological factors. This lends some support to the hypothesis that abnormal people are, first of all, people like everyone else, but they have some additional traits that happen to be pathological (Cattell, 1979–1980).

SECOND-ORDER TRAITS

Because Cattell assumed an intercorrelation among the primary source traits, he was able to factor analyze the results of the original factor analysis and determine which of the first-order traits tend to cluster together. His results have consistently identified

Table 13.2 Cattell's 12 Abnormal Primary Source Traits

Factor	Low Score Description	High Score Description
D_1	**Low Hypochondriasis** Is happy, mind works well, does not find ill health frightening	**High Hypochondriasis** Shows overconcern with bodily functions, health, or disabilities
D_2	**Zestfulness** Is contented about life and surroundings, has no death wishes	**Suicidal Disgust** Is disgusted with life, harbors thoughts or acts of self-destruction
D_3	**Low Brooding Discontent** Avoids dangerous and adventurous undertakings, has little need for excitement	**High Brooding Discontent** Seeks excitement, is restless, takes risks, tries new things
D_4	**Low Anxious Depression** Is calm in emergency, confident about surroundings, poised	**High Anxious Depression** Has disturbing dreams, is clumsy in handling things, tense, easily upset
D_5	**High Energy Euphoria** Shows enthusiasm for work, is energetic, sleeps soundly	**Low Energy Depression** Has feelings of weariness, worries, lacks energy to cope
D_6	**Low Guilt and Resentment** Is not troubled by guilt feelings, can sleep no matter what is left undone	**High Guilt and Resentment** Has feelings of guilt, blames self for everything that goes wrong, is critical of self
D_7	**Low Bored Depression** Is relaxed, considerate, cheerful with people	**High Bored Depression** Avoids contact and involvement with people, seeks isolation, shows discomfort with people
Pa	**Low Paranoia** Is trusting, not bothered by jealousy or envy	**High Paranoia** Believes is being persecuted, poisoned, controlled, spied on, mistreated
Pp	**Low Psychopathic Deviation** Avoids engagement in illegal acts or breaking rules, sensitive	**High Psychopathic Deviation** Has complacent attitude toward own and others' antisocial behavior, is not hurt by criticism, likes crowds
Sc	**Low Schizophrenia** Makes realistic appraisals of self and others, shows emotional harmony and absence of regressive behavior	**High Schizophrenia** Hears voices or sounds without apparent source outside self, retreats from reality, has uncontrolled and sudden impulses
As	**Low Psychasthenia** Is not bothered by unwelcome thoughts and ideas or compulsive habits	**High Psychasthenia** Suffers insistent, repetitive ideas and impulses to perform certain acts
Ps	**Low General Psychosis** Considers self as good, dependable, and smart as most others	**High General Psychosis** Has feelings of inferiority and unworthiness, timid, loses head easily

SOURCE: From *The Manual for the Clinical Analysis Questionnaire* (CAQ). Copyright © 1975 Institute for Personality and Ability Testing, Inc. All rights reserved. Reprinted by permission.

Table 13.3 Cattell's Second-Order Source Traits

Factor	Name	Primary Factors		Descriptive Label
QI	Exvia (Extraversion)	A	Affectia	Sociable
		F	Surgency	Enthusiastic
		H	Parmia	Adventurous
		Q_2—	Group dependency	Dependent
QII	Anxiety	C —	Low ego strength	Easily upset
		H —	Threctia	Shy, timid
		L	Protension	Suspicious
		O	Guilt proneness	Apprehensive
		Q_3—	Low self-sentiment	Uncontrolled
		Q_4	High ergic tension	Tense
QIII	Corteria (Cortical Alertness)	A —	Sizia	Unsociable
		I —	Harria	Insensitive
		M	Praxernia	Practical
QIV	Independence	E	Dominance	Dominant
		F	Surgency	Enthusiastic
		H	Parmia	Adventurous
		L	Protension	Suspicious
QV	Discreetness	A	Affectia	Sociable
		N	Shrewdness	Astute, socially aware
QVI	Subjectivity	M	Autia	Unconcerned
		Q_1	Radicalism	Radical
QVII	Intelligence	B	Intelligence	Intelligent
QVIII	Good upbringing	E —	Submissive	Obedient, docile
		F —	Desurgency	Taciturn
		G	High superego strength	Emotionally stable
		Q_3	High self-sentiment	Controlled

SOURCE: From R. B. Cattell, *Personality and Learning Theory*, Vol. 1, 1979. Copyright © 1978 Springer Publishing Company, New York, NY 10012. Used by permission.

eight second-order traits and tentatively isolated at least seven more. Because these last seven still need more cross-validation, we will discuss only the more firmly established original eight second-order factors and the primary factors that contribute most heavily to their makeup. Second-order factors are assigned roman numerals and the Q preface signifies Q data (questionnaire).

Table 13.3 shows Cattell's eight second-order factors and the primary factors that contribute to each, with their appropriate descriptive label. For example, four primary factors contribute to second-order Factor QI (exvia). Primary Factors A, F, and H are positively correlated with QI, whereas primary Factor Q_2 (group dependency) is negatively correlated with it. Exvia (extraversion), of course, has an opposite pole called invia (introversion), and it would be negatively related to primary Factors A, F, and H and positively related to Factor Q_2. Again, second-order source traits are numbered in descending order of magnitude, so that QI (exvia/invia) and QII (anxiety) are the strongest and most readily identified of these factors. This is consistent with other personality theorists such as Jung who, using clinical methods, identified extraversion and introversion as basic types, and with Freud, Sullivan, and others who noted the importance of anxiety in shaping different personalities. Likewise, Eysenck, employing a different factor analytic technique, has recognized the importance of extraversion/introversion plus an anxiety factor he terms "neuroticism."

MEASUREMENT OF TRAITS

To measure normal traits, Cattell (1949) developed several forms of the 16 PF: the Pre-School Personality Questionnaire (PSPQ) for ages 4–6; the Early School Personality Questionnaire (ESPQ) for ages 6–8; the Child Personality Questionnaire (CPQ) for ages 8–12; and the High School Personality Questionnaire (HSPQ) for ages 12–18. These questionnaires ask young people to select one of two alternatives such as, "Can you spell as well as other children or do most children spell better?" and "Would you rather play with your toys or with friends?"

In addition, Delhees and Cattell (1971) have constructed the Clinical Analysis Questionnaire (CAQ), an instrument designed to assess the 12 abnormal traits along with the 16 normal personality traits and nine second-order factors. Scores are reported in terms of *stens*, that is, a 10-unit scale ranging from low scores of 1 to high scores of 10. The profile of a 24-year-old woman is shown in Figure 13.4.

DYNAMIC TRAITS

Besides temperament, Cattell recognizes motivation traits that underlie the *dynamics of personality*. The general personality traits discussed earlier include ability (Factor B, intelligence), and some generalized dynamic traits (Cattell, 1979–1980). However, they are largely temperament traits. We turn now to a more specific discussion of motivation, that is, the dynamics of personality, which includes *attitudes*, *ergs*, and *sems*.

ATTITUDES

The cornerstone of Cattell's dynamic traits is the concept of **attitude.** An attitude is not an opinion for or against something, but a concept with a much more basic definition. It is a specific course of action, or desire to act, in response to a given situation (Cattell & Child, 1975). For example, let us consider a college student, Monica, whose desire to study French with a particular classmate would be an attitude. Like all attitudes, hers includes a particular stimulus or situation, an interest (intensity level of the desire), the response, and an object. In this example, it makes no difference whether Monica actually studies with the classmate. The attitude is present in either case and serves as a motive for behavior.

Cattell assumes that motivation is complex and that a network of motives, or **dynamic lattice,** is involved with nearly any attitude. A variety of motives, not all of which are conscious, would doubtless enter into our example. Monica may desire to do well in French in order to maintain her reputation as a good student, she may wish to spend time with a potential sexual partner, or she may be lonely and simply desire the company of another person. In addition to this network of motives, a **subsidiation chain** underlies nearly all motivation. This simply means that some motives are subsidiary to others; that is, they are directed toward subgoals that must be reached in order to attain the next goal. Assuming motivation to be conscious (which is not always

NORMAL PERSONALITY TRAITS

Trait	Low Score Description	High Score Description	raw	sten
A: WARMTH	reserved, detached, aloof	warm, personable, easygoing	9	5
B: INTELLIGENCE	concrete-thinking	abstract-thinking	7	6
C: EMOTIONAL STABILITY	easily upset, emotional	emotionally stable, calm	13	7
E: DOMINANCE	submissive, accommodating	dominant, assertive, competitive	12	8
F: IMPULSIVITY	prudent, sober, serious	impulsive, happy-go-lucky	11	7
G: CONFORMITY	expedient, disregards rules	conforming, conscientious, persistent	7	3
H: BOLDNESS	shy, timid, threat-sensitive	bold, venturesome	10	7
I: SENSITIVITY	tough-minded, insensitive	sensitive, tender-minded, unrealistic	10	6
L: SUSPICIOUSNESS	trusting, adaptable	suspicious, hard-to-fool, jealous	12	8
M: IMAGINATION	practical, "down-to-earth"	imaginative, absent-minded	13	8
N: SHREWDNESS	forthright, unpretentious	shrewd, polished, calculating	5	3
O: INSECURITY	confident, self-satisfied	insecure, apprehensive	9	6
Q_1: RADICALISM	conservative, traditional	experimenting, innovative	12	9
Q_2: SELF-SUFFICIENCY	group-adherent, sociable	self-sufficient, resourceful	13	8
Q_3: SELF-DISCIPLINE	undisciplined, uncontrolled	self-disciplined, controlled, precise	6	3
Q_4: TENSION	relaxed	tense, frustrated, driven	8	6

THE CLINICAL FACTORS

Factor	Low Score Description	High Score Description	raw	sten
D_1: HYPOCHONDRIASIS	few somatic complaints	obsessed by ill health	0	2
D_2: SUICIDAL DEPRESSION	contented	despondent, thinks of self-destruction	0	2
D_3: AGITATION	restrained	craves excitement, hypomanic	15	8
D_4: ANXIOUS DEPRESSION	composed	shaky, frightened, clumsy	6	5
D_5: LOW ENERGY DEPRESSION	energetic	gloomy, worn out, sad	5	5
D_6: GUILT & RESENTMENT	untroubled	guilty, self-critical, resentful	4	4
D_7: BOREDOM & WITHDRAWAL	seeks relationships with others	seclusive, feels useless	10	8
Pa: PARANOIA	reasonable	unreasonable, feels persecuted	9	8
Pp: PSYCHOPATHIC DEVIATION	inhibited	uninhibited, unsocialized	22	10
Sc: SCHIZOPHRENIA	reality-oriented	retreats from reality, withdrawn	5	6
As: PSYCHASTHENIA	noncompulsive	obsessive, compulsive	7	6
Ps: PSYCHOLOGICAL INADEQUACY	feels competent, has sense of self-worth	feels inferior and unworthy	6	6

Figure 13.4 Profile for a 24-year-old female on the Clinical Analysis Questionnaire (CAQ).

so), a subsidiation chain could be revealed by asking the person a series of "Why" questions. In our example with Monica, the first question would be "Why do you want to study French with Glenn?" Answer: To pass French. "Why?" To graduate from college. "Why?" To get a job. "Why?" To be able to eat. At this point, an innate drive (hunger) is reached and no further questions are needed. Each motive in this chain is subsidiary to the next and all eventually lead to the innate drive for food.

ERGS

Innate drives or motives are called **ergs** (Cattell, 1983). The term erg refers to the energy inherent in primary or unlearned drives such as sex, hunger, curiosity, anger, and other motives, most of which are not limited to humans, but also are found in the primates and other higher mammals. In identifying dynamic traits, Cattell began with no preconceived biases as to their nature or their number. Unlike other personality theorists such

Table 13.4 List of Experimentally Mapped Human Ergs

Goal Title	Emotion	Status of Evidence
Food-seeking	Hunger	
Mating	Sex	
Gregariousness	Loneliness	
Parental protectiveness	Pity	
Exploration	Curiosity	
Escape to security	Fear	Consistently identified
Self-assertion	Pride	
Narcissistic sex	Sensuousness	
Pugnacity	Anger	
Acquisitiveness	Greed	
Appeal	Despair	
Rest-seeking	Sleepiness	
Constructiveness	Creativity	Uncertain independence
Self-abasement	Humility	
Disgust	Disgust	
Laughter	Amusement	Questionable factors

SOURCE: From R. B. Cattell and P. Kline, *The Scientific Analysis of Personality and Motivation*, 1977. Copyright © 1977 by Academic Press. Reprinted by permission.

as Freud (Chapter 2), Cattell did not presuppose the existence of basic primary drives or instincts. Rather, he started with a heterogeneous array of objective test items (T data), administered them to children and adults in different cultures, factor analyzed the results, and thereby mapped out human motivation mathematically rather than logically.

As a consequence of this approach, Cattell has extracted some 10 ergs, most of which are also found in the other mammals. Cattell (1979–1980) saw this as a reason to believe that these dynamic traits are not acquired through enculturation. In fact, he suggested that ergic factors are the human equivalents of animal instinctual patterns. The presently mapped human ergic goals and their corresponding emotions are shown in Table 13.4. The first 10 have been consistently identified as independent factors; the next four are of uncertain independence; and the final two are even more questionable as factors.

SEMS

The third component in Cattell's theory of motivation are **sems,** which are learned or acquired dynamic traits. Sems (an acronym for "socially shaped ergic manifolds") receive their energy from the ergs and give some organization and stability to the attitudes. Sems are socially acquired and, ordinarily, satisfy several ergs at the same time. Recall that an attitude is an action or desire to act in response to a particular situation, and that attitudes ordinarily can be traced to primary, innate drives called ergs. The intermediate goals between attitudes and ergs are the sems. In the earlier example of our student Monica and her desire to study French with a classmate, we saw that her strong wish to study represented her attitude and that her ultimate goal of food was an erg. The network of subgoals bridging the span between attitude and erg comprise various sems (see Figure 13.5). For example, Monica's wish to maintain her reputation as a diligent student is part of her self-sentiment and her motivation to study French with

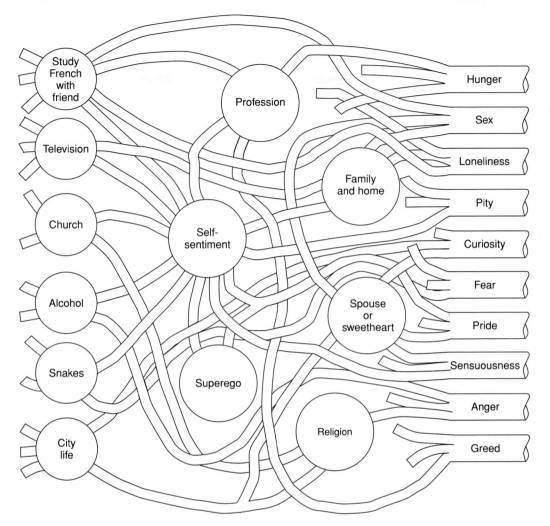

Figure 13.5 Fragments of a person's dynamic lattice, illustrating subsidiation chains and their component attitudes, sems, and ergs.

a friend connects directly with the loneliness erg. This example shows that several sems can be subsidiated in one erg. For example, self and superego are both connected to pride. With the complexity of human motivation, it is also quite likely that several ergs will be involved with one sem. For example, the family and home sem may relate to the ergs of sex and loneliness.

Because sems are culturally acquired, their number differs with different cultures and among various age groups. Cattell has thus far identified a number of sems, but the strongest mathematically and most important clinically are those shown in the center of Figure 13.5, namely profession, family and home, spouse or sweetheart, self-sentiment, superego, and religion. The *self-sentiment* has some special importance because of its crucial position in integrating other sems. The self-sentiment is the psychometric equivalent of the clinically derived term of self-concept. However, it is no different from the other sems in quality and origin. Like the others, it is peculiarly human and learned through one's culture.

THE DYNAMIC LATTICE

The interrelationships among the dynamic traits of an individual can be expressed pictorially by the dynamic lattice (see Figure 13.5), which consists of a complex network of attitudes, ergs, and sems underlying a person's motivational structure. To understand the dynamic lattice shown in Figure 13.5, begin with the ergs—the innate human drives—on the right side of the diagram. Each erg affects one or more of the sems (depicted in large circles in the center). Recall that sems are learned dynamic traits that can satisfy one or more ergs. Notice that the profession sem is subsidiary to—that is, receives its basic energy from—both hunger and greed. The small circles at the left of the diagram represent attitudes, or a person's tendency to action in a particular situation. Monica's attitude toward studying French with Glenn is energized directly by the sex erg, indirectly by hunger, through the profession sem, and also indirectly by pride, through the self-sentiment.

THE DYNAMIC CALCULUS

In the broad sense of the word, Cattell is a behaviorist; that is, his ultimate aim is to understand and predict behavior. Traits of temperament, ability, and motivation are measured not in terms of properties owned by an individual but rather in terms of behavior. How can behavior be predicted most accurately? Cattell's response is to employ the **dynamic calculus,** a complex procedure for determining the strength and direction of attitudes.

In the dynamic calculus, ergs and sems are considered to be the roots of all motivation and they enter into the **behavioral equation,** which allows one to predict the behavior of a given individual (Cattell & Child, 1975). Cattell's early work of identifying various source traits as well as the different ergs and sems simply provided the structure of personality. As Cattell (1982) put it, "This unitary trait structure research yields a description of the pieces on the chess board, but not of the rules of the game" (p. 14).

The dynamic calculus provides those rules. It allows for the prediction of strength of attitudes and is sufficiently practical to enable the clinician, for example, to recommend equally satisfying but less destructive and fatiguing ways of behaving. It also permits the specific calculation of such previously amorphous concepts as conflict, repression, and decision making. Through precise mathematical means, the investigator can determine the exact weights attached to the various ergs and sems, and then fit these weights into the behavioral formulas, thereby yielding an accurate prediction of people's attitudes, that is, their specific course of action or desire to act (Cattell, 1982, 1985).

GENETIC BASIS OF TRAITS

Cattell has long been interested in behavior genetics and the heritability of various source traits such as intelligence, ego strength, and superego strength. Using factor analytic methods and a sample of more than 3,000 related and unrelated subjects, Cattell and his associates have provided tentative estimates of the heritability of such traits as intelligence, ego strength, superego strength, and introversion/extraversion.

The heritability (H) of a trait is the ratio of the genetically determined variance to the total variance. For example, an H of .60 for intelligence would mean that 60% of the total variance of intelligence is accounted for by genetic factors. Variance refers to the extent to which scores spread out over the entire scale. If everyone in a sample obtained the same score, then variance for those scores would be zero. If people do not all score the same, the difference must be due to something—heredity, environment, or an interaction of the two. Cattell's H is simply an estimate of the extent to which the variance of a given trait is due to heredity. The statistical technique used to obtain an H is Multiple Abstract Variance Analysis, or MAVA (Cattell, 1979–1980, 1983).

Cattell (1993) feels that MAVA is superior to the older, twin methods, which simply compared differences among identical twins, fraternal twins, and siblings. MAVA has the advantage, among other things, of being sensitive to differences in the environment for identical twins as compared to fraternal twins. It also allows analysis within families as well as between families. The technique has the capacity to measure genetic, environmental, and total variances for pairs of children (or other people) in the following family constellations: (1) identical twins reared together; (2) fraternal twins reared together; (3) siblings reared together; (4) half siblings reared together; (5) unrelated children reared together; (6) siblings reared apart; (7) unrelated children (adopted) reared apart; and so on. Identical twins reared apart could also be included, but due to their relative scarcity (MAVA only utilizes large sample sizes), this constellation has not been included by Cattell.

Cattell and his associates have published several studies that have used some or all of a total sample of more than 3,000 boys aged 12 to 18. All must be of the same sex because identical twins are necessarily of the same sex. In one study, Cattell, Schuerger, and Klein (1982) investigated the heritability of three primary source traits: ego strength (Factor C), superego strength (Factor G), and self-sentiment (Factor Q_3). These three factors, sometimes called the "controlling triumvirate," were chosen because of their substantial interest to clinicians. The researchers administered a 10-hour battery of tests to 94 identical twins reared together, 124 fraternal twins reared together, 470 brothers reared together, and 2,973 unrelated children reared apart. This latter category was considered a general population group. Using the MAVA method, the authors found, as one might expect, that very little of the variance for superego strength (Factor G) was accounted for by heredity. For the general population, the H was .05, which indicates that superego is mostly a function of education or environment. For ego strength (Factor C) and self-sentiment (Factor Q_3), however, the H values were considerably higher. For the general population, heritability of ego strength was about .40, whereas the within-family H was a little lower, between .30 and .40. For self-sentiment, the heritability for the general population was even higher, .63, an interesting finding in view of Cattell's assumption that sems are culturally acquired. However, in looking at the H values for within- and between-families, the authors found that self-sentiment has a higher heritability for between-families (.65) than for within-families (.46). This suggests that brothers have a similar exposure to cultural influences within the family, at least as far as self-sentiment (self-concept) is concerned.

Cattell (1979–1980) has averaged results from earlier studies and has compiled estimates of H for 18 primary- and 13 second-stratum source traits. Interestingly, the H for both sizia/affectia and exvia/invia is estimated at 50%. Sizia/affectia is a basic primary source trait that describes people in terms of reserved and detached vs. outgoing and warmhearted. Exvia/invia is a second-stratum source trait roughly equivalent to Jung's concept of extraversion/introversion. For both these strong traits, Cattell estimated that approximately half the variance is accounted for by heritability factors and about half by the environment.

Before looking at the controversial issue of the heritability of intelligence, we should understand that Cattell differentiates between fluid and crystallized intelligence. *Fluid intelligence* is that which enables one to adapt to new kinds of material regardless of previous experiences with it. *Crystallized intelligence*, on the other hand, is that which depends on previous learnings to solve present problems. Primary Factor B is considered to be crystallized intelligence, and Cattell estimates that it has a heritability value of 60%. For fluid intelligence, a second-stratum trait, the estimate is .65 (Cattell, 1979–1980). These relatively high heritability values suggest that intelligence is due more to heredity than to environment, an observation that Cattell (1993) claimed was consistent with the assumptions of psychologists in the early part of the 20th century.

EYSENCK'S FACTOR THEORY

Hans Eysenck's approach to theory building differs from Cattell's in several respects. First, he is more likely to use the *hypothetico-deductive* method of theorizing *before* factor analyzing data. Second, he has only three basic *types*, rather than 35 traits. Third, Eysenck uses factor analysis as only one means of answering important questions on personality theory. In an interview with Richard Evans, he said,

> I think probably of all the factor analysts you may know, I'm the one who thinks least of it. I regard it as a useful adjunct, a technique that was invaluable under certain circumstances, but one which we must leave behind as soon as possible in order to get a proper causal type of understanding of the factors and to know just what they mean. (Evans, 1976, p. 259)

Eysenck, then, is a generalist, not merely a factor analyst. His range of interests is broad; his willingness to step into a controversy is legendary. He has been a gadfly to the conscience of psychology since he first entered its ranks. He upset many psychoanalysts and other therapists in the early 1950s with his contention that no evidence exists to suggest that psychotherapy is more effective than spontaneous remission. In other words, those people who receive no therapy are just as likely to get better as are those who undergo expensive, painful, prolonged psychotherapy with expertly trained psychoanalysts and psychologists (Eysenck, 1952a). Eysenck is not afraid to take an unpopular stand, as witnessed by his defense of Arthur Jensen, whose contention is that IQ cannot be significantly increased by well-intentioned social programs but is largely genetically determined. Eysenck's book *The IQ Argument* (1971) was so controversial that elements in the United States "threatened booksellers with arson if they dared to stock the book; well-known 'liberal' newspapers refused to review it; and the outcome was that it was largely impossible in the land of free speech to discover the existence of the book or to buy it" (Eysenck, 1980, p. 175).

In England, he was attacked and beaten up by left-wing thugs while preparing to deliver a speech on a separate topic. Eysenck's enemies and critics, however, do not only come from the political left; his battles with the fascist right go back even further.

BIOGRAPHY OF HANS J. EYSENCK

Hans Jurgen Eysenck was born in Berlin, Germany, on March 4, 1916, the child of a theatrical family. His mother was Ruth Werner, a starlet at the time of Hans's birth who later became a German silent film star under the stage name of Helga Molander. His father, Anton Eduard Eysenck, was a comedian, singer, and actor. Eysenck (1991a, p. 40) recalled that he "saw very little of my parents, who divorced when I was 4, and who had little feeling for me, an emotion I reciprocated." After his parents' divorce, Hans went to live with his maternal grandmother, who had also been in the theater, but whose promising career in opera was cut short by a crippling fall (Eysenck, 1982). Eysenck (1991a) described his grandmother as "unselfish, caring, altruistic, and altogether too good for this world" (p. 40). Although his grandmother was a devout Catholic, neither parent was religious, and Hans grew up without any formal religious commitment (Gibson, 1981).

He also grew up with little parental discipline and few strict controls over his behavior. Neither parent seemed interested in curtailing his actions, and his grandmother had a quite permissive attitude toward him. This benign neglect is exemplified by two incidents. In the first, his father had bought Hans a bicycle and had promised to teach him to ride. "He took me to the top of a hill, told me that I had to sit on the saddle and pump the pedals and make the wheels go round. He then went off to release some balloons . . . leaving me to learn how to ride all by myself" (Eysenck, 1990c, p. 12). In the second incident, an adolescent Eysenck told his grandmother that he was going to buy some cigarettes, expecting her to forbid it. However, his grandmother simply said: " 'If you like it, do it by all means'" (p. 14). According to Eysenck, environmental experiences, such as these two, have little to do with personality development. To him, genetic factors have a greater impact on subsequent behavior than do childhood experiences. Thus, his permissive upbringing neither helped nor hindered him in becoming a famous scientist.

Even as a schoolboy, Eysenck was not afraid to take an unpopular stand, often challenging his teachers, especially those with militaristic leanings. He was skeptical of much of what they taught and was not always reluctant to embarrass them with his superior knowledge. In his autobiography, he described himself as "a sanctimonious prig . . . who didn't suffer fools (or even ordinarily bright people) gladly" (Eysenck, 1990c, p. 31).

Eysenck suffered the deprivation of many post–World War I Germans who were faced with astronomical inflation, mass unemployment, and near starvation, and his future appeared no brighter after Hitler came to power. As a condition of studying physics at the University of Berlin, he was told that he would have to join the Nazi secret police, an idea he found so repugnant that he decided to leave Germany.

This encounter with the fascist right and his later battles with the radical left suggested to him that the trait of tough-mindedness, or authoritarianism, was equally prevalent in both extremes of the political spectrum. He later found some scientific support for this hypothesis in a study that demonstrated that although communists were radical and fascists were conservative on one dimension of personality, on the tough-minded vs. tender-minded dimension, both groups were more authoritarian, rigid, and intolerant of ambiguity (tough-minded) than a control group was (Eysenck, 1954; Eysenck & Coulter, 1972).

As a consequence of Nazi tyranny, Eysenck, at age 18, left Germany and eventually settled in England, where he tried to enroll in the University of London. He was an avid reader, interested in both the arts and the sciences, but his first choice of curriculum was physics. However, a chance event altered the flow of his life and, consequently, the course of the history of psychology. In order to be accepted at the university, he was required to pass an entrance examination, which he took after a year's study at a commercial college. After passing the exam in 1935, he confidently enrolled in the University of London, intending to major in physics. However, he was told that he had taken the wrong subjects in his exam and therefore was not eligible to pursue a course in physics. Rather than waiting another year to take the right subjects, he asked if there was some scientific subject that he was qualified to pursue. When told he could always take psychology, he replied, "What on earth is psychology?" (Eysenck, 1982, p. 290).

At that time, the psychology department at the University of London was basically pro-Freudian, but it was also psychometrically oriented, with Charles Spearman having just left and with Cyril Burt still presiding. Eysenck received a bachelor's degree in 1938, about the same time that he married Margaret Davies, a Canadian woman with a degree in mathematics. In 1940, he was awarded a Ph.D. from the University of London, but by this time England and most of Europe were at war.

As a German national, he was considered an enemy alien and not allowed to enter the Royal Air Force (his first choice) or any other branch of the military. Instead, with no training as a psychiatrist or as a clinical psychologist, he went to work at the Mill Hill Emergency Hospital, treating patients who were suffering from a variety of psychological symptoms, including anxiety, depression, and hysteria. Eysenck, however, was not comfortable with most of the traditional clinical diagnostic categories. Using factor analysis, he found that two major personality factors—neuroticism and extraversion/introversion—could account for all the traditional diagnostic groups. These early theoretical ideas led to the publication of his first book, *Dimensions of Personality* (Eysenck, 1947). After the war, he became director of the Psychology Department at Maudsley Hospital and later became a reader in psychology at the University of London.

In 1949, Eysenck traveled to North America to examine the clinical psychology programs in the United States and Canada with the idea of setting up a clinical psychology profession in Great Britain. He obtained a visiting professorship at the University of Pennsylvania for the year 1949–1950, but he spent much of that year traveling throughout the United States and Canada looking over clinical psychology programs, which he found to be totally unscientific (Eysenck, 1980, 1990c).

Eysenck and his wife had been growing steadily apart, and his marriage was not improved when his traveling companion to Philadelphia was Sybil Rostal, a beautiful quantitative psychologist and the daughter of a famous violinist. On returning to England, Eysenck obtained a divorce from his first wife, and on October 30, 1950, he married Sybil. Hans and Sybil Eysenck have coauthored several publications, and their marriage has produced three sons and a daughter. Eysenck's son from his first marriage, Michael, is a widely published author of psychology articles and books.

After returning from North America, Eysenck established a clinical psychology department at the University of London and in 1955, became professor of psychology. While in the United States, he had begun *The Structure of Human Personality* (1952b), in which he argued for the efficacy of factor analysis as the best method of representing the known facts of human personality.

Eysenck surpasses even Cattell for volume of published works. Along with nearly 800 journal articles or book chapters, he has published more than 75 books, several of which have titles with popular appeal such as *Uses and Abuses of Psychology* (1953); *Sense and Nonsense in Psychology* (1956); *Fact and Fiction in Psychology* (1965); *Psychology Is About People* (1972b); *You and Neurosis* (1977b); *Sex, Violence and the Media* (with D. K. B. Nias, 1978); *Smoking, Personality, and Stress* (1991c), and *Genius: The Natural History of Creativity* (1995).

In 1983, Eysenck retired as professor of psychology at the Institute of Psychiatry, University of London, and as senior psychiatrist at the Maudsley and Bethlehem Royal hospitals. He then served as professor emeritus at the University of London until his death from cancer on September 4, 1997. During his later years, his research continued to reflect a variety of topics, including creativity (Eysenck, 1993, 1995; Frois & Eysenck, 1995) and behavioral interventions in cancer and heart disease (Eysenck, 1991c; Eysenck & Grossarth-Maticek, 1991).

MEASUREMENT OF PERSONALITY

Three people—Cyril Burt, Charles Spearman, and Ivan Pavlov—have had the greatest influence on Eysenck's theory of personality. Burt, his professor, and Spearman, whose lectures he attended, showed him that personality could best be investigated psychometrically. Pavlov, whom he never knew personally, taught him that there is a biological basis for personality structure (Cohen, 1977). Thus, Eysenck's theory has strong psychometric and biological components.

CRITERIA FOR IDENTIFYING FACTORS

Eysenck (1977a) contended that psychometric sophistication alone is not sufficient to measure the structure of human personality, and that types arrived at through factor analytic methods are sterile and meaningless unless they have been shown to possess a biological existence. In fact, he listed four criteria for the identification of a factor. First, *psychometric evidence* for the factor's existence must be established. A corollary to this criterion is that the factor must be reliable and replicable. Other investigators, from separate laboratories, must also be able to find the factor. A second criterion is that the factor must also possess *heritability* and must fit an established genetic model. This criterion eliminates learned characteristics, such as the ability to mimic the voices of well-known people or a religious or political belief. Third, the factor must *make sense from a theoretical view*. Eysenck employs the **deductive method** of investigation, beginning with a theory and then gathering data that are logically consistent with that theory. The final criterion for the existence of a factor is that it must *possess social relevance*; that is, it must be demonstrated that mathematically derived factors have a relationship (not necessarily causal) with such socially relevant variables as drug addiction, accident proneness, outstanding performance in sports, psychotic behavior, criminality, and so on.

HIERARCHY OF MEASURES

Eysenck (1947, 1994c) has long recognized a four-level hierarchy of behavior organization. At the lowest level are *specific acts or cognitions*, individual behaviors or thoughts that may or may not be characteristic of the person. A student finishing a reading assignment would be an example of a specific response. At the second level are the *habitual acts or cognitions*, that is, responses that recur under similar conditions. For example, if a student frequently keeps at an assignment until it is finished, this behavior becomes a habitual response. As opposed to specific responses, habitual responses must be reasonably reliable or consistent.

Several related habitual responses form a *trait*—the third level of behavior. Eysenck (1981) defined traits as "important semi-permanent personality disposition" (p. 3). For example, students would have the trait of persistence if they habitually complete class assignments and keep working at other endeavors until they are finished. Although traits can be identified intuitively, trait and factor theorists rely on a more systematic approach, namely factor analysis. Trait-level behaviors are extracted through factor analysis of habit-level responses just as habitual responses are mathematically extracted through factor analysis of specific responses. Traits, then, are "defined in terms of significant intercorrelations between different habitual behaviors" (Eysenck, 1990a, p. 244). Most of Cattell's 35 normal and abnormal primary source traits are at

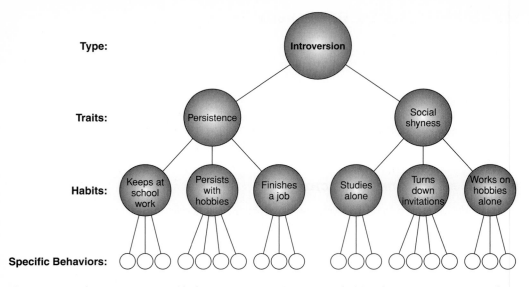

Type: Introversion

Traits: Persistence   Social shyness

Habits: Keeps at school work   Persists with hobbies   Finishes a job   Studies alone   Turns down invitations   Works on hobbies alone

Specific Behaviors:

***Figure* 13.6** The organization of behavior into specific actions, habitual responses, traits, and types. Besides persistence and social shyness, other traits such as inferiority, low activity, and serious-mindedness contribute to introversion.

this third (trait) level of organization, which accounts for the fact that he has identified far more personality factors than Eysenck.

In contrast to Cattell, Eysenck has concentrated on the fourth level, that of **types** or superfactors. A type is made up of several interrelated traits. For example, persistence may be related to inferiority, poor emotional adjustment, social shyness, and several other traits, with the entire cluster forming the *introverted type*. These four levels of behavior organization are shown in Figure 13.6. Remember that Eysenck's structure of personality rests on the more generalized type level factors, whereas Cattell's theory is based largely on trait level factors.

To better understand the difference between the approaches of Cattell and Eysenck, let's compare Cattell and Eysenck to two cartographers who have set out to map the earth. One cartographer may decide to chart the entire globe—every mountain, river, hill, and stream. This mapmaker would be like Cattell, who assigned himself the task of measuring the entire sphere of human personality.

The second cartographer may decide to measure more obvious features of the earth—the continents and the oceans. This mapmaker would be analogous to Eysenck, who has looked at the more global features of personality.

In addition, the tools of the cartographers might differ, just as Cattell and Eysenck used different factor analytic techniques. Cattell's inductive method can be compared to a mapmaker who uses a variety of surveying instruments with no preconceived notion of what he is going to find. On the other hand, Eysenck's deductive method would be more like a cartographer who takes aerial photos of preselected locations and then interprets these pictures from a predetermined view. With these vastly different approaches, we would expect differences in what the two explorers find.

Thus, the work of Cattell and Eysenck has produced different results because each man has mapped different parts of the sphere of human personality. Moreover, Cattell and Eysenck have arrived at a different number of factors because they are working at different levels of factoring. Cattell's 35 traits cannot be directly compared with Eysenck's three types, because traits are at the third level of the hierarchical structure and types are at the fourth level.

TYPES

How many general types or superfactors exist? Eysenck has extracted three general types or superfactors—**extraversion** (E), **neuroticism** (N), and **psychoticism** (P), although he does not rule out "the possibility that further dimensions may be added later" (Eysenck, 1994c, p. 151). Figure 13.7 shows the hierarchical structure of Eysenck's P, E, and N.

Neuroticism and psychoticism are not limited to pathological individuals, although disturbed people tend to score higher than normal people on scales measuring these two factors. Eysenck regards all three types as part of normal personality structure. All three types are bipolar, with extraversion being at one end of Factor E and **introversion** occupying the opposite pole. Similarly, Factor N includes neuroticism at one pole and **stability** at the other, and Factor P has psychoticism at one pole and the **superego function** at the other.

The bipolarity of Eysenck's factors does not imply that most people are at one end or the other of the three main poles. Each type is unimodally, rather than bimodally, distributed. Extraversion, for example, is fairly normally distributed in much the same fashion as intelligence or height. Most people are near the center of a bell-shaped distribution, which means that Eysenck (1994c) does not believe that people can be neatly divided into mutually exclusive types.

Eysenck contends that each of these types meets his four criteria for identifying personality dimensions. First, strong psychometric evidence exists for each, especially Factors E and N. The P factor (psychoticism) emerged later in Eysenck's work and currently has less confirming evidence from other researchers. Extraversion and neuroticism (or anxiety) are basic types or superfactors in nearly all factor analytic studies of human personality. For example, Royce and Powell (1983) compared Eysenck's E and N to Cattell's second-stratum traits and found that Eysenck's E (extraversion) appears to be comparable to Cattell's QI (exvia/invia), and his N (neuroticism) may be the same factor as Cattell's QII (anxiety).

Second, Eysenck (1994b, 1994c) has argued that a strong biological base exists for each of his three superfactors. At the same time, he has claimed that traits such as agreeableness and conscientiousness, which are part of the "Big Five" taxonomy (John, 1990; Norman, 1963; Tupes & Christal, 1961), do not have an underlying biological foundation. (We discuss the Big Five traits in Chapter 19.)

Third, Eysenck's three types, especially E and N, make sense theoretically. Jung, Freud, and others have recognized the powerful effect on behavior of extraversion/introversion and anxiety/emotional stability. Eysenck (1994b) has proposed a theory underlying the P factor (psychoticism) that assumes a continuous range of psychological health among the general population. At one end of this bell-shaped distribution are such healthy qualities as altruism, good socialization, and empathy. At the other end are such qualities as hostility, aggression, and schizophrenic reactions. People may score at any point along this range and never be regarded as psychotic. Eysenck, however, adopts a **diathesis-stress model** of psychiatric illness, which suggests that some people are vulnerable to illness because they have either a genetic or an acquired weakness that predisposes them to an illness. This predisposition (diathesis) may interact with stress to produce a psychotic episode. Eysenck assumes that people at the healthy

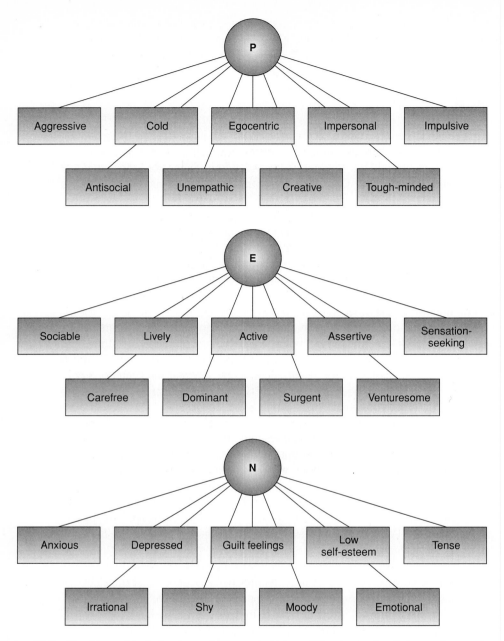

Figure 13.7 The hierarchical structure of (P) psychoticism, (E) extraversion-introversion, and (N) neuroticism.

Source: From Biological dimensions of personality by H. J. Eysenck. In L. A. Pervin (Ed.), *Handbook of personality: Theory and research* (pp. 244–276). New York: Guilford Press. Reprinted by permission of Guilford Press.

end of the P scale will resist a psychotic break, even in periods of extreme stress. On the other hand, people at the unhealthy end of the scale may suffer a psychotic reaction as a result of minimal stress. In other words, the higher the psychoticism score, the lower the level of stress necessary to precipitate a psychotic reaction.

Fourth, Eysenck has repeatedly demonstrated that his three types relate to such social issues as drugs (Eysenck, 1983), sexual behaviors (Eysenck, 1976), criminality

(Eysenck, 1964, Eysenck & Gudjonsson, 1989), preventing cancer and heart disease (Eysenck, 1991b, 1991c; Grossarth-Maticek, Eysenck, & Vetter, 1988), and creativity (Eysenck, 1993). (We review some of this research on creativity later.)

EXTRAVERSION

In Chapter 3, we saw that Jung conceptualized two broad personality types, called "extraversion" and "introversion." We also noted some differences between his definitions and the prevailing notion of these two terms. Jung saw extraverted people as having an objective or nonpersonalized view of the world, whereas introverts have essentially a subjective or individualized way of looking at things. Eysenck's concepts of extraversion and introversion are closer to the popular usage. Extraverted types are characterized primarily by sociability and impulsiveness, but also by jocularity, liveliness, quick-wittedness, optimism, and other traits indicative of people who are rewarded for their association with others (Eysenck & Eysenck, 1969).

Introverts are characterized by traits opposite those of extraverts. They can be described as quiet, passive, unsociable, careful, reserved, thoughtful, pessimistic, peaceful, sober, and controlled (Eysenck, Nias, & Cox, 1982). According to Eysenck (1982), however, the principal differences between extraversion and introversion are not behavioral, but rather biological and genetic in nature.

Eysenck (1990a) believes that the primary cause of differences between extraverts and introverts is one of *cortical arousal level*, a physiological condition that is largely inherited rather than learned. Because extraverts have a lower level of cortical arousal than introverts, they have higher sensory thresholds and thus lesser reactions to sensory stimulation. Introverts, conversely, are characterized by a higher level of arousal, and as a result of a lower sensory threshold, they experience greater reactions to sensory stimulation. To maintain an optimal level of stimulation, introverts, with their congenitally low sensory threshold, avoid situations that will cause too much excitement. Hence, introverts shun such activities as wild social events, downhill skiing, sky diving, competitive sports, leading a fraternity or sorority, or playing practical jokes.

On the other hand, because extraverts have a habitually low level of cortical arousal, they need a high level of sensory stimulation to maintain an optimal level of stimulation. Therefore, extraverts participate more often in exciting and stimulating activities. They may enjoy such activities as mountain climbing, sky diving, driving fast cars, drinking alcohol, and smoking marijuana. In addition, Eysenck (1976) hypothesized that extraverts, as opposed to introverts, will engage in sexual intercourse earlier, more frequently, with more different partners, in more different positions, and with a greater variety of sexual behaviors, and will indulge in longer precoital love play. Because extraverts have a lower level of cortical arousal, however, they become more quickly accustomed to strong stimuli (sexual or otherwise) and respond less and less to the same stimuli, whereas introverts are less likely to become bored and uninterested in routine activities carried on with the same people.

NEUROTICISM

The second type extracted by Eysenck is neuroticism/stability (N). Like extraversion/introversion, Factor N has a strong hereditary component. Eysenck (1967) reported several studies that have found evidence of a genetic basis for such neurotic traits as anxiety, hysteria, and obsessive-compulsive disorders. In addition, he has found a much

Extraverts enjoy exciting and stimulating activities.

greater agreement among identical twins than among fraternal twins on a number of antisocial and asocial behaviors such as adult crime, childhood behavior disorders, homosexuality, and alcoholism (Eysenck, 1964).

People who score high on neuroticism often have a tendency to overreact emotionally and to have difficulty returning to a normal state after emotional arousal. They frequently complain of physical symptoms such as headache and backache and of vague psychological problems such as worries and anxieties. Neuroticism, however, does not necessarily suggest a neurosis in the traditional meaning of that term. People can score high on neuroticism and be free of any debilitating psychological symptoms. However, Eysenck accepts the *diathesis-stress model*, which suggests that high N scorers are more likely than low N scorers to develop neurotic disorders during times of high stress.

Because neuroticism can be combined with different points on the extraversion scale, no single syndrome can define neurotic behavior. Eysenck's factor analytic technique assumes the independence of types, which means that the neuroticism scale is at right angles (signifying zero correlation) to the extraversion scale. Thus several people can all score high on the N scale, yet display quite different symptoms, depending on their degree of introversion or extraversion. Figure 13.8 shows the extraversion/introversion pole with zero correlation with the neuroticism/stability pole. Consider persons A, B, and C, all equal on the neuroticism scale, but representing three distinct points on the extraversion scale. Person A, an introverted neurotic, is characterized by anxiety, depression, phobias, and obsessive-compulsive symptoms; Person B is neither introverted nor extraverted and is likely to be characterized by hysteria (a neurotic disorder associated with emotional instability), suggestibility, and somatic symptoms; Person C, an extraverted neurotic, will probably manifest psychopathic qualities such as criminality and delinquent tendencies (Eysenck, 1967). Consider, also, Persons A, D, and E, all equally introverted, but with three different levels of emotional stability. Person A is the introverted neurotic described above; B is equally introverted, but is neither severely neurotic nor emotionally stable; and E is both extremely introverted and psychologically healthy.

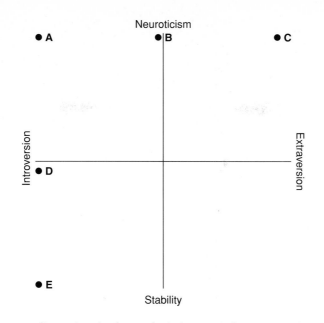

Figure 13.8 Two-dimensional scheme depicting several extreme points on Eysenck's E and N scales.

Figure 13.8 shows only five people, all of whom have at least one extreme score. Most other people, of course, would score near the mean on both scales. As scores move toward the outer limits of the diagram, they become increasingly less and less frequent, just as scores on the ends of a bell-shaped curve are less frequent than those near the midpoint.

PSYCHOTICISM

Eysenck's original theory of personality was based on only two types—extraversion and neuroticism. After several years of alluding to psychoticism (P) as an independent personality type, Eysenck finally elevated it to a position equal to E and N (Eysenck & Eysenck, 1976). Eysenck (1992) sees psychoticism as a unitary concept rather than separate, unrelated disorders such as schizophrenia, manic-depression, and so forth. Also, psychoticism/superego is a continuous variable that approximates a normal, bell-shaped curve. High P scorers are often egocentric, cold, nonconforming, aggressive, impulsive, hostile, suspicious, and antisocial. People low on psychoticism (in the direction of superego function) tend to be empathic, caring, cooperative, and highly socialized (Eysenck, Nias, & Cox, 1982).

People high on the psychoticism variable are not necessarily suffering from a psychosis, but they do have a high *"predisposition* to succumb to stress and develop a psychotic illness" (Eysenck, 1994b, p. 20). In other words, high P scorers are genetically more vulnerable than low P scorers. During periods of low stress, high P scorers may function normally, but high levels of stress can interact with their high vulnerability to produce a psychotic breakdown (Eysenck, 1994b, 1994c).

Like extraversion and neuroticism, psychoticism has a large genetic component. Eysenck (1990a) has estimated that about three fourths of the variance of all three factors can be accounted for by heredity and about one fourth by environmental factors.

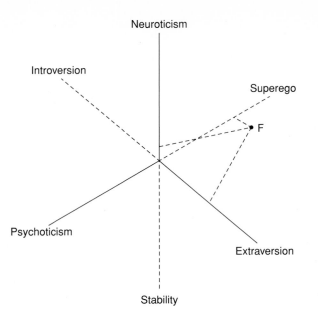

Figure 13.9 Three-dimensional scheme depicting one individual's scores on each of Eysenck's major dimensions of personality.

Eysenck has summarized much of the evidence for a strong biological component in personality. First, nearly identical factors have been found among people in various parts of the world, "from Uganda and Nigeria to Japan and mainland China, from the capitalist countries of the West and the American continent to Eastern-bloc countries such as the Soviet Union, Hungary, Czechoslovakia, Bulgaria, and Yugoslavia" (Eysenck, 1990a, pp. 245–246). Second, evidence suggests that individuals tend to maintain their position over time on the three dimensions of personality. And third, studies of twins show a higher concordance between identical twins than between same-gender fraternal twins reared together, suggesting that genetic factors play a dominant part in determining individual differences in personality.

Psychoticism/superego (P) is independent of both E and N. Figure 13.9 shows each of the three factors at right angles with the other two. (Because three-dimensional space cannot be faithfully produced on a two-dimensional plane, the reader is asked to look at Figure 13.9 as if the solid lines represent the corner of a room where two walls meet the floor. Each line can then be seen as perpendicular to the other two.) Eysenck's view of personality, therefore, allows each person to be measured on three independent factors and resultant scores to be plotted in space having three coordinates. Person F in Figure 13.9, for example, is very high on superego, somewhat high on extraversion, and near the midpoint on the neuroticism/stability scale. In similar fashion, scores of each person can be plotted in three-dimensional space.

Eysenck has evolved four personality inventories that measure his superfactors. The first, the Maudsley Personality Inventory, or MPI (Eysenck, 1959), assessed only E and N and yielded some correlation between these two factors. For this reason, he developed another test, the Eysenck Personality Inventory, or EPI. The EPI contains a lie (L) scale to detect faking, but more importantly, it measures extraversion and neuroticism independently, with a near zero correlation between E and N (Eysenck & Eysenck, 1964, 1968). The EPI was still a two-factor inventory, so consequently, Eysenck and Eysenck (1975) published the third of his personality tests, namely, the

Eysenck Personality Questionnaire (EPQ), which was a revision of the still-published EPI and which included a psychoticism (P) scale. Subsequent criticisms of the P scale led to yet another revision, the Eysenck Personality Questionnaire-Revised (Eysenck & Eysenck, 1993).

RELATED RESEARCH

The trait-oriented perspectives of Cattell and Eysenck have been among the most fruitful theories of personality in generating testable hypotheses and wide-ranging research programs. Both Cattell and Eysenck have developed widely used personality inventories, namely Cattell's Sixteen Personality Factor Questionnaire (16 PF) (Cattell, 1949) and its offshoots, and Eysenck's various inventories (Eysenck, 1959; Eysenck & Eysenck, 1964, 1968, 1975, 1993). Furthermore, Eysenck ranks among the top 10 psychologists of all time in terms of number of publications. During his 45-year professional career, Eysenck has written on a vast array of topics, including politics, sexual behavior, personality assessment, cancer and smoking, hypnosis, humor, personality and heart disease, personality and cancer, behavior therapy, intelligence, and creative genius. Furthermore, in all these writings, Eysenck has taken a biological and genetic perspective. He and Cattell are two of the few major personality theorists to emphasize the biological foundation of behavior and personality. Of the myriad topics discussed by Cattell and Eysenck, we have chosen to review only research spawned by their work on the creative personality.

CREATIVE SCIENTISTS

Beginning with Cattell's own research in the mid-1950s, a number of studies have used the 16 PF to examine the unique personality characteristics of creative scientists. For instance, Cattell and J. E. Drevdahl (1955) reported that creative scientists, relative to the general population, were significantly more intelligent, outgoing, adventurous, and sensitive; they were somewhat more radical and self-sufficient; and they had greater ego-strength and dominance but less free-floating anxiety. In 1964, Jack Chambers used the 16 PF to compare the personalities of creative scientists (chemists and psychologists) to their less creative peers and found that the creative scientists were more self-sufficient, dominant, and driven. Later, Louise Bachtold and Emmy Werner (1972) used the 16 PF to examine personality traits in creative female scientists. They collected personality data on female biologists and chemists listed in *Who's Who in America* and *Who's Who of American Women* and compared them to female norms. Bachtold and Werner found that the female scientists were more dominant, confident, intelligent, radical, and adventurous than women in general. Furthermore, the personality profile of female scientists was quite consistent with that of male scientists.

Researchers have also used the Eysenck Personality Questionnaire (EPQ) to assess creativity among scientists and have found that conscientiousness appears to distinguish scientists from nonscientists. For example, Paul Kline and Sharon Lapham (1992) used the EPQ to measure the personality characteristics of undergraduate science majors and art majors and found that the science majors were much more conscientious than the art majors. In addition, creative scientists appear to score high on Eysenck's introversion scale. In one study, Glenn Wilson and Chris Jackson (1994) administered the EPQ to male and female physicists and compared their scores to the population norms. They found that both male and female physicists scored much lower on the sociable dimension than did people in general. Moreover, creative scientists scored higher than other people on the psychoticism scale and also showed higher levels of drive and ambition (Ikpaahindi, 1987; Rushton, 1990; Rushton, Murray, & Paunonen, 1983).

To summarize, research using Cattell's 16 PF and Eysenck's EPQ has demonstrated that creative scientists are consistently more intelligent, introverted, conscientious, driven, dominant, self-sufficient, open, and adventurous than their less creative peers.

CREATIVE ARTISTS

Drevdahl and Cattell (1958) were also among the first researchers to use the 16 PF to examine the unique personality traits of creative artists. They found that, in comparison with people in general, writers and artists were more intelligent, dominant, adventurous, emotionally sensitive, radical, and self-sufficient. In addition, creative artists were less concerned with norms and group standards and less socially outgoing. Later, David Payne, W. Gerald Halpin, Chad Ellett, and Joyce Dale (1975) found that gifted high school students in drama, music, and art were more "experimenting, assertive, self-sufficient, tender-minded [sensitive], and expedient [persevering]" (p. 107) than other high school students were. Furthermore, in a study of more than 1,000 music students, Anthony Kemp (1981) reported the highest levels of neuroticism and introversion among the most creative musicians. Finally, Louise Buttsworth and Glen Smith (1994) administered the 16 PF to college music students and to undergraduate psychology students and found that the music students were more stable, sensitive, suspicious, and independent, but less intelligent, radical, and anxious than the psychology students were.

A number of studies have examined the unique personality traits of creative artists using Eysenck's EPQ, and a consistent set of findings has emerged. Creative artists tend to be higher on neuroticism (anxious, sensitive, obsessive) and psychoticism (impulsive, hostile, risk-taking) than nonartist controls. For instance, Susan Marchant-Haycox and Glenn Wilson (1992) administered the Eysenck Personality Profile (EPP; an offshoot of the EPQ) to performing artists (actors, dancers, musicians, and singers) and reported elevated scores on emotional instability and sensitivity (neuroticism). In addition, these performing artists scored low on sociability and all except the actors were high on caution. Comparing the different art groups, the actors were the most extraverted and the musicians were the most introverted. Compared with people in general, writers (Mohan & Tiwana, 1986) and musicians (Wills, 1983) appear to be higher on both neuroticism and psychoticism.

CAUSE OR EFFECT?

These findings suggest that highly creative people, whether they are artists or scientists, are more introverted, open, dominant, driven, impulsive, hostile, and sensitive than less creative people. As is true with the trait perspective in general, such a conclusion is merely descriptive of the creative personality and reveals little about whether these traits are causes or effects of creativity. Do highly creative people develop these traits or do people with these traits become creative? To date, the development and causal path of personality traits on creative behavior remain unanswered and in need of further investigation.

CRITIQUE OF TRAIT AND FACTOR THEORIES

The trait and factor theories of Cattell and Eysenck are examples of a strictly empirical approach to personality investigation. Both theories were built by collecting as much data as possible on a large number of people, intercorrelating the scores, factor analyzing correlation matrices, and applying appropriate psychological significance to the resultant factors. Psychometrics, rather than clinical judgment, is the cornerstone of trait and factor theories. Nevertheless, like other theories, those of Cattell and Eysenck must be judged by six criteria of a useful theory.

First, do trait and factor theories *generate research*? On this criterion, the theories of Cattell and Eysenck must be rated very high. Cattell, especially, has built his theory inductively, without relying on any preconceived notion of what personality ought to be. This highly empirical procedure may appear to be atheoretical, but it is actually a sound method of building a theory. In this manner, theory and observation never become estranged. Factor analytic methods not only create hypotheses, they are capable of testing them as well. Cattell and Eysenck have each constructed several personality inventories that have generated a prodigious amount of research. Although many of these investigations are not direct tests of the theory on which the inventories are based, trait and factor theories have generated an impressive amount of research.

Second, are trait and factor theories *falsifiable*? On this criterion, trait and factor theories receive only a moderate rating. Although both Cattell and Eysenck built a theory on sound psychometric principles, the two theories are quite different from each other, and neither lends itself easily to falsification. Indeed, both Eysenck (1972a) and Cattell (1972) have attempted to falsify each other's theory. Moreover, both theories have come under heavy attack by proponents of the Big Five (see, for example, Goldberg, 1993). In her father's defense, Heather Cattell (1993) has attempted to show that Cattell's second-order traits "line up fairly well" (p. 1302) with the Big Five factors, while Eysenck (1994a) continues to insist that his three-factor system is more theoretically sound than the five-factor model or Cattell's multi-factor theory. This continuing debate suggests that trait and factor theories may be falsifiable if each theorist had begun with the same set of rules, but that the theoretical models derived from factor analytic procedures are themselves quite difficult to falsify.

Third, trait and factor theories are rated high on their ability to *organize knowledge*. Anything that is truly known about personality should be reducible to some quantity. Anything that can be quantified can be measured and anything that can be measured can be factor analyzed. The extracted factors then provide a convenient and accurate description of personality in terms of traits. These traits, in turn, can present a framework for organizing many disparate observations about human personality. Traits possess a high level of versatility. They can be viewed as highly specific factors, not much broader than a habit, or they can be clustered to form generalized dispositions or types; they can be seen as individual traits (peculiar to one person) or as common traits (shared by many); and they can be viewed as unitary (unrelated to other traits). In addition, people can be seen in terms of normal or pathological traits and also in terms of learned or inherited traits. Trait and factor theories, then, have the power to give meaning to much of what is known about personality.

A fourth criterion of a useful theory is its power to *guide the actions of practitioners*. On this criterion, trait and factor theories receive mixed reviews. In general, they provide a comprehensive and structured taxonomy or classification. A taxonomy, though impotent in generating testable hypotheses, is a necessary condition for theory and for science. The classification system provided by trait theorists, particularly Cattell, serves as a useful guide to the researcher and the theory builder, but it is somewhat less useful to psychotherapists, teachers, and parents who look toward a sound theoretical system to answer many of their everyday questions.

Are trait and factor theories *internally consistent*? Again, the rating must be equivocal. Each theory alone is a model of consistency, but the two theories taken together are somewhat inconsistent. This presents a problem, especially because factor analysis is a precise mathematical procedure, and because factor theories are heavily empirical.

The final criterion of a useful theory is *parsimony*. Ideally, trait and factor theories should receive an excellent rating on this standard, because factor analysis is predicated on the idea of the fewest number of explanatory factors possible. In other words, the very purpose of factor analysis is to reduce a large number of variables to as few as possible. This is the essence of parsimony. Eysenck, with only three factors, certainly has epitomized parsimony. Cattell, on the other hand, has not only extracted many more factors but has also applied neologistic labels to most of them, thus rendering his language troublesome for the uninitiated.

CONCEPT OF HUMANITY

How do trait and factor theorists view humanity? Cattell and Eysenck are not concerned with traditional themes such as *determinism vs. free choice, optimism vs. pessimism*, and *teleological vs. causal* influences. In fact, their theories do not even lend themselves to speculation of these topics. What, then, can we say concerning their view of humanity?

First, we know that Cattell and Eysenck see humans as being different from other animals. From a psychometric view, people can be differentiated from other beings on the basis of their ability to report data about themselves. Nonhuman animal data can be collected by life records (L data) and by objective measurement of performance (T data). However, only humans are capable of answering questions about themselves (Q data). From this fact, it can be inferred that Cattell and Eysenck believe that humans possess not only *consciousness*, but self-consciousness as well. People are also able to evaluate their performance and to render reasonably reliable reports concerning their attitudes, temperament, needs, interests, and behaviors.

Second, both Cattell and Eysenck place heavy emphasis on *genetic factors* of personality. Eysenck insists that the traits of extraversion, neuroticism, and psychoticism all have strong hereditary components, but he does not dismiss social factors altogether. Instead, he says that humans are biosocial organisms whose behaviors are "determined equally by biological factors such as hunger, thirst, sexual appetite, etc., and by social constraints enforced by the government . . . or by public approval and disapproval" (Eysenck, 1990c, p. 64). Nevertheless, on the dimension of *biological vs. social* influences, trait and factor theories strongly favor biology as a determinant of personality.

On the dimension of *individual differences vs. similarities*, trait and factor theories lean toward individual differences. Factor analysis rests on the premise of differences among individuals and thus variability in their scores. If scores on individuals did not differ, correlations would be impossible and factor analysis unthinkable. Even though common factors are ordinarily derived from factor analysis, trait theorists still place heavy emphasis on individual differences. Eysenck (1981), for instance, stated that "people are above all else *individuals*" (p. xi), and Cattell has pioneered the use of the P technique, which begins with a large pool of scores obtained from a single individual and results in the identification of individual traits. Thus, trait theorists are more concerned with individual differences than with similarities among people.

Chapter Summary

The trait and factor theories of Raymond B. Cattell and Hans J. Eysenck have been derived from a mathematical procedure called *factor analysis*. This procedure assumes that people differ from one another on semipermanent personality dispositions, or traits, and that these traits can be measured by correlational studies. More than any other personality theorists, Cattell and Eysenck emphasize genetic, or hereditary, factors underlying personality. Whereas Cattell identified 35 first-order personality traits, Eysenck based his theory on only three broad factors: extraversion/introversion, neuroticism/stability, and psychoticism/superego.

Cattell's theory of personality is psychometrically rather than clinically based. He began with no preconceived ideas on the structure of human personality; proceeded inductively to gather quantified information from life reports (L data), self reports (Q data), and objective test performance (T data); obtained intercorrelations of scores; and then extracted *primary factors* from the correlation matrices. These factors emerged as psychologically meaningful traits within three modalities of personality—*temperament*, *ability*, and *motivation*.

In all, Cattell identified 35 *first-order personality traits*—23 within the realm of normal personality plus 12 pathological traits. These factors are themselves intercorrelated, thus allowing for further factoring and the extraction of at least eight *second-order factors*. These primary and secondary factors are called "general personality traits," but they are largely traits of temperament.

Cattell has also been able to classify ability and motivation traits. Motivation or *dynamic traits* are divided into innate drives, or *ergs*, and culturally acquired motives, called *sems*. Both are part of the *dynamic lattice*, which also includes the more fundamental concept of *attitudes*. After nearly 60 years of work, Cattell, who set out to explore the entire sphere of human personality, has succeeded in mapping a comprehensive taxonomy of personality structure and in suggesting possible means of predicting behavior.

In contrast, Eysenck has had more modest goals. Relying more on a *hypothetico-deductive approach*, he has extracted only three bipolar factors—extraversion/introversion, neuroticism/stability, and psychoticism/superego.

Extraversion is characterized by sociability and impulsiveness—*introversion*, by passivity and thoughtfulness; *neuroticism*, by anxiety and compulsivity—*stability*, by their absence; *psychoticism*, by antisocial behavior—*superego*, by empathy and cooperation.

Both Cattell and Eysenck place heavy emphasis on *biological components of personality*, and both have produced personality inventories that have generated prodigious amounts of research.

Suggested Readings

Cattell, R. B. (1974a). An autobiography. In G. Lindzey (Ed.), A *history of psychology in autobiography* (Vol. 6, pp. 61–100). Englewood Cliffs, NJ: Prentice-Hall.
This autobiography provides an interesting account of Cattell's early life in England, his settling in the United States, and his lengthy search for various components of personality.

Cattell, R. B. (1990). Advances in Cattellian personality theory. In L. A. Pervin (Ed.), *Handbook of personality: Theory and research* (pp. 101–110). New York: Guilford Press.

Cattell provides a brief look at his theory and research, including a description of the dynamic calculus and a guide for future research.

Eysenck, H. J. (1982). Personality. In H. J. Eysenck, *Personality, genetics, and behavior: Selected papers* (pp. 49–109). New York: Praeger.

Eysenck presents a selection of six papers on personality, including a brief discussion of the three superfactors—extraversion, neuroticism, and psychoticism.

Eysenck, H. J. (1990c). *Rebel with a cause: The autobiography of H. J. Eysenck*. London: W. H. Allen.

Although literary expression is not one of Eysenck's principal strengths, this autobiography is consistently informative, interesting, and witty.

Allport

Chapter

14

Allport: Psychology of the Individual

Biography of Gordon Allport
Allport's Approach to Personality Study
Personality Defined
Structure of Personality
    Personal Dispositions
    Proprium
Motivation
    Reactive and Proactive Theories
      of Motivation
    Functional Autonomy
    Conscious and Unconscious Motivation
Growth of Personality
    The Developing Person
    The Psychologically Healthy
      Personality
The Study of the Individual
    Morphogenic Science
    Letters from Jenny
Related Research
Critique of Allport
Concept of Humanity
Chapter Summary
Suggested Readings

ordon W. Allport developed a theory of personality that emphasized the *uniqueness* of *psychologically healthy individuals* who strive *proactively* toward goals that they have *consciously* set. He criticized older theories of personality for losing sight of the normal, psychologically healthy individual and for overemphasizing unconsciously determined behaviors.

As a reaction to psychoanalysis and animal-derived behaviorism, Allport's psychology of the individual often seems to adopt a position diametrically opposed to these and other "reactive" theories. However, Allport's intention was to swing the pendulum back to a middle position—a position that even he might have found more balanced than the individualistic one he sometimes appeared to advocate. His goal was to supplement rather than supplant the findings of psychoanalysis, stimulus-response theories, operant conditioning, and social psychology.

Allport was *eclectic* in his acceptance of certain observations cited by these older schools, but he objected to their tendencies to overlook the essence of the individual person. He believed that a comprehensive personality theory should be based on insights gathered from psychoanalysis, learning theory, social psychology, and trait theory as well as his own psychology of the individual. Many of his writings therefore are controversial and overstated, but that was his intention. He once wrote, "I know in my bones that my opponents are partly right" (Allport, 1968, p. 405).

BIOGRAPHY OF GORDON ALLPORT

Gordon Willard Allport was born on November 11, 1897, in Montezuma, Indiana, the fourth and youngest son of John E. Allport and Nellie Wise Allport. His father had engaged in a number of business ventures before becoming a physician at about the time of Gordon's birth. Lacking adequate outside facilities, Dr. Allport turned the household into a miniature hospital, with both patients and nurses occupying the home. In his autobiography, Allport (1967) wrote that his early life "was marked by plain Protestant piety" (p. 4). Floyd, his older brother by 7 years and who also became a famous psychologist, described their mother as a very pious woman who placed heavy emphasis on religion (F. Allport, 1974). As a former schoolteacher, she taught young Gordon the virtues of clean language and proper conduct as well as the importance of searching for ultimate religious answers.

By the time Gordon was 6 years old, the family had moved three time—finally settling in Cleveland, Ohio. Young Allport developed an early interest in philosophical and religious questions and had more facility for words than for games. He described himself as a social "isolate," who fashioned his own circle of activities. Although he graduated second in his high school class of 100, he did not consider himself an inspired scholar (Allport, 1967).

In the fall of 1915, Allport entered Harvard, following in the footsteps of his brother Floyd, who had graduated 2 years earlier and who at that time was a graduate assistant in psychology. In his autobiography, Gordon Allport (1967) wrote: "Almost overnight my world was remade. My basic moral values, to be sure, had been fashioned at home. What was new was the horizon of intellect and culture I was now invited to explore" (p. 5). His enrollment at Harvard also marked the beginning of a 50-year association with that university, which was only twice briefly interrupted. When he received his bachelor's degree in 1919 with a major in philosophy and economics, he was still uncertain about a future career. He had taken undergraduate courses in psychology and social ethics, and both disciplines had made a lasting impression on him. When he received an opportunity to teach in Turkey, he saw it as a chance to find out whether he would enjoy teaching. He spent the academic year 1919–1920 in Europe teaching English and sociology at Robert College in Istanbul.

While in Turkey, Allport was offered a fellowship for graduate study at Harvard. He also received an invitation from his brother Fayette to stay with him in Vienna, where Fayette was working for the U.S. trade commission. In Vienna, Allport had an interesting meeting with Sigmund Freud that greatly influenced his later ideas on personality. With a certain audacity, the 22-year-old Allport wrote to Freud announcing that he was in Vienna and offered the father of psychoanalysis an opportunity to meet with him. The encounter proved to be a fortuitous life-altering event for Allport. Not knowing what to talk about, the young visitor told Freud about seeing a small boy on the tram car going to Freud's home. The boy, about 4 years old, had displayed an obvious dirt phobia, complaining constantly to his well-starched mother about the filthy conditions on the car. Allport claimed that he chose this particular incident to get Freud's reaction to a dirt phobia in a child so young, but he was quite flabbergasted when Freud "fixed his kindly therapeutic eyes on [him] and said, "And was that little boy you?" (Allport, 1967, p. 8). Allport said he felt a bit guilty and quickly changed the subject.

Allport told this story many times, seldom changing many words, and never revealing the rest of his lone encounter with Freud. However, Alan Elms (1994) has uncovered Allport's written description of what happened next. After realizing that Freud was expecting a professional consultation, Allport then talked about his dislike of cooked raisins.

> I told him I thought it due to the fact that at the age of three, a nurse had told me they were "bugs." Freud asked, "When you recalled this episode, did your dislike vanish?" I said, "No." He replied, "Then you are not at the bottom of it." (Elms, 1994, p. 77)

After that discussion, Allport "spoke of a common sexual problem of youthful males of my age" (Elms, 1994, p. 77). And finally, Allport asked Freud to recommend a psychoanalyst in America. Freud suggested A. A. Brill (an early disciple and translator of Freud). Allport wrote that he "then departed with a vivid feeling of respect and liking for Freud, even though our short conversation had started at cross purposes" (Elms, 1994, p. 77).

Back at Harvard, Allport quickly finished his work, receiving a Ph.D. in psychology in 1922 at age 24. Harvard offered him a traveling fellowship, so he spent the following 2 years in Europe studying under the great German psychologists Max Wertheimer, Wolfgang Kohler, William Stern, Heinz Werner, and others in Berlin and Hamburg. The latter half of his European experience was spent in Cambridge, England, where he had a chance to absorb what he had learned in Germany.

In 1924, he returned again to Harvard to teach, among other classes, a new course in the psychology of personality. After 2 years, he took a position at Dartmouth College, but 4 years later he returned to Harvard where he remained until his death. On October 9, 1967, Allport, a heavy smoker, died of lung cancer.

In 1925, Allport married Ada Lufkin Gould, whom he had met when both were graduate students in psychology and who later became a clinical psychologist. Their son, Robert, became a pediatrician, thus sandwiching Allport between two generations of physicians, a fact that seemed to have pleased him in no small measure (Allport, 1967). Allport's awards and honors were many. In 1939, he was elected president of the American Psychological Association (APA). In 1963, he received the Gold Medal Award of the APA; in 1964, he was awarded the Distinguished Scientific Contribution Award of the APA; and in 1966, he was honored as the first Richard Clarke Cabot Professor of Social Ethics at Harvard.

ALLPORT'S APPROACH TO PERSONALITY STUDY

Allport's approach to the study of personality is characterized by several key terms: (1) *conscious motivation*, (2) *psychologically healthy individuals*, (3) *proactive behavior*, (4) *uniqueness of each individual*, and (5) *an eclectic attitude* toward other theories.

Allport traced his emphasis on *conscious motivation* to his single encounter with Freud, who surprised the 22-year-old Allport when he asked: "And was that little boy you?" Frued's question was to have great meaning for Allport. Although not an anti-Freudian, he later evolved a personality theory about the importance of conscious motivation that was almost diametrically opposed to psychoanalysis. Whereas Freud assumed an underlying unconscious meaning to such stories, Allport was inclined to accept self-reports at face value. Allport (1967) reported that "this experience taught me that depth psychology, for all its merits, may plunge too deep, and that psychologists would do well to give full recognition to manifest motives before probing the unconscious" (p. 8). Most people, Allport believed, are motivated by present drives rather than by past events and are aware of what they are doing and have some understanding of why they are doing it.

Allport, perhaps, was the first personality theorist to study the *psychologically healthy individual*. Long before Abraham Maslow made the concept of self-actualization popular, Gordon Allport (1937) hypothesized in depth about the attributes of the mature personality. Psychologically healthy people have the potential to learn new patterns of behavior and to grow during any period of their lives. Later in this chapter, we discuss in some detail Allport's conception of the healthy personality.

Psychologically mature personalities are characterized by **proactive behavior,** that is, they not only *react* to external stimuli, but they are capable of consciously acting on their environment in new and innovative ways and causing their environment to react to them. Proactive behavior is not merely directed at reducing tensions but also at establishing new ones. Again, we discuss proactive behavior in more detail later.

A fourth key term in Allport's approach to the study of personality is *uniqueness of the individual*. Indeed, Allport himself is rather unique among personality theorists in his insistence that each person is, in some manner, unlike any other individual. Any attempts to describe people in terms of general traits robs them of their unique individuality. For this reason, Allport objected to the trait and factor theories of Cattell and Eysenck (see Chapter 13) that tended to reduce individual behaviors to common traits. He would insist, for example, that one person's miserliness is different from any other person's miserliness and the manner in which one person's miserliness interacts with his or her introversion is duplicated by no other individual.

Consistent with Allport's emphasis on each person's uniqueness was his willingness to study in depth a single individual. He called the study of the individual **morphogenic science** and contrasted it with the **nomothetic** methods used by most other psychologists. Morphogenic methods are those that gather data on a single individual, whereas nomothetic methods gather data on groups of people. Morphogenic methods can reveal a great deal of information about one person, which then may generalize to other individuals; nomothetic methods reveal information about a group of people, which then may have some significance for a particular individual. We discuss morphogenic science more fully in a later section.

Finally, Allport advocated an **eclectic** approach to theory building. He argued against particularism, or theories that emphasize a single approach, and he went on to warn theorists not to "forget what you have decided to neglect" (Allport, 1968, p. 23). In other words, no theory is completely comprehensive, and one should always realize that much of human nature is not included in any single theory. Allport accepted the contributions of Freud, Cattell, Skinner, and others, but he believed that these theorists were unable to explain the growing, changing personality. The growth theories of Maslow, Rogers, and Allport himself add to the earlier foundation formed by psychoanalysis and learning theory, but none is complete by itself. Allport (1968), therefore, favored eclecticism over particularism because it is less restrictive and offers more hope in understanding the complete and unique person. Broader theories, even when they do not generate specific testable hypotheses, are preferable to narrow ones, because they organize known facts from all kinds of research as well as from intuition.

PERSONALITY DEFINED

Few psychologists have been as painstaking and exhaustive as Allport in defining terms. His pursuit of a definition of personality is a classic. He traced the etymology of the word *persona* back to early Greek roots, including the Old Latin and Etruscan meanings. As we saw in Chapter 1, the word personality probably comes from *persona*, which refers to the theatrical mask used in ancient Greek drama by Roman actors during the first and second centuries before Christ. After tracing the history of the term, Allport spelled out 49 definitions of personality as used in theology, philosophy, law, sociology, and psychology. He then offered a 50th definition, which in 1937 was *"the dynamic organization within the individual of those psychophysical systems that determine his unique adjustments to his environment"* (Allport, 1937, p. 48).

In 1961, he had changed the last phrase to read *"that determine his characteristic behavior and thought"* (Allport, 1961, p. 28). The change was significant and reflected Allport's penchant for accuracy. By 1961, he realized that the phrase "adjustments to his environment" could imply that people merely adapt to their environment. In his later definition, Allport conveyed the idea that behavior is *expressive* as well as adaptive. People not only adjust to their environment, but also reflect on it and interact with it in such a way as to cause their environment to adjust to them.

Allport chose each phrase of his definition carefully so that each word conveys precisely what he wanted to say. The term *dynamic organization* implies an integration or interrelatedness of the various aspects of personality. Personality is organized and patterned. However, the organization is always subject to change, hence the qualifier "dynamic." Personality is not a static organization; it is constantly growing or changing.

The term *psychophysical* emphasizes the importance of both the psychological and the physical aspects of personality.

Another word in the definition that implies action is *determine*, which suggests that "personality is something and does something" (Allport, 1961, p. 29). In other words, personality is not merely the mask we wear; nor is it simply behavior. It refers to the person behind the facade, the organism behind the action.

By *characteristic*, Allport wished to imply individual or unique. The word "character" originally meant a marking or engraving, terms that give flavor to what Allport meant by "characteristic." All persons stamp their unique mark or engraving on their personality, and their characteristic behavior and thought set them apart from all other people. Characteristics are marked with a unique engraving, a stamp or marking, that no one else can duplicate.

The words *behavior and thought* simply refer to anything the person does. They are omnibus terms meant to include internal behaviors (thoughts) as well as external behaviors such as words and actions.

Allport's comprehensive definition of personality suggests that human beings are both product and process; people have some organized structure while, at the same time, they possess the capability of change. Pattern coexists with growth, order with diversification.

In summary, personality is everything, both physical and psychological; it includes both overt behaviors and covert thoughts; it not only *is* something, but it *does* something. Personality is both substance and change; both product and process; both structure and growth.

STRUCTURE OF PERSONALITY

The structure of personality refers to its basic units or building blocks. To Freud, the basic units were instincts; to Cattell and Eysenck, they are traits. To Allport, the most important structures are those that permit the description of the person in terms of individual characteristics. Thus, the two basic units of personality are *personal dispositions* and the *proprium*.

PERSONAL DISPOSITIONS

In a conversation with Richard Evans (1976), Allport rejected the label of trait psychologist, because he believed that the term *trait* implies a general characteristic held in common by several people. Allport was careful to distinguish between *common traits* and individual traits, which he called *personal dispositions*. **Common traits** are those aspects of human personality that lend themselves to interindividual comparisons. They provide the means by which the characteristics of people within a given culture can be compared. Whereas common traits are important for studies that make comparisons among people, personal dispositions are of even greater importance because they permit researchers to study a single individual.

Allport used the term "personal dispositions" rather than individual traits because it is more descriptive and less likely to be confused with common traits. He defined a **personal disposition** as "a generalized neuropsychic structure (peculiar to the individual), with the capacity to render many stimuli functionally equivalent, and to initiate and guide consistent (equivalent) forms of adaptive and stylistic behavior" (Allport, 1961, p. 373). The most important distinction between a personal disposition and a common trait is indicated by the parenthetical phrase "peculiar to the individual." Personal dispositions are individual; common traits are shared by several people.

To identify personal dispositions, Allport and Odbert (1936) counted approximately 18,000 personally descriptive words in the 1925 edition of *Webster's New International Dictionary*, about a fourth of which described personality characteristics. Some of these terms, usually referred to as *traits*, describe relatively stable characteristics such as "sociable" or "introverted"; others, usually referred to as *states*, describe temporary characteristics such as "happy" or "angry"; others described evaluative characteristics such as "unpleasant" or "wonderful"; and still others referred to physical characteristics such as "tall" or "obese".

How many personal dispositions does one individual have? This question cannot be answered without reference to the degree of dominance that each personal disposition has in the individual's life. If we count those personal dispositions that are central to a person, each person probably has 10 or fewer. However, if all tendencies are included, then each person may have hundreds of personal dispositions.

Levels of Personal Dispositions

Allport placed personal dispositions on a continuum from those that are most central to those that are of only peripheral importance to a person.

Cardinal Dispositions

Some people possess an eminent characteristic or ruling passion so outstanding that it dominates their lives. Allport (1961) called these PDs **cardinal dispositions.** They are so obvious that they cannot be hidden; nearly every action in a person's life revolves around this one cardinal disposition. Most people do not have a cardinal disposition, but those few people who do are often known by that single characteristic.

Allport identified several historical people and fictional characters who possessed a disposition so outstanding that they have given our language a new word. Some examples of these cardinal dispositions include quixotic, chauvinistic, narcissistic, sadistic, a Don Juan, and so forth. Because personal dispositions are individual and not shared with any other person, only Don Quixote was truly quixotic; only Narcissus was completely narcissistic; only the Marquis de Sade possessed the cardinal disposition of sadism. When these names are used to describe characteristics in others, they become common traits.

Central Dispositions

Few people have cardinal dispositions, but everyone has several **central dispositions,** which include the 5 to 10 most outstanding characteristics around which a person's life focuses. Allport (1961) described central dispositions as those that would be listed in an accurate letter of recommendation written by someone who knew the person quite well. Later, we will look at a series of letters written to Gordon and Ada Allport by a woman they called Jenny. The contents of these letters constitute a rich source of information about their writer. We will also see that two separate analysis of these letters revealed that Jenny could be described by about eight central dispositions, that is, characteristics sufficiently strong to be detected by each of these two separate procedures. Similarly, most of us, Allport believed, have 5 to 10 central dispositions that our friends and close acquaintances would agree are descriptive of our personality.

Secondary Dispositions

Less conspicuous but far greater in number than central dispositions are the **secondary dispositions.** Everyone has many secondary dispositions, which are not central to the personality yet which occur with some regularity and are responsible for much of one's specific behaviors.

The three levels of personal dispositions are, of course, arbitrary points on a continuous scale from most appropriate to least appropriate. Cardinal dispositions, which are exceedingly prominent in a person, shade into central dispositions, which are less dominating, but which nevertheless mark the person as unique. Central dispositions, which guide much of a person's adaptive and stylistic behavior, blend into secondary dispositions, which are less descriptive of that individual. We cannot say, however, that one person's secondary dispositions are less intense than another person's central dispositions. Interperson comparisons are inappropriate to personal dispositions, and any attempt to make such comparison transforms the personal dispositions into common traits (Allport, 1961).

Motivational and Stylistic Dispositions

All personal dispositions are dynamic in the sense that they have motivational power. Nevertheless, some are much more strongly felt than others, and Allport called these intensely experienced dispositions *motivational dispositions*. These strongly felt dispositions receive their motivation from basic needs and drives. Allport referred to personal dispositions that are less intensely experienced as *stylistic dispositions*, even though these dispositions possess some motivational power. Stylistic dispositions *guide* action, whereas motivational dispositions *initiate* action. An example of a stylistic disposition might be impeccable personal appearance. People are motivated to dress because of a basic need to stay warm, but the *manner* in which they attire themselves is determined by their stylistic personal dispositions (Allport, 1961).

No sharp line exists between motivational and stylistic personal dispositions, because both have some motivational power. Although some dispositions are clearly stylistic, others are obviously based on a strongly felt need and are thus motivational. Politeness, for example, is a stylistic disposition, whereas eating is more motivational. How people eat (their style) depends at least partially on how hungry they are, but it also depends on the strength of their stylistic dispositions. A usually polite but hungry person may forego manners while eating alone, but if the politeness disposition is strong enough and if others are present, then that person may eat with etiquette and courtesy despite being famished.

Whether motivational or stylistic, some personal dispositions are close to the core of personality, whereas others are more on the periphery. Those that are at the center of personality are experienced by the person as being an important part of self. They are the ones an individual refers to in such terms as, "That is me," or "This is mine." All characteristics that are "peculiarly mine" belong to the *proprium* (Allport, 1955).

PROPRIUM

Allport used the term **proprium** to refer to those behaviors and characteristics that we regard as warm, central, and important in our lives. The proprium is not the whole personality, because many characteristics and behaviors of a person are not warm and central; rather, they exist on the periphery of personality. These nonpropriate behaviors include (1) basic drives and needs that are ordinarily met and satisfied without much trouble; (2) tribal customs such as saying "hello" to people, wearing clothes, and driving on the right side of the road; and (3) habitual behaviors, such as smoking and brushing one's teeth, that are performed automatically and that are not crucial to the person's sense of self.

As the warm center of personality, the proprium includes those aspects of a person that are regarded as important to a sense of self-identity and self-enhancement (Allport, 1955). The proprium includes a person's values as well as that part of the conscience that is personal and consistent with one's adult beliefs. A generalized conscience (one shared by most people within a given culture) may be only peripheral to a person's sense of personhood and thus outside that person's proprium.

MOTIVATION

Allport (1961) contended that theories of motivation must consider the differences between peripheral motives and propriate strivings. Peripheral motives are those that *reduce a need*, whereas propriate strivings seek to *maintain tension and disequilibrium*. Adult behavior is both reactive and proactive, and an adequate theory of motivation must be able to explain both.

REACTIVE AND PROACTIVE THEORIES OF MOTIVATION

Allport believed that a useful theory of personality rests on the assumption that people not only react to their environment but also shape their environment and cause it to react to them. Personality is a growing system, allowing new elements constantly to enter into and change the person.

Many older theories of personality, Allport (1960) believed, do not allow for possibilities of growth. Psychoanalysis and the various learning theories are basically homeostatic, or **reactive,** theories because they treat human personalities as reactive; that is, they see people being motivated primarily by needs to reduce tension and to return to a state of equilibrium.

An adequate theory of personality, Allport contended, must allow for *proactive behavior*. It must view people as consciously acting on their environment in a manner that permits growth toward psychological health. It must also be able to incorporate the explanation of reactive theories while at the same time making allowances for proactive theories that stress change and growth. In other words, Allport argued for a psychology that, on one hand, studies behavioral patterns and general laws (the subject matter of traditional psychology) and, on the other, growth and individuality.

Allport claimed that theories of unchanging motives are incomplete because they are limited to an explanation of reactive behavior. The mature person, however, is not motivated merely to seek pleasure and reduce pain but to acquire new systems of motivation that are functionally independent from their original motives.

FUNCTIONAL AUTONOMY

The concept of **functional autonomy** represents Allport's most distinctive and, at the same time, most controversial postulate. It is Allport's (1961) explanation for the myriad human motives that seemingly are not accounted for by hedonistic or drive-reduction principles. Functional autonomy represents a theory of changing rather than unchanging motives and is the capstone of Allport's ideas on motivation.

In general, the concept of functional autonomy holds that some, but not all, human motives are functionally independent from the original motive responsible for the behavior. If a motive is functionally autonomous, it is the explanation for behavior, and we need not look beyond it for hidden or primary causes. In other words, if hoarding money is a functionally autonomous motive, then the miser's behavior is *not* traceable to childhood experiences with toilet training or with rewards and punishments. Rather, the miser simply *likes* money, and this is the only explanation necessary. This idea that much of our behavior is based on present interests and on conscious preferences is in harmony with the commonsense belief of many people who hold that they do things simply because they like to do them.

Functional autonomy is a reaction to what Allport called theories of unchanging motives, namely, Freud's pleasure principle and the drive-reduction hypothesis of stimulus-response psychology. Allport held that both theories are concerned with *historical facts* rather than *functional facts*. He believed that adult motives are built primarily on conscious, self-sustaining, contemporary systems. Functional autonomy represents his attempt to explain these conscious, self-sustaining contemporary motivations.

Admitting that some motivations are unconscious and others are the result of drive reduction, Allport contended that, because some behavior is functionally autonomous, theories of unchanging motives are inadequate. He listed four requirements of an adequate theory of motivation. Functional autonomy, of course, meets each criterion.

1. An adequate theory of motivation *"will acknowledge the contemporaneity of motives."* In other words, "Whatever moves us must move now" (Allport, 1961, p. 220). The past per se is unimportant. The history of an individual is significant only when it has a present effect on motivation.

2. *"It will be a pluralistic theory—allowing for motives of many types"* (Allport, 1961, p. 221). On this point, Allport was critical of Freud and his two-instinct theory, Adler and the single striving for success, and all theories that emphasize self-actualization as the ultimate motive. Allport was emphatically opposed to reducing all human motivation to one master drive. He contended that adults' motives are basically different from those of children and that the motivations of neurotic individuals are not the same as those of normal people. In addition, some motivations are conscious, others unconscious; some are transient, others recurring; some are peripheral, others propriate; and some are tension reducing, others tension maintaining. Motives that appear to be different really are different, not only in form but also in substance.

3. *"It will ascribe dynamic force to cognitive processes—e.g., to planning and intention"* (Allport, 1961, p. 222). Allport argued that most people are busy living their lives into the future, but that many psychological theories are "busy tracing these lives backward into the past. And while it seems to each of us that we are spontaneously *active*, many psychologists are telling us that we are only *reactive*" (p. 206). Although intention is involved in all motivation, this third requirement refers more generally to long-range intention. A young woman declines an offer to see a movie because she *prefers* to study anatomy. This preference is consistent with her *purpose* of making good grades at college and relates to her *plans* of being admitted to medical school, which is necessary in order for her to fulfill her *intention* of being a doctor. The lives of healthy adults are future-oriented, involving preferences, purposes, plans, and intentions. These, of course, are not always completely rational processes, as when we allow our anger to dominate our plans and intentions.

4. An adequate theory of motivation is one that *"will allow for the concrete uniqueness of motives"* (Allport, 1961, p. 225). A concrete unique motive is different from an abstract generalized one, the latter being based on a preexistent theory rather than the actual motivation of a real person. An example of a concrete unique motive would be Derrick, who is interested in improving his bowling game. His motive is concrete, and his manner of seeking improvement is unique to him. Some theories of motivation may ascribe Derrick's behavior to an aggressive need, others to an inhibited

sexual drive, and still others to a secondary drive learned on the basis of a primary drive. Allport would simply say that Derrick wants to improve his bowling game because he wants to improve his bowling game. This is Derrick's unique, concrete, and functionally autonomous motive.

In summary, a functionally autonomous motive is contemporary, self-sustaining, growing out of an earlier motive but functionally independent of it. Allport (1961) defined functional autonomy as *"any acquired system of motivation in which the tensions involved are not of the same kind as the antecedent tensions from which the acquired system developed"* (p. 229). In other words, what begins as one motive may grow into a new one that is historically continuous with the original but functionally autonomous from it. For example, a person may originally plant a garden to satisfy a hunger drive but eventually become interested in gardening for its own sake.

Allport (1961) recognized two levels of functional autonomy— perseverative and propriate.

Perseverative Functional Autonomy

The more elementary of the two levels of functional autonomy is **perseverative functional autonomy.** Allport borrowed this term from the word "perseveration," which is the tendency of an impression to leave an influence on subsequent experience. Perseverative functional autonomy is found in animals as well as humans and is based on simple neurological principles. An example of perseverative functional autonomy would be a rat that has learned to run a maze in order to be fed but then continues to run the maze even after it has become satiated. Why does it continue to run? Allport would say that the rat runs the maze just for the fun of it.

Allport (1961) listed other examples of perseverative functional autonomy that involve human rather than animal motivation. The first is an addiction to alcohol, tobacco, or other drugs when there is no physiological hunger for them. Alcoholics continue to drink although their current motivation is functionally independent from their original motive.

Another example concerns uncompleted tasks. A problem once started but then interrupted will perseverate, creating a new tension to finish the task. This new tension is different from the initial motivation. For example, college students are offered 10 cents for every piece of a 500-piece jigsaw puzzle they successfully put together. Assume that these students do not have a preexisting interest in solving jigsaw puzzles and that their original motivation is solely for the money. Also assume that their monetary reward is limited to $45.00, so that after they have completed 450 pieces, they have maximized their pay. Will these students finish the remaining 50 pieces in the absence of monetary reward? If they do, then a new tension has been created, and their motive to complete the task is functionally autonomous from the original motive of getting paid.

Propriate Functional Autonomy

The master system of motivation that confers unity on personality is **propriate functional autonomy,** which refers to those self-sustaining motives that are related to the proprium. Jigsaw puzzles and alcohol are seldom regarded as "peculiarly mine." They are not part of the proprium, but exist only on the periphery of personality. On the other hand, occupations, hobbies, and interests are closer to the core of personality, and

A person might begin running to lose weight but continue because running is enjoyable. The motive for continuing to run is then functionally autonomous from the motive for beginning to run.

many of our motivations concerning them become functionally autonomous. For example, a woman may originally take a job because she needs money. At first, the work is uninteresting, perhaps even distasteful. As the years pass, however, she develops a consuming passion for the job itself, spending some vacation time at work and, perhaps, even developing a hobby that is closely related to her occupation.

Criterion for Functional Autonomy

In general, *a present motive is functionally autonomous to the extent that it seeks new goals*, meaning that the behavior will continue even as the motivation for it changes. For example, children first learning to walk are perhaps motivated by some maturational drive, but later they may walk to increase mobility or to build self-confidence. Similarly, scientists may be dedicated to searching for answers to difficult problems. Their satisfaction comes more from the search than from the solution, and their method of searching may vary as the problem changes. As one problem is solved, scientists search for another area of inquiry even though the new field may be somewhat different from the previous one. New tensions are established that are separate and autonomous from the antecedent ones. Each new finding leads to higher levels of aspiration and to the setting of new goals.

Limitations of Functional Autonomy

Functional autonomy is not an explanation for all human motivation. Allport (1961) listed several processes that are not functionally autonomous. These include (1) biological drives, such as eating, breathing, and sleeping; (2) motives directly linked to the reduction of basic drives; (3) reflex actions such as an eye blink; (4) constitutional equipment, namely physique, intelligence, and temperament; (5) habits in the process of being formed; (6) patterns of behavior that require primary reinforcement; (7) nonproductive behaviors, such as compulsions, fixations, and regressions; and (8) sublimations that can be tied to childhood sexual desires.

Not all pathological symptoms, however, lie beyond the range of functional autonomy. Some serve a contemporary lifestyle and are presently independent of an earlier trauma that may have instigated the pathology. Many symptoms, however, are traceable to childhood experiences and, therefore, are not functionally autonomous. Compulsions may seem similar to perseverative functional autonomy, but they are not self-sustaining and can be eliminated through behavior modification or some other method of therapy. In contrast, functionally autonomous symptoms cannot be extinguished through psychotherapy and do not change as the self-concept changes.

CONSCIOUS AND UNCONSCIOUS MOTIVATION

More than any other personality theorist, Allport emphasized the importance of conscious motivation; healthy adults are generally aware of what they are doing and their reasons for doing it. His emphasis on conscious motivation goes back to his meeting in Vienna with Freud and his emotional reaction to Freud's question: "And was that little boy you?" Freud's response carried the implication that his 22-year-old visitor was unconsciously talking about his own fetish for cleanliness in revealing the story of the clean little boy on the tram car. Allport (1967) insisted that his motivation was quite conscious—he simply wanted to know Freud's ideas about dirt phobia in a child so young.

However, Allport (1961) did not ignore the existence or even the importance of unconscious processes. He recognized the fact that some motivation is driven by hidden impulses and sublimated drives. He believed, for example, that most symptomatic behaviors are automatic repetitions, usually self-defeating, and motivated by unconscious tendencies. They often originate in childhood and retain a childish flavor into adult years.

For the healthy individual, however, consciousness is in control of behavior. Allport insisted that normal behavior is functionally autonomous and is motivated by conscious processes that are not only separate from unconscious motivation, but have their own ignition and spark. In summary, psychologically mature adults are motivated mostly by conscious thoughts, with unconscious processes playing only a minor role in their behavior.

GROWTH OF PERSONALITY

Allport's theory of personality rests on a dual system of motivation. People are driven both by the need *to adjust* to their environment *and* by the tendency *to grow* or to become more and more self-actualized. Adjustment needs and growth needs exist side by side within the same person, and any adequate theory of personality, Allport said, must take into consideration the fact that people are both reactive and proactive.

THE DEVELOPING PERSON

Allport (1961) believed that the sense of self evolves from birth to adulthood in seven overlapping and cumulative stages. At birth, Allport contended, infants do not have a personality because they possess no characteristic modes of behavior and thought. Thus they have only potential personality, one based on genetic endowment. Unlike most psychologists, Allport believed that the first year of life is the *least* important one.

An infant's developing selfhood includes a growing sense of "me" and "not me."

The first 3 or 4 years of life comprise the three earliest aspects of selfhood—the bodily sense, self-identity, and ego-esteem. The first aspect of selfhood to evolve is the *bodily sense* (Allport, 1961). Throughout our lives, our bodies provide us with a reference for self-awareness. If I scrape my arm, I know that the blood and the pain are "peculiarly mine." They belong to no other person and give me a bodily sense of self.

A second early aspect of the developing proprium is the sense of continuing *self-identity* (Allport, 1961). This feeling of who I am includes my thoughts and actions as well as my memory of them and the acceptance of them as mine. At first, the sense of self-identity is weak and children may accept imaginary characteristics as their own. Their self-identity is closely bound to their social surroundings, especially the family. "This is my house" or "That tricycle is mine." The words "I," "me," and "mine" dominate the vocabulary of young children.

The third aspect of early self is ego-enhancement, or *self-esteem* (Allport, 1961). Self-esteem, which can be both positive and negative, is that property of the proprium that involves pride, selfishness, narcissism, and other behaviors and sentiments related to exaltation of the ego.

From 4 to 6 years of age, children are extremely egocentric. While their bodily sense, self-identity, and self-esteem continue to grow during this period, a fourth and fifth stage of the proprium begin to emerge. The fourth is the *extension of self* and the fifth is the *self-image*. Children broaden their sense of self to include possessions (clothes, toys, and pets) as well as mother, father, sisters, and brothers. Self-image refers to one's view of present abilities, status, and roles and also to one's aspirations or future goals. It consists largely of the child's image of self as a "good" or "bad" person—in Freudian terms, one's ego-ideal and conscience (Allport, 1961).

The years from age 6 to 12 are important because school extends a child's life beyond the family. During this period of reality testing, challenges by classmates and teachers modify the child's self-identity, self-esteem, and self-image. The sixth stage, the *rational-self*, which develops during these early school years, is capable of rationalization and denials, but it is also capable of reasoning correctly and finding solutions to the problems of living. The rational-self is responsible for formal and reflective thought and reconciling inner needs with demands of the external world (Allport, 1961).

Adolescence brings about a seventh and final aspect of the self as object, namely **propriate strivings.** At this level, a person emerges as a truly unique individual with a clearly defined sense of personhood and a well-developed proprium, which unifies the other six aspects of self. Propriate strivings also lead to some consistency in actions and thoughts and allow the person to set goals that maintain tension rather than merely reduce it. (Allport, 1961).

Propriate strivings are those that are close to the person; that is, they are experienced as "peculiarly mine." They rely on memory of past experiences, but they also include thoughts of the future in the form of realistic planning and intention. The problems of selecting a mate and choosing a career can be successfully pursued only through propriate strivings, although some people stumble into choosing a spouse or a job without any sense of purpose. When people drift into decisions, their striving is called "opportunistic," because it is not part of the proprium and exists only on the periphery of personality (Allport, 1961). In a real sense, the goals of propriate strivings are not attainable because people constantly seek to maintain tension and to strive for goals they may never reach (Allport, 1955).

In addition to these seven stages, Allport (1961) identified an eighth aspect of self called the *self as knower*, or the subjective self. However, only the first seven aspects of self belong to the proprium. The self as knower is the "I" that is aware of the objective "me." When I think of my self, I can think only of my objective self; that is, my physical self, my reputation, my self-image, and so on. But who is the "I" doing the thinking? This is also my self, but it is the self as knower and cannot be part of my proprium.

Personality and proprium are not synonymous, because personality includes many habits, emotions, traits, tribal customs, opportunistic strivings, adjustment patterns, and chance factors that are not warm and central to the person. Some skills such as typing or driving a car may be propriate in the beginning, but later they lose their central importance and become opportunistic. Others, such as language, are not ordinarily propriate, but when denied to a person or when accomplished only through great difficulty, they can become part of the proprium.

THE PSYCHOLOGICALLY HEALTHY PERSONALITY

Allport's interest in the psychologically healthy person predated Maslow's (see Chapter 17) study of self-actualizing people and probably goes back to 1922 when he finished his Ph.D. Not having any particular skills in mathematics, biology, medicine, or laboratory manipulations, Allport (1967) was forced to "find [his] own way in the humanistic pastures of psychology" (p. 8). Such pastures led to a study of the psychologically mature personality.

Allport saw a dichotomy between the psychologically healthy or mature personality and the one who is unhealthy or neurotic. Because healthy individuals are motivated by conscious processes, they are more flexible and autonomous than unhealthy people, who remain dominated by unconscious motives that spring from childhood experiences. Mature people are also characterized by activity, security, and freedom of choice. Ordinarily, they have experienced a relatively trauma-free childhood, even though their later years may be tempered by conflict and suffering. Psychologically healthy individuals are not without foibles and idiosyncrasies. In fact, individuality and uniqueness would be expected. Age is not a requisite for maturity, although healthy persons seem to become more mature as they get older.

Sometimes people are motivated to seek tension, not merely reduce it.

What are the requirements for psychological health? Allport (1961) identified six criteria for the mature personality. The number is somewhat arbitrary, yet the list is descriptive of the healthy personality as seen by Allport.

The first criterion of psychological health is an *extension of the sense of self*. Mature people continually seek to identify with and participate in events outside themselves. They are not self-centered but are able to become involved in problems and activities that are not centered on themselves. They develop a nonegotistical interest in work, play, and recreation. Social interest, family, and spiritual life are important to them. Eventually, these outside activities become part of the proprium. Allport (1961) summed up this first criterion by saying: "Everyone has self-love, but only self-extension is the earmark of maturity" (p. 285).

Second, mature personalities are characterized by a *"warm relating of self to others"* (Allport, 1961, p. 285). They have the capacity to love others in an intimate and compassionate manner. Warm relating, of course, is dependent on the ability to extend the sense of self. Only by looking beyond themselves can mature people love others nonpossessively and unselfishly. Psychologically healthy individuals treat other people with respect, and they realize that the needs, desires, and hopes of others are not completely foreign to their own. In addition, they have a healthy sexual attitude and do not exploit others for personal gratification.

A third criterion is *emotional security* or *self-acceptance*. Mature individuals accept themselves for what they are, and they possess what Allport (1961) called emotional poise. These psychologically healthy people are not overly upset when things do not go as planned or when they are simply "having a bad day." They do not dwell on minor irritations, and they recognize that frustrations and inconveniences are a part of living.

Psychologically healthy people also possess a *realistic perception* of their environment. They do not live in a fantasy world or bend reality to fit their own wishes. They are problem-oriented rather than self-centered; they are in touch with the world as most others see it and are capable of supporting themselves economically (Allport, 1961).

A fifth criterion is *insight and humor*. Mature people know themselves and, therefore, have no need to attribute their own sins and weaknesses to others. They also have a nonhostile sense of humor, which gives them the capacity to laugh at themselves rather than relying on sexual or aggressive themes to elicit laughter from others. Allport (1961) believed that insight and humor are closely related and may be aspects of the same thing, namely self-objectification. Healthy individuals see themselves objectively. They are able to perceive the incongruities and absurdities in life and have no need to pretend or to put on airs.

The final criterion of maturity is *a unifying philosophy of life*. Healthy people have a clear view of the purpose of life. Without this, their insight would be empty and barren, and their humor would be trivial and cynical. The unifying philosophy of life may or may not be religious, but Allport (1954, 1963), on a personal level, seemed to have felt that a mature religious orientation is a crucial ingredient in lives of most mature individuals. Although many churchgoing people have an immature religious philosophy and narrow racial and ethnic prejudices, a deeply held religious orientation is free of these prejudices and is often a mark of psychological maturity. Allport was never far from a consideration of religion and published six lectures on the subject under the title *The Individual and His Religion* (Allport, 1950). The person with a mature religious attitude and a unifying philosophy of life has a well-developed conscience and, quite likely, a strong desire to serve others.

THE STUDY OF THE INDIVIDUAL

Because psychology has historically dealt with general laws and characteristics that people have in common, Allport repeatedly advocated the development and use of research methods that study the individual. To balance the predominant normative or group approach, he suggested that psychologists employ methods that study the motivational and stylistic behaviors of the single case.

MORPHOGENIC SCIENCE

Early in his writings, Allport distinguished between two scientific approaches: the *nomothetic*, which seeks general laws; and the **idiographic,** which refers to that which is peculiar to the single case. Because the term "idiographic" was so often misused, misunderstood, and misspelled (being confused with "ideographic," or the representation of ideas by graphic symbols), Allport (1968) abandoned the term in his later writings and spoke of *morphogenic procedures*. Both idiographic and morphogenic pertain to the individual, but idiographic does not suggest structure or pattern. In contrast, morphogenic refers to patterned properties of the whole organism and allows for intraperson comparisons. The pattern or structure of one's personal dispositions are important. For example, Tyrone may be intelligent, introverted, and strongly motivated by achievement needs, but the unique manner in which his intelligence is related to his introversion and his needs for achievement form a structured pattern. These individual patterns are the subject matter of morphogenic science.

What are the methods of morphogenic psychology? Allport (1962) listed many; some completely morphogenic, some partly so. Examples of wholly morphogenic, first-person methods are verbatim recordings, including interviews, dreams, and confessions; diaries and letters; personalized questionnaires and self-anchoring scales; and expressive and projective documents, including literary works, art forms, automatic writings, doodles, handshakes, voice patterns, body gestures, handwriting, gait, and autobiographies.

When Allport met Hans Eysenck, the famous British factor analyst and believer in nomothetic science (see Chapter 13), he told Eysenck that one day he (Eysenck) would write his autobiography. Eventually, Eysenck (1990c) did indeed publish an autobiography in which he admitted that Allport was right and that morphogenic methods such as one's description of one's own life and work can have validity.

Semimorphogenic approaches include self-rating scales, such as the adjective checklist; standardized tests using **ipsative scores** in which people are compared to themselves rather than a norm group; the Allport-Vernon-Lindzey *Study of Values* (1960); and the Q sort technique of Stephenson (1953), which we discuss in Chapter 16.

Consistent with common sense, but contrary to many psychologists, Allport was willing to accept at face value the self-disclosure statements of most participants in a study. A psychologist who wishes to learn the personal dynamics of people need simply ask them what they think of themselves. Answers to direct questions should be accepted as valid unless the person is a young child, psychotic, or extremely defensive. Allport (1962) said that, "Too often we fail to consult the richest of all sources of data, namely, the subject's own self-knowledge" (p. 413).

LETTERS FROM JENNY

Allport's morphogenetic approach to the study of lives is best illustrated in his famous *Letters from Jenny*. The letters from Jenny Gove Masterson (a fictitious name) reveal the story of an older woman and her intense love/hate feelings toward her son, Ross. Between March 1926 (when she was 58) and October 1937 (when she died), Jenny wrote a series of 301 letters to Ross's former college roommate Glenn and his wife Isabel. (In 1993, David Winter presented compelling evidence that "Glenn" and "Isabel" were in reality Gordon and Ada Allport and that Allport's early possession of these letters may have suggested to him the value of morphogenetic material.) Allport originally published parts of these letters anonymously in 1946 (Anonymous, 1946) and then later published them in more detail (Allport, 1965).

Jenny was the oldest in a family of seven children that included five sisters and a brother. When she was 18, her father died and Jenny was forced to quit school and go to work to help support her family. After her brothers and sisters became self-supporting, Jenny, who had always been considered rebellious, married a divorced man. This further alienated her from her conservatively religious family.

After only 2 years of marriage, her husband died, and her son, Ross, was born a month later. The next 17 years were somewhat contented ones for Jenny. Her world revolved around her son, and she worked hard to ensure that he had everything he wanted. She told Ross that, aside from art, the world was a miserable place and that it was her duty to sacrifice for him because she was responsible for his existence.

When Ross moved away to attend college, Jenny continued to scrimp in order to pay all his bills. As Ross began to be interested in women, his idyllic relationship with his mother came to an end. The two quarreled often and bitterly over his female friends. Jenny referred to each of them as prostitutes or whores, including the woman Ross married. With that marriage, Jenny and Ross became temporarily estranged.

At about that same time, Jenny began an 11½-year correspondence with Glenn and Isabel (Gordon and Ada) in which she revealed much about both her life and her personality. The early letters showed that she was deeply concerned with money, death, and Ross. She felt that Ross was ungrateful and that he had abandoned her for another woman, a prostitute at that. She continued her bitterness toward him until he and his wife were divorced. She then moved into the apartment next to Ross's, and for a short time, Jenny was happy. But soon Ross was seeing other women, and Jenny inevitably found something wrong with each. Her letters were filled again with animosity for Ross, a suspicious and cynical attitude toward others, and a morbid yet dramatic approach to life.

Three years into the correspondence, Ross suddenly died. After his death, Jenny's letters expressed a somewhat more favorable attitude toward him. Now she did not have to share him with anyone. Now he was safe—no more prostitutes.

For the next 8 years, Jenny continued writing to Glenn and Isabel, and they usually answered her. However, they served mostly as neutral listeners and not as advisors or confidantes. Jenny continued to be overly concerned with death and money. She increasingly blamed others for her misery and intensified her suspicions and hostility toward her caregivers. After Jenny died, Isabel (Ada) commented that, in the end, Jenny was "the same only more so."

These letters represent an unusually rich source of morphogenic material. For years they were subjected to close analysis and study by Allport and his students, who sought to build the structure of a single personality by identifying personal dispositions that were central to that person. One of Allport's students, Alfred Baldwin (1942), developed a technique called *personal structure analysis*, which he used to analyze approximately one third of the letters. The purpose of this technique was to analyze the structure of Jenny's personality from her letters. Baldwin used two strictly morphogenic procedures, frequency and contiguity, for gathering evidence. The first simply involves a notation of the frequency with which an item appears in the case material. For example, how often did Jenny mention Ross, or money, or herself? Contiguity refers to the proximity of two items in the letters. How often did the category "Ross—unfavorable" occur in close correspondence with "herself—self-sacrificing"? Freud and other psychoanalysts intuitively used this technique of contiguity to discover an association between two items in a patient's unconscious mind. Baldwin, however, refined it by determining statistically those correspondences that occur more frequently than could be expected by chance alone.

Using the personal structure analysis, Baldwin identified three clusters of categories in Jenny's letters. The first related to *Ross, women, the past, and herself—self-sacrificing*. The second dealt with Jenny's *search for a job*, and the third cluster revolved around her attitude toward *money and death*. The three clusters are independent of each other even though a single topic, such as money, may appear in all three clusters.

The reader will note that Baldwin's original clusters resembled those that might be found in factor analysis (see Chapter 13). Indeed, Jeffrey Paige (1966), another student of Allport, later published a factor analytic study of Jenny's letters. He extracted and identified a total of eight factors: aggression, possessiveness, affiliation, autonomy, familial acceptance, sexuality, sentience, and martyrdom.

Paige's study is interesting for two reasons. First, he identified eight factors, a number that corresponds very well with the number of central dispositions—5 to 10—that Allport had earlier hypothesized would be found in most people. Second, the results are quite similar to those that Allport (1965) found when he used a somewhat commonsense approach.

In Allport's 1965 study, 36 judges had listed what they thought were Jenny's essential characteristics. They recorded 198 descriptive adjectives, many of which were synonymous and overlapping. Allport then grouped the terms into eight clusters: quarrelsome-suspicious; self-centered; independent-autonomous; dramatic-intense; aesthetic-artistic; aggressive; cynical-morbid; and sentimental.

Comparing this commonsense, clinical approach with Paige's factorial study, Allport (1966) presented some interesting parallels (see Table 14.1). Through Jenny's

Table 14.1 *Jenny's Central Dispositions Revealed by Clinical and Factor Analytic Techniques*

Clinical Technique (Allport)	Factor Analytic Technique (Paige)
Quarrelsome-suspicious	Aggression
Aggressive	
Self-centered (possessive)	Possessiveness
Sentimental	Need for affiliation
	Need for family acceptance
Independent-autonomous	Need for autonomy
Aesthetic-artistic	Sentience
Self-centered (self-pitying)	Martyrdom
(No parallel)	Sexuality
Cynical-morbid	(No parallel)
Dramatic-intense	("Overstate," that is, the tendency to be dramatic and to overstate her concerns)

letters, then, we find that she possessed about eight central traits that characterized the last 12 years of her life, if not her entire life. She was aggressive, suspicious, possessive, aesthetic, sentimental, morbid, dramatic, and self-centered. These central dispositions were sufficiently powerful that she was described in similar terms both by Isabel, who knew her well, and by independent researchers, who studied her letters (Allport, 1965).

The close agreement between the clinical, commonsense approach and the factor analytic method does not prove the validity of either. It does, however, indicate the feasibility of morphogenic studies. Psychologists can analyze one person and identify central dispositions with consistency even when they use different procedures.

RELATED RESEARCH

Allport was one of the most influential figures in the history of personality psychology. He founded the academic discipline of personality psychology at Harvard, wrote the first textbook on personality, and was the intellectual grandfather of the "trait" perspective and its offshoot, the "Big Five." However, Allport's theoretical ideas have generated only a moderate amount of empirical research, more than Fromm or Horney but less than Skinner or Eysenck.

More than any other personality theorist, Allport maintained a lifelong active interest in the scientific study of religion (Allport, 1950). On a personal level, Allport was a devout Episcopalian, and from 1938 to 1966, he offered a series of 33 meditations in Appleton Chapel, Harvard University (Allport, 1978).

Allport believed that a deep religious commitment was a mark of a mature individual. However, not all churchgoers have a mature religious orientation. Some, in fact, are highly prejudiced. Allport and J. Michael Ross (1967) looked at earlier studies that had found that some people who attended church were highly prejudiced, while others had very little prejudice.

To understand this relationship, Allport and Ross (1967) developed the Religious Orientation Scale (ROS), which assumes both an extrinsic and an intrinsic orientation toward religion. People with an *extrinsic orientation* have a utilitarian view of religion; that is, they see it as a means to an end. Theirs is a self-serving religion of comfort and social convention. Their beliefs are lightly held and easily reshaped when convenient. On the other hand, people with an *intrinsic orientation* live their religion and find their master motive in their religious faith. Rather than using religion for some end, they bring other needs into harmony with their religious values. They have an internalized creed and follow it fully.

With this distinction in mind, Allport and Ross (1967) developed two subscales for the ROS—one consisting of Extrinsic (E) items and the other of Intrinsic (I) items. Examples of Extrinsic items are, "What religion offers me most is comfort when sorrow and misfortune strike" and "One reason for my being a church member is that such membership helps to establish a person in the community" (p. 436). People who definitely disagree or tend to disagree with these type of statements are scored in the direction of an Intrinsic orientation. People who definitely agree or tend to agree with these items are scored in an Extrinsic direction. Examples of Intrinsic items are, "My religious beliefs are what really lie behind my whole approach to life" and "I try hard to carry my religion over into all my other dealings in life" (p. 436). A person who agrees with statements of this nature scores high on the Intrinsic scale, whereas a person who disagrees with these statements scores high on the Extrinsic scale.

Although Allport originally thought that religious orientation would be a bipolar trait, he soon realized that not everyone could easily be fit into either the Extrinsic or the Intrinsic pole. Some people endorsed *both* the Extrinsic and the Intrinsic statements. These people formed a third group called *indiscriminately proreligious*. Others tended to *disagree with both* the Extrinsic and the Intrinsic items, and these people made up a fourth group called *indiscriminately antireligious* or nonreligious. More recently, a few studies of the psychometric qualities of the ROS have suggested that the Extrinsic dimension should be separated into two dimensions: social reward (Social-Extrinsic or Es) and gaining personal relief, protection, and comfort (Personal-Extrinsic or Ep) (Genia, 1993; Kirkpatrick, 1989; Kirkpatrick & Hood, 1990).

Many of the refinements of the ROS have been suggested by Ralph W. Hood, Jr. (1970), who has been interested in religious orientation for 30 years. Hood and his colleagues at the University of Tennessee at Chattanooga have also conducted dozens of studies on religious commitment. Some of Hood's research has examined Allport's assumption that an intrinsic religious orientation is part of psychological maturity and altruistic behavior. In one study, Hood and his associates (Watson, Morris, & Hood, 1990) found that people who score high on the Intrinsic scale are characterized by good mental health, whereas those who score high on the Extrinsic scale have many more personal problems. Interestingly, indiscriminately proreligious as well as antireligious people tend to have mixed mental health.

In addition, Allen Bergin, Kevin Masters, and P. Scott Richards (1987) found that the Intrinsic scale was negatively related to anxiety and positively related to self-control and better personal functioning, whereas the Extrinsic scale was positively related to anxiety and negatively related to self-control and healthy personal functioning. Also, Kim Van Haitsma (1986) examined the relationship between intrinsic religious orientation and personal adjustment in the elderly and found that highly intrinsic elderly people are generally more satisfied with their lives compared with extrinsically religious elderly people. Futhermore, David Hansen, Brian Vandenberg, and Miles Patterson (1995) reported that intrinsically religious students, compared with extrinsically religious students, were more likely to report participating in volunteer work. These studies tend to support Allport's notion of differing types of religiousness and to obviate the argument that strongly religious people are generally neurotic. Some are, others are not, depending on their personal view of religion.

A few studies have examined whether being intrinsically religious is related to having an internal locus of control (see Chapter 12). Using Allport's ROS and Rotter's I-E Scale, Ralph Hood and his associates (Watson, Milliron, Morris, & Hood, 1995) reported that people with an intrinsic religious orientation were no more likely to believe that their behavior was under their control than were those with an extrinsic religious orientation; that is, the researchers found no relationship between religious orientation and locus of control. However, an earlier study by Ed Edmonds, Margaret Shipman, and Delwin Cahoon (1992) compared intrinsically religious, extrinsically religious, and indiscriminately proreligious orientations in each of three measures of control: (1) personal efficacy, (2) sociopolitical control, and (3) interpersonal control. They found that intrinsics scored slightly higher than extrinsics on the combined spheres of control. However, all the difference was accounted for by a single measure, namely, interpersonal control. These findings suggest that people with an intrinsic religious orientation are more socially assertive than either people with an extrinsic orientation or those with an indiscriminately proreligious orientation.

Based on previous work (Leak & Fish, 1989; Watson, Hood, Morris, & Hall, 1984) that had suggested a relationship between religious orientation and impression management, that is, the desire to make a favorable impression on others, P. Scott Richards (1994) asked the following question: Are devoutly religious people more likely to maintain socially favorable impressions of themselves? Richards used the ROS to measure religious orientation and Snyder's Self-Monitoring Scale (1974) to assess impression management. The Self-Monitoring Scale measures the extent to which people monitor and change their behavior. Richards also used the Marlowe-Crowne Social Desirability Scale (Marlowe & Crowne, 1961) to measure participants' desire to present themselves to others in the most desirable and positive manner. His sample consisted of 70 Lutherans, 65 Roman Catholics, 32 non-Lutheran Protestants, one Jew, and seven who had no religious preference. Overall, the sample was a relatively faithful one: 87% believed in a supreme being, 9% were agnostic, and only 3% were atheistic. Richards found inconsistent support for the relationship between impression management and religious orientation. The Intrinsic scale of the ROS was positively correlated with the Marlowe-Crowne social desirability scale, but not with self-monitoring. Indeed, intrinsic religious orientation and self-monitoring were negatively related, suggesting that intrinsically religious people are *less* concerned with making a favorable impression on other people.

Allport, undoubtedly, would be pleased that in recent years, psychology and religion have become less estranged. In its infancy, psychology had an intimate relationship with both religion and philosophy, but later, during the behaviorist influence, religion ceased to be regarded as an important psychological variable. Gorsuch (1988) has traced psychologists' interest in religion and found that, whereas the psychology of religion is still not well integrated within psychology in general, there has been a resurgence of research activity. Much of the activity is due to Allport's passionate interest in both psychology and religion.

CRITIQUE OF ALLPORT

Allport's theory is based more on philosophical speculation and common sense than on original scientific investigations. Unlike Bandura and Cattell, Allport did not conduct a vast number of investigations testing hypotheses drawn from his own theory. Nevertheless, he was quite familiar with much of the literature, and his theorizing never ventured too far beyond what was then known about human personality. Remember, it was not Allport's intention to construct a completely new theory of personality. He was eclectic, carefully borrowing from older theories those elements that were consistent with his conviction that most people are best thought of as conscious, forward-looking, tension-seeking individuals. To people who are offended by the deterministic theories of Freud and Skinner, Allport's view of humanity is philosophically refreshing. As with any other theory, however, it must be evaluated on a scientific basis.

The first consideration is whether or not Allport's approach is truly a theory of personality. It certainly deals with personality. In fact, Allport probably did more than any other psychologist to define personality and to categorize other definitions of the term. But did he have a *theory* in the sense of stating a set of related assumptions that generate testable hypotheses? On this criterion, Allport's exhortations rate a qualified "Yes." It is a limited theory, offering explanations for a fairly narrow scope of personality, namely, certain kinds of motivation. The functionally autonomous motives of psychologically healthy adults are covered quite adequately by Allport's theory. But what of the motives of children and of psychotic and neurotic adults? What moves them and why? What about ordinarily healthy adults who uncharacteristically behave in a strange manner? What accounts for these inconsistencies? What explanation did Allport offer for the bizarre dreams, fantasies, and hallucinations of mature individuals? Unfortunately, his account of personality is not broad enough to adequately answer these questions.

Despite its limitations as a useful theory, Allport's approach to personality is both stimulating and enlightening. Anyone interested in building a theory of personality should first become familiar with Allport's writings. Few other psychologists have made as much effort to place personality theory in perspective; few have been as careful in defining terms, in categorizing previous definitions, or in questioning what units should be employed in personality theory. The work of Allport has set a standard for clear thinking and precision that future theorists would do well to emulate.

Has the theory *generated research*? On this criterion, Allport's theory receives a moderate rating. His Religious Orientation Scale and the Study of Values have led to multiple studies on the scientific study of religion and of values. In addition to these areas of inquiry, Allport's advocacy of morphogenic studies remains a steady influence on many current researchers.

On the criterion of *falsifiability*, Allport's theory must receive a low rating. The concept of four somewhat independent religious orientations can be verified or falsified, but most of Allport's other insights lie beyond the ability of science to determine whether some other explanation might be equally appropriate.

A useful theory provides an *organization for observations*. Does Allport's theory meet this criterion? Again, only for a narrow range of adult motives does the theory offer a meaningful organization for observations. Much of what is known about human personality cannot be easily integrated into Allport's theory. Specifically, behaviors motivated by unconscious forces as well as those that are stimulated by primary drives were not adequately explained by Allport. He recognized the existence of these kinds of motivations, but seemed content to allow the psychoanalytic and behavioral explanations to stand without further elaboration. This limitation, however, does not devastate Allport's theory. To accept the validity of other theoretical concepts is a legitimate approach to theory building. Nevertheless, Allport might have been more specific in identifying those elements of earlier theories that he accepted and those that he rejected.

As a *guide for the practitioner*, Allport's theory has moderate usefulness. It certainly serves as a beacon to the teacher and the therapist, illuminating the view of personality that suggests that people should be treated as individuals. The details, unfortunately, are left unspecified.

On the final two criteria of a useful theory, Allport's psychology of the individual is highly rated. His precise language renders the theory both *internally consistent* and *parsimonious*.

CONCEPT OF HUMANITY

Allport had a basically *optimistic* and hopeful view of life. He rejected the psychoanalytic and behavioral views of humanity as being too deterministic and too mechanistic. He believed that our fates and our traits are not determined by unconscious motives originating in early childhood but by conscious choices we make in the present. We are not simply automatons blindly reacting to the forces of reward and punishment. Instead, we are able to interact with our environment and make it reactive to us. This view is similar to that of Bandura (see Chapter 11), the social-cognitive theorist, who believes that cognition is at least partially responsible for shaping behavior.

Allport believed that people not only seek to reduce tensions but to establish new ones. Healthy individuals desire both change and challenge. They are active, purposive, flexible, and enjoy the new and the unexpected.

Because people have the potential to learn a variety of responses in many situations, psychological growth can take place at any age. Personality is not established in early childhood, even though for some people infantile influences remain strong. Early childhood experiences are important only to the extent that they exist in the present. Although early security and love leave lasting marks, children need more than love: They need an opportunity to shape their own existence creatively, to resist conformity, and to be free, self-directed individuals.

Although society has some power to mold personality, Allport believed that it does not hold the answer to the nature of humanity. The factors shaping personality, Allport held, are not as important as personality itself. Heredity, environment, and the nature of the organism are important, but people are essentially proactive and free to follow the prevailing dictates of society or to chart their own life course.

People, however, are not completely free. Allport (1961) adopted a *limited-freedom* approach. He was often critical of those views that allow for absolute freedom, but he also opposed the psychoanalytic and behavioral views, which he regarded as denying free will. Allport's position was somewhere in the middle. Although free will exists, some people are more capable of making choices than are others. A healthy person has more freedom than a child or a severely disturbed adult. The intelligent, reflective person has more capacity for free choice than the nonreflective, mentally deficient one. Again, this stance is similar to the one adopted by Bandura (1986), who holds that people are partially free and that different individuals have different degrees of freedom.

Even though freedom is limited, Allport maintained that it can be expanded. The more self-insight a person develops, the greater that person's freedom of choice. The more objective a person becomes, that is, the more the blindfolds of self-concern and egotism are removed, the greater that person's degree of freedom. As serious compulsions and restrictive habits are overcome (as in successful psychotherapy or some other growth process), a person becomes more and more free to engage in spontaneous and flexible behavior.

Education and knowledge also expand the amount of freedom we have. The greater our knowledge of a particular area, the broader becomes our freedom in that area. To have a broad general education means that, to some extent, one has a wider choice of jobs, recreational activities, reading materials, and friends. Finally, our freedom can be expanded by our mode of choosing. If we stubbornly adhere to a familiar course of action simply because it is more comfortable, our freedom remains largely restricted. On the other hand, if we adopt an open-minded mode of solving problems, then we broaden our perspective and increase our alternatives; that is, we expand our freedom to choose (Allport, 1955).

Allport's view of humanity is more *teleological* than causal. Personality, to some extent, is influenced by past experiences, but the behaviors that make us human are those that are motivated by our expectations of the future. In other words, we are healthy individuals to the extent that we set and seek future purposes and aspirations. Those factors that make one person different from another are not so much the basic drives, but rather self-erected goals and intentions.

The growth of personality always takes place within a social setting, but Allport placed only moderate emphasis on *social factors*. He recognized the importance of environmental influences in helping to shape personality, but he insisted that personality has some life of its own. Culture can influence our language, our morals, our values, our fashions, and so forth, but how each of us reacts to cultural forces depends on our unique personality and our basic motivation.

In summary, Allport held an optimistic view of humanity, maintaining that people have at least limited freedom. Human beings are goal-oriented, proactive, and motivated by a variety of forces, most of which are within their realm of *consciousness*. Early childhood experiences are of relatively minor importance and are significant only to the exten that they exist in the present. Both differences and similarities among people are important, but *individual differences* and *uniqueness* receive far greater emphasis in Allport's psychology.

Chapter Summary

Allport attempted to restore balance to the study of personality by emphasizing the uniqueness of the individual, a stance opposed to most of the existing approaches to personality theory. He did not discount the insights from psychoanalysis and learning theory; he was *eclectic* in his acceptance of ideas from a variety of sources. Most of these earlier theories, however, were reactive, and he wished to advocate a *proactive* position, one that emphasized the notion that people have much conscious control over their lives. Allport's psychology of the individual suggests that people desire *growth and change* and are motivated to *seek new tensions* as well as to maintain the status quo and to reduce tensions.

His emphasis on uniqueness led him to de-emphasize common traits and to espouse *individual traits or personal dispositions*. Three levels of personal dispositions are (1) cardinal dispositions, (2) central dispositions, and (3) secondary dispositions. Few people have a *cardinal* disposition, that is, a personal disposition so outstanding that it cannot be hidden. Most of us have 6 to 10 *central dispositions*, characteristics that would be used in an honest description of us by people who know us very well. Central dispositions, blend into *secondary dispositions* which are less reliable but far more numerous.

All personal dispositions are dynamic, but those that initiate actions are called *motivational*, whereas those that guide actions are called *stylistic*.

The *proprium* refers to those behaviors and personal dispositions that we regard as peculiarly our own. Not all personality belongs to the proprium, only those aspects that are warm, central, and important to our lives.

Childhood is relatively unimportant in Allport's theory. Ordinarily, not until adolescence do people develop a clearly defined sense of personhood and a well-developed proprium that leads them to be motivated by *propriate strivings*.

Probably Allport's most controversial concept is that of *functional autonomy*, which holds that the motivation for some behavior is functionally independent from the motives that were originally responsible for that behavior. *Perseverative functional autonomy* refers to those habits and behaviors that are not part of one's proprium; *propriate functional autonomy* includes all those self-sustaining motivations that are related to the proprium.

Allport believed that *psychologically healthy people* are motivated largely by conscious processes, have an extended sense of self, relate warmly to others, accept themselves for who they are, have a realistic perception of the world, and possess insight, humor, and a unifying philosophy of life.

Research methods that emphasize general laws, Allport insisted, must be balanced by morphogenic procedures that stress the study of the individual. Personal documents, such as the famous *Letters from Jenny* (Allport, 1965), provide insights into the whole of humanity by revealing outstanding characteristics of the single individual.

Allport's psychology of the individual receives high ratings for its internal consistency and parsimony, but on its capacity to organize knowledge, its ability to generate research, it falsifiability, and its usefulness to the practitioner, its ratings are somewhat lower.

Allport's concept of humanity is optimistic and is welcomed by those who believe that common sense has been abandoned by some of the earlier personality theorists. Throughout our lifetime, Allport insisted, we have some freedom to grow and to seek new challenges.

Suggested Readings

Allport, G. W. (1955). *Becoming: Basic considerations for a psychology of personality.* New Haven, CT: Yale University Press.
> Allport's perceptive thinking and cogent writing are evidenced in this brief book that discusses a wide range of topics pertinent to personality.

Allport, G. W. (1961). *Pattern and growth in personality.* New York: Holt, Rinehart and Winston.
> A completely revised edition of Allport's classic 1937 book on personality, this volume once again focuses on the study of the individual. The book is essential to an understanding of Allport's conception of personality.

Allport, G. W. (1965). *Letters from Jenny.* New York: Harcourt, Brace & World.
> This is a fascinating account of Jenny as seen through her eyes and from the view of others who knew her.

Allport, G. W. (1967). An autobiography. In E. G. Boring & G. Lindzey (Eds.), A *history of psychology in autobiography* (Vol. 5). New York: Appleton-Century-Crofts.
> Allport writes an interesting account of his life, including his encounter with Sigmund Freud.

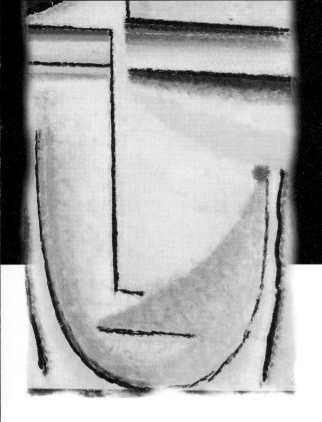

Kelly

Chapter

15

Kelly:
Psychology of Personal Constructs

George Kelly's theory of personal constructs is like no other personality theory. It has been variously called a cognitive theory, a behavioral theory, an existential theory, and a phenomenological theory. Yet it is none of these. Perhaps the most appropriate term would be "metatheory," or a theory about theories. According to Kelly, all people (including those who build personality theories) anticipate events by the meanings or interpretations they place on those events. These meanings or interpretations are called *constructs*. People exist in a real world, but their behavior is shaped by their gradually expanding interpretation or *construction* of that world. They construe the world in their own way, and every construction is open to revision or replacement. People are not victims of circumstances, because alternative constructions are always available. Kelly called this philosophical position *constructive alternativism*.

Constructive alternativism is implied by Kelly's theory of personal constructs, a theory he expressed in one basic postulate and 11 supporting corollaries. The basic postulate assumes that people are constantly active and that their activity is guided by the way they anticipate events.

BIOGRAPHY OF GEORGE KELLY

George Alexander Kelly was born April 28, 1905, on a farm near Perth, Kansas, a small town 35 miles south of Wichita. George was the only child of Theodore V. Kelly, an ordained Presbyterian minister, and Elfleda M. Kelly, a former schoolteacher. By the time George was born, his father had given up the ministry in favor of becoming a Kansas farmer. Both parents were well-educated and both helped in the formal education of their son, a fortunate circumstance because George's schooling was rather erratic.

When George was four years old, the family moved to eastern Colorado, where his father staked a claim on some of the last free land in that part of the country. While in Colorado, George attended school only irregularly, seldom for more than a few weeks at a time (Thompson, 1968).

Lack of water drove the family back to Kansas, where George attended four different high schools in four years. At first, he commuted to high school, but at age 13, he was sent away to school in Wichita. From that time on, he mostly lived away from home. After graduation, he spent three years at Friends University in Wichita and 1 year at Park College in Parkville, Missouri. Both schools had religious affiliations, which may explain why many of Kelly's later writings are sprinkled with biblical references.

Kelly was a man of many and varied interests. His undergraduate degree was in physics and mathematics, but he was also a member of the college debate team and, as such, became intensely concerned with social problems. This interest led him to the University of Kansas, where he received a master's degree with a major in educational sociology and a minor in labor relations and sociology.

During the next few years, Kelly moved several times and held a variety of positions. First, he went to Minneapolis, where he taught soapbox oratory at a special college for labor organizers, conducted classes in speech for the American Bankers Association, and taught government to an Americanization class for prospective citizens (Kelly, 1969a). Then in 1928, he moved to Sheldon, Iowa, where he taught at a junior college and coached drama. While there, he met his future wife, Gladys Thompson, an English teacher at the same school. After a year and a half, he moved back to Minnesota, where he taught a summer session at the University of Minnesota.

Next, he returned to Wichita to work for a few months as an aeronautical engineer. From there, he went to the University of Edinburgh in Scotland as an exchange student, receiving an advanced professional degree in education.

At this point in his life, Kelly "had dabbled academically in education, sociology, economics, labor relations, biometrics, speech pathology, and anthropology, and had majored in psychology for a grand total of nine months" (Kelly, 1969a, p. 48). After returning from Edinburgh, however, he began in earnest to pursue a career in psychology. He enrolled at the State University of Iowa in 1930 and the following year completed a Ph. D. with a dissertation on common factors in speech and reading disabilities.

Once again, Kelly returned to Kansas, beginning his academic career in 1931 at Fort Hays State College in Hays, Kansas, by teaching physiological psychology. With the dust bowl and the Great Depression, however, he soon became convinced that he should "pursue something more humanitarian than physiological psychology" (Kelly, 1969a, p. 48). Consequently, he decided to become a psychotherapist, counseling college and high school students in the Hays community. True to his psychology of personal constructs, Kelly pointed out that *circumstances* did not dictate his decision, but rather his *interpretation* of events; that is, his own construction of reality altered his life course.

> Everything around us "calls," if we choose to heed. Moreover, I have never been completely satisfied that becoming a psychologist was even a very good idea in the first place. . . . The only thing that seems clear about my career in psychology is that it was I who got myself into it and I who have pursued it. (p. 49)

Now a psychotherapist, Kelly obtained legislative support for a program of traveling psychological clinics in Kansas. He and his students traveled widely throughout the state, providing psychological services during those hard economic times. During this period, he evolved his own approach to therapy, abandoning the Freudian techniques that he had previously used.

During World War II, Kelly joined the Navy as an aviation psychologist. After the war, he taught at the University of Maryland for a year and then, in 1946, joined the faculty at Ohio State University as a professor and director of the Psychological Clinic. There he worked with Julian Rotter (see Chapter 12), who succeeded him as director of the clinic. Kelly had been gradually formulating his theory of personality, and in 1955, his most important work, *The Psychology of Personal Constructs*, was published in two volumes.

Many of his summers were spent as a visiting professor at such schools as the University of Chicago, the University of Nebraska, the University of Southern California, Northwestern University, Brigham Young University, Stanford University, and City College of New York. During those postwar years, Kelly became a major force in clinical psychology in the United States. He was president of both the Clinical and the Consulting Divisions of the American Psychological Association and was also head of the American Board of Examiners in Professional Psychology.

In 1965, he accepted a position at Brandeis University, where, for a brief time, he was a colleague of A. H. Maslow (see Chapter 17). Kelly died on March 6, 1967, before he could complete revisions of his theory of personal constructs.

Although Kelly's popularity with American psychologists has waned somewhat since his death, his ideas are widely known among psychologists in England. The late Donald Bannister was instrumental in spreading Kelly's theories throughout Britain (Bannister, 1970, 1975, 1977; Bannister & Fransella, 1966, 1971; Bannister & Mair, 1968), and Fay Fransella in London helped open the Center of Personal Construct Psychology, with a mission to train clinicians in the theory and practice of personal construct psychology. In addition, Nigel Beail (Beail, 1985; Beail & Parker, 1991) has helped apply personal construct theory to clinical and educational settings, and other British psychologists have applied Kelly's ideas to industrial and organizational settings. In the United States, Alvin Landfield of the University of Nebraska has championed personal construct theory (Landfield, 1971; Landfield & Epting, 1987; Landfield & Leitner, 1980; Landfield, Stefan, & Dempsey, 1990).

Kelly's diverse life experiences, from the wheat fields of Kansas to some of the major universities of the world, from education to labor relations, from drama and debate to psychology, are consistent with his theory of personality, which emphasizes the possibility of interpreting events from many possible angles.

KELLY'S PHILOSOPHICAL POSITION

Is human behavior based on reality or on our perception of reality? George Kelly would say *both*. He did not accept Skinner's (see Chapter 10) position that behavior is shaped by the environment, that is, reality. On the other hand, he also rejected a strictly **phenomenological** approach (see Combs & Snygg, 1959), which holds that the only reality is what we perceive. Kelly (1955) believed that the universe is real, but that different people construe it in different ways. Thus, our **personal constructs,** or ways of interpreting and explaining events, hold the key to predicting our behavior.

Personal construct theory does not try to explain nature. Rather, it is a theory of our *construction* of events, that is, our personal inquiry into our world. It is "a psychology of the human quest. It does not say what has or will be found, but proposes rather how we might go about looking for it" (Kelly, 1970, p. 1).

PERSON AS SCIENTIST

When you decide what foods to eat for lunch, what television shows to watch, or what occupation to enter, you are acting in much the same manner as a scientist. That is, you ask questions, formulate hypotheses, test them, draw conclusions, and try to predict future events. Like all other people (including scientists), your perception of reality is colored by your *personal constructs*—your way of looking at, explaining, and interpreting events in your world.

Consider the case of Arlene, a 21-year-old engineering major whose heavy schedule of classes and work became even more hectic when her 10-year-old car broke down. Now she faces a problem not unlike those you encounter with regard to eating lunch, watching television, or choosing an occupation. Arlene has several choices. She could have her old car repaired; she could borrow money to purchase a nearly new used car; she could walk to and from school and work; she could ask friends for transportation; she could quit school and move back home with her parents; or she could choose among several other options.

Kelly believed that the process by which Arlene (or any of us) makes a decision is comparable to those processes followed by scientists when they approach a problem. Like a good scientist, Arlene observed her environment ("I see that my car won't run"); asked questions ("How can I stay in school and keep my job if my car won't run?" "Should I have my old car repaired?" "Should I buy a newer car?" "What other options do I have?"); anticipated answers ("I can have my old car fixed, buy a newer one, rely on friends for transportation, or quit school"); perceived relationships between events ("Quitting school would mean moving back home, postponing or giving up my goal of becoming an engineer, and losing much of my independence"); hypothesized about possible solutions to her dilemma ("If I have my old car repaired, it might cost more than the car is worth, but if I buy a late-model used one, I'll have to borrow money"); asked more questions ("If I buy a different car, what make, model, and color do I want?"); predicted potential outcomes ("If I buy a reliable car, I will be able to stay in school and continue my job"); and attempted to control events ("By purchasing this car, I will be free to drive to work and earn enough money to stay in school").

In a similar manner, all of us, in our quest for meaning, make observations, construe relationships among events, formulate theories, generate hypotheses, test those that are plausible, and reach conclusions from our experiments. As with those of any scientist, our conclusions are not fixed or final. They are open to reconsideration and reformulation. Kelly was hopeful that people individually, as well as humanity in general, will find better ways of restructuring their lives through imagination and foresight.

Scientist as Person

If people can be seen as scientists, then scientists can also be seen as people. Therefore, the pronouncements of scientists should be regarded with the same skepticism with which we view any behavior. Every scientific observation can be looked at from a different perspective. Every theory can be slightly tilted and viewed from a new angle. This means, of course, that Kelly's theory is not exempt from restructuring. Kelly (1969b) presented his theory as a set of half-truths and recognized the inaccuracy of its constructions. Like Carl Rogers (see Chapter 16), Kelly hoped that his theory would be overthrown and replaced by a better one. Indeed, Kelly, more than other personality theorists, formulated a theory that encourages its own demise. Just as all of us can use our imagination to see everyday events differently, personality theorists can use their ingenuity to construe better theories.

Constructive Alternativism

As already mentioned, Kelly began with the assumption that the universe really exists and that it functions as an integral unit, with all its parts interacting precisely with each other. Moreover, the universe is constantly changing so that something is happening all the time. Added to these basic assumptions is the notion that people's thoughts also really exist and that people strive to make sense out of their continuously changing world. Different people construe reality in different ways, and the same person is capable of changing his or her view of the world.

In other words, people always have alternative ways of looking at things. Kelly (1963) assumed *that all of our present interpretations of the universe are subject to revision or replacement"* (p. 15). He referred to this assumption as **constructive alternativism** and summed up the notion with these words: "The events we face today are subject to as great a variety of constructions as our wits will enable us to contrive" (Kelly, 1970, p. 1). The philosophy of constructive alternativism assumes that the piece by piece accumulation of facts does not add up to truth, but rather that facts can be looked at from different perspectives. Kelly agreed with Adler (see Chapter 4) that our interpretation of events is more important than the events themselves. In contrast to Adler, however, Kelly stressed the notion that interpretations have meaning in the dimension of time, and what is valid at one time becomes false when construed differently at a later time. For example, when Freud (see Chapter 2) originally heard his patients' accounts of childhood seduction, he believed that early sexual experiences were responsible for later hysterical reactions. If Freud had continued to construe his patients' reports in this fashion, the entire history of psychoanalysis would have been quite different. But then, for a variety of reasons, Freud restructured his data and gave up his seduction hypothesis. Shortly thereafter, he tilted the picture a little and saw a very different view. With this new view, he concluded that these seduction reports were merely childhood fantasies. His alternative hypothesis was the Oedipus complex, a concept that permeates current psychoanalytic theory, and one that is 180 degrees removed from his original seduction theory. If we view Freud's observations from yet another angle, such as Erikson's perspective (see Chapter 9), then we might reach a still different conclusion.

Kelly believed that the *person*, not the facts, holds the key to an individual's future. Facts and events do not dictate conclusions, but rather they carry meanings for us to discover. We are all constantly faced with alternatives, which we can explore if we choose, but in any case, we must assume responsibility for how we construe our worlds. We are victims neither of our history nor our present circumstances. That is not to say that we can make of our world whatever we wish. We are "limited by our feeble wits and our timid reliance upon what is familiar" (Kelly, 1970, p. 3). We do not always welcome new ideas. Like scientists in general and personality theorists in particular, we often find restructuring disturbing and thus hold on to ideas that are comfortable and theories that are well-established.

PERSONAL CONSTRUCTS

Kelly's philosophy assumes that our interpretation of a unified, ever-changing world constitutes our reality. Arlene's perception of her transportation problem is not a static one. As she talked to a mechanic, a used car dealer, a new car dealer, a banker, her parents, and others, she was constantly changing her interpretation of reality. In similar fashion, we all continually create our own view of the world. Some people are quite inflexible and seldom change their way of seeing things. They cling to their view of reality even as the real world changes. For example, people with **anorexia nervosa** continue to see themselves as fat while their weight continues to drop to a life-threatening level. Some people construe a world that is substantially different from the world of other people. For example, psychotic patients in mental hospitals may talk to people whom no one else can see, or they may see things that no one else can. Kelly (1963) would insist that these people, along with everyone else, are looking at their world through "transparent patterns or templates" that they have created in order to cope with the world's realities. Although these patterns or templates do not always fit accurately, they are the means by which people make sense out of the world. Kelly referred to these patterns as *personal constructs*:

> They are ways of construing the world. They are what enables man, and lower animals too, to chart a course of behavior, explicitly formulated or implicitly acted out, verbally expressed or utterly inarticulate, consistent with other courses of behavior or inconsistent with them, intellectually reasoned or vegetatively sensed. (p. 9)

A personal construct is our way of seeing how things (or people) are alike and yet different from other things (or people). For example, we may see how Betty and Jane are alike and how they are different from Carol. The comparison and the contrast must occur within the same context. For example, to say that Betty and Jane are attractive and Carol is religious would not constitute a personal construct, because attractiveness is one dimension and religiosity is another. A construct would be formed if we see that Betty and Jane are attractive and Carol is unattractive, or if we view Betty and Jane as irreligious and Carol as religious. Both the comparison and the contrast are essential.

Whether they are clearly perceived or dimly felt, personal constructs shape an individual's behavior. As an example, consider Arlene, the engineering student with the broken-down car. After her old car stopped running, her personal constructs molded her subsequent course of action, but not all constructs were clearly defined. For instance, she may have decided to buy a late-model automobile because she interpreted the car dealer's friendliness and persuasiveness as meaning that the car was reliable. Arlene's personal constructs may be accurate or inaccurate, but in either case, they are her means of predicting and controlling her environment.

Arlene tried to increase the accuracy of her predictions (that the car would provide reliable, economical, and comfortable transportation) by increasing her store of information. She researched her purchase, asked others' opinions, tested the car, and had it checked by a mechanic. In much the same manner, all of us attempt to validate our constructs. We look for better fitting templates and thus try to improve our personal constructs. However, personal improvement is not inevitable, because the investment we make in our established constructs blocks the path of forward development. The world is constantly changing so that what is accurate at one time may not be accurate at another. The reliable blue bicycle Arlene rode during childhood should not mislead her to construe that all blue vehicles are reliable.

Kelly's basic theory is expressed in one fundamental postulate or assumption and elaborated by means of 11 supporting corollaries.

BASIC POSTULATE

The fundamental postulate of personal construct theory is that *"a person's processes are psychologically channelized by the ways in which he [or she] anticipates events"* (Kelly, 1955, p. 46).

This statement assumes that our behavior (thoughts and actions) are directed by the way we see the future. This postulate is not intended as an absolute statement of truth but is a tentative assumption open to question and scientific testing.

Kelly (1955, 1970) clarified this fundamental assumption by defining its key terms. First, the phrase *person's processes* refers to a living, changing, moving human being. Kelly was not concerned here with animals, with society, or with any part or function of the person. He did not recognize motives, needs, drives, or instincts as forces underlying motivation. Life itself accounts for our movement. "The person is not an object which is temporarily in a moving state but is himself a form of motion" (Kelly, 1955, p. 48).

Kelly chose the term *channelized* to suggest that people move with a direction through a network of pathways or channels. The network, however, is flexible, both facilitating and restricting one's range of action. In addition, the term avoids the implication that some sort of energy is being transformed into action. People are already in movement; they merely channelize or direct their processes toward some end or purpose.

The next key phrase is *ways of anticipating events*, which suggests that people guide their actions according to the ways they predict the future. Neither the past nor the future per se determine behavior. Rather, our present view of the future shapes our actions. Arlene did not buy a blue car because she had a blue bicycle when she was a child, although that fact may have helped her construe the present so that she anticipated that her blue late-model car would be a reliable one in the future. "It is the future which tantalizes man, not the past. Always he reaches out to the future through the window of the present" (Kelly, 1955, p. 49).

Supporting Corollaries

To elaborate his theory of personal constructs, Kelly proposed 11 supporting corollaries, all of which can be inferred from his basic postulate.

Similarities Among Events

No two events are exactly alike, yet we construe similar events so that they are perceived as being the same. One sunrise is never identical to another, but our construct *dawn* conveys our recognition of some similarity or some replication of events. Two dawns are never exactly alike, although they may be similar enough for us to construe them as the same event. Kelly (1955, 1970) referred to this similarity among events as the **construction corollary.**

The construction corollary states that *"a person anticipates events by construing their replications"* (Kelly, 1955, p. 50). This corollary again points out that people are forward-looking; their behavior is molded by their anticipation of future events. It also emphasizes the notion that people construe or interpret future events according to recurrent themes or replications.

The construction corollary may seem little more than common sense. We see similarities among events and use a single concept to describe the common properties. Kelly, however, felt that it was necessary to include the obvious when building a theory.

Differences Among People

Kelly's second corollary is equally obvious. *"Persons differ from each other in their construction of events"* (Kelly, 1955, p. 55). Kelly called this emphasis on individual differences the **individuality corollary.**

People have different experiences and construe things in different ways, so that even when two constructions appear the same, they are not seen in an identical manner to two different individuals. In addition, no two people put an experience together in exactly the same way. In other words, both the substance and the form of the construct are different. For example, a philosopher may subsume the construct *truth* under the rubric of eternal values; a lawyer may view truth as a relative concept, useful for a particular purpose; and a scientist may construe truth as an ever-elusive goal, something to be sought, but never attained. For the philosopher, the lawyer, and the scientist, *truth* has a different substance, a different meaning. Moreover, each person arrived at his or her particular construction in a different manner and thus gives it a different form.

Even identical twins living in nearly identical environments do not construe events exactly the same. For example, part of Twin A's environment includes Twin B, an experience not shared by Twin B. In addition, each twin experiences a unique self as the central figure of life.

Although Kelly (1955) emphasized individual differences, he pointed out that experiences can be shared and that people can find a common ground for construing

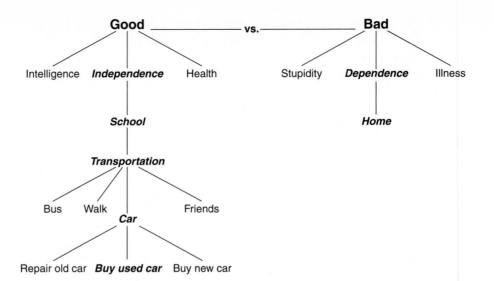

Figure 15.1 Complexity of relationships among constructs.

experiences. This allows people to communicate both verbally and nonverbally. However, due to individual differences, the communication is never perfect.

Relationships Among Constructs

Kelly's third corollary, the **organization corollary,** emphasizes relationships among constructs and states that people *"characteristically evolve, for [their] convenience in anticipating events, a construction system embracing ordinal relationships between constructs"* (Kelly, 1955, p. 56).

The first two corollaries assume similarities among events and differences among people. The third emphasizes that different people organize similar events in a manner that minimizes incompatibilities and inconsistencies. We arrange our constructions so that we may move from one to another in an orderly fashion, which allows us to anticipate events in ways that transcend contradictions and avoid needless conflicts.

The organization corollary also assumes an ordinal relationship of constructs so that one construct may be subsumed under another. Figure 15.1 illustrates a hierarchy of constructs as they might apply to Arlene, the engineering major. In deciding a course of action after her car broke down, Arlene may have seen her situation in terms of dichotomous superordinate constructs such as good vs. bad. At that point in her life, Arlene regarded *independence* (of friends or parents) as good and *dependence* as bad. However, her personal construct system undoubtedly included a variety of constructs subsumed under good and bad. For example, Arlene probably construed intelligence and health as good and stupidity and illness as bad. Furthermore, Arlene's views of independence and dependence (like her constructs of good and bad) would have had a multitude of subordinate constructs. In this situation, Arlene construed continuation in school as independence and returning home as dependence. In order to remain in school and continue her job, Arlene needed transportation. There were many possible means of transportation, but Arlene considered only four: riding a public bus, walking, relying on friends, or driving her own car. Subsumed under the construct of car were three subordinate constructs: repairing her old car, buying a new one, or purchasing a

People choose between alternatives based on their anticipation of future events.

late-model used car. This example not only suggests that constructs have a complex ordinal relationship with each other but a dichotomous one as well.

Dichotomy of Constructs

Now we come to a corollary that is not so obvious. The **dichotomy corollary** states that *"a person's construction system is composed of a finite number of dichotomous constructs"* (Kelly, 1955, p. 59).

Kelly insisted that a construct is an either/or proposition—black or white, with no shades of gray. In nature, things may not be either/or, but natural events have no meanings other than those attributed to them by an individual's personal construct system. In nature, the color blue may have no opposite pole (except on a color chart), but people attribute contrasting qualities to blue, such as *light* blue vs. *dark* blue or *pretty* vs. *ugly*.

In order to form a construct, we must be able to see similarities between events, but we must also contrast those events with their opposite pole. Kelly (1955) stated it this way: "In its minimum context a construct is a way in which at least two elements are similar and contrast with a third" (p. 61). As an example, let us return to Figure 15.1. How are *intelligence* and *independence* alike? Their common element has no meaning without contrasting it to an opposite. Intelligence and independence have no overlapping element when compared to purple or modern. By contrasting intelligence with stupidity and independence with dependence, we see how they are alike and how they can be organized under the construct "good" as opposed to "bad."

Choice Between Dichotomies

If people construe events in dichotomized fashion, then it follows that they have some choice in following alternative courses of action. This is Kelly's **choice corollary,** paraphrased as follows: *People choose for themselves that alternative in a dichotomized construct through which they anticipate the greater possibility for extension and definition of future constructs.*

This corollary assumes much of what is stated in Kelly's basic postulate and in the preceding corollaries. People make choices on the basis of how they anticipate events, and those choices are between dichotomous alternatives. In addition, the choice corollary assumes that people choose those actions that are most likely to extend their future range of choices.

Arlene's decision to buy a used car was based on a series of previous choices, each of which was between dichotomized alternatives and each of which broadened her range of future choices. First she chose the *independence* of school over the *dependence* of going home to live with her parents. Next, buying a car offered more freedom than relying on friends or on bus schedules or walking (which she perceived as time consuming). Repairing her old car was *financially risky* compared to the greater *safety* of buying a used one. Purchasing a new car was too *expensive* compared to the relatively *inexpensive* used car. Each choice was between alternatives in a dichotomized construct, and with each choice, Arlene anticipated the greater possibility for extending and defining future constructs.

Range of Convenience

Kelly's **range corollary** assumes that personal constructs are finite and not relevant to everything. "A *construct is convenient for the anticipation of a finite range of events only*" (Kelly, 1955, p. 68). In other words, a construct is limited to a particular *range of convenience*.

The construct *independence* was within Arlene's range of convenience when she was deciding to buy a car, but on other occasions, independence would be outside those boundaries. Independence carries with it the notion of *dependence*. Arlene's freedom to remain in school, freedom to continue her job, and freedom to move quickly from place to place without relying on others all fall within her independence/dependence range of convenience. However, Arlene's construct of independence excludes all irrelevancies such as up/down, light/dark, or wet/dry; that is, it is convenient only for a finite range of events.

The range corollary allowed Kelly to distinguish between a *concept* and a *construct*. A concept includes all elements having a common property, and it excludes those that do not have that property. The concept tall includes all those people and objects having extended height and excludes all other concepts, even those that are outside its range of convenience. Therefore, *fast* or *independent* or *dark* are all excluded from the concept *tall* because they do not have extended height. But such exclusions are both endless and needless. The idea of construct contrasts tall with short, thus limiting its range of convenience. "That which is outside the range of convenience of the construct is not considered part of the contrasting field but simply an area of irrelevancy" (Kelly, 1955, p. 69). Thus we see that dichotomies limit a construct's range of convenience.

Experience and Learning

Basic to personal construct theory is the anticipation of events. We look to the future and make guesses as to what will happen. Then, as events become revealed to us, we either validate our existing constructs or restructure them to match our experience. The restructuring of events allows us to learn from our experiences.

The **experience corollary** states: "A *person's construction system varies as he [or she] successively construes the replications of events*" (Kelly, 1955, p. 72). Kelly used the word "successively" to point out that we pay attention to only one thing at a time. "The events of one's construing march single file along the path of time" (p. 73).

Experience consists of the successive construing of events. The events themselves do not constitute experience—it is the meaning we attach to them that changes our lives. To illustrate this point, let us return to Arlene and her personal construct of independence. When her old car (a high school graduation gift from her parents) broke down, Arlene decided to remain in school rather than to return to the security and dependent status of living at home. As Arlene subsequently encountered successive events, she had to make decisions without benefit of parental consultation, a task that forced her to restructure her notion of independence. Earlier, she had construed independence as freedom from outside interference. After deciding to go into debt for a used car, she began to alter her meaning of independence to include responsibility and anxiety. The events themselves did not force a restructuring. Arlene could have become a spectator to the events surrounding her. Instead, her existing constructs were flexible enough to allow her to adapt to experience.

Adaptation to Experience

Arlene's flexibility illustrates Kelly's **modulation corollary.** *"The variation in a person's construction system is limited by the permeability of the constructs within whose range of convenience the variants lie"* (Kelly, 1955, p. 77). This corollary follows from and expands the experience corollary. It assumes that the extent to which we revise our constructs is related to the degree of **permeability** of our existing constructs. A construct is permeable if new elements can be added to it. Impermeable or concrete constructs do not admit new elements. If a man believes that women are inferior to men, then contradictory evidence will not find its way into his range of convenience. Instead, he will attribute the achievements of women to luck or unfair social advantage. A change in events means a change in constructs only if those constructs are permeable.

Arlene's personal construct of *independence vs. dependence* was sufficiently permeable to take in new elements. When, without parental consultation, she made the decision to buy a used car, the construct of *maturity vs. childishness* penetrated *independence vs. dependence* and added a new flavor to it. Previously the two constructs had been separated and Arlene's notion of independence was limited to the idea of doing as she chose, while dependence was associated with parental domination. Now she construed independence as meaning mature responsibility and dependence as signifying a childish leaning on parents. In such a manner, we all modulate or adjust our personal constructs.

Incompatible Constructs

Although Kelly assumed an overall stability or consistency of a person's construction system, his **fragmentation corollary** allows for the incompatibility of specific elements. *"A person may successively employ a variety of constructive subsystems which are inferentially incompatible with each other"* (Kelly, 1955, p. 83).

At first it may seem as if personal constructs must be compatible, but if we look to our own behavior and thinking, we can easily see some inconsistencies. In Chapter 12, we saw that Walter Mischel (a student of Kelly's) believed that behavior is usually more inconsistent than trait theorists would have us believe. Children are often patient in one situation, yet impatient in another. Similarly, a person may be brave while confronting a vicious dog, but cowardly when confronting a boss or teacher. Although our behaviors often seem inconsistent, Kelly saw underlying stability in most of our actions. For example, a man might be protective of his wife, yet encourage her to be more independent. Protection and independence may be incompatible with each other on one level, but on a larger level, both are subsumed under the construct of *love.* Thus, the man's actions to protect his wife and to encourage her to be more independent are consistent with a larger, superordinate construct.

Superordinate systems may also change, but those changes take place within a still larger system. In our previous example, for instance, the man's love for his wife may gradually shift to hatred, but that change remains within a larger construct of *self-interest*. The previous love for his wife and the present hatred are both consistent with his view of self-interest. If incompatible constructs could not coexist, people would be locked into a fixed construct, which would make change nearly impossible.

Similarities Among People

Recall that Kelly's second supporting corollary assumed that people are different from each other. Now we see that he also assumed similarities among people. His slightly revised **commonality corollary** reads: *"To the extent that one person employs a construction of experience which is similar to that employed by another, his [or her] processes are psychologically similar to those of the other person"* (Kelly, 1970, p. 20).

Two people need not experience the same event or even similar events for their processes to be psychologically similar; they must merely *construe* their experiences in a similar fashion. Because people actively construe events by asking questions, forming hypotheses, drawing conclusions, and then asking more questions, different people with widely different experiences may construe events in very similar ways. For example, two people might arrive at similar political views although they come from disparate backgrounds. One may have come from a wealthy family, having lived a life of leisure and contemplation, while the other may have survived a destitute childhood, struggling constantly for survival. Yet both adopt a conservative political view.

Although people of different backgrounds can have similar constructs, people with similar experiences are more likely to construe events along similar lines. Americans tend to construe *democracy* in a somewhat similar manner, and one that differs from the construction of democracy held by people in India.

Within a given social group, people may employ similar constructions, but it is always the individual, never society, who construes events. Moreover, no two people ever interpret experiences exactly the same. Americans may have a similar construction of *democracy*, but no two Americans see it in identical terms.

Social Processes

"People belong to the same cultural group, not merely because they behave alike, nor because they expect the same things of others, but especially because they construe their experience in the same way" (Kelly, 1955, p. 94).

The final supporting corollary, the **sociality corollary** states: *"To the extent that one person construes the construction processes of another, he [or she] may play a role in a social process involving the other person"* (Kelly, 1955, p. 95).

We do not communicate with one another simply on the basis of common experiences or even similar constructions; we communicate because we construe the constructions of each other. In our interpersonal relations, we not only observe the behavior of the other person, we also interpret what that behavior means to that person. When Arlene was negotiating with the used car dealer, she was not only aware of his words and actions, but also their meanings. She realized that to him she was a potential buyer, someone who might provide him with a substantial commission. She construed his words as exaggerations and, at the same time, realized that he construed her indifference as an indication that she construed his motivations differently from her own.

In our interpersonal relationships, we observe not only the behavior of the other person, but we also interpret what that behavior means to that person.

All this seems rather complicated, but Kelly is simply suggesting that we are actively involved in interpersonal relations and realize that we are part of the other person's construction system.

Kelly also introduced the notion of **role** with his sociality corollary. A role refers to a pattern of behavior that results from a person's understanding of the constructs of others with whom that person is engaged in a task. For example, when Arlene was negotiating with the used car dealer, she construed her role as that of a potential buyer because she understood that was his expectation of her. At other times and with other people, she construes her role as student, employee, daughter, girlfriend, and so on.

Kelly construed roles from a psychological rather than a sociological perspective. One's role does not depend on one's place or position in a social setting but rather on how one interprets that role. Kelly also stressed the point that one's construction of a role need not be accurate in order for the person to play that role.

Arlene's roles as student, employee, and daughter would be considered *peripheral roles*. More central to her existence would be her *core role*. With our **core role,** we define ourselves in terms of who we really are. It gives us a sense of identity and provides us with guidelines for everyday living.

APPLICATIONS OF PERSONAL CONSTRUCT THEORY

Like most personality theorists, Kelly evolved his theoretical formulations from his practice as a psychotherapist. He spent more than 20 years conducting therapy before he published *The Psychology of Personal Constructs* in 1955. In this section, we look at his views of abnormal development, his approach to psychotherapy, and finally, his Role Construct Repertory (Rep) Test.

ABNORMAL DEVELOPMENT

In Kelly's view, psychologically healthy people validate their personal constructs against their experiences with the real world. They are like competent scientists who test reasonable hypotheses, accept the results without denial or distortion, and then willingly alter their theories to match available data. Healthy individuals not only anticipate events but are also able to make satisfactory adjustments when things do not turn out as they expected.

Unhealthy people, on the other hand, stubbornly cling to outdated personal constructs, fearing validation of any new constructs that would upset their present comfortable view of the world. Such people are similar to incompetent scientists who test unreasonable hypotheses, reject or distort legitimate results, and refuse to amend or abandon old theories that are no longer useful. Kelly (1955) defined a disorder as *"any personal construction which is used repeatedly in spite of consistent invalidation"* (p. 831).

A person's construction system exists in the present—not the past or future. Psychological disorders, therefore, also exist in the present; they are caused neither by childhood experiences nor by future events. Because construction systems are *personal*, Kelly objected to traditional classifications of abnormalities. Labeling a person as a manic-depressive or a paranoid schizophrenic is likely to result in misconstruing the person's unique constructions.

Psychologically unhealthy people, like everyone else, possess a complex construction system. Their personal constructs, however, often fail the test of permeability in one of two ways: They may be too impermeable, or they may be too flexible. In the first instance, new experiences do not penetrate the construction system so that the person fails to adjust to the real world. For example, an abused child may construe intimacy with parents as bad and solitude as good. Psychological disorders result when the child's construction system rigidly denies the value of any intimate relationship and clings to the notion that either withdrawal or attack is a preferred mode of solving interpersonal problems. Another example would be a man seriously dependent on alcohol who refuses to see himself as an alcoholic even as his drinking escalates and his job and marriage suffer.

On the other hand, a construction system that is too loose or flexible leads to disorganization, an inconsistent pattern of behavior, and a transient set of values. Such an individual is too easily "shaken by the impact of unexpected minor daily events" (Kelly, 1955, p. 80).

Although Kelly did not use traditional labels in describing psychopathology, he did identify four common elements in most human disturbance: threat, fear, anxiety, and guilt.

Threat

Threat is experienced when people perceive that the stability of their basic constructs is likely to be shaken. Kelly (1955) defined threat as *"the awareness of imminent comprehensive change in one's core structures"* (p. 489). We can be threatened by either people or events, and sometimes the two cannot be separated. For example, during psychotherapy, clients often feel threat from the prospect of change, even change for the better. If they see a therapist as a possible instigator of change, they will view that therapist as a threat. Clients frequently resist change and construe their therapist's behavior in a negative fashion. Such resistance and "negative transference" are means of reducing threat and maintaining existing personal constructs.

Fear

By Kelly's definition, threat involves a *comprehensive* change in a person's core structures. **Fear,** on the other hand, is more *specific* and *incidental*. Kelly (1955) illustrated the difference between threat and fear with the following example. A man may drive his car dangerously as the result of anger or exuberance. These impulses become *threatening* when the man realizes that he may run over a child or be arrested for reckless driving and end up as a criminal. In this case, a comprehensive portion of his personal constructs is threatened. However, if he is suddenly confronted with the probability of crashing his car, he will experience *fear*. Threat demands a comprehensive restructuring—fear an incidental one. Psychological disturbance results when either threat or fear persistently prevents a person from feeling secure.

Anxiety

Kelly (1955) defined **anxiety** as *"the recognition that the events with which one is confronted lie outside the range of convenience of one's construct system"* (p. 495). We are likely to feel anxious when we are experiencing a new event. For example, when Arlene, the engineering student, was bargaining with the used car dealer, she was not sure what to do or say. She had never before negotiated over such a large amount of money, and therefore this experience was outside the range of her convenience. As a consequence, she felt anxiety, but it was a normal level of anxiety and did not result in incapacitation.

Pathological anxiety exists when incompatible constructs can no longer be tolerated and one's construction system breaks down. Recall that Kelly's fragmentation corollary assumes that people can evolve construction subsystems that are incompatible with one another. For example, when a person who has erected the rigid construction that all people are trustworthy is blatantly cheated by a colleague, that person may for a time tolerate the ambiguity of the two incompatible subsystems. However, when evidence of the untrustworthiness of others becomes overwhelming, the person's construct system may break down. The result is a relatively permanent and debilitating experience of anxiety.

Guilt

Kelly's sociality corollary assumes that people construe a core role that gives them a sense of identity within a social environment. When that core role is weakened or dissolved, they develop a feeling of guilt. Kelly (1970) defined **guilt** as *"the sense of having lost one's core role structure"* (p. 27). In other words, people feel guilty when they behave in ways that are inconsistent with their sense of who they are.

People who have never developed a core role do not feel guilty. They may be anxious or confused, but without a sense of personal identity, they do not experience guilt. For example, people with an underdeveloped conscience have little or no integral sense of self and a weak or nonexistent core role structure. Such people have no stable guidelines to violate and hence feel little or no guilt regardless of their behavior.

PSYCHOTHERAPY

Psychological distress exists whenever people have difficulty validating their personal constructs, anticipating future events, and controlling their present environment. When distress becomes unmanageable, they may seek outside help in the form of psychotherapy.

In Kelly's view, people should be free to choose those courses of action most consistent with their prediction of events. In therapy, this means that clients, not the therapist, select the goal. Clients are active participants in the therapeutic process, and the therapist's role is to assist them to alter their construct systems in order to improve efficiency in making predictions.

As a technique for altering the clients' constructs, Kelly used a procedure called *fixed-role therapy*. The purpose of fixed-role therapy is to help clients change their outlook on life (personal constructs) by acting out a predetermined role, first within the relative security of the therapeutic setting and then in the environment beyond therapy where they enact the role continuously over a period of several weeks. Together with the therapist, clients work out a role, one that includes attitudes and behaviors not currently part of their core role. In writing the fixed-role sketch, the client and therapist are careful to include the construction systems of other people. How will the client's spouse or parents or boss or friends construe and react to this new role? Will their reactions help the client reconstrue events more productively?

This new role is then tried out in everyday life in much the same manner that a scientist tests a hypothesis—cautiously and objectively. In fact, the fixed-role sketch is typically written in the third person, with the actor assuming a new identity. The client is not trying to be another person but is merely playing the part of someone who is worth knowing. The role should not be taken too seriously; it is only an act, something that can be altered as evidence warrants.

Fixed-role therapy is not aimed at solving specific problems or "repairing" obsolete constructs. It is a creative process that allows clients to gradually discover previously hidden aspects of themselves. In the early stages, clients are introduced only to peripheral roles, but then, after they have had time to become comfortable with minor changes in personality structure, they try out new core roles, which permit more profound personality change (Kelly, 1955).

Prior to developing the fixed-role approach, Kelly (1969a) stumbled on an unusual procedure that strongly resembles fixed-role therapy. After becoming uncomfortable with Freudian techniques, he decided to offer his clients "preposterous interpretations" for their complaints. Some were far-fetched Freudian interpretations, but nevertheless, most clients accepted these "explanations" and used them as guides to future action. For example, Kelly might tell a client that strict toilet training has caused him to construe his life in a dogmatically rigid fashion, but that he need not continue to see things in this way. To Kelly's surprise, many of his clients began to function better! The key to change was the same as with fixed-role therapy—clients must begin to interpret their lives from a different perspective and see themselves in a different role.

THE REP TEST

Another procedure used by Kelly, both inside and outside therapy, was the *Role Construct Repertory (Rep) Test*. The purpose of the Rep Test is to discover ways in which people construe significant people in their lives.

With the Rep Test, a person is given a Role Title List and asked to designate people who fit the role titles by writing their names on a card. For example, for "a teacher you liked," the person must supply a particular name. The number of role titles can vary, but Kelly (1955) listed 24 on one version (see Table 15.1). Next, the person is given three names from the list and asked to judge which two people are alike and yet different from the third. Recall that a construct requires both a similarity and a contrast, so that three is the minimum number for any construct. Say, for example, that a person construes Number 1 ("A teacher you liked") and Number 6 ("Your mother") as similar and Number 9 ("Your sister nearest your age") as different. Then the person is asked how mother and favorite teacher are alike and yet different from sister. The *reason* a

Table 15.1 *Example of a List of Role Titles Used for the Rep Test*

1. A teacher you liked. (Or the teacher of a subject you liked.)
2. A teacher you disliked. (Or the teacher of a subject you disliked.)
3a. (for men) Your wife or present girl friend.
3b. (for women) Your husband or present boy friend.
4. An employer, supervisor, or officer under whom you worked or served and whom you found hard to get along with. (Or someone under whom you worked in a situation you did not like.)
5. An employer, supervisor, or officer under whom you worked or served and whom you liked. (Or someone under whom you worked in a situation you liked.)
6. Your mother. (Or the person who has played the part of a mother in your life.)
7. Your father. (Or the person who has played the part of a father in your life.)
8. Your brother nearest your age. (Or the person who has been most like a brother.)
9. Your sister nearest your age. (Or the person who has been most like a sister.)
10. A person with whom you have worked who was easy to get along with.
11. A person with whom you have worked who was hard to understand.
12. A neighbor with whom you get along well.
13. A neighbor whom you find hard to understand.
14. A boy you got along well with when you were in high school. (Or when you were 16.)
15. A girl you got along well with when you were in high school. (Or when you were 16.)
16. A boy you did not like when you were in high school. (Or when you were 16.)
17. A girl you did not like when you were in high school. (Or when you were 16.)
18. A person of your own sex whom you would enjoy having as a companion on a trip.
19. A person of your own sex whom you would dislike having as a companion on a trip.
20. A person with whom you have been closely associated recently who appears to dislike you.
21. The person whom you would most like to be of help to. (Or whom you feel most sorry for.)
22. The most intelligent person whom you know personally.
23. The most successful person whom you know personally.
24. The most interesting person whom you know personally.

SOURCE: From G. A. Kelly, *The Psychology of Personal Constructs*. Copyright © 1955 by W. W. Norton & Company. Reprinted by permission of Mrs. Gladys Kelly.

person gives for the similarity and contrast constitutes the construct. If the person gives a superficial response such as "They're both old, and my sister is young," the examiner will say, "That's one way they are alike. Can you think of another?" The person might then say, "My mother and my favorite teacher are both unselfish, and my sister is very self-centered." The examiner records the construct and then asks the person to sort three more cards. Not all combinations of sorts are elicited, and the examiner has some latitude in determining which combinations to use.

After a number of sorts are completed, the examiner transfers the information to a repertory grid (see Figure 15.2 for an example). In this particular grid, 19 role titles are listed along the horizontal axis and 22 personal constructs along the vertical axis. On Sort Number 1, the person who filled out this grid construed Persons 17 and 18 alike because they don't believe in God and Person 19 as being different because he or she is very religious. The examinee also checked Persons 7, 10, and 12 because they are construed as similar to the two people in the emergent pole, that is, they too do not believe in God. Similarly, the person checks each row until the entire grid is completed.

There are several versions of the Rep Test and the repertory grid, but all are designed to assess personal constructs. For example, a woman can see how her father

	Self	Mother	Father	Brother	Sister	Spouse	Ex-flame	Pal	Ex-pal	Rejecting Person	Pitied Person	Threatening Person	Attractive Person	Accepted Teacher	Rejected Teacher	Boss	Successful Person	Happy Person	Ethical Person	SORT NO.	EMERGENT POLE	IMPLICIT POLE
	1	2	3	4	5	6	7	8	9	10	11	12	13	14	15	16	17	18	19		CONSTRUCTS	
						✓		✓		✓						⊗	⊗	○		1	Don't believe in God	Very religious
			✓	✓		✓						⊗	⊗	○	✓					2	Same sort of education	Complete different education
	✓		✓	✓	✓		✓	⊗	○	✓	⊗	✓			✓					3	Not athletic	Athletic
		✓		⊗	⊗	○						✓								4	Both girls	A boy
	✓	⊗	⊗	○	✓	✓		✓			✓	✓	✓	✓	✓	✓				5	Parents	Ideas different
		✓	○			✓					⊗	✓			⊗					6	Understand me better	Don't understand at all
	⊗	✓	✓				○				⊗	✓	✓				✓			7	Teach the right thing	Teach the wrong thing
	✓	○	✓								✓		⊗	⊗	✓	✓				8	Achieved a lot	Hasn't achieved a lot
		⊗	✓		✓		○				✓	⊗	✓	✓						9	Higher education	No education
		⊗		✓		⊗						○								10	Don't like other people	Like other people
	✓	✓	✓		⊗	✓				○	✓		✓	✓		✓	✓	⊗		11	More religious	Not religious
	✓	✓	✓	⊗			✓	✓	○	✓	✓	⊗	✓	✓	✓	✓	✓	✓	✓	12	Believe in higher education	Not believing in too much education
	✓		✓		○				✓	✓	⊗		✓		✓		⊗			13	More sociable	Not sociable
	○			⊗	⊗									✓						14	Both girls	Not girls
	✓	○		⊗	⊗								✓							15	Both girls	Not girls
	✓	✓	✓	✓	✓		⊗	○			⊗	✓	✓		✓	✓	✓			16	Both have high morals	Low morals
	⊗		⊗	○	✓		✓		✓		✓	✓	✓	✓			✓	✓		17	Think alike	Think differently
		✓	✓								✓	⊗	⊗	✓	○	○				18	Same age	Different ages
	⊗	⊗		✓					✓	○			✓	✓	✓	✓	✓	✓		19	Believe the same about me	Believe differently about me
		✓			✓	⊗	⊗	✓	✓	✓	○									20	Both friends	Not friends
				○	✓						⊗	⊗	✓	✓	✓	✓	✓			21	More understanding	Less understanding
	⊗		✓		○	✓	⊗						✓		✓		✓		✓	22	Both appreciate music	Don't understand music

Figure 15.2   Example of a repertory grid.

and boss are alike or different; whether or not she identifies with her mother; how her boyfriend and father are alike; or how she construes men in general. Also, the test can be given early in therapy and then again at the end. Changes in personal constructs reveal the nature and degree of movement made during therapy.

Kelly and his colleagues have used the Rep Test in a variety of forms, and no set scoring rules apply. Reliability and validity of the instrument are not very high and its usefulness depends largely on the skill and experience of the examiner (Adams-Webber, 1970; Fransella & Bannister, 1977).

RELATED RESEARCH

Considering that George Kelly wrote only one seminal work (1955), his impact on personality psychology is remarkable. His personal construct theory has generated a sizable number of empirical investigations, including almost 500 empirical studies on his repertory test between 1967 and 1996. Whereas this number does not place him with Skinner, Eysenck, or Bandura, it does suggest that his theory has fared quite well on the criterion of generating testable hypotheses and research.

Personal construct theory has been used to investigate a large number of psychological constructs, including physical health and illness, grief, depression, marital relationships, attitudes and beliefs, management, and the arts and education (Fransella & Thomas, 1988; Hammond & Romney, 1995).

A number of studies have used the Rep Test, or modification of it, to examine the cognitive structures of children or adolescents. For example, Wayne Hammond and David Romney (1995) found that self-constructs of depressed adolescents mirror those of adults and are characterized by low self-esteem, pessimism, polarized construing, increased interpersonal isolation, and a more external locus of control. In another study, James Middleton, Joan Littlefield, and Richard Lehrer (1992) looked at the personal constructs of 10- to 14-year-old gifted children with regard to academic subjects. They assumed that students who enjoyed doing a task for its own sake would also be motivated to do the task well. They used Kelly's personal construct theory to argue that constructs of "fun" would be important to understanding what academic subjects students find intrinsically motivating. Furthermore, they suggested that students attempt to match activities with what they consider to be "fun." For example, if students do not find an academic subject to be fun, they will not be interested in working hard or in doing well in that subject. Finally, Middleton et al. argued that gifted students would be ideal participants because they are energetic and seek out challenging, stimulating tasks.

Middleton et al. first determined why students saw an activity as fun (for example, "I am good at it" or "It is exciting") by having them rate 12 school activities (art, math, science, high technology/computers, recess, and so forth). This procedure yielded 20 constructs as to why an activity was fun. Next, they administered a specially designed repertory test to gifted students in grades 4, 5, 6, 7, and 8 to see how these students construed fun activities. They found that: (1) children construe activities to be fun based on how interesting it is, how much it arouses their imagination, and how much control they have over it; (2) boys construed physical education and high technology/computers as more fun than girls did; (3) both boys and girls experienced a decreased interest in math with increased age.

Eileen Donahue (1994) conducted another study of children's construct systems that revolved around the question of what domains of personality children use to evaluate themselves and others. More specifically, she was interested in whether children conceptualize themselves and others in terms of the Big Five dimensions of personality. (The Big Five personality factors include surgency or extraversion; agreeableness; conscientiousness; emotional stability; and culture/intellect.) Using Rep Test scores from Jeanne Block and Jack Block's (1980) longitudinal sample of 11-year-old participants, Donahue asked children to nominate individuals who fit one of nine roles in their lives: self, opposite sex peer, best friend, a disliked peer, mother or mother figure, father or father figure, a liked teacher, the ideal self, and a disliked adult. Then she presented the children with *Role Triads* and asked them to distinguish how two of the people were alike but differed from the third. Each child rated a total of nine triads. Once these constructs were made, they were coded and categorized by independent judges into different categories such as traits, trends, skills, habits, and relationships. Moreover, each statement that had any relevance to personality was categorized on the Big Five dimensions. The primary purpose of the study was to investigate whether children used the same dimensions as adults did to describe themselves and others. Results showed that children did, in fact, use the Big Five dimensions to describe themselves and others, but the five dimensions were not all used with the same frequency. For instance, agreeableness was the most frequently used construct (73%), whereas emotional stability was the least frequently used (16%). There were no gender differences in how frequently the Big Five categories were used. These findings are important because they counteract the criticism that five personality dimensions all come from existing personality tests. It appears that the Big Five dimensions are not dependent on methodology and the structured format of personality tests; they also emerge from a free response format of the Rep Test. Children apparently construe themselves and others in terms of agreeableness, surgency, conscientiousness, emotional stability, and culture/intellect.

Greg Neimeyer and Alison Gold Hall (1988) investigated how adults' personal constructs relate to marital satisfaction. Participants in this study were 31 married women classified into having a "Satisfied," "Dissatisfied," or "Abused" relationship. The Satisfied group consisted of 10 women who lived in university married housing; the Dissatisfied group consisted of 10 women who were receiving counseling for marital dissatisfaction; and the Abused group consisted of 11 residents of a women's shelter who had been physically abused by their husbands. Each participant was administered the 32-item Dyadic Adjustment Scale (DAS), which is a measure of overall marital adjustment. In addition, each participant completed a Rep Test, rating intimate friends or relatives as well as "myself in my current marriage," "myself as I would be if I were OUT of my current marriage," and "myself as I would LIKE to be in a marriage." The constructs were then coded on three dimensions: (a) *Desired Identity Enactment*, which was calculated as the difference between the self construct scores in current marriage and the ideal marriage; (b) *Organization*, which was measured by how highly similar the scores were across the different constructs; and *Threat*, which was measured by comparing constructs from "myself in my current marriage" to "myself out of this marriage," with the greater discrepancy representing a greater threat to self-image. Results showed that happily married women had identities that were closer to their ideal or preferred image. Abused women had significantly lower organization scores than satisfied or dissatisfied women. Finally, abused and dissatisfied women were significantly more threatened than satisfied women. Taken together, these findings suggest that happily married women are in relationships that validate their identity and self-image, whereas unhappily married women are in relationships that invalidate and threaten their self-constructs.

Another example of current research using the Rep Test with adults was conducted by Frances James and Robert Large (1992). This study concerned constructs of people with chronic pain and their "closest others." Chronic pain is an important psychological process for construct theory, because, in contrast to people who experience temporary illness or disease, those who experience chronic pain must learn to live with constant and often excruciating pain. They must to some extent learn to reappraise pain as something normal in their lives rather than as something abnormal that will go away in a few hours or days. Moreover, chronic pain also severely affects the lives of those closest to the pain patient, whether this is a caregiver, spouse, friend, or family member. James and Large wanted to see how the constructs of "closest others" had been affected by their relationships with chronic pain patients and whether the closest others understood what those with chronic pain were going through. A total of 15 pairs of participants completed a Rep Test designed for the study of illness, namely the Illness Self-Construct Repertory Grid (ISCRG). The ISCRG asks respondents to describe themselves "As I am," "As I would like to be," "As the person closest to me sees me," "As my doctor sees me," "Like a hypochondriac," and "Like a physically ill person." The closest other completed the same ISCRG, except instead of "As I am" they rated "As they imagined the person who has pain would be." The similarity of this response to the chronic person's "As I am" response was the index of how well the closest other understood what the person with chronic pain was going through. In general, closest others perceived the pain as more central to the life of the person with chronic pain than did the person with chronic pain, suggesting an incongruity of construct systems between the person with chronic pain and their closest other. By somewhat exaggerating the level of pain, the closest others may be construing the situation in such a way that bolsters their view of themselves as the "helper" and "protector," and this in turn allows them to behave consistently with their personal constructs of the world.

CRITIQUE OF KELLY

Kelly's personal construct theory is like no other personality theory discussed in this book. We have included it with the humanistic theories, but it could easily be placed among the cognitive theorists. Indeed, Kelly has probably had more influence on cognitive theorists than on humanistic theorists. Both Rotter and Bandura have been indirectly influenced by him, and Mischel's theory has borrowed even more directly from Kelly's personal construct theory. Cantor and Zirkel (1990) believe that "Kelly and Rotter have influenced almost all of what has come to be known as 'cognitive personality theory,' but this influence is most clearly seen among those researchers [who] emphasize the role played by perception and mental transformations of experiences" (pp. 137–138).

On the surface, Kelly seems to be remarkably open-minded. He repeatedly stated that all theories, including his own, should be open to reconstruction. He insisted that events can always be construed differently, and that alternative ways of looking at things always exist. Contrary to this broad-minded stance, however, was Kelly's lack of toleration for existing theories. As Holland (1970) pointed out, Kelly frequently attacked Freudian theory, behavior theories, cognitive theories, existentialism, and phenomenology. He seemed to have been rather nonacceptant of these constructive alternatives.

Most of Kelly's professional career was spent working with relatively normal, intelligent college students. Understandably, his theory seems most applicable to these people. He made no attempt to elucidate early childhood experiences (as did Freud) or maturity and old age (as did Erikson). To him, people live solely in the present, with one eye always on the future. This view, though somewhat optimistic, fails to account for developmental and cultural influences on personality.

How does his theory rate on the six criteria of a useful theory? First, personal construct theory receives a moderate rating on the amount of *research* it has generated. The Rep Test and the repertory grid have generated a sizable number of studies, especially in Great Britain, although these instruments are used less frequently by psychologists in the United States.

Despite the relative parsimony of Kelly's basic postulate and 11 supporting corollaries, the theory does not lend itself easily to either verification or falsification. Therefore, we rate personal construct theory low on *falsifiability*.

Third, does personal construct theory *organize knowledge* about human behavior? On this criterion, the theory must be rated very low. Kelly's avoidance of the problems of motivation, developmental influences, and cultural forces limits his theory's ability to give meaning to much of what is currently known about the complexity of personality.

The theory also falls short as a *guide to action*. Kelly's ideas on psychotherapy are rather innovative and suggest to the practitioner some interesting techniques. Playing the role of a fictitious person, someone the client would like to know, is indeed an unusual and practical approach to therapy. Kelly relied heavily on "common sense" in this therapeutic practice and what worked for him might not work for someone else. That would be quite acceptable to Kelly, however, because he viewed therapy as a scientific experiment. The therapist is like a scientist, using imagination to test a variety of hypotheses, that is, to try out new techniques and to explore alternate ways of looking at things. Nevertheless, Kelly's theory offers few specific suggestions to parents, therapists, researchers, and others who are trying to understand human behavior.

Fifth, is the theory *internally consistent*, with a set of *operationally defined terms*? On the first part of this question, personal construct theory rates very high. Kelly was exceptionally careful in choosing terms and concepts to explain his fundamental postulate and the 11 corollaries. His language, although frequently difficult, is both elegant and precise. *The Psychology of Personal Constructs* (Kelly, 1955) contains more than 1,200 pages, but the entire theory is pieced together like a finely woven fabric. Kelly seemed to have constantly been aware of what he had already said and what he was going to say.

On the second half of this criterion, personal construct theory falls short, because like most theorists discussed in this book, Kelly did not define his terms operationally. However, he was exemplary in writing comprehensive and exacting definitions of nearly all terms used in the basic postulate and supporting corollaries.

Finally, is the theory *parsimonious*? Despite the length of Kelly's two-volume book, the theory of personal constructs is exceptionally straightforward and economical. The basic theory is stated in one fundamental postulate and then elaborated by means of 11 corollaries. All other concepts and assumptions can be easily related to this relatively simple structure.

CONCEPT OF HUMANITY

Kelly had an essentially *optimistic* view of human nature. He saw people as anticipating the future and living their lives in accordance with those anticipations. People are capable of changing their personal constructs at any time of life, but those changes are seldom easy. Kelly's modulation corollary suggests that constructs are permeable or resilient, meaning that new elements can be admitted. Not all people, however, have equally permeable constructs. Some accept new experiences and restructure their interpretations accordingly, whereas others possess concrete constructs that are very difficult to alter. Nevertheless, Kelly was quite optimistic in his belief that therapeutic experiences can help people live more productive lives.

On the dimension of *determinism vs. free choice*, Kelly's theory leans toward free choice. The environment, although it has a real existence, can never make us free; that is, no one can grant us freedom, no event can unloose our chains. Only within our own personal construct system are we free to make a choice (Kelly, 1980). We choose between alternatives within a construct system that we ourselves have built. We make those choices on the basis of our anticipation of events. But more than that, we choose those alternatives that appear to offer us the greater opportunity for further elaboration of our anticipatory system. Kelly referred to this as the **elaborative choice,** that is, in making present choices, we look ahead and pick the alternative that will increase our range of future choices.

Kelly adopted a *teleological* as opposed to a causal view of human personality. He repeatedly insisted that childhood events per se do not shape current personality. Our present construction of past experiences may have some influence on present behavior, but the influence of past events is quite limited. Personality is much more likely to be guided by our present anticipation of future events. Kelly's fundamental postulate—the one on which all corollaries and assumptions stand—is that all human activity is directed by the way that we anticipate events (Kelly, 1955). There can be no question, then, that Kelly's theory is essentially teleological.

Kelly emphasized *conscious processes* more than unconscious ones. However, he did not stress conscious *motivation* because motivation plays no part in personal construct theory. Kelly speaks of levels of cognitive awareness. High levels of awareness refer to those psychological processes that are easily symbolized in words and can be accurately expressed to other people. Low-level processes are incompletely symbolized and are difficult or impossible to communicate.

There are several reasons why some processes are at low levels of awareness. First, some constructs are preverbal because they were formed before a person acquired meaningful language, and hence, they are not capable of being symbolized even to oneself. Second, some processes are at a low level of awareness because a person sees only similarities and fails to make meaningful contrasts. For example, a person may construe all people as trustworthy. However, the implicit pole of untrustworthiness is denied. Because the person's superordinate construction system is rigid, he or she fails to adopt a realistic construct of trustworthy/untrustworthy and tends to see the actions of others as completely trustworthy. Third, some subordinate constructs may remain at a low level of awareness as superordinate constructs are changing. In the above example, for instance, even after changing one's view to the notion that not all people are trustworthy, the person may be reluctant to construe one particular individual as untrustworthy. This means that a subordinate construct has not yet caught up to a superordinate one. Finally, some events may lie outside our range of convenience, so that certain experiences do not become part of our construct system. For example, such automatic processes as heartbeat, blood circulation, eye blink, and digestion are ordinarily outside our range of convenience, and we are usually not aware of them.

On the issue of *biological vs. social influences*, Kelly was inclined more toward the social, but his emphasis on social forces was not strong. His sociality corollary assumes that, to some extent, we are influenced by others and in turn have some impact on them. When we accurately construe the constructions of another person, we may play a role in a social process involving that other person. Kelly assumed that our interpretation of the construction systems of important other people (such as parents, spouse, and friends) may have some influence on our future constructions. Recall that in fixed-role therapy, clients adopt the identity of a fictitious person, and by trying out that role in various social settings, they may come to experience some change in their personal constructs. However, the actions of others do not mold their behavior; rather, their interpretation of events changes their behavior.

On the final dimension for a conception of humanity—*uniqueness vs. similarities*—Kelly emphasized the uniqueness of personality. This emphasis, however, was tempered by his commonality corollary, which assumes that people from the same sociocultural background tend to have had some of the same kinds of experience and therefore construe events similarly. Nevertheless, Kelly held that our individual interpretations of events are crucial and that no two persons ever have precisely the same personal constructs.

Chapter Summary

According to Kelly, our personality is shaped by our idiosyncratic interpretation of events. Although the outside world is real, it does not directly influence our behavior. Instead, our actions are guided by the way we anticipate events, and we anticipate events by our *personal constructs*, that is, the meanings or interpretations we place on our experience.

Kelly sees people as scientists, asking questions, testing hypotheses, formulating theories, asking additional questions, and making interpretations.

Basic to Kelly's theory is the idea of *constructive alternativism*, or the notion that our present interpretations are subject to change.

Kelly's theory can be summarized in his one fundamental postulate and 11 supporting corollaries. His *basic postulate* assumes that all our psychological processes are directed by the ways in which we anticipate events. The 11 corollaries derive from and elaborate the one fundamental postulate.

1. *Construction Corollary*. We anticipate future events according to our interpretations of recurrent themes.
2. *Individuality Corollary*. People have different experiences and therefore construe events in different ways.

3. *Organization Corollary.* We organize our personal constructs in a hierarchical system, with some constructs in superordinate positions and others subordinate to them. This organization allows us to minimize incompatible constructs.

4. *Dichotomy Corollary.* All personal constructs are dichotomous; that is, we construe events in an either/or manner.

5. *Choice Corollary.* We choose the alternative in a dichotomized construct that we see as extending our range of future choices.

6. *Range Corollary.* Constructs are limited to a particular range of convenience; that is, they are not relevant to all situations.

7. *Experience Corollary.* We continually revise our personal constructs as the result of experience.

8. *Modulation Corollary.* Not all new experiences lead to a revision of personal constructs. To the extent that constructs are permeable, they are subject to change through experience. Concrete or impermeable constructs resist modification regardless of our experience.

9. *Fragmentation Corollary.* Our behavior is sometimes inconsistent because our construct system can readily admit incompatible elements.

10. *Commonality Corollary.* To the extent that we have had experiences similar to others, our personal constructs tend to be similar to the construction systems of those people.

11. *Sociality Corollary.* We are able to communicate with others because we can construe their constructions. We not only observe the behavior of others, but we also interpret what that behavior means to them.

The application of Kelly's theory can be divided into (1) *abnormal development,* (2) *psychotherapy,* and (3) *the Role Construct Repertory (Rep) Test.*

In Kelly's view, unhealthy people are like incompetent scientists who test unreasonable hypotheses and refuse to modify their constructs in the light of contradictory evidence. They persist in using personal constructs that have consistently failed the test of validation.

Kelly's psychotherapeutic approach relies heavily on the clients' ability to actively participate with the therapist in restructuring their construct systems and making them more efficient predictors of future events. *Fixed-role therapy* calls for clients to act out predetermined roles continuously for a couple of weeks. Clients' peripheral and core roles may gradually change as significant others begin reacting differently to them.

The purpose of the *Rep Test* is to discover ways in which people construe important people in their lives.

Unfortunately, personal construct theory falls short on the most crucial standards for a useful theory. Aside from the Rep Test, it has generated very little research, and its ability to organize knowledge is limited by Kelly's avoidance of developmental issues and his rejection of such concepts as learning and motivation.

Kelly had an optimistic view of humanity and saw people as forward-looking and ultimately in charge of their lives.

Suggested Readings

Button, E. (1985). Personal construct theory: The concepts. In E. Button (Ed.), *Personal construct theory & mental health* (pp. 3–30). Cambridge, MA: Brookline Books.
   In this chapter, Button presents an excellent summary of Kelly's personal construct theory, including fresh examples of the various corollaries and ways of looking at psychological disorders and mental health from the view of personal constructs.

Kelly, G. A. (1963). A *theory of personal constructs: The psychology of personal constructs*. New York: Norton.
   This small paperback contains the first three chapters of Kelly's *The Psychology of Personal Constructs* (1955). These three chapters present the essence of Kelly's theory—constructive alternativism, the basic theory, and the nature of personal constructs.

Kelly, G. A. (1969a). The autobiography of a theory. In B. Maher (Ed.), *Clinical psychology and personality: The selected papers of George Kelly* (pp. 46–65). New York: Wiley.
   Perhaps the most interesting of all of Kelly's writings, this chapter combines personal glimpses with theoretical insights to produce the story of how personal construct theory came into being.

Kelly, G. A. (1970). A brief introduction to personal construct theory. In D. Bannister (Ed.), *Perspectives in personal construct theory* (pp. 1–29). London: Academic Press.
   Written the year preceding Kelly's death, this chapter was originally intended as an introduction to a book Kelly never finished. It presents an updated but briefer version of his 1955 book.

Landfield, A. W. , & Epting, F. R. (1987). *Personal construct psychology: Clinical and personality assessment*. New York: Human Sciences Press.
   Although intended mainly for the clinician, this book can be easily understood by students interested in the practical applications of personal construct theory.

Rogers

Chapter

16

Rogers: Person-Centered Theory

lthough he is best known as the founder of **client-centered therapy,** Carl Rogers developed a humanistic theory of personality, which grew out of his experiences as a practicing psychotherapist and which gave his practice a theoretical foundation. Unlike Freud, who was primarily a theorist and secondarily a therapist, Rogers was a consummate therapist but only a reluctant theorist (Rogers, 1959). He was more concerned with helping people than with discovering why they behaved as they did. He was more likely to ask, How can I help this other person grow and develop? rather than to ponder the question, What caused this person to develop in this manner?

Even though he formulated a rigorous, internally consistent theory of personality, Rogers did not feel comfortable with the notion of theory. His personal preference was to be a helper of people and not a constructor of theories. To him, theories seemed to make things too cold and external, and he worried that his theory might imply a measure of finality.

During the 1950s, at a midpoint in his career, Rogers was invited to write what was then called the "client-centered" theory of personality, and his original statement is found in Volume 3 of Sigmund Koch's *Psychology: A Study of a Science* (see Rogers, 1959). Even at that time, Rogers realized that 10 or 20 years hence, his theories would be different, but unfortunately, throughout the intervening years, he never systematically reformulated his theory of personality. Although many of his subsequent experiences altered some of those earlier ideas, his final theory of personality rests on that original foundation, spelled out in the Koch series.

BIOGRAPHY OF CARL ROGERS

Carl Ransom Rogers was born on January 8, 1902, in Oak Park, Illinois, the fourth of six children born to Walter and Julia Cushing Rogers. Carl was closer to his mother than to his father who, during the early years, was often away from home working as a civil engineer. Walter Rogers eventually became a successful civil engineer and contractor, so Carl was truly a product of upper-middle class, midwestern America. Walter and Julia Rogers were both devoutly religious, and Carl became interested in the Bible, reading from it and other books even as a preschool child. From his parents, Rogers also learned the value of hard work—a value that, unlike religion, stayed with him through his life.

As a child in Oak Park, Carl attended school with Ernest Hemingway, who was two years older, and with the children of Frank Lloyd Wright, the great American architect. Carl was an excellent student, but he was also a dreamer who loved adventure books. Although he was from a large family, he was a loner and quite unsocial at school. A sensitive boy, he was easily hurt by the teasing he received from classmates and siblings.

At the beginning of his high school years, Carl moved with his family to a farm 25 miles west of Chicago. His father was not a farmer but by this time was running a successful construction company. Carl's parents hoped the move to the farm would provide a more wholesome and religious atmosphere for their children. The house was more of a mansion than a farmhouse, having eight bedrooms, five baths, a tile roof, and a tennis court. In this environment, young Carl developed a passionate interest in nature and adopted a scientific attitude toward farming, taking detailed notes of his observations of both plants and animals. This scientific attitude was to remain with him for a lifetime, and his early interest in plants became a satisfying hobby in his later years.

Rogers had intended to become a farmer, and after he graduated from high school in 1919, he entered the University of Wisconsin with agriculture as his major. During his freshman year at the university, he made the first close friendships outside his family. That year also marked the beginning of a more intense interest in religion and a lessening of his desire to become a farmer.

By his third year at Wisconsin, he was deeply involved with religious activities on campus and spent six months during his junior year traveling to China to attend a student religious conference. This trip made a lasting impression on Rogers. The interaction with other young religious leaders changed him into a more liberal thinker and moved him toward independence from the religious views of his parents. These experiences with his fellow leaders also gave him more self-confidence in social relationships. Unfortunately, he returned from the journey with an ulcer. Although his illness prevented him from immediately going back to the university, it did not keep him from working; he spent a year recuperating by laboring on the farm and at a local lumberyard before eventually returning to Wisconsin. There, he joined a fraternity, displayed more self-confidence, and, in general, was a changed student from his pre-China days.

However, Rogers paid a price for his new-found freedom and self-confidence. Robert Dolliver (1995) cited an unpublished segment of an interview in which Rogers said that his parents had nearly disowned him when he broke from their fundamentalist religious beliefs. In that same interview (conducted when Rogers was 82), Paul Heppner asked him if he would like to communicate his accomplishments to his parents. Rogers replied:

> I guess I don't think they would understand now. All I could communicate would be the outward signs of success. That wouldn't have any particular meaning to me—it might to them, but it wouldn't to me. I really don't think with their values and viewpoints that they would have any real understanding of what I'm about. Some of the most fundamental aspects of my point of view and my approach are sort of the reciprocal of what my parents believed. (Heppner, Rogers, & Lee, 1984, p. 18)

Rogers went on to describe his mother's attitude in even more derogatory terms:

> I asked my next younger brother, "How did you think of mother?" He said, "Well, she was a person you never told anything to." And that really is true. I would have never thought of telling anything significant to my mother, because I know that she would have a judgment about it and it probably would be negative. (Heppner et al., 1984, p. 18)

It seems, then, that the empathic understanding that Rogers later regarded as essential to psychological growth was absent in his own relationships with his parents.

As an adolescent, Rogers was extremely shy, had no close friends, and was "socially incompetent in any but superficial contacts" (Rogers, 1973, p. 4). This shyness and social incompetency greatly restricted his experiences with women and girls. When he originally entered Wisconsin, he had only enough courage to ask out a young lady whom he had known in elementary school in Oak Park. This young lady was Helen Elliott, whom Carl married in 1924. Carl and Helen had two children—David, born in 1926, and Natalie, born in 1928.

After their marriage, Carl and Helen traveled to New York, where Carl entered the Union Theological Seminary with the intention of becoming a minister. While at the seminary, Rogers enrolled in several psychology and education courses at neighboring Columbia University. He was influenced by the progressive education movement of John Dewey, which was then strong at Teachers College, Columbia. Gradually, he became disenchanted with the doctrinaire attitude of religious work. Even though Union Theological Seminary was quite liberal, Rogers decided that he did not wish to express a fixed set of beliefs but desired more freedom to explore new ideas. Finally, in the fall of 1926, he crossed the street to attend Teachers College on a full-time basis with a major in clinical and educational psychology. From that point on, he never returned to formal religion. His life would now take a new direction—toward psychology and education.

In 1927, Rogers served as a fellow at the new Institute for Child Guidance in New York City and continued to work there while completing his doctoral degree. At the institute, he gained an elementary knowledge of Freudian psychoanalysis, but he was not much influenced by it, even though he tried it out in his practice. He also attended a lecture by Alfred Adler, who shocked Rogers and the other staff members with his contention that an elaborate case history was unnecessary for psychotherapy. Rogers received a Ph.D. from Columbia in 1931 after having already moved to Rochester, New York, to work with the Rochester Society for the Prevention of Cruelty to Children.

During the early phase of his professional career, Rogers was strongly influenced by the ideas of Otto Rank, who had been one of Freud's closest associates before his dismissal from Freud's inner circle. Rogers had always credited Rank with helping to shape his ideas on therapy, but he denied any Rankian influence on this theory (Evans, 1981). Nevertheless, Robert Kramer (1995) has recently presented a convincing argument that Rank had considerable impact on both Rogers's practice *and* his theory. In 1936, Rogers invited Rank to Rochester for a three-day seminar to present his new post-Freudian practice of psychotherapy. Although no record of Rank's remarks remain, it seems likely that he discussed many of the same ideas found in *Truth and Reality: A Life History of the Human Will* (Rank, 1978a) and *Will Therapy: An Analysis of the Therapeutic Process in Terms of Relationship* (Rank, 1978b), two books published by Rank at about that same time. According to Kramer's account, Rank not only originated the term *client-centered*, but provided Rogers with the notion that therapy is an emotional growth-producing relationship, nurtured by the therapist's empathic listening and unconditional acceptance of the client. However, Rogers was not much concerned with theoretical formulations at that time, so his denial of Rankian influence on his later theories may have been a reflection of his contemporary disinterest in theory.

Rogers spent 12 years at Rochester, working at a job that might easily have isolated him from a successful academic career. He had harbored a desire to teach in a university after a rewarding teaching experience during the summer of 1935 at Teachers College and after having taught courses in sociology at the University of Rochester. During this period, he wrote his first book, *The Clinical Treatment of the Problem Child* (1939), the publication of which led to a teaching offer from Ohio State University. Despite his fondness for teaching, he might have turned down the offer if his wife had not urged him to accept and if Ohio State had not agreed to start him at the top, with the academic rank of full professor. In 1940, at the age of 38, Rogers moved to Columbus to begin a new career.

Pressed by his graduate students at Ohio State, Rogers gradually conceptualized his own ideas on psychotherapy, not intending them to be unique and certainly not controversial. These ideas were put forth in *Counseling and Psychotherapy*, published in 1942. In this book, which was a reaction to the older approaches to therapy, Rogers minimized the causes of disturbances and the identification and labeling of disorders. Instead, he emphasized the importance of growth within the patient (called by Rogers the "client").

In 1944, as part of the war effort, Rogers took a leave from Ohio State to move back to New York as director of counseling services for the United Services

Organization. After one year, he took a position at the University of Chicago, where he established a counseling center and was allowed more freedom to do research on the process and outcome of psychotherapy. The years 1945 to 1957 at Chicago were the most productive and creative of his career. His therapy evolved from one that emphasized methodology, or what in the early 1940s was called the "nondirective" technique, to one in which the sole emphasis was on the client/therapist relationship. Always the scientist, Rogers, along with his students and colleagues, produced the most original and sophisticated research on the process and effectiveness of psychotherapy published to that date.

Wanting to expand his research and his ideas to psychiatry, Rogers accepted a position at the University of Wisconsin in 1957. However, he was disappointed with his stay at Wisconsin because he was unable to unite the professions of psychiatry and psychology, and because he felt that some members of his own research staff had engaged in dishonest and unethical behavior (Kirschenbaum, 1979). Nevertheless, he did have an opportunity to influence both psychiatry and psychology and also to work with both normal and psychotic individuals as opposed to the largely neurotic clients he encountered at Chicago and Ohio State.

Disappointed with his job at Wisconsin, Rogers moved to California in 1964, where he joined the Western Behavioral Sciences Institute (WBSI) and became increasingly interested in encounter groups. He also became interested in expanding the "person-centered" approach to education and to larger social issues, including politics and international affairs (Heppner et al., 1984; Rogers, 1982b).

He resigned from WBSI when he felt it was becoming less democratic and, along with about 75 others from the institute, formed the Center for Studies of the Person. He continued to work with encounter groups but extended his person-centered methods to education (including the training of physicians) and to international politics. During the last years of his life, he led workshops in such countries as Hungary, Brazil, South Africa, and the former Soviet Union (Gendlin, 1988). He died on February 4, 1987, following surgery for a broken hip.

The personal life of Carl Rogers was characterized by change and openness to experience. As a youth, he was a shy loner with an active fantasy life, which he later believed probably would have been diagnosed as "schizoid" (Rogers, 1980, p. 30). A socially inept youngster, Rogers grew to become a leading proponent of the notion that the interpersonal relationship between two individuals is a powerful ingredient that cultivates psychological growth within both persons. The transition, however, was not easy. He abandoned the formalized religion of his parents, gradually shaping a humanistic, and then an existential, philosophy that he hoped would bridge the gap between Eastern and Western thought.

Rogers received many honors during his long professional life. He was the first president of the American Association for Applied Psychology and helped bring that organization and the American Psychological Association (APA) back together. He served as president of APA for the year 1946–1947 and served as first president of the American Academy of Psychotherapists. In 1956, he was co-winner, along with Kenneth Spence and Wolfgang Kohler, of the first Distinguished Scientific Contribution Award presented by APA. This award was especially satisfying to Rogers because it highlighted his skill as a researcher, a skill he learned well as a farm boy in Illinois (O'Hara, 1995). In both time and self-image, Rogers was first a scientist, second a psychotherapist, and third a theorist.

Rogers originally saw little need for a theory of personality. But under pressure from others and also to satisfy an inner need to be able to explain the phenomena he was observing, he evolved his own theory, which was first tentatively expressed in his

APA presidential address (Rogers, 1947). His theory was more fully espoused in *Client-Centered Therapy* (1951) and was expressed in even greater detail in the Koch series (Rogers, 1959). However, Rogers always insisted that the theory should remain tentative, and it is with this thought that one should approach a discussion of Rogerian personality theory.

PERSON-CENTERED THEORY

The therapy and theory of Rogers underwent several changes in name, but no substantive changes in philosophy occurred from the early years when the therapy was known as "nondirective" until the final years when the theory was called "person-centered." During the intervening years, his approach was variously termed "client-centered," "student-centered," "group-centered," and "person to person." We use the label *client-centered* in reference to Rogers's *therapy* and the more inclusive term **person-centered** to refer to Rogerian personality *theory*.

Person-centered theory is a holistic theory, and like other holistic theories, it can be outlined and divided only arbitrarily. Each assumption is interrelated with every other concept and cannot be considered apart from the whole of the theory. Rogers, however, was able to state many of the assumptions of his theory in an if-then framework. A general example would be: *if* certain conditions exist, *then* a process will occur; *if* this process occurs, *then* certain outcomes can be expected. A more specific example is found in therapy: *If* the therapist possesses unconditional positive regard (a concept to be discussed in the section on therapy), *then* therapeutic change will occur; *if* therapeutic change occurs, *then* the client will experience more self-acceptance, greater trust of self, and so on. Person-centered theory is one of very few personality theories stated in such a precise fashion (see Rogers, 1959).

BASIC ASSUMPTIONS

What are the basic assumptions of person-centered theory? Rogers postulated two broad assumptions—the formative tendency and the actualizing tendency.

Formative Tendency

Rogers (1978, 1980) believed that there is a tendency for all matter, both organic and inorganic, to evolve from simpler to more complex forms. For the entire universe, a creative process, rather than a disintegrative one, is in operation. Rogers called this the **formative tendency** and pointed to many examples from nature. For instance, complex galaxies of stars form from a less well-organized mass; crystals such as snowflakes emerge from formless vapor; complex organisms develop from single cells; and human consciousness evolves from a primitive unconsciousness to a highly organized awareness.

Actualizing Tendency

An interrelated and more pertinent assumption is the **actualizing tendency,** the tendency within all human beings to move toward completion or fulfillment of potentials

(Rogers, 1980). Individuals have within themselves the creative power to solve problems, to alter their self-concepts, and to become increasingly self-directed. The source of psychological growth and maturity resides within the individual and is not found in outside forces. Individuals perceive their experiences as reality, and they know their reality better than anyone else. They do not need to be directed, controlled, exhorted, or manipulated in order to spur them toward actualization.

Although we have a variety of needs and behave in many different ways, all our behavior is relative to this single actualizing tendency. Because we operate as one complete organism, actualization involves our whole person—physiological and intellectual, rational and emotional, conscious and unconscious. The need to satisfy our hunger drive, to express deep emotions when they are felt, and to accept our self, are all examples of the single motive of actualization.

The actualization tendency is not limited to humans. Other animals and even plants have an inherent tendency to grow toward reaching their genetic potential— provided certain conditions are present. For example, in order for a bell pepper plant to reach its full productive potential, it must have water, sunlight, and a nutrient soil. Similarly, our actualization tendency is realized only under certain *conditions*. Specifically, we must be involved in a relationship with a partner who is *genuine* or *authentic*, and who demonstrates *empathy* and *unconditional positive regard* or *acceptance* toward us. (We discuss genuineness, empathy, and unconditional acceptance more fully in the section on therapy.)

Rogers (1961) emphasized that our partner's possession of these three qualities does not *cause* us to move toward constructive personal change. It does, however, permit us to actualize our own tendency toward self-fulfillment. In fact, Rogers contended that when these three conditions are present in a relationship, psychological growth will invariably occur. For this reason, Rogers regarded genuineness, unconditional positive regard, and empathy as both *necessary* and *sufficient* conditions for becoming a fully-functioning or self-actualizing person. Although people share the actualizing tendency with plants and other animals, only humans have a concept of self and thus a potential for *self-actualization*.

THE SELF AND SELF-ACTUALIZATION

A vague concept of self begins to emerge during early infancy when a portion of experience becomes personalized and differentiated in *awareness* as "I" or "me" experiences. Infants gradually become aware of their own identity as they learn what tastes good and what tastes bad, what feels pleasant and what does not. They then begin to evaluate experiences as positive or negative using as a criterion the actualizing tendency. Because nourishment is a requirement for actualization, infants value food and devalue hunger. They also value sleep, fresh air, physical contact, and health because each of these is needed for actualization (Rogers, 1959).

Once the self structure is established, the tendency to actualize the self begins to evolve. **Self-actualization** is a subsystem of the actualization tendency and is therefore not synonymous with it. The *actualization tendency* refers to organismic experiences of the individual, that is, to the whole person—conscious and unconscious, physiological and cognitive. On the other hand, *self-actualization* is the tendency to actualize the self as *perceived in awareness*. When the organism and the perceived self are in harmony, the two actualization tendencies are identical; but when one's organismic experiences are not in harmony with one's view of self, a discrepancy exists between the actualization tendency and the self-actualization tendency. For example, if a man's organismic experience is one of anger toward his wife, and if anger toward spouse is contrary to his perception of self, then his actualization tendency and his self-actualization are incongruent and he will experience conflict and inner tension (Rogers, 1959).

Rogers (1959) postulated that the self has two subsystems, the *self-concept* and the *ideal self*.

The Self-Concept

The **self-concept** includes all those aspects of one's being and one's experiences that are perceived in awareness (though not always accurately) by the individual. The self-concept is not identical with the **organismic self.** Portions of the organismic self may be beyond our awareness or simply not owned by us. For example, your stomach is part of your organismic self, but unless it malfunctions and causes concern, it is not likely to be part of your self-concept. Similarly, people can disown certain aspects of their self, such as experiences of dishonesty, when such experiences are not consistent with their self-concept.

Thus, once we form our self-concept, we find change and significant learnings quite difficult. Experiences that are inconsistent with our self-concept usually are either denied or accepted only in distorted forms (Rogers, 1959). Take, for example, a woman who sees herself as a faithful wife who could not possibly be attracted to any man other than her husband. If, on an organismic level, she experiences sexual feelings for another man, she will either deny the feelings to her awareness or reshape them, possibly by projecting them onto the man.

An established self-concept does not make change impossible, merely difficult. Change most readily occurs in an atmosphere of acceptance by others, which allows a person to reduce anxiety and threat and to take ownership of previously rejected experiences.

The Ideal Self

The second subsystem of the self is the **ideal self,** defined as one's view of self as one wishes to be. The ideal self contains all those attributes, usually positive, that people aspire to possess. Operationally, both the self-concept and the ideal self can be measured by such psychometric devices as the Q *sort technique* (an instrument that will be more fully discussed later). A wide gap between the ideal self and the self-concept indicates **incongruence** and an unhealthy personality. Psychologically healthy individuals perceive little discrepancy between their self-concept and what they ideally would like to be.

AWARENESS

Without awareness, the self-concept and the ideal self would not exist. Rogers (1959) defined *awareness* as "the symbolic representation (not necessarily in verbal symbols) of some portion of our experience" (p. 198). He used the term synonymously with both consciousness and symbolization.

Levels of Awareness

Rogers (1959) recognized three levels of symbolization or awareness. First, some events are experienced below the threshold of awareness and are either *ignored* or

Incongruence between the ideal self and the perceived self can result in conflict and unhappiness.

denied. An ignored experience can be illustrated by a woman walking down a busy street, an activity that presents many potential stimuli, particularly of sight and sound. Because she cannot attend to all of them, many remain *ignored*. An example of *denied* experience might be seen in a mother who never wanted children, but out of guilt she becomes overly solicitous to them. Her anger and resentment toward her children may be hidden to her for years, never reaching consciousness but yet remaining a part of her experience and coloring her conscious behavior toward them. Rogers (1959) also used the term *subceived* to refer to experiences that are perceived but yet not accepted into awareness. **Subception** refers to the process of perceiving stimuli without an awareness of the perception. Denied experiences are examples of subception.

Second, Rogers (1959) hypothesized that some experiences are *accurately symbolized* and freely admitted to the self-structure. Such experiences are both nonthreatening and consistent with the existing self-concept. For example, if a pianist who has full confidence in his piano-playing ability is told by a friend that his playing is excellent, he may hear these words, accurately symbolize them, and freely admit them to his self-concept.

A third level of awareness involves experiences that are perceived in a *distorted* form. When our experience is not consistent with our view of self, we reshape or distort the experience so that it can be assimilated into our existing self-concept. If the gifted pianist from the above example were to be told by a distrusted competitor that his playing was excellent, he might react very differently than he did when he heard the same words from a trusted friend. He may hear the remarks but distort their meaning because he feels threatened. "Why is this person trying to flatter me? This doesn't make sense." His experiences are inaccurately symbolized in awareness and therefore can be distorted so that they conform to an existing self-concept that, in part, says, "I am a person who does not trust my piano-playing competitors, especially those who are trying to trick me."

Denial of Positive Experiences

From the preceding example, we can see that it is not only the negative or derogatory experiences that are distorted or denied to awareness; many people have difficulty accepting genuine compliments and positive feedback, even when deserved. A student who feels inadequate but yet makes a superior grade might say to herself, "I know this grade should be evidence of my scholastic ability, but somehow I just don't feel that way. This class was the easiest one on campus. The other students just didn't try. My teacher did not know what she was doing." Compliments, even those genuinely dispensed, seldom have a positive influence on the self-concept of the recipient (Rogers, 1961). They may be distorted because the person distrusts the giver, or they may be denied because the recipient does not feel deserving of them; in all cases, a compliment from another also implies the right of that person to criticize or condemn, and thus the compliment carries an implied threat.

NEEDS

As we have seen, Rogers believed that people possess an inherent tendency to move toward actualization. Experiences that are seen as either maintaining or enhancing that movement are positively valued; those that are not, are negatively valued. The basic needs of all of us, therefore, are *maintenance* and *enhancement*, but we also have a need for *positive regard* and for *positive self-regard*.

Maintenance

The need for **maintenance** of our organismic self involves the satisfaction of basic needs such as food, air, and safety, but it also includes the tendency to resist change and to seek the status quo. The conservative nature of maintenance needs finds expression in our desire to protect our current, comfortable self-concept. We fight against new ideas; we distort experiences that do not quite fit; we find change painful and growth frightening.

Enhancement

Even though we have a strong desire to maintain the status quo, we are still willing to learn and to change. This need to become more, to develop, and to achieve growth is called **enhancement.**

The need for enhancing the self is manifested in our willingness to learn things that are not immediately rewarding. Other than enhancement, what motivation does a child have in learning to walk? Crawling can satisfy the need for mobility, whereas walking is associated with falling and with pain. Rogers's position is that we are willing to face threat and pain because of a biologically based tendency for the organism to fulfill its basic nature.

Enhancement needs are expressed in a variety of forms, including curiosity, playfulness, self-exploration, maturation, and friendship. Even food and sex are usually expressions of the organism's need to enhance itself. Both might also be maintenance needs, particularly when they are largely unsatisfied. However, for most people, the pursuit of food and sex is conducted in ways that enhance the self-concept.

Positive Regard

As the awareness of self emerges, the infant begins to develop a need to be loved, liked, or accepted by another person, a need Rogers (1959) referred to as **positive regard.** The need for positive regard is found in all human beings and remains a strong and persistent motivator throughout our lives. We value those experiences that satisfy our needs for positive regard. Unfortunately, the positive regard we receive from a significant other may be more powerful than the reward we receive by meeting our organismic needs. For example, a child who on an organismic level is afraid of a large dog may hear his father say, "Show me how brave you are. Go ahead and touch the dog." The child may then deny or distort his fear in order to receive the praise (positive regard) from his father.

Positive Self-Regard

After the self emerges, we begin to develop the need for **self-regard** as the result of our experiences with the satisfaction or frustration of our need for positive regard. In the above example, when the child receives praise from his father for courageous behavior, he may acquire positive self-regard for being brave and negative self-regard for acting cowardly. If the child generally dislikes himself, he will develop feelings of negative self-regard. But if he likes himself independently of others' attitudes toward him, he will continue to have *positive self-regard*. Positive self-regard includes feelings of self-confidence and self-worth.

How do we acquire positive self-regard? Originally, the need is dependent on the perception that others, especially significant others, care for, prize, or value us. If we perceive that we are liked or loved by others, then our need to receive positive regard is at least partially satisfied. Positive regard is a prerequisite for positive self-regard, but once positive self-regard is established, it becomes independent of the continual need to be loved (Rogers, 1959). This conception is quite similar to Maslow's (see Chapter 17) notion that we must satisfy our love and belongingness needs before self-esteem needs can become active, but once we begin to feel confident and worthy, we no longer require a replenishing supply of love and approval from others.

The source of positive self-regard, then, lies in the positive regard we receive from others, but once established, it is autonomous and self-perpetuating. As Rogers (1959) stated it, the person then "becomes in a sense his own significant social other" (p. 224).

CONDITIONS OF WORTH

Unfortunately, instead of unconditional positive regard, most of us receive **conditions of worth;** that is, we perceive that others love and accept us only if we meet their expectations and approval. "A condition of worth arises when the positive regard of a significant other is conditional, when the individual feels that in some respects he is prized and in others not" (Rogers, 1959, p. 209).

Conditions of worth become the criterion by which we accept or reject our experiences. We gradually assimilate into our self-structure the attitudes we perceive others as expressing toward us, and eventually we come to evaluate our experiences on this basis.

As the self begins to evolve during early childhood, we learn to attach worth and value to those experiences that we see as meeting the approval of our parents and significant others. If we perceive that our behavior is disapproved, we feel rejected. But our feelings of rejection are not limited to that specific behavior—they permeate our entire person because we feel that *we* are rejected. Eventually, we come to believe those reflected appraisals of others that are consistent with our view of self. We ignore our own primary sensory and visceral perceptions and gradually become less acquainted with our real or organismic self.

Acceptance by others is so important that when it is not forthcoming we desperately seek it, even at the expense of our own enhancement. From early childhood forward, most of us, to some extent, learn to disregard our own organismic valuations and, instead, look beyond ourselves for direction and guidance. To the degree that we introject the values of others, that is, accept conditions of worth, we tend to be incongruent or out of balance. Other people's values can be assimilated only in distorted fashion or at the risk of creating disequilibrium and conflict within the self (Rogers, 1959).

Inner conflict and incongruence, then, are due to the disparity between one's own values, which are formed from direct organismic experience, and the more or less distorted values that one has introjected from others. **External evaluations,** either positive or negative, do not foster psychological health, but rather, prevent us from being completely open to our own experiences. For example, we may reject organismically pleasurable experiences because we believe that other people do not approve of them. When our own experiences are distrusted, we distort our awareness of them, thus solidifying the discrepancy between our organismic evaluation and the values we have introjected from others. As a result, we may become psychologically stagnated (Rogers, 1959).

PSYCHOLOGICAL STAGNATION

To understand Rogers's view of abnormal development, remember that the organism and the self are two separate entities that may or may not be congruent with one another. Also recall that actualization refers to the organism's tendency to move toward fulfillment, whereas self-actualization is the desire of the perceived self to reach fulfillment. These two tendencies are sometimes at variance with one another.

Incongruence

Psychological disequilibrium begins when we fail to recognize our organismic experiences as self-experiences, that is, when we do not accurately symbolize organismic experiences into awareness because they appear to be inconsistent with our emerging self-concept. This *incongruence* between our self-concept and our organismic experience is the source of psychological stagnation. Conditions of worth that we received during early childhood lead to a somewhat false self-concept, one based on distortions and denials. The self-concept that emerges includes subceived perceptions that are not in harmony with our organismic experiences, and this incongruence between self and experience leads to discrepant and seemingly inconsistent behaviors. Sometimes we behave in ways that maintain or enhance our actualizing tendency, and at other times, we may behave in a manner designed to maintain or enhance a self-concept founded on other people's expectations and evaluations of us.

Vulnerability

The greater the incongruence between our perceived self (self-concept) and our organismic experience, the more vulnerable we are. Rogers (1959) believed that people are

vulnerable when they are unaware of the discrepancy between their organismic self and their significant experience. Lacking awareness of their incongruence, vulnerable people often behave in ways that are incomprehensible not only to others but also to themselves. For example, a person may say, "I don't know why I say such childish things to my boss. I know she must think I'm an idiot. I don't want to do it, but every time I open my mouth I say something stupid." The person fails to understand her own behavior because she is completely unaware of the incongruence between her organismic self and her perceived self.

Anxiety and Threat

If vulnerability exists when we have no awareness of the incongruence within our self, then anxiety and threat are experienced as we become more and more aware of such an incongruence. When we become dimly aware or subceive that the discrepancy between our organismic experience and our self-concept may become conscious, we feel anxious. Rogers (1959) defined **anxiety** as "a state of uneasiness or tension whose cause is unknown" (p. 204). As we become even more aware of the incongruence between our organismic experience and our perception of self, our anxiety begins to evolve into **threat,** that is, an awareness that our self is no longer whole or congruent. Although anxiety and threat can represent steps toward psychological health, they are not pleasant or comfortable feelings, because they signal to us that our organismic experience is inconsistent with our self-concept.

Defensiveness

In order to prevent this inconsistency between our organismic experience and our perceived self, we react in a defensive manner. **Defensiveness** is the protection of the self-concept against anxiety and threat by the denial or distortion of experiences inconsistent with it (Rogers, 1959). Because the self-concept consists of many self-descriptive statements, it is a many-faceted phenomenon. When one of our experiences is inconsistent with one part of our self-concept, we will behave in a defensive manner in order to protect the current structure of our self-concept.

The two chief defenses are *distortion* and *denial*. With **distortion,** we misinterpret an experience in order to fit it into some aspect of our self-concept. We perceive the experience in awareness, but we fail to understand its true meaning. With **denial,** we refuse to perceive an experience in awareness, or at least we keep some aspect of it from reaching symbolization. Denial is not as common as distortion because most experiences can be twisted or reshaped to fit the current self-concept. According to Rogers (1959), both distortion and denial serve the same purpose—they keep our perception of our organismic experiences consistent with our self-concept.

Distortion and denial can lead to behaviors similar to several Freudian concepts. For example, distortions usually result in rigid behaviors designed to protect the status quo (compulsions); they can also take the form of giving reasonable-sounding but invalid explanations for our behavior (rationalizations), making up for feelings of inadequacy by pretending to be somebody other than what we truly are (compensations), projecting our own organismic experiences onto others (paranoia), and believing ourselves to be either more or less competent than we really are (delusions). Denials, on the other hand, block out reality more completely and can result in behaviors similar to those that spring from Freud's concept of repression. Both denial and repression protect people from having to deal with painful reality by ignoring or blocking out experiences that otherwise would cause unpleasant anxiety or threat.

Behavior can become disorganized or even psychotic when one's defenses fail to operate properly.

Disorganization

Defensiveness is characteristic of so-called normal and neurotic individuals. When people's defenses fail to operate properly, their behavior becomes disorganized or psychotic. But why would defenses fail to function?

To answer this question, we must trace the course of disorganized behavior, which has the same origins as both normal defensive and neurotic behaviors, namely discrepancy between our organismic experience and our view of self. In normal and neurotic cases, denial and distortion prevent us from recognizing this discrepancy. In contrast, disorganization occurs when the incongruence between people's perceived self and their organismic experience is either too obvious or occurs too suddenly to be denied or distorted. Because people are forced into an awareness of this inconsistency, their previously unified self-structure becomes broken. The resulting disorganization can occur suddenly, or it can take place gradually over a long period of time. Ironically, people are particularly vulnerable to disorganization during therapy, especially if a therapist accurately interprets their actions and also insists that they face the experience prematurely (Rogers, 1959).

In a state of disorganization, people sometimes behave consistently with their organismic experience and sometimes in accordance with their shattered self-concept. An example of the first case is a previously prudish and proper woman who suddenly begins to use language explicitly sexual and scatological. The second case can be illustrated by a man who, because his self-concept is no longer a gestalt or unified whole, begins to behave in a confused, inconsistent, and totally unpredictable manner. In both cases, behavior is still consistent with the self-concept, but the self-concept has been broken and thus the behavior appears bizarre and confusing.

Although Rogers was even more tentative than usual when he first put forth his views of disorganized behavior in 1959, he made no important revisions in this portion of his theory. He never wavered in his disdain for using diagnostic labels to describe people. Traditional classifications such as those found in the *Diagnostic and Statistical Manual of Mental Disorders, Fourth Edition* (DSM-IV) (American Psychiatric Association, 1994) have never been part of the vocabulary of person-centered theory. In fact, Rogers always remained uncomfortable with the terms "neurotic" and "psychotic," preferring instead to speak of "defensive" and "disorganized" behaviors, terms that more accurately convey the idea that psychological maladjustment is on a continuum from the slightest discrepancy between self and experience to the most incongruent.

PSYCHOTHERAPY

Client-centered therapy is deceptively simple in statement but decidedly difficult in practice. Briefly, the client-centered approach holds that in order for vulnerable or anxious people to grow psychologically, they must come into contact with a therapist who is congruent and whom they perceive as providing an atmosphere of unconditional acceptance and accurate empathy. But therein lies the difficulty. The counselor qualities of congruence, unconditional positive regard, and empathic understanding are not easily obtainable.

The client-centered counseling approach can be stated in an if-then fashion. If the *conditions* of therapist congruence, unconditional positive regard, and empathic listening are present in a client/counselor relationship, then the *process* of therapy will transpire. If the process of therapy takes place, then certain predictable *outcomes* can be noted. Rogerian therapy, therefore, can be viewed in terms of conditions, process, and outcomes.

CONDITIONS

Rogers (1959) postulated that in order for therapeutic growth to take place, the following conditions are necessary and sufficient. First, an anxious or vulnerable client must come into contact with a congruent therapist who also possesses empathy and unconditional positive regard for that client. Second, the client must perceive these characteristics in the therapist. Third, contact between client and therapist must be of some duration.

The significance of the Rogerian hypothesis is revolutionary. With nearly any psychotherapy, the first and third conditions are present; that is, the client, or patient, is motivated by some sort of tension to seek help, and the relationship between the client and the therapist will last for some period of time. Client-centered therapy is unique in its insistence that the conditions of *counselor congruence, unconditional positive regard*, and *empathic listening* are both necessary and sufficient (Rogers, 1957).

Even though all three conditions are necessary for psychological growth, Rogers (1980) believed that congruence is more basic than either unconditional positive regard or empathic listening. Congruence is a general quality possessed by the therapist, whereas the other two conditions are specific feelings or attitudes that the therapist has for an individual client.

Counselor Congruence

The first necessary and sufficient condition for therapeutic change is a congruent therapist. **Congruence** exists when a person's organismic experiences are matched by an awareness of them and by an ability and willingness to openly express these feelings (Rogers, 1980). To be congruent means to be real or genuine, to be whole or integrated, to be what one truly is. Rogers (1995) spoke about congruence in these words:

Effective client-centered therapy requires a congruent counselor who feels empathy and unconditional positive regard for the client.

> *In my relationships with persons I have found that it does not help, in the long run, to act as though I were something that I am not* . . . It does not help to act calm and pleasant when actually I am angry and critical. It does not help to act as though I were permissive when I am really feeling that I would like to set limits. . . . It does not help to act as though I were acceptant of another person when underneath that exterior I feel rejection. (p. 9)

A congruent counselor, then, is not simply a kind and friendly person but rather a complete human being with feelings of joy, anger, frustration, confusion, and so on. When these feelings are experienced, they are neither denied nor distorted but flow easily into awareness and are freely expressed. A congruent therapist, therefore, is not passive, not aloof, and definitely *not* "nondirective."

Congruent therapists are not static. Like most other people, they are constantly exposed to new organismic experiences, but unlike most people, they accept these experiences into awareness, which contributes to their psychological growth. They wear no mask, do not attempt to fake a pleasant facade, and avoid any pretense of friendliness and affection when these are not truly felt. Also, they do not fake anger, toughness, or ignorance, nor do they cover up feelings of joy, elation, or happiness. In addition, they are able to match feelings with awareness and both with honest expression.

Because congruence involves feelings, awareness, and expression, incongruence can arise from either of two points. First, there can be a breakdown between feelings and awareness. A person may be feeling angry, and the anger may be obvious to others, but the angry person is unaware of the feeling. ("I'm not angry. How dare you say I'm angry!") The second source of incongruence is a discrepancy between awareness of an experience and the ability or willingness to express it to another. ("I know I'm feeling bored by what is being said, but I don't dare verbalize my disinterest, because my client will think that I am not a good therapist.") Rogers (1961) stated that therapists will be more effective if they communicate genuine feelings, even when those feelings are negative or threatening. To do otherwise would be dishonest, and clients will detect (but not necessarily consciously) any significant indicators of incongruence.

Although congruence is a necessary ingredient in successful therapy, Rogers (1980) did not believe that it is essential that a therapist be congruent in all relationships outside the therapeutic process. One can be less than perfect and yet become an effective psychotherapist. Also, a therapist need not be absolutely congruent in order to facilitate some growth within a client. As with unconditional positive regard and empathic listening, different degrees of congruence exist. The more the client perceives each of these qualities as characterizing the therapist, the more successful will be the therapeutic process.

Unconditional Positive Regard

Positive regard is the need to be liked, prized, or accepted by another person. When this need exists without any conditions or qualifications, **unconditional positive regard** occurs (Rogers, 1980). Therapists have unconditional positive regard when they are "experiencing a warm, positive and accepting attitude toward what *is* the client" (Rogers, 1961, p. 62). The attitude is without possessiveness, without evaluations, and without reservations.

A therapist with unconditional positive regard toward a client will show a non-possessive warmth and acceptance, not an effusive, effervescent persona. To have non-possessive warmth means to care about another without smothering or owning that person. It includes the attitude "Because I care about you, I can permit you to be autonomous and independent of my evaluations and restrictions. You are a separate person with your own feelings and opinions regarding what is right or wrong. The fact that I care for you does not mean that I must guide you in making choices, but that I can allow you to be yourself and to decide what is best for you." This kind of permissive attitude earned for Rogers the undeserved reputation of being passive or nondirective in therapy, but, as seen above, a client-centered therapist must be actively involved in a relationship with the client.

Therapists with unconditional positive regard do not evaluate a client, nor do they accept one action and reject another. External evaluation, whether positive or negative, is always restricting and leads to client defensiveness rather than growth. "My therapist thinks I'm so brilliant. However, I don't feel very smart so I'm having a hard time fitting together her evaluation of me and my own feelings about myself." When a client-centered therapist experiences unconditional positive regard for a client, no conditions of worth exist and no evaluations are made.

Unconditional positive regard means that therapists accept clients without any restrictions or reservations. Regardless of their clients' behavior, therapists continue to prize them. Although therapists may value some client behaviors more than others, their positive regard remains constant and unwavering whether their clients are frightened, obnoxious, angry, or loving (Rogers, 1959).

Although "unconditional positive regard" is a somewhat awkward term, all three words are important. "Regard" means that there is a close relationship and that the therapist sees the client as an important person; "positive" indicates that the direction of the relationship is toward warm and caring feelings; and "unconditional" suggests that the positive regard is no longer dependent on specific client behaviors and does not have to be continually earned.

Empathic Listening

The third necessary and sufficient condition of psychological growth is **empathic listening.** Empathy exists when therapists accurately sense the feelings of their clients and are able to communicate these perceptions so that the clients know that another person has entered their world of feelings without prejudice, projection, or evaluation.

To Rogers (1980), empathy "means temporarily living in the other's life, moving about in it delicately without making judgments" (p. 142). Empathy does not involve interpreting clients' meanings or uncovering their unconscious feelings, procedures that would entail an external frame of reference and a threat to clients. In contrast, empathy suggests that a therapist sees things from the client's point of view and that the client feels safe and unthreatened.

Client-centered therapists do not take empathy for granted; they check the accuracy of their sensings by trying them out on the client. "You seem to be telling me that you feel a great deal of resentment toward your father." Valid empathic understanding is often followed by an exclamation from the client along these lines: "Yes, that's it exactly! I really do feel resentful."

Empathic listening is a powerful tool, which, along with genuineness and caring, facilitates personal growth within the client. What, precisely, is the role of empathy in psychological change? How does an empathic therapist help a client move toward wholeness and psychological health? Rogers's (1980) own words provide the best answer to these questions.

> When persons are perceptively understood, they find themselves coming in closer touch with a wider range of their experiencing. This gives them an expanded referent to which they can turn for guidance in understanding themselves and directing their behavior. If the empathy has been accurate and deep, they may also be able to unblock a flow of experiencing and permit it to run its uninhibited course. (p. 156)

Empathy is effective because it enables clients to listen to themselves and, in effect, become their own therapists.

Empathy should not be confused with sympathy. The latter term suggests a feeling *for* the client, whereas empathy connotes a feeling *with* another. Sympathy is never therapeutic, because it stems from external evaluation and usually leads to clients feeling sorry for themselves. Self-pity is a deleterious attitude that threatens the self-concept and creates disequilibrium within the self-structure. Also, empathy does not mean that a therapist has the same feelings as the client. A therapist does not feel anger, frustration, confusion, resentment, or sexual attraction at the same time a client experiences them. Rather, a therapist is experiencing the depth of the client's feeling while permitting the client to be a separate person. A therapist has an emotional as well as a cognitive reaction to a client's feelings, but *the feelings belong to the client*, not the therapist. A therapist does not take ownership of a client's experiences but is able to convey to the client an understanding of what it means to be the client at that particular moment (Rogers, 1961).

PROCESS

If the conditions of therapist congruence, unconditional positive regard, and empathy are present, then the process of therapeutic change will be set in motion. Although each person seeking psychotherapy is unique, Rogers (1959) believed that a certain lawfulness characterizes the process of therapy.

The process of constructive personality change can be placed on a continuum from most defensive to most integrated. Rogers (1961) has arbitrarily divided this continuum into seven stages.

Stage One is characterized by an unwillingness to communicate anything about oneself. People at this stage ordinarily do not seek help, but if for some reason they come to therapy, they are extremely rigid and resistant to change. They do not recognize any problems and refuse to own any personal feelings or emotions.

In *Stage Two*, clients become slightly less rigid. They discuss external events and other people, but they still disown or fail to recognize their own feelings. However, they may talk about personal feelings as if such feelings were objective phenomena.

As clients enter into *Stage Three*, they can more freely talk about self, although still as an object. "I'm doing the best I can at work, but my boss still doesn't like me." Clients talk about feelings and emotions in the past or future tense and avoid present feelings. They refuse to accept their emotions, keep personal feelings at a distance from the here and now situation, only vaguely perceive that they can make personal choices, and deny individual responsibility for most of their decisions.

Clients in *Stage Four* begin to talk of deep feelings but not ones presently felt. "I was really burned up when my teacher accused me of cheating." When clients do express present feelings, they are usually surprised by this expression. They deny or distort experiences, although they may have some dim recognition that they are capable of feeling emotions in the present. They begin to question some values that have been introjected from others, and they start to see the incongruence between their perceived self and their organismic experience. They accept more freedom and responsibility than they did in Stage Three and begin to tentatively allow themselves to become involved in a relationship with the therapist.

By the time clients reach *Stage Five*, they have begun to experience significant change and growth. They can express feelings in the present, although they have not yet accurately symbolized those feelings. They are beginning to rely on an internal locus of evaluation for their feelings and to make fresh and new discoveries about themselves. They also experience a greater differentiation of feelings and develop more appreciation for nuances among them. In addition, they begin to make their own decisions and to accept responsibility for their choices.

Stage Six is characterized by dramatic growth, with people at this stage moving irreversibly closer to becoming fully functioning or self-actualizing individuals. They freely allow into awareness those experiences that they had previously denied or distorted. They become more congruent and are able to match their present experiences with awareness and with open expression. They no longer evaluate their own behavior from an external viewpoint but rely on their organismic self as the criterion for evaluating experiences. They begin to develop unconditional self-regard, which means that they have a feeling of genuine caring and affection for the person they are becoming.

An interesting concomitant to this stage is a physiological loosening. These people experience their whole organismic self, as their muscles relax, tears flow, circulation improves, and physical symptoms disappear.

In many ways Stage Six signals an end to therapy. Indeed, if therapy were to be terminated at this point, clients would still progress to the next level.

Stage Seven can occur outside the therapeutic encounter, because growth at Stage Six seems to be irreversible. Clients who reach Stage Seven become fully functioning "persons of tomorrow" (a concept more fully explained later). They are able to generalize their in-therapy experiences to their world beyond therapy. They possess the confidence to be themselves at all times, to own and to feel deeply the totality of their experiences, and to live those experiences in the present. Their organismic self, now unified with the self-concept, becomes the locus for evaluating their experiences. People at Stage Seven receive pleasure in knowing that these evaluations are fluid and that change and growth will continue. In addition, they become congruent, possess *unconditional positive self-regard*, and are able to be loving and empathic toward others.

Persons of tomorrow are confident in themselves and comfortable with change.

Now that we have described the dynamics of therapeutic change, we must look at the theoretical formulations evoked to explain this process. Rogers's (1980) explanation follows this line of reasoning. When persons come to experience themselves as prized and unconditionally accepted, they realize, perhaps for the first time, that they are lovable. The example of the therapist enables them to prize and accept themselves, to have unconditional positive self-regard. As clients perceive that they are emphatically understood, they are freed to listen to themselves more accurately, to have empathy for their own feelings. As a consequence, when persons come to prize themselves and to accurately understand themselves, their perceived self becomes more congruent with their organismic experiences. They now possess the same three therapeutic characteristics as any effective helper, and in effect, they become their own therapist.

Outcomes

If the process of therapeutic change is set in motion, then certain observable outcomes can be expected. Rogers (1959) elaborated these predictable outcomes with enough precision to allow for research on the effectiveness of psychotherapy.

The most basic outcome of successful client-centered therapy is a congruent client who is less defensive and more open to experience. Each of the remaining outcomes is a logical extension of this basic one.

As a result of being more congruent and less defensive, clients have a clearer picture of themselves and a more realistic view of the world. They are better able to assimilate experiences into the self on the symbolic level; they are more effective in solving problems; and they have a higher level of positive self-regard.

Being realistic, they have a more accurate view of their potentials, which permits them to narrow the previously wide gap between their self-ideal and their real self. Typically, this gap is narrowed because both the ideal self and the true self show some movement. Clients, because they are more realistic, lower their expectations of what they should be or would like to be, and because they have an increase in positive self-regard, they raise their view of what they really are.

Table 16.1 Rogers's Theory of Therapeutic Change

If These Conditions Exist	Then Therapeutic Change Occurs and the Client Will

• A vulnerable or anxious client
• contacts a counselor who possesses
  1. **congruence in the relationship,**
  2. **unconditional positive regard for the client, and**
  3. **empathic understanding for the client's internal frame of reference,**
• and the client perceives Conditions 1, 2, and 3—the necessary and sufficient conditions for therapeutic growth
	1. **become more congruent**
	2. **be less defensive**
	3. **become more open to experiences**
	4. have a more realistic view of the world
	5. develop positive self-regard
	6. close the gap between ideal self and real self
	7. be less vulnerable to threat
	8. become less anxious
	9. take ownership of experiences
	10. become more accepting of others
	11. become more congruent in relationships with others

Note: Boldfaced terms represent the key therapeutic conditions and the most basic outcomes.

Because their ideal self and their real self are more congruent, clients experience less physiological and psychological tension, are less vulnerable to threat, and have less anxiety. They are less likely to look to others for direction and less likely to use others' opinions and values as the criteria for evaluating their own experiences. Instead, they become more self-directed and more likely to perceive that the locus of evaluation resides within themselves. They no longer feel compelled to please other people and to meet external expectations. They feel sufficiently safe to take ownership of an increasing number of their experiences and comfortable enough with themselves to lessen the need for denial and distortion.

Their relationships with others are also changed. They become more accepting of others, make fewer demands, and simply allow others to be themselves. Because they have less need to distort reality, they have less desire to force others to meet their expectations. They are also perceived by others as being more mature, more likable, and more socialized. Their genuineness, positive self-regard, and empathic understanding are extended beyond therapy, and they become better able to participate in other growth-facilitating relations (Rogers, 1959, 1961). Table 16.1 illustrates Rogers's theory of therapy.

THE PERSON OF TOMORROW

The interest shown by Rogers in the psychologically healthy individual is rivaled only by that of Maslow (see Chapter 17). Whereas Maslow was primarily a researcher, Rogers was first of all a psychotherapist, whose concern with the psychologically healthy people grew out of his general theory of therapy. In 1951, Rogers first briefly put forward his "characteristics of the altered personality," then he enlarged on the concept of the **fully functioning person** in an unpublished paper (Rogers, 1953). In 1959, his theory of the healthy personality was expounded in the Koch series, and he returned to this topic frequently during the early 1960s (Rogers, 1961, 1962, 1963). Somewhat later, he described both the world of tomorrow and the **person of tomorrow** (Rogers, 1980).

CHARACTERISTICS

If the three necessary and sufficient therapeutic conditions of congruence, unconditional positive regard, and empathy are optimal, what kind of theoretically possible person would emerge? Rogers (1961, 1980) listed five characteristics.

First, persons of tomorrow would be in a *constant state of change*. They would not be end products, but emerging, evolving individuals. They would have self-structures that are fluid and flexible, and they would be comfortable with change and confident that the present, for all its richness of feeling, is not the final goal. They would realize that they have not "arrived" and that life will continue to open before them, bringing new and unexpected experiences and an accompanying change in the self-structure.

Second, persons of tomorrow would be *open to their experiences*, accurately symbolizing them in awareness rather than denying or distorting them. This simple statement is pregnant with meaning. For people who are open to experience, all stimuli, whether stemming from within the organism or from the external environment, are freely received by the self. Fully functioning people can openly accept their experiences, which allows their self-structure to be in a continual state of change and growth. For the average person, this might be a rather frightening situation, because it signifies that outside events cannot be completely controlled.

A related characteristic of persons of tomorrow is a *freshness of attitude and approach*. Because these people are open to their experiences, they are in a constant state of fluidity and change. What they experience in each moment is new and unique, something never before experienced by their evolving self. They see each experience with a new freshness, and they appreciate fully the present moment. Their experience may not be pleasant or even welcome, but they openly live it in the here and now.

Rogers (1961) referred to this tendency to live in the moment as **existential living.** This freshness of attitude and approach to each new situation becomes possible as the need for defensiveness declines. Persons of tomorrow would permit even undesirable and repugnant experiences to be symbolized in consciousness, because they have no need to deceive themselves and no reason to impress others. They are young in mind and spirit, with no preconceptions about how the world should be. They discover what an experience means to them by living that experience without the prejudice of prior expectations. They do not live by "shoulds" and "oughts" but by what is. They are unique and creative in their search for new means of adapting new solutions to problems and new ways of being.

A fourth characteristic of psychologically healthy people is a *trust in their organismic selves*. Persons of tomorrow do not depend on others for guidance because they realize that their own experiences are the best criteria for making choices; they do what feels right for them because they trust their own inner feelings more than the pontifications of parents or the rigid rules of society. However, they perceive clearly the rights and feelings of other people, which they take into consideration when making decisions.

Unlike most people who have a cloudy view of themselves and whose memories and expectations are colored by wishful thinking, persons of tomorrow would assimilate experiences without denial and distortion. Thus, their own perceptions would be their most reliable guide to action. The meanings they have discovered in their own experiences, although not infallible, would be more trustworthy than the values or opinions of any other person. Nevertheless, they would value other people and seek harmonious relationships with them.

Finally, persons of tomorrow would remain confident of their own ability to experience *harmonious relations with others*. They would feel no need to be liked or loved by everyone, because they already know that they are unconditionally prized and accepted by someone. They would seek intimacy with another person who is probably equally healthy, and such a relationship itself would contribute to the continual growth of each partner.

Persons of tomorrow would be authentic in their relations with others. They would be what they appear to be, without deceit or fraud, without defenses and facades, without hypocrisy and sham. They would care about others, but in a nonjudgmental manner. They would seek meaning beyond themselves and would yearn for the spiritual life and inner peace (Rogers, 1980).

IMPLICATIONS

Rogers believed that when people experience the necessary conditions for growth, they become more and more fully functioning and eventually emerge as persons of tomorrow. What implications does this hypothesis have for the individual and for society? Rogers (1961, 1962, 1980) listed at least four.

Persons of tomorrow become *more integrated*, more whole, more "all one piece" (Rogers, 1962). They no longer have an artificial boundary between conscious processes and unconscious ones. Because they are able to accurately symbolize all their experiences in awareness, they clearly see the difference between what is and what should be; because they use their organismic feelings as criteria for evaluating their experiences, they bridge the gap between their real self and their ideal self; because they have no need for self-importance and taking pleasure in simply being themselves, they present no facades to other people; and because they have confidence in who they are, they can openly express whatever feelings they are experiencing.

Second, psychologically healthy people are *more adaptable*. Thus, from an evolutionary viewpoint, they are more likely to survive—hence the title, "persons of tomorrow." They are not conformists and do not adjust to a static environment. They realize that conformity and adjustment to a fixed condition have little long term survival value. Persons of tomorrow can afford to be adaptable because they feel comfortable with change. They live in harmony with other people and balance their contributions to society with the satisfaction of their own needs.

A third implication of Rogers's description of persons of tomorrow is the *basic trustworthiness of human nature*. Psychologically healthy people will not harm others merely for personal gain. They care about others and are ready to help when needed, even though "they are suspicious of the professional 'helpers'" (Rogers, 1980, p. 351). They experience anger, but they can be trusted not to strike out unreasonably against others when they are angry. They feel aggression, but they can channel it in appropriate directions (Rogers, 1961).

Finally, because persons of tomorrow are open to all their experiences, they enjoy a *greater richness in life* than do other people. They neither distort internal stimuli nor buffer their emotions. Consequently, they feel more deeply than others. They are able to experience both negative and positive emotions to the fullest extent. They vividly feel anger, pain, and sorrow, but they are also capable of intense joy, elation, pleasure, and love. They live in the present and thus participate more richly in the ongoing moment. The high level of confidence they have in themselves allows them to enjoy a life that is "enriching, exciting, rewarding, challenging, meaningful" (Rogers, 1961, p. 32).

Rogers (1961) summed up the implications of fully functioning living with these words:

> This process of healthy living is not, I am convinced, a life for the faint-hearted. It involves the stretching and growing of becoming more and more one's potentials. It involves the courage to be. It means launching

oneself fully into the stream of life. Yet the deeply exciting thing about human beings is that when the individual is inwardly free, he chooses this process of becoming. (p. 32)

PHILOSOPHY OF SCIENCE

As we have seen, Rogers was first a scientist, second a therapist, and third a personality theorist. Because his scientific attitude permeates both his therapy and his theory of personality, we look briefly at his philosophy of science.

According to Rogers (1968), science begins and ends with the subjective experience. Scientists must have many of the characteristics of the person of tomorrow. They must be inclined to look within, to be in tune with internal feelings and values, to be intuitive and creative, to be open to experiences, to be able to change, to have a fresh outlook, and to possess a solid trust in themselves.

In addition, scientists should be completely involved in the phenomena being studied. They must not view those phenomena too objectively, as detached outsiders. Rogers (1968) believed that people who conduct research on psychotherapy, for example, must first have had long careers as therapists. Scientists must care about and care for newly born ideas and nurture them lovingly through their fragile infancy.

Science begins when an intuitive scientist starts to perceive patterns among phenomena. At first, these dimly seen relationships may be too vague to be communicated to others, but they are nourished by a caring scientist until eventually they can be formulated into testable hypotheses. These hypotheses, then, are the consequence of the open-minded personal experiences of the scientist and not the result of preexisting stereotypical thought. The scientist formulates hypotheses not to fit existing tools of measurement, but in accordance with the phenomena being investigated.

At this point, methodology enters the picture. Although the creativity of a scientist may yield innovative methods of research, these procedures themselves must be rigorously controlled, empirical, and objective. Precise methods prevent the scientist from self-deception and from intentionally or unintentionally manipulating the observations. But this precision should not be confused with science. It is only the *method* of science that is precise and objective.

The scientist then communicates findings from that method to others, but the communication itself is subjective. The people receiving the communication bring their own degrees of open-mindedness or defensiveness into this process. They have varying levels of readiness to receive the findings, depending on the prevailing climate of scientific thought and the personal subjective experiences of each individual.

THE CHICAGO STUDY

Consistent with his philosophy of science, Rogers did not permit methodology to dictate the nature of his research. In his investigations of the outcomes of client-centered psychotherapy, first at the Counseling Center of the University of Chicago (Rogers & Dymond, 1954) and then with schizophrenic patients at the University of Wisconsin (Rogers, Gendlin, Kiesler, & Truax, 1967), he and his colleagues allowed the problem to take precedence over methodology and measurement. They did not formulate hypotheses simply because the tools for testing them were readily available. Instead, they began by sensing vague impressions from clinical experience and gradually forming these into testable hypotheses. It was only then that Rogers and his colleagues dealt with the task of finding or inventing instruments by which these hypotheses could be tested.

The purpose of the Chicago Study was to investigate both the process and the outcomes of client-centered therapy. The therapists were of a "journeyman" level. They included Rogers and other faculty members, but graduate students also served as therapists. Although they ranged widely in experience and ability, all were basically client-centered in approach (Rogers, 1961; Rogers & Dymond, 1954).

HYPOTHESES

Research at the University of Chicago Counseling Center was built around the basic client-centered hypothesis, which states that all persons have within themselves the capacity, either active or latent, for self-understanding as well as the capacity and tendency to move in the direction of self-actualization and maturity. This tendency will become realized provided the therapist creates the proper psychological atmosphere (Rogers, 1954). More specifically, Rogers hypothesized that during therapy, clients would assimilate into their self-concepts those feelings and experiences previously denied to awareness; the discrepancy between real self and ideal self would lessen as a concomitant of therapy; the observed behavior of clients would become more socialized and mature as a result of therapy; during and after therapy, clients would become both more self-accepting and more accepting of others. These hypotheses, in turn, became the foundation for several more specific hypotheses, which were operationally stated and then tested.

METHOD

Because the hypotheses of the study dictated that subtle subjective personality changes be measured in an objective fashion, the selection of measurement instruments was a difficult one. To assess change from an external viewpoint, the researchers used the Thematic Apperception Test (TAT), the Self-Other Attitude Scale (S-O Scale), and the Willoughby Emotional Maturity Scale (E-M Scale). The TAT, a projective personality test developed by Henry Murray (1938), was used to test hypotheses that called for a standard clinical diagnosis; the S-O Scale, an instrument compiled at the Counseling Center from several earlier sources, measures antidemocratic trends and ethnocentrism; the E-M Scale was used to compare descriptions of clients' behavior and emotional maturity as seen by two close friends and by the clients themselves.

To measure change from the client's point of view, the researchers relied on the **Q sort** technique developed by William Stephenson of the University of Chicago (Stephenson, 1953). The Q sort technique begins with a universe of 100 self-referent statements printed on 3 × 5 cards, which participants are requested to sort into nine piles from "most like me" to "least like me." Researchers asked the participants to sort the cards into piles of 1, 4, 11, 21, 26, 21, 11, 4, and 1. The resulting distribution approximates a normal curve and allows for statistical analysis. At various points throughout the study, participants were requested to sort the cards to describe the self, the ideal self, and the ordinary person.

Participants for the study were 18 men and 11 women who had sought therapy at the Counseling Center at the University of Chicago. More than half were university students and the others were from the surrounding community. These clients, called the

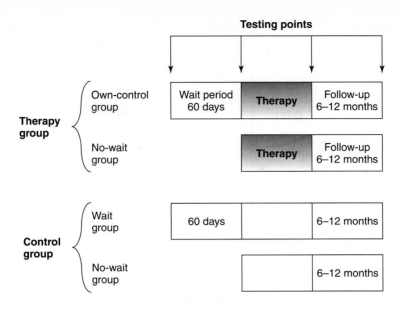

Testing points

| | | Wait period 60 days | Therapy | Follow-up 6–12 months |

Therapy group
- Own-control group
- No-wait group

Control group
- Wait group
- No-wait group

Figure **16.1**   Design of the Chicago Study.
SOURCE: From C. R. Rogers and R. F. Dymond, *Psychotherapy and Personality Change*, 1954. Copyright © 1954 The University of Chicago Press, Chicago, IL. Reprinted by permission.

experimental or *therapy group*, received at least six therapeutic interviews and each session was electronically recorded and transcribed, a procedure Rogers had pioneered as early as 1938.

The researchers used two different methods of control. First, they asked half the people in the therapy group to wait 60 days before they would receive therapy. These participants, known as the own-control or *wait group*, were required to wait before receiving therapy in order to determine if motivation to change rather than the therapy itself might cause people to get better. The other half of the therapy group, called the *no-wait group*, received therapy immediately.

The second control consisted of a separate group of "normals," who had volunteered to serve as participants in a "research on personality" study. Researchers needed this comparison group to determine the effects of such variables as passage of time, knowledge that one is part of an experiment (the **placebo effect**), and the impact of repeated testing. The participants in this *control group* were divided into a *wait group* and a *no-wait group*, which corresponded to the wait and no-wait therapy groups. Researchers tested both the therapy wait group and the control wait group four times, at the beginning of the 60-day wait period, prior to therapy, immediately after therapy, and after a 6- to 12-month follow-up period. They administered the no-wait groups the same tests on the same occasions, except, of course, prior to the wait period. The overall design of the study is shown in Figure 16.1.

FINDINGS

As hypothesized, the therapy group showed less discrepancy between self and ideal self after therapy than before, and they retained almost all those gains throughout the follow-up period. As expected, the "normal" controls had a higher level of congruence than the therapy group at the beginning of the study, but, in contrast to the therapy group, they showed almost no change in congruence between self and self-ideal from the initial testing until the final follow-up.

The researchers also found that the self concept of the therapy group changed more than their perception of the ordinary person, meaning that, although clients showed little change in their notion of what the average person was like, they manifested marked change in their perceptions of self. This finding suggests that intellectual insight does not result in psychological growth (Rudikoff, 1954).

Does therapy bring about noticeable changes in clients' behavior as perceived by close friends? Participants in both the therapy and the control groups were asked to supply the experimenters with names of two intimate friends who would be in a position to judge overt behavioral changes. Researchers used letters to contact these friends, who did not know the true nature of the study.

In general, the friends reported no significant behavioral changes in the clients from the pretherapy period to posttherapy. However, this global rating of no change was due to a counterbalancing effect. Clients judged by their therapists as being most improved received higher posttherapy maturity scores from their friends, whereas those rated as least improved received lower scores from their friends. Interestingly, before therapy, clients typically rated themselves less mature than their friends rated them, but as therapy progressed, they began to rate themselves higher and, therefore, more in agreement with their friends' ratings. Participants in the control group showed no changes throughout the study in emotional maturity as judged by friends (Rogers & Dymond, 1954).

SUMMARY OF RESULTS

The Chicago Study continues as some of the best-designed investigations of the outcomes of psychotherapy. It demonstrated that people receiving client-centered therapy, in general, show some growth or improvement. However, improvement fell short of the optimum. The therapy group began treatment as less healthy than the control group, showed growth during therapy, and retained most of that improvement throughout the follow-up period. However, they never attained the level of psychological health demonstrated by people in the control group.

Looking at these outcomes another way, the typical person receiving client-centered therapy probably never approaches Stage Seven hypothesized by Rogers and discussed earlier. A more realistic expectation might be for the client to advance to Stage Three or Four. Client-centered therapy is effective, but it does not result in the fully functioning person.

RELATED RESEARCH

Since the Chicago Study, Rogers's three facilitative conditions have been investigated by others (Truax & Carkhuff, 1967), but the person currently most actively researching these nurturing qualities is Duncan Cramer in Great Britain. Cramer has investigated Rogers's "necessary and sufficient" conditions in interpersonal relationships outside of therapy. Typically, Cramer administers the Rosenberg (1965) Self-Esteem Scale and the revised Relationship Inventory (Barrett-Lennard, 1964) to a group of participants to determine the relationship between Rogers's facilitative conditions and self-esteem.

The Barrett-Lennard (1962, 1964) Relationship Inventory was developed to assess clients' perceptions of therapists' congruence, unconditional positive regard, and empathy, but it divides unconditional positive regard into two separate components, namely, level of regard and unconditionality of regard. Thus, the revised Relationship Inventory measures four facilitative conditions, but it is not limited to clients' perception of their therapist—it can be used to describe any relationship. The four scales contain 16 items each. Examples include: "She/he cares for me" (level of regard); "Her/his feelings toward me don't depend on how I feel toward him/her" (unconditionality of regard); "She/he almost always knows exactly what I mean" (empathy); and "She/he is comfortable and at ease in our relationship" (congruence). Cramer employs the revised Relationship Inventory to assess people's perception of various close relationships.

In one study, for example, Cramer (1985) used the Rosenberg Self-Esteem Scale as a measure of psychological health and the revised Relationship Inventory as an assessment of Rogerian facilitative conditions. Rather than requiring participants to use a therapist as the target person, Cramer asked participants for their descriptions of a close friend. He found significant positive correlations for female students between their level of self-esteem and all four facilitative conditions, suggesting that women with high self-esteem perceive their close friends as being congruent and as providing unconditional positive regard and empathy. For men, the correlations were positive, but because the sample size was small, they were significant only for level of regard and for the combination of all four facilitative conditions.

Because he tested few men in his 1985 study, Cramer (1987) conducted a similar investigation using a larger sample size. Besides including more men, he also used a statistical analysis that allowed him to determine which of four facilitative conditions was most directly related to self-esteem, and he also tested the hypothesis that advice from a close friend would be negatively related to self-esteem. In this study, Cramer asked 232 female students and 87 male students to describe their relationship with their closest friend. He also constructed a 16-item scale for measuring the importance of advice received from a friend and incorporated this scale into the Relationship Inventory. Again, he used the Rosenberg Self-Esteem Scale as a measure of self-esteem and psychological health.

Cramer (1987) found significant positive correlations between self-esteem and all four facilitative variables for women, and between self-esteem and level of regard, congruence, and empathy for men. Thus, the only condition that did not attain significance was unconditionality of regard for male students. The correlations, however, were only low to moderate, and when the influence of level of regard was controlled for, the correlations between the three remaining facilitative conditions and self-esteem failed to reach significance. This finding tends to support Rogers's hypothesis that all three conditions are necessary; that is, the therapist must be perceived as exhibiting all the conditions, not just one or two.

Contrary to Rogers, however, Cramer could find no negative correlation between self-esteem and providing advice. In fact, he found that both female and male students saw their closest friend as giving them advice, and that friends who provide advice are the ones who are seen as exhibiting positive regard, unconditionality of regard, empathy, and congruence.

In 1988, Cramer conducted a similar study, except that he introduced the element of time; that is, he asked college students to respond to the Self-Esteem Scale and the Barrett-Lennard Relationship Inventory near the beginning of the school year and then again 15 weeks later. For the first testing, self-esteem was related only to level of regard, perhaps because students did not yet know one another well, or because they named friends from whom they were separated. For the second testing session, however, Cramer found significant and positive correlations between self-esteem and level of regard, empathy, congruence, and total score. Thus, unconditionality of regard had the weakest relationship with self-esteem.

Cramer (1989) expanded his study once more—this time to include parents as well as close friends. He asked 16- to 18-year-old participants to fill out the Self-Esteem Scale and the revised Relationship Inventory, which targeted their mother, father, closest friend of the same sex, and closest friend of the opposite sex. Again, he found positive relationships between self-esteem and the facilitative conditions, but more importantly, he found no differences in the size of the correlations for the four facilitative conditions among any of the four relationships, which suggests that young people with positive self-esteem tend to have growth-producing relationships with more than one person.

Next, Cramer (1990a) determined the correlations among self-esteem, disclosure of personal problems, and the facilitative conditions of unconditional acceptance, empathy, and congruence. He administered the Rosenberg Self-Esteem Scale and the revised Barrett-Lennard Relationship Inventory along with an index of disclosure of personal problems to 104 young women and 19 young men and asked them to target four different relationships—a casual friend, the closest friend of the same sex, the closest friend of the opposite sex, and a romantic partner. Cramer found that self-esteem was most closely associated with the facilitative conditions in the romantic partner. Interestingly, the second highest correlations were for self-esteem and the facilitative qualities in the casual friend. In addition, Cramer found that disclosure of personal problems was positively related to the facilitative conditions, meaning that people were willing to reveal important aspects of themselves to friends whom they perceived as being congruent and as possessing empathy and unconditional positive regard.

More recently, Cramer has attempted to demonstrate the direction of the relationship between Rogers's therapeutic conditions and positive self-esteem; that is, he has tried to show that the facilitative conditions *precede* elevations in self-esteem. As Cramer (1990b) correctly pointed out, the only way that researchers can conclusively demonstrate that the therapeutic conditions *cause* increases in self-esteem would be to manipulate these conditions, that is, to raise and lower counselor congruence, empathy, level of regard, and conditionally of regard and then to observe their effects. Such a procedure, however, would encounter both ethical and practical difficulties. Instead of manipulating the independent variables (the four facilitative conditions), Cramer and Roelf Takens (1992) looked at therapists' empathy and acceptance and clients' progress at both Session 2 and Session 6 for 37 clients treated weekly with individual psychoanalytic and client-centered therapy.

High correlations between level of therapists' facilitative qualities and clients' status (as judged by both therapists and clients) would not indicate direction of cause and effect. Clients may be improving because they perceive greater levels of therapists' empathy and acceptance, or therapists may become more empathic and acceptant because they see their clients improving, or some other factor may be confounding the relationship. However, if the correlation between the therapeutic conditions at Session 2 and client status at Session 6 is significantly higher than the correlation between client status at Session 2 and the therapeutic conditions at Session 6, then one can infer that the quality of the therapists' acceptance and empathy determines therapeutic status. Cramer and Takens, however, found no support for this hypothesis, although they did find that therapists' acceptance and empathy at Session 2 was positively associated with client progress at Session 6, suggesting some evidence for the notion that counselor empathy and acceptance are at least *related* to therapeutic growth.

Cramer has presented further evidence that the four facilitative conditions exist before clients experience an increase in self-esteem. In one study, Cramer (1993) found that clients who saw their therapists as possessing a combination of congruence, empathy, level of regard, and unconditionality of regard after Session 1 had higher self-esteem and lower need for approval after Session 3. Later, Cramer (1994) studied college students on two occasions 15 weeks apart. Students who at the beginning of the study felt that they had a close friend who was unconditionally accepting, empathic, and congruent tended to have high self-esteem 15 weeks later.

These studies suggest that Rogers's necessary and sufficient conditions are related to self-esteem and psychological health and that the direction of the relationship is from the facilitative conditions to increasingly higher levels of self-esteem. However, only experimental designs are able to prove conclusively that congruence, unconditional positive regard, and empathy *cause* people to move toward becoming fully functioning.

CRITIQUE OF ROGERS

How well does Rogerian theory satisfy the six criteria of a useful theory? The first criterion of a useful theory is the ability to *generate research* and testable hypotheses. Although Rogerian theory has generated much research in the realm of psychotherapy and classroom learning (see Rogers, 1983), it has been only moderately productive outside these two areas and thus receives only an average rating on its ability to spark research activity within the general field of personality.

Nevertheless, Rogerian theory rates high on *falsification*. Rogers was one of very few theorists who spelled out his theory in an if/then framework, and such a paradigm lends itself to either confirmation or disconfirmation. His precise language facilitated research at the University of Chicago and later at the University of Wisconsin that exposed his theory of therapy to falsification. Unfortunately, since Rogers's death, many humanistically oriented followers have failed to put his more general theory to test. Maureen O'Hara (1995) has suggested that "the time is ripe for humanistic psychology to once more pick up the scientific trail and begin to submit some of Carl Rogers's later ideas to critical evaluation" (p. 51).

Third, does Rogerian theory *organize knowledge* into a meaningful framework? Although much of the research generated by the theory has been limited to interpersonal relations, the theory nevertheless can be extended to a relatively wide range of human personality. Rogers's interests went beyond the consulting room and included group dynamics, classroom learning, social problems, and international relations. Thus, person-centered theory receives a high rating on its ability to explain what is currently known about human behavior.

Fourth, how well does person-centered theory serve as a *guide for the solution of practical problems*? For the psychotherapist, the answer is unequivocal. To bring about personality change, the therapist must possess congruence and be able to demonstrate empathic understanding and unconditional positive regard for the client. Rogers suggested that these three conditions are both necessary and sufficient to effect growth in any interpersonal relationship, including those outside of therapy.

The fifth criterion of a useful theory is *internal consistency* and a set of operational definitions. Person-centered theory must receive a very high rating for its consistency and its carefully worked-out operational definitions. Future theory builders can learn a valuable lesson from Rogers's pioneering work in constructing a theory of personality.

Finally, is Rogerian theory *parsimonious* and free from cumbersome concepts and difficult language? The theory itself is unusually clear and economical, but some of the language seems needlessly awkward and vague. Concepts such as "unconditional positive regard," "organismic experiencing," "becoming," "symbolization," and "fully functioning" are too broad and imprecise to have any scientific meaning. This is a small criticism, however, in comparison with the overall tightness and parsimony of person-centered theory.

CONCEPT OF HUMANITY

Rogers's concept of humanity was clearly stated in his famous debates with B.F. Skinner during the mid-1950s and early 1960s. Perhaps the most famous debates in the history of American psychology, these debates consisted of three face-to-face confrontations between Rogers and Skinner regarding the issue of freedom and control (Rogers & Skinner, 1956). Skinner (see Chapter 10) argued that people are always controlled, whether they realize it or not. Because we are controlled mostly by haphazard contingencies that have no grand design or plan, we often have the illusion that we are free (Skinner, 1971).

Rogers, however, contended that people have some degree of *free choice* and some capacity to be self-directed. Admitting that some portion of human behavior is controlled, predictable, and lawful, Rogers argued that the important values and choices that people make are outside the realm of science and within the scope of personal control.

Throughout his long career, Rogers remained cognizant of the human capacity for great evil, yet his concept of humanity is realistically *optimistic*. He believed that people are essentially forward moving and that, under proper conditions, they will grow toward self-actualization. People are basically trustworthy, socialized, and constructive. They ordinarily know what is best for themselves and will strive for completion provided they are prized and understood by another healthy individual. However, Rogers was also aware that people can be quite brutal, nasty, and neurotic:

> I do not have a Pollyanna view of human nature. I am quite aware that out of defensiveness and inner fear individuals can and do behave in ways which are horribly destructive, immature, regressive, anti-social, hurtful. Yet, one of the most refreshing and invigorating parts of my experience is to work with such individuals and to discover the strongly positive directional tendencies which exist in them, as in all of us, at the deepest levels. (Rogers, 1995, p. 21)

This tendency toward growth and self-actualization has a biological basis. Just as plants and animals have in their basic nature some tendency toward growth and fulfillment, so, too, do human beings. All organisms actualize themselves, but only humans can become self-actualizing. Humans are different from plants and animals primarily because they have self-awareness. To the extent that we have awareness, we are able to make free choices and to play an active role in forming our personalities.

Rogers's person-centered theory is also rated high on *teleology* because it holds that people strive with purpose toward goals that they freely set for themselves. Again, under proper therapeutic conditions, people consciously desire to become more fully functioning, more open to their experiences, and more accepting of self and others.

Rogers placed more emphasis on individual differences and *uniqueness* than on similarities. If plants have individual potential for growth, people have even greater uniqueness and individuality. Within a nurturant environment, people can grow in their own fashion toward the process of being more fully functioning. Although common elements can be extracted from an analytical study of this process, people themselves are becoming more unique and more completely themselves as this process continues.

Although Rogers did not deny the importance of unconscious processes, his primary emphasis was on the ability of people to *consciously* choose their own course of action. Fully functioning people are ordinarily aware of what they are doing and have some understanding of their reasons for doing it.

On the dimension of *biological vs. social influences*, Rogers favored the latter. Psychological growth is not automatic. In order to move toward actualization, one must experience empathic understanding and unconditional positive regard from another person who is genuine or congruent. Rogers firmly held that, although much of our behavior is determined by heredity and environment, we have within us the capacity to choose and to become self-directed. Not only do we possess the ability to choose, but under nurturant conditions "choice always seems to be in the direction of greater socialization, improved relationships with others" (Rogers, 1982a, p. 8).

People are not by nature ego-centered, socially dangerous, or evil, but neither do they possess an innate morality. Rogers (1982a) did not claim that, if left alone, people would be righteous, virtuous, or honorable. However, in an atmosphere without threat, people are free to become what they potentially can be. This is neither good nor bad, because these terms imply some standard of evaluation. No evaluation in terms of morality applies to the nature of humanity. People simply have the potential for growth, the need for growth, and the desire for growth. By nature they will strive for completion even under unfavorable conditions, but under poor conditions they do not realize their full potential for psychological health. However, under the most nurturant and favorable conditions, people will become more self-aware, trustworthy, congruent, and self-directed. They will become psychologically adjusted, rational, realistic, and will move toward becoming the persons of tomorrow.

Chapter Summary

Person-centered theory of personality grew out of Rogers's experiences as a client-centered therapist and is an expression of his fundamental belief that, under proper conditions, people will move inevitably toward psychological growth and fulfillment. This assumption follows from a more general notion that all matter, both organic and inorganic, tends to evolve from simple to more complex forms. Rogers called this the *formative tendency*.

Somewhat more specific is the *actualizing tendency*, or people's movement toward completion or fulfillment. During early infancy, a person begins to evolve a self-system, which eventually includes a *self-concept* (perceived self). At that point, the person seeks *self-actualization*, or fulfillment of the self as perceived. *Incongruence* develops when the organismic (real) self and the perceived self do not match. In order to bring the organismic self and the perceived self together, people distort or deny certain aspects of their experience.

Rogers postulated that we are guided by two basic needs—*maintenance* and *enhancement* of our perceived selves. In addition, we need positive regard, first from others, then from ourselves. Conditions of worth and external evaluation prevent us from experiencing unconditional positive regard and may lead to psychological maladjustment.

Psychologically unhealthy people are characterized by incongruence between self and experience; *vulnerability*, or an unawareness of their incongruence; and *anxiety*, *threat*, and *defensiveness*. When their defenses of *denial* and *distortion* are insufficient to block out incongruence, they become *disorganized*.

Rogerian therapy can be stated quite simply. If clients receive certain *conditions*, then they will undergo the *process* of therapy, which will have certain predictable *outcomes*. The three necessary and sufficient therapeutic *conditions* are (1) *counselor congruence*, (2) *unconditional positive regard*, and (3) *empathic listening*.

The *process* of therapeutic personality change ranges from extreme defensiveness, or unwillingness to talk about self, to the final stage, in which clients are their own therapists and are able to continue psychological growth outside the therapeutic setting.

The basic *outcomes* of client-centered counseling are congruent clients who are open to experiences and who have no need to be defensive. They approach Rogers's concept of a *fully functioning person*, or the *person of tomorrow*. They are characterized by (1) a constant state of change, (2) an increasing openness to experience, (3) a fresh attitude and approach toward life, (4) trust in self, and (5) harmonious relations with others.

Rogerian theory rates high on its ability to generate research and its exposure to falsification. It is also quite able to organize knowledge, especially that which relates to therapy, education, and interpersonal relations. In these three areas, it receives a very high rating as a practical guide to action, but a lower rating in human endeavors beyond therapy, education, and interpersonal relations. On the criteria of self-consistency and parsimony, person-centered theory rates very high.

The Rogerian view of humanity is basically positive and optimistic, because it holds that through proper conditions people will move toward becoming more open to their experiences and more self-actualizing.

Suggested Readings

Kirschenbaum, H. (1979). O*n becoming Carl Rogers.* New York: Delacorte Press.
    The best and most complete source for biographical information on Rogers, Kirschenbaum's book adopts a highly favorable attitude toward the father of client-centered therapy and person-centered theory.
Rogers, C. R. (1959). A theory of therapy, personality, and interpersonal relationships, as developed in the client-centered framework. In S. Koch (Ed.), P*sychology: A study of a science* (Vol. 3) (pp. 184–246). New York: McGraw-Hill.
    Although this chapter is included in the Kirschenbaum and Henderson (1989) book of readings, it is important enough to recommend again in the event that the Kirschenbaum and Henderson book is not available. Rogers remained disappointed that this frequently referenced chapter was not more widely read.
Rogers, C. R. (1961). O*n becoming a person: A therapist's view of psychotherapy.* Boston: Houghton Mifflin.
    Rogers's most popular book, this volume is actually a collection of papers written during the decade preceding its publication.

Rogers, C. R. (1980). *A way of being*. Boston: Houghton Mifflin.

Reflecting changes that occurred in his life and work during the decade of the 1970s, this book presents Rogers's latest thoughts on client-centered therapy and person-centered education.

Rogers, C. R. (1995). What understanding and acceptance mean to me. *Journal of Humanistic Psychology*, 35, 7–22.

This recently published article is from a previously unknown transcript of a talk Rogers delivered to the 12th annual conference of the Illinois Guidance and Personnel Association in October of 1956. Rogers discusses his ideas on acceptance, empathy, and genuineness in a typically personal manner.

Thorne, B. (1992). *Carl Rogers*. London: Sage.

In this brief book, Thorne presents an overview of Rogers's life, his theoretical contributions, and his views on psychotherapy. Thorne also includes a critique of Rogers and a summary of his contributions to the creation of a person-centered society.

Maslow

Maslow: Holistic-Dynamic Theory

he concept of **self-actualization** and the name Abraham Maslow have been closely associated for many years. Although Maslow did not coin the term and was not the only personality theorist to use it, he did more than any other psychologist to popularize the notion of self-actualization.

Maslow's theory of personality, however, goes far beyond a consideration of self-actualization. His **holistic-dynamic theory** holds that people are constantly being motivated by one need or another. Few of us ever reach self-actualization but, instead, are motivated by lower level needs such as hunger, safety, love, and self-esteem. In addition, other dimensions of needs, namely, cognitive and aesthetic, help shape our behavior. Moreover, some of us are driven by neurotic needs to perpetuate the status quo rather than to move in the direction of psychological health or self-actualization.

Although sometimes thought of as the father of the **third force** in psychology (the first force was psychoanalysis and its modifications; the second was behaviorism), Maslow (1971) did not regard himself as either anti-Freudian or antibehavioristic. In fact, he perceived himself to be both a psychoanalyst and a behaviorist. He repudiated neither and saw much of value in both of these earlier theories. However, he held that both psychoanalysis and behaviorism had a limited view of humanity and that neither dealt adequately with the normal healthy person. Maslow believed that humans have a higher nature than was formerly thought, and he spent the last years of his life trying to discover what it is like to achieve the ultimate in psychological health.

BIOGRAPHY OF ABRAHAM H. MASLOW

Abraham Harold Maslow was born on April 1, 1908, in Brooklyn, New York. The oldest of seven children, he was not especially close to either parent but felt more affection toward his father, a Russian-Jewish immigrant from Kiev. Toward his mother, he felt hatred and deep-seated animosity, not only during his childhood, but until the day she died just a couple of years before Maslow's own death. His mother was a very religious woman who often threatened young Abe with punishment from God. From such threats, Maslow learned to hate and mistrust religion. Although never a practicing Jew, he felt the sting of anti-Semitism from a young age onward. Possibly as a defense against the anti-Semitic attitudes of his classmates, he turned to books and scholarly pursuits.

Throughout early childhood, Abe was extremely lonely, shy, and socially introverted, even more so than Carl Rogers (see Chapter 16). In addition, Maslow felt ugly, inferior, and depressed. He later described himself as being neurotic during his childhood (Wilson, 1972). During Abe's early years, however, the Maslow family gradually rose from the slums to lower-middle-class respectability. Abe's three younger brothers later became financially independent as owners of the Maslow Cooperage Corporation.

Maslow's father wanted him to be a lawyer, and while attending the City College of New York, Maslow also enrolled in law school. However, he walked out of law classes one night, leaving his books behind. Significantly, he felt that law dealt too much with evil people and was not sufficiently concerned with the good. His father, although initially disappointed, eventually accepted Abe's decision to quit law school (Hall, 1968).

Maslow was a mediocre student at CCNY, and after three semesters, he transferred to Cornell University. There, too, his scholastic work was poor. His introductory psychology professor was Edward B. Titchener, a renowned pioneer in psychology who taught all his classes in full academic robes. Titchener's "bloodless" approach to psychology left Maslow cold and indifferent (Hoffman, 1988).

After one semester, Maslow returned to the City College of New York, partly to be nearer his first cousin, Bertha Goodman. He loved Bertha in a distant, bashful sort of way, having never touched her nor expressed his feelings. Then, suddenly a fortuitous event changed his life. While visiting his Aunt Pearl (Bertha's mother), his cousin Anna (Bertha's older sister) shoved Abe toward Bertha, saying, "For the love of Pete, kiss her, will ya!" (Hoffman, 1988, p. 29). He did, and to his surprise, Bertha did not fight back. She kissed him, and from that time on, his life became meaningful.

Abe and Bertha were married during Christmas recess, 1928, when he was 20 and she 19. Maslow's parents stubbornly resisted the marriage, fearing hereditary defects in any possible offspring. This resistance was ironic in light of the fact that Abe's parents themselves were first cousins and had seven healthy children!

Maslow had earlier enrolled at the University of Wisconsin, and after his marriage, Bertha went west to join him. At Wisconsin, Maslow became interested in psychology and his grades showed a marked improvement. His life, by his own reckoning, began at this time (Hall, 1968).

As a student, Maslow was greatly influenced by two forces that, at first glance, seem far removed from the holistic and humanistic leanings that so strongly characterize his later works. The first of these was behaviorism. The influence of John B. Watson was strong on American campuses during the 1930s and Maslow became excited about the potential of behaviorism to remake the world. The second influence was Harry Harlow and his experiments with monkeys. Maslow not only worked in Harlow's laboratories, but made some important discoveries on dominance and sexual behavior among monkeys.

Although Maslow's later researches on self-actualizing people seem far removed from either behaviorism or experiments with monkeys, these two early experiences played an important role in the evolution of his thinking. For example, after studying the sexual behavior of monkeys, Maslow moved easily to the field of human sexuality and made important contributions to that area several years before Alfred Kinsey's (Kinsey, Pomeroy, & Martin, 1948) landmark research appeared. The destruction wrought by World War II moved him to devote his life to the study of the best in human beings, and the experiences he gained from interviewing people on sexual behavior proved useful in interviewing healthy individuals.

After receiving a Ph.D. from Wisconsin in 1934, Maslow could not find an academic position due in part to the Great Depression and to anti-Semitic prejudice still strong on many American campuses in those years. Consequently, he continued to teach at Wisconsin for a short time and even enrolled in medical school there. However, medical school bored him, and he felt that, like law school, it reflected a dispassionate and negative view of people. Whenever Maslow became bored with something, he usually quit it, and medical school was no exception.

In 1935, he returned to New York to become E. L. Thorndike's research assistant at Teachers College, Columbia University. Because Maslow scored 195 on Thorndike's intelligence test, Thorndike, demonstrating confidence in both Maslow and his own test, gave his assistant free reign to do as he wished. Maslow's fertile mind thrived in this situation, but after a year and a half of doing research on human sexuality, he left Columbia to join the faculty of Brooklyn College.

Living in New York during the 1930s and 1940s afforded Maslow an opportunity to come into contact with many of the European psychologists who had escaped Nazi rule. Among others, he met Erich Fromm, Karen Horney, Max Wertheimer, and Kurt Goldstein. Maslow was influenced by each of these as well as by Alfred Adler, who was living in New York at that time. Adler held seminars in his home on Friday nights, and

Maslow was a frequent visitor to these sessions, as was Julian Rotter (see Chapter 12). In a personal letter to Frank Goble, Maslow wrote:

> I think it's fair to say that I have had the best teachers, both formal and informal, of any person who ever lived, just because of being in New York City when the cream of European intellect was migrating away from Hitler . . . I learned from all of them.
>
> . . . So I could not be said to be a Goldsteinian nor a Frommian nor an Adlerian or whatever. . . . I never accepted any of the invitations to join any of these parochial and sectarian organizations. I learned from all of them and refused to close any doors. (Goble, 1970, pp. 11–12)

While at Brooklyn College, Maslow underwent a partial psychoanalysis with Emil Oberholzer, a New York psychiatrist. Despite this and later psychoanalytic treatments, Maslow never lost his hatred for his mother and even refused to attend her funeral.

During the mid-1940s, Maslow's health began to deteriorate. In 1946, at age 38, he suffered a strange illness that left him weak, faint, and "barely able to stand for more than a few minutes at a time" (Hoffman, 1988, p. 176). In 1947, he took a medical leave and, with Bertha and their two daughters, moved to Pleasanton, California, where, in name only, he was plant manager of a branch of the Maslow Cooperage Corporation. His light work schedule enabled him to read biographies and histories in a search for information on self-actualizing people. By 1949, his health had improved and he went back to teaching at Brooklyn College.

In 1951, Maslow took a position as chairman of the psychology department at the recently established Brandeis University in Waltham, Massachusetts. During his Brandeis years, he began writing extensively in his journals, jotting down at irregular intervals his thoughts, opinions, feelings, social activities, important conversations, and concerns for his health (Maslow, 1979).

Despite achieving fame during the 1960s, Maslow was not happy with his work during this time. He became increasingly disenchanted with students and faculty at Brandeis. Some students rebelled against his teaching methods, demanding more experiential involvement and less of an intellectual and scientific approach. In addition, he suffered a severe but nonfatal heart attack in December of 1967. He then learned that his strange malady more than 20 years earlier had been an undiagnosed heart attack.

In poor health and disappointed with the academic atmosphere at Brandeis, Maslow accepted an offer to join the Saga Administrative Corporation in Menlo Park, California. He had no particular job there and was free to think and write as he wished. He enjoyed that freedom, but on June 8, 1970, while slowly jogging in place, he suddenly collapsed and died of a massive heart attack. He was 62.

Maslow received many honors during his lifetime, including his election to the presidency of the American Psychological Association for the year 1967–1968. At the time of his death, he was well known, not only within the profession of psychology, but among educated people generally, particularly in business management, marketing, theology, counseling, education, nursing, and other health-related fields.

Maslow's personal life was filled with pain, both physical and psychological. As an adolescent, he was terribly shy, unhappy, isolated, and self-rejecting. His love for Bertha made him miserable because he did not know how to act or what Bertha felt toward him. Those problems were solved by his marriage, but he continued to be painfully shy. He was terrified of public speaking and was past 50 before he was able to overcome some of his stage fright. He never overcame the intense hatred of his mother, and in 1969 he wrote in his journal these thoughts concerning her.

> What I had reacted against and totally hated and rejected was not only her physical appearance, but also her values and world view, her stinginess, her total selfishness, her lack of love for anyone else in the world, even her own husband and children . . . her assumption that anyone was wrong who disagreed with her, her lack of concern for her grandchildren, her lack of friends, her sloppiness and dirtiness, her lack of family feeling for her own parents and siblings. . . . I've always wondered where my Utopianism, ethical stress, humanism, stress on kindness, love, friendship, and all the rest came from. I knew certainly of the direct consequences of having no mother-love. But the whole thrust of my life-philosophy and all my research and theorizing also has its roots in a hatred for and revulsion against everything she stood for. (Maslow, 1979, p. 958)

Maslow's physical health was never robust, and he suffered from a series of ailments, including chronic fatigue, hypoglycemia, an arthritic hip, and chronic heart problems. His journals (Maslow, 1979) are sprinkled with references to ill health. In his last journal entry (May 7, 1970) a month before his death, he complained about people expecting him to be a courageous leader and spokesperson. He wrote: "I am not temperamentally 'courageous.' My courage is really an overcoming of all sorts of inhibitions, politeness, gentleness, timidities—and it always cost me a lot in fatigue, tension, apprehension, bad sleep" (p. 1307).

MASLOW'S VIEW OF MOTIVATION

Maslow's theory of personality rests on several basic assumptions regarding motivation. First, Maslow (1970) adopted a *holistic approach to motivation*, repeatedly pointing out that the whole person, not any single part or function, is motivated.

Second, *motivation is usually complex*, meaning that a person's behavior may spring from several separate motives. For example, the desire for sexual union may be motivated not only by a genital need but also by needs for dominance, companionship, love, and self-esteem. Moreover, the motivation for a behavior may be unconscious or unknown to the person. For example, the motivation to use a telephone may actually be to satisfy one's needs for love or belongingness. Maslow's acceptance of the importance of unconscious motivation represents one important way in which he differed from Allport (Chapter 14). Whereas Allport might say that a person plays golf just for the fun of it, Maslow would look beneath the surface for underlying and often complex reasons for playing.

A third assumption is that *people are continually motivated by one need or another*. When one need is satisfied, it ordinarily loses its motivational power and is thus replaced by another need. For example, as long as people's hunger needs are frustrated, they will strive for food, but when they do have enough to eat, they move on to other needs such as safety, friendship, and self-worth.

Another assumption is that *all people everywhere are motivated by the same basic needs*. The *manner* in which people in different cultures obtain food, build shelter, express friendship, and so forth may vary widely, but the fundamental needs for food, safety, and friendship are common to the entire species.

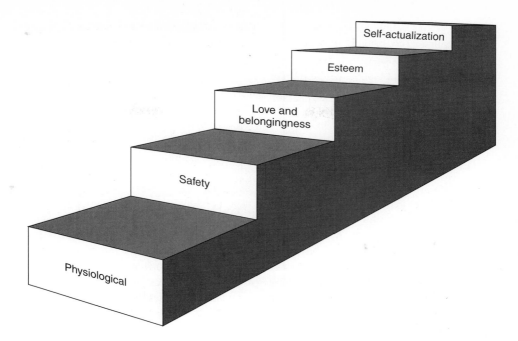

Figure 17.1 Maslow's hierarchy of needs. One must reach self-actualization one step at a time.

A final assumption concerning motivation is that *needs can be arranged on a hierarchy* (Maslow, 1943, 1970).

HIERARCHY OF NEEDS

Maslow's **hierarchy of needs** concept assumes that basic or lower level needs must be satisfied or at least relatively satisfied before higher level needs become motivators. Needs can be arranged on a hierarchy or staircase, with each ascending step representing a higher need but one less basic to survival (see Figure 17.1). The hierarchy of needs is also referred to as the *theory of prepotent needs*. Lower level needs have prepotency over higher level needs, meaning that lower needs must be satisfied in order for people to strive for higher needs. For example, an artist at work in her studio may be satisfying higher level needs such as esteem or self-actualization, but eventually she will become hungry and leave her work to find food (a lower level need). Hunger, then, has prepotency over both esteem and self-actualization.

Maslow (1970) listed the following needs in order of their prepotency: physiological, safety, love and belongingness, esteem, and self-actualization.

Physiological Needs

The most basic needs of any person are **physiological needs,** including food, water, oxygen, maintenance of body temperature, and so on. Physiological needs are the most prepotent of all. Perpetually hungry people are motivated to eat—not to make friends or gain self-esteem. They do not see beyond food, and as long as this need remains unsatisfied, their primary motivation is to obtain something to eat.

In affluent societies, most people satisfy their hunger needs as a matter of course. They usually have enough to eat, so when they say they are hungry, they are really speaking of appetites, not hunger. A truly hungry person will not be overly particular about taste, smell, temperature, or texture of the food.

Maslow (1970) said: "It is quite true that man lives by bread alone—when there is no bread" (p. 38). When people do not have their physiological needs satisfied, they live primarily for those needs and strive constantly to satisfy them. Starving people become preoccupied with food and are willing to do nearly anything to obtain it (Keys, Brozek, Henschel, Mickelsen, & Taylor, 1950).

Physiological needs differ from other needs in at least two important respects. First, they are the only needs that can be completely satisfied or even overly satisfied. One can get enough to eat so that food completely loses its motivational power. For someone who has just finished a large meal, the thought of more food can even have a nauseating effect. A second characteristic peculiar to physiological needs is their recurring nature. After we have eaten, we will eventually become hungry again; we constantly need to replenish our water supply; and one breath of air must be followed by another. Other level needs do not constantly recur. For example, once love and esteem needs are relatively met, they remain satisfied, but physiological needs continually reappear.

Safety Needs

When our physiological needs are satisfied or relatively well satisfied, we become motivated by **safety needs,** including physical security, stability, dependency, protection, and freedom from such threatening forces as illness, fear, anxiety, danger, and chaos. The need for law, order, and structure are also safety needs (Maslow, 1970).

Safety needs differ from physiological needs in that they cannot be overly satiated; we can never have too much safety. We can never be completely protected from meteorites, fires, floods, or the dangerous acts of others.

In societies not at war, most healthy adults satisfy their safety needs most of the time, thus making these needs relatively unimportant. Children, however, are more often motivated by safety needs because they live with such threats as darkness, animals, strangers, and punishments from parents. Neurotic adults also feel relatively unsafe because they retain irrational fears from childhood, which cause them to act as if they were afraid of parental punishment. They imagine their physical well-being to be threatened and therefore constrict themselves to the safe and the familiar. They spend far more energy than do healthy people trying to satisfy safety needs, and when they are not successful in their attempts, they suffer from what Maslow (1970) called **basic anxiety.**

For both healthy and unhealthy people, safety needs become activated during emergency situations such as natural disasters, injury, accidents, and war. During periods of immediate danger or threats to physical well-being, higher level needs—love, esteem, and self-actualization—lose their potency and people become motivated primarily by safety needs.

Love and Belongingness Needs

For most of us, physiological and safety needs are fairly well satisfied and do not dominate our lives. **Love and belongingness needs,** however, are a different matter. Most of us get stuck at this level and strive more or less constantly to be accepted and loved by other people (Maslow, 1970).

In addition to physiological and safety needs, children have love and belongingness needs.

After we partially satisfy our physiological and safety needs, we become motivated by love and belongingness needs, such as the desire for friendship, the wish for a mate and children, the need to belong to a family, a club, a neighborhood, or a nation. Love and belongingness also includes some aspects of sex and human contact, as well as the need to both give and receive love.

Motivation for love is ordinarily strongest when the need is only partially satisfied. People who have never received love, who have never been kissed or cuddled, can go for long periods without these things and not panic. They take absence of love for granted and eventually devalue this need. Conversely, people who have had love and belongingness needs adequately satisfied from early years also will not panic when denied love. These people have confidence that they are accepted by those who are important to them, so if other people reject them, they do not feel devastated.

On the other hand, people who have tasted love only in small doses will be strongly motivated to seek satisfaction of love and belongingness needs. In other words, people who have received only a little amount of love have stronger needs for affection and acceptance than do people who have received either a healthy amount of love or none at all (Maslow, 1970).

Children need love in order to grow psychologically, and their attempts to satisfy this need are usually straightforward and direct. Adults, too, need love, but their attempts to attain it are sometimes cleverly disguised. They often engage in self-defeating behaviors, such as pretending to be aloof from other people or adopting a cynical, cold, and calloused manner in their interpersonal relationships. They may give the appearance of self-sufficiency and independence, but in reality they have a strong need to be accepted and loved by other people. Other adults whose love needs remain largely unsatisfied adopt more obvious ways of trying to satisfy them, but they undermine their own success by striving too hard. Their constant supplications for acceptance and affection leave others suspicious, unfriendly, and impenetrable.

If people have had love needs gratified from childhood, they gain a feeling of self-esteem, and they may even become self-actualizing adults who are no longer dependent on the continual love and acceptance of other people. As self-actualizing adults, they maintain their feelings of self-esteem even when scorned, rejected, and dismissed by other people. In other words, esteem and self-actualization are no longer dependent on the satisfaction of love and belonging needs; that is, they are now *functionally autonomous* from the lower level needs that gave them birth (see Chapter 14 for Allport's discussion of functional autonomy).

Esteem Needs

To the extent that people satisfy their love and belongingness needs, they are free to pursue **esteem needs,** such as self-respect, confidence, competence, and the esteem of others. Maslow (1970) identified two levels of esteem needs—reputation and self-esteem. Reputation is the perception of the prestige, recognition, or fame people have achieved in the eyes of others, whereas self-esteem is the person's own feelings of worth and confidence. Self-esteem is based on more than reputation or prestige; it reflects a "desire for strength, for achievement, for adequacy, for mastery and competence, for confidence in the face of the world, and for independence and freedom" (p. 45). In other words, self-esteem is based on real competence and not merely on others' opinions. Once people meet their esteem needs, they stand on the threshold of self-actualization, the highest need recognized by Maslow.

Self-Actualization Needs

When lower level needs are satisfied, people proceed more or less automatically to the next level. However, once esteem needs are met, they do not always move to the level of self-actualization. Originally, Maslow assumed that self-actualization needs become potent whenever esteem needs have been met. However, during the 1960s, he came to realize that many of the young students at Brandeis and other campuses around the country had all their basic needs gratified, including reputation and self-esteem, and yet they did not become self-actualizing (Frick, 1971, 1982; Maslow, 1967, 1971). Why some people step over the threshold from esteem to self-actualization and others do not is a matter of whether or not they embrace the B-values (B-values will be discussed later). People who hold in high respect such values as truth, beauty, justice, and the other B-values become self-actualizing after their esteem needs are met, whereas those who do not embrace these values are frustrated in their self-actualization needs even though they have satisfied each of their other basic needs.

Self-actualization needs include the desire for self-fulfillment, to realize all of one's potential, to become everything that one can, and to become creative in the full sense of the word (Maslow, 1970). People who have reached the level of self-actualization become fully human, satisfying needs that others merely glimpse or never view at all. They are natural in the same sense that animals and infants are natural; that is, they express their basic human needs and do not allow them to be suppressed by culture. (A more complete sketch of self-actualizing people follows the present discussion of needs.)

The five needs composing this hierarchy are **conative needs,** which Maslow often referred to as *basic needs*. However, he also identified other needs, *aesthetic* and *cognitive*, which are sometimes preconditions for satisfying basic needs but nevertheless operate on a separate dimension. In addition to these needs are the *neurotic needs*, which tend to oppose basic needs and block psychological health.

AESTHETIC NEEDS

Unlike conative needs, **aesthetic needs** are not universal, but at least some people in every culture seem to be motivated by the need for beauty and aesthetically pleasing experiences (Maslow, 1967). Historically, humanity has produced art for art's sake from the days of the cave dweller down to the present time.

People with strong aesthetic needs desire beautiful and orderly surroundings, and when these needs are not met, they become sick in the same way that they become sick when their conative needs are frustrated. People prefer beauty to ugliness, and they may even become physically and spiritually ill when forced to live in squalid, disorderly environments.

Because the various needs overlap, we cannot always identify the true bases of a particular need. For example, the needs for order and symmetry may be aesthetic needs, but they might also satisfy the conative need for safety. Then again, they could also satisfy cognitive needs, especially those involving mathematics and numbers (Maslow, 1970).

COGNITIVE NEEDS

In addition to conative and aesthetic needs, people also possess **cognitive needs,** that is, a desire to know, to solve mysteries, to understand, and to be curious (Maslow, 1970). Although cognitive needs have an interdependence with conative needs, they belong to a different dimension. When cognitive needs are blocked, all other needs are threatened. Knowledge is necessary to satisfy each of the five conative needs. People can gratify their physiological needs by knowing how to secure food; safety needs by knowing how to build a shelter; love needs by knowing how to relate to people; esteem needs by attaining some knowledge and acquiring some level of self-confidence with that knowledge; and they can achieve self-actualization by fully using their cognitive potentials (although self-actualizing people need not have outstanding innate intellectual powers).

When people cannot satisfy their cognitive needs, they become pathological, just as they become sick when their conative and aesthetic needs are thwarted (Maslow, 1970). Ignorance, dishonesty, and secrecy all frustrate our need to know and therefore undermine our psychological health. We become sick, paranoid, and depressed when we are consistently lied to, denied knowledge, or deprived of curiosity. Our physical health may suffer when our work does not challenge our intellectual capacities, and we may become skeptical, disillusioned, and cynical when we do not hear the whole truth.

Besides having a synergistic relationship with conative needs, cognitive needs have a separate existence. The need to know is important in itself and is not always specifically related to the satisfaction of another need. Knowledge brings with it the desire to know more, to theorize, to test hypotheses, or to find out how something works just for the satisfaction of knowing (Maslow, 1968b).

NEUROTIC NEEDS

The satisfaction of conative, aesthetic, and cognitive needs is basic to one's physical and psychological health, and their frustration leads to some level of illness. On the other hand, a fourth category of needs—**neurotic needs**—leads only to stagnation and pathology, whether or not these needs are satisfied (Maslow, 1970).

By definition, neurotic needs are nonproductive. They perpetuate an unhealthy style of life and have no value in the striving for self-actualization. Neurotic needs are usually reactive; that is, they serve as compensation for unsatisfied basic needs. People who do not satisfy their safety needs, for example, may develop a strong desire to hoard money or property. The hoarding drive is a neurotic need, worthless as a motivator toward health. Then again, when love and belongingness needs are not fulfilled, people may become overly aggressive and hostile toward others. Aggressive and hostile needs are also neurotic and play no positive role in one's movement toward self-actualization.

As we have seen, neurotic needs are distinguishable from basic needs in that their satisfaction does not foster health. As Maslow (1970) said,

> Giving a neurotic power seeker all the power he wants does not make him less neurotic, nor is it possible to satiate his neurotic need for power. However much he is fed he still remains hungry (because he's really looking for something else). It makes little difference for ultimate health whether a neurotic need be gratified or frustrated. (p. 274)

GENERAL DISCUSSION OF NEEDS

Maslow (1970) estimated that the hypothetical average person has his or her needs satisfied to approximately these levels: physiological, 85%; safety, 70%; love and belongingness, 50%; esteem, 40%; and self-actualization, 10%. The more a lower level need is satisfied, the greater the emergence of the next level need. For example, if love needs are only 10% satisfied, esteem needs may not be active at all. But if love needs are 25% satisfied, esteem may emerge 5% as a need. If love is 75% satisfied, then esteem may emerge 50%, and so on. Needs, therefore, emerge gradually, and a person may be simultaneously motivated by needs from two or more levels. For example, a self-actualizing person may be the honorary guest at a dinner given by close friends in a peaceful restaurant. The act of eating gratifies a physiological need, but at the same time, the guest of honor may be satisfying safety, love, esteem, and self-actualization needs.

Reversed Order of Needs

Even though needs are generally satisfied in the same order, occasionally they are reversed. For some people, the drive for creativity (a self-actualization need) may take precedence over safety and physiological needs. An enthusiastic artist may risk safety and health to complete an important work. For years, the late sculptor Korczak Ziolkowski endangered his health and abandoned companionship to work on carving a mountain in the Black Hills into a monument to Chief Crazy Horse.

Reversals, however, are usually more apparent than real, and some seemingly obvious deviations in the order of needs are not variations at all. If we understood the *unconscious motivation* underlying the behavior, we would recognize that the needs are not reversed.

Unmotivated Behavior

Maslow believed that, even though all behaviors have a cause, some behaviors are not motivated. In other words, not all determinants are motives. Some behavior is not caused by needs, but by other factors such as conditioned reflexes, maturation, or drugs. Motivation is limited to the striving for the satisfaction of some need. Much of what Maslow (1970) called "expressive behavior" is unmotivated.

Expressive and Coping Behavior

Maslow (1970) distinguished between expressive behavior, which is often unmotivated, and coping behavior, which is always motivated and aimed at satisfying a need.

Expressive behavior is often an end in itself and serves no other purpose than to be. It is often unconscious and usually takes place naturally and with little effort. It has no goals or aim but is merely the person's mode of expression. Expressive behavior includes such actions as slouching, looking stupid, being relaxed, showing anger, and expressing joy. Expressive behavior can continue even in the absence of reinforcement or reward. For example, a frown, a blush, or a twinkle of the eye are not ordinarily specifically reinforced.

Expressive behaviors also include one's gait, gestures, voice, and smile (even when alone). A person, for example, may express a methodical, compulsive personality simply because he is what he is and not because of any need to do so. Other examples of expression include art, play, enjoyment, appreciation, wonder, awe, and excitement. Expressive behavior is usually unlearned, spontaneous, and determined by forces within the person rather than by the environment.

On the other hand, *coping behavior* is usually conscious, effortful, learned, and determined by the external environment. It involves the individual's attempts to cope with the environment, to secure food and shelter, to make friends, and to receive acceptance, appreciation, and prestige from others. Coping behavior serves some aim or goal (although not always conscious or known to the person), and it is always motivated by some deficit need (Maslow, 1970).

Deprivation of Needs

Lack of satisfaction of any of the basic needs leads to some kind of pathology. Deprivation of physiological needs results in fatigue, loss of energy, malnutrition, obsession with sex, and so on. Threat to safety leads to fear, insecurity, and dread. When love needs go unfulfilled, a person becomes defensive, overly aggressive, or socially shy. Lack of esteem also results in the illnesses of self-doubt, self-depreciation, and lack of confidence. Deprivation of self-actualization needs likewise leads to pathology, or more accurately, **metapathology.** Maslow (1967) defined metapathology as the absence of values, lack of fulfillment, and the loss of meaning in life.

If deprived needs cause us to become ill, then satisfied needs move us toward physical and psychological health. In fact, Maslow (1967) considered the satisfaction of needs to be the definition of health. Traditionally, many philosophers and even psychologists have held the opposite view, believing that health and happiness come from the renunciation of basic needs. For example, some religious leaders have advocated fasting and other forms of self-sacrifice as a means of self-control and spiritual growth. Maslow, however, insisted that self-actualization (the essence of psychological health) is characterized by the full enjoyment of food, sex, and other sensuous pleasures.

Instinctoid Nature of Needs

Maslow (1970) rejected the classical instinct theories of Freud and William McDougall (1933), but he also refused to accept the newer, anti-instinct concepts of the behaviorists. Instead, he proposed a middle position, which hypothesizes that some human needs are innately determined even though they can be modified by learning. These are called **instinctoid needs.**

One criterion for separating instinctoid from noninstinctoid needs is the level of pathology upon frustration. The thwarting of instinctoid needs produces pathology; the frustration of other needs does not. For example, when people are denied sufficient love, they become sick and are blocked from achieving psychological health. Likewise, when people are frustrated in satisfying their physiological, safety, esteem, and self-actualization needs, they become sick. Therefore, these needs are instinctoid. On the other hand, the need to comb one's hair or to speak one's native tongue are learned, and their frustration does not ordinarily produce illness. If people would become psychologically ill as the result of not being able to comb their hair or to speak their native language, then the frustrated need is actually a basic instinctoid need, perhaps love and belongingness or possibly esteem.

A second criterion for distinguishing between the two types of needs is that instinctoid needs are persistent and their satisfaction leads to psychological health. Noninstinctoid needs, in contrast, are usually temporary and their satisfaction is not a prerequisite for health.

Instinctoid needs are basic and not the result of reinforcement. Moreover, instinctoid behavior is species-specific, and therefore animal instincts cannot be used as a model for their study. On the other hand, not all instinctoid needs are unchangeable. Some can be molded, inhibited, or altered by environmental influences. Because many instinctoid needs (for example, love) are weaker than cultural forces (for example, aggression in the form of crime or war), Maslow (1970) insisted that society should "protect the weak, subtle, and tender instinctoid needs if they are not to be overwhelmed by the tougher more powerful culture" (p. 82). Stated another way, even though instinctoid needs are basic and unlearned, they can be changed and even destroyed by the more powerful forces of civilization. Hence, a healthy society should seek ways in which its members can receive satisfaction not only for physiological and safety needs but for love, esteem, and self-actualization needs as well.

Comparison of Higher and Lower Needs

Important similarities and differences exist between higher level needs (love, esteem, and self-actualization) and lower level needs (physiological and safety). Higher needs are similar to lower ones in that they are instinctoid. Maslow (1970) insisted that love, esteem, and self-actualization are just as biological as thirst, sex, and hunger.

Differences between higher needs and lower ones are those of degree and not of kind. First, higher level needs are later on the phylogenetic or evolutionary scale. For instance, only humans (a relatively recent species) have the need for self-actualization. Also, higher needs appear later during the course of individual development; lower level needs must be cared for in infants and children before higher level needs become operative.

Second, higher level needs produce more happiness and more peak experiences (although satisfaction of lower level needs may produce a degree of pleasure). Hedonistic pleasure, however, is usually temporary and not comparable to the quality of happiness produced by the satisfaction of higher needs. Also, the satisfaction of higher level needs is more subjectively desirable to those people who have experienced both higher and lower level needs. In other words, a person who has reached the level of self-actualization would have no motivation to return to a lower stage of development (Maslow, 1970).

SELF-ACTUALIZATION

Maslow's devotion to the study of health rather than illness is most clearly visible in his research on self-actualizing people. His ideas on self-actualization began soon after he received his Ph.D., when he became puzzled as to why two of his teachers in New York City—Ruth Benedict and Max Wertheimer—were so different from average people. His love and admiration for each of these two unusual people led him to take notes describing fundamental characteristics of each. Soon, he realized that, although the two were different from each other, a single pattern seemed to characterize their lives. He began to look for others who fit this pattern and found several. To Maslow, these people represented the highest level of human development, and he called that level "self-actualization," a term borrowed from Kurt Goldstein, another New York mentor who was then at Columbia University.

VALUES OF SELF-ACTUALIZERS

Maslow (1971) held that self-actualizing people are motivated by the "external verities," what he called **B-values.** These "Being" values are indicators of psychological health and are opposed to deficiency needs, which motivate non-self-actualizers. B-values are not needs in the same sense as food, shelter, or companionship. Maslow termed them "metaneeds" to indicate that they are the ultimate level of needs. He distinguished between ordinary need motivation and the motives of self-actualizing people, which he called **metamotivation.**

Metamotivation is characterized by expressive rather than coping behavior and is associated with the B-values. It differentiates self-actualizing people from those who are not. In other words, metamotivation was Maslow's tentative answer to the problem of why some people have their lower needs satisfied, are capable of giving and receiving love, possess a great amount of confidence and self-esteem, and yet fail to pass over the threshold to self-actualization. The lives of these people are meaningless and lacking in B-values. Only people who live among the B-values are self-actualizing, and they alone are capable of metamotivation.

Maslow identified 14 B-values, but the exact number is not important, because ultimately all become one, or at least all are highly correlated. The values of self-actualizing people include *truth, goodness, beauty, wholeness or the transcendence of dichotomies, aliveness, uniqueness, perfection, completion, justice and order, simplicity, richness or totality, effortlessness, playfulness and humor,* and *self-sufficiency or autonomy* (see Figure 17.2).

These values distinguish self-actualizing people from those whose psychological growth is stunted after they reach esteem needs. Maslow (1971) hypothesized that when our metaneeds are not met, we experience illness, an existential sickness. We all have a holistic tendency to move toward completeness or totality, and when this movement is thwarted, we suffer feelings of inadequacy, disintegration, and unfulfillment. Absence of the B-values leads to pathology just as surely as lack of food results in malnutrition. When denied the truth, we suffer from paranoia; when we live in ugly surroundings, we become physically ill; without justice and order we experience fear and

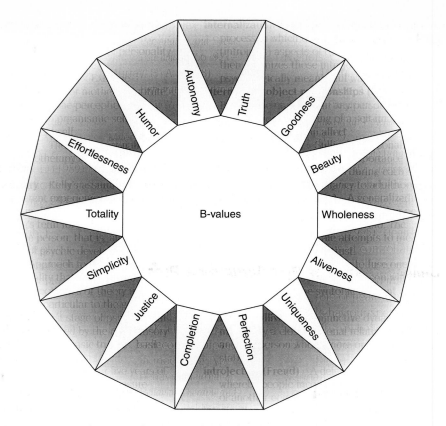

Figure 17.2 Maslow's B-values: A single jewel with many facets.

anxiety; without playfulness and humor, we become stale, rigid, and somber. Deprivation of any of the B-values results in *metapathology,* or the lack of a meaningful philosophy of life.

DEFINITION AND DESCRIPTION

Using research methods described later, Maslow (1970) identified a self-actualizing **syndrome** while studying healthy people. These individuals, to a greater or lesser extent, possessed characteristics consistent with that syndrome, so that eventually a pattern of self-actualization emerged. Maslow defined self-actualization as the "full use and exploitation of talents, capacities, potentialities, etc." (p. 150).

In identifying self-actualizing people, Maslow used both negative and positive criteria. First, *these people must be free from psychopathology.* They must not be neurotic or psychotic or have a tendency toward these psychological disturbances. This is an important negative criterion because some neurotic and psychotic individuals have some things in common with self-actualizing people, namely, such characteristics as a heightened sense of reality, mystical experiences, creativity, and detachment from other people. Maslow eliminated from the list of possible self-actualizing people anyone who showed clear signs of psychopathology—excepting some psychosomatic illnesses.

Second, *self-actualizing people have progressed through the hierarchy of needs* and therefore live above the subsistence level of existence and have no ever-present threat to their safety. But more importantly, they must also have experienced love and have a well-rooted sense of self-worth and esteem. Because they have had their lower level needs satisfied, self-actualizing people are better able to tolerate the frustration of these needs. Even when hungry, self-actualizing people do not panic when food is not immediately available. They do not have the desperate need for money or security often found in people operating at the level of physiological and safety needs. Because they feel loved, they have no neurotic need to have everyone love them. They can tolerate rejection, and their esteem remains intact even in the face of criticism and scorn. They are capable of loving a wide variety of people but feel no obligation to love everyone they meet.

The third criterion for self-actualization is the *full realization of one's needs to grow, to develop, and to increasingly become what one is capable of becoming*. This, in essence, is Maslow's definition of self-actualization. However, in order to fully utilize their capacities, self-actualizing people must embrace the B-values.

CHARACTERISTICS OF SELF-ACTUALIZING PEOPLE

Most people identified by Maslow as being self-actualizing were private individuals, not widely known to the general public. However, he did study some historical and several then-living public persons whom he regarded as self-actualizing. These included Thomas Jefferson, Abraham Lincoln (in his later years), Albert Einstein, Jane Addams, William James, Albert Schweitzer, Aldous Huxley, Benedict de Spinoza, and Eleanor Roosevelt.

What characteristics do these and other self-actualizing people tend to have in common? In his 1970 book, *Motivation and Personality*, Maslow listed 15 tentative qualities that characterize these people to at least some degree.

More Efficient Perception of Reality

Self-actualizing people can more easily detect phoniness in others. They can discriminate between the genuine and the fake not only in people but also in literature, art, and music. They are not fooled by facades and can see both positive and negative underlying traits in others, which are not readily apparent to most people. They perceive ultimate values more clearly than other people and are less prejudiced and less likely to see the world as they wish it to be.

Also, self-actualizing people are less afraid and more comfortable with the unknown. They not only have a greater tolerance of ambiguity, they actively seek it and feel comfortable with problems and puzzles that have no definite right or wrong solution. They welcome doubt, uncertainty, indefiniteness, and uncharted paths, a quality that makes self-actualizing people particularly well suited to be philosophers, explorers, or scientists.

Acceptance of Self, Others, and Nature

Self-actualizing people can accept themselves the way they are. They lack defensiveness, phoniness, and self-defeating guilt; have good hearty animal appetites for food, sleep, and sex; are not overly critical of their own shortcomings; and are not burdened by undue anxiety or shame. In similar fashion, they are accepting of others. They have no compelling need to instruct, inform, or convert. They can tolerate weaknesses in others and are not threatened by others' strengths. They accept nature, including human nature, as it is and do not expect perfection in either themselves or in others. They realize that people suffer, grow old, and die.

> As the child looks out upon the world with wide, uncritical, undemanding, innocent eyes, simply noting and observing what is the case, without either arguing the matter or demanding that it be otherwise, so does the self-actualizing person tend to look upon human nature in himself and in others. (Maslow 1970, p. 156)

Spontaneity, Simplicity, and Naturalness

Self-actualizing people are spontaneous, simple, and natural. They are unconventional but not compulsively so; they are highly ethical but may appear unethical or nonconforming. They usually behave conventionally, either because the issue is not of great importance or out of deference to others. But when the situation warrants it, they can be unconventional and uncompromising even at the price of ostracism and censure. The similarity between self-actualizing people and children and animals is in their spontaneous and natural behavior. They ordinarily live simple lives in the sense that they have no need to erect a complex veneer designed to deceive the world. They are unpretentious and not afraid or ashamed to express joy, awe, elation, sorrow, anger, or other deeply felt emotions.

Problem-Centered

A fourth characteristic of self-actualizing people is their interest in problems outside themselves. Neurotics and, to a lesser extent, average people are self-centered, tending to see all the world's problems in relation to themselves. Self-actualizing people, however, are task-oriented and concerned with problems outside themselves. This interest allows them to develop a mission in life, a purpose for living that spreads beyond self-aggrandizement. Their occupation is not merely a means to earning a living but a vocation, a calling, an end in itself.

Self-actualizing people extend their frame of reference far beyond self. They are concerned with eternal problems and adopt a solid philosophical and ethical basis for handling these problems. They are unconcerned with the trivial and the petty. Their realistic perception enables them to clearly distinguish between the important and the unimportant issues in life.

The Need for Privacy

Self-actualizing people have a quality of detachment that allows them to be alone without being lonely. Unlike neurotics, who often have difficulty with interpersonal relations but must be surrounded by others, healthy individuals feel relaxed and comfortable when they are either with people or alone. They enjoy solitude and privacy and have no desperate need for others, having already satisfied their love and belongingness needs.

Unfortunately, this quality of detachment is not always understood or accepted by others. Self-actualizing people may be seen as aloof or uninterested, but, in fact, their disinterest is limited to minor matters. They have a global concern for the welfare of others without becoming entangled in minute and insignificant problems. Because they spend little energy attempting to impress others or trying to gain love and acceptance, they have more ability to make responsible choices. They are self-movers, resisting society's attempts to make them adhere to convention.

Autonomy

A related characteristic is autonomy, or the ability to be independent of culture and environment. Self-actualizing people depend on themselves for growth even though at some time in their past they had to have received love and security from others. No one is born autonomous, and therefore no one is completely independent of people. Autonomy can be achieved only through satisfactory relations with others.

However, the confidence that one is loved and accepted for what one is, without conditions or qualifications, can be a powerful force in contributing to feelings of self-worth. Once that confidence is attained, a person no longer depends on others for self-esteem. Self-actualizing people have that confidence—and therefore a large measure of autonomy—that allows them to be not only unperturbed by criticism but also unmoved by flattery. This independence also gives them an inner peace and serenity not enjoyed by those who live for the approval of others.

Continued Freshness of Appreciation

Maslow (1970) wrote that "self-actualizing people have the wonderful capacity to appreciate again and again, freshly and naively, the basic goods of life, with awe, pleasure, wonder, and even ecstasy" (p. 163). The most intense of these feelings comes only occasionally, but they are experienced most often by self-actualizers who are constantly aware of their good physical health, friends and loved ones, economic security, and political freedom. Unlike others who take their blessings for granted, self-actualizing individuals see with a fresh vision such everyday phenomena as flowers, food, and friends. They have an appreciation of their possessions and do not waste time complaining about a boring, uninteresting existence. In short, they "retain their constant sense of good fortune and gratitude for it" (Maslow, 1970, p. 164).

The Peak Experience

As Maslow's study of self-actualizers continued, he made the unexpected discovery that many of his people had experiences that were mystical in nature and that somehow gave them a feeling of transcendence. Originally, he thought that these so-called **peak experiences** were far more common among self-actualizers than among non-self-actualizers. Later, however, Maslow (1971) stated that "most people, or almost all people, have peak experiences, or ecstasies" (p. 175).

Peak experiences are not spiritual or supernatural, although they are religious in their core (Maslow, 1964). Also, they are not all of equal intensity; some are only mildly sensed, others moderately felt, and some are quite intensely experienced. In their mild form, these peak experiences probably occur in everyone, although they are seldom noticed. For example, long-distance runners often report a sort of transcendence, a loss of self, or a feeling of being separated from their body. Sometimes, during periods of intense pleasure or satisfaction, people will experience mystical or peak experiences. Viewing a sunset or some other grandeur of nature may precipitate a peak experience, but these experiences cannot be brought on by an act of the will; often they occur at unexpected, quite ordinary moments (Maslow, 1970).

What is it like to have a peak experience? Maslow (1964) described several guidelines that may help answer this question. First, although peak experiences have a religious core, they are not supernatural events. They are quite natural and are part of our human makeup. Second, people having a peak experience see the whole universe as unified or all in one piece, and they see clearly their place in that universe. Also, during this mystical time, peakers feel both more humble and more powerful at the same time. They feel passive, receptive, more desirous of listening, and more capable of hearing. Simultaneously, they feel more responsible for their activities and perceptions, more active, and more self-determined. Peakers experience a loss of fear, anxiety, and conflict and become more loving, accepting, and spontaneous. Although peakers often report such emotions as awe, wonder, rapture, ecstasy, reverence, humility, and surrender, they are not likely to want to get something practical from the experience. They often experience a disorientation in time and space, a loss of self-consciousness, an unselfish attitude, and an ability to transcend everyday polarities.

The peak experience is unmotivated, nonstriving, and nonwishing, and during such an experience, a person experiences no needs, wants, or deficiencies. In addition, Maslow (1964) says "the peak experience is seen only as beautiful, good, desirable, worthwhile, etc., and is never experienced as evil or undesirable" (p. 63). Maslow also believed that the peak experience often has a lasting effect on a person's life.

Gemeinschaftsgefühl

Self-actualizing people possess *Gemeinschaftsgefühl*, Adler's term for social interest, community feeling, or a sense of oneness with all humanity. Maslow found that his self-actualizers had a kind of caring attitude toward other people. Although they often feel like aliens in a foreign land, self-actualizers nevertheless identify with all other people and have a genuine interest in helping others—strangers as well as friends.

Self-actualizers may become angry, impatient, or disgusted with others, but they retain a feeling of affection for human beings in general. More specifically, Maslow (1970) stated that self-actualizing people are "often saddened, exasperated, and even enraged by the shortcomings of the average person" (p. 166), but nevertheless, they continue to feel a basic kinship with that person.

Profound Interpersonal Relations

Related to *Gemeinschaftsgefühl* is a special quality of interpersonal relations that involves deep and profound feelings for individuals. Self-actualizers have a nurturant feeling toward people in general, but their close friendships are limited to only a few. They have no desperate need to be friends with everyone, but the few important interpersonal relationships they do have are quite deep and intense. They tend to choose other very healthy people as friends and avoid intimate interpersonal relationships with dependent or neurotic people, although their social interest allows them to have a special feeling of empathy for these less healthy persons.

We have seen that self-actualizers are often misunderstood and sometimes despised by others. On the other hand, many are greatly loved and attract a large group of admirers and even worshipers, especially if they have made a notable contribution to their business or professional field. Those healthy people studied by Maslow (1970) felt uneasy and embarrassed by this veneration, preferring instead relationships that were mutual rather than one-sided.

Democratic Character Structure

Maslow found that all his self-actualizers possessed democratic values. They could be friendly and considerate with other people regardless of class, color, age, or gender, and, in fact, they seemed to be quite unaware of superficial differences among people.

> They are all quite well aware of how little they know in comparison with what *could* be known and what *is* known by others. Because of this it is possible for them without pose to be honestly respectful and even humble before people who can teach them something that they do not know or who have a skill they do not possess.
>
> They are more likely rather than less likely to counterattack against evil [people] and evil behavior. They are far less ambivalent, confused or weak-willed about their own anger than average [people] are. (Maslow, 1970, p. 168)

Discrimination Between Means and Ends

Self-actualizing people have a clear sense of right and wrong conduct and have little conflict about basic values. They set their sights on ends rather than means and have an unusual ability to distinguish between the two. What other people consider to be a means (for example, eating or exercise), self-actualizing people often see as an end in itself. They enjoy doing something for its own sake and not just because it is a means to some other end. Maslow (1970) described his self-actualizing people by saying that "they can often enjoy for its own sake the getting to some place as well as the arriving. It is occasionally possible for them to make out of the most trivial and routine activity an intrinsically enjoyable game" (p. 169).

Philosophical Sense of Humor

Another distinguishing characteristic of self-actualizing people is their philosophical, nonhostile sense of humor. Most of what passes for humor or comedy is basically hostile, sexual, or scatological. The laugh is usually at someone else's expense. Healthy people see little humor in put-down jokes. They may poke fun at themselves, but not masochistically so. They make fewer tries at humor than others, but their attempts serve a purpose beyond making people laugh. They amuse, inform, point out ambiguities, provoke a smile rather than a guffaw.

The humor of a self-actualizing person is intrinsic to the situation rather than contrived; it is spontaneous rather than planned. Because it is situation-dependent, it usually cannot be repeated. For those who look for examples of a philosophical sense of humor, disappointment is inevitable. A retelling of the incident almost invariably loses its original quality of amusement. One must "be there" to appreciate it.

Creativeness

All self-actualizing people studied by Maslow (1970) were creative in some sense of the word. In fact, Maslow suggested that creativity and self-actualization may be one and the same. However, not all self-actualizers are talented or creative in the arts, but all are creative in their own way. They have a keen perception of truth, beauty, and reality—ingredients that form the foundation of true creativity.

Although not necessarily artistic, self-actualizers are creative in their own ways.

Self-actualizing people need not be poets or artists to be creative. In speaking of his mother-in-law (who was also his aunt), Maslow (1968a) vividly pointed out that creativity can come from almost anywhere. He said that, whereas his self-actualizing mother-in-law had no special talents as a writer or artist, she was truly creative in preparing homemade soup. Maslow remarked that first-rate soup was more creative than second-rate poetry!

Resistance to Enculturation

A final characteristic identified by Maslow was resistance to enculturation. Self-actualizing people have a sense of detachment from their surroundings and are able to transcend a particular culture. They are neither antisocial nor consciously noncon-forming. Rather, they are autonomous, following their own standards of conduct and not blindly obeying the rules of others.

Self-actualizing people do not waste energy fighting against insignificant cus-toms and regulations of society. Such folkways as dress, hair style, and traffic laws are relatively arbitrary, and self-actualizing people do not make a conspicuous show of defying these conventions. Because they accept conventional style and dress, they are not too different in appearance from anyone else. However, on important matters, they can become strongly aroused to seek social change and to resist society's attempts to enculturate them. Self-actualizing people do not merely have different social mores but, Maslow (1970) hypothesized, they are "less enculturated, less flattened out, less molded" (p. 174).

For this reason, these healthy people are more individualized and less homoge-nized than others. They are not all alike. In fact, the term "self-actualization" means to become everything that one can become, to actualize or fulfill all of one's potentials. When people can accomplish this, they become more unique, more heterogeneous, and less shaped by a given culture (Maslow, 1970).

LOVE, SEX, AND SELF-ACTUALIZATION

Before people can become self-actualizing, they must satisfy their love and belonging-ness needs. It follows then that self-actualizing people are capable of both giving and receiving love and are no longer motivated by the kind of deficiency love **(D-love)** that characterizes people motivated by lower level needs. Self-actualizing people are capable of **B-love,** which is love for the essence or "Being" of the other. B-love is mutually felt and shared and not motivated by a deficiency or incompleteness within the lover. In fact, it is unmotivated, expressive behavior. Self-actualizing people do not love because they expect something in return. They simply love and are loved. Their love is never harmful. It is the kind of love that allows lovers to be relaxed, open, and nonse-cretive (Maslow, 1970).

Because self-actualizers are capable of a deeper level of love, Maslow (1970) believed that sex between two B-lovers often becomes a kind of mystical experience. Although they are lusty people, fully enjoying sex, food, and other sensuous pleasures, self-actualizers are not dominated by sex. They can more easily tolerate the absence of sex (as well as other basic needs), because they have no deficiency need for it. Sexual activity between B-lovers is not always a heightened emotional experience; sometimes it is taken quite lightly in the spirit of playfulness and humor. But this is to be expected, because playfulness and humor are B-values, and like the other B-values, they characterize all aspects of a self-actualizer's life, including sexual relationships.

PHILOSOPHY OF SCIENCE

Maslow's philosophy of science and his research methods are integral to an understanding of how he arrived at his concept of self-actualization. Value-free science, Maslow (1966) contended, has been too limited to properly study human personality. Such a science does not help us to understand people, because its philosophy is without value and its methodology is sterile and nonemotional. Maslow argued for a different philosophy of science, a humanistic, holistic approach that is not value-free and that has scientists who *care* about the people and topics they investigate.

Maslow agreed with Allport (see Chapter 14) that psychological science should stress the importance of individual procedures as opposed to the study of groups. Subjective reports should be favored over rigidly objective ones, and people should be allowed to tell about themselves in a holistic fashion instead of the more orthodox approach that studies people in bits and pieces. Traditional psychology has dealt with sensations, intelligence, attitudes, stimuli, reflexes, test scores, and hypothetical constructs from an external point of view. It has not been much concerned with the whole person as seen from that person's subjective view.

Maslow was critical of scientists who have **"desacralized"** science, that is, removed the emotion, joy, wonder, awe, and rapture from their study in order to purify and objectify it. Orthodox science has no ritual or ceremony. Maslow believed that scientists should put values, emotion, and ritual back into their work and be creative in their pursuit of knowledge. They must be willing to **"resacralize"** science or to instill it with human values, emotion, and ritual. Astronomers must not only study the stars, they must be awestruck by them; psychologists must not only study human personality, they must do so with enjoyment, excitement, wonder, and affection.

Maslow (1966) argued for a **Taoistic attitude** for psychology, one that would be noninterfering, passive, and receptive. This new psychology would abolish prediction and control as the major goals of science and replace them with sheer fascination and the desire to release people from controls so that they can grow and become less predictable. The proper response to mystery, Maslow said, is not analysis but awe.

The new scientific psychologists must themselves be healthy people, able to tolerate ambiguity and uncertainty. They must be intuitive, nonrational, insightful, and courageous enough to ask the right questions. They must also be willing to flounder, to be imprecise, to question their own procedures, and to take on the important problems of psychology. Maslow (1966) contended that there is no need to do well that which is not worth doing. Rather, it is better to do poorly that which is important.

RESEARCH METHODS

In his study of self-actualizing people and peak experiences, Maslow employed research methods consistent with his philosophy of science. He began intuitively, often "skating on thin ice," then attempted to verify his hunches using idiographic and subjective methods. He often left to others the technical work of gathering evidence. His personal preference was to "scout out ahead," leaving one area when he grew tired of it and going on to explore new ones (Hall, 1968).

Maslow's (1970) approach to studying self-actualizing people was to begin by selecting from among friends, acquaintances, and public and historical persons those people who appeared to him to be healthy, strong, creative, saintly, and wise. In addition, he attempted to study 3,000 college students, but found only one who was definitely self-actualizing. He later searched for relatively self-actualizing people, arbitrarily defined as the healthiest 1% of Brandeis University students.

After selecting his original sample on the basis of somewhat arbitrary and unscientific definitions, Maslow carefully studied these people to establish a *syndrome for psychological health*. Next, he refined the original definition and then reselected potential self-actualizers, retaining some, eliminating others, and adding new ones. Then he repeated the entire procedure with the second group, making some changes in the definition and criteria of self-actualization. Maslow continued this cyclical process to a third or fourth selection group or until he was satisfied that he had refined a vague, unscientific concept into a precise operational definition and that his study of self-actualization was indeed scientific.

Maslow's methods of investigation, however, are subject to severe criticism. In his study of self-actualizers, he selected people from among personal acquaintances, friends, and public and historical persons. Therefore, most were from the middle and upper classes, highly intelligent, and well educated.

In addition, Maslow has left unanswered several important questions concerning self-actualization. First, is self-actualization limited to highly intelligent individuals? Are feeble-minded people capable of full use of their capacities and talents? Maslow, in an interview with Willard Frick (1971), said that he did not know what self-actualization means in feeble-minded people.

A second question not fully answered involves the possibility of intentionally striving toward self-actualization. Can people consciously and willfully move themselves in the direction of high-level motivation? In the same interview, Maslow alluded to certain people who consciously set metamotivation as a goal, but added that "they're doing it stupidly and inefficiently and incapably and they want it *now*" (Frick, 1971, p. 36).

Another question concerns replication, a critical ingredient in scientific methodology. Because Maslow failed to give us an operational definition of self-actualization and a full description of his sampling procedures, researchers cannot be certain that they are repeating Maslow's original study or that they are identifying the same syndrome of self-actualization.

MEASUREMENT OF SELF-ACTUALIZATION

Everett L. Shostrom (1974) avoided some of these criticisms by developing a standardized inventory that attempts to assess self-actualization. Shostrom's **Personal Orientation Inventory (POI)** has adequate reliability and validity and purports to be a comprehensive measure of the values and behaviors of self-actualizing people. It consists of 150 forced-choice items, such as: (a) "I can feel comfortable with less than a perfect performance" versus (b) "I feel uncomfortable with anything less than a perfect performance"; (a) " Two people will get along best if each concentrates on pleasing the other" versus (b) "Two people can get along best if each person feels free to express himself"; (a) "I live in terms of my wants, likes, dislikes and values" versus (b) "I do not live in terms of my wants, likes, dislikes and values"; and (a) "My moral values are dictated by society" versus (b) "My moral values are self-determined" (Shostrom, 1963). Respondents are asked to choose either statement (a) or statement (b), but they may leave the answer blank if neither statement applies to them or if they do not know anything about the statement.

The POI has two major scales and 10 subscales. The first major scale—the Time Competence/Time Incompetence scale—measures the degree to which people are present oriented. The second major scale—the Support scale—is "designed to measure whether an individual's mode of reaction is characteristically 'self' oriented or 'other' oriented" (Shostrom, 1974, p. 4). The 10 subscales assess levels of: (1) self-actualization values, (2) flexibility in applying values, (3) sensitivity to one's own needs and feelings, (4) spontaneity in expressing feelings behaviorally, (5) self-regard, (6) self-acceptance, (7) positive view of humanity, (8) ability to see opposites of life as meaningfully related, (9) acceptance of aggression, and (10) capacity for intimate contact. High scores on these 12 scales indicate some level of self-actualization; low scores do not necessarily suggest pathology but give clues concerning a person's self-actualizing values and behaviors.

Research indicates that the POI is extremely resistant to faking—unless one is familiar with Maslow's description of a self-actualizing person. In the POI manual, Shostrom (1974) cited several studies in which the examinees were asked to "fake good" or "make a favorable impression" in filling out the inventory. When participants followed these instructions, they generally scored lower (in the direction away from self-actualization) than they did when responding honestly to the statements.

This, indeed, is an interesting finding. Why should people lower their scores when trying to look good? The answer lies in Maslow's concept of self-actualization. Statements that might be true for self-actualizers are not necessarily socially desirable and do not always conform to cultural standards. For example, items such as: "I can overcome any obstacles as long as I believe in myself" or "My basic responsibility is to be aware of others' needs" may seem like desirable goals to someone trying to simulate self-actualization, but an actualizing person probably would not endorse either of these items. On the other hand, a truly self-actualizing person may choose such items as: "I do not always need to live by the rules and standards of society" or "I do not feel obligated when a stranger does me a favor" (Shostrom, 1974, p. 22). Because one of the characteristics of self-actualizing people is resistance to enculturation, it should not be surprising that attempts to make a good impression will usually result in failure.

Interestingly, Maslow himself seemed to have answered the questions honestly when he filled out the inventory. Despite the fact that he helped in the construction of the POI, Maslow's own scores were only in the direction of self-actualization and not nearly as high as the scores of people who were definitely self-actualizing (Shostrom, 1974).

APPLICATIONS OF MASLOW'S THEORY

Maslow's personality theory can be applied to the study of the abnormal personality and to the process of psychotherapy.

ABNORMAL DEVELOPMENT

According to Maslow (1970), everyone is born with a will toward health, a tendency to grow toward self-actualization. Failure of personal growth results in neuroses and abnormal development. Strictly considered, anything less than self-actualization is abnormal. That which is usually considered "normal" in psychology is merely descriptive of the majority. The average person falls short of full human potential and is thus "abnormal." The normal human condition is health; the usual condition is somewhat less.

If the normal human condition is self-actualization, what prevents people from reaching this level? Growth toward normal healthy personality is blocked by an absence of basic need gratification. If people cannot provide for food and shelter, they cannot reach their full potential for psychological growth. Many people, however, have their physiological and safety needs relatively satisfied, and yet they remain blocked at the level of love and belongingness needs. They find it difficult to give and receive love and to develop feelings of belongingness because, as children, they did not experience healthy parental love. Even when people satisfy their love needs and gain self-esteem, they do not automatically reach self-actualization (Maslow, 1970).

One abnormal syndrome that often blocks people's growth toward self-actualization is the **Jonah complex,** or the fear of being one's best. The Jonah complex is characterized by attempts to run away from one's destiny just as the biblical Jonah tried to escape from his fate. The Jonah complex, which is found in nearly everyone, represents a fear of success, a fear of being one's best, and a feeling of awesomeness in the presence of beauty and perfection (Maslow, 1971).

Why do people run away from greatness and self-fulfillment? Maslow (1971) offered the following rationale. First, the human body is simply not strong enough to endure the ecstasy of fulfillment for any length of time, just as peak experiences and sexual orgasms would be overly taxing if they lasted too long. Therefore, the intense emotion that accompanies perfection and fulfillment carries with it a shattering sensation such as: "This is too much" or "I can't stand it anymore."

A second explanation for the evasion of growth is the necessity of humility. Maslow (1971) reasoned that most of us have a private ambition to be great, to write a great novel, to be a movie star, to become a world famous scientist, and so on. However, when we compare ourselves with those who have accomplished greatness, we are appalled by our own arrogance. "Who am I to think I could do as well as this great person?" As a defense against this grandiosity or "sinful pride," we lower our aspirations, feel stupid and humble, and adopt the self-defeating approach of running away from the realization of our full potentials.

Although the Jonah complex stands out most sharply in neurotic people, nearly all of us have some timidity toward seeking perfection and greatness. We allow false humility to stifle creativity, and thus we prevent ourselves from becoming self-actualizing.

PSYCHOTHERAPY

Although not known as a practicing psychotherapist, Maslow (1970) considered how his personality theory could be applied to psychotherapy. First, the hierarchy of needs concept suggests that, because physiological and safety needs are prepotent, people operating on these levels will not ordinarily be motivated to seek psychotherapy. Instead, they will strive to obtain nourishment and protection.

Most people who come for therapy have these two lower level needs relatively well satisfied but have some difficulty satisfying love and belongingness needs. Therefore, psychotherapy is largely an interpersonal process. Through a warm, loving interpersonal relationship with the therapist, the client gains satisfaction of love and belongingness needs and thereby acquires feelings of confidence and self-worth. A healthy interpersonal relationship between client and therapist is therefore the best psychological medicine. This accepting relationship gives clients a feeling of being worthy of love and facilitates their ability to establish other healthy relationships outside of therapy. This view of psychotherapy is nearly identical to that of Carl Rogers, as we discussed in Chapter 16.

To Maslow (1970), the aim of therapy would be to free clients from their dependency on others so that their natural impulse toward growth and self-actualization could become active. Psychotherapy cannot be value-free but must take into consideration the fact that everyone has an inherent tendency to move toward a better, more enriching condition, namely self-actualization.

RELATED RESEARCH

Maslow's holistic-dynamic theory continues to attract interest not only among psychologists but also among business managers, educators, marketers, and nurses. Whereas much of this influence has been due to the hierarchy of needs model, Maslow's notion of self-actualization has also spawned a moderate amount of empirical investigation. Much of this research has been aided by the development of two self-report inventories of self-actualization: the Personal Orientation Inventory (POI) (Shostrom, 1963, 1974; Knapp, 1976) and the Short Index of Self-Actualization (SI) (Jones & Crandall, 1986).

Even though the POI has demonstrated reasonable reliability and validity (Crandall, McCown, & Robb, 1988; Fogarty, 1994; Hattie & Cooksey, 1984; Jones & Crandall, 1986; Knapp, 1976; Shostrom, 1974), some researchers have criticized the inventory for failing to distinguish between known self-actualizers and non-self-actualizers (Ray, 1984; Weiss, 1991; Whitson & Olczak, 1991). Furthermore, the POI has two practical problems: first, it is long, taking most participants 30 to 45 minutes to complete; and second, the two-item forced-choice format can engender hostility in the participants, who feel frustrated by the limitations of a forced-choice option. To overcome these two practical limitations, Alvin Jones and Rick Crandall (1986) created the Short Index (SI) of the POI. The SI borrows 15 items from the POI that are most strongly correlated with the total self-actualization score and places them on a 6-point Likert scale (from strongly disagree to strongly agree).

If self-actualization is a valid concept, it must be able to predict healthy interpersonal relationships. Recall that Maslow listed profound and close interpersonal relationships as one criterion of self-actualization. Recently, Michael Sheffield, James Carey, William Patenaude, and Michael Lambert (1995) conducted a study that examined the relationship between self-actualization and the presence of close interpersonal relationships. These researchers used the POI to measure self-actualization and the Inventory of Interpersonal Problems (IIP) to assess such relationship problems as being domineering, vindictive, cold, socially avoidant, nonassertive, exploitable, overly nurturant, and intrusive. As predicted, they found that interpersonal problems were negatively related to the POI scales of inner directedness, time competence, acceptance of aggression, and capacity for intimate contact. In other words, people with interpersonal problems were not inner directed, did not live in the present, denied feelings of aggression, and had problems with close interpersonal relationships.

Another study that used the POI was conducted by Gerard Fogarty (1994) in Australia. Fogarty was interested in whether a group of socially and economically disadvantaged non-self-actualizing people would increase their self-actualization scores after participating in a 10-week course designed to increase basic math and language skills and to improve self-confidence. Compared with their pretest scores, participants in the course scored higher on the POI subscales of spontaneity and self-acceptance. Spontaneity is "the freedom to react spontaneously, or to be oneself" (Knapp, 1976, p. 6), whereas self-acceptance is "the affirmation or acceptance of oneself in spite of one's weaknesses or deficiencies" (p. 7). These findings suggest that the POI can predict changes in competence and self-esteem that occur from an intervention program intended to bolster feelings of competence.

As with the POI, most of the studies using the Short Index (SI) have been efforts to demonstrate its congruence with Maslow's theory of self-actualization. According to Maslow's concept, self-actualization should relate positively to healthy interpersonal relationships, creativity, self-esteem, openness, and having a sense of purpose in life. In addition, it should relate negatively to maladjustment and anxiety.

Mark Runco, Peter Ebersole, and Wayne Mraz (1991) studied what Maslow believed may be *the* definitive characteristic of self-actualizing people: high levels of creativity. Maslow (1959) made a distinction between the specialized creativity of artists and scientists and the self-actualizing creativity of people at everyday life tasks, such as that displayed by his own mother-in-law, who was quite creative in making first-rate soup. In other words, Maslow did not believe that self-actualizing people would be creative artists and scientists, but rather that they would solve everyday problems of living in a creative and adaptive way.

Using a group of college students, Runco and his colleagues administered the SI and two creativity measures that assess general rather than specialized creativity. The first measure of creativity was the How Do You Think (HDYT) inventory, which contains 100 statements indicative of a creative personality and lifestyle. Example items include: "I am very conscious of aesthetic considerations" and "I often become engrossed in a new idea." These statements are scored on four subscales: (1) Interest, (2) Confidence and Flexibility, (3) Energetic Originality, and (4) Arousal and Risk Taking. The second creativity measure used by Runco et al. was the Creative Personality Scale of the Adjective Check List (Gough & Heilbrun, 1980). This scale consists of trait terms that highly creative people tend to use in describing themselves, such as "autonomous," "original," or "interests wide." The results showed significantly positive correlations between each of the four subscales of the HDYT and the SI, with the Energetic Originality subscale being the best predictor of self-actualization. The Creative Personality Scale was positively, but insignificantly, correlated to the Short Index. These results suggest that creativity is at least partly related to self-actualization.

A number of different studies have examined the extent to which purpose in life, close interpersonal relationships, self-esteem, and openness are positively related to self-actualization as measured by the SI. For example, Peter Ebersole and Pat Humphreys (1991) found that college students who scored high on the SI also tended to have high scores on a purpose in life scale. In addition, Deborah Rowan, William Compton, and James Rust (1995) examined close interpersonal relationships and SI self-actualization. They found that for men, but not for women, the SI was positively related to marital satisfaction and affection in marriage.

Furthermore, Maslow's prediction that self-actualizing people are also able to accept themselves has been studied mostly with self-esteem inventories. For example, William Compton, Maggie Smith, Kim Cornish, and Donald Qualls (1996) administered the SI along with other measures of mental health—including self-esteem and openness—to college students and found that those who scored high on self-esteem also tended to score high on the SI measure of self-actualization. These results are consistent with those reported earlier by Rick Richard and Steve Jex (1991), who found that SI scores were negatively related to anxiety. In addition, Compton and his colleagues found that self-actualization related to openness to experience. People who scored high on the SI were likely to seek out new and highly arousing experiences.

In summary, Maslow's description of the self-actualizing person appears to match constructs measured by both the POI and the SI; that is, self-actualizing people seem to have high self-esteem, be creative, have close interpersonal relationships, be open to new and varied experiences, and have a sense of purpose in life.

CRITIQUE OF MASLOW

A useful theory of personality must generate relevant research, lend itself to falsification, organize what is known about a particular discipline, serve as a guide to action, have internal consistency, and be parsimonious. How does Maslow's theory rate on these six criteria?

First, on its ability to *generate research*, Maslow's personality theory has been somewhat fruitful in stimulating research on self-actualization. However, much of the theory's assumptions regarding motivation and the hierarchy of needs remains unexamined. Therefore, we rate Maslow's theory about average on this criterion.

On the criterion of falsifiability, however, Maslow's theory receives a low rating. Maslow left future researchers with few clear guidelines to follow when attempting to replicate his studies on self-actualization. Lacking operational definitions of such terms as the Jonah complex, metamotivation, love, belongingness, esteem, and self-actualization, researchers are able to neither verify nor falsify much of Maslow's basic theory.

Nevertheless, Maslow's hierarchy of needs framework gives his theory excellent flexibility to *organize what is known about human behavior*. Maslow's theory is also quite consistent with common sense. For example, common sense suggests that a person must have enough to eat before being motivated by other matters. Starving people care little about political philosophy. Their primary motivation is to obtain food, not to sympathize with one political philosophy or another. Similarly, people living under threat to their physical well-being will be motivated mostly to secure safety, and people who have physiological and safety needs relatively satisfied will strive to be accepted and to establish a love relationship.

Does Maslow's theory serve as *a guide to the practitioner*? On this criterion, the theory is rated as highly useful. Psychotherapists adhering to Maslow's theory know that if clients believe that their safety needs are threatened, then they must provide a safe and secure environment for those clients. Once clients have satisfied physiological and safety needs, the therapist can work to provide them with feelings of love and belongingness. Likewise, personnel managers in business and industry can use Maslow's theory to motivate workers. The theory suggests that increases in pay cannot satisfy any needs beyond the physiological and safety levels. Because physiological and safety needs are already largely gratified for the average worker in the United States, wage increases per se will not permanently increase worker morale and productivity. Pay raises can satisfy higher level needs only when workers see them as recognition for a job well done. Maslow's theory suggests that business executives should allow workers more responsibility and freedom, tap into their ingenuity and creativity in solving problems, and encourage them to use their intelligence and imagination on the job.

Is the theory *internally consistent*? Unfortunately, Maslow's arcane and often unclear language makes important parts of his theory ambiguous and inconsistent. Apart from the problem of idiosyncratic language, however, Maslow's theory ranks high on the criterion of internal consistency. The hierarchy of needs concept follows a logical progression, and Maslow hypothesized that the order of needs is the same for everyone, although he does not overlook the possibility of certain reversals. Aside from some deficiencies in his scientific methods, Maslow's theory has a consistency and precision that give it popular appeal.

Is Maslow's theory *parsimonious*, or does it contain superfluous fabricated concepts and models? At first glance, the theory seems quite simplistic. A hierarchy of needs model with only five steps gives the theory a deceptive appearance of simplicity. A full understanding of Maslow's total theory, however, suggests a far more complex model. Overall, the theory receives a moderate rating on parsimony.

CONCEPT OF HUMANITY

In Maslow's view, people have a natural tendency to move toward self-actualization, and the basic needs that motivate them are precisely those that ultimately result in positive growth and health. Human nature is structured in such a way that our activated needs are exactly what we desire most. For example, children first want food, then protection, love, praise, and finally self-fulfillment.

Although Maslow was generally *optimistic* and hopeful, he recognized that people are capable of great evil and destruction. Evil, however, stems from the frustration or thwarting of basic needs, not from the essential nature of people. When basic needs are not met, people may steal, cheat, lie, or kill. Although Maslow believed that human perfection is not possible, he insisted that certain individuals are capable of far greater growth and improvement than is generally supposed. Society, too, can be improved although not perfected. Growth, both individually and culturally, is slow and painful, but it seems to be part of our evolutionary history. Maslow insisted on the ultimate improvability of humans, but he also realized that "most men are doomed to wish for what they do not have" (Maslow, 1970, p. 70). In other words, although all people have the potential for self-actualization, most will live out their lives struggling for food, safety, or love. Most societies, Maslow believed, emphasize these lower level needs and base their educational and political systems on an invalid concept of humanity.

Truth, love, beauty, and the like are instinctoid and are just as basic to our nature as hunger, sex, and aggression. All people have the potential to strive toward self-actualization just as they have the motivation to seek food and protection. Because Maslow held that basic needs are structured the same for all people and that people satisfy these needs at their own rate, his holistic-dynamic theory of personality places moderate emphasis on both *uniqueness* and *similarities*.

From both a historical and an individual point of view, humans are an evolutionary animal, in the process of becoming more and more fully human. That is, as evolution progresses, humans gradually become more motivated by metamotivations and by the B-values. High-level needs exist, at least as potentiality, in everyone. Because people aim toward self-actualization, Maslow's view can be considered *teleological and purposive*.

Maslow's view of humanity is difficult to classify on such dimensions as determinism vs. free choice, conscious vs. unconscious, or biological vs. social determinants of personality. In general, the behavior of people motivated by physiological and safety needs is *determined by outside forces*, whereas the behavior of self-actualizing people is at least partially shaped by *free choice*.

On the dimension of *consciousness vs. unconsciousness*, Maslow held that self-actualizing people are ordinarily more aware than others of what they are doing and why. However, motivation is so complex that people may be driven by several needs at the same time, and even healthy people are not always fully aware of all the reasons underlying their behavior.

As for *biological vs. social influences*, Maslow would have insisted that this is a false dichotomy. Individuals are shaped by both biology *and* society, and the two cannot be separated. Inadequate genetic endowment does not condemn a person to an unfulfilled life, just as a poor social environment does not preclude growth. When people achieve self-actualization, they experience a wonderful synergy among the biological, social, and spiritual aspects of their lives. Self-actualizers receive more physical enjoyment from the sensuous pleasures; they experience deeper and richer interpersonal relationships; and they receive pleasure from spiritual qualities such as beauty, truth, goodness, justice, and perfection.

Chapter Summary

Maslow's holistic-dynamic theory of personality is largely a theory of human motivation. It assumes that (1) the *whole person* is motivated, (2) *motivation is complex* and often *unconscious*, (3) people are *continually motivated* by one need or another, and (4) the *same basic needs apply to all people*.

Maslow recognized four major dimension of needs: (1) the *conative needs*; (2) *cognitive needs*, including knowledge; (3) *aesthetic needs*, including love of beauty and order; and (4) *neurotic needs*, which produce neuroses whether or not they are satisfied.

The conative needs can be arranged on a *hierarchy*, meaning that one need must be relatively satisfied before the next one can become active. The most basic needs are *physiological*, including food, water, oxygen, and so forth. After physiological needs are at least partially satisfied, people are motivated to seek *safety*. When safety needs are relatively satisfied, *love and belongingness* needs become motivators. To the extent that people satisfy their needs for love, they acquire self-esteem. When *esteem* needs are adequately met, people will either remain on that level or cross the threshold to *self-actualization*.

Occasionally, needs on the hierarchy can be *reversed*, but ordinarily people from all cultures proceed in the same order through the hierarchy. *Unconscious motivation* frequently blurs one's view of the true need underlying a particular behavior.

Maslow believed that all behavior has a cause but not all behavior is motivated. *Coping behavior*, which stems from basic needs, is motivated, whereas expressive behavior frequently is not. *Expressive behavior* has no goal; it is simply our way of expressing ourselves.

Conative needs, including self-actualization, are *instinctoid*; that is, their deprivation leads to pathology. The frustration of self-actualization needs results in *metapathology*.

Self-actualizing people are motivated by the B-*values*. In fact, acceptance of B-values (truth, beauty, humor, and so forth) is the criterion that separates self-actualizing people from those who are merely healthy but mired at the level of self-esteem.

In addition, self-actualizers are characterized by (1) a more efficient perception of reality; (2) acceptance of self, others, and nature; (3) spontaneity, simplicity, and naturalness; (4) a problem-centered approach to life; (5) the need for privacy; (6) autonomy; (7) freshness of appreciation; (8) peak experiences; (9) social interest; (10) profound interpersonal relations; (11) a democratic attitude; (12) the ability to discriminate means from ends; (13) a philosophical sense of humor; (14) creativeness; and (15) resistance to enculturation.

Also, self-actualizers are capable of B-*love*, or love for the essence of another. Maslow also hypothesized that sex between two self-actualizers is both more mystical and more pleasurable than sex between non-self-actualizers.

In his *philosophy of science*, Maslow argued for a *Taoistic attitude*, one that is noninterfering, passive, receptive, and subjective. The subject matter of psychology must be viewed with joy, wonder, awe, and affection. Maslow's own *research methods* followed a Taoistic approach, but he was less than careful in reporting his procedures.

The Personal Orientation Inventory (POI) is a standardized test designed to measure self-actualizing values and behavior. *Abnormal development* arises when people are frustrated in any of their basic needs, but especially love and belongingness. The *Jonah complex* is the fear of being or doing one's best. *Psychotherapy* to rectify abnormal development should be directed at the need level currently being thwarted.

Despite difficulties with verification or falsification, Maslow's holistic-dynamic theory is quite useful in generating research, organizing knowledge, and serving as a guide to the practitioner. Maslow's language is not always clear, but his theory is rated adequate on both internal consistency and parsimony.

Maslow's view of humanity is both realistic and optimistic. If lower level needs are thwarted, people will live difficult lives of frustration and desperation. However, If they are able to satisfy their needs, they will move naturally toward self-fulfillment.

Suggested Readings

Cleary, T. S., & Shapiro, S. I. (1995). The plateau experience and the post-mortem life: Abraham H. Maslow's unfinished theory. *Journal of Transpersonal Psychology, 27,* 1–23.

These authors discuss Maslow's interesting concept of a "high plateau" experience, one that, unlike the peak experience, is serene and calm and can be intentionally experienced. Cleary and Shapiro believe that the plateau experience enabled Maslow to transcend his fear of death and to become more peaceful during the last months of his life.

Hoffman, E. (1988). *The right to be human: A biography of Abraham Maslow.* Los Angeles: Tarcher.

Hoffman interviewed dozens of Maslow's family members, friends, and associates to write this fascinating biography. The result is a very readable, informative, and comprehensive book.

Maslow, A. H. (1964). *Religions, values, and peak-experiences.* Columbus: Ohio State University Press.

In this brief book, Maslow discusses the differences between personalized and institutionalized religious experiences and also describes the religious aspects of the peak experience.

Maslow, A. H. (1970). *Motivation and personality* (2nd ed.). New York: Harper & Row.

Maslow's basic theory of motivation and self-actualization are presented. This book should be required reading for anyone interested in Maslow's holistic-dynamic theory.

Maslow, A. H. (1993). *The farther reaches of human nature.* New York: Viking Press.

Originally published in 1971, this paperback reprint is an extension of Maslow's (1968b) *Toward a Psychology of Being.* Among other topics, Maslow discusses B-values, metamotivation, creativeness, and peak experiences.

May

May:
Existential Psychology

Biography of Rollo May
Background of Existentialism
    What Is Existentialism?
    Basic Concepts
The Case of Philip
Anxiety
    Normal Anxiety
    Neurotic Anxiety
Guilt
Intentionality
Care, Love, and Will
    Union of Love and Will
    Forms of Love
Freedom and Destiny
    Freedom Defined
    Forms of Freedom
    Destiny Defined
    Philip's Destiny
The Power of Myth
Psychopathology
Psychotherapy
Related Research
Critique of May
Concept of Humanity
Chapter Summary
Suggested Readings

Shortly after World War II, a new psychology—existential psychology—began to spread from Europe to the United States. Existential psychology is rooted in the philosophy of Soren Kierkegaard, Friedrich Nietzsche, Martin Heidegger, Jean-Paul Sartre, and other European writers. The first existential psychologists and psychiatrists were also Europeans, and these included Ludwig Binswanger, Medard Boss, Victor Frankl, and others.

For more than 40 years, the foremost spokesperson for existential psychology in the United States was Rollo May. During his years as a psychotherapist, May evolved a new way of looking at human beings. His approach was not based on any controlled scientific research, but rather on clinical experience. He saw people as living in the world of present experiences and ultimately being responsible for who they become. May's penetrating insights and profound analyses of the human condition made him a popular writer among laypeople as well as professional psychologists.

Many people, May believed, lack the courage to face their destiny, and in the process of fleeing from it, they give up much of their freedom. Having negated their freedom, they likewise run away from their responsibility. Not being willing to make choices, they lose sight of who they are and develop a sense of insignificance and alienation. Healthy people, on the other hand, challenge their destiny, cherish their freedom, and live authentically with other people and with themselves. They recognize the inevitability of death and have the courage to live life in the present.

BIOGRAPHY OF ROLLO MAY

Rollo Reese May was born April 21, 1909, in Ada, Ohio, the first son of the six children born to Earl Tittle May and Matie Boughton May. Neither parent was very well educated, and May's early intellectual climate was virtually nonexistent. In fact, when his older sister had a psychotic breakdown some years later, May's father attributed it to too much education (Bilmes, 1978)!

At an early age, May moved with his family to Marine City, Michigan, where he spent most of his childhood. As a young boy, Rollo was not particularly close to either of his parents, who often argued with each other and eventually separated. May's father, a secretary for the Young Men's Christian Association, moved frequently during Rollo's youth. May's mother often left the children to care for themselves and, according to May's description, was a "bitch-kitty on wheels" (Rabinowitz, Good, & Cozad, 1989, p. 437). May attributed his own two failed marriages to his mother's unpredictable behavior and to his older sister's psychotic episode.

During his childhood, May found solitude and relief from family strife by playing on the shores of the St. Clair River. The river became his friend, a serene place to swim during the summer and to ice skate during the winter. He claimed to have learned more from the river than from the school he attended in Marine City (Rabinowitz et al., 1989). As a youth, he acquired an interest in art and literature, interests that never left him. He attended college at Michigan State University, where he majored in English. However, he was asked to leave school soon after he became editor of a radical student magazine. May then transferred to Oberlin College in Ohio, from which he received a bachelor's degree in 1930.

For the next three years, May followed a course very similar to the one traveled by Erik Erikson (see Chapter 9) some 10 years earlier. He roamed throughout eastern and southern Europe as an artist, painting pictures and studying native art (Harris, 1969). Actually, the nominal purpose for May's trip was to tutor English at Anatolia

College, in Saloniki, Greece. This job provided him time to work as an itinerant artist in Turkey, Poland, Austria, and other countries. However, by his second year, May was beginning to become lonely. As a consequence, he poured himself into his work as a teacher, but the harder he worked, the less effective he became.

> Finally in the spring of that second year I had what is called, euphemistically, a nervous breakdown. Which meant simply that the rules, principles, values, by which I used to work and live simply did not suffice anymore. I got so completely fatigued that I had to go to bed for two weeks to get enough energy to continue my teaching. I had learned enough psychology at college to know that these symptoms meant that something was wrong with my whole way of life. I had to find some new goals and purposes for my living and to relinquish my moralistic, somewhat rigid way of existence. (May, 1985, p. 8)

From that point on, May began to listen to his inner voice, the one that spoke to him of beauty. "It seems it had taken a collapse of my whole former way of life for this voice to make itself heard" (p. 13).

A second experience in Europe also left a lasting impression on him, namely, his attendance at Alfred Adler's 1932 summer seminars at a resort in the mountains above Vienna. May greatly admired Adler and learned much about human behavior and about himself during that time (Rabinowitz et al., 1989).

After May returned to the United States in 1933, he enrolled at Union Theological Seminary in New York, the same seminary Carl Rogers had attended 10 years earlier. Unlike Rogers, however, May did not enter the seminary to become a minister but rather to ask the ultimate questions concerning the nature of human beings (Harris, 1969). While at the Union Theological Seminary, he met the renowned existential theologian and philosopher Paul Tillich, then a recent refugee from Germany and a faculty member at the seminary. May learned much of his philosophy from Tillich, and the two men remained friends for more than 30 years.

Although May had not gone to the seminary to be a preacher, he was ordained as a Congregational minister in 1938 after receiving a Master of Divinity degree. He then served as a pastor for two years, but finding parish work meaningless, he quit to pursue his interest in psychology. He studied psychoanalysis at the William Alanson White Institute of Psychiatry, Psychoanalysis, and Psychology while working as a counselor to male students at City College of New York. At about this time, he met Harry Stack Sullivan (see Chapter 8), president and cofounder of the William Alanson White Institute. May was impressed with Sullivan's notion that the therapist is a participant observer and that therapy is a human adventure capable of enhancing the life of both patient and therapist. He also met and was influenced by Erich Fromm (see Chapter 7), who at that time was a faculty member at the William Alanson White Institute.

In 1946, May opened his own private practice and, two years later, joined the faculty of the William Alanson White Institute. In 1949, at the relatively advanced age of 40, he earned the first Ph.D. in clinical psychology awarded by Columbia University. He continued to serve as assistant professor of psychiatry at the William Alanson White Institute until 1974.

Prior to receiving his doctorate, May underwent the most profound experience of his life. While still in his early thirties, he contracted tuberculosis and spent three years at the Saranac Sanitarium in upstate New York. At that time, no medication for tuberculosis was available, and for a year and a half, May did not know whether he would live or die. He felt helpless and had little to do except wait for the monthly X-ray that would tell whether the cavity in his lung was getting larger or smaller (May, 1972).

At that point, he began to develop some insight into the nature of his illness. He realized that the disease was taking advantage of his helpless and passive attitude. He saw that the patients around him who accepted their illness were the very ones who tended to die, whereas those who fought against their condition tended to survive. "Not until I developed some 'fight,' some sense of personal responsibility for the fact that it was I who had the tuberculosis, an assertion of my own will to live, did I make lasting progress" (May, 1972, p. 14).

As May learned to listen to his body, he discovered that healing is an active, not a passive, process. The person who is sick, be it physiologically or psychologically, must be an active participant in the therapeutic process. May realized this truth for himself as he recovered from tuberculosis, but it was only later that he was able to see that his psychotherapy patients also had to fight against their disturbance in order to get better (May, 1972).

During his illness and recovery, May was writing a book on anxiety. To better understand the subject, he read both Freud and Søren Kierkegaard, the great Danish existential philosopher and theologian. He admired Freud, but he was more deeply moved by Kierkegaard's view of anxiety as a struggle against *nonbeing*, that is, loss of consciousness (May, 1969a).

After May recovered from his illness, he wrote his dissertation on the subject of anxiety and the next year published it under the title *The Meaning of Anxiety* (May, 1950). Three years later, he wrote *Man's Search for Himself* (May, 1953), the book that gained him some recognition, not only in professional circles, but among other educated people as well. In 1958, he collaborated with Ernest Angel and Henri Ellenberger to publish *Existence: A New Dimension in Psychiatry and Psychology*. This book introduced American psychotherapists to the concepts of existential therapy and continued the popularity of the existential movement. May's best-known work, *Love and Will* (1969b), became a national best-seller and won the 1970 Ralph Waldo Emerson Award for humane scholarship. In 1971, he won the American Psychological Association's Award for Distinguished Contribution to the Science and Profession of Clinical Psychology. In 1972, the New York Society of Clinical Psychologists presented him with the Dr. Martin Luther King, Jr., Award for his book *Power and Innocence* (1972), and in 1987, May received the American Psychological Foundation Gold Medal Award for Lifetime Contributions to Professional Psychology.

During his career, May was a visiting professor at both Harvard and Princeton and lectured at such institutions as Yale, Dartmouth, Columbia, Vassar, Oberlin, and the New School for Social Research. In addition, he was an adjunct professor at New York University, chairman for the Council for the Association of Existential Psychology and Psychiatry, president of the New York Psychological Association, and a member of the Board of Trustees of the American Foundation for Mental Health.

In 1969, May and his first wife, Florence DeFrees, were divorced after 30 years of marriage. He later married Ingrid Kepler Scholl, but that marriage too ended in divorce. On October 22, 1994, after two years of declining health, May died in Tiburon, California, where he had made his home since 1975. He was survived by his third wife, Georgia Lee Miller Johnson (a Jungian analyst whom he married in 1988), son Robert, and twin daughters Allegra and Carolyn.

Through his books, articles, and lectures, May was the best-known American representative of the existential movement. Nevertheless, he spoke out against the tendency of some existentialists to slip into an antiscientific or even anti-intellectual posture (May, 1962). He was critical of any attempt to dilute existential psychology into a painless method of reaching self-fulfillment. People can aspire to psychological health only through coming to grips with the unconscious core of their existence. Although he was philosophically aligned with Carl Rogers (see Chapter 16), May took issue with what he saw as Rogers's naive view that evil is a cultural phenomenon. May (1982) regarded human beings as both good and evil and capable of creating cultures that are both good and evil.

BACKGROUND OF EXISTENTIALISM

Modern existential psychology has its roots in the writings of Søren Kierkegaard (1813–1855), Danish philosopher and theologian. Kierkegaard was concerned with the increasing trend in modern societies toward the dehumanization of people. He opposed any attempt to see people merely as objects, but at the same time, he opposed the view that subjective perceptions are one's only reality. Instead, Kierkegaard was concerned with *both* the experiencing person and the person's experience. He wished to understand people as they exist in the world as thinking, active, and willing beings. As May (1967) put it, "Kierkegaard sought to overcome the dichotomy of reason and emotion by turning men's attentions to the reality of the immediate experience which underlies both subjectivity and objectivity" (p. 67).

Kierkegaard, like later existentialists, emphasized a balance between *freedom* and *responsibility*. People acquire freedom of action through expanding their self-awareness and then by assuming responsibility for their actions. The acquisition of freedom and responsibility, however, is achieved only at the expense of anxiety. As people realize that, ultimately, they are in charge of their own destiny, they experience the burden of freedom and the pain of responsibility.

Kierkegaard's views had little effect on philosophical thought during his comparatively short lifetime (he died at age 42), but the work of two German philosophers, Friedrich Nietzsche (1844–1900) and Martin Heidegger (1899–1976), helped carry existential philosophy into the 20th century. Heidegger exerted considerable influence on two Swiss psychiatrists, Ludwig Binswanger and Medard Boss. Binswanger and Boss, along with Karl Jaspers, Victor Frankl, and others, adapted the philosophy of existentialism to the practice of psychotherapy.

Existentialism has also permeated modern literature through the work of the French writer Jean-Paul Sartre and the French-Algerian novelist Albert Camus; religion through the writings of Martin Buber, Paul Tillich, and others; and the world of art through the work of Cezanne, Matisse, and Picasso, whose paintings break through the boundaries of realism and demonstrate a freedom of being rather than the freedom of doing (May, 1981).

After World II, European existentialism in its various forms spread to the United States and became even more diversified as it was taken up by an assorted collection of writers, artists, dissidents, college professors and students, playwrights, clergy, and others. The variety of interpretations threatened the existence of existentialism as a meaningful entity. In more recent years, however, existentialism has lost some of its popularity and, paradoxically, has strengthened its position as an alternate means of understanding humanity.

What Is Existentialism?

Although philosophers and psychologists still interpret existentialism in a variety of ways, some common elements are found among most existential thinkers. First, *existence* takes precedence over *essence*. Existence means to emerge or to become; essence implies a static immutable substance. Existence suggests process; essence refers to a product. Existence is associated with growth and change; essence signifies stagnation and finality. Western civilization, and particularly Western science, has traditionally valued essence over existence. It has sought to understand the essential composition of things, including humans. Existentialists, on the other hand, affirm that people's essence is their power to continually redefine themselves through the choices they make.

Second, existentialism opposes the split between subject and object. May (1958b) defined existentialism as *"the endeavor to understand man by cutting below the cleavage between subject and object"* (p. 11). As we have seen, Kierkegaard opposed those who saw the person only as a subjective thinking being. May (1969a) quoted Kierkegaard as saying, "Truth exists for the individual only as he himself produces it in action" (p. 6). In other words, people find the truth by living honest and authentic lives and not by armchair contemplation. On the other hand, Kierkegaard also criticized those who wished to make people into machines or objects. Each individual is a unique being and must not be viewed as a mere cog in the machinery of an industrialized society.

Third, people search for some meaning to their lives. They ask (though not always consciously) the important questions concerning their being. Who am I? Is life worth living? Does it have a meaning? How can I realize my humanity?

Fourth, existentialists hold that ultimately each of us is responsible for who we are and what we become. We cannot blame parents, teachers, employers, God, or circumstances. As Sartre (1957) said, "Man is nothing else but what he makes of himself. Such is the first principle of existentialism" (p. 15). Although we may associate with others in productive and healthy relationships, in the end, we are each alone. We can choose to become what we can be, or we can choose to avoid commitment and choice, but ultimately, it is our choice.

Fifth, existentialists are basically antitheoretical. To them, theories further dehumanize people and render them as objects. As we saw in Chapter 1, theories are constructed, in part, to explain phenomena. Existentialists are generally opposed to this approach. Authentic experience takes precedence over artificial explanations. When experiences are molded into some preexisting theoretical model, they lose their authenticity and become divorced from the individual who experienced them.

BASIC CONCEPTS

Before proceeding to Rollo May's view of humanity, we pause to look at two basic concepts of existentialism, namely, being-in-the-world and nonbeing.

Being-in-the-World

Existentialists adopt a phenomenological approach to understanding humanity. To them, we exist in a world that can be best understood from our own perspective. When scientists study people from an external frame of reference, they violate both the subjects and their existential world. The basic unity of person and environment is expressed in the German word **Dasein,** meaning to exist there. Hence, *Dasein* literally means to exist in the world and is generally written as **being-in-the-world.** The hyphens in this term imply a oneness of subject and object, of person and world.

Many people suffer from anxiety and despair brought on by their alienation from themselves and/or from their world. They either have no clear image of themselves, or they feel isolated from a world that seems distant and foreign. They have no sense of *Dasein*, no unity of self and world. As people strive to gain power over nature, they lose touch with their relationship to the natural world. As they come to rely on the products of the industrial revolution, they become more alienated from the stars, the soil, and the sea. Alienation from the world includes being out of touch with one's own body as well. Recall that Rollo May began his recovery from tuberculosis only after realizing that it was he who had the illness.

This feeling of isolation and alienation of self from the world is suffered not only by pathologically disturbed individuals but also by most individuals in modern societies. Alienation is the illness of our time, and it manifests itself in three areas: (1) separation from nature, (2) lack of meaningful interpersonal relations, and (3) alienation from one's authentic self. Thus, three simultaneous aspects or modes of the world characterize people in their being-in-the-world. The first of these is **Umwelt,** or the environment around us. The second is **Mitwelt** (literally, with the world), or our relations with other people. Third is **Eigenwelt,** or our relationship with our self.

Umwelt is the world of objects and things and would exist even if people had no awareness. It is the world of nature and natural law and includes our biological drives, such as hunger and sleep, and such natural phenomena as birth and death. We cannot escape *Umwelt*; we must learn to live in the world around us and to adjust to changes within this world. Freud's theory, with its emphasis on biology and instincts, deals mostly with *Umwelt*.

But we do not live only in *Umwelt*. We also live in the world with people, that is, *Mitwelt*. We must relate to people as people, not as things. If we treat people as objects, then we are living solely in *Umwelt*. The difference between *Umwelt* and *Mitwelt* can be seen by contrasting sex with love. If a person uses another as an instrument for sexual gratification, then *Umwelt* dominates his or her life in relation to the other person. However, love demands that one make a commitment to the other person. Love means respect for the other person's being-in-the-world, an unconditional acceptance of that person, and living in *Mitwelt* in relation to that person. Not every *Mitwelt* relationship, however, necessitates love. The essential criterion is that the *Dasein* of the other person is respected. The theories of Sullivan and Rogers, with their emphasis on interpersonal relations, deal mostly with *Mitwelt*.

Eigenwelt refers to our relationship with our self. It is a world not usually explored by other personality theorists. To live in *Eigenwelt* means to be aware of our self as a human being and to grasp who we are as we relate to the world of things and to the world of people. What does this sunset mean to *me*? How is this other person a part of *my* life? What characteristics of *mine* allow me to love this person? How do I perceive this experience?

Healthy people live in *Umwelt*, *Mitwelt*, and *Eigenwelt* simultaneously (see Figure 18.1). They adapt to the natural world, relate to others as humans, and have a keen awareness of what all these experiences mean to them (May, 1958a).

Nonbeing

Being-in-the-world necessitates an awareness of self as a living, emerging being. This awareness, in turn, leads to the dread of not being, that is, **nonbeing** or **nothingness.** May (1958a) wrote that

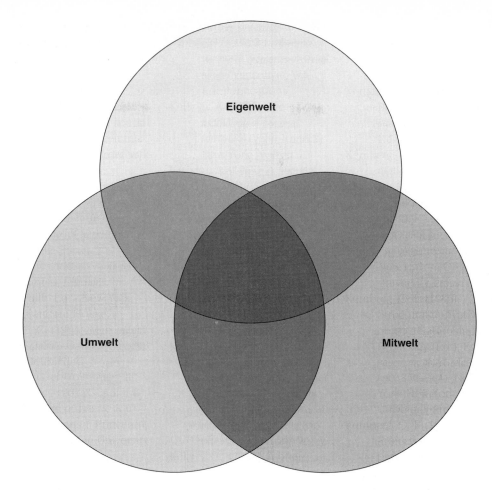

Figure 18.1   Healthy people live simultaneously in U*mwelt*, M*itwelt*, and E*igenwelt*.

to grasp what it means to exist, one needs to grasp the fact that he might not exist, that he treads at every moment on the sharp edge of possible annihilation and can never escape the fact that death will arrive at some unknown moment in the future. (pp. 47–48)

Death is not the only avenue of nonbeing, but it is the most obvious one. Life becomes more vital, more meaningful when we confront the possibility of our death. Nearly 40 years before his own death, May (1958a) spoke of death as "the one fact of my life which is not relative but absolute, and my awareness of this gives my existence and what I do each hour an absolute quality" (p. 49).

When we do not courageously confront our nonbeing through contemplation of our death, nonbeing will manifest itself in a variety of other forms, including addiction to alcohol or other drugs, promiscuous sexual activity, and other compulsive behaviors. Our nonbeing can also be expressed by a blind conformity to society's expectations and by a generalized hostility that pervades our relations to others.

The fear of death or nonbeing often provokes us to live defensively and to receive less from life than if we would confront the issue of our nonexistence. As May (1991) said, "we are afraid of nonbeing and so we shrivel up our being" (p. 202). We

The dread of nonbeing can take the form of isolation and alienation.

flee from making active choices, that is, choices based on a consideration of who we are and what we want. We may try to avoid the dread of nonbeing by dimming our self-awareness and denying our individuality, but such choices leave us with feelings of despair and emptiness. Thus, we escape the dread of nonbeing at the expense of a constricted existence. A healthier alternative is to face the inevitability of death and to realize that nonbeing is an inseparable part of being.

THE CASE OF PHILIP

Existential theory is concerned with the individual's struggle to work through life's experiences and to grow toward becoming more fully human. May (1981) described this struggle in a report on one of his patients—a successful architect in his mid-fifties named Philip. Here, we present a brief account of Philip's story, and later we use his experiences to illustrate May's concepts of anxiety, intentionality, destiny, psychopathology, and psychotherapy.

Twice married, twice divorced, Philip was struggling through yet another difficult relationship, this time with Nicole, a writer in her mid-forties. Philip could offer Nicole both love and financial security, but their relationship did not seem to be working.

Six months after Philip met Nicole, the two spent an idyllic summer together at his retreat. Nicole's two small sons were with their father and Philip's three children were by then young adults who could care for themselves. At the beginning of the summer, Nicole talked about the possibility of marriage, but Philip replied that he was against it, citing his two previous unsuccessful marriages as his reason. Aside from this brief disagreement, the time they spent together that summer was completely pleasurable. Their intellectual discussions were gratifying to Philip and their lovemaking was the most satisfying he had ever experienced, often bordering on ecstasy. In addition to the intellectual and sexual stimulation, both Philip and Nicole were able to work productively—he on his architectural designs, she on her writing.

At the end of this romantic summer, Nicole returned home alone to put her children in school. The day after she arrived home, Philip telephoned her, but somehow her voice seemed strange. The next morning he called again and got the feeling that someone else was with Nicole. That afternoon he called several more times but kept getting a busy signal. When he finally got through, he asked her if someone had, indeed, been with her that morning. Without hesitation, Nicole reported that Craig, an old friend from her college days, had been staying with her and that she had fallen in love with him. Moreover, she planned to marry Craig at the end of the month and move to another part of the country.

Philip was devastated. He felt betrayed and abandoned. He lost weight, resumed smoking, and suffered from insomnia. When he saw Nicole again, he expressed his anger at her "crazy" plan. This outburst of rage was rare for Philip. He seldom showed anger, perhaps for fear of losing the one he loved. To complicate matters, Nicole said she still loved Philip and continued to see him whenever Craig was not available. Eventually, Nicole lost her infatuation for Craig and told Philip that, as he well knew, she could never leave him. This confused Philip because he knew no such thing. Nevertheless, he accepted her statement because he needed to be desired by Nicole.

About a year later, Philip learned that Nicole had another affair, but before he could confront her and break off their relationship, he had to leave for a five-day business trip. By the time he returned, Philip was able to reason that perhaps he could accept Nicole's right to sleep with other men. Also, Nicole convinced him that the other man didn't mean anything to her and that she loved only Philip.

A little later, Nicole had a third affair, one which she made sure Philip would discover. Once again, Philip was filled with anger and jealousy. But once again, Nicole reassured him that the man meant nothing to her.

On one level, Philip wished to accept Nicole's behavior, but on another, he felt betrayed by her affairs. Yet, he did not seem to be able to leave her and to search for some other woman to love. He was paralyzed—unable to change his relationship with Nicole, but also unable to break it off. At this point in Philip's life, he sought therapy from Rollo May.

ANXIETY

Philip was suffering from neurotic anxiety. Like others who experience neurotic anxiety, he behaved in a nonproductive, self-defeating manner. Although he was deeply hurt by Nicole's unpredictable and "crazy" behavior, he became paralyzed with inaction and could not break off their relationship. Nicole's actions seemed to engender in Philip a sense of duty toward her. Because she obviously needed him, he felt obligated to take care of her.

Before May published *The Meaning of Anxiety* in 1950, most theories of anxiety held that high levels of anxiety were indicative of neuroses or other forms of psychopathology. Just prior to publishing this book, May had experienced a great deal of anxiety while recovering from tuberculosis. He and his first wife and their young son were basically penniless, and he was unsure of his own recovery. In *The Meaning of Anxiety*, May claimed that much of human behavior is motivated by an underlying sense of dread and anxiety. The failure to confront death serves as a temporary escape from the anxiety or dread of nonbeing. But the escape cannot be permanent. Death is the one absolute of life that sooner or later everyone must face.

We experience **anxiety** when we become aware that our existence or some value identified with it might be destroyed. May (1958a) defined anxiety as "the subjective state of the individual's becoming aware that his existence can be destroyed, that he can become 'nothing'" (p. 50). At another time he defined anxiety as a threat to some important value. Anxiety, May (1967) said, is *the apprehension cued off by a threat to some value which the individual holds essential to his existence as a self*" (p. 72).

Anxiety, then, can spring either from an awareness of our nonbeing or from a threat to some value essential to our existence. It exists when we confront the issue of fulfilling our potentialities (May, 1958a). This confrontation can lead to stagnation and decay, but it can also result in growth and change.

The acquisition of freedom inevitably leads to anxiety. Freedom cannot exist without anxiety, nor can anxiety exist without an awareness of the possibility of freedom. May (1981) quoted Kierkegaard as saying that "anxiety is the dizziness of freedom" (p. 185). Anxiety, like dizziness, can be either pleasurable or painful, constructive or destructive. It can give us energy and zest, but it can also paralyze and panic us. Moreover, anxiety can be either normal or neurotic.

NORMAL ANXIETY

We live in an age of anxiety. No one can escape its effects. To grow and to change one's values means to experience constructive or normal anxiety. May (1967) defined **normal anxiety** as that "which is proportionate to the threat, does not involve repression, and can be confronted constructively on the conscious level" (p. 80).

As we grow from infancy to old age, our values change, and with each step, we experience normal anxiety. "All growth consists of the anxiety-creating surrender of past values" (May, 1967, p. 80). Normal anxiety is also experienced during those creative moments when an artist, a scientist, or a philosopher suddenly achieves an insight that leads to a recognition that one's life, and perhaps the lives of countless others, will be permanently changed. For example, scientists who witnessed the first atomic bomb tests in Alamogordo, New Mexico, experienced normal anxiety with the realization that from that moment forward, everything had been changed (May, 1981).

NEUROTIC ANXIETY

Normal anxiety, the type experienced during periods of growth or of threat to one's values, is experienced by everyone. It can be constructive provided it remains proportionate to the threat. But anxiety can become neurotic or sick. May (1967) defined **neurotic anxiety** as "a reaction which is disproportionate to the threat, involves repression and other forms of intrapsychic conflict, and is managed by various kinds of blocking-off of activity and awareness" (p. 80).

Whereas normal anxiety is felt whenever values are threatened, neurotic anxiety is experienced whenever values become transformed into dogma. To be absolutely right in our beliefs provides us with temporary security, but it is security "bought at the price of surrendering [our] opportunity for fresh learning and new growth" (May, 1967, p. 80).

Philip's neurotic anxiety was evident in his attachment to unpredictable and "crazy" women, an attachment that began in early childhood. During the first two years of his life, his world was inhabited primarily by just two other people—his mother and a sister two years older than Philip. His mother was a borderline schizophrenic whose behavior toward Philip alternated between tenderness and cruelty. His sister was definitely schizophrenic, and later spent some time in a mental hospital.

> Thus, Philip endured his first years in the world learning to deal with two exceedingly unpredictable women. Indeed, he must have had inescapably imprinted on him that he needed not only to rescue women, but that one of his functions in life was to stick by them, especially when they acted their craziest. Life, then, for Philip would understandably not be free, but rather would require that he be continuously on guard or on duty. (May, 1981, p. 30)

We return to Philip later in this chapter, but at this point, his story can be used to illustrate how neurotic anxiety blocks growth and productive action. Philip could find no new way of behaving toward Nicole. His approach seemed to be a recapitulation of childhood behaviors toward his mother and sister.

GUILT

We have said that anxiety arises when we are faced with the problem of fulfilling our potentialities. **Guilt** arises when we deny our potentialities, fail to accurately perceive the needs of our fellow humans, or remain oblivious to our dependence on the natural world (May, 1958a). Just as May used the term "anxiety" to refer to large issues dealing with our being-in-the-world, so, too, did he employ the concept of guilt. In this sense, both anxiety and guilt are *ontological*; that is, they refer to the nature of being and not to feelings arising from specific situations or transgressions.

In all, May (1958a) recognized three forms of ontological guilt, each corresponding to one of the three modes of being-in-the-world: U*mwelt*, M*itwelt*, and E*igenwelt*. To understand the form of guilt that corresponds to U*mwelt*, we should recall that ontological guilt need not stem from our own actions or failures to act; it can arise from a lack of awareness of our being-in-the-world. As civilization advances technologically and scientifically, we become more and more removed from nature, that is, from U*mwelt*. This alienation leads to a form of ontological guilt that is especially prevalent in "advanced" societies where people live in heated or cooled dwellings, use motorized means of transportation, and consume food gathered and prepared by others. Our undiscerning reliance on other people for these and other needs contributes to our first form of ontological guilt. Because this type of guilt is a result of our separation from nature, May (1958a) also referred to it as *separation guilt*, a concept similar to Fromm's notion of the human dilemma (see Chapter 7).

The second form of guilt stems from our inability to perceive accurately the world of others (M*itwelt*). We can see other people only through our own eyes and can never perfectly judge their needs. Thus, we do violence to their true identity. Because we cannot unerringly anticipate the needs of others, we feel inadequate in our relations with them. This then leads to a pervasive condition of guilt, one experienced by all of us to some extent. May (1958a) wrote that "this is not a question of moral failure . . . it is an inescapable result of the fact that each of us is a separate individuality and has no choice but to look at the world through [our] own eyes" (p. 54).

The third form of ontological guilt is associated with our denial of our own potentialities or with our failure to fulfill them. In other words, it is grounded in our relationship with self (E*igenwelt*). Again, this form of guilt is universal, because none of us can completely fulfill all our potentials. This third type of guilt is reminiscent of Maslow's concept of the J*onah complex*, or the fear of being one's best (see Chapter 17).

Like anxiety, ontological guilt can have either a positive or a negative effect on personality. We can use it to develop a healthy sense of humility, to improve our relations with others, and to creatively use our potentialities. However, when we refuse to accept ontological guilt, it becomes neurotic or morbid. Neurotic guilt, like neurotic anxiety, leads to nonproductive or neurotic symptoms such as sexual impotency, depression, cruelty to others, or inability to make a choice.

INTENTIONALITY

The ability to make a choice implies some underlying structure upon which that choice is made. The structure that gives meaning to our experience and allows us to make decisions about the future is called **intentionality** (May, 1969b). Without intentionality, we could neither choose nor act on our choice. Action implies intentionality, just as intentionality implies action. The two are inseparable: "The act is in the intention, and the intention in the act" (p. 242).

May used the term "intentionality" to bridge the gap between subject and object. Intentionality is "the structure of meaning which makes it possible for us, subjects that we are, to see and understand the outside world, objective that it is. In intentionality, the dichotomy between subject and object is partially overcome" (May, 1969b, p. 225).

To illustrate how intentionality partially bridges the gap between subject and object, May (1969b) used a simple example of a man (the subject) seated at his desk observing a piece of paper (the object). The man can write on the paper, fold it into a paper airplane for his grandson, or sketch a picture on it. In all three instances, the subject (man) and object (paper) are identical, but the man's actions depend on his intentions and on the meaning he gives to his experience. That meaning is a function of both himself (subject) and his environment (object).

Intentionality is not always conscious. It "goes below levels of immediate awareness, and includes spontaneous, bodily elements and other dimensions which are usually called 'unconscious' " (May, 1969b, p. 234). Unconscious intentionality can be illustrated with the case of Philip, who felt a duty to take care of Nicole despite her unpredictable and "crazy" behavior. Philip did not see that his actions were in some way connected to his early experiences with his unpredictable mother and his "crazy" sister. He was trapped in his unconscious belief that unpredictable and "crazy" women must be cared for, and this intentionality made it impossible for him to discover new ways of relating to Nicole.

CARE, LOVE, AND WILL

Philip had a history of taking care of others, especially women. He had given Nicole a "job" with his company that permitted her to work at home and earn enough money to live on. In addition, after she ended her affair with Craig and gave up her "crazy" plan to move across country, Philip gave her several thousand dollars. He previously had felt a duty to take care of his two wives and, before that, his mother and sister.

In spite of Philip's pattern of taking care of women, he never really learned to care *for* them. To care for someone means to recognize that person as a fellow human being, to identify with that person's pain or joy, guilt or pity. Care is an active process, the opposite of apathy. "Care is a state in which something does *matter*" (May, 1969b, p. 289).

Care is not the same as love, but it is the source of love. To love means to care, to recognize the essential humanity of the other person, to have an active regard for that person's development. May (1953) defined **love** as a "delight in the presence of the other person and an affirming of his value and development as much as one's own" (p. 206). Without care there can be no love—only empty sentimentality or transient sexual arousal.

Care is also the source of will. May (1969b) defined **will** as "the capacity to organize one's self so that movement in a certain direction or toward a certain goal may take place" (p. 218). He distinguished between will and wish, the latter simply meaning "*the imaginative playing with the possibility* of some act or state occurring" (p. 218). More forcefully he stated:

> "Will" requires self-consciousness; "wish" does not. "Will" implies some possibility of either/or choice; "wish" does not. "Wish" gives the warmth, the content, the imagination, the child's play, the freshness, and the richness to "will." "Will" gives the self-direction, the maturity to "wish." "Will" protects "wish," permits it to continue without running risks which are too great. (p. 218)

Union of Love and Will

Modern society, May (1969b) claimed, is suffering from an unhealthy division of love and will. Love has become associated with sensual love or sex, whereas will has come to mean a dogged determination or will power. Neither concept captures the true meaning of these two terms. When love is seen as sex, it becomes temporary and lacking in commitment; there is no will, but only wish. When will is seen as will power, it becomes self-serving and lacking in passion; there is no care, but only manipulation.

Love and will "are not united by automatic biological growth but must be part of our conscious development" (May, 1969b, p. 283). In fact, there are biological reasons why love and will are separated. When we first come into the world, we are at one with the universe (U*mwelt*), our mother (M*itwelt*), and ourself (E*igenwelt*). "Our needs are met without self-conscious effort on our part, as, biologically, in the early condition of nursing at the mother's breast. This is the first freedom, the first 'yes' " (May, 1969b, p. 284).

Then, when will begins to develop, it manifests itself as opposition, the first "no." The blissful existence of early infancy is now opposed by the emerging willfulness of late infancy. The "no" should not be seen as a statement against the parents, but rather a positive assertion of self. Unfortunately, parents often interpret the "no" negatively and therefore stifle the child's self-assertion. As a result, children learn to disassociate will from the blissful love they had previously enjoyed.

Our task, said May, is to unite love and will. This is not easy, but it is possible. Neither blissful love nor self-serving will have a role in the uniting of love and will. For the mature person, both love and will mean a reaching out toward another person. Both involve care, both necessitate choice, both imply action, and both require responsibility (May, 1969b, 1990c).

Forms of Love

Love is obviously more than sex, but sex is one form of love. May (1969b) identified four kinds of love in Western tradition—sex, eros, philia, and agape.

Sex

Sex is a biological function that can be satisfied through sexual intercourse or some other release of sexual tension. Although it has become cheapened in modern Western societies, "it still remains the power of procreation, the drive which perpetuates the race, the source at once of the human being's most intense pleasure and his most pervasive anxiety" (May, 1969b, p. 38).

May (1969b) believed that in ancient times sex was taken for granted, just as eating and sleeping were taken for granted. In modern times, sex has become a problem. First, during the Victorian period, Western societies generally denied sexual feelings, and sex was not a topic of conversation in polite company. Then, during the 1920s, people reacted against this sexual suppression and sex suddenly came into the open. From that time until the 1980s, Western society's preoccupation with sex has caused it to become trivialized. During the past decade, however, the spread of the human immunodeficiency virus (HIV) and deaths from AIDS have rekindled the ashes of sexual anxiety. May pointed out that our society went from a period when having sex was fraught with guilt and anxiety to a time when not having it brought about guilt and anxiety. Now, he would probably say that the threat of HIV infection has once again associated sexual behaviors with feelings of anxiety for many people.

Eros

In our society, sex is frequently confused with eros. Sex is a physiological need that seeks gratification through the release of tension. **Eros** is a psychological desire that seeks procreation or creation through an enduring union with a loved one. In comparing eros to sex, May (1969b) wrote:

> Eros, on the other hand, takes wings from human imagination and is forever transcending all techniques, giving the laugh to all the "how to" books by gaily swinging into orbit above our mechanical rules, making love rather than manipulating organs. (p. 74).

Eros is built on care and tenderness. It longs to establish an enduring union with the other person, such that both partners experience delight and passion and both are broadened and deepened by the experience. Eros is the kind of love that draws two people together to form a lasting relationship, for example, in marriage. Because the human species could not survive without desire for a lasting union, eros can be regarded as the salvation of sex.

Philia

Eros, the salvation of sex, is built on the foundation of **philia,** that is, an intimate nonsexual friendship between two people. Philia cannot be rushed; it takes time to grow, to develop, to sink its roots, like, for example, the slowly evolving love between siblings or between lifelong friends. "Philia does not require that we do anything for the beloved except accept him, be with him, and enjoy him. It is friendship in the simplest, most direct terms" (May, 1969a, p. 31).

In Chapter 8, we saw that Harry Stack Sullivan placed great importance on preadolescence, that developmental epoch characterized by the need for a chum, someone who is more or less like oneself. According to Sullivan, chumship or philia is a necessary requisite for healthy erotic relationships during early and late adolescence. May, who was influenced by Sullivan at the William Alanson White Institute, agreed that

Agape is altruistic love that requires nothing in return.

philia makes eros possible. The gradual, relaxed development of true friendship is a prerequisite for the enduring union of two people.

Agape

Just as eros depends on philia, so philia needs agape. May (1969b) defined **agape** as "esteem for the other, the concern for the other's welfare beyond any gain that one can get out of it; disinterested love, typically, the love of God for man" (p. 319).

Agape is altruistic love. It is a kind of spiritual love that carries with it the risk of playing God. It does not depend on any behaviors or characteristics of the other person. In this sense, it is undeserved and unconditional.

Healthy adult relationships, May believed, blend all four forms of love. They are based on sexual satisfaction, a desire for an enduring union, genuine friendship, and an unselfish concern for the welfare of the other person. Such authentic love, unfortunately, is quite difficult. It requires self-affirmation and the assertion of oneself. "At the same time it requires tenderness, affirmation of the other, relaxing of competition as much as possible, self-abnegation at times in the interests of the loved one, and the age-old virtues of mercy and forgiveness" (May, 1981, p. 147).

FREEDOM AND DESTINY

We have seen that a blend of the four forms of love requires both self-assertion and an affirmation of the other person. It also requires an assertion of one's *freedom* and a confrontation with one's *destiny*. Healthy individuals are able both to assume their freedom and to face their destiny.

FREEDOM DEFINED

In an early definition, May (1967) said that "freedom is the individual's capacity to *know that he is the determined one*" (p. 175). The word "determined" in this definition is synonymous with what May (1981) would later call *destiny*. Freedom, then, comes from an understanding of our destiny: an understanding that death is a possibility at any moment, that we are male or female, that we have inherent weaknesses, that early childhood experiences dispose us toward certain patterns of behavior.

Freedom is the possibility of changing, although we may not know what those changes might be. Freedom "entails being able *to harbor different possibilities in one's mind even though it is not clear at the moment which way one must act*" (May, 1981, pp. 10–11). This condition often leads to increases in anxiety, but it is normal anxiety, the kind that healthy people welcome and are able to manage.

FORMS OF FREEDOM

May (1981) recognized two forms of freedom—freedom of doing and freedom of being. The first he called *existential freedom*; the latter, *essential freedom*.

Existential Freedom

Existential freedom, May insisted, should not be identified with existential philosophy or existential psychology. It is the freedom of action—the freedom of doing. Most middle-class adult Americans enjoy large measures of existential freedom. They are free to travel across state lines, to choose their associates, to vote for their representatives in government, and so on. On a more trivial scale, they are free to push their shopping carts through a supermarket and select from among thousands of items. Existential freedom, then, is the freedom to act on the choices that one makes.

Essential Freedom

Freedom of action, however, does not ensure freedom of being. At times, in fact, it seems that existential freedom makes **essential freedom** more difficult. May (1981) cited several examples of prisoners and inmates in concentration camps who spoke enthusiastically of their "inner freedom." Perhaps solitary confinement or the denial of liberty allows people to face their destiny and to gain their freedom of being. May framed this question in these words: "Do we get to essential freedom only when our everyday existence is interrupted?" (p. 60)

May's own answer was: "No." One need not be imprisoned to attain essential freedom, that is, freedom of being. Destiny itself is our prison—our concentration camp that allows us to be less concerned with freedom of doing and more concerned with essential freedom.

> Does not the engaging of our destiny—which is the design of our life—hedge us about with the confinement, the sobriety, indeed, often the cruelty, which forces us to look beyond the limits of day-to-day action? Is not the inescapable fact of death . . . the concentration camp of us all? Is not the fact that life is a joy and a bondage at the same time enough to drive us to consider the deeper aspect of being? (May, 1981, p. 61)

Destiny is our "concentration camp" that paradoxically defines our essential freedom.

DESTINY DEFINED

May (1981) defined destiny as "the pattern of limits and talents that constitutes the 'givens' in life" (p. 89). Destiny is *the design of the universe speaking through the design of each one of us*" (p. 90). Our ultimate destiny is death, but on a lesser scale our destiny includes other biological properties such as intelligence, gender, size and strength, and genetic predisposition toward certain illnesses. In addition, psychological and cultural factors contribute to our destiny.

Destiny does not mean preordained or foredoomed. It is our destination, our terminus, our goal. Within the boundaries of our destiny we have the power to choose, and this freedom allows us to confront and challenge our destiny. It does not, however, permit any change we wish. We cannot be successful at any job, conquer any illness, enjoy a fulfilling relationship with any person. "Our destiny cannot be canceled out; we cannot erase it or substitute anything else for it. But we can choose how we shall respond, how we shall live out our talents which confront us" (May, 1981, p. 89).

May suggested that freedom and destiny, like love-hate, or life-death, are not antithetical but rather a normal paradox of life. "The paradox is that freedom owes its vitality to destiny, and destiny owes its significance to freedom" (May, 1981, p. 17). Freedom and destiny are thus inexorably intertwined; one cannot exist without the other. Freedom without destiny is license. Ironically, license leads to anarchy and the ultimate destruction of freedom. Without destiny, then, we have no freedom, but without freedom, our destiny is meaningless.

Freedom and destiny give birth to each other. As we challenge our destiny, we gain freedom, and as we achieve freedom, we push at the boundaries of destiny.

PHILIP'S DESTINY

When Philip, the architect immobilized by his relationship with Nicole, first walked into Rollo May's office, he was paralyzed with inaction because he refused to accept his destiny. He saw no connection between his adult pattern of relating to women and the strategy that, as an infant, he had adopted to survive in an unpredictable and "crazy" world. His destiny was not fixed by those early experiences. Philip, like other people, had the freedom to change his destiny, but first he had to recognize his biological, social, and psychological limitations, and then he had to possess the courage to make choices within those limitations.

Philip lacked both the understanding and the courage to confront his destiny. Up to the point of seeking therapy, he had tried to compensate for his destiny, to consciously deny it. "He had been searching for someone who would make up for his having been born into an unwelcoming world consisting of a disturbed mother and a schizophrenic sister, a destiny that he did not in the slightest choose" (May, 1981, p. 88). Philip's denial of his destiny "only contributed to resentment, a longing and yearning that he could not understand" (p. 89).

Philip's inability or unwillingness to face his destiny robbed him of personal freedom and kept him tied to his mother. He treated his wives and Nicole in the same way that earlier had proven successful with his mother and sister. He could not dare express his anger to women, but instead, he adopted a charming though somewhat possessive and protective attitude toward them. May (1981) insisted that "the freedom of each of us is in proportion to the degree with which we confront and live in relation to our destiny" (p. 89). After several weeks of psychotherapy, Philip was able to stop blaming his mother for not doing what he thought she should have done. When he began to see the positive things she *did* do, he began to change his attitude toward her. The objective facts of his childhood had not changed, but his subjective perceptions had. As Philip came to terms with his destiny, he began to be able to express his anger, to feel less trapped in his relationship with Nicole, and to become more aware of his possibilities. In other words, he gained his freedom of being.

THE POWER OF MYTH

For many years, May was concerned with the powerful effects of **myths** on individuals and cultures—a concern that culminated in his book *The Cry for Myth* (1991). May contended that the people of Western civilization have an urgent need for myths at this time. Lacking myths to believe in, they turn to religious cults, drug addiction, and popular culture in a vain effort to find meaning in their lives. Myths are not falsehoods; rather, they are conscious and unconscious belief systems that provide explanations for personal and social problems. May wrote that "myths are like the beams in a house; not exposed to outside view, they are the structure which holds the house together so people can live in it" (p. 15).

From earliest times and in diverse civilizations, people have found meaning in their lives by the myths they share with others in their culture. Myths are the stories that unify a society; "they are essential to the process of keeping our souls alive and bringing us new meaning in a difficult and often meaningless world" (May, 1991, p. 20).

May believed that people communicate with one another on two levels. The first is rationalistic language, and on this level, truth takes precedence over the people who are communicating. The second is through myths, and on this level, the total human experience is more important than the empirical accuracy of the communication. We

The Oedipus myth holds meaning for us even today because it deals with existential crises common to us all.

use myths and symbols to transcend the immediate concrete situation, to expand self-awareness, and to search for identity.

May (1990a, 1991) held that the Oedipus story is a powerful myth in our culture because it contains elements of existential crises common to us all. These crises include birth, separation or exile from parents and home, sexual union with one parent and hostility toward the other, the assertion of independence and the search for identity, and finally, death. The Oedipus myth has meaning for us because it deals with all these crises. Like Oedipus, we are removed from our mother and father and are driven by the need to know who we are. Our struggle for self-identity, however, is not easy, and it may even result in tragedy, as it did for Oedipus when he insisted on knowing the truth about his origins. After being told that he had killed his father and married his mother, Oedipus put out his eyes, depriving himself of the ability to see, that is, to be aware, to be conscious.

But the Oedipus narration does not end with denial of consciousness. At this point in Sophocles's trilogy, Oedipus once again is exiled, an experience May saw as symbolic of our own isolation and ostracism. As an old man, Oedipus is seen contemplating his tragic suffering and accepting responsibility for killing his father and marrying his mother. His late life meditations bring him peace and understanding and the ability to accept death with grace. The central themes of Oedipus's life—birth, exile and separation, identity, incest and patricide, repression of guilt, and finally, conscious meditation and death—touch us all and make this myth a potentially powerful healing force in our lives.

May's concept of myths is comparable to Jung's idea of a collective unconscious in that myths are archetypal patterns in the human experience; they are avenues to universal images that lie beyond our individual experience. And like archetypes, myths can contribute to our psychological growth if we will embrace them and allow them to open up for us a new reality. On the other hand, if we deny our universal myths or see only their regressive functions, we risk alienation, apathy, and emptiness—the principal ingredients of psychopathology.

PSYCHOPATHOLOGY

According to May, apathy and emptiness—not anxiety and guilt—are the malaise of our time. When people deny their destiny or abandon their myths, they lose their purpose for being, they become directionless. Without some goal or destination, people become sick and engage in a variety of self-defeating and self-destructive behaviors. "The human being cannot live in a condition of emptiness for very long: if he is not growing toward something, he does not merely stagnate; the pent-up potentialities turn into morbidity and despair, and eventually into destructive activities" (May, 1953, p. 24).

Many people in modern Western societies feel alienated from the world (U*mwelt*); from others (M*itwelt*); and especially from themselves (E*igenwelt*). They experience a sense of helplessness to prevent natural disasters, to reverse industrialization, or to make contact with another human being. They feel insignificant in a world that increasingly dehumanizes the individual. This sense of insignificance leads to *apathy* and to a state of diminished consciousness (May, 1967).

May saw psychopathology as lack of communicativeness. It is the "inability to participate in the feelings and thoughts of others or to share oneself with others" (May, 1981, p. 21). Psychologically disturbed individuals deny their destiny and, in the process, lose their freedom. They erect a variety of neurotic symptoms, not to regain their freedom but to renounce it. Symptoms narrow the person's phenomenological world to the size that makes coping easier. The compulsive person adopts a rigid routine, thereby making new choices unnecessary.

Symptoms may be temporary, as when stress produces a headache, or they may be relatively permanent and stem from early childhood experiences. Philip's psychopathology was tied to his early environment with a disturbed mother and a schizophrenic sister. These experiences did not *cause* his pathology in the sense that they alone produced it. However, they did set up Philip to learn to adjust to his world by containing his anger, by developing a sense of apathy, and by trying to be a "good little boy." Neurotic symptoms, therefore, do not represent a failure of adjustment, but rather a proper and necessary adjustment by which one's *Dasein* can be preserved. Philip's behavior toward his two wives and Nicole represents a denial of his freedom and a self-defeating attempt to escape from his destiny.

PSYCHOTHERAPY

Unlike Freud, Adler, Rogers, and other clinically oriented personality theorists, May did not establish a school of psychotherapy with avid followers and identifiable techniques. Nevertheless, he wrote extensively on the subject.

As noted earlier, May did not regard anxiety and guilt as the primary ingredients in psychopathology and, consistent with this view, he did not believe that the goal of therapy should be their alleviation. In fact, he did not think that psychotherapy should be aimed at curing patients of a particular disorder or eliminating a specific problem. Instead, he suggested that the purpose of therapy is to make people more human, to help them expand and develop their consciousness so that they will be in a better position to make choices (Hall, 1967). These choices, then, lead to the simultaneous growth of freedom and responsibility.

May (1981) stated that *"the purpose of psychotherapy is to set people free. . . . I believe that the therapist's function should be to help people become free to be aware of and to experience their possibilities"* (pp. 19–20). May (1990c) argued that therapists who concentrate on a patient's symptoms are missing the more important picture. Neurotic symptoms are simply ways of running away from freedom and an indication that patients' inner possibilities are not being used. When patients become more free, more human, their neurotic symptoms usually disappear, their neurotic anxiety gives way to normal anxiety, and their neurotic guilt is replaced by normal guilt. But these are secondary gains and not the central purpose of therapy. May insisted that psychotherapy must be concerned with helping people experience their existence, and that "any cure of symptoms which will last must be a by-product of that" (May, 1967, p. 86).

How does a therapist help patients become free, responsible human beings? May did not offer many specific directions for therapists to follow. Existential therapists have no special set of techniques or methods that can be applied to all patients. Instead, they have only themselves, their own humanity to offer. They must establish a one-to-one relationship (*Mitwelt*) that enables patients to become more aware of themselves and to live more fully in their own world (*Eigenwelt*). This may mean challenging patients to confront their destiny, to experience despair, anxiety, and guilt. But it also means establishing an I-thou encounter where both therapist and patient are viewed as subjects rather than objects. "In this encounter I have to be able, to some extent, to experience what the patient is experiencing. My job as a therapist is to be open to his world" (May, 1967, p. 108).

May (1991) also described therapy as partly religion, partly science, and partly friendship. The friendship, however, is not an ordinary social relationship; rather, it calls for the therapist to be confronting and to challenge the patient. May believed that the relationship itself is therapeutic, and its transforming effects are independent of anything therapists might say or any theoretical orientation they might have.

> *Our task is to be guide, friend, and interpreter to persons on their journeys through their private hells and purgatories.* Specifically our task is to help patients get to the point where they can decide whether they wish to remain victims . . . or whether they choose to leave this victim-state and venture through purgatory with the hope of achieving some sense of paradise. Our patients often, toward the end, are understandably frightened by the possibility of freely deciding for themselves whether to take their chances by completing the quest they have bravely begun. (May, 1991, p. 165)

Philosophically, May held many of the same beliefs as Carl Rogers (see Chapter 16). Basic to both approaches is the notion of therapy as a human encounter; that is, an I-thou relationship with the potential to facilitate growth within both therapist and patient (May, 1990b). In practice, however, May was much more likely to ask questions, to delve into a patient's early childhood, and to suggest possible meanings of current behavior.

For example, he explained to Philip that his relationship with Nicole was an attempt to hold on to his mother. Rogers would have rejected such a technique because it emanated from an external (that is, the therapist's) frame of reference. May, however, believed that these kinds of interpretations can be an effective means of confronting patients with information that they have been hiding from themselves.

Another technique May used with Philip was the suggestion that he hold a fantasy conversation with his dead mother. In this conversation, Philip spoke for both himself and his mother. When talking for his mother, he was able for the first time to empathize with her, to see himself from her point of view. Speaking for his mother, he said that she was very proud of him and that he had always been her favorite child. Then talking for himself, he told his mother that he appreciated her courage and recalled an incident when her courage saved his eyesight. When Philip finished the fantasy conversation, he said, "'I never in a thousand years would have imagined *that* would come out'" (May, 1981, p. 39).

May also asked Philip to bring a photo of himself when he was a little boy. Philip then had a fantasy conversation with "Little Philip." As the conversation ensued, "Little Philip" explained that he had triumphed over the problem that had most troubled grown Philip, namely, the fear of abandonment. "Little Philip" became Philip's friendly companion and helped him overcome his loneliness and allay his jealousy of Nicole.

At the end of therapy, Philip did not become a new person, but he did become more conscious of a part of himself that had been there all the time. An awareness of new possibilities allowed him to move in the direction of personal freedom. For Philip, the end of therapy was the beginning of "the uniting of himself with that early self that he had to lock up in a dungeon in order to survive when life was not happy but threatening" (May, 1981, p. 41).

RELATED RESEARCH

Rollo May's existential theory has been moderately influential as a method of psychotherapy, but to date, it has sparked almost no direct empirical research. In fact, it ranks with the theories of Erich Fromm and Karen Horney for being the least empirically validated of all the theories of personality covered in this book. This state of affairs is no doubt related to the critical stance that May adopted toward objective and quantitative measurement. Any theory that emphasizes the connection between subject and object and the uniqueness of each individual will not be conducive to large sample research with experimental or questionnaire design. In fact, May argued that modern science is too rationalistic, too objective, and that a new science is needed in order to grasp the total, living person.

May, along with Kelly, Rogers, Maslow, and other humanistically oriented theorists, suggested that human agency (free will or volition) exerts some influence on behavior. This suggestion has prompted George S. Howard and his associates at the University of Notre Dame to study the effects of human agency, or self-determination, on a variety of dependent variables such as eating peanuts (Howard & Conway, 1986), snacking on carrot and celery sticks (Lazarick, Fishbein, Loiello, & Howard, 1988), and alcohol and milk consumption (Howard, Curtin, & Johnson, 1991). Howard believes that humans are not free to behave in any manner they please, but neither are their actions completely determined by environmental forces or by physiological factors such as hunger or thirst. "Thus, although each person may be the captain of his or her own ship (agency), the ship is subject to all the nonagentic natural processes (like wind and currents) that influence any ship's course" (Howard & Myers, 1990).

A study by Howard and Myers (1990) gives a flavor of the research conducted on self-determination, or agency. In one phase of this study, participants' own volition served as the independent variable. In other words, participants' free will was the intervention. Participants told themselves to "try to exercise" on some days or to "try not to exercise" on other days. The experimenters selected exercise because it is a behavior that seemingly can be controlled both by external factors, such as the weather, school and social obligations, and daily schedule (nonagentic factors), and also by a person's desire to exercise (an agentic factor).

In a complex analysis, Howard and Myers found that the interventions chosen by the participants were better predictors of how much exercise a person would do than were the interventions chosen by the experimenters. In other words, this study demonstrated that volition, or self-determination, is not only an accurate predictor of behavior, but it may have superior predictive value than external interventions chosen by other people.

Although this and other studies reviewed by Howard (1994) were not specifically conducted to test hypotheses from May's theory, they are philosophically consistent with the existential emphasis on the uniqueness of the individual and on the impact of a person's ability to choose.

In addition to human agency, another existential topic to receive some empirical attention has been existential anxiety. Recall that May (1967) defined anxiety as "the apprehension cued off by a threat to some value which the individual holds essential to his existence as a self" (p. 72). When events threaten our physical or psychological existence, we experience existential anxiety, and strongest among the threats to our existence is death. Indeed, May and Yalom (1989) argued that "a major developmental task is to deal with the terror of obliteration" (p. 367). In a sense, life is the process of coping with and confronting death. Alida Westman (1992) has demonstrated that existential anxiety (fear of death, freedom of choice, personal isolation, and meaning of life) is positively related to (1) having a confused identity, (2) fearing interpersonal closeness, and (3) viewing death as cold. On the other hand, Westman found that existential anxiety was unrelated to one's degree of religiosity.

Recently, Jeff Greenberg, Sheldon Solomon, and their colleagues have developed "terror management theory," which is based on the notion of existential anxiety. In addition, they have conducted a number of ingenious studies to test the theory. Consistent with existential psychology, terror management theory assumes that: (1) thoughts of death lead to anxiety and (2) anxiety is buffered by *faith* in a cultural worldview and by *self-esteem*. More specifically, faith in a worldview lessens anxiety by giving meaning, order, and permanence to our world; self-esteem lessens anxiety by bolstering our belief that we are living up to and perhaps exceeding the standards of the cultural worldview.

In one study, Greenberg and his colleagues (Greenberg, Simon, Pyszczynski, Solomon, & Chatel, 1992) predicted that making one's mortality salient—that is, increasing one's thoughts of one's death—would lead to an increase in the need to preserve one's worldview. Such a need was measured by the degree of negativity shown to people who threaten and oppose one's worldview and by how positively one reacted to those who agree with it. In a set of studies, Greenberg and colleagues had some participants describe the feelings aroused in them by the thought of their own death (mortality salient) and had other participants describe their feelings while watching TV (control condition). Greenberg et al. chose either very conservative or very liberal participants, with the assumption that liberals would be more tolerant of other people's point of view. They predicted that thinking about one's own death—compared with watching TV—would lead to greater liking of those people who share one's political views and a greater disliking of those who oppose one's political views. Results supported the prediction, but only for conservative participants. That is, conservatives who thought about their death rated other conservatives more favorably than did conservatives who thought about watching TV. Liberals, however, did not become more favorable toward liberals, but they did become less unfavorable toward conservatives. The authors explained these findings in terms of tolerance toward opposing beliefs. An important tenet of liberalism is tolerance of a diversity of customs and beliefs. Thus, thoughts of one's mortality should not strengthen a liberal's generally negative view of conservatives nor lessen their generally positive view of other liberals.

In another set of studies, Greenberg, Pyszczynski, Solomon, Simon, and Breus (1994) replicated the finding that mortality salience leads to a greater liking of those supporting our worldview and a greater disliking of those who oppose it. In these studies, Greenberg et al. also established that the effect holds only when the thoughts of death are subtle and somewhat unconscious rather than consciously processed. On the surface, it may seem paradoxical that only subtle thoughts of one's mortality lead to a need to preserve one's worldview. However, this hypothesis is consistent not only with existential theory but also with psychoanalytic theory, which holds that unconscious motives often are stronger influences on behavior than conscious ones. The authors argued that when people think deeply and consciously about their own death, they develop strong defenses that ultimately allow them to deny their vulnerability or construe it as being far in the future. However, if their thoughts of death are more subtle, the defense mechanisms are not as clearly set into motion, and people will console themselves by defending their worldview.

The findings by Greenberg and colleagues are intriguing and quite consistent with May's definition of existential anxiety as apprehension of threats to our existence. However, although these findings are consistent with May's theory, they do not directly confirm it.

CRITIQUE OF MAY

Existentialism in general and May's psychology in particular have been criticized as being anti-intellectual and antitheoretical. May acknowledged the claim that his views did not conform to the traditional concept of theory, but he staunchly defended his psychology against the charge of being anti-intellectual or antiscientific. He pointed to the sterility of conventional scientific methods and their inability to unlock the ontological character of willing, caring, and acting human beings.

May held that a new scientific psychology must recognize such human characteristics as uniqueness, personal freedom, destiny, phenomenological experiences, and especially our capacity to relate to ourselves as both object and subject. A new science of humans must also include ethics. "The actions of living, self-aware human beings are never automatic, but involve some weighing of consequences, some potentiality for good or ill" (May, 1967, p. 199).

May concluded his position on a new psychology with these words:

> The outlines of a science of man we suggest will deal with man as the symbol-maker, the reasoner, the historical mammal who can participate in his community and who possesses the potentiality of freedom and ethical action. The pursuit of this science will take no less rigorous thought and wholehearted discipline than the pursuit of experimental and natural science at their best, but it will place the scientific enterprise in a broader context. Perhaps it will again be possible to study man scientifically and still see him whole. (May, 1967, p. 199)

Until this new science acquires greater maturity, we must evaluate May's views by the same criteria used for each of the other personality theorists.

Have May's ideas *generated scientific research*? May did not formulate his views in a theoretical structure, and a paucity of hypotheses are suggested by his writings. Some research, such as that conducted by Jeff Greenberg et al. and George Howard, which we discussed earlier, relate generally to existential psychology, but these studies do not specifically flow from May's theory. On this first criterion of a useful theory, therefore, May's existential psychology receives a very low score.

Second, can May's ideas be verified or *falsified*? Again, existential psychology in general and May's theory in particular must be rated very low on this criterion. The theory is too amorphous to suggest specific hypotheses that could either confirm or disconfirm its major concepts.

Third, does May's philosophically oriented psychology help *organize what is currently known about human nature*? On this criterion, May would receive an average rating. Compared with most theorists discussed in this book, May has more closely followed Allport's dictum, "Do not forget what you have decided to neglect" (Allport, 1968, p. 23). May did not forget that he excluded discourses on developmental stages, basic motivational forces, and other factors that tend to segment the human experience. May's philosophical writings have reached deep into the far recesses of the human experience and have explored aspects of humanity not examined by other personality theorists. His popularity has been due in part to his ability to touch individual readers, to connect with their humanity. Although his ideas may affect people in ways that other theorists do not, his use of certain concepts were at times inconsistent and confusing. Moreover, he decided to neglect several important topics in human personality, for example, development, cognition, learning, and motivation.

As a *practical guide to action*, May's theory is quite weak. Although he possessed a keen understanding of human personality, May's writings are more philosophical than scientific. In fact, he had no objection to being called a philosopher and frequently referred to himself as a philosopher-therapist.

On the criterion of *internal consistency*, May's existential psychology, again, falls short. He offered a variety of definitions for such concepts as anxiety, guilt, intentionality, will, and destiny. Unfortunately, he never presented operational definitions of these terms. This imprecise terminology has contributed to the lack of research on May's ideas.

The final criterion of a useful theory is *parsimony*, and on this standard, May's psychology receives a moderate rating. His writings, at times, were cumbersome and awkward, but to his credit, he dealt with complex issues and did not attempt to oversimplify human personality.

CONCEPT OF HUMANITY

Like Erik Erikson (see Chapter 9), May offered a new way of looking at things. His view of humanity is both broader and deeper than those of most other personality theorists. He saw people as complex beings, capable of both tremendous good and immense evil.

According to May, people have become estranged from the natural world, from other people, and, most of all, from themselves. As people become more alienated from other people and from themselves, they surrender portions of their consciousness. They become less aware of themselves as a subject, that is, the person who is aware of the experiencing self. As the subjective self becomes obscured, people lose some of their capacity to make choices. This progression, however, is not inevitable. May believed that people, within the confines of their destiny, have the ability to make free choices. Each choice pushes back the boundaries of determinism and permits new choices. People generally have much more potential for freedom than they realize. However, free choice does not come without anxiety. Choice demands the courage to confront one's destiny, to look within and to recognize the evil as well as the good.

Choice also implies action. Without action, choice is merely a wish, an idle desire. With action comes responsibility. Freedom and responsibility are always commensurable. A person cannot have more freedom than responsibility, nor can one be shackled with more responsibility than freedom. Healthy individuals welcome both freedom and responsibility, but they realize that choice is often painful, anxiety-provoking, and difficult.

May believed that many people have surrendered some of their ability to choose, but that capitulation itself, he insisted, is a choice. Ultimately, each of us is responsible for the choices we make and those choices define us as unique human beings. May, therefore, must be rated high on the dimension of *free choice*.

Is May's theory *optimistic* or *pessimistic*? Although he sometimes painted a rather gloomy picture of humanity, May was not pessimistic. He saw the present age as merely a plateau in humanity's quest for new symbols and new myths that will engender the species with renewed spirit.

Although May recognized the potential impact of childhood experiences on adult personality, he clearly favored *teleology* over causality. In a comment on Clement Reeves's (1977) book, May stated: "I believe in a teleological approach—that each person, by virtue of his being a person, has certain potentialities that he is required, by life itself, to live out" (May 1977, pp. 303–304). Each of us has a particular destiny that we must discover and challenge or else risk alienation and neurosis.

May assumed a moderate stance on the issue of *conscious* vs. *unconscious* forces in personality development. By their nature, people have enormous capacity for self-awareness, but often that capacity remains fallow. People sometimes lack the courage to face their destiny or to recognize the evil that exists within their culture as well as within themselves. Consciousness and choices are interrelated. As people make more free choices, they gain more insight into who they are; that is, they develop a greater sense of being. This sharpened sense of being, in turn, facilitates the ability to make further choices. Awareness of self and capacity for free choice are hallmarks of psychological health.

May also took an intermediate position on *social* vs. *biological* influences. Society contributes to personality principally through interpersonal relationships. Our relations with other people can have either a freeing or an enslaving effect. Sick relationships, such as those Philip experienced with his mother and sister, can stifle personal growth and leave us with an inability to participate in a healthy encounter with another person. Without the capacity to relate to people as people, life becomes meaningless and we develop a sense of alienation not only from others but from ourselves as well. Biology also contributes to personality. Biological factors such as gender, physical size, predisposition to illnesses, and ultimately death itself, shape a person's destiny. Everyone must live within the confines of destiny, even though those confines can be expanded.

On the dimension of *uniqueness* vs. *similarities*, May's view of humanity definitely leans toward uniqueness. Each of us is responsible for shaping our own personality within the limits imposed by destiny. No two of us make the same sequence of choices and no two develop identical ways of looking at things. May's emphasis on phenomenology implies individual perceptions and therefore unique personalities.

Chapter Summary

During the past 45 years, existential psychology, which began in Europe, has secured a hold in the United States. Rooted in the philosophy of Kierkegaard, Nietzsche, Sartre, and others, existential psychology holds that people are largely responsible for their own personalities. Existence is given priority over essence; growth and change are seen as being more important than stable and fixed characteristics; and process receives preference over product.

Until his death in 1994, Rollo May was at the vanguard of existential psychology in the United States. May, a philosophically oriented psychologist, came to existentialism from a background of art and psychotherapy. Like other existentialists, May believed that (1) existence precedes essence, meaning that what people *do* is more important than what they *are*; (2) people are both subjective and objective; that is, they are thinking as well as acting beings; (3) people are motivated to search for answers to important questions regarding the meaning of life; (4) *freedom* and *responsibility* are always balanced; so that people cannot have one without the other; and (5) fixed personality theories tend to dehumanize people and turn them into objects or things to be observed.

Existentialists generally take a *phenomenological* approach to understanding humanity, insisting that people can best be studied from their own point of view. The unity of people and their phenomenological world is expressed by the term *Dasein*, or being-in-the-world.

There are three modes of being-in-the-world: *Umwelt*, our relationship with the world of objects or things; *Mitwelt*, our world with people; and *Eigenwelt*, our relationship with ourselves. Healthy people live in all three worlds simultaneously.

If people are aware of their being-in-the-world, then they are also aware of the possibility of *nonbeing* or nothingness. Life becomes more meaningful when we confront the inevitability of death or nonbeing.

The awareness of nonbeing contributes to the experience of *anxiety*, but anxiety is also increased when people realize that they are free to choose and have responsibility for their actions. *Normal anxiety* is experienced by everyone. It is proportionate to the threat and can be managed constructively on a conscious level. *Neurotic anxiety* is disproportionate to the threat, involves repression, and is handled in a self-defeating manner.

Just as anxiety is a normal aspect of the human condition, so too is *guilt*. People experience guilt as a result of their (1) separation from the natural world; (2) inability to judge the needs of others; and (3) denial of their own potentials.

Intentionality is the underlying structure that gives meaning to experience and allows people to make decisions about the future. Intentionality implies action, not merely idle wishing.

Both *love* and *will* involve *care*, both necessitate choice, and both require responsibility. Love means taking delight in the presence of the other person and affirming that person's value as much as one's own; will calls for a conscious commitment to action. May identified four aspects of love: (1) *sex*, which is a physiological function; (2) *eros*, which seeks an enduring union with a loved one; (3) *philia*, or nonsexual friendship between two people; and (4) *agape*, or an altruistic love that demands nothing in return.

May held that freedom comes with one's confrontation with *destiny* and with an understanding that death or nonbeing is a possibility at any moment. Many people have *freedom of action*, but a deeper, more rare kind of freedom is *freedom of being*. People can be free within themselves even though they may be physically imprisoned. May also believed that a breakdown in our cultural myths has contributed to social upheaval and personal feelings of alienation.

Although May was a psychotherapist for many years, he did not write extensively on techniques or methods of existential therapy. Because psychopathology is the result of alienation from nature, others, and self, May asserted that the purpose of therapy is to help people expand their consciousness so that they can make free choices and be at one with nature, other people, and self.

In his concept of humanity, May placed high emphasis on uniqueness, free choice, and teleology. Existential psychology receives high marks for its ability to organize that which is known about human personality, but it falls short as a scientific theory, having little heuristic value either in generating research or in guiding the practitioner.

Suggested Readings

Hall, M. H. (1967, September). An interview with "Mr. Humanist": Rollo May. *Psychology Today*, pp. 25–29, 72–73.
> Although this article is more than 30 years old, it reflects many ideas that are appropriate today.

May, R. (1958b). The origins and significance of the existential movement in psychology. In R. May, E. Angel, & H. F. Ellenberger (Eds.), *Existence: A new dimension in psychiatry and psychology* (pp. 3–36). New York: Basic Books.
> With this chapter, May introduced existential psychology to many American readers. The philosophical background, rationale, and terminology of existential psychology are presented.

May, R. (1969a). The emergence of existential psychology. In R. May (Ed.), *Existential psychology* (2nd ed.) (pp. 1–48). New York: Random House.
> Another introductory chapter, in which May discusses the meaning of existentialism and the implications of existential psychology for science and psychotherapy.

May, R. (1969b). *Love and will*. New York: Norton.
> May's most popular book, this volume discusses the failure of modern culture to understand the meaning of love and will. Included are chapters on intentionality and care.

May, R. (1991). *The cry for myth*. New York: Norton.
> In this book, May argues for the importance of durable myths and discusses their therapeutic impact on people's lives.

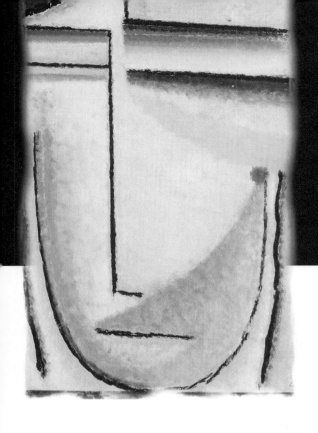

Part

Conclusions

Concepts of Humanity Summarized
Evaluation of Personality Theories
Theorists of Personality
Future Directions

I n the years since Sigmund Freud began seriously formulating the first modern theory of personality, the world has seen unprecedented change. When Breuer and Freud published *Studies in Hysteria* in 1895, Henry Ford had not yet mass-produced the automobile, the Wright brothers had not flown at Kitty Hawk, Marconi had not yet built the wireless radio, and bleeding was a treatment sometimes still used in medicine.

What progress has personality theory made in the intervening decades? Obviously, the advances have not been as dramatic as those in technology. Some observers may believe that few if any major advances have been made since Freud's fascinating description of human personality.

From a scientific view, however, considerable progress has been made. Consider, for example, the work of Bandura and Mischel, currently the most active theory builders discussed in these pages. Bandura and Mischel's cautious mixture of research and theoretical speculation serve as a model for correct theory building. Although their theories may lack the breadth and the colorful appeal of Freud's psychoanalysis, they are, nevertheless, several steps in front as rigorous scientific theories. If personality theory is to serve as a tool for explaining, predicting, and controlling human behavior, it must be modeled more on the pattern of current theorists rather than on the highly speculative formulations of the original triumvirate, namely, Freud, Adler, and Jung.

CONCEPTS OF HUMANITY SUMMARIZED

In the opening chapter, we pictured Sigmund Freud as a young Viennese neurologist contemplating the nature of human nature, something philosophers had done for thousands of years. However, Freud added an important ingredient to the speculations of philosophers—controlled observation. Freud checked his hunches derived from clinical practice with subsequent clinical experiences, including an interpretation of his own dreams and the dreams of his patients. These crude scientific observations eventually led to a field of psychology called personality theory. In the more than 100 years since Freud's early contemplations, many other observers of personality have contributed their ideas and their research to this field, and in the previous 17 chapters, we have discussed 23 different theories constructed by some of these people.

Return once more to the young Dr. Freud and his thinking about human personality. In Chapter 1, we listed several questions that Freud eventually considered, either explicitly or implicitly. What motivates people? Do people strive toward some goal, or is behavior without purpose? What accounts for similarities and differences among people? What makes people act in predictable or unpredictable ways? Do dreams have a meaning? What unconscious forces underlie human behavior? What are the causes of mental disturbances? Is personality determined more by hereditary and biological forces or by environmental and social factors? What is the nature of human nature? Some of these questions have endured to the present time and currently spark both debate and research. Others, such as the meaning of dreams, no longer hold a central place in personality theory.

We have formulated the more durable questions into six broad and somewhat overlapping dimensions and then rated the various personality theorists on each of these dimensions. These basic questions reflect theorists' philosophical stance as well as their scientific perspective.

The first dimension for a concept of humanity concerns the theorist's belief that behavior is determined either by forces outside the individual or by the individual's ability to freely choose. Interestingly, two theories that have little else in common—Freud's psychoanalysis and Skinner's behavioral analysis—are the only ones rated very high on determinism, that is, very low on free choice (see Table 19.1). Humanistically oriented theorists, including Kelly, Rogers, Maslow, and May, are all rated high on the free choice dimension.

The second dimension involves an optimistic view of humanity versus a pessimistic one. Some people—philosophers, novelists, playwrights, and personality theorists—see human existence as a hopeless and perpetual struggle against powerful internal or external forces. Others see people as having the capacity to conquer these forces and to live satisfying and fulfilling lives. The most optimistic of our personality theorists have been Adler and Rogers, whereas Freud was probably the most pessimistic.

The third dimension of a concept of humanity is causality versus teleology. Theorists rated high on causality emphasize past experiences as critical determinants of present behavior, whereas those high on teleology believe that present expectations of future goals shape our behavior. Freud and Skinner are both rated very high on causality, because both believed that our past determines our present. For Freud, early childhood experiences, many of which have been repressed, greatly influence personality. For Skinner, our previous experiences with reinforcement and, to a lesser extent, punishment, along with genetics and culture, shape present behavior. Adler's goal-oriented theory and Kelly's personal construct theory receive the highest ratings on teleology, because both theorists saw personality as being molded by a person's beliefs concerning the future.

A fourth question concerns the role of conscious vs. unconscious forces in shaping personality. All personality theorists believe that some of our behaviors and the motives behind them can be unconscious. Even Allport, who placed the highest emphasis on consciousness, believed that psychologically disturbed individuals are at least partly motivated by forces beyond their awareness. In addition to Allport, the cognitive theorists (Bandura, Rotter, and Mischel), and the humanistic/existential theorists (except May) all emphasize conscious motivation over unconscious drives. Freud, of course, is rated very high on unconscious determinants, as is Jung with his concept of the collective unconscious. Not quite so obvious is the very high rating that Skinner receives on unconscious influences. Skinner believed that people seldom have any conscious knowledge of the complex of genetic, cultural, and environmental contingencies responsible for their behaviors.

The fifth dimension concerns biological factors (largely heredity) and social factors (that is, environmental influences). This is no longer an issue of nature *versus* nurture; all personality theorists recognize that personality results form an interaction of hereditary and environmental factors. The question now is one of emphasis. We have rated Freud high on biology (low on social influences), but Eysenck and Cattell put even greater weight on genetic influences. Theorists on the social end of this dimension include Sullivan, Bandura, Rotter, and Mischel.

And finally, can personality best be conceptualized in terms of unique patterns of behavior or in terms of similar elements among people? Although Adler, the learning and cognitive theorists, and the humanistic/existential theorists all placed high emphasis on uniqueness among people, none could rival Allport for dedication to individuality.

These six dimensions relate more to philosophical positions than to scientific issues. Lawrence Pervin (1990a) has listed 10 largely scientific issues that have endured throughout the history of personality study. Many of these issues are the same as or similar to our six philosophical dimensions, underscoring personality theory's debt to both philosophical speculation and scientific observations.

Table 19.1 Summary of Major Personality Theorists' Concepts of Humanity

	Free Choice	Optimism	Causality	Unconscious Influences	Social Influences	Uniqueness
Freud	VL	L	VH	VH	L	M
Jung	M	M	H	VH	L	L
Adler	H	VH	VL	M	H	H
Klein	L	M	H	H	H	L
Horney	H	H	M	M	H	L
Fromm	M	M	L	M	H	M
Sullivan	M	M	M	H	VH	L
Erikson	M	H	H	M	H	H
Skinner	VL	M	VH	VH	H	H
Bandura	M	M	M	L	VH	H
Rotter	H	M	L	L	VH	M
Mischel	H	M	L	L	VH	H
Cattell/Eysenck	NA	NA	NA	M	VL	H
Allport	M	H	L	VL	M	VH
Kelly	H	H	VL	L	M	H
Rogers	H	VH	L	L	H	H
Maslow	H	H	L	M	M	H
May	H	M	L	M	M	H

VH = Very High;   H = High;   M = Moderate;   L = Low;   VL Very Low;   NA = Not Applicable

Pervin's first enduring issue is the definition of personality. Not all theorists have been concerned with defining personality, but all have worked around at least an implicit definition. Second, personality has an important relationship with and is deeply embedded within general psychology. Such has not always been true. Introductory psychology textbooks of 45 and 50 years ago seldom contained a chapter devoted to "theories of personality." Now all do. Personality also has an established relationship with other subspecialties within psychology, such as clinical, developmental, and social psychology. Pervin's third issue is the view of science within psychology and personality. Although people who studied personality did not always use the same scientific tools as those of other psychologists, Pervin advocates methods of science that both personality psychologists and other psychologists can employ.

Pervin's fourth issue concerns the basic nature of people. Are people naturally good, evil, or neither? This is a philosophical issue that, perhaps, can never be settled by science. Fifth, is personality best studied from a nomothetic perspective that emphasizes universal laws and procedures or from an idiographic view that considers the single individual? Pervin correctly pointed out that Allport, Freud, and Skinner all favored idiographic research. The sixth issue regards the problem of person versus situation. This, too, is no longer an either/or issue, because all people who study personality see behavior as flowing from an interaction of person and situation. As Pervin (1990a) said, "although we are all pretty much interactionists at this point, there remains considerable disagreement about *what* in the person interacts *how* with *what* in the situation" (p. 14).

Pervin's seventh issue, perhaps the oldest issue of all, is nature versus nurture, a question we discussed in our philosophical dimensions and one that involves heredity and environment as well as biological and social factors.

Pervin calls his eighth issue the time dimension, by which he means past influences versus future expectations. Only present factors can motivate us, but as we have

Table 19.2 Ratings of Personality Theorists on the Criteria for a Useful Theory

	Generate Research	Falsifiable	Organize Knowledge	Guide Action	Internally Consistent	Parsimonious
Freud	H	VL	M	M	L	M
Jung	M	VL	M	L	L	L
Adler	H	L	H	H	L	M
Klein	L	L	L	H	H	M
Horney	VL	L	L	L	M	M
Fromm	VL	VL	H	L	L	L
Sullivan	L	VL	M	M	M	L
Erikson	M	M	H	M	H	M
Skinner	VH	H	M	VH	VH	H
Bandura	VH	H	H	H	VH	VH
Rotter	H	M	M	M	H	H
Mischel	M	M	L	M	H	H
Cattell/Eysenck	VH	M	H	M	M	H
Allport	M	L	L	M	H	H
Kelly	L	L	VL	L	VH	VH
Rogers	M	H	H	M	VH	VH
Maslow	M	L	VH	H	M	M
May	VL	VL	M	VL	L	M

VH = Very High;   H = High;   M = Moderate;   L = Low;   VL Very Low

seen, personality theorists differ greatly on whether present factors are shaped by people's past experiences or by their anticipation of future events. Ninth is persistence and change in personality. Does personality persist throughout the years, or do people grow psychologically and change their basic personality? Finally, Pervin addresses the issue of conscious versus unconscious processes, a dimension we have already discussed. Because these issues have endured for a number of years, we expect that most will continue to be important problems in the years to come.

EVALUATION OF PERSONALITY THEORIES

In the first chapter, we defined scientific theory as a set of related assumptions from which, by logical deductive reasoning, testable hypotheses can be drawn. Chapters 2 through 18 examined in some detail a number of theories of personality and evaluated each theory on the basis of six criteria of a useful theory. Table 19.2 presents a summary of our evaluation of these theories.

First, how well do current personality theories generate research? Although much current psychological research is without theoretical focus, a significant portion has been stimulated by attempts to test hypotheses drawn from established theories, including those within the scope of personality. Of the personality theories discussed in this book, those of Freud, Jung, Adler, Erikson, Skinner, Bandura, Rotter, Cattell, Eysenck, Allport, Rogers, and Maslow have produced the most research, but the three that clearly outdistance the others during the past 30 years are those of Skinner, Eysenck, and Rotter (see Figure 19.1). For example, a search of PsychINFO from the

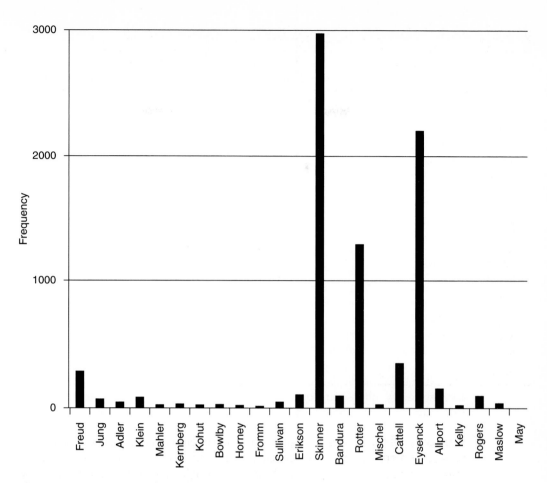

***Figure* 19.1** Frequency of mention in research articles by last name of theorist (PsychINFO, 1967–1996)

years 1967 to 1996 revealed that Skinner's name and his concept of operant condition-ing appeared nearly 3,000 times in research articles. Eysenck's name appeared in the psychology literature largely in reference to the Eysenck Personality Inventory and the Eysenck Personality Questionnaire, whereas Rotter's name is usually associated with his concepts of locus of control and interpersonal trust. Taken as a totality, personality theory has sparked a substantial amount of research and is responsible for much of what is now known about human behavior.

The second criterion of a useful theory is falsifiability, but by this standard, per-sonality theories generally do not fare well. For example, Freud's theory alone has gen-erated thousands of research studies over the decades, most of which have been nei-ther experimental nor subject to falsification. Thus, a weakness of Freud's theory, as well as other philosophically based theories, is a lack of falsifiability or verifiability. Although these theories have **heuristic** value in generating research, results of that research can usually be explained in other ways and thus do not specifically support the parent theory.

Third, how well do personality theories organize knowledge? Most findings from psychological research can be explained by one or more of these theories. Human behavior, from the most mundane to the most fanciful, from the simplest to the most complex, from the most altruistic to the most sadistic, from the most healthy to the most psychotic, can be explained by at least one, but usually most, of these theories. Not all explanations, of course, would be the same, and some may be quite unsatisfactory to some readers. This situation is understandable, because readers have their own personal preference and can reject explanations not compatible with their philosophical orientation.

Explanation is precisely what personality theories do best. Personality theories are considerably more useful and accurate in explaining behavior than they are in predicting or controlling behavior. Encouragingly, the more recently developed theories are becoming more sophisticated at predicting human behavior, and they are also more effective at suggesting the means to control it. The earlier theories, especially those of Freud and Adler, are sufficiently comprehensive and flexible to explain what is already known about human behavior, but they are less proficient at predicting it. Although Freud's psychoanalysis can accommodate nearly anything human, we gave it only a moderate rating on its ability to organize knowledge, because it often offers the same explanation for contradictory findings and contradictory explanations for the same finding. However, we gave Adler's theory a high rating on this criterion because nearly all behavior can be seen as either useless or useful attempts to gain superiority or success. The only very high rating on this criterion was that given to Maslow, whose theory is able to organize most behavior in terms of the hierarchy of needs concept and to offer an explanation for a wide range of human activity.

The fourth criterion for evaluating personality theory is the extent to which it serves as a guide for the practitioner. Also included in this criterion is the extent to which the theory fertilizes thought and action in other disciplines, such as art, literature, sociology, philosophy, business administration, education, and psychotherapy. The majority of our theories receive at least a moderate rating on this criterion. However, this rating presupposes that practitioners, be they psychotherapist, plant manager, parent, politician, or teacher, have extensive knowledge of at least one theory. Without that knowledge, the theory has no value as a practical tool, and even with that knowledge, practitioners will face problems for which contemporary personality theory offers no ready-made solutions. Despite these shortcomings, knowledge of the various personality theories serves as a practical guide for those who must understand, explain, control, or predict human behavior. Table 19.2 reveals that Skinner's behavioral analysis receives a very high rating as a guide to the practitioner, and that the theories of Adler, Klein, Bandura, and Maslow all receive a high rating. Freud's psychoanalysis, Jung's Analytical Psychology, and Fromm's humanistic psychoanalysis receive moderate, low, and low ratings respectively, and these ratings would be even lower if we included only their current influence in psychology. However, these theories continue to guide the actions of some artists, writers, and philosophers.

This fourth criterion of a useful theory is sometimes overlooked by those who believe that theory and practice are necessarily antithetical and that theory exists only in some abstract realm far removed from practical concerns. For the person making daily decisions about human behavior, knowledge of one or more personality theories can eliminate endless floundering and serve as a practical guide to action.

The fifth criterion of a useful theory is internal consistency. In general, older theories are less internally consistent than later ones, partly because they employ terminology that is difficult to define operationally. Later personality theorists, such as Bandura and Mischel, have been more precise in defining terms in ways that suggest testable hypotheses. Several other theories, including those of Erikson, Klein, Skinner, Rotter, Allport, Kelly, and Rogers receive a high or very high rating on internal consistency.

Finally, are current personality theories parsimonious? A review of Table 19.2 reveals that no theory is rated very low on this criterion, despite the tremendous diversity and complexity of human personality. Several, however, are probably needlessly cumbersome, notably those of Jung, Sullivan, Horney, Fromm, and Klein. All these theorists introduced terms or concepts that have detracted from their theory's simplicity.

The ratings in Table 19.2, of course, are not chiseled in stone; indeed, they differ slightly even from those in the previous edition of this book. They merely represent our current judgment of where each theory falls on the six criteria of a useful theory. Also, the table is but a synopsis of the ratings. A more detailed discussion is found in the Critique section of each of the 17 preceding chapters. Notice also that these personality theories receive the highest marks on their ability to organize knowledge and to explain what is known about human behavior. Only Horney, Klein, Mischel, Allport, and Kelly fail to receive at least a moderate rating on this criterion. In summary, useful theories are practical. Not only do they explain data and offer guidance to the researcher, but they also help the clinician, teacher, parent, and administrator make decisions that involve human behavior.

THEORISTS OF PERSONALITY

In this text, we have devoted a little more space to the lives of the theorists than is typically found in personality textbooks. One reason for this is that personality differences among the theorists account, at least in part, for differences in their theories. Differences in birth order, family size, religious and socioeconomic backgrounds, closeness to mother or father, and training and education account for differences in the manner in which these theorists view the world and also in their concepts of humanity.

On the other hand, these theorists are also similar in some respects. For example, each of these persons has been motivated to construct and publish a personal view of human personality. Not every observer of human behavior is so disposed.

What other characteristics do these theorists have in common? Without indulging in too much groundless speculation, we can say that all of them have possessed superior intelligence, nearly all have been highly creative, and most have had outstanding literary skills. Several of the theorists have been unusually romantic, almost to the point of sentimentality. Many were lonely, at least at one time or another during their lives. Freud remained somewhat distrustful of outsiders throughout his life; Jung retreated into extreme isolation during his late 30s; Klein had difficulties with many of her colleagues and waged a bitter and endless war with her own daughter; Eysenck was not close to either parent and was literally a man without a country for some time; Maslow was painfully shy during his youth and retained a deep hatred for his mother; Rogers, who like Maslow came from a large family, spent most of his childhood and adolescence as a loner and never felt close to his mother; and Sullivan, an only child, had difficulties with interpersonal relationships during most of his life. Another characteristic shared by most of these theorists is the fervent belief that they were scientists and were making observations and constructing theories within the framework of science. As scientists, they shared some of the characteristics of most creative scientists. For example, Greg Feist (1993, 1994) found that eminent scientists were highly creative, independent, flexible, self-confident, arrogant, hostile, open to new experiences, and mostly introverted.

FUTURE DIRECTIONS

Perhaps the only accurate statement one can make about the future is this: "No accurate statements can be made about the future." Nevertheless, we venture a few guesses about the future direction of personality theory, guesses that do not require prophetic vision, because most of these forecasts simply call for extending current trends.

First, recent years have seen a shift away from practicing clinicians formulating grand, all-encompassing theories based largely on their therapeutic experiences. This was the procedure followed by many early theorists—Freud, Jung, Adler, Klein, Horney, Fromm, Sullivan, Erikson, Kelly, and Rogers. Personality theories are now being built piece by piece on the foundation of empirical research, and it appears that this trend will continue. These newer theories are less inclusive, less speculative, and less philosophical than those that emanated from the consulting rooms and libraries of the previously mentioned theorists.

These smaller, lower-level theories are being developed by academic, research-oriented psychologists studying one variable at a time and developing a limited model to explain that variable. Being less philosophical, these theories will be less concerned with such topics as causality versus teleology. They will avoid postulating a single master motive, such as self-actualization or striving for success. Conscious versus unconscious motivation and human agency versus determinism will be matters for empirical research, not personal opinion. Empirical observations will replace philosophical speculation as the cornerstone of future personality theories.

Although these newer theories may be less global than the older ones, they nevertheless will borrow data from a variety of related fields. Pervin (1990b) pointed out that progress in the study of personality is closely tied to developments in other fields of psychology. He went on to predict that progress in other disciplines, such as biopsychology, neuropsychology, computer science, sociology, and anthropology may facilitate developments in personality theory, provided personality theorists keep up with progress in these other fields and do not allow such progress to destroy the identity of personality study.

Another trend in personality theory is the greater reliance on team effort rather than on the work of a single person. The vast research on which future theories will be constructed can only be conducted by a well-coordinated group effort. Carl Rogers initiated this procedure nearly 50 years ago by relying on graduate students and colleagues for assistance in conducting research on client-centered psychotherapy. Albert Bandura has refined this approach, but has been much more empirical. Bandura is building a social-cognitive theory in small increments as he gathers data from studies carried out by him and his colleagues.

No single individual will be able to conduct enough research to support an adequate theory of personality. At the very least, a lifetime of solid empirical research by one person would be needed before a theory could begin to have firm underpinnings. For one person to come up with insightful, comprehensive, consistent, and researchable ideas concerning the nature of human personality is one thing; but for that same person to single-handedly conduct research, compile data, and publish results covering the full range of personality would seem to be impossible. Only a cooperative team approach can provide sufficient data for even a moderately comprehensive theory of personality.

Currently, the leading example of an empirically developed, lower-level theory has been the development of the Big Five personality traits. The history of the Big Five goes back nearly 40 years, when Tupes and Christal (1961) reanalyzed studies that had used Cattell's 35 scales or revisions of them and found "five relatively strong and recurrent factors and nothing more of any consequence" (p. 14). They labeled these factors (I) Surgency, (II) Agreeableness, (III) Dependability, (IV) Emotional Stability, and (V) Culture. Two years later, Warren Norman (1963), using peer nominations, extracted nearly identical factors. Norman's five factors, which subsequently have been called the Big Five, included: (I) *Extroversion* vs. *Surgency*; (II) *Agreeableness*; (III) *Conscientiousness*; (IV) *Emotional Stability*; and (V) *Culture*. Since then, evidence for Norman's Big Five has been found in a variety of studies. Perhaps the most comprehensive of these studies has been Lewis Goldberg's (1990, 1993) work, which has supported the notion of five and only five basic dimensions of personality. In the Netherlands, Willem K. Hofstee and his associates (Brokken, 1978; de Raad, Mulder, Kloosterman, & Hofstee, 1988; Hofstee, de Raad, & Goldberg, 1992) have consistently found that factor analyses of Dutch language adjectives yield five dimensions, each easily identifiable as one of the Big Five. Oliver John and his associates (John, Goldberg, & Angleitner, 1984) reported on a study in which German American bilingual people provided personality descriptions in both German and English. Results from this ongoing project suggest high cross-language correlations between German and English versions of the Big Five dimensions. In addition, Eileen Donahue (1994) found that children conceptualize themselves and others in terms of the Big Five dimensions of personality. These studies suggest that researchers using a variety of methods with a variety of people in a variety of cultures support the notion that five major traits can be used to describe most human personalities.

Agreement that personality has five basic dimensions is a step toward understanding the structure of personality. However, the structure of personality tells us little about its causes, developments, and goals. The task of future personality psychologists will be to explain why certain individuals exhibit their particular combination of consistent and unique personality dimensions. Description of personality is but the first step in explaining and predicting future behavior. Predicting future behavior must still be left to the future.

Glossary

A

accusation   Adlerian safeguarding tendency whereby one protects magnified feelings of self-esteem by blaming others for one's own failures.

active imagination   Technique used by Jung to uncover collective unconscious material. Subjects are asked to concentrate on an image until a series of fantasies are produced.

actualizing tendency (Rogers)   Tendency within all people to move toward completion or fulfillment of potentials.

adolescence (Erikson)   An important psychosocial stage when ego identity should be formed. Adolescence is characterized by puberty and the crisis of identity vs. identity confusion.

adulthood (Erikson)   The stage from about ages 31 to 60 that is characterized by the psychosexual mode of procreativity and the crisis of generativity vs. stagnation.

aesthetic needs (Maslow)   Needs for art, music, beauty, and the like. Although they may be related to the basic conative needs, aesthetic needs are a separate dimension.

agape   Altruistic love.

aggression (Adler)   Safeguarding tendencies that may include depreciation or accusation of others as well as self-accusation, all designed to protect exaggerated feelings of personal superiority by striking out against other people.

aggression (Freud)   One of two primary instincts or drives that motivate people. Aggression is the outward manifestation of the death instinct and is at least a partial explanation for wars, personal hostility, sadism, masochism, and murder.

anal character   Freudian term for a person characterized by compulsive neatness, stubbornness, and miserliness.

anal phase (Freud)   Sometimes called the anal-sadistic phase; second stage of the infantile period, characterized by a child's attempts to gain pleasure from the excretory function and by such related behaviors as destroying or losing objects, stubbornness, neatness, and miserliness. Corresponds roughly to the second year of life.

anal triad (Freud)   The three traits of compulsive neatness, stubbornness, and miserliness that characterize the anal character.

anal-urethral-muscular   Erikson's term for the young child's psychosexual mode of adapting.

Analytical Psychology   Theory of personality and approach to psychotherapy founded by Carl Jung.

anima   Jungian archetype that represents the feminine component in the personality of males and originates from men's inherited experiences with women.

animus   Jungian archetype that represents the masculine component in the personality of females and originates from women's inherited experiences with men.

anorexia nervosa   Eating disorder characterized by intentional starvation, distorted body image, excessive amounts of energy, and an intense fear of gaining weight.

anxiety   A felt, affective, unpleasant state accompanied by the physical sensation of uneasiness.

anxiety (Kelly)   The recognition that the events with which one is confronted lie outside the range of convenience of one's construct system.

anxiety (May)   The experience of the threat of imminent nonbeing.

anxiety (Rogers)   Feelings of uneasiness or tension with an unknown cause.

apathy (Sullivan)   Dynamism that reduces tensions of needs through the adoption of an indifferent attitude.

archetypes   Jung's concept that refers to the contents of the collective unconscious. Archetypes, also called primordial images or collective symbols, represent psychic patterns of inherited behavior and are thus distinguished from instincts, which are physical impulses toward action. Typical archetypes are the anima, animus, and shadow.

attitude (Cattell)   A motivational trait that refers to a specific course of action in response to a given situation. In Cattell's definition, an attitude includes a particular situation, interest, response, and object.

attitude (Jung)   A predisposition to act or react in a characteristic manner, that is, in either an introverted or an extraverted direction.

authoritarianism (Fromm)   The tendency to give up one's independence and to unite with another person or persons in order to gain strength. Takes the form of masochism or sadism.

autistic language (Sullivan)   Private or parataxic language, which makes little or no sense to other people.

B

basic anxiety (Fromm)   The feeling of being alone and isolated, separated from the natural world.

basic anxiety (Horney)   Feelings of isolation and helplessness in a potentially hostile world.

basic anxiety (Maslow)   Anxiety arising from inability to satisfy physiological and safety needs.

basic conflict (Horney)   The incompatible tendency to move toward, against, and away from people.

basic hostility (Horney)   Repressed feelings of rage that originate during childhood when a child fears that its parents will not satisfy its needs for safety and satisfaction.

basic strength   The ego quality that emerges from the conflict between antithetical elements in Erikson's stages of development.

behavior potential (Rotter)   The possibility of a particular response occurring at a given time and place as calculated in relation to the reinforcement of that response.

behavioral analysis   Skinner's approach to studying behavior that assumes that human conduct is shaped primarily by the individual's personal history of reinforcement and secondarily by natural selection and cultural practices.

behavioral equation   Cattell's basic formula for representing and predicting behavior.

behaviorism   A "school" of psychology that limits its subject matter to observable behavior. John B. Watson is usually credited with being the founder of behaviorism, with B. F. Skinner its most notable proponent.

being-in-the-world   (see *Dasein*)

biophilia   Love of life.

bipolar traits   Traits with two poles; that is, traits scaled from a minus point to a positive point, with zero representing the midpoint.

B-love (Maslow)   Love between self-actualizing people and characterized by the love for the *being* of the other.

B-values (Maslow)   The values of self-actualizing people, including beauty, truth, goodness, justice, wholeness, and the like.

C

cardinal traits (Allport)   (see **disposition, cardinal**)

care (Erikson)   A commitment to take care of the people and things that one has learned to care for.

castration anxiety (Freud)   (see **castration complex**)

castration complex (Freud)   Condition that accompanies the Oedipus complex, but takes different forms in the two sexes. In boys, it takes the form of *castration anxiety*, or fear of having one's penis removed, and is responsible for shattering the Oedipus complex. In girls, it takes the form of *penis envy*, or the desire to have a penis, and it precedes and instigates the Oedipus complex.

causality   An explanation of behavior in terms of past experiences.

central traits (Allport)   (see **disposition, central**)

chance encounters (Bandura)   An unintended meeting of persons unfamiliar to each other.

character (Fromm)   Relatively permanent acquired qualities through which people relate themselves to others and to the world.

character orientation (Fromm)   Productive or nonproductive patterns of reacting to the world of things and the world of people.

choice corollary   Kelly's assumption that people choose the alternative in a dichotomized construct that they perceive will extend their range of future choices.

client-centered therapy   Approach to psychotherapy originated by Rogers, which is based on respect for the person's capacity to grow within a nurturing climate.

cognitive-affective personality system   Mischel's theory that views people as active, goal-directed individuals capable of exerting influence on both their situation and themselves.

cognitive needs (Maslow)   Needs for knowledge and understanding; related to basic or conative needs, yet operating on a different dimension.

collective efficacy (Bandura)   The confidence people have that their combined efforts will produce social change.

collective unconscious   Jung's idea of an inherited unconscious, which is responsible for many of our behaviors, ideas, and dream images. The collective unconscious lies beyond our personal experiences and originates with repeated experiences of our ancestors.

common traits (Allport)   (see **trait, common**)

commonality corollary   Kelly's theory that the personal constructs of people with similar experiences tend to be similar.

competencies (Mischel)   People's cognitive and behavioral construction of what they can and cannot do, based on their observations of the world, themselves, and others.

complex (Jung)   An emotionally toned conglomeration of ideas, which comprises the contents of the personal unconscious. Jung originally used the Word Association Test to uncover complexes.

conative needs   Needs that pertain to willful and purposive striving, for example, Maslow's hierarchy of needs.

conditioned reinforcer (Skinner)   Environmental event that is not by nature satisfying but becomes so because it is associated with unlearned or unconditioned reinforcers such as food, sex, and the like.

conditions of worth (Rogers) Restrictions or qualifications attached to one person's regard for another.

conformity (Fromm) Means of escaping from isolation and aloneness by giving up one's self and becoming whatever others desire.

congruence (Rogers) The matching of organismic experiences with awareness and with the ability to express those experiences. One of three "necessary and sufficient" therapeutic conditions.

conscience (Freud) The part of the superego that results from experience with punishment and that, therefore, tells a person what is wrong or improper conduct.

conscious (Freud) Those mental elements in awareness at any given time.

conscious (Jung) Mental images that are sensed by the ego and that play a relatively minor role in Jungian theory.

consistency paradox Mischel's term for the observation that clinical intuition and the perceptions of laypeople suggest that behavior is consistent, whereas research finds that it is not.

constructing obstacles (Adler) Safeguarding tendency in which people create a barrier to their own success, thus allowing them to protect their self-esteem by either using the barrier as an excuse for failure or by overcoming it.

construction corollary Kelly's assumption that people anticipate events according to their interpretations of recurrent themes.

constructive alternativism Kelly's view that events can be looked at (construed) from a different (alternative) perspective.

continuous schedule (Skinner) The reinforcement of an organism for every correct trial; opposed to the intermittent schedule in which only certain selected responses are reinforced.

core pathology (Erikson) A psychosocial disorder at any of the eight stages of development that results from too little basic strength.

core role (Kelly) People's construction of who they really are; their sense of identity that provides a guide for living.

correlation coefficient A mathematical index used to measure the direction and magnitude of the relationship between two variables.

cosmology The realm of philosophy dealing with the nature of causation.

countertransference Strong undeserved feelings that the therapist develops toward the patient during the course of treatment. These feelings can be either positive or negative and are considered by most writers to be a hindrance to successful psychotherapy.

creative power Adler's term for what he believed to be an inner freedom that empowers each of us to create our own style of life.

curvilinear relationship A relationship between two variables in which scores on the first variable increase with increases of scores on the second, but only to a certain point at which they then begin to decrease.

D

Dasein An existential term meaning a sense of self as a free and responsible person whose existence is embedded in the world of things, of people, and of self-awareness.

death instinct (Freud) One of two primary drives or impulses, the death instinct takes the form of destruction or aggression.

deductive method Approach to factor analytical theories of personality that gathers data on the basis of previously determined hypotheses or theories. Reasoning from the general to the particular.

defense mechanisms (Freud) Techniques such as repression, reaction formation, sublimation, and the like, whereby the ego defends itself against the pain of anxiety.

defensiveness (Rogers) Protection of the self-concept against anxiety and threat by denial and distortion of experiences that are inconsistent with it.

delay of gratification A reference to the observation that some people some of the time will prefer more valued delayed rewards over lesser valued immediate ones.

denial (Rogers) The blocking of an experience or some aspect of an experience from awareness because it is inconsistent with the self-concept.

depreciation Adlerian safeguarding tendency whereby another's achievements are undervalued and one's own are overvalued.

depressive position (Klein) Feelings of anxiety over losing a loved object coupled with a sense of guilt for wanting to destroy that object.

desacralization (Maslow) The process of removing respect, joy, awe, and rapture from an experience, which then purifies or objectifies that experience.

destructiveness (Fromm) Method of escaping from freedom by eliminating people or objects, thus restoring feelings of power.

diathesis-stress model A theory of stress that suggests that some individuals are vulnerable to stress-related illnesses because they are genetically predisposed to those illnesses.

dichotomy corollary Kelly's assumption that people construe events in an either/or (dichotomous) manner.

differential R (dR) technique Correlational procedure pioneered by Cattell, which correlates scores of a large number of people on many tests obtained at two different occasions. The dR technique measures consistency of the scores.

disengagement of internal control (Bandura) The displacement or diffusion of responsibility for the injurious effects of one's actions.

displacement A Freudian defense mechanism in which unwanted urges are redirected onto other objects or people in order to disguise the original impulse.

disposition, cardinal (Allport) Personal traits so dominating in an individual's life that they cannot be hidden. Most people do not have a cardinal disposition.

disposition, central (Allport) The five to ten personal traits around which a person's life focuses.

disposition, secondary (Allport) The least characteristic and reliable personal traits that still appear with some regularity in an individual's life.

dissociation (Sullivan) The process of separating unwanted impulses, desires, and needs from the self-system.

distortion (Rogers) Misinterpretation of an experience so that it is seen as fitting into some aspect of the self-concept.

D-love (Maslow) Deficiency love or affection (attachment) based on the lover's specific deficiency and the loved one's ability to satisfy that deficit.

dynamic calculus Cattell's complex procedure for determining the strength and direction of attitudes. The dynamic calculus includes the more specific behavioral equation, which permits the specific prediction of behavior.

dynamic lattice Cattell's term for a network of motives that includes attitudes, sems, and ergs.

dynamisms (Sullivan) Relatively consistent patterns of action that characterize the person throughout a lifetime. Similar to traits or habit patterns.

dystonic Erikson's term for the negative element in each pair of opposites that characterizes the eight stages of development.

E

earliest recollections Technique proposed by Adler to understand the pattern or theme that runs throughout a person's style of life.

early childhood (Erikson) The second stage of psychosocial development, characterized by the anal-urethral-muscular psychosexual mode and by the crisis of autonomy vs. shame and doubt.

eclectic Approach that allows selection of usable elements from different theories or approaches and combines them in a consistent and unified manner.

ego (Freud) The province of the mind that refers to the "I" or those experiences that are owned (not necessarily consciously) by the person. As the only region of the mind in contact with the real world, the ego is said to serve the reality principle.

ego (Jung) The center of consciousness. In Jungian psychology, the ego is of lesser importance than the more inclusive self and is limited to consciousness.

ego-ideal (Freud) The part of the superego that results from experiences with reward and that, therefore, teaches a person what is right or proper conduct.

eidetic personifications (Sullivan) Imaginary traits attributed to real or imaginary people in order to protect one's self-esteem.

Eigenwelt An existentialist term meaning the world of one's relationship to self. One of three simultaneous modes of being-in-the-world.

elaborative choice (Kelly) Making choices that will increase a person's range of future choices.

empathic listening (Rogers) The accurate sensing of the feelings of another and the communication of these perceptions. One of three "necessary and sufficient" therapeutic conditions.

empathy (Sullivan) An indefinite process through which anxiety is transferred from one person to another, for example, from mother to infant.

empirical Based on experience, systematic observation, and experiment rather than on logical reasoning or philosophical speculation.

empirical law of effect (Rotter) The assumption that behaviors that move people in the direction of their goals are more likely to be reinforced.

encoding strategies (Mischel) People's ways of transforming stimulus inputs into information about themselves, other people, and the world.

energy transformations (Sullivan) Overt or covert actions designed to satisfy needs or reduce anxiety.

enhancement needs (Rogers) The need to develop, to grow, and to achieve.

entropy Principle that states that when objects of differing temperatures meet, heat flows from the hotter to the colder, bringing about an equalization of temperature. Jung emphasized that tension is generated by the meeting of opposites.

epigenetic principle Erikson's term meaning that one component grows out of another in its proper time and sequence.

epistemology The branch of philosophy that deals with the nature of knowledge.

equivalence Principle that states that when a given quantity of energy is expended in the performance of an activity, an equal amount of energy will appear elsewhere. Jung emphasized that psychic energy is not destroyed but merely displaced.

ergs Energy inherent in primary or innate drives or motives. In Cattell's theory, ergs are contrasted to sems, which are learned motives.

erogenous zones Organs of the body that are especially sensitive to the reception of pleasure. In Freudian theory, the three principal erogenous zones are the mouth, anus, and genitals.

eros The desire for an enduring union with a loved one.

essential freedom (May) The freedom of being or the freedom of the conscious mind. Essential freedom cannot be limited by chains or bars.

esteem needs The fourth level on Maslow's hierarchy of needs; they include self-respect, competence, and the perceived esteem of others.

ethology The scientific study of the characteristic behavior patterns of animals.

excuses Adlerian safeguarding tendencies whereby the person, through the use of reasonable sounding justifications, becomes convinced of the reality of self-erected obstacles.

existential freedom (May) The freedom of doing one's will. Existential freedom can be limited by chains or bars.

existential living Rogers's term indicating a tendency to live in the moment.

existential needs (Fromm) Peculiarly human needs aimed at moving people toward a reunification with the natural world. Fromm listed relatedness, transcendence, rootedness, a sense of identity, and a frame of orientation as existential, or human, needs.

expectancy The subjective probability held by a person that any specific reinforcement or set of reinforcements will occur in a given situation.

experience corollary Kelly's view that people continually revise their personal constructs as the result of experience.

exploitative characters (Fromm) People who take from others, either by force or cunning.

external evaluations (Rogers) Conditions of worth placed on a person, which may then serve as a criterion for evaluating one's own conduct. Conditions of worth block growth and interfere with one's becoming fully functioning.

external reinforcement (Rotter) The positive or negative value of any reinforcing event as seen from the view of societal or cultural values.

extinction The tendency of a previously acquired response to become progressively weakened upon nonreinforcement.

extraversion (E) (Eysenck) One of three types of superfactors identified by Eysenck and

consisting of two opposite poles—extraversion and introversion. *Extraverts* are characterized behaviorally by sociability and impulsiveness and physiologically by a low level of cortical arousal. *Introverts*, by contrast, are characterized by unsociability and caution and by a high level of cortical arousal.

extraversion (Jung) An attitude or type marked by the turning outward of psychic energy so that a person is oriented toward the objective world.

F

factor A unit of personality derived through factor analysis. However, the term is sometimes used more generally to include any underlying aspect of personality.

factor analysis A mathematical procedure for reducing a large number of variables to a few. Used by Cattell and Eysenck to identify personality traits.

factor loadings The amount of correlation that a score contributes to a given factor.

falsifiable An attribute of a theory that allows research to either support or fail to support that theory's major tenets. A falsifiable theory is accountable to experimental results.

fear (Kelly) A specific threat to one's personal constructs.

feeling (Jung) A rational function that tells us the value of something. The feeling function can be either extraverted (directed toward the objective world) or introverted (directed toward the subjective world).

fiction (Adler) A belief or expectation of the future that serves to motivate present behavior. The truthfulness of a fictional idea is immaterial, because the person acts as if the idea were true.

fixation A defense mechanism that arises when psychic energy is blocked at one stage of development, thus making change or psychological growth difficult.

fixation (Fromm) The nonproductive form of rootedness marked by a reluctance to grow beyond the security provided by one's mother.

fixed-interval (Skinner) Intermittent reinforcement schedule whereby the organism is reinforced for its first response following a designated period of time (for example, FI 10 means that the animal is reinforced for its initial response after 10 minutes have elapsed since its previous reinforcement).

fixed-ratio (Skinner) Reinforcement schedule in which the organism is reinforced intermittently according to a specified number of responses it makes (for example, FR 7 means that the organism is reinforced for every seventh response).

formative tendency (Rogers)   Tendency in all matter to evolve from simpler to more complex forms.

fortuitous events (Bandura)   Environmental events that are unexpected and unintended.

fragmentation corollary   Kelly's assumption that behavior is sometimes inconsistent because one's construct systems can admit incompatible elements.

frame of orientation (Fromm)   The need for humans to develop a unifying philosophy or consistent way of looking at things.

free association   Technique used in Freudian psychotherapy in which the therapist instructs the patient to verbalize every thought that comes to mind, no matter how irrelevant or repugnant it may appear.

freedom of movement (Rotter)   The mean expectancy of being reinforced for performing all those behaviors that are directed toward the satisfaction of some general need.

fully functioning person (Rogers)   (see **person of tomorrow**)

functional autonomy (Allport)   The tendency for some motives to become independent from the original motive responsible for the behavior.

G

Gemeinschaftsgefühl   (see **social interest**)

generalization   The transfer of the effects of one learning situation to another.

generalized expectancy (Rotter)   Expectation based on similar past experiences that a given behavior will be reinforced.

generalized reinforcer (Skinner)   A conditioned reinforcer that has been associated with several primary reinforcers. Money, for example, is a generalized reinforcer because it is associated with food, shelter, and other primary reinforcers.

genital-locomotor   Erikson's term for the preschool child's psychosexual mode of adapting.

genital stage (Freud)   Period of life beginning with puberty and continuing through adulthood and marked by full sexual identity.

genital stage (Klein)   Comparable to Freud's phallic stage, that is, the time around ages three to five when the Oedipus complex reaches its culmination.

genitality (Erikson)   The psychosexual mode of young adulthood characterized by mutual trust and a sharing of sexual satisfactions.

great mother   Jungian archetype of the opposing forces of fertility and destruction.

guilt (Kelly)   The sense of having lost one's core role structure.

guilt (May)   An ontological characteristic of human existence arising from our separation

from the natural world (U*mwelt*), from other people (M*itwelt*), or from our self (E*igenwelt*).

H

hero   A Jungian archetype representing the myth of the godlike man who conquers or vanquishes evil, usually in the form of a monster, dragon, or serpent.

hesitating (Adler)   Safeguarding tendency characterized by vacillation or procrastination designed to provide a person with the excuse "It's too late now."

heuristic   Pertaining to a method or theory that leads to the discovery of new information.

hierarchy of needs   Maslow's concept that needs are ordered in such a manner that those on a lower level must be satisfied before higher level needs become activated.

hoarding characters (Fromm)   People who seek to save and not let go of material possessions, feelings, or ideas.

holistic-dynamic   Maslow's theory of personality, which stresses both the unity of the organism and the motivational aspects of personality.

humanistic psychoanalysis   Fromm's personality theory that combines the basics of both psychoanalysis and humanistic psychology.

hypochondriasis   Exaggerated attention to and anxiety about one's health.

hypothesis   An assumption or educated guess that can be scientifically tested.

hysteria (Freud)   A mental disorder marked by the conversion of repressed psychical elements into somatic symptoms such as impotency, paralysis, or blindness, when no physiological bases for these symptoms exist.

I

id (Freud)   The region of personality that is alien to the ego because it includes experiences that have never been owned by the person. The id is the home base for all the instincts, and its sole function is to seek pleasure regardless of consequences.

ideal self (Rogers)   One's view of self as one would like to be.

idealistic principle (Freud)   A reference to the demands of the superego that the ego must oppose the pleasure-seeking id and instigate, instead, behaviors consistent with the child's perception of parental standards.

idealized self-image (Horney)   An attempt to solve basic conflicts by adopting a belief in one's godlike qualities.

identity crisis   Erickson's term for a crucial period or turning point in the life cycle that may result in either more or less ego strength. Identity crises can be found in those Eriksonian stages that follow the development of identity, ordinarily during adolescence.

idiographic   Approach to the study of personality that is based on the single case.

incestuous symbiosis (Fromm)   Extreme dependence on a mother or mother substitute.

incongruence (Rogers)   The perception of discrepancies between organismic self, self-concept, and ideal self.

Individual Psychology   Theory of personality and approach to psychotherapy founded by Alfred Adler.

individuality corollary   Kelly's assumption that people have different experiences and therefore construe events in different ways.

individuation   Jung's term for the process of becoming a whole person, that is, an individual with a high level of psychic development.

inductive method   Approach to factor analytic theories of personality that gathers data with no preconceived hypotheses or theory in mind. Reasoning from the particular to the general.

infancy (Erikson)   The first stage of psychosocial development—one marked by the oral-sensory mode and by the crisis of basic trust vs. basic mistrust.

infantile stage (Freud)   First four or five years of life characterized by autoerotic or pleasure-seeking behavior and consisting of the oral, anal, and phallic substages.

instinct (Freud)   From the German *Trieb* meaning drive or impulse; refers to an internal stimulus that impels action or thought. The two primary instincts are sex and aggression.

instinct (Jung)   An unconscious physical impulse toward action. Instincts are the physical counterpart of archetypes.

instinctoid needs (Maslow)   Needs that are innately determined but that can be modified through learning. The frustration of instinctoid needs leads to various types of pathology.

intentionality (May)   The underlying structure that gives meaning to our experience.

interactionist   One who believes that behavior results from an interaction of environmental variables and person variables, including cognition.

intermittent schedule (Skinner)   The reinforcement of an organism on only certain selected occurrences of a response; opposed to a continuous schedule in which the organism is reinforced for every correct trial. The four most common intermittent schedules are: fixed-ratio, variable-ratio, fixed-interval, and variable-interval.

internal reinforcement (Rotter)   The individual's perception of the positive or negative value of any reinforcing event.

internalization (object relations theory)   A process in which the person takes in (introjects) aspects of the external world and then organizes those introjections in a psychologically meaningful way.

internalized object relationships (Kernberg)   Basic structural units in any personality organization, consisting of a self-image, an object-image, and an affect.

interpersonal theory   Sullivan's personality theory that emphasizes the importance of interpersonal relationships during each stage of development from infancy to adulthood.

interpersonal trust (Rotter)   A generalized expectancy held by a person that other people can be relied on to keep their word. The Interpersonal Trust Scale attempts to measure degree of interpersonal trust.

intimacy (Erikson)   The ability to fuse one's identity with that of another person without fear of losing it. The syntonic element of young adulthood.

intimacy (Sullivan)   Conjunctive dynamism marked by a close personal relationship with another person who is more or less of equal status.

introjection (Freud)   A defense mechanism whereby people incorporate positive qualities of another person into their ego.

introjection (Klein)   Fantasizing taking external objects, such as the mother's breast, into one's own body.

introversion (Eysenck)   (see **extraversion, Eysenck**)

introversion (Jung)   An attitude or type characterized by the turning inward of psychic energy with an orientation toward the subjective.

intuition (Jung)   An irrational function that involves perception of elementary data that are beyond our awareness. Intuitive people "know" something without understanding how they know.

ipsative   A method of measurement that uses the person's own behavior or scores as a standard of reference; opposed to the normative method, which compares a person's scores to those obtained by a norm group.

irrational functions (Jung)   Methods of dealing with the world without evaluation or thinking. Sensing and intuiting are the two irrational functions.

isolation (Erikson)   The inability to share true intimacy or to take chances with one's identity. The dystonic element of young adulthood.

J

Jonah complex   The fear of being one's best.

L

L data   Cattell's term for life record, or information collected on a person by objective observation.

latency (Erikson)   The psychosexual mode of the school-age child. A period of little sexual development.

latency stage (Freud)   The time between infancy and puberty when psychosexual growth is at a standstill.

latent dream content (Freud)   The underlying, unconscious meaning of a dream. Freud held that the latent content, which can only be revealed through dream interpretation, was more important than the surface or manifest content.

law of effect   Thorndike's principle that responses to stimuli followed immediately by a satisfier tend to strengthen the connection between those responses and stimuli; that is, they tend to be learned.

libido (Freud)   Psychic energy of the life instinct; sexual drive or energy.

life instinct (Freud)   One of two primary drives or impulses, the life instinct is also called Eros or sex.

locus of control (Rotter)   The belief people have that their attempts to reach a goal are within their control (internal locus of control) or are primarily due to powerful events such as fate, chance, or other people (external locus of control). Locus of control is measured by the Internal-External Control Scale.

love (Erikson)   The basic strength of young adulthood that emerges from the crisis of intimacy vs. isolation.

love (Fromm)   A union with another person in which a person retains separateness and integrity of self.

love (May)   To delight in the presence of the other person and to affirm that person's value and development as much as one's own.

love and belongingness needs   The third level on Maslow's hierarchy of needs; they include both the need to give love and the need to receive love.

lust (Sullivan)   Isolating dynamism in which one person has an impersonal sexual interest in another.

M

maintenance needs (Rogers)   Those basic needs that protect the status quo. They may be either physiological (for example, food) or interpersonal (for example, the need to maintain the current self-concept).

malevolence   Sullivan's term for those destructive behavior patterns dominated by the attitude that people are evil and harmful and that the world is a bad place to live.

malignant aggression (Fromm)   The destruction of life for reasons other than survival.

mandala (Jung)   Symbol representing the striving for unity and completion. It is often seen as a circle within a square or a square within a circle.

manifest dream content (Freud)   The surface or conscious level of a dream. Freud believed that the manifest level of a dream has no deep psychological significance and that the unconscious or latent level holds the key to the dream's true meaning.

marketing characters (Fromm)   People who see themselves as commodities, with their personal value dependent on their ability to sell themselves.

masculine protest   Adler's term for the neurotic and erroneous belief held by some men and women that men are superior to women.

masochism   A condition characterized by the reception of sexual pleasure from suffering pain and humiliation inflicted either by self or by others.

maturity (Freud)   The final psychosexual stage following infancy, latency, and the genital period. Hypothetically, maturity would be characterized by a strong ego in control of the id and the superego and by an ever-expanding realm of consciousness.

meta-analysis   A statistical technique that collects results from multiple studies and quantifies the magnitude of the effect, thus allowing for conclusions on the basis of many findings rather than a single one.

metamotivation (Maslow)   The motives of self-actualizing people, including especially the B-values.

metapathology (Maslow)   Illness characterized by absence of values, lack of fulfillment, and loss of meaning that results from deprivation of self-actualization needs.

Mitwelt   An existentialist term meaning the world of one's relationship to other people. One of three simultaneous modes of being-in-the-world.

modeling (Bandura)   One of two basic sources of learning; involves the observation of others and thus learning from their actions. More than simple imitation, modeling entails the addition and subtraction of specific acts and the observation of consequences of others' behavior.

modulation corollary (Kelly)   Theory that states that personal constructs are permeable (resilient), they are subject to change through experience.

moral anxiety (Freud)   Anxiety that results from the ego's conflict with the superego.

moral hypochondriasis (Fromm) Preoccupation with guilt about things one has done wrong.

moralistic principle (Freud) A reference to the conscience, a subsystem of the superego that tells people what they should not do.

morphogenic science Allport's concept of science, which deals with various methods of gathering on a single individual.

moving against people One of Horney's neurotic trends in which neurotics protect themselves against the hostility of others by adopting an aggressive strategy.

moving away from people One of Horney's neurotic trends in which neurotics protect themselves against feelings of isolation by adopting a detached attitude.

moving backward (Adler) Safeguarding inflated feelings of superiority by reverting to a more secure period of life.

moving toward people One of Horney's neurotic trends in which neurotics develop a need for others as a protection against feelings of helplessness.

myth (May) Belief system that provides explanations for personal and social problems.

N

narcissism Love of self or the attainment of erotic pleasure from viewing one's own body.

necrophilia Love of death.

need potential (Rotter) A reference to the possible occurrence of a set of functionally related behaviors directed toward the satisfaction of the same goal or a similar set of goals.

need value (Rotter) The degree to which a person prefers one set of reinforcements to another.

negative reinforcer Any aversive stimulus that, when removed from a situation, increases the probability that the immediately preceding behavior will occur.

negative transference Strong, hostile, and undeserved feelings that the patient develops toward the analyst during the course of treatment.

neurosis Somewhat dated term signifying mild personality disorders as opposed to the more severe psychotic reactions. Neuroses are generally characterized by one or more of the following: anxiety, hysteria, phobias, obsessive-compulsive reactions, depression, chronic fatigue, and hypochondriacal reactions.

neurotic anxiety (Freud) An apprehension about an unknown danger facing the ego but originating from id impulses.

neurotic anxiety (May) A reaction that is disproportionate to the threat and that leads to repression and defensive behaviors.

neurotic claims (Horney) Unrealistic demands and expectations of neurotics to be entitled to special privilege.

neurotic needs (Horney) Original 10 defenses against basic anxiety.

neurotic needs (Maslow) Nonproductive needs that are opposed to the basic needs and that block psychological health whether or not they are satisfied.

neurotic pride (Horney) A false pride based on one's idealized image of self.

neurotic search for glory Horney's concept for the comprehensive drive toward actualizing the ideal self.

neurotic trends Horney's term for the three basic attitudes toward self and others—moving toward people, moving against people, and moving away from people; a revision of her original list of 10 neurotic needs.

neuroticism (N) (Eysenck) One of three types or superfactors identified by Eysenck. Neuroticism is a bipolar factor consisting of neuroticism at one pole and stability at the other. High scores on N may indicate anxiety, hysteria, obsessive-compulsive disorders, or criminality.

nomothetic An approach to the study of personality that is based on general laws or principles.

nonbeing The awareness of the possibility of one's not being, through death or loss of awareness.

normal anxiety (May) The experience of threat that accompanies growth or change in one's values.

normal autism (Mahler) The stage in an infant's development when all its needs are satisfied automatically, that is, without the infant having to deal with the external world.

normal symbiosis (Mahler) The second developmental stage marked by a dual unity of infant and mother.

nothingness (see **nonbeing**)

O

object Psychoanalytic term referring to the person or part of a person that can satisfy an instinct or drive.

object relations theory A reference to the work of Melanie Klein and others who have extended Freudian psychoanalysis with their emphasis on early relations to parents (objects) that influence later interpersonal relationships.

oblique rotation A method of rotating the axes in factor analysis that assumes some intercorrelation among primary factors.

obsession A persistent or recurrent idea, usually involving an urge toward some action.

Oedipus complex Term used by Freud to indicate the situation in which the child of either sex develops feelings of love and/or hostility for the parent. In the simple male Oedipus complex, the boy has incestuous feelings of love for the mother and hostility toward the father. The simple female Oedipus complex exists when the girl feels hostility for the mother and sexual love for the father.

old age (Erikson)   The eighth and final stage of the life cycle, marked by the psychosocial crisis of integrity vs. despair and the basic strength of wisdom.

old wise man   Jungian archetype of wisdom and meaning.

operant conditioning (Skinner)   A type of learning in which reinforcement, which is contingent upon the occurrence of a particular response, increases the probability that the same response will occur again.

operant discrimination   Skinner's observation that an organism, as a consequence of its reinforcement history, learns to respond to some elements in the environment but not to others. Operant discrimination does not exist within the organism but is a function of environmental variables and the organism's previous history of reinforcement.

operant extinction (Skinner)   The loss of an operantly conditioned response due to the systematic withholding of reinforcement.

operational definition   A definition of a concept in terms of specific operations to be carried out.

oral phase (Freud)   The earliest stage of the infantile period, characterized by attempts to gain pleasure through the activity of the mouth, especially sucking, eating, and biting; corresponds roughly to the first 12–18 months of life.

oral-sensory   Erikson's term for the infant's first psychosexual mode of adapting.

organ dialect (Adler)   The expression of a person's underlying intentions or style of life through a diseased or dysfunctional bodily organ.

organismic self (Rogers)   A more general term than self-concept; refers to the entire person, including those aspects of existence beyond awareness.

organization corollary   Kelly's notion that people arrange their personal constructs in a hierarchical system.

orthogonal rotation   A method of rotating the axes in factor analysis that assumes the independence of primary factors.

P

P technique   Correlational procedure pioneered by Cattell that utilizes variables or scores taken from one person on many different occasions.

paranoia   Mental disorder characterized by unrealistic feelings of persecution, grandiosity, and a suspicious attitude toward others.

paranoid-schizoid position (Klein)   A tendency of the infant to see the world as having the same destructive and omnipotent qualities that it possesses.

parapraxes   Freudian slips such as slips of the tongue or pen, misreading, incorrect hearing, temporary forgetting of names and intentions, and the misplacing of objects.

parataxic (Sullivan)   Mode of cognition characterized by attribution of cause and effect when none is present; private language not consensually validated (that is, not able to be accurately communicated to others).

parataxic distortion (Sullivan)   The process of seeing a cause and effect relationship between two events in close proximity when there is no such relationship.

parsimony   Criterion of a useful theory, which states that when two theories are equal on other criteria, the simpler one is preferred.

peak experience (Maslow)   An intense, mystical experience, often characteristic of self-actualizing people but not limited to them.

penis envy (Freud)   (see **castration complex**)

perceptual conscious (Freud)   The system that perceives external stimuli through sight, sound, taste, and the like and that communicates them to the conscious system.

permeability (Kelly)   A quality of personal constructs that allows new information to revise our way of viewing things.

perseverative functional autonomy (Allport)   Functionally independent motives that are not part of the proprium; includes addictions, the tendency to finish uncompleted tasks, and other acquired motives.

person of tomorrow (Rogers)   The psychologically healthy individual in the process of evolving into all that he or she can become.

persona   Jungian archetype that represents the side of personality that one shows to the rest of the world. Also, the mask worn by ancient Roman actors in the Greek theater and thus the root of the word "personality."

personal constructs (Kelly)   A person's way of interpreting, explaining, and predicting events.

personal disposition (Allport)   A relatively permanent neuropsychic structure peculiar to the individual, which has the capacity to render different stimuli functionally equivalent and to initiate and guide personalized forms of behavior.

Personal Orientation Inventory (POI)   Test designed by E. L. Shostrom to measure Maslow's concept of self-actualizing tendencies in people.

personal unconscious   Jung's term for those repressed experiences that pertain exclusively to one particular individual; opposed to the collective unconscious, which pertains to unconscious experiences that originate with repeated experiences of our ancestors.

personality   A global concept referring to all those relatively permanent traits, dispositions, or characteristics within the individual that give some degree of consistency to that person's behavior.

personality signature (Mischel)   An individual's unique and stable pattern of behaving differently in different situations.

person-centered   The theory of personality founded by Carl Rogers as an outgrowth of his client-centered psychotherapy.

personifications (Sullivan)   Images a person has of self or others, such as "good-mother," "bad-mother," "good-me," and "bad-me."

phallic phase (Freud)   The third and final stage of the infantile period, characterized by the Oedipus complex. Although anatomical differences between the sexes are responsible for important differences in the male and female Oedipal periods, Freud used the term "phallic phase" to signify both male and female development.

phenomenology   A philosophical position emphasizing that behavior is caused by one's perceptions rather than by external reality.

philia   Brotherly or sisterly love; friendship.

phylogenetic endowment   Freud's term for those unconscious inherited images that have been passed down to us through many generations of repetition.

physiological needs   The most basic level on Maslow's hierarchy of needs; they include food, water, air, and so on.

placebo effect   Changes in behavior or functioning brought about by one's beliefs or expectations.

play age (Erikson)   The third stage of psychosocial development, encompassing the time from about ages three to five and characterized by the genital-locomotor psychosexual mode and the crisis of initiative vs. guilt.

play construction   Erikson's projective technique for assessing personality dynamics in children through the use of toys.

pleasure principle (Freud)   A reference to the motivation of the id to seek immediate reduction of tension through the gratification of instinctual drives.

positions (Klein)   Ways in which an infant organizes its experience in order to deal with its basic conflict of love and hate. The two positions are the paranoid-schizoid position and the depressive position.

positive freedom (Fromm)   Spontaneous activity of the whole, integrated personality; signals a reunification with others and with the world.

positive regard (Rogers)   The need to be loved, liked, or accepted by another.

positive reinforcer   Any stimulus that, when added to a situation, increases the probability that a given behavior will occur.

post-Freudian theory   Erikson's theory of personality that extended Freud's developmental stages into old age. At each age, a specific psychosocial struggle contributes to the formation of personality.

preconscious (Freud)   Those mental elements that are currently not in awareness, but that can become conscious with varying degrees of difficulty.

primary narcissism (Freud)   The infant's investment of libido in its own ego; self-love or autoerotic behavior of the infant (see **narcissism**).

primary process (Freud)   A reference to the id, which houses the primary motivators of behavior, called instincts.

primary traits   First-order traits extracted through factor analysis of more specific behaviors.

principle of entropy (Jung)   (see **entropy**)

principle of equivalence (Jung)   (see **equivalence**)

proactive (Allport)   Concept that presupposes that people are capable of consciously acting upon their environment in new and innovative ways, which then feed new elements into the system and stimulate psychological growth.

procreativity (Erikson)   The drive to have children and to care for them.

progression (Jung)   The forward flow of psychic energy; involves the extraverted attitude and movement toward adaptation to the external world.

projection   A defense mechanism whereby the ego reduces anxiety by attributing an unwanted impulse to another person.

projective identification (Klein)   A psychic defense mechanism in which infants split off unacceptable parts of themselves, project them onto another object, and then introject them in a distorted form.

propriate functional autonomy (Allport)   Allport's concept of a master system of motivation that confers unity on personality by relating self-sustaining motives to the proprium.

propriate strivings (Allport)   Motivation toward goals that are consistent with an established proprium and that are uniquely one's own.

proprium (Allport)   All those characteristics that people see as peculiarly their own and that are regarded as warm, central, and important.

prototaxic (Sullivan) Primitive, presymbolic, undifferentiated mode of experience that cannot be communicated to others.

pseudospecies (Erikson) The illusion held by a particular society that it is somehow chosen to be more important than other societies.

psychoanalysis Theory of personality, approach to psychotherapy, and method of investigation founded by Freud.

psychoanalytical social theory Horney's theory of personality that emphasizes cultural influence in shaping both normal and neurotic development.

psychological situation (Rotter) That part of the external and internal world to which an individual is responding.

psychology of science A subdiscipline of psychology that studies both science and the behavior of scientists.

psychoses Severe personality disorders, as opposed to the more mild neurotic reactions. Psychoses interfere seriously with the usual functions of life and include both organic brain disorders and functional (learned) conditions.

psychoticism (P) (Eysenck) One of three superfactors or types identified by Eysenck. Psychoticism is a bipolar factor consisting of psychoticism at one pole and superego function at the other. High P scores indicate hostility, self-centeredness, suspicion, and nonconformity.

punishment The presentation of an aversive stimulus or the removal of a positive one. Punishment sometimes, but not always, weakens a response.

Q

Q data Cattell's term for questionnaire information or self-report data.

Q sort Inventory technique originated by William Stephenson in which the subject is asked to sort a series of self-referent statements into several piles, the size of which approximates a normal curve.

R

radical behaviorism Skinner's view that psychology as a science can only advance when psychologists stop attributing behavior to hypothetical constructs and begin writing and talking strictly in terms of observable behavior.

range corollary Kelly's assumption that personal constructs are limited to a finite range of convenience.

rational functions (Jung) Methods of dealing with the world that involve thinking and feeling (valuing).

reaction formation A defense mechanism in which a person represses one impulse and adopts the exact opposite form of behavior, which ordinarily is exaggerated and ostentatious.

reactive (Allport) Term for those theories that view people as being motivated by tension reduction and by the desire to return to a state of equilibrium.

realistic anxiety (Freud) An unpleasant, nonspecific feeling resulting from the ego's relationship with the external world.

reality principle (Freud) A reference to the ego, which must realistically arbitrate the conflicting demands of the id, the superego, and the external world.

receptive characters (Fromm) People who relate to the world through receiving love, knowledge, and material possessions.

reciprocal determinism (Bandura) Scheme that includes environment, behavior, and person as mutually interacting to determine personal conduct.

regression (Freud) A defense mechanism whereby a person returns to an earlier stage in order to protect the ego against anxiety.

regression (Jung) The backward flow of psychic energy. Regression involves the introverted attitude and movement toward adaptation to the internal world.

reinforcement (Skinner) Any condition within the environment that strengthens a behavior (see also **negative reinforcer** and **positive reinforcer**).

reinforcement-reinforcement sequences Rotter's term indicating that the value of an event is a function of one's expectation that a reinforcement will lead to future reinforcements.

reinforcement value (Rotter) The preference a person attaches to any reinforcement when the probabilities are equal for the occurrence of a number of different reinforcements.

relatedness (Fromm) The need for union with another person or persons. Expressed through submission, power, or love.

reliability The extent to which a test or other measuring instrument yields consistent results.

repetition compulsion (Freud) The tendency of an instinct, especially the death instinct, to repeat or recreate an earlier condition, particularly one that was frightening or anxiety-arousing.

repression (Freud) The forcing of unwanted, anxiety-laden experiences into the unconscious in order to defend a person against the pain of that anxiety.

resacralization (Maslow) The process of returning respect, joy, awe, and rapture to an experience in order to make that experience more subjective and personal.

resistance A variety of unconscious responses by patients designed to block therapeutic progress.

respondent conditioning Often called *classical conditioning* and sometimes *Pavlovian conditioning*. In respondent conditioning, a neutral (conditioned) stimulus is paired with, that is, immediately precedes, an unconditioned stimulus a number of times until it is capable of bringing about a previously unconditioned response, now called the conditioned response.

role (Kelly) A pattern of behavior that results from people's understanding of the constructs of others with whom they are engaged in some task.

role repudiation (Erikson) The inability to synthesize different self-images and values into a workable identity.

rootedness (Fromm) The human need to establish roots, that is, to find a home again in the world.

S

sadism A condition in which a person receives sexual pleasure by inflicting pain or humiliation on another person.

safeguarding tendencies (Adler) Protective mechanisms such as aggression, withdrawal, and the like that maintain exaggerated feelings of superiority.

safety needs The second level on Maslow's hierarchy of needs; they include physical security, protection, and freedom from danger.

school age (Erikson) The fourth stage of psychosocial development; covers the period from about ages 6 to 12 or 13 and is characterized by psychosexual latency and the psychosocial crisis of industry vs. inferiority.

science A branch of study concerned with observation and classification of data and with the verification of general laws through the testing of hypotheses.

secondary narcissism (Freud) Self-love or autoerotic behavior in an adolescent (see **narcissism**).

secondary process (Freud) A reference to the ego, which chronologically is the second region of the mind (after the id or primary process). Secondary process thinking is in contact with reality.

secondary traits (Allport) (see **disposition, secondary**)

security operations (Sullivan) Behaviors aimed at reducing interpersonal tension.

selective activation Bandura's belief that self-regulatory influences are not automatic but rather operate only if they are activated.

selective inattention (Sullivan) The control of focal awareness, which involves a refusal to see those things that one does not wish to see.

self (Jung) The most comprehensive of all archetypes, the self includes the whole of personality, although it is mostly unconscious. The self is often symbolized by the mandala motif.

self-system (Bandura) Cognitive structure of personality that provides reference for perceiving, evaluating, and regulating behavior.

self-accusation Adlerian safeguarding tendency whereby a person aggresses indirectly against others through self-torture and guilt.

self-actualization needs (Maslow) The highest level of human motivation; they include the need to fully develop all one's psychological capacities.

self-actualization (Rogers) A subsystem of the actualizing tendency. The tendency to actualize the self as perceived.

self-concept Those aspects of one's experiences that are perceived by the individual.

self-efficacy (Bandura) People's expectation that they are capable of performing those behaviors that will produce desired outcomes in any particular situation.

self-hatred (Horney) The powerful tendency for neurotics to despise their real self.

self-objects (Kohut) Parents or other significant adults in a child's life who eventually become incorporated into the child's sense of self.

self-realization (Jung) The highest possible level of psychic maturation; necessitates a balance between conscious and unconscious, ego and self, masculine and feminine, and introversion and extraversion. All four functions (thinking, feeling, sensing, and intuiting) would be fully developed by self-realized people.

self-regard (Rogers) The need to accept, like, or love oneself.

self-regulatory strategies (Mischel) Techniques used to control one's own behavior through self-imposed goals and self-produced consequences.

self-system (Sullivan) Complex of dynamisms that protect a person from anxiety and maintain interpersonal security.

sems (Cattell) Learned dynamic traits.

sensation (Jung) An irrational function that receives physical stimuli and transmits them to perceptual consciousness. People may rely on either extraverted sensing (outside perceptions) or on introverted sensing (internal perceptions).

sense of identity (Fromm) The distinctively human need to develop a feeling of "I."

separation anxiety Reactions of infants upon losing sight of their primary caregiver; at first infants protest, then despair, and finally become emotionally detached.

separation-individuation (Mahler) The third major stage of development, marked by the child's becoming an individual, separate from its mother; spans the period from ages four or five months to about 30 to 36 months.

shadow Jungian archetype representing the inferior or dark side of personality.

shaping Conditioning a response by first rewarding gross approximations of the behavior, then closer approximations, and finally the desired behavior itself.

social cognitive theory Bandura's assumption that personality is molded by an interaction of behavior, personal factors, and one's environment.

social interest (Adler) Translation of the German *Gemeinschaftsgefühl*, meaning a community feeling or a sense of feeling at one with all human beings.

sociality corollary Kelly's notion that people can communicate with others because they are able to construe their constructions.

somnolent detachment (Sullivan) Dynamism that protects a person from increasingly strong and painful effects of severe anxiety.

splitting (object relations theory) A psychic defense mechanism in which the child subjectively separates incompatible aspects of an object.

stability (Eysenck) (see **neuroticism, Eysenck**)

standing still (Adler) Safeguarding tendency characterized by lack of action as a means of avoiding failure.

states Temporary conditions within an individual such as anger, stress, sexual arousal, or fear; opposed to traits, which are more permanent.

stimulus generalization (see **generalization**)

style of life (Adler) A person's individuality that expresses itself in any circumstance or environment; the "flavor" of a person's life.

subception (Rogers) The process of perceiving stimuli without an awareness of the perception.

sublimation A defense mechanism that involves the repression of the genital aim of Eros and its substitution by a cultural or social aim.

subsidiation chain Cattell's term for the complex of subgoals underlying motivation. A subsidiation chain generally traces motivation to some innate drive.

successive approximations Procedure used to shape an organism's actions by rewarding behaviors as they become closer and closer to the target behavior.

superego (Freud) The moral or ethical processes of personality; the superego has two subsystems—the conscience, which tells us what is wrong, and the ego-ideal, which tells us what is right.

superego function (Eysenck) (see **psychoticism, Eysenck**)

suppression The blocking or inhibiting of an activity either by a conscious act of the will or by an outside agent such as parents or other authority figures. It differs from repression, which is the unconscious blocking of anxiety-producing experiences.

syndrome A group of concurrent symptoms or characteristics.

syntaxic (Sullivan) Consensually validated experiences that represent the highest level of cognition and that can be accurately communicated to others, usually through language.

syntonic Erikson's term for the positive element in each pair of opposites that characterize his eight stages of development.

systematic desensitization A behavior therapy technique used to inhibit or extinguish phobias and fears through the use of relaxation.

T

T data Cattell's term for test scores or objective information obtained from observation of performance.

Taoistic attitude (Maslow) Noninterfering, passive, receptive attitude that includes awe and wonder toward that which is observed.

taxonomy A system of classification of data according to their natural relationships.

teleology An explanation of behavior in terms of future goals or purposes.

tenderness (Sullivan) Tension within the mothering one that is aroused by the manifest needs of the infant. The child feels tenderness as the need to receive care.

tension (Sullivan) The potentiality for action, which may or may not be experienced in awareness.

theory A set of related assumptions from which, by logical deductive reasoning, testable hypotheses can be drawn.

thinking (Jung) A rational function that tells us the meaning of an image that originates either from the external world (extraverted) or from the internal world (introverted).

third force Somewhat vague term referring to those approaches to psychology that have reacted against the older psychodynamic and behavioristic theories. The third force is usually thought to include humanistic, existential, and phenomenological theories.

threat (Kelly) The anticipation of danger to the stability of one's personal constructs.

threat (Rogers) Feeling that results from the perception of an experience that is inconsistent with one's organismic self.

trait A relatively permanent disposition of an individual, which is inferred from behavior. Cattell, Eysenck, and Allport each have slightly different definitions of traits.

trait, common (Allport) Relatively permanent neuropsychic structure with the capacity to render disparate stimuli functionally equivalent and to initiate and guide action.

transcendence (Fromm) The need for humans to rise above their passive animal existence through either creating or destroying life.

transference Strong, undeserved feelings that the patient develops toward the analyst during the course of treatment. These feelings may be either sexual or hostile, but they stem from the patient's earlier experiences with parents.

transformation Psychotherapeutic approach used by Jung in which the therapist is transformed into a healthy individual who can aid the patient in establishing a philosophy of life.

types (factor theorists) A cluster of primary traits. Eysenck recognized three general types—extraversion (E), neuroticism (N), and psychoticism (P).

types (Jung) Classification of people based on the two-dimensional scheme of attitudes and functions. The two attitudes of extraversion and introversion and the four functions of thinking, feeling, sensing, and intuiting combine to produce eight possible types.

tyranny of the should (Horney) A key element in the neurotic search for glory; includes an unconscious and unrelenting drive for perfection.

U

Umwelt An existentialist term meaning the world of things or objects. One of three simultaneous modes of being-in-the-world.

unconditional positive regard (Rogers) The need to be accepted and prized by another without any restrictions or qualifications. One of three "necessary and sufficient" therapeutic conditions.

unconscious (Freud) All those mental elements of which a person is unaware. Two levels of the unconscious are the unconscious proper and the preconscious. Unconscious ideas can become conscious only through great resistance and difficulty.

unconscious (Jung) All those psychic processes not related to the ego. Jung divides the unconscious into personal (individual) and collective (inherited).

unipolar traits Traits with only one pole; that is, those scaled from zero to some large amount, as opposed to bipolar traits that are scaled from a minus point, through zero, to a positive point.

V

validity The extent to which a test or other measuring instrument measures what it is supposed to measure; accuracy.

variable-interval (Skinner) Intermittent reinforcement schedule in which the organism is reinforced after a lapse of random and varied periods of time (for example, VI 10 means that the animal is reinforced for its first response following random-length intervals that average 10 minutes).

variable-ratio (Skinner) Intermittent reinforcement schedule in which the organism is reinforced for every *nth* response on the average (for example, VR 50 means that the animal is reinforced on the average of one time for every 50 responses).

vicarious experience Learning by observing the consequences of others' behavior.

vulnerable (Rogers) A condition that exists when people are unaware of the discrepancy between their organismic self and their significant experiences. Vulnerable people often behave in ways incomprehensible to themselves and to others.

W

will (May) A conscious commitment to action.

withdrawal (Adler) Safeguarding one's exaggerated sense of superiority by establishing a distance between oneself and one's problems.

Y

young adulthood (Erikson) The stage from about ages 18 to 30 during which a person gains mature genitality and experiences the crisis of intimacy vs. isolation.

References

Adams-Webber, J. R. (1970). An analysis of the discriminant validity of several repertory grid indices. *British Journal of Psychology, 60,* 83–90.

Adler, A. (1907/1917). *Study of organ inferiority and its psychical compensation.* New York: Nervous and Mental Disease Publishing.

Adler, A. (1925/1968). *The practice and theory of Individual Psychology.* Totowa, NJ: Littlefield Adams.

Adler, A. (1927). *Understanding human nature.* New York: Greenberg.

Adler, A. (1929/1964). *Problems of neurosis.* New York: Harper Torchbooks.

Adler, A. (1929/1969). *The science of living.* New York: Anchor Books.

Adler, A. (1930). Individual Psychology. In C. Murchinson (Ed.), *Psychologies of 1930.* Worcester, MA: Clark University Press.

Adler, A. (1931). *What life should mean to you.* New York: Capricorn Books.

Adler, A. (1956). *The Individual Psychology of Alfred Adler: A systematic presentation in selections from his writings* (H. L. Ansbacher & R. R. Ansbacher, Eds.). New York: Basic Books.

Adler, A. (1964). *Superiority and social interest: A collection of later writings* (H. L. Ansbacher & R. R. Ansbacher, Eds.). New York: Norton.

Ainsworth, M., Blehar, M., Waters, E., & Wall, S. (1978). *Patterns of attachment.* Hillsdale, NJ: Erlbaum.

Alexander, I. E. (1990). *Personology: Method and content in personality assessment and psychobiography.* Durham, NC: Duke University Press.

Allers, C. T., White, J., & Hornbuckle, D. (1990). Early recollections: Detecting depression in the elderly. *Individual Psychology, 46,* 61–66.

Allport, F. (1974). An autobiography. In G. Lindzey (Ed.), *A history of psychology in autobiography* (Vol. 6, pp. 1–29). Englewood Cliffs, NJ: Prentice-Hall.

Allport, G. W. (1937). *Personality: A psychological interpretation.* New York: Henry Holt.

Allport, G. W. (1950). *The individual and his religion.* New York: Macmillan.

Allport, G. W. (1954). *The nature of prejudice.* Reading, MA: Addison Wesley.

Allport, G. W. (1955). *Becoming: Basic consideration for a psychology of personality.* New Haven, CT: Yale University Press.

Allport, G. W. (1960). The open system in personality theory. *Journal of Abnormal and Social Psychology, 61,* 301–310.

Allport, G. W. (1961). *Pattern and growth in personality.* New York: Holt, Rinehart and Winston.

Allport, G. W. (1962). The general and the unique in psychological science. *Journal of Personality, 30,* 405–422.

Allport, G. W. (1963). Behavioral science, religion and mental health. *Journal of Religion and Health, 2,* 187–197.

Allport, G. W. (1965). *Letters from Jenny.* New York: Harcourt, Brace & World.

Allport, G. W. (1966). Traits revisited. *American Psychologist, 21,* 1–10.

Allport, G. W. (1967). An autobiography. In E. G. Boring & G. Lindzey (Eds.), *A history of psychology in autobiography* (Vol. 5, pp. 1–27). New York: Appleton-Century-Crofts.

Allport, G. W. (1968). *The person in psychology.* Boston: Beacon Press.

Allport, G. W. (1978). *Waiting for the Lord: 33 meditations on God and man.* New York: Macmillan.

Allport, G. W., & Odbert, H. S. (1936). Trait-names: A psycho-lexical study. *Psychological Monographs, 47,* 1–171.

Allport, G. W., & Ross, J. M. (1967). Personal religious orientation and prejudice. *Journal of Personality and Social Psychology, 5,* 432–443.

Allport, G. W., Vernon, P. E., & Lindzey, G. (1960). A *study of values.* Boston: Houghton Mifflin.

American Psychiatric Association. (1987). *Diagnostic and statistical manual of mental disorders* (3rd ed.). Washington, DC: Author.

American Psychiatric Association. (1994). *Diagnostic and statistical manual of mental disorders* (4th ed.). Washington, DC: Author.

Anonymous. (1946). Letters from Jenny. *Journal of Abnormal and Social Psychology, 41,* 315–350, 449–480.

Ansbacher, H. L. (1985). The significance of Alfred Adler for the concept of narcissism. *American Journal of Psychiatry, 142,* 203–207.

Arehart, D. M., & Smith, P. H. (1990). Identity in adolescence: Influences of dysfunction and psychosocial task issues. *Journal of Youth and Adolescence, 19,* 63–72.

Axtell, A., & Newlon, B. J. (1993). An analysis of Adlerian life themes of bulimic women. *Individual Psychology, 49,* 58–67.

Bachofen, J. J. (1861/1967). *Myth, religion, and mother right: Selected writings of Johann Jacob Bachofen* (R. Manheim, Trans.). Princeton, NJ: Princeton University Press.

Bachtold, L. M., & Werner, E. E. (1972). Personality characteristics of women scientists. *Psychological Reports, 31,* 391–396.

Bailey, W. T. (1992). Psychological development in men: Generativity and involvement with young children. *Psychological Reports, 71,* 929–930.

Baker, L., Silk, K. R., Westen, D., Nigg, J. T., & Lohr, N. E. (1992). Malevolence, splitting, and parental ratings by borderlines. *The Journal of Nervous and Mental Disease, 180,* 258–264.

Balay, J., & Shevrin, H. (1988). The subliminal psychodynamic activation method. *American Psychologists, 43,* 161–174.

Baldwin, A. F. (1942). Personal structure analysis: A statistical method for investigating the single personality. *Journal of Abnormal and Social Psychology, 37,* 163–183.

Balmary, M. (1979/1982). *Psychoanalyzing psychoanalysis: Freud and the hidden fault of the father.* Baltimore: Johns Hopkins University Press.

Bandura, A. (1977). *Social learning theory.* Englewood Cliffs, NJ: Prentice-Hall.

Bandura, A. (1978a). On paradigms and recycled ideologies. *Cognitive Therapy and Research, 2,* 79–103.

Bandura, A. (1978b). The self system in reciprocal determinism. *American Psychologist, 33,* 344–358.

Bandura, A. (1981). Self-referent thought: A developmental analysis of self-efficacy. In J. H. Flavell & L. D. Ross (Eds.), *Cognitive social development: Frontiers and possible futures.* New York: Cambridge University Press.

Bandura, A. (1982a, July). *Model of causality in social learning theory.* Paper presented at the meeting of the Japanese Psychological Association, Kyoto.

Bandura, A. (1982b). The psychology of chance encounters and life paths. *American Psychologist, 37,* 747–755.

Bandura, A. (1982c). Self-efficacy mechanisms in human agency. *American Psychologist, 37,* 122–147.

Bandura, A. (1986). *Social foundations of thought and action: A social cognitive theory.* Englewood Cliffs, NJ: Prentice-Hall.

Bandura, A. (1988a, August). *Human agency in social cognitive theory.* Paper presented at the XXIV International Congress of Psychology, Sydney, Australia.

Bandura, A. (1988b). Self-regulation of motivation and action through goal systems. In V. Hamilton, G. H. Bower, & N. H. Fryda (Eds.), *Cognitive perspectives on emotion and motivation*. Dordrecht: Kluwer Academic Publishers.

Bandura, A. (1989). Human agency in social cognitive theory. *American Psychologist, 44*, 1175–1184.

Bandura, A. (1991a). Social cognitive theory of moral thought and action. In W. M. Kurtiness & J. L. Gewirtz (Eds.), *Handbook of moral behavior and development: Vol. 1. Theory* (pp. 45–103). Hillsdale, NJ: Erlbaum.

Bandura, A. (1991b). Social cognitive theory of self-regulation. *Organizational Behavior and Human Decision Processes, 50*, 248–287.

Bandura, A. (1994a). Social cognitive theory and exercise of control over HIV infection. In R. J. DiClemente & J. L. Peterson (Eds.), *Preventing AIDS: Theories and methods of behavioral interventions* (pp. 25–59). New York: Plenum Press.

Bandura, A. (1994b). Social cognitive theory and mass communication. In J. Bryant & D. Zillmann (Eds.), *Media effects: Advances in theory and research* (pp. 61–90). Hillsdale, NJ: Erlbaum.

Bandura, A. (1995a). Exercise of personal and collective efficacy in changing societies. In A. Bandura (Ed.), *Self-efficacy in changing societies* (pp. 1–45). Cambridge,

England: Cambridge University Press.

Bandura, A. (1995b). On rectifying conceptual ecumenism. In J. E. Maddux (Ed.), *Self-efficacy, adaptation, and adjustment: Theory, research, and application* (pp. 347–375). New York: Plenum Press.

Bandura, A., Adams, N. E., Hardy, A. B., & Howells, G. N. (1980). Tests of the generality of self-efficacy theory. *Cognitive Therapy and Research, 4*, 39–66.

Bandura, A., Blanchard, E. B., & Ritter, B. (1969). The relative efficacy of desensitization and modeling approaches for inducing behavioral, affective, and attitudinal changes. *Journal of Personality and Social Psychology, 13*, 173–199.

Bandura, A., & Mischel, W. (1965). Modification of self-imposed delay of reward through exposure to live and symbolic models. *Journal of Personality and Social Psychology, 2*, 698–705.

Bandura, A., Ross, D., & Ross, S. A. (1963). Imitation of film-mediated aggressive models. *Journal of Abnormal and Social Psychology, 66*, 3–11.

Bandura, A., & Walters, R. H. (1959). *Adolescent aggression*. New York: Ronald Press.

Bannister, D. (1970). *Perspectives in personal construct theory*. London: Academic Press.

Bannister, D. (Ed.). (1975). *Issues and approaches in the psychological therapies*. London: Wiley.

Bannister, D. (1977). *New perspectives in personal construct theory*. London: Academic Press.

Bannister, D., & Fransella, F. (1966). A grid test of schizophrenic thought disorder. *British Journal of Social and Clinical Psychology, 5*, 95–102.

Bannister, D., & Fransella, F. (1971). *Inquiring man: The theory of personal constructs*. Harmondsworth, England: Penguin Books.

Bannister, D., & Mair, J. M. M. (1968). *The evaluation of personal constructs*. London: Academic Press.

Barrett-Lennard, G. T. (1962). Dimensions of therapist response as causal factors in therapeutic change. *Psychological Monographs: General and Applied, 76* (43, Whole No. 562).

Barrett-Lennard, G. T. (1964). *The Relationship Inventory. Forms OS-M-64 and MO-M-64 plus MO-F-64.* Unpublished manuscript, University of New England, Biddeford, ME.

Bass, E., & Davis, L. (1988). *The courage to heal*. New York: Harper & Row.

Beail, N. (Ed.). (1985). *Repertory Grid technique and personal constructs: Applications in clinical & educational settings*. Cambridge, MA: Brookline.

Beail, N., & Parker, S. (1991). Group fixed-role therapy: A clinical application. *International Journal of Personal Construct Psychology, 4,* 85–95.

Bell, M. D., Billington, R., & Becker, B. (1986). A scale for the assessment of object relationships: Reliability, validity, and factorial invariance. *Journal of Clinical Psychology, 42,* 733–741.

Bell, M. D., Billington, R., Cicchetti, D., & Gibbons, J. (1988). Do object relations deficits distinguish BPD from other diagnostic groups? *Journal of Clinical Psychology 44,* 511–576.

Bender, L., & Vogel, B. F. (1941). Imaginary companions of children. *American Journal of Orthopsychiatry, 11,* 56–65.

Benjamin, L. S. (1974). Structural analysis of social behavior. *Psychological Review, 81,* 392–425.

Benson, R. M., & Pryor, D. B. (1973). When friends fall out: Developmental interference with the function of some imaginary companions. *Journal of the American Psychoanalytic Association, 21,* 457–468.

Bergin, A. E., Masters, K. S., & Richards, P. S. (1987). Religiousness and mental health reconsidered: A study of an intrinsically religious sample. *Journal of Counseling Psychology, 34,* 197–204.

Berndt, T. J., & Hanna, N. A. (1995). Intimacy and self-disclosure in friendships. In K. J. Rotenberg (Ed.), *Disclosure processes in children and adolescents* (pp. 57–77). New York: Cambridge University Press.

Bettelheim, B. (1982, March 1). Freud and the soul. *The New Yorker,* pp. 52–93.

Bettelheim, B. (1983). *Freud and man's soul.* New York: Knopf.

Bilmes, M. (1978). Rollo May. In R. S. Valle & M. King (Eds.), *Existential-phenomenological alternatives for psychology* (pp. 290–294). New York: Oxford University Press.

Bjork, D. W. (1993). *B. F. Skinner: A life.* New York: Basic Books.

Blatt, S., & Homann, E. (1992). Parent-child interaction in the etiology of dependent and self-critical depression. *Clinical Psychology Review, 12,* 47–91.

Block, J. H., & Block, J. (1980). The role of ego-control and ego-resiliency in the organization of behavior. In W. A. Collins (Ed.), *Minnesota symposium on child psychology* (Vol. 13, pp. 39–101). Hillsdale, NJ: Erlbaum.

Bottome, P. (1939). *Alfred Adler: Apostle of freedom.* London: Faber & Faber.

Bowlby, J. (1969/1982). *Attachment and loss: Vol. 1. Attachment* (2nd ed.). New York: Basic Books.

Bowlby, J. (1973). *Attachment and loss: Vol. 2. Separation: Anxiety and anger.* New York: Basic Books.

Bowlby, J. (1980). *Attachment and loss: Vol. 3. Loss: Sadness and depression.* New York: Basic Books.

Brannon, L. (1996). *Gender: Psychological perspectives.* Boston: Allyn and Bacon.

Breuer, J., & Freud, S. (1895/1955). *Studies on hysteria.* In J. Strachey (Ed. and Trans.), *The standard edition of the complete psychological works of Sigmund Freud* (Vol. 2). London: Hogarth Press.

Brokken, F. B. (1978). *The language of personality.* Meppel, The Netherlands: Krips.

Brome, V. (1978). *Jung.* New York: Atheneum.

Brosschot, J. F., Gebhardt, W. A., & Godaert, G. L. (1994). Internal, powerful others and chance locus of control: Relationships with personality, coping, stress and health. *Personality and Individual Differences, 16,* 839–852.

Brown, I., Jr., & Inouye, D. K. (1978). Learned helplessness through modeling: The role of perceived similarity in competence. *Journal of Personality and Social Psychology, 36,* 900–908.

Buchanan, L. P., Kern, R., & Bell-Dumas, J. (1991). Comparison of content in created versus actual early recollections. *Individual Psychology, 47,* 348–355.

Bunch, J. M., & Schneider, H. G. (1991). Smoking-specific locus of control. *Psychological Reports, 69,* 1075–1081.

Burston, D. (1991). *The legacy of Erich Fromm.* Cambridge, MA: Harvard University Press.

Butler, T. L., & Newlon, B. J. (1992). Children of trauma: Adlerian personality characteristics. *Individual Psychology, 48,* 313–318.

Button, E. (Ed.). (1985). *Personal construct theory & mental health: Theory, research and practice.* Cambridge, MA: Brookline.

Buttsworth, L. M., & Smith, G. A. (1994). Personality of Australian performing musicians by gender and by instrument. *Personality and Individual Differences, 18,* 595–603.

Byck, R. (Ed.). (1974). *Cocaine papers by Sigmund Freud.* New York: Meridian.

Cantor, N., & Zirkel, S. (1990). Personality, cognition, and purposive behavior. In L. A. Pervin (Ed.), *Handbook of personality: Theory and research* (pp. 135–164). New York: Guilford Press.

Caper, R. (1988). *Immaterial facts: Freud's discovery of psychic reality and Klein's development of his work.* Northvale, NJ: Aronson.

Carey, J. C., Hamilton, D. L., & Shanklin, G. (1986). Does personality similarity affect male roommates' satisfaction? *Journal of College Student Personnel, 27,* 63–69.

Carlson, R. (1980). Studies of Jungian topology: II, Representation of the personal world. *Journal of Personality and Social Psychology, 38,* 801–810.

Carroll, W. R., & Bandura, A. (1982). The role of visual monitoring in observational learning of action patterns: Making the observable observable. *Journal of Motor Behavior, 14,* 153–167.

Carroll, W. R., & Bandura, A. (1985). Role of timing of visual monitoring and motor rehearsal in observational learning of action patterns. *Journal of Motor Behavior, 17,* 269–281.

Cashdan, S. (1988). *Object relations therapy: Using the relationship.* New York: Norton.

Cattell, H. E. P. (1993). Comment on Goldberg. *American Psychologist, 48,* 1302–1303.

Cattell, R. B. (1949). *Manual for Forms A and B: Sixteen Personality Factors Questionnaire.* Champaign, IL: IPAT.

Cattell, R. B. (1950). *Personality: A systematic, theoretical and factual study.* New York: McGraw-Hill.

Cattell, R. B. (1957). *Personality and motivation structure and measurement.* Yonkers-on-Hudson, NY: World Book.

Cattell, R. B. (1971). *Abilities: Their structure, growth, and action.* Boston: Houghton Mifflin.

Cattell, R. B. (1972). The 16 P.F. and basic personality structure: A reply to Eysenck. *Journal of Behavioral Science, 1,* 169–187.

Cattell, R. B. (1973). A check on the 29-factor Clinical Analysis Questionnaire structure on normal and pathological subjects. *Journal of Multivariate Experimental Personality and Clinical Psychology, 1,* 3–12.

Cattell, R. B. (1974a). An autobiography. In G. Lindzey (Ed.), *A history of psychology in autobiography* (Vol. 6, pp. 59–100). Englewood Cliffs, NJ: Prentice-Hall.

Cattell, R. B. (1974b). Travels in psychological hyperspace. In T. S. Krawiec (Ed.), *The Psychologists* (Vol. 2). New York: Oxford University Press.

Cattell, R. B. (1979–1980). *Personality and learning theory: Vol. 1. The structure of personality in its environment. Vol. 2. A systems theory of maturation and structure learning.* New York: Springer.

Cattell, R. B. (1982). The development of Cattellian structured systems theory of personality. The VIDAS model. *Zeitschrift fur Differentielle und Diagbostische Psychologie 3,* 7–25.

Cattell, R. B. (1983). *Structured personality—learning theory: A wholistic multivariate research approach*. New York: Praeger.

Cattell, R. B. (1985). *Human motivation and the dynamic calculus*. New York: Praeger.

Cattell, R. B. (1990). Advances in Cattellian personality theory. In L. A. Pervin (Ed.), *Handbook of personality: Theory and research* (pp. 101–110). New York: Guilford Press.

Cattell, R. B. (1993). Planning basic clinical research. In C. E. Walker (Ed.), *The history of clinical psychology in autobiography:* (Vol. 2, pp. 101–111). Pacific Grove, CA: Brooks/Cole.

Cattell, R. B., & Cattell, H. E. P. (1995). Personality structure and the new fifth edition of the 16PF. *Educational and Psychological Measurement, 55,* 926–937.

Cattell, R. B., & Child, D. (1975). *Motivation and dynamic structure*. New York: Halsted Press.

Cattell, R. B., & Drevdahl, J. E. (1955). A comparison of the personality profile (16PF) of eminent researchers with that of eminent teachers and administrators, and the general population. *British Journal of Psychology, 46,* 248–261.

Cattell, R. B., & Kline, P. (1977). *The scientific analysis of personality and motivation*. New York: Academic Press.

Cattell, R. B., Schuerger, J. M., & Klein, T. W. (1982). Heritabilities of ego strength (Factor C), superego strength (Factor G), and self-sentiment (Factor Q_3) by multiple abstract variance analysis. *Journal of Clinical Psychology, 38,* 769–779.

Chambers, J. (1964). Creative scientists of today. *Science, 145,* 1203–1205.

Chambliss, C. A., & Murray, E. J. (1979). Cognitive procedures for smoking reduction: Symptom attribution versus efficacy attribution. *Cognitive Therapy and Research, 3,* 91–95.

Chaplin, M. P., & Orlofsky, J. L. (1991). Personality characteristics of male alcoholics as revealed through their early recollections. *Individual Psychology, 47,* 356–371.

Chapman, A. H. (1976). *Harry Stack Sullivan: His life and his work*. New York: Putnam.

Chodorow, N. J. (1989). *Feminism and psychoanalytic theory*. New Haven, CT: Yale University Press.

Chodorow, N. J. (1991). Freud on women. In J. Neu (Ed.). *The Cambridge companion to Freud: Cambridge companions to philosophy* (pp. 224–248). New York: Cambridge University Press.

Chodorow, N. J. (1994). *Femininities, masculinities, sexualities: Freud and beyond*. Lexington, KY: University of Kentucky Press.

Clark, R. W. (1980). *Freud: The man and the cause*. New York: Random House.

Cleary, T. S., & Shapiro, S. I. (1995). The plateau experience and the post-mortem life: Abraham H. Maslow's unfinished theory. *Journal of Transpersonal Psychology, 27,* 1–23.

Clements, L. B., York, R. O., & Rohrer, G. E. (1995). The interaction of parental alcoholism and alcoholism as a predictor of drinking-related locus of control. *Alcoholism Treatment Quarterly, 12,* 97–110.

Cohen, D. (1977). *Psychologists on psychology*. New York: Taplinger.

Cohen, J. (1992). Spouse type similarity and prediction accuracy: Testing a theory of mate selection. *Journal of Psychological Type, 24,* 45–53.

Coles, R. (1970). *Erik H. Erikson: The growth of his work*. Boston: Little, Brown.

Combs, A. W., & Snygg, D. (1959). *Individual behavior: A perceptual approach to behavior*. New York: Harper & Row.

Compton, W. C., Smith, M. L., Cornish, K. A., & Qualls, D. L. (1996). Factor structure of mental health measures. *Journal of Personality and Social Psychology, 71,* 406–413.

Cooper, H., & Hedges, L. V. (Eds.). (1994). *The handbook of research synthesis*. New York: Sage.

Coram, G. J., & Shields, D. J. (1987). Early recollections of criminal justice majors and nonmajors. *Psychological Reports*, 60, 1287–1290.

Cramer, D. (1985). Psychological adjustment and the facilitative nature of close personal relationships. *British Journal of Medical Psychology*, 58, 165–168.

Cramer, D. (1987). Self-esteem, advice-giving, and the facilitative nature of close personal relationships. *Person-Centered Review*, 2, 99–110.

Cramer, D. (1988). Self-esteem and facilitative close relationships: A cross-lagged panel correlation analysis. *British Journal of Social Psychology*, 27, 115–126.

Cramer, D. (1989). Self-esteem and the facilitativeness of parents and close friends. *Person-Centered Review*, 4, 61–76.

Cramer, D. (1990a). Disclosure of personal problems, self-esteem, and the facilitativeness of friends and lovers. *British Journal of Guidance and Counseling*, 18, 186–196.

Cramer, D. (1990b). Toward assessing the therapeutic value of Rogers's core conditions. *Counselling Psychology Quarterly*, 3, 57–68.

Cramer, D. (1993). Therapeutic relationship and outcome seen by clients in first and third session of individual therapy. *Counselling Psychology Quarterly*, 6, 13–15.

Cramer, D. (1994). Self-esteem and Rogers' core conditions in close friends: A latent variable path analysis of panel data. *Counselling Psychology Quarterly*, 7, 327–337.

Cramer, D., & Takens, R. J. (1992). Therapeutic relationship and progress in the first six sessions of individual psychotherapy: A panel analysis. *Counselling Psychology Quarterly*, 5, 25–36.

Crandall, J. E. (1975). A scale for social interest. *Journal of Individual Psychology*, 31, 187–195.

Crandall, J. E. (1981). *Theory and measurement of social interest: Empirical tests of Alfred Adler's concept*. New York: Columbia University Press.

Crandall, R., McCown, D. A., & Robb, Z. (1988). The effects of assertiveness training on self-actualization. *Small Group Behavior*, 19, 134–145.

Crews, F. (1995). *The memory wars: Freud's legacy in dispute*. New York: The New York Review of Books.

Crews, F. (1996). The verdict on Freud. *Psychological Science*, 7, 63–68.

Critelli, J. W. (1977). Romantic attraction and happiness. *Psychological Reports*, 41, 721–722.

Delhees, K. H., & Cattell, R. B. (1971). *Manual for the Clinical Analysis Questionnaire* (CAQ). Champaign, IL: IPAT.

Demorest, A. P., & Siegel, P. F. (1996). Personal influences on professional work: An empirical case study of B. F. Skinner. *Journal of Personality*, 64, 243–261.

de Raad, B., Mulder, E., Kloosterman, K., & Hofstee, W. K. (1988). Personality-descriptive verbs. *European Journal of Personality*, 2, 81–96.

Dollard, J., & Miller, N. E. (1950). *Personality and psychotherapy: An analysis in terms of learning, thinking, and culture*. New York: Knopf.

Dolliver, R. H. (1995). Carl Rogers personality theory and psychotherapy as a reflection of his life experience and personality. *Journal of Humanistic Psychology*, 35, 111–128.

Donahue, E. M. (1994). Do children use the Big Five, too? Content and structural form in personality description. *Journal of Personality*, 62, 45–66.

Drevdahl, J. E., & Cattell, R. B. (1958). Personality and creativity in artists and writers. *Journal of Clinical Psychology*, 14, 107–111.

Dunst, C. J., & Lingerfelt, B. (1985). Maternal ratings of temperament and operant learning in two-

and three-month-old infants. *Child Development,* 56, 555–563.

Duttweiler, P. C. (1984). The internal control index: A newly developed measure of locus of control. *Educational and Psychological Measurement,* 44, 209–211.

Ebersole, P., & Humphreys, P. (1991). The Short Index of Self-Actualization and purpose in life. *Psychological Reports,* 69, 550.

Edmonds, E. M., Shipman, M., & Cahoon, D. D. (1992). Religious orientation and locus of control. *Psychology: A Journal of Human Behavior,* 29, 17–19.

Ellenberger, H. F. (1970). *The discovery of the unconscious.* New York: Basic Books.

Elliot, W. N., Fakouri, M. E., & Hafner, J. L. (1993). Early recollections of criminal offenders. *Individual Psychology,* 49, 68–75.

Elms, A. C. (1981). Skinner's dark year and *Walden Two. American Psychologist,* 36, 470–479.

Elms, A. C. (1994). *Uncovering lives: The uneasy alliance of biography and psychology.* New York: Oxford University Press.

Epstein, S. (1979). The stability of behavior: I. On predicting most of the people most of the time. *Journal of Personality and Social Psychology,* 37, 1097–1126.

Epstein, S. (1980). The stability of behavior. II. Implications for

psychological research. *American Psychologist,* 35, 790–806.

Erik Erikson, 91, psychoanalyst who reshaped views of human growth, dies. (1994, May 13). *The New York Times,* p. B9.

Erikson, E. H. (1950). *Childhood and society.* New York: Norton.

Erikson, E. H. (1958). *Young man Luther: A study in psychoanalysis and history.* New York: Norton.

Erikson, E. H. (1963). *Childhood and society.* (2nd ed.). New York: Norton.

Erikson, E. H. (1968). *Identity: Youth and crisis.* New York: Norton.

Erikson, E. H. (1969). *Gandhi's truth: On the origins of militant nonviolence.* New York: Norton.

Erikson, E. H. (1974). *Dimensions of a new identity: The 1973 Jefferson Lectures in the Humanities.* New York: Norton.

Erikson, E. H. (1975). *Life history and the historical moment.* New York: Norton.

Erikson, E. H. (1977). *Toys and reasons: Stages in the ritualization of experience.* New York: Norton.

Erikson, E. H. (1980). *Identity and the life cycle.* New York: Norton.

Erikson, E. H. (1982). *The life cycle completed: A review.* New York: Norton.

Erikson, E. H. (1985). *Childhood and society* (3rd ed.). New York: Norton.

Erikson, E. H. (1989). Elements of psychoanalytic theory of

psychosocial development. In S. I. Greenspan & G. H. Pollock (Eds.), *The course of life: Vol. 1. Infancy* (pp. 15–83). Madison, CT: International Universities Press.

Erikson, E. H., Erikson, J. M., & Kivnick, H. Q. (1986). *Vital involvement in old age.* New York: Norton.

Erikson, J. M. (1988). *Wisdom and the senses: The way of creativity.* New York: Norton.

Esterson, A. (1993). *Seductive mirage: An exploration of the work of Sigmund Freud.* Chicago: Open Court.

Evans, R. I. (1966). *Dialogue with Erich Fromm.* New York: Harper & Row.

Evans, R. I. (1967). *Dialogue with Erik Erikson.* New York: Harper & Row.

Evans, R. I. (1976). *The making of psychology: Discussion with creative contributors.* New York: Knopf.

Evans, R. I. (1981). *Dialogue with Carl Rogers.* New York: Praeger.

Evans, R. I. (1989). *Albert Bandura: The man and his ideas—A dialogue.* New York: Praeger.

Eysenck, H. J. (1947). *Dimensions of personality.* London: Routledge & Kegan Paul.

Eysenck, H. J. (1952a). The effects of psychotherapy: An evaluation. *Journal of Consulting Psychology,* 16, 319–324.

Eysenck, H. J. (1952b). *The structure of human personality.* London: Methuen.

Eysenck, H. J. (1953). *Uses and abuses of psychology.* Baltimore: Penguin.

Eysenck, H. J. (1954). *The psychology of politics.* London: Routledge & Kegan Paul.

Eysenck, H. J. (1956). *Sense and nonsense in psychology.* London: Penguin.

Eysenck, H. J. (1959). *Manual for the Maudsley Personality Inventory.* London: University of London Press.

Eysenck, H. J. (1964). *Crime and personality.* Boston: Houghton Mifflin.

Eysenck, H. J. (1965). *Fact and fiction in psychology.* London: Penguin.

Eysenck, H. J. (1967). *The biological basis of personality.* Springfield, IL: Charles C Thomas.

Eysenck, H. J. (1971). *The IQ argument.* New York: Library Press. (British edition: *Race, intelligence and education.* London: Maurice Temple Smith, 1971).

Eysenck, H. J. (1972a). Primaries or second-order factors: A critical consideration of Cattell's 16 PF Battery. *British Journal of Social and Clinical Psychology, 11,* 265–269.

Eysenck, H. J. (1972b). *Psychology is about people.* London: Allen Lane.

Eysenck, H. J. (1976). *Sex and personality.* Austin: University of Texas Press.

Eysenck, H. J. (1977a). Personality and factor analysis: A reply to Guilford. *Psychological Bulletin, 84,* 405–411.

Eysenck, H. J. (1977b). *You and neurosis.* London: Temple Smith.

Eysenck, H. J. (1980). An autobiography. In G. Lindzey (Ed.), *A history of psychology in autobiography* (Vol. 7). San Francisco: Freeman.

Eysenck, H. J. (Ed.). (1981). *A model for personality.* New York: Springer.

Eysenck, H. J. (1982). *Personality, genetics and behavior: Selected papers.* New York: Praeger.

Eysenck, H. J. (1983). Psychopharmacology and personality. In W. Janke (Ed.), *Response variability to psychotropic drugs* (pp. 127–154). Oxford, England: Pergamon Press.

Eysenck, H. J. (1990a). Biological dimensions of personality. In L. A. Pervin (Ed.), *Handbook of personality: Theory and research* (pp. 244–276). New York: Guilford Press.

Eysenck, H. J. (1990b). *Decline and fall of the Freudian empire.* Washington, DC: Scott-Townsend.

Eysenck, H. J. (1990c). *Rebel with a cause: The autobiography of H. J. Eysenck.* London: W. H. Allen.

Eysenck, H. J. (1991a). Hans J. Eysenck: Maverick psychologist. In C. E. Walker (Ed.), *The history of clinical psychology in autobiography* (Vol. 2, pp. 39–86). Pacific Grove, CA: Brooks/Cole.

Eysenck, H. J. (1991b). Personality as a risk factor in coronary heart disease. *European Journal of Personality, 5,* 81–92.

Eysenck, H. J. (1991c). *Smoking, personality and stress: Psychosocial factors in the prevention of cancer and coronary heart disease.* New York: Springer-Verlag.

Eysenck, H. J. (1992). The definition and measurement of psychoticism. *Personality and Individual Differences, 13,* 757–785.

Eysenck, H. J. (1993). Creativity and personality: Suggestions for a theory. *Psychological Inquiry, 4,* 147–179.

Eysenck, H. J. (1994a). The big five or giant three: Criteria for a paradigm. In C. F. Halverson, Jr., G. A. Kohnstamm, & R. P. Martin (Eds.), *The developing structure of temperament and personality from infancy to adulthood* (pp. 37–51). Hillsdale, NJ: Erlbaum.

Eysenck, H. J. (1994b). Normality-abnormality and the three-factor model. In S. Strack & M. Lorr (Eds.), *Differentiating normal and abnormal personality* (pp. 3–25). New York: Springer.

Eysenck, H. J. (1994c). Personality: Biological foundations. In P. A. Vernon (Ed.), *The neuropsychology of individual differences* (pp. 151–207). San Diego, CA: Academic Press

Eysenck, H. J. (1995). *Genius: The natural history of creativity.* Cambridge, England: Cambridge University Press.

Eysenck, H. J., & Coulter, T. (1972). The personality and attitudes of working class British Communists and Fascists. *Journal of Social Psychology, 87,* 59–73.

Eysenck, H. J., & Eysenck, S. B. G. (1964). *Manual of the Eysenck Personality Inventory.* London: University of London Press.

Eysenck, H. J., & Eysenck, S. B. G. (1968). *Manual for the Eysenck Personality Inventory.* San Diego, CA: Educational and Industrial Testing Service.

Eysenck, H. J., & Eysenck, S. B. G. (1969). *Personality structure and measurement.* San Diego: R. R. Knapp.

Eysenck, H. J., & Eysenck, S. B. G. (1975). *Manual of the Eysenck Personality Questionnaire (Junior and Adult).* London: Hodder & Stoughton.

Eysenck, H. J., & Eysenck, S. B. G. (1976). *Psychoticism as a dimension of personality.* London: Hodder & Stoughton.

Eysenck, H. J., & Eysenck, S. B. G. (1993). *The Eysenck Personality Questionnaire— Revised.* London: Hodder & Stoughton.

Eysenck, H. J., & Grossarth-Maticek, R. (1991). Creative novation behaviour therapy as a prophylactic treatment for cancer and coronary heart disease: Part II— Effects of treatment. *Behaviour Research Therapy, 29,* 17–31.

Eysenck, H. J., & Gudjonsson, G. (1989). *The causes and cures of criminality.* New York: Plenum Press.

Eysenck, H. J., & Nias, D. K. B. (1978). *Sex, violence and the media.* New York: Harper & Row.

Eysenck, H. J., Nias, D. K. B., & Cox, D. N. (1982). Sport and personality. *Advances in behavior research and therapy, 4,* 1–56.

Eysenck, H., & Wilson, G. D. (1976). *Know your own personality.* New York: Barnes and Noble Books.

Fakouri, M. E., & Hafner, J. L. (1984). Early recollections of first-borns. *Journal of Clinical Psychology, 40,* 209–213.

Fakouri, M. E., Hartung, J. R., & Hafner, J. L. (1985). Early recollections of neurotic depressive patients. *Psychological Reports, 57,* 783–786.

Federn, E. (1988). Psychoanalysis—The fate of a science in exile. In E. Timms & N. Segal (Eds.), *Freud in exile: Psychoanalysis and its vicissitudes* (pp. 156–162). New Haven, CT: Yale University Press.

Feist, G. J. (1993). A structural model of scientific eminence. *Psychological Science, 4,* 366–371.

Feist, G. J. (1994). Personality and working style predictors of integrative complexity: A study of scientists' thinking about research and teaching. *Journal of Personality and Social Psychology, 67,* 474–484.

Feist, G. J., & Gorman, M. E. (1996). *The psychology of science: Review and integration of a nascent discipline.* Manuscript submitted for publication.

Fern, T. L. (1991). Identifying the gifted child humorists. *Roeper Review, 14,* 30–34.

Ferster, C. B., & Skinner, B. F. (1957). *Schedules of reinforcement.* New York: Appleton-Century-Crofts.

Fischer, J. L. (1981). Transitions in relationship style from adolescence to young adulthood. *Journal of Youth and Adolescence, 10,* 11–23.

Fogarty, G. J. (1994). Using the Personal Orientation Inventory to measure change in student self-actualization. *Personality and Individual Differences, 17,* 435–439.

Fourqurean, J. M., Meisgeier, C., & Swank, P. (1990). The link between learning style and Jungian psychological type: A finding of two bipolar preference dimensions. *Journal of Experimental Education, 58,* 225–237.

Fransella, F., & Bannister, D. (1977). *A manual for repertory grid technique.* London: Academic Press.

Fransella, F., & Thomas, L. (Eds.). (1988).

Experimenting with personal construct psychology. New York: Routledge & Kegan Paul.

Freud, A. (1946). The ego and the mechanisms of defense. New York: International Universities Press.

Freud, S. (1896/1962). The aetiology of hysteria. In J. Strachey (Ed. and Trans.), The standard edition of the complete psychological works of Sigmund Freud (Vol. 3). London: Hogarth Press.

Freud, S. (1900/1953). The interpretation of dreams. In Standard edition (Vols. 4 & 5).

Freud, S. (1901/1953). On dreams. In Standard edition (Vol. 5).

Freud, S. (1901/1960). Psychopathology of everyday life. In Standard edition (Vol. 6).

Freud, S. (1905/1953a). Fragment of an analysis of a case of hysteria. In Standard edition (Vol. 7).

Freud, S. (1905/1953b). On psychotherapy. In Standard edition (Vol. 7).

Freud, S. (1905/1953c). Three essays on the theory of sexuality. In Standard edition (Vol. 7).

Freud, S. (1905/1960). Jokes and their relation to the unconscious. In Standard edition (Vol. 8).

Freud, S. (1910/1957). Leonardo da Vinci and a memory of his childhood. In Standard edition (Vol. 11).

Freud, S. (1911/1958). Formulations on the two principles of mental functioning. In Standard edition (Vol. 12).

Freud, S. (1913/1953). Totem and taboo. In Standard edition (Vol. 13).

Freud, S. (1914/1953). The Moses of Michelangelo. In Standard edition (Vol. 13).

Freud, S. (1914/1957). On narcissism: An introduction. In Standard edition (Vol. 14).

Freud, S. (1915/1957a). Instincts and their vicissitudes. In Standard edition (Vol. 14).

Freud, S. (1915/1957b). The unconscious. In Standard edition (Vol. 14).

Freud, S. (1917/1955a). A difficulty in the path of psycho-analysis. In Standard edition (Vol. 17).

Freud, S. (1917/1955b). On transformations of instinct as exemplified in anal erotism. In Standard edition (Vol. 17).

Freud, S. (1917/1963). Introductory lectures on psychoanalysis. In Standard edition (Vols. 15 & 16).

Freud, S. (1920/1955a). Beyond the pleasure principle. In Standard edition (Vol. 18).

Freud, S (1920/1955b). The psychogenesis of a case of homosexuality in a woman. In Standard edition (Vol. 18).

Freud, S. (1922/1955). Some neurotic mechanisms in jealousy, paranoia and homosexuality. In Standard edition (Vol. 18).

Freud, S. (1923/1961a). The ego and the id. In Standard edition (Vol. 19).

Freud, S. (1923/1961b). The infantile genital organization: An interpolation into the theory of sexuality. In Standard edition (Vol. 19).

Freud, S. (1924/1961). The dissolution of the Oedipus complex. In Standard edition (Vol. 19).

Freud, S. (1925/1959). An autobiographical study. In Standard edition (Vol. 20).

Freud, S. (1925/1961). Some psychical consequences of the anatomical distinction between the sexes. In Standard edition (Vol. 19).

Freud, S. (1926/1959a). Inhibitions, symptoms and anxiety. In Standard edition (Vol. 20).

Freud, S. (1926/1959b). The question of lay analysis. In Standard edition (Vol. 20).

Freud, S. (1931/1961). Female sexuality. In Standard edition (Vol. 21).

Freud, S. (1933/1964). New introductory lectures on psychoanalysis. In Standard edition (Vol. 22).

Freud, S. (1950/1966). Project for a scientific psychology. In Standard edition (Vol. 1).

Freud, S. (1960). Letters of Sigmund Freud (E. L. Freud, Ed.; T. Stern & J. Stern, Trans.). New York: Basic Books.

Freud, S. (1985). The complete letters of Sigmund Freud to Wilhelm Fleiss, 1887–1904 (J. M. Masson, Ed. and Trans.). Cambridge, MA: Harvard University Press.

Freud, S., & Bullitt, W. C. (1967). Thomas Woodrow Wilson: A psychological study. Boston: Houghton Mifflin.

Frick, W. B. (1971). *Humanistic psychology: Interviews with Maslow, Murphy, and Rogers*. Columbus, OH: Merrill.

Frick, W. B. (1982). Conceptual foundations of self-actualization: A contribution to motivation theory. *Journal of Humanistic Psychology, 22*, 33–52.

Friedrich-Cofer, L., & Huston, A. C. (1986). Television violence and aggression: The debate continues. *Psychological Bulletin, 100*, 364–371.

Frois, J. P., & Eysenck, H. J. (1995). The Visual Aesthetic Sensitivity Test applied to Portuguese children and fine arts students. *Creativity Research Journal, 8*, 277–284.

Fromm, E. (1941). *Escape from freedom*. New York: Holt, Rinehart and Winston.

Fromm, E. (1947). *Man for himself: An inquiry into the psychology of ethics*. New York: Holt, Rinehart and Winston.

Fromm, E. (1950). *Psychoanalysis and religion*. New Haven, CT: Yale University Press.

Fromm, E. (1951). *The forgotten language: An introduction to the understanding of dreams, fairy tales and myths*. New York: Rinehart.

Fromm, E. (1955). *The sane society*. New York: Holt, Rinehart and Winston.

Fromm, E. (1956). *The art of loving*. New York: Harper & Brothers.

Fromm, E. (1959). *Sigmund Freud's mission*. New York: Harper & Brothers.

Fromm, E. (1961). *Marx's concept of man*. New York: Ungar.

Fromm, E. (1962). *Beyond the chains of illusion*. New York: Simon and Schuster.

Fromm, E. (1963). *The dogma of Christ and other essays on religion, psychology, and culture*. New York: Holt, Rinehart and Winston.

Fromm, E. (1964). *The heart of man*. New York: Harper & Row.

Fromm, E. (1973). *The anatomy of human destructiveness*. New York: Holt, Rinehart and Winston.

Fromm, E. (1976). *To have or be*. New York: Harper & Row.

Fromm, E. (1981). *On disobedience and other essays*. New York: Seabury Press.

Fromm, E. (1986). *For the love of life* (H. J. Schultz, Ed.; Robert Kimber & Rita Kimber, Trans.). New York: Free Press. (Original works published 1972, 1974, 1975, 1983)

Fromm, E. (1992). *The revision of psychoanalysis*. Boulder, CO: Westview Press.

Fromm, E. (1994a). *The art of listening*. New York: Continuum.

Fromm, E. (1994b). *On being human*. New York: Continuum.

Fromm, E., & Maccoby, M. (1970). *Social character in a Mexican village*. Englewood Cliffs, NJ: Prentice-Hall.

Garner, D. M., Olmstead, M. P., & Polivy, J. (1983). Development and validation of a multidimensional eating disorder inventory for anorexia nervosa and bulimia. *International Journal of Eating Disorder, 2*, 15–34.

Garry, M., Loftus, E. F., & Brown, S. W. (1994). Memory: A river runs through it. *Consciousness and Cognition, 3*, 438–451.

Gay, P. (1988). *Freud: A life for our time*. New York: Norton.

Gendlin, E. T. (1988). Carl Rogers (1902–1987). *American Psychologist, 43*, 127–128.

Genia, V. (1993). A psychometric evaluation of the Allport-Ross I/E Scales in a religiously heterogeneous sample. *Journal for the Scientific Study of Religion, 32*, 284–290.

Gholson, B., Shadish, W. R., Neimeyer, R. A., & Houts, A. C. (Eds.) (1989). *The psychology of science: Contributions to metascience*. Cambridge, England: Cambridge University Press.

Gibson, H. B. (1981). *Hans Eysenck: The man and his work*. London: Peter Owen.

Goble, F. G. (1970). *The third force: The psychology of Abraham Maslow*. New York: Grossman.

Gold, J. M., & Rogers, J. D. (1995). Intimacy and isolation: A validation study of Erikson's theory. *Journal of*

Humanistic Psychology, 35(1), 78–86.

Goldberg, L. R. (1990). An alternative "description of personality": The Big-Five factor structure. *Journal of Personality and Social Psychology, 59,* 1216–1229.

Goldberg, L. R. (1993). The structure of phenotypic personality traits. *American Psychologist, 48,* 26–34.

Goldwert, M. (1992). *The wounded healers: Creative illness in the pioneers of depth psychology.* Lantham, MD: University Press of America.

Gorsuch, R. L. (1988). Psychology of religion. *Annual Review of Psychology, 39,* 201–221.

Gough, H. G., & Heilbrun, A. B. (1980). *Adjective Check List manual.* Palo Alto, CA: Consulting Psychologists Press.

Greenberg, J., Pyszczynski, T., Solomon, S., Simon, L., & Breus, M. (1994). Role of consciousness and accessibility of death-related thoughts in mortality salience effects. *Journal of Personality and Social Psychology, 67,* 627–637.

Greenberg, J., Simon, L., Pyszczynski, T., Solomon, S., & Chatel, D. (1992). Terror management and tolerance: Does mortality salience always intensify negative reactions to others who threaten one's worldview? *Journal of Personality and Social Psychology, 63,* 212–220.

Greever, K. B., Tseng, M. S., & Friedland, B. U. (1973). Development of the social interest index. *Journal of Consulting and Clinical Psychology, 41,* 454–458.

Grossarth-Maticek, R., Eysenck, H. J., & Vetter, H. (1988). Personality type, smoking habit and their interaction as predictors of cancer and coronary heart disease. *Personality and Individual Differences, 9,* 479–495.

Grosskurth, P. (1986). *Melanie Klein: Her world and her work.* New York: Knopf.

Gupta, B. S., & Gupta, U. (1984). Dextroamphetamine and individual susceptibility to reinforcement in verbal operant conditioning. *British Journal of Psychology, 75,* 201–206.

Gupta, S., & Shukla, A. P. (1989). Verbal operant conditioning as a function of extraversion and reinforcement. *British Journal of Psychology, 80,* 39–44.

Gupta, U. (1984). Phenobarbitone and the relationship between extraversion and reinforcement in verbal operant conditioning. *British Journal of Psychology, 75,* 499–506.

Haaken, J. (1995). Viewpoint: The debate over recovered memory of sexual abuse: A feminist-psychoanalytic perspective. *Psychiatry, 58,* 189–198.

Hafner, J. L., & Fakouri, M. E. (1984). Early recollections of individuals preparing for careers in clinical psychology, dentistry, and law. *Journal of Vocational Behavior, 24,* 236–241.

Hafner, J. L., Fakouri, M. E., & Chesney, S. M. (1988). Early recollections of alcoholic women. *Journal of Clinical Psychology, 44,* 302–306.

Hall, E. (1983, June). A conversation with Erik Erikson. *Psychology Today,* pp. 22–30.

Hall, M. H. (1967, September). An interview with "Mr. Humanist": Rollo May. *Psychology Today,* pp. 25–29, 72–73.

Hall, M. H. (1968, July). A conversation with Abraham Maslow. *Psychology Today,* pp. 35–37, 54–57.

Hammond, W. A., & Romney, D. M. (1995). Cognitive factors contributing to adolescent depression. *Journal of Youth and Adolescence, 24,* 667–683.

Hampes, W. P. (1993). Relation between humor and generativity. *Psychological Reports, 73,* 131–136.

Hansen, D. E., Vandenberg, B., & Patterson, M. L. (1995). The effects of religious orientation on spontaneous and nonspontaneous helping behaviors. *Personality and Individual Differences, 19,* 101–104.

Harris, A. S. (1996). *Living with paradox: An introduction to Jungian psychology*. Pacific Grove, CA: Brooks/Cole.

Harris, T. G. (1969, August). The devil and Rollo May. *Psychology Today*, pp. 13–16.

Harrist, R. S., Quintana, S. M., Strupp, H. H., & Henry, W. P. (1994). Internalization of interpersonal process in time-limited dynamic psychotherapy. *Psychotherapy*, 31, 49–57.

Hart, J. J. (1982). Psychology of the scientists: XLVI: Correlation between theoretical orientation in psychology and personality type. *Psychological Reports*, 50, 795–801.

Harter, S., & Chao, C. (1992). The role of competence in children's creation of imaginary friends. *Merrill-Palmer Quarterly*, 38, 350–363.

Hartshorne, H., & May, M. A. (1928). *Studies in the nature of character: Vol. 1. Studies in deceit*. New York: Macmillan.

Hathaway, S. R., & McKinley, J. C. (1951). *The Minnesota Multiphasic Personality Inventory Manual* (Revised). New York: Psychological Corp.

Hattie, J., & Cooksey, R. W. (1984). Procedures for assessing the validities of tests using the "known-groups" method. *Applied Psychological Measurement*, 8, 295–305.

Hausdorff, D. (1972). *Erich Fromm*. New York: Twayne.

Havens, L. (1987). *Approaches to the mind: Movement of psychiatric schools from sects toward science*. Cambridge, MA: Harvard University Press.

Haynes, S. G., Feinleib, M., & Kannel, W. B. (1980). The relationship of psychosocial factors to coronary heart disease in the Framingham study: III. Eight-year incidence of coronary heart disease. *American Journal of Epidemiology*, 111, 37–58.

Hazan, C., & Shaver, P. R. (1987). Romantic love conceptualized as an attachment process. *Journal of Personality and Social Psychology*, 52, 511–524.

Heesacker, R. S., & Neimeyer, G. J. (1990). Assessing object relations and social cognitive correlates of eating disorders. *Journal of Counseling Psychology*, 37, 419–426.

Henry, W. P., Schacht, T. E., & Strupp, H. H. (1990). Patient and therapist introject, interpersonal process, and differential psychotherapy outcome. *Journal of Consulting and Clinical Psychology*, 58, 768–774.

Heppner, P. L., Rogers, M. E., & Lee, L. A. (1984). Carl Rogers: Reflections on his life. *Journal of Counseling and Development*, 63, 14–20.

Higgins, S. T., Budney, A. J., Bickel, W. K., Badger, G. J., Foerg, F. E., & Ogden, D. (1995). Outpatient behavioral treatment for cocaine dependence: One-year outcome. *Experimental and Clinical Psychopharmacology*, 3, 205–212.

Higgins, S. T., Delaney, D. D., Budney, A. J., Bickel, W. K., Hughes, J. R., Foerg, F., & Fenwick, J. W. (1991). A behavioral approach to achieving initial cocaine abstinence. *American Journal of Psychiatry*, 148, 1218–1224.

Hillman, J. (1985). *Anima: An anatomy of a personified notion*. Dallas, TX: Spring.

Hinshelwood, R. D. (1994). *Clinical Klein: From theory to practice*. New York: Basic Books.

Hoffman, E. (1994). *The drive for self: Alfred Adler and the founding of Individual Psychology*. Reading, MA: Addison-Wesley.

Hoffman, E. (1988). *The right to be human: A biography of Abraham Maslow*. Los Angeles: Tarcher.

Hofstee, W. K. B., de Raad, B., & Goldberg, L. R. (1992). Integration of the Big Five and circumplex approaches to trait structure. *Journal of Personality and Social Psychology*, 61, 146–163.

Holder, A. (1988). Reservations about the Standard Edition. In E. Timms & N. Segal (Eds.), *Freud in exile:*

Psychoanalysis and its vicissitudes (pp. 210–214). New Haven, CT: Yale University Press.

Holland, R. (1970). George Kelly: Constructive innocent and reluctant existentialist. In D. Bannister (Ed.), *Perspectives in personal construct theory*. London: Academic Press.

Holt, R. R. (1989). *Freud reappraised: A fresh look at psychoanalytic theory*. New York: Guilford Press.

Homans, P. (1995). *Jung in context: Modernity and the making of a psychology*. Chicago: University of Chicago Press.

Hood, R. W., Jr. (1970). Religious orientations and the report of religious experiences. *Journal for the Scientific Study of Religion*, 9, 285–291.

Horney, K. (1917/1968). The technique of psychoanalytic therapy. *American Journal of Psychoanalysis*, 28, 3–12.

Horney, K. (1937). *The neurotic personality of our time*. New York: Norton.

Horney, K. (1939). *New ways in psychoanalysis*. New York: Norton.

Horney, K. (1942). *Self-analysis*. New York: Norton.

Horney, K. (1945). *Our inner conflicts: A constructive theory of neurosis*. New York: Norton.

Horney, K. (1950). *Neurosis and human growth: The struggle toward self-realization*. New York: Norton.

Horney, K. (1967). The flight from womanhood: The masculinity-complex in women as viewed by men and women. In H. Kelman (Ed.), *Feminine psychology* (pp. 54–70). New York: Norton.

Horney, K. (1987). *Final lectures* (D. H. Ingram, Ed.). New York: Norton.

Horney, K. (1994). Woman's fear of action. In B. J. Paris, *Karen Horney: A psychoanalyst's search for self-understanding* (pp. 233–238). New Haven, CT: Yale University Press.

Howard, G. S. (1994). Some varieties of free will worth practicing. *Journal of Theoretical and Philosophical Psychology*, 14, 50–61.

Howard, G. S., & Conway, C. G. (1986). Can there be an empirical science of volitional action? *American Psychologist*, 41, 1241–1251.

Howard, G. S., Curtin, T. D., & Johnson, A. J. (1991). Point estimation techniques in psychological research: Studies on the role of meaning in self-determined action. *Journal of Counseling Psychology*, 38, 219–226.

Howard, G. S., & Myers, P. R. (1990). Predicting human behavior: Comparing ideographic, nomothetic, and agentic methodologies. *Journal of Counseling Psychology*, 37, 227–233.

Huesmann, L. R., & Miller, L. S. (1994). Long-term effects of repeated exposure to media violence in childhood. In L. R. Huesmann (Ed.), *Aggressive behavior: Current perspectives*. Plenum series in social/clinical psychology (pp. 153–186). New York: Plenum Press.

Hughes, J. M. (1989). *Reshaping the psychoanalytic domain: The work of Melanie Klein, W. R. D. Fairbairn, and D. W. Winnicott*. Berkeley, CA: University of California Press.

Ikpaahindi, L. (1987). The relationship between the needs for achievement, affiliation, power, and scientific productivity among Nigerian veterinary surgeons. *The Journal of Social Psychology*, 127, 535–537.

Irigaray, L. (1986). This sex which is not one. In H. Cixous & C. Clement (Eds.), *The newly born woman*. Minneapolis: University of Minnesota Press.

Isbister, J. N. (1985). *Freud: An introduction to his life and work*. Cambridge, England: Polity Press.

Jacobs, M. (1992). *Sigmund Freud*, London: Sage.

James, F. R., & Large, R. G. (1992). Chronic pain, relationships and illness self-construct. *Pain*, 50, 263–271.

James, W. H. (1957). *Internal versus external control of reinforcement as a basic variable in learning theory*. Unpublished doctoral dissertation, Ohio State University.

Janeway, E. (1971). *Man's world, woman's place*. New York: Morrow.

Jih, C.-S., Sirgo, V. I., & Thomure, J. C. (1995). Alcohol consumption, locus of control, and self-esteem of high school and college students. *Psychological Reports*, 76, 851–857.

John, O. P. (1990). The "Big Five" factor taxonomy: Dimensions of personality in the natural language and in questionnaires. In L. A. Pervin (Ed.), *Handbook of personality: Theory and research* (pp. 66–100). New York: Guilford Press.

John, O. P., Goldberg, L. R., & Angleitner, A. (1984). Better than the alphabet: Taxonomies of personality-descriptive terms in English, Dutch, and German. In H. Bonarius, G. van Heck, & N. Smid (Eds.), *Personality psychology in Europe: Theoretical and empirical developments* (pp. 83–100). Berwyn, PA: Swets North America.

Johnson, J. A., Germer, C. K., Efran, J. S., & Overton, W. F. (1988). Personality as the basis for theoretical predilections. *Journal of Personality and Social Psychology*, 55, 824–835.

Jones, A., & Crandall, R. (1986). Validation of a Short Index of Self-Actualization. *Personality and Social Psychology Bulletin*, 12, 63–73.

Jones, E. (1953, 1955, 1957). *The life and work of Sigmund Freud* (Vols. 1–3). New York: Basic Books.

Jorgensen, J. A., & Newlon, B. J. (1988). Life-style themes of unwed, pregnant adolescents who chose to keep their babies. *Individual Psychology*, 44, 466–471.

Jung, C. G. (1916/1953). The structure of the unconscious. In H. Read, M. Fordham, & G. Adler (Eds.) (R. F. C. Hull, Trans.), *The collected works of C. G. Jung* (Vol. 7). New York: Pantheon Books.

Jung, C. G. (1916/1960). General aspects of dream psychology. In *Collected works* (Vol. 8).

Jung, C. G. (1921/1971). Psychological types. In *Collected works* (Vol. 6).

Jung, C. G. (1928/1960). On psychic energy. In *Collected works* (Vol. 8).

Jung, C. G. (1931/1954). Problems of modern psychotherapy. In *Collected works* (Vol. 16).

Jung, C. G. (1931/1960a). The stages of life. In *Collected works* (Vol. 8).

Jung, C. G. (1931/1960b). *The structure of the psyche*. In *Collected works* (Vol. 8).

Jung, C. G. (1934/1954a). The development of personality. In *Collected works* (Vol. 17).

Jung, C. G. (1934/1954b). The practical use of dream-analysis. In *Collected works* (Vol. 16).

Jung, C. G. (1934/1960). The soul and death. In *Collected works* (Vol. 8).

Jung, C. G. (1935/1968). The Tavistock lectures. In *Collected works* (Vol. 18).

Jung, C. G. (1937/1959). The concept of the collective unconscious. In *Collected works* (Vol. 9, Pt. 1).

Jung, C. G. (1939/1959). Conscious, unconscious, and individuation. In *Collected works* (Vol. 9, Pt. 1).

Jung, C. G. (1943/1953). *The psychology of the unconscious*. In *Collected works* (Vol. 7).

Jung, C. G. (1945/1953). *The relations between ego and the unconscious*. In *Collected works* (Vol. 7).

Jung, C. G. (1948/1960a). Instinct and the unconscious. In *Collected works* (Vol. 8).

Jung, C. G. (1948/1960b). On the nature of dreams. In *Collected works* (Vol. 8).

Jung, C. G. (1950/1959). Concerning rebirth. In *Collected works* (Vol. 9, Pt. 1).

Jung, C. G. (1951/1959a). Aion: *Researches into the phenomenology of the self*. In *Collected works* (Vol. 9, Pt. 2).

Jung, C. G. (1951/1959b). The psychology of the child archetype. In *Collected works* (Vol 9, Pt. 1).

Jung, C. G. (1952/1956). *Symbols of transformation*. In *Collected works* (Vol. 5).

Jung, C. G. (1952/1968). *Psychology and alchemy* (2nd ed.). In *Collected works* (Vol. 12).

Jung, C. G. (1954/1959a). *Archetypes and the collective unconscious*. In *Collected works* (Vol. 9, Pt. 1).

Jung, C. G. (1954/1959b). Concerning the archetypes, with special reference to the anima concept. In *Collected works* (Vol. 9, Pt. 1).

Jung, C. G. (1954/1959c). Psychological aspects of the mother archetype. In *Collected works* (Vol. 9, Pt. 1).

Jung, C. G. (1961). *Memories, dreams, reflections*. (A. Jaffé, Ed.). New York: Random House.

Jung, C. G. (1964). *Man and his symbols*. Garden City, NY: Doubleday.

Jung, C. G. (1976). *Letters: II. 1951–1961* (G. Adler & A. Jaffé, Eds.) (R. F. C. Hull, Trans.). Princeton, NJ: Princeton University Press.

Jung, C. G. (1979). *Word and image* (A. Jaffé, Ed.). Princeton, NJ: Princeton University Press.

Jung, C. G., & Riklin, F. (1904/1973). The associations of normal subjects. In *Collected works* (Vol. 2).

Kaczor, L. M., Ryckman, R. M., Thornton, B., & Kuehnel, R. H. (1991). Observer hypercompetitiveness and victim participation of rape. *Journal of Social Psychology*, 131, 131–134.

Keene, K. K., & Wheeler, M. S. (1994). Substance use in college freshmen and Adlerian life-style themes. *Individual Psychology*, 50, 97–109.

Kelley, C. R., & Kelley, E. C. (1994). *Now I remember: Recovered memories of sexual abuse*. Vancouver, WA: K/R Publications.

Kelly, G. A. (1955). *The psychology of personal constructs* (Vols. 1 and 2). New York: Norton.

Kelly, G. A. (1963). *A theory of personality: The psychology of personal constructs*. New York: Norton.

Kelly, G. A. (1969a). The autobiography of a theory. In B. Maher (Ed.), *Clinical psychology and personality: The selected papers of George Kelly* (pp. 46–65). New York: Wiley.

Kelly, G. A. (1969b). Man's construction of his alternatives. In B. Maher (Ed.), *Clinical psychology and personality: The selected papers of George Kelly* (pp. 66–93). New York: Wiley.

Kelly, G. A. (1970). A brief introduction to personal construct theory. In D. Bannister (Ed.), *Perspectives in personal construct theory*. London: Academic Press. Also in J. C. Mancuso (Ed.), *Readings for a cognitive theory of personality*. New York: Holt, Rinehart and Winston.

Kelly, G. A. (1980). A psychology of the optimal man. In A. W. Landfield & L. M. Leitner (Eds.), *Personal construct psychology: Psychotherapy and personality*. New York: Wiley.

Kemp, A. (1981). The personality structure of the musician: I. Identifying a profile of traits for the performer. *Psychology of Music*, 9, 3–14.

Kernberg, O. F. (1975). *Borderline conditions and pathological narcissism*. New York: Aronson.

Kernberg, O. F. (1976). *Object-relations theory and clinical psychoanalysis*. New York: Aronson.

Kernberg, O. F. (1984). *Severe personality disorders: Psychotherapeutic strategies*. New Haven, CT: Yale University Press.

Kernberg, O. F. (1986). Structural derivatives of object relationships. In P. Buckley (Ed.), *Essential papers on object relations* (pp. 350–384). New York: New York University Press.

Kernberg, O. F. (1993). Projection and projective identification: Developmental and clinical aspects. In G. H. Pollock (Ed.), *Pivotal papers on identification* (pp. 405–425). Madison, CT: International Universities Press.

Kernberg, O. F. (1995). *Love relations: Normality and pathology*. New Haven, CT: Yale University Press.

Kerr, J. (1993). *A most dangerous method: The story of Jung, Freud, and Sabina Spielrein*. New York: Knopf.

Keys, A., Brozek, J., Henschel, A., Mickelsen, O., & Taylor, H. L. (1950). *The biology of human starvation* (Vols. 1 and 2).

Minneapolis: *University of Minnesota Press.*

King, P. (1991). Conclusions. In P. King & R. Steiner (Eds.), *The Freud-Klein controversies 1941–1945* (pp. 920–931). London: Tavistock/Routledge.

King, P., & Steiner, R. (Eds.). (1991). *The Freud-Klein controversies 1941–1945.* London: Tavistock/Routledge.

Kinsey, A. C., Pomeroy, W., & Martin, C. (1948). *Sexual behavior in the human male.* Philadelphia: Saunders.

Kirkpatrick, L. A. (1989). A psychometric analysis of the Allport-Ross and Feagin measures of intrinsic-extrinsic religious orientation. In M. L. Lynn & D. O. Moberg (Eds.), *Research in the social scientific study of religion: A research annual* (Vol. 1, pp.1–31). Greenwich, CT: JAI Press.

Kirkpatrick, L. A., & Hood, R. W. Jr. (1990). Intrinsic-extrinsic religious orientation: The boon or bane of contemporary psychology of religion? *Journal for the Scientific Study of Religion, 29,* 442–462.

Kirsch, I. (1982). Efficacy expectation or response predictions: The meaning of efficacy ratings as a function of task characteristics. *Journal of Personality and Social Psychology, 42,* 132–136.

Kirsch, I. (1985). Self-efficacy and expectancy: Old wine with new labels. *Journal of Personality and Social Psychology, 49,* 824–830.

Kirsch, I. (1986). Early research on self-efficacy: What we already know without knowing we know. Special Issue: Self-efficacy theory in contemporary psychology. *Journal of Social and Clinical Psychology, 4,* 339–358.

Kirsch, I. (1995). Self-efficacy and outcome expectancies: A concluding commentary. In J. E. Maddux (Ed.), *Self-efficacy, adaptation, and adjustment: Theory research and application* (pp. 331–345). New York: Plenum.

Kirschenbaum, H. (1979). *On becoming Carl Rogers.* New York: Delacorte Press.

Kirschenbaum, H., & Henderson, V. L. (Eds.). (1989). *The Carl Rogers reader.* Boston: Houghton Mifflin.

Klein, M. (1930). The importance of symbol-formation in the development of the ego. In M. Klein (1964). *Contributions to psycho-analysis, 1921–1945* (pp. 236–250). New York: McGraw-Hill.

Klein, M. (1932). *The Psycho-analysis of children.* London: Hogarth Press.

Klein, M. (1933). The early development of conscience in the child. In M. Klein (1964). *Contributions to psycho-analysis, 1921–1945* (pp. 267–277). New York: McGraw-Hill.

Klein, M. (1935). A contribution to the psychogenesis of manic-depressive states. In J. Mitchell (Ed.). (1986) *The selected Melanie Klein* (pp. 166–145). New York: Free Press.

Klein, M. (1943). Memorandum on her technique by Melanie Klein. In P. King & R. Steiner (Eds.). (1991). *The Freud-Klein controversies 1941–45* (pp. 635–638). London: Tavistock/Routledge.

Klein, M. (1945). The Oedipus complex in the light of early anxieties. In M. Klein (1984). *Love, guilt and reparation and other works, 1921–1945* (pp. 370–419). New York: Macmillan.

Klein, M. (1946). Notes on some schizoid mechanism. In M. Klein (1975). *Envy and gratitude and other works, 1946–1963* (pp. 1–24). New York: Delta Books.

Klein, M. (1948). *Contributions to psycho-analysis, 1921–45.* London: Hogarth.

Klein, M. (1952). *Envy and gratitude.* London: Tavistock.

Klein, M. (1955). The psycho-analytic play technique: Its history and significance. In J. Mitchell (Ed.). (1986). *The selected Melanie Klein* (pp. 35–54). New York: Free Press.

Klein, M. (1959). Our adult world and its roots in infancy. In M. Klein

(1984). *Envy and gratitude and other works, 1946–1963* (pp. 247–263). New York: Macmillan.

Klein, M. (1991). The emotional life and ego-development of the infant with special reference to the depressive position. In P. King & R. Steiner (Eds.), *The Freud-Klein controversies 1941–45* (pp. 752–577). London: Tavistock/Routledge.

Kline, P. (1984). *Psychology and Freudian theory: An introduction*. London: Methuen.

Kline, P., & Lapham, S. L. (1992). Personality and faculty in British universities. *Personality and Individual Differences, 13*, 855–857.

Knapp, G. P. (1989). *The art of living: Erich Fromm's life and works*. New York: Peter Lang.

Knapp, R. A. (1976). *Handbook for the Personal Orientation Inventory*. San Diego, CA: Educational and Industrial Testing Service.

Kobak, R. R., & Hazan, C. (1991). Attachment in marriage: Effects of security and accuracy of working models. *Journal of Personality and Social Psychology, 60*, 861–869.

Kohut, H. (1971). *The analysis of the self: A systematic approach to the treatment of narcissistic personality disorders*. New York: International Universities Press.

Kohut, H. (1977). *The restoration of the self*. New York: International Universities Press.

Kohut, H. (1987). *The Kohut Seminars on self psychology and psychotherapy with adolescents and young adults* (M. Elson, Ed.). New York: Norton.

Koski-Jannes, A. (1994). Drinking-related locus of control as a predictor of drinking after treatment. *Addictive Behaviors, 19*, 491–495.

Kothera, L., Fudin, R., & Nicastro, R. (1990). Effects of subliminal psychodynamic activation on dart-throwing performance: Another non-replication. *Perceptual and Motor Skills, 71*, 1015–1022.

Kramer, R. (1995). The birth of client-centered therapy: Carl Rogers, Otto Rank, and "the beyond". *Journal of Humanistic Psychology, 35*, 54–110.

Krausz, E. O. (1994). Freud's devaluation of women. *Individual Psychology: Journal of Adlerian Theory, Research and Practice, 50*, 298–313.

Krug, S. (1994). Personality: A Cattellian perspective. In S. Strack & M. Lorr (Eds.), *Differentiating normal and abnormal personality* (pp. 65–78). New York: Springer.

Kunzendorf, R. G., Jesses, M., Dupille, L., & Butler, W. (1991). Subliminal activation of intrapsychic conflicts: Subconscious realms of mind vs. subconscious processes of mentation. *Imagination, Cognition, and Personality, 10*, 117–128.

Kurzweil, E. (1989). *The Freudians: A comparative perspective*. New Haven, CT: Yale University Press.

Landfield, A. W. (1971). *Personal construct systems in psychotherapy*. Chicago: Rand-McNally.

Landfield, A. W., & Epting, F. R. (1987). *Personal construct psychology: Clinical and personality assessment*. New York: Human Sciences Press.

Landfield, A. W., & Leitner, L. M. (Eds.). (1980). *Personal construct psychology: Psychotherapy and personality*. New York: Wiley.

Landfield, A. W., Stefan, R., & Dempsey, D. (1990). Single and multiple self implications for change grids: Studies of consistency. *International Journal of Personal Construct Psychology, 3*, 423–436.

Landis, B., & Tauber, E. S. (1971). Erich Fromm: Some biographical notes. In B. Landis & E. S. Tauber (Eds.), *In the name of life: Essays in honor of Erich Fromm*. New York: Holt, Rinehart and Winston.

Laser, E. D. (1984). The relationship between obesity, early recollections, and adult life-style. *Individual Psychology, 40*, 29–35.

Last, J. M. (1983). *Comprehensive early memory scoring system manual.* Unpublished manuscript.

Last, J. M., & Bruhn, A. R. (1983). The psychodiagnostic value of children's early memories. *Journal of Personality Assessment, 47,* 597–603.

Lazarick, D. L., Fishbein, S. S., Loiello, M. A., & Howard, G. S. (1988). Practical investigations of volition. *Journal of Counseling Psychology, 35,* 15–26.

Leak, G. K., & Fish, S. (1989). Religious orientation, impression management, and self-deception: Toward a clarification of the link between religiosity and social desirability. *Journal for the Scientific Study of Religion, 28,* 355–359.

Lerman, H. (1986). A *mote in Freud's eye: From psychoanalysis to the psychology of women.* New York: Springer.

Levenson, H. (1973). Multidimensional locus of control in psychiatric patients. *Journal of Consulting and Clinical Psychology, 41,* 397–404.

Levenson, H. (1974). Activism and powerful others: Distinction within the concept of internal-external control. *Journal of Personality Assessment, 38,* 377–383.

Levenson, H. (1981). Differentiating among internality, powerful others, and chance. In H. M. Lefcourt (Ed.), *Research with the locus of control construct: Vol. 1. Assessment methods* (pp. 15–63). New York: Academic Press.

Levy, N., & Ridley, S. E. (1987). Stability of Jungian personality types within a college population over a decade. *Psychological Reports, 60,* 419–422.

Loftus, E. F. (1993). The reality of repressed memories. *American Psychologist, 48,* 518–537.

Loftus, E. F. (1994). The repressed memory controversy. *American Psychologist, 49,* 443–445.

Loftus, E. F., & Ketcham, K. (1994). *The myth of repressed memory: False memories and allegations of sexual abuse.* New York: St. Martin's Press.

Loftus, E. F., Polonsky, S., & Fullilove, M. T. (1994). Memories of childhood sexual abuse: Remembering and repressing. *Psychology of Women Quarterly, 18,* 67–84.

Lonky, E., Kaus, C. R., & Roodin, P. A. (1984). Life experience and mode of coping: Relation to moral judgment in adulthood. *Developmental Psychology, 20,* 1159–1167.

Lyon, D., & Greenberg, J. (1991). Evidence of codependency in women with an alcoholic parent: Helping out Mr. Wrong. *Journal of Personality and Social Psychology, 61,* 435–439.

Maccoby, M. (1972). Emotional attitudes and political choices. *Politics and Society, 2,* 209–241.

Macmillan, M. (1991). *Freud evaluated: The completed arc.* Amsterdam: Elsevier.

Mahler, M. S. (1952). On child psychosis and schizophrenia: Autistic and symbiotic infantile psychoses. *Psychoanalytic Study of the Child, 7,* 286–305.

Mahler, M. S. (1967). On human symbiosis and the vicissitudes of individuation. *Journal of the American Psychoanalytic Association, 15,* 740–762.

Mahler, M. S. (1972). On the first three subphases of the separation-individuation process. *International Journal of Psycho-Analysis, 53,* 333–338.

Mahler, M. S., Pine, F., & Bergman, A. (1975). *The psychological birth of the human infant.* New York: Basic Books.

Manaster, G. J., & Perryman, T. B. (1974). Early recollections and occupational-choice. *Journal of Individual Psychology, 30,* 232–237.

Manaster, G. J., & Perryman, T. B. (1979). Manaster-Perryman manifest content early recollection scoring manual. In H. Olson (Ed.), *Early recollections: Their use in diagnosis and psychotherapy* (pp. 347–350). Springfield, IL: Charles C. Thomas.

Manosevitz, M., Fling, S., & Prentice, N. M. (1977). Imaginary companions in young children: Relationships with intelligence, creativity and waiting ability. *Journal of Child Psychology and Psychiatry and Applied Disciplines, 18,* 73–78.

Mansager, E., Barnes, M., Boyce, B., Brewster, J. D., Lertora, H. J., III, Marais, F., Santos, J., & Thompson, D. (1995). Interactive discussion of early recollections: A group technique with adolescent substance abusers. *Individual Psychology, 51,* 413–421.

Marchant-Haycox, S. E., & Wilson, G. D. (1992). Personality and stress in performing artists. *Personality and Individual Differences, 13,* 1061–1068.

Marcia, J. E. (1966). Development and validation of ego-identity status. *Journal of Personality and Social Psychology, 3,* 551–558.

Marcia, J. E. (1976). Identity six years after: A follow-up study. *Journal of Youth and Adolescence, 5,* 145–160.

Marcia, J. E. (1980). Identity in adolescence. In J. Adelson (Ed.), *Handbook of adolescent psychology* (pp. 159–187). New York: Wiley.

Marcia, J. E. (1987). The identity status approach to the study of ego identity development. In T. Honess & K. Yardley (Eds.), *Self and identity:*
Perspectives across the lifespan (pp. 161–171). Boston: Routledge & Kegan Paul.

Marcia, J. E. (1994). The empirical study of ego identity. In H. A. Bosma, T. L. G. Graafsma, H. D. Grotevant, & D. J. de Levita (Eds.), *Identity and development: An interdisciplinary approach* (pp. 67–80). Thousands Oaks, CA: Sage.

Marlowe, D., & Crowne, D. P. (1961). Social desirability and response to perceived situational demands. *Journal of Consulting Psychology, 25,* 109–115.

Maslow, A. H. (1943). A theory of human motivation. *Psychological Review, 50,* 370–396.

Maslow, A. H. (1959). Creativity in self-actualizing people. In H. H. Anderson (Ed.), *Creativity and its cultivation* (pp. 83–95). New York: Harper.

Maslow, A. H. (1964). *Religions, values, and peak-experiences.* Columbus: Ohio State University Press.

Maslow, A. H. (1966). *The psychology of science.* New York: Harper & Row.

Maslow, A. H. (1967). A theory of metamotivation: The biological rooting of the value-life. *Journal of Humanistic Psychology, 7*(2), 93–127.

Maslow, A. H. (1968a). Self-actualization [Film]. Santa Ana, CA: Psychological Films.

Maslow, A. H. (1968b). *Toward a psychology of being* (2nd
ed.). New York: Van Nostrand.

Maslow, A. H. (1970). *Motivation and personality* (2nd ed.). New York: Harper & Row.

Maslow, A. H. (1971). *The farther reaches of human nature.* New York: Viking.

Maslow, A. H. (1979). *The journals of A. H. Maslow* (Vols. 1–2) (R. J. Lowry, Ed.). Monterey, CA: Brooks/Cole.

Maslow, A. H. (1993). *The farther reaches of human nature.* New York: Arkana/Penguin Books

Masson, J. M. (1984). *The assault on truth: Freud's suppression of the seduction theory.* New York: Farrar, Straus and Giroux.

May, R. (1950). *The meaning of anxiety.* New York: Ronald Press.

May, R. (1953). *Man's search for himself.* New York: Norton.

May, R. (1958a). Contributions of existential psychotherapy. In R. May, E. Angel, & H. F. Ellenberger (Eds.), *Existence: A new dimension in psychiatry and psychology* (pp. 57–91). New York: Basic Books.

May, R. (1958b). The origins and significance of existential movement in psychology. In R. May, E. Angel, & H. F. Ellenberger (Eds.), *Existence: A new dimension in psychiatry and psychology* (pp. 3–56). New York: Basic Books.

May, R. (1962). Dangers in the relation of existentialism to psychotherapy. In. H. M. Ruitenbeek (Ed.), *Psychoanalysis and existential philosophy.* New York: Dutton.

May, R. (1967). *Psychology and the human dilemma.* Princeton, NJ: Van Nostrand.

May, R. (1969a). The emergence of existential psychology. In R. May (Ed.), *Existential psychology* (2nd ed., pp. 1–48). New York: Random House.

May, R. (1969b). *Love and will.* New York: Norton.

May, R. (1972). *Power and innocence: A search for the sources of violence.* New York: Norton.

May, R. (1977). Reflections and commentary by Rollo May. In C. Reeves, *The psychology of Rollo May* (pp. 295–309). San Francisco: Jossey-Bass.

May, R. (1981). *Freedom and destiny.* New York: Norton.

May, R. (1982). The problem of evil: An open letter to Carl Rogers. *Journal of Humanistic Psychology, 22*(3), 10–21.

May, R. (1985). *My quest for beauty.* San Francisco: Saybrook.

May, R. (1990a). The meaning of the Oedipus myth. *Review of Existential Psychology and Psychiatry: 1986–87. Special Issue, 20,* 169–177.

May, R. (1990b). On the phenomenological bases of therapy. *Review of Existential Psychology and Psychiatry: 1986–87. Special Issue, 20,* 49–61.

May, R. (1990c). Will, decision and responsibility. *Review of Existential Psychology and Psychiatry: 1986–87. Special Issue, 20,* 269–278.

May, R. (1991). *The cry for myth.* New York: Norton.

May, R., Angel, E., & Ellenberger, H. F. (Eds.). (1958). *Existence: A new dimension in psychiatry and psychology.* New York: Basic Books.

May, R., & Yalom, I. (1989). Existential psychotherapy. In R. J. Corsini & D. Wedding (Eds.), *Current psychotherapies* (pp. 354–391). Itasca, IL: Peacock.

McAdams, D. P. (1980). A thematic coding system for the intimacy motive. *Journal of Research in Personality, 14,* 413–432.

McAdams, D. P., & de St. Aubin, E. (1992). A theory of generativity and its assessment through self-report, behavioral acts, and narrative themes in autobiography. *Journal of Personality and Social Psychology, 62,* 1003–1015.

McAdams, D. P., de St. Aubin, E., & Logan, R. L. (1993). Generativity among young, midlife, and older adults. *Psychology and Aging, 8,* 221–230.

McCain, G., & Segal, E. M. (1988). *The game of science* (5th ed.). Pacific Grove, CA: Brooks/Cole.

McCaulley, M. H. (1990). The Myers-Briggs Type Indicator: A measure for individuals and groups. *Measurement and Evaluation in Counseling and Development, 22,* 181–195.

McCrae, R. R., & Costa, P. T. (1989). Reinterpreting the Myers-Briggs Type Indicator from the perspective of the five-factor model of personality. *Journal of Personality, 57,* 17–40.

McDougall, W. (1933). *The energies of men.* New York: Scribner's.

McGuire, W. (Ed.). (1974). *The Freud/Jung letters: The correspondence between Sigmund Freud and C. G. Jung* (R. Manheim & R. F. C. Hull, Trans.). Princeton, NJ: Princeton University Press.

McGuire, W., & McGlashan, A. (Eds.). (1994). *The Freud/Jung letters: The correspondence between Sigmund Freud and C. G. Jung* (abridged ed.). (R. Manheim & R. F. C. Hull, Trans.). Princeton, NJ: Princeton University Press.

Mellor, S. (1989). Gender differences in identity information as a function of self-other relationships. *Journal of Youth and Adolescence, 4,* 361–375.

Menninger, K. A. (1920). *The human mind.* New York: Knopf.

Middleton, J. A., Littlefield, J., & Lehrer, R. (1992). Gifted students' conceptions of academic fun: An examination of a critical construct for gifted education. *Gifted Child Quarterly, 36*, 38–44.

Miller, N. E., & Dollard, J. (1941). *Social learning and imitation*. New Haven, CT: Yale University Press.

Mischel, H. N., & Mischel, W. (Eds.). (1973). *Readings in personality*. New York: Holt, Rinehart and Winston.

Mischel, W. (1958). Preference for delayed reinforcement: An experimental study of cultural observation. *Journal of Abnormal and Social Psychology, 56*, 57–61.

Mischel, W. (1961a). Delay of gratification, need for achievement, and acquiesce in another culture. *Journal of Abnormal and Social Psychology, 62*, 543–552.

Mischel, W. (1961b). Preference for delayed reinforcement and social responsibility. *Journal of Abnormal and Social Psychology, 62*, 1–7.

Mischel, W. (1965). Predicting success of Peace Corps volunteers in Nigeria. *Journal of Personality and Social Psychology, 1*, 510–517.

Mischel, W. (1968). *Personality and assessment*. New York: Wiley.

Mischel, W. (1971). *Introduction to personality*. New York: Holt, Rinehart and Winston.

Mischel, W. (1973). Toward a cognitive social learning reconceptualization of personality. *Psychological Review, 80*, 252–283.

Mischel, W. (1976). *Introduction to personality* (2nd ed.). New York: Holt, Rinehart and Winston.

Mischel, W. (1979). On the interface of cognition and personality: Beyond the person-situation debate. *American Psychologist, 34*, 740–754.

Mischel, W. (1981). *Introduction to personality* (3rd ed.). New York: Holt, Rinehart and Winston.

Mischel, W. (1986). *Introduction to personality: A new look* (4th ed.). New York: Holt, Rinehart and Winston.

Mischel, W. (1990). Personality dispositions revisited and revised: A view after three decades. In L. A. Pervin (Ed.), *Handbook of personality: Theory and research* (pp. 111–134). New York: Guilford Press.

Mischel, W. (1993). *Introduction to personality* (5th ed.). Fort Worth: Harcourt Brace Jovanovich.

Mischel, W., & Baker, N. (1975). Cognitive appraisals and transformations in delay behavior. *Journal of Personality and Social Psychology, 31*, 254–261.

Mischel, W., & Ebbesen, E. B. (1970). Attention in delay of gratification. *Journal of Personality and Social Psychology, 16*, 329–337.

Mischel, W., Ebbesen, E. B., & Zeiss, A. R. (1972). Cognitive and attentional mechanisms in delay of gratification. *Journal of Personality and Social Psychology, 21*, 204–218.

Mischel, W., & Metzner, R. (1962). Preference for delayed reward as a function of age, intelligence, and length of delay interval. *Journal of Abnormal and Social Psychology, 64*, 425–431.

Mischel, W., & Mischel, H. N. (1976). A cognitive social learning approach to morality and self-regulation. In T. Lickona (Ed.), *Moral development and behavior: Theory, research, and social issues*. New York: Holt, Rinehart and Winston.

Mischel, W., & Mischel, H. N. (1983). Development of children's knowledge of self-control strategies. *Child Development, 54*, 603–619.

Mischel, W., & Moore, B. (1973). Effects of attention to symbolically presented rewards upon self-control. *Journal of Personality and Social Psychology, 28*, 172–179.

Mischel, W., & Shoda, Y. (1994). Personality psychology has two goals: Must it be two fields? *Psychological Inquiry, 5*, 156–158.

Mischel, W., & Shoda, Y. (1995). A cognitive-affective system theory of personality: Reconceptualizing situations, dispositions, dynamics, and invariance in personality structure. *Psychological Reports, 102*, 246–268.

Mischel, W., Shoda, Y., & Peake, P. K. (1988). The nature of adolescent competencies predicted by preschool delay of gratification. *Journal of Personality and Social Psychology, 54,* 687–696.

Mischel, W., Shoda, Y., & Rodriquez, M. L. (1989). Delay of gratification in children. *Science, 244,* 933–938.

Mischel, W., & Staub, E. (1965). Effects of expectancy on working and waiting for larger rewards. *Journal of Personality and Social Psychology, 2,* 625–633.

Mitchell, S. A., & Black, M. J. (1995). *Freud and beyond: A history of modern psychoanalytic thought.* New York: Basic Books.

Mohan, J., & Tiwana, M. (1986). Personality and alienation of creative writers: A brief report. *Personality and Individual Differences, 8,* 449.

Moore, S., & Boldero, J. (1991). Psychosocial development and friendship function in adolescence. *Sex Roles, 25,* 521–536.

Morrison, J. W., Ispa, J. M., & Thornburg, K. R. (1994). African American college students' psychosocial development as related to care arrangements during infancy. *Journal of Black Psychology, 20,* 418–429.

Moskowitz, D. S. (1994). Cross-situational generality and the interpersonal circumplex. *Journal of Personality and Social Psychology, 66,* 921–933.

Murray, H. A. (1938). *Explorations in personality.* New York: Oxford University Press.

Myers, I. B. (1962). *Myers-Briggs Type Indicator Manual.* Palo Alto, CA: Consulting Psychologists Press.

Myers, I. B., & McCaulley, M. H. (1985). *Manual: A guide to the development and use of the Myers-Briggs Type Indicator.* Palo Alto, CA: Consulting Psychologists Press.

Nakano, K. (1990). Operant self-control procedure in modifying Type A behavior. *Journal of Behavior Therapy and Experimental Psychiatry, 21,* 49–255.

Neimeyer, G. J., & Hall, A. G. (1988). Personal identity in disturbed marital relationships. In F. Fransella & L. Thomas (Eds.), *Experimenting with personal construct psychology* (pp. 297–307). London: Routledge & Kegan Paul.

Neisser, U., and Harsch, N. (1992). Phantom flashbulbs: False recollections of hearing the news about *Challenger.* In E. Winograd & U. Neisser (Eds.), *Affect and accuracy in recall: Studies of "flashbulb" memories* (pp. 9–31). New York: Cambridge University Press.

Newton, P. M. (1995). *Freud: From youthful dream to mid-life crisis.* New York: Guilford.

Nichols, C. C., & Feist, J. (1994). Explanatory style as a predictor of earliest recollections. *Individual Psychology, 50,* 31–39.

Noll, R. (1994). *The Jung cult: Origins of a charismatic movement.* Princeton, NJ: Princeton University Press.

Norman, P. (1995). Health locus of control and health behaviour: An investigation into the role of health value and behaviour-specific efficacy beliefs. *Personality and Individual Differences, 18,* 213–218.

Norman, W. T. (1963). Toward an adequate taxonomy of personality attributes. Replicated factor structure in peer nomination personality ratings. *Journal of Abnormal and Social Psychology, 66,* 574–583.

O'Connell, A. N. (1990). Karen Horney (1885-1952). In A. N. O'Connell & N. F. Russo (Eds.), *Women in psychology: A bio-bibliographic sourcebook* (pp. 185–196). New York: Greenwood Press.

Ogden, T. H. (1990). *The matrix of the mind: Object relations and the psychoanalytic dialogue.* Northvale, NJ: Aronson.

O'Hara, M. (1995). Carl Rogers: Scientist and mystic. *Journal of Humanistic Psychology 35,* 40–53.

Paige, J. M. (1966). Letters from Jenny: An

approach to the clinical analysis of personality structure by computer. In P. J. Stone (Ed.), *The general enquirer: A computer approach to content analysis.* Cambridge, MA: M.I.T. Press.

Paik, H., & Comstock, G. (1994). The effects of television violence on antisocial behavior: A meta-analysis. *Communication Research, 21,* 516–546.

Palenzuela, D. L. (1988). Refining the theory and measurement of expectancy of internal vs. external control of reinforcement. *Personality and Individual Differences, 9,* 607–629.

Paris, B. J. (1994). *Karen Horney: A psychoanalyst's search for self-understanding.* New Haven, CT: Yale University Press.

Payne, D. A., Halpin, W. G., Ellett, C. D., & Dale, J. B. (1975). General personality correlates of creative personality in academically and artistically gifted youth. *Journal of Special Education, 9,* 105–108.

Pendse, S. G. (1978). An empirical validity test of Fromm's personality orientation. *Journal of General Psychology, 99,* 133–139.

Perry, H. S. (1982). *Psychiatrist of America: The life of Harry Stack Sullivan.* Cambridge, MA: Belknap Press.

Pervin, L. A. (1990a). A brief history of modern personality theory. In L. A. Pervin (Ed.), *Handbook of personality: Theory and research* (pp. 3–18). New York: Guilford.

Pervin, L. A. (1990b). Personality theory and research; Prospects for the future. In L. A. Pervin (Ed.), *Handbook of personality: Theory and research* (pp. 723–727). New York: Guilford.

Peterson, B. E., & Stewart, A. J. (1993). Generativity and social motives in young adults. *Journal of Personality and Social Psychology, 65,* 186–198.

Petot, J.-M. (1990). *Melanie Klein: Volume I. First discoveries and first system: 1919–1932* (C. Trollop, Trans.). Madison, CT: International Universities Press. (Original work published 1979)

Phares, E. J. (1955). *Changes in expectancy in skill and chance situations.* Unpublished doctoral dissertation, Ohio State University.

Pines, M. (1978, September). Invisible playmates. *Psychology Today,* pp. 38–42, 106.

Polanyi, M. (1958). *Personal knowledge: Toward a post-critical philosophy.* New York: Harper.

Popper, K. R. (1963). *Conjectures and refutations: The growth of scientific knowledge.* New York: Harper & Row.

Powell, R. A., & Boer, D. P. (1994). Did Freud mislead patients to confabulate memories of abuse? *Psychological Reports, 74,* 1283–1298.

Quinlan, D. M., Blatt, S. J., Chevron, E. S., & Wein, S. J. (1992). The analysis of descriptions of parents: Identification of a more differentiated factor structure. *Journal of Personality Assessment, 59,* 340–351.

Quinn, S. (1987). *A mind of her own: The life of Karen Horney.* New York: Summit Books.

Quinn, S. (1994). Awakened to life: Sources of independence in the girlhood of Karen Horney. In M. M. Berger (Ed.), *Women beyond Freud: New concepts of feminine psychology* (pp. 1–14). New York: Brunner/Mazel.

Rabinowitz, F. E., Good, G., & Cozad, L. (1989). Rollo May: A man of meaning and myth. *Journal of Counseling and Development, 67,* 436–441.

Rank, O. (1978a). *Truth and reality: A life history of the human will* (J. Taft, Trans.). New York: Norton. (Original work published 1936)

Rank, O. (1978b). *Will therapy: An analysis of the therapeutic process in terms of relationship* (J. Taft, Trans.). New York: Dover. (Original work published 1936)

Rattner, J. (1983). *Alfred Adler* (H. Zohn, Trans.). New York: Frederick Ungar. (Original work published 1983)

Ray, J. J. (1984). A caution against the use of the Shostrom Personal Orientation Inventory. *Personality and Individual Differences*, 5, 755.

Ray, J. J., & Lovejoy, F. H. (1982). Conservatism, attitude to abortion, and Maccoby's biophilia. *Journal of Social Psychology*, 118, 143–144.

Ray, J. J., & Lovejoy, F. H. (1984). Attitude toward the environment as a special case of attitude toward all living things. *Journal of Social Psychology*, 123, 285–286.

Reeves, C. (1977). *The psychology of Rollo May*. San Francisco: Jossey-Bass.

Rehfish, J. M. (1958). A scale for personality rigidity. *Journal of Consulting Psychology*, 22, 11–15.

Rest, J. R. (1979). *Revised manual for the Defining Issues Test*. Minneapolis: Minnesota Moral Research Projects.

Richard, R. L., & Jex, S. M. (1991). Further evidence for the validity of the Short Index of Self-Actualization. *Journal of Social Behavior and Personality*, 6, 331–338.

Richards, P. S. (1994). Religious devoutness, impression management, and personality functioning in college students. *Journal of Research in Personality*, 28, 14–26.

Roazen, P. (1976). *Erik H. Erikson: The power and limits of a vision*. New York: Free Press.

Roazen, P. (1993). *Meeting Freud's family*. Amherst: University of Massachusetts Press.

Roazen, P. (1996). Erich Fromm's courage. In M. Cortina & M. Maccoby (Eds.), A *prophetic analyst: Erich Fromm's contribution to psychoanalysis* (pp. 427–453). Northvale, NJ: Aronson.

Robinson, P. (1993). *Freud and his critics*. Berkeley: University of California Press.

Rogers, C. R. (1939). *The clinical treatment of the problem child*. Boston: Houghton Mifflin.

Rogers, C. R. (1942). *Counseling and psychotherapy: Newer concepts in practice*. Boston: Houghton Mifflin.

Rogers, C. R. (1947). Some observations on the organization of personality. *American Psychologist*, 2, 358–368.

Rogers, C. R. (1951). *Client-centered therapy: Its current practice, implications, and theory*. Boston: Houghton Mifflin.

Rogers, C. R. (1953). *A concept of the fully functioning person*. Unpublished manuscript, University of Chicago Counseling Center, Chicago.

Rogers, C. R. (1954). Introduction. In C. R. Rogers & R. F. Dymond (Eds.), *Psychotherapy and personality change: Co-ordinated research studies in the client-centered approach* (pp. 3–11). Chicago: University of Chicago Press.

Rogers, C. R. (1957). The necessary and sufficient conditions of therapeutic personality change. *Journal of Consulting Psychology*, 21, 95–103.

Rogers, C. R. (1959). A theory of therapy, personality, and interpersonal relationships, as developed in the client-centered framework. In S. Koch (Ed.), *Psychology: A study of a science* (Vol. 3). New York: McGraw-Hill.

Rogers, C. R. (1961). *On becoming a person: A therapist's view of psychotherapy*. Boston: Houghton Mifflin.

Rogers, C. R. (1962). Toward becoming a fully functioning person. In A. W. Combs (Ed.), *Perceiving, behaving, becoming: Yearbook* (pp. 21–33). Washington, DC: Association for Supervision and Curriculum Development.

Rogers, C. R. (1963). The concept of the fully functioning person. *Psychotherapy: Theory, Research, and Practice*, 1(1), 17–26.

Rogers, C. R. (1968). Some thoughts regarding the current presuppositions of the behavioral sciences. In W. R. Coulson & C. R. Rogers (Eds.), *Man and the science of man*. Columbus, OH: Merrill.

Rogers, C. R. (1973). My philosophy of interpersonal

relationships and how it grew. *Journal of Humanistic Psychology*, 13, 3–15.

Rogers, C. R. (1978). The formative tendency. *Journal of Humanistic Psychology*, 18(1), 23–26.

Rogers, C. R. (1980). A *way of being*. Boston: Houghton Mifflin.

Rogers, C. R. (1982a). Notes on Rollo May. *Journal of Humanistic Psychology*, 22(3), 8–9.

Rogers, C. R. (1982b). A psychologist looks at nuclear war: Its threat; its possible prevention. *Journal of Humanistic Psychology*, 22(4), 9–20.

Rogers, C. R. (1983). *Freedom to learn for the 80's*. Columbus, OH: Merrill.

Rogers, C. R. (1995). What understanding and acceptance mean to me. *Journal of Humanistic Psychology*, 35, 7–22.

Rogers, C. R., & Dymond, R. F. (Eds.). (1954). *Psychotherapy and personality change: Co-ordinated research studies in the client-centered approach*. Chicago: University of Chicago Press.

Rogers, C. R., Gendlin, E., Kiesler, D., & Truax, C. (Eds.). (1967). *The therapeutic relationship and its impact: A study of psychotherapy with schizophrenics*. Madison: University of Wisconsin Press.

Rogers, C. R., & Skinner, B. F. (1956). Some issues concerning the control of human behavior. *Science*, 124, 1057–1066.

Rosen, D. H., Smith, S. M., Huston, H. L., & Gonzalez, G. (1991). Empirical study of associations between symbols and their meaning: Evidence of collective unconscious (archetypal) memory. *Journal of Analytical Psychology*, 36, 211–228.

Rosenberg, M. (1965). *Society and the adolescent self-image*. Princeton, NJ: Princeton University Press.

Rosenthal, D. A., Gurney, R. M., & Moore, S. M. (1981). From trust to intimacy: A new inventory for examining Erikson's stages of psychosocial development. *Journal of Youth and Adolescence*, 10, 525–537.

Rosenthal, T. L., & Bandura, A. (1978). Psychological modeling: Theory and practice. In S. L. Garfield & A. E. Bergin (Eds.), *Handbook of psychotherapy and behavior change: An empirical analysis*. New York: Wiley.

Ross, C. A., Heber, S., Norton, G. R., & Anderson, G. (1989). Differences between multiple personality disorder and diagnostic groups on structured interview. *Journal of Nervous and Mental Disease*, 177, 489–491.

Rotter, J. B. (1954). *Social learning and clinical psychology*. Englewood Cliffs, NJ: Prentice-Hall.

Rotter, J. B. (1964). *Clinical psychology*. Englewood Cliffs, NJ: Prentice-Hall.

Rotter, J. B. (1966). Generalized expectancies for internal versus external control of reinforcement. *Psychological Monographs*, 80 (Whole No. 609).

Rotter, J. B. (1967). A new scale for the measurement of interpersonal trust. *Journal of Personality*, 35, 651–665.

Rotter, J. B. (1970). Some implications of a social learning theory for the practice of psychotherapy. In D. J. Levis (Ed.), *Learning approaches to therapeutic behavior change*. Chicago: Aldine.

Rotter, J. B. (1975). Some problems and misconceptions related to the construct of internal vs. external control of reinforcement. *Journal of Consulting and Clinical Psychology*, 43, 56–67.

Rotter, J. B. (1978). Generalized expectancies for problem solving and psychotherapy. *Cognitive Therapy and Research*, 2, 1–10.

Rotter, J. B. (1980). Interpersonal trust, trustworthiness, and gullibility. *American Psychologist*, 35, 1–7.

Rotter, J. B. (1982). *The development and applications of social learning theory: Selected papers*. New York: Praeger.

Rotter, J. B. (1990). Internal versus external control of reinforcement: A case history of a variable. *American Psychologist, 45,* 489–493.

Rotter, J. B. (1992). Cognates of personal control: Locus of control, self-efficacy, and explanatory style: Comment. *Applied and Preventive Psychology,* 1, 127–129.

Rotter, J. B. (1993). Expectancies. In C. E. Walker (Ed.), *The history of clinical psychology in autobiography* (Vol. 2, pp. 273–284). Pacific Grove, CA: Brooks/Cole.

Rotter, J. B., Chance, J. E., & Phares, E. J. (1972). *Applications of a social learning theory of personality.* New York: Holt, Rinehart and Winston.

Rotter, J. B., & Hochreich, D. J. (1975). *Personality.* Glenview, IL: Scott, Foresman.

Rowan, D. G., Compton, W. C., & Rust, J. O. (1995). Self-actualization and empathy as predictors of marital satisfaction. *Psychological Reports, 77,* 1011–1016.

Royce, J. R., & Powell, A. (1983). *Theory of personality and individual differences: Factors, systems and processes.* Englewood Cliffs, NJ: Prentice-Hall.

Rudikoff, E. C. (1954). A comparative study of the changes in the concepts of the self, the ordinary person, and the ideal in eight cases. In C. R. Rogers & R. F. Dymond (Eds.), *Psychotherapy and personality change: Co-ordinated research studies in the client-centered approach* (pp. 85–98). Chicago: University of Chicago Press.

Runco, M. A., Ebersole, P., & Mraz, W. (1991). Creativity and self-actualization. *Journal of Social Behavior and Personality, 6,* 161–167.

Rushton, J. P. (1990). Creativity, intelligence, and psychoticism. *Personality and Individual Differences,* 11, 1291–1298.

Rushton, J. P., Murray, H. G., & Paunonen, S. V. (1983). Personality, research creativity, and teaching effectiveness in university professors. *Scientometrics, 5,* 93–116.

Ryckman, R. M., Hammer, M., Kaczor, L. M., & Gold, J. A. (1990). Construction of a Hypercompetitive Attitude Scale. *Journal of Personality Assessment, 55,* 630–639.

Ryckman, R. M., Thornton, B., & Butler, J. C. (1994). Personality correlates of the Hypercompetitive Attitude Scale: Validity tests of Horney's theory of neurosis. *Journal of Personality Assessment, 62,* 84–94.

Ryckman, R. M., Van den Borne, H. W., & Syroit, J. E. (1992). Differences in hypercompetitive attitudes between American and Dutch university students. *Journal of Social Psychology,* 132, 331–334.

St. Clair, M. (1986). *Object relations and self psychology: An introduction.* Monterey, CA: Brooks/Cole.

Sartre, J. P. (1957). *Existentialism and human emotions.* New York: Wisdom Library.

Savill, G. E., & Eckstein, D. G. (1987). Changes in early recollections as a function of mental status. *Individual Psychology, 43,* 3–17.

Sayers, J. (1991). *Mothers of psychoanalysis: Helene Deutsch, Karen Horney, Anna Freud, Melanie Klein.* New York: Norton.

Schacht, A. J., & Howe, H. E. (1989). Psychologists' theoretical orientation and MBTI personality type. *Journal of Psychological Type, 18,* 39–42.

Schaefer, C. E. (1969). The self-concept of creative adolescents. *Journal of Psychology, 72,* 233–242.

Schlein, S. (Ed.). (1987). *A way of looking at things: Selected papers of Erik Erikson.* New York: Norton.

Schur, M. (1972). *Freud: Living and dying.* New York: International Universities Press.

Schurr, K. T., & Ruble, V. (1988). Psychological type and the second year of college achievement: Survival and the gravitation toward appropriate and manageable major fields. *Journal of*

Psychological Type, 14, 57–59.

Segal, H. (1979). Melanie Klein. New York: Viking Press.

Segal, H. G., Westen, D., Lohr, N. E., Silk, K. R., & Cohen, R. (1992). Assessing object relations and social cognition borderline personality disorders from stories told to the picture arrangement subtest of the WAIS-R. Journal of Personality Disorders, 6, 458–470.

Segal, J. (1992). Melanie Klein. London: Sage.

Seiffge-Krenke, I. (1993). Close friendship and imaginary companions in adolescence. In B. Laursen (Ed.), Close friendships in adolescence. New directions for child development (No. 60, pp. 73–87). San Francisco: Jossey-Bass.

Sheffield, M., Carey, J., Patenaude, W., & Lambert, M. J. (1995). An exploration of the relationship between interpersonal problems and psychological health. Psychological Reports, 76, 947–956.

Shelburne, W. A. (1988). Mythos and logos in the thought of Carl Jung: The theory of the collective unconscious in scientific perspective. Albany: State University of New York Press.

Shoda, Y., & Mischel, W. (1993). Cognitive social approach to dispositional inferences: What if the perceiver is a cognitive social theorist? Personality and Social Psychology Bulletin, 19, 574–585.

Shoda, Y., Mischel, W., & Peake, P. K. (1990). Predicting adolescent cognitive and self-regulatory competencies from preschool delay of gratification: Identifying diagnostic conditions. Developmental Psychology, 26, 978–986.

Shoda, Y., Mischel, W., & Wright, J. C. (1993). Links between personality judgments and contextualized behavior patterns: Situation-behavior profiles of personality prototypes. Social Cognition 11, 399–429.

Shoda, Y., Mischel, W., & Wright, J. C. (1994). Intraindividual stability in the organization and patterning of behavior: Incorporating psychological situations into the ideographic analysis of personality. Journal of Personality and Social Psychology, 67, 674–687.

Shostrom, E. L. (1963). Personal Orientation Inventory. San Diego: Educational and Industrial Testing Service.

Shostrom, E. L. (1974). Manual for the Personal Orientation Inventory. San Diego: Educational and Industrial Testing Service.

Silverman, L. H. (1983). The subliminal psychodynamic activation method: Overview and comprehensive listing of studies. In J. Masling (Ed.), Empirical studies of psychoanalytic theories (pp. 69–100). Hillsdale, NJ: Erlbaum.

Silverman, L. H., Ross, D. L., Adler, J. M., & Lustig, D. A. (1978). Simple research paradigm for demonstrating subliminal psychodynamic activation: Effects of Oedipal stimuli on dart-throwing accuracy in college males. Journal of Abnormal Psychology, 87, 341–357.

Silverman, L. H., & Weinberger, J. (1985). Mommy and I are one: Implications for psychotherapy. American Psychologist, 40, 1296–1308.

Singer, J. (1994). Boundaries of the soul: The practice of Jung's psychology (2nd ed.). New York: Doubleday.

Skinner, B. F. (1938). The behavior of organisms: An experimental analysis. Englewood Cliffs, NJ: Prentice-Hall.

Skinner, B. F. (1945). The operational analysis of psychological terms. Psychological Review, 52, 270–277, 291–294.

Skinner, B. F. (1948). Walden two. New York: Macmillan.

Skinner, B. F. (1953). Science and human behavior. New York: Macmillan.

Skinner, B. F. (1954). The science of learning and

the art of teaching. *Harvard Educational Review, 24,* 86–97.

Skinner, B. F. (1956). A case history in scientific method. *American Psychologist, 11,* 221–233.

Skinner, B. F. (1967). An autobiography. In E. G. Boring & G. Lindzey (Eds.), *A history of psychology in autobiography* (Vol. 5). New York: Appleton-Century-Crofts.

Skinner, B. F. (1971). *Beyond freedom and dignity.* New York: Knopf.

Skinner, B. F. (1974). *About behaviorism.* New York: Knopf.

Skinner, B. F. (1976). *Particulars of my life.* New York: Knopf.

Skinner, B. F. (1978). *Reflections on behaviorism and society.* Englewood Cliffs, NJ: Prentice-Hall.

Skinner, B. F. (1979). *The shaping of a behaviorist.* New York: Knopf.

Skinner, B. F. (1983). *A matter of consequences.* New York: Knopf.

Skinner, B. F. (1987a). *Upon further reflection.* Englewood Cliffs, NJ: Prentice-Hall.

Skinner, B. F. (1987b). Whatever happened to psychology as the science of behavior? *American Psychologist, 42,* 780–786.

Skinner, B. F. (1988). The operant side of behavior therapy. *Journal of Behavior Therapy and Experimental Psychiatry, 19,* 171–179.

Skinner, B. F. (1989a). The origins of cognitive thought. *American Psychologist, 44,* 13–18.

Skinner, B. F. (1989b). *Recent issues in the analysis of behavior.* Columbus, OH: Merrill.

Skinner, B. F. (1990a). Can psychology be a science of the mind? *American Psychologist, 45,* 1206–1210.

Skinner, B. F. (1990b). To know the future. *Behavior Analyst, 13,* 103–106.

Skinner, B. F., & Vaughan, M. E. (1983). *Enjoy old age: A program for self-management.* New York: Norton.

Slife, B.D., & Rychlak, J. F. (1982). Role of affective assessment in modeling aggressive behavior. *Journal of Personality and Social Psychology, 43,* 861–868.

Snyder, M. (1974). Self monitoring of expressive behavior. *Journal of Personality and Social Psychology, 30,* 526–537.

Sobel, D. (1980, March 19). Erich Fromm. *The New York Times,* p. B11.

Solomon, I. (1995). *A primer of Kleinian therapy.* Northvale, NJ: Aronson.

Somers, J. U., & Yawkey, T. D. (1984). Imaginary play companions: Contributions of creative and intellectual abilities of young children. *Journal of Creative Behavior, 18,* 77–89.

Sroufe, L. A., Carlson, E., & Shulman, S. (1993).

Individuals in relationships: Development from infancy through adolescence. In D. C. Funder, R. D. Parke, C. Tomlinson-Keasey, & K. Widaman (Eds.), *Studying lives through time: Personality and development.* APA *science volume* (pp. 315–342). Washington, DC: American Psychological Association.

Stanovich, K. E. (1996). *How to think straight about psychology* (4th ed.). Glenview, IL: Scott, Foresman.

Statton, J. E., & Wilborn, B. (1991). Adlerian counseling and the early recollections of children. *Individual Psychology, 47,* 338–347.

Steele, R. S., & Kelley, T. J. (1976). Eysenck Personality Questionnaire and Jungian Myers-Briggs Type Indicator correlations of extraversion-introversion. *Journal of Consulting and Clinical Psychology, 44,* 690–691.

Steiger, H., & Houle, L. (1991). Defense styles and object-relations disturbances among university women displaying varying degrees of "symptomatic" eating. *International Journal of Eating Disorders, 10,* 145–153.

Steiger, H., Leung, F., & Thibaudeau, J. (1993). Prognostic value of pretreatment social adaptation in bulimia nervosa. *International Journal of Eating Disorders, 14*, 269–278.

Steiner, R. (1985) Some thoughts about tradition and change arising from an examination of the British Psycho-Analytical Society's controversial discussions (1943–1944). *International Review of Psycho-Analysis, 12*, 27–71.

Stephenson, W. (1953). *The study of behavior: Q-technique and its methodology*. Chicago: University of Chicago Press.

Stevens, A. (1994). *On Jung*. Oxford, England: Oxford University Press.

Strasburger, V. (1995). *Adolescents and the media: Medical and psychological impact*. New York: Sage.

Sulliman, J. R. (1973). The development of a scale for the measurement of "social interest." Unpublished doctoral dissertation, Florida State University.

Sullivan, H. S. (1953a). *Conceptions of modern psychiatry*. New York: Norton.

Sullivan, H. S. (1953b). *The interpersonal theory of psychiatry*. New York: Norton.

Sullivan, H. S. (1954). *The psychiatric interview*. New York: Norton.

Sullivan, H. S. (1956). *Clinical studies in psychiatry*. New York: Norton.

Sullivan, H. S. (1962). *Schizophrenia as a human process*. New York: Norton.

Sullivan, H. S. (1964). *The fusion of psychiatry and social science*. New York: Norton.

Sulloway, F. J. (1992). *Freud, biologist of the mind: Beyond the psychoanalytical legend* (Rev. ed.). Cambridge, MA: Harvard University Press.

Sulloway, F. J. (1996). *Born to rebel: Birth order, family dynamics, and creative lives*. New York: Pantheon Books.

Thompson, G. G. (1968). George A. Kelly (1905–1967). *Journal of General Psychology, 79*, 19–24.

Thorndike, E. L. (1898). Animal intelligence: An experimental study of the associative processes in animals. *Psychological Monographs, 2* (Whole No. 8).

Thorndike, E. L. (1913). *The psychology of learning*. New York: Teachers College.

Thorndike, E. L. (1931). *Human learning*. New York: Appleton-Century.

Thorne, B. (1992). *Carl Rogers*. London: Sage.

Thorton, P. I., Igleheart, H. C., & Silverman, L. H. (1987). Subliminal stimulation of symbiotic fantasies as an aid in the treatment of drug abusers. *International Journal of the Addictions, 22*, 751–765.

Truax, C. B., & Carkhuff, R. R. (1967). *Toward effective counseling and psychotherapy*. Chicago: Aldine.

Tupes, E. C., & Christal, R. E. (1961). *Recurrent personality factors based on trait ratings* (Technical Report No. ASD-TR-61-97). Lackland, TX: U.S. Air Force.

Vaihinger, H. (1911/1925). *The philosophy of "as if."* New York: Harcourt, Brace & Co.

Van Haitsma, K. (1986). Intrinsic religious orientation: Implications in the study of religiosity and personal adjustment in the aged. *Journal of Social Psychology, 126*, 685–687.

Vitz, P. C. (1988). *Sigmund Freud's Christian unconscious*. New York: Guilford Press.

Walker, S. F. (1995). *Jung and the Jungians on myth: An introduction*. New York: Garland.

Watkins, C. E. (1994). Measuring social interest. *Individual Psychology, 50*, 69–96.

Watkins, C. E., & Blazina, C. (1994). Reliability of the Sulliman Scale of Social Interest. *Individual Psychology, 50*, 164–165.

Watkins, C. E., & St. John, C. (1994). Validity of the Sulliman Scale of Social Interest. *Individual Psychology, 50*, 166–169.

Watkins, C. E., Jr. (1992a). Adlerian-oriented early memory research: What does it tell us? *Journal of Personality Assessment, 59*, 248–263.

Watkins, C. E., Jr. (1992b). Birth-order research and

Adler's theory: A critical review. *Individual Psychology, 48,* 357–368.

Watkins, C. E., Jr. (1992c). Research activity with Adler's theory. *Individual Psychology, 48,* 107–108.

Watson, J. B. (1913). Psychology as the behaviorist views it. *Psychological Review, 20,* 158–177.

Watson, J. B. (1925). *Behaviorism.* New York: Norton.

Watson, J. B., & Rayner, R. (1920). Conditioned emotional reactions. *Journal of Experimental Psychology, 3,* 1–14.

Watson, P. J., Hood, R. W., Jr., Morris, R. J., & Hall, J. R. (1984). Empathy, religious orientation, and social desirability. *Journal of Psychology, 117,* 211–216.

Watson, P. J., Milliron, J. T., Morris, R. J., & Hood, R. W., Jr. (1995). Locus of control within a religious ideological surround. *Journal of Psychology and Christianity, 14,* 239–249.

Watson, P. J., Morris, R. J., & Hood, R. W., Jr. (1990). Extrinsic Scale factors: Correlations and construction of religious orientation types. *Journal of Psychology and Christianity, 9,* 35–46.

Webster, R. (1995). *Why Freud was wrong: Sin, science, and psychoanalysis.* New York: Basic Books.

Weinberger, J., & Silverman, L. H. (1990). Testability and empirical verification of psychoanalytic dynamic propositions through subliminal psychodynamic activation. *Psychoanalytic Psychology, 7,* 299–339.

Weiss, A. S. (1991). The measurement of self-actualization: The quest for the test may be as challenging as the search for the self. *Journal of Social Behavior and Personality, 6,* 265–290.

Westen, D. (1990). Psychoanalytic approaches to personality. In L. A. Pervin, *Handbook of personality: Theory and research* (pp. 21–65). New York: Guilford Press.

Westen, D., Lohr, N., Silk, K. R., Gold, L., & Kerber, K. (1990). Object relations and social cognition in borderlines, major depressives, and normals: A thematic Apperception Test analysis. *Psychological Assessment, 2,* 355–364.

Westen, D., Ludolph, P., Block, M. J., Wixom, J., & Wiss, F. C. (1990). Developmental history and object relations in psychiatrically disturbed adolescent girls. *American Journal of Psychiatry, 147,* 1061–1068.

Westen, D., Ludolph, P., Misle, B., Ruffins, S., & Block, J. (1990). Physical and sexual abuse in female adolescents with borderline personality disorder. *American Journal of Orthopsychiatry, 60,* 55–66.

Westman, A. S. (1992). Existential anxiety as related to conceptualization of self and of death, denial of death, and religiosity. *Psychological Reports, 71,* 1064–1066.

Wheeler, M. S., Kern, R. M., & Curlette, W. L. (1982). *Wheeler-Kern-Curlette Life Style Personality Inventory.* Unpublished manuscript.

Wheeler, M. S., Kern, R. M., & Curlette, W. L. (1986). Factor analytic scales designed to measure Adlerian life style themes. *Individual Psychology, 42,* 1–16.

Wheeler, M. S., Kern, R. M., & Curlette, W. L. (1991). Life-style can be measured. *Individual Psychology, 47,* 229–240.

Wheelwright, J. B., Wheelwright, J. A., & Buehler, J. A. (1964). *Jungian Type Survey Manual.* San Francisco: Society of Jungian Analysts of Northern California.

Whitbourne, S. K., Zuschlag, M. Z., Elliot, L. B., & Waterman, A. S. (1992). Psychosocial development in adulthood: A 22-year sequential study. *Journal of Personality and Social Psychology, 63,* 260–271.

Whitson, E. R., & Olczak, P. V. (1991). The use of the POI in clinical situations: An evaluation. *Journal of*

Social Behavior and Personality, 6, 291–310.

Wiegman, O., Kuttschreuter, M., & Baarda, B. (1992). A longitudinal study of the effects of television viewing on aggressive and prosocial behaviours. British Journal of Social Psychology, 31, 147–164.

Williams, E. L., & Manaster, G. J. (1990). Restricter anorexia, bulimic anorexia, and bulimic women's early recollection and Thematic Apperception Test response. Individual Psychology, 45, 98–107.

Wills, G. I. (1983). A personality study of musicians working in the popular field. Personality and Individual Differences, 5, 359–360.

Wilson, C. (1972). New pathways in psychology: Maslow and the post-Freudian revolution. New York: Taplinger.

Wilson, G. D., & Jackson, C. (1994). The personality of physicists. Personality and Individual Differences, 16, 187–189.

Winter, D. G. (1993). Gordon Allport and "Letters from Jenny." In K. H. Craik, R. Hogan, & R. N. Wolfe (Eds.), Fifty years of personality psychology (pp. 147–163). New York: Plenum Press.

Wittig, A. F., Schurr, K. T., Ruble, V. E., & Ellen, A. (1994). Relationship of

Myers-Briggs Type Indicator thinking-feeling preferences with physical activity choices. Journal of Psychological Type, 28, 21–28.

Woehlke, P. A., & Piper, R. B. (1980). Factorial validity of the Jungian Type Survey. Educational and Psychological Measurement, 40, 1051–1058.

Wolpe, J. (1973). The practice of behavior therapy. New York: Pergamon Press.

Wright, J. C., & Mischel, W. (1987). A conditional approach to disposition constructs: The local predictability of social behavior. Journal of Personality and Social Psychology, 53, 1159–1177.

Wright, J. C., & Mischel, W. (1988). Conditional hedges and the intuitive psychology of traits. Journal of Personality and Social Psychology, 55, 454–469.

Wulfert, E., Greenway, D. E., Farkas, P., Hayes, S. C., & Dougher, M. J. (1994). Correlation between self-reported rigidity and rule-governed insensitivity to operant contingencies. Journal of Applied Behavior Analysis, 27, 659–671.

Yeakley, F. R. (1982). Communication style preferences and adjustments as an

approach for studying effects of similarity in psychological type. Research in Psychological Type, 5, 30–48.

Zachar, P., & Leong, F. T. L. (1992). A problem of personality: Scientist and practitioner differences in psychology. Journal of Personality, 60, 665–677.

Zimmerman, B. J., & Bandura, A. (1994). Impact of self-regulatory influences on writing course attainment. American Educational Research Journal, 31, 845–862.

Zimmerman, B. J., Bandura, A., & Martinez-Pons, M. (1992). Self-motivation for academic attainment: The role of self-efficacy beliefs and personal goal setting. American Educational Research Journal, 29, 663–676.

Zuriff, G. E. (1995). Continuity over change within the experimental analysis of behavior. In J. T. Todd & E. K. Morris (Eds.), Modern perspectives on B. F. Skinner and contemporary behaviorism (pp. 171–183). Westport, CT: Greenwood Press.

Zuroff, D. C., & Rotter, J. B. (1985). A history of the expectancy construct in psychology. In J. B. Dusek (Ed.), Teacher expectancies (pp. 7–36). Hillsdale, NJ: Erlbaum.

Credits

Chapter 1
Opener: © Alexej von Jawlensky/Superstock, Inc.; p. 4: © David Frazier Photolibrary.

Chapter 2
Opener: © Archive Photos; p. 19: Freud Museum, London; p. 37: © C & W Shields, Inc.; p. 50: Freud Museum, London.

Chapter 3
Opener: Courtesy Clark University Archives; p. 88: © Archive Photos.

Chapter 4
Opener: © Bettman Archive; p. 107: © Ken Fisher/Tony Stone Images p. 116: Digital Stock.

Chapter 5
Opener: © The Wellcome Institute Library, London; p. 139: © American Psychiatric Association; p. 142: Courtesy of Dr. Otto Kernberg; p. 144: © Institute for Psychoanalysis, Courtesy Jerome Kavka, M.D.; p. 145: © The American Psychological Association.

Chapter 6
Opener: © Bettmann Archive; p. 165: © Christopher Bissell/Tony Stone Images; p. 169: © David Grossman/Photo Researchers, Inc.

Chapter 7
Opener: © Rene Burri/Magnum Photos; p. 182: © SuperStock, Inc.; p. 195: © Stock Montage.

Chapter 8
Opener: Historical Pictures/Stock Montage, Inc.; p. 208: © SuperStock, Inc.; p. 216: © David Frazier Photolibrary; p. 218: © David Frazier Photolibrary.

Chapter 9
Opener: The Bettmann Archive; p. 242: © Sacha Ajbeszyc/The Image Bank; p. 247: © Deborah Davis/PhotoEdit; p. 250: AP/Wide World Photos.

Chapter 10
Opener: © Christopher S. Johnson/Stock Boston; p. 265: © Archives of the History of American Psychology, Akron, OH; p. 266: Archives of the History of American Psychology, University of Akron; p. 271: © David Frazier Photolibrary; p. 276: © Bob Daemmrich/The Image Works; p. 280: © Alex Farnsworth/The Image Works; p. 285: © David Powers/Stock Boston.

Chapter 11
Opener: Courtesy, Albert Bandura; p. 309: © David Frazier Photolibrary; p. 310: © David Frazier Photolibrary; p. 314: © Alice Kandell/Photo Researchers, Inc.

Chapter 12
Opener Left: © Courtesy of Julian Rotter; Opener RIght: Courtesy of Walter Mischel; p. 333: © David Frazier Photolibrary; p. 341: © Steven E. Sutton/The Image Bank; p. 354: © Nat Antman/The Image Works.

Chapter 13
Opener Left: Courtesy of Dr. Raymond B. Cattell; Opener Right: © Topham/The Image Works; p. 392: © SuperStock, Inc.

Chapter 14
Opener: © Archives of the History of American Psychology, Akron, OH; p. 412: © Robert Aschenbrenner/Stock Boston; p. 414: © PhotoEdit; p. 416: © David Frazier Photolibrary.

Chapter 15
Opener: By permission of Brandeis University; p. 437: © Rhoda Sidney/Stock Boston; p. 441: © Gary W. Nolton/Tony Stone Images p. 446: *The psychology of personal constructs*, by G. A. Kelly, 1955, p. 270. New York: Norton. Copyright 1955 by W. W. Norton & Company. Used by permission.

Chapter 16
Opener: Carl Rogers Memorial Library, Center for Study of the Person; p. 462: © David Stewart/Tony Stone Images; p. 467: © SuperStock, Inc.; p. 469: © Rhoda Sidney/PhotoEdit; p. 473: © Howard Dratch/The Image Works.

Chapter 17
Opener: © Bettmann Archive; p. 495: © David Hanover/Tony Stone Images p. 508: © Kathy McLaughlin/The Image Works.

Chapter 18
Opener: Courtesy of Georgia M. Johnson-May; p. 528: © Jean-Claude Lejeune/Stock Boston; p. 535: UPI/Bettmann; p. 537: © Michel Tcherevkoff/The Image Bank; p. 539: © Stock Montage.

Chapter 19
Opener: © Alexej von Jawlensky/Superstock, Inc.

Name Index

A

Abraham, K., 129, 156, 157
Abrahamsen, K., 230
Achilles, 71
Adams, N. E., 310
Adams-Webber, J. R., 446
Addams, J., 503
Adler, Alexandria, 99
Adler, Alfred, 3, 10, 13, 21, 75,
        96–126, 128, 158, 225,
        230, 241, 261, 288, 302,
        307, 312, 328, 410, 432,
        457, 490–91, 506, 522,
        540, 551–56, 558
Adler, J. M., 52
Adler, K., 99
Adler, L., 97
Adler, P., 97
Adler, Raissa E., 99
Adler, Rudoff, 97
Adler, S., 97, 99
Ainsworth, M., 146, 150
Alexander, I. E., 61
Allers, C. T., 120
Allport, A. L., 403, 407, 418–19
Allport, Fayette, 403
Allport, Floyd, 402
Allport, G., 3, 277, 302, 303, 347,
        365, 370, 371, 401–26,
        492, 496, 509, 545,
        552–57
Allport, J. E., 402
Allport, N. W., 402
Allport, R., 403
Amos, 178
Anderson, G., 224
Angel, E., 523
Angleitner, A., 559
Ansbacher, H. L., 108, 123, 126
Ansbacher, R. R., 123, 126
Arehart, D. M., 253
Aristotle, 268
Axtell, A., 122

B

Baarda, B., 321
Bachofen, J. J., 180, 183–84
Bachtold, L. M., 395
Bailey, W. T., 255
Baker, L., 148
Baker, N., 357–58
Balay, J., 53

Baldwin, A., 419
Balmary, M., 41, 45–46, 55
Bandura, A., 3, 296–326, 328, 347,
        352, 357, 360, 422, 424,
        446, 449, 551–56, 558
Bandura, C., 298
Bandura, M., 298
Bandura, V. V., 298
Bannister, D., 430, 446
Barnes, C. See Rotter, C. B.
Barrett-Lennard, G. T., 480–83
Bass, E., 53
Baum, F., 71
Beall, N., 431
Becker, B., 148
Beethoven, L., 104
Bell, M. D., 148, 149
Bell-Dumas, J., 120, 121–22
Bellinger, C., 203
Bender, L., 223
Benedict, R., 231, 501
Benson, R. M., 223
Bergin, A. E., 421
Bergman, A., 140
Berndt, T. J., 224
Bettelheim, B., 55
Billington, R., 148, 149
Binswanger, L., 521, 524
Bjork, D. W., 262, 275, 295
Black, M. J., 152
Blanchard, E. B., 319
Blatt, S. J., 149
Blazina, C., 122
Bleuler, E., 62
Block, Jack, 148, 447
Block, Jeanne, 447
Blos, P., 231
Blue, Y. See Skinner, Y. B.
Boer, D., 45
Boldero, J., 225, 253
Bonaparte, N. See Napoleon
Boss, M., 521, 524
Bottome, P., 97
Bowlby, J., 3, 128, 130, 139,
        145–46, 147,
        150–52, 555
Brannon, L., 41
Breuer, J., 18, 19–20, 551
Breus, M., 543
Brill, A. A., 403
Brokken, F. B., 559
Brome, V., 63, 64
Brosschot, J. F., 356

Brown, S. W., 54
Brozek, J., 494
Bruhn, A. R., 120
Bryan, W. J., 71
Buber, M., 524
Buchanan, L. P., 120, 121–22
Buddha, 73
Buehler, J., 89
Bullitt, W., 250
Bunch, J. M., 355
Burlingham, D. T., 231
Burston, D., 200
Burt, C., 386, 387
Butler, J. C., 173
Butler, T. L., 122
Butler, W., 53
Button, E., 453
Buttsworth, L. M., 396
Byck, R., 18

C

Caesar, J., 287
Cahoon, D. D., 422
Campbell, J., 10
Camus, A., 524
Cantor, N., 449
Caper, R., 151
Carey, J., 514
Carey, J. C., 90
Carkhuff, R. R., 480
Carlson, E., 150
Carlson, R., 89
Carroll, W. R., 315
Cashdan, S., 152
Cattell, A. S., 366, 370
Cattell, H. E. P., 367, 373, 397
Cattell, M. R., 366
Cattell, R. B., 3, 13, 345, 347,
        364–84, 386, 387–89,
        395–400, 404–6, 422,
        552–55, 558
Cezanne, P., 524
Chambers, J., 395
Chambliss, C. A., 310
Chance, J. E., 329, 332, 336,
        337, 345
Chao, C., 224
Chaplin, M. P., 120
Chapman, A. H., 203, 228
Charcot, J. M., 18, 19, 21, 62
Chatel, D., 543
Chesney, J. M., 120
Chevron, E. S., 149

Garry, M., 54
Gay, P., 3, 21, 59
Gebhardt, W. A., 356
Gendlin, E. T., 458, 477
Genia, V., 421
Germer, C. K., 8
Gholson, G., 8
Gibbons, J., 149
Gibson, H. B., 385
Glover, E., 130
Goble, F., 491
Godaert, G. L., 356
Goethe, J. W., 61, 99
Gold, J. A., 172–73
Gold, J. M., 255
Gold, L., 148
Goldberg, L. R., 397, 559
Goldstein, K., 490, 491, 501
Goldwert, M., 63
Gonzalez, G., 91
Good, G., 521
Goodman, A., 490
Goodman, B. See Maslow, B. G.
Goodman, P., 490, 508
Gorky, M., 248
Gorman, M. E., 8
Gorsuch, R. L., 422
Gough, H. G., 514
Gould, A. L. See Allport, A. L.
Graf, M. (Little Hans), 129
Greenberg, J., 172, 543–44
Greenway, D. E., 291
Greever, K. B., 122
Grossarth-Maticek, R., 386, 391
Grosskurth, P., 129
Gudjonsson, G., 390
Gupta, G., 290
Gupta, S., 290
Gurland, H. See Fromm, H. G.
Gurney, R. M., 253

H

Haaken, J., 46
Hafner, J. L., 120
Hall, A. G., 448
Hall, E., 246, 258
Hall, J. R., 422
Hall, M. H., 490, 510, 540, 548
Halpin, W. G., 396
Hamilton, D. L., 90
Hammer, M., 172–73
Hammond, W. A., 446–47
Hampes, W. P., 255
Hanna, N. A., 224
Hansen, D. E., 421
Hardy, A. B., 310
Harlow, H., 490
Harris, A. S., 91
Harris, T. G., 521, 522

Harrist, S., 223
Harsh, N., 54
Hart, J. J., 8
Harter, S., 224
Hartshorne, H., 348
Hartung, J. R., 120
Hathaway, S. R., 375
Hattie, J., 513
Hausdorff, D., 179
Haven, L., 202
Hayes, S. C., 291
Haynes, S. G., 290
Hazan, C., 150
Heber, S., 224
Hedges, L. V., 321
Heesacker, R. S., 149
Heidegger, M., 521, 534
Heilbrun, A. B., 514
Hemingway, E., 455
Henderson, V. L., 486
Henry, W. P., 223
Henschel, A., 596
Heppner, P. L., 456, 458
Higgins, S. T., 289–90
Hillman, J., 69
Hinselwood, R. D., 154
Hitler, A., 184, 191, 193, 194–96, 197, 248, 385
Hochreich, D. J., 329, 330–31, 335, 338, 339, 343
Hoffman, E., 97, 98, 100, 118, 301, 489–91, 519
Hofstee, W. K., 559
Holder, A., 55
Holland, R., 449
Holt, R. R., 55
Homann, E., 149
Homans, P., 91
Homburger, E. See Erikson, E. H.
Homburger, T., 230
Hood, R. W., 421, 422
Hornbuckle, D., 120
Horney, K. D., 3, 100, 129, 155–76, 177, 180, 186, 191, 204, 225, 230, 231, 420, 490, 542, 553–55, 557, 558
Horney, O., 157
Hosea, 178
Houle, L., 149
Houts, A. C., 8
Howard, G. S., 542–43, 544
Howe, H., 90
Howells, G. N., 310
Huesmann, L. R., 321
Hughes, J. M., 130
Humphreys, P., 515
Huston, A. C., 321
Huston, H. L., 91
Huxley, A., 503

I

Igleheart, H. C., 52
Ikpaahindi, L., 396
Inouye, D. K., 310
Inscoe, J., 205
Irigaray, L., 41
Isaiah, 176
Isbister, J. N., 21
Ispa, J. M., 153–54

J

Jackson, C., 395–96
Jacobs, M., 59
Jaffe, A., 94
James, F. R., 448
James, W., 503
James, W. H., 339
Janet, P., 62
Janeway, E., 252
Jasper, K., 524
Jefferson, T., 503
Jensen, A., 384
Jesses, M., 53
Jesus, 73, 197, 287
Jex, S. M., 515
Jih, C. S., 356
John, O., 389, 559
Johnson, G. L. M., 523
Johnson, J. A., 8
Jones, A., 513, 514
Jones, E., 18, 20, 21, 129
Jorgensen, J. A., 122
Juan, D., 225, 407
Jung, C. G., 3, 13, 21, 22, 23, 60–95, 99, 100, 122, 128, 158, 205, 225, 226, 230, 261, 539, 551, 553–58
Jung, Emilie P., 61–62
Jung, Emma R., 62, 64, 77
Jung, P., 61–62

K

Kaczor, L. M., 172–73
Kahane, M., 21
Kannel, W. B., 290
Kaus, C. R., 196–97
Keene, K. K., 122
Kelley, C. R., 46
Kelley, E. C., 46
Kelley, T. J., 89
Kelly, E. M., 429
Kelly, George A., 3, 329, 346, 428–52, 542, 553–58
Kelly, Gladys T., 429
Kelly, T. V., 429

Nicastro, R., 53
Nichols, C., 120–21
Nietzsche, F., 521, 524, 546
Nigg, J. T., 148
Noll, R., 91
Norman, P., 356
Norman, W., 389, 559
Norton, G. R., 224

O

Oberholzer, E., 491
O'Connell, A. N., 176
Odbert, H. S., 371, 406
Oedipus, King of Thebes, 39, 539
Ogden, T. H., 133
O'Hara, M., 458, 483
Olczak, P. V., 513
Olmstead, M. P., 149
Orlofsky, J. L., 120
Overton, W. F., 8

P

Paige, J., 419, 420
Paik, H., 321
Paris, B., 156, 157, 170, 173, 176
Park, R. E., 204
Parker, S., 431
Pasteur, L., 292
Patterson, M. L., 421
Paunonen, S. V., 396
Pavlov, I., 262, 387
Payne, D. A., 396
Peake, P. K., 358
Pendse, S. G., 196
Perry, H. S., 203, 204, 205, 228
Perryman, T., 120, 121
Pervin, L. A., 552–54, 558
Petanaude, W., 514
Peterson, B. E., 254–55
Petot, J-M., 129
Phares, E. J., 329, 332, 336, 337,
    339, 345
Picasso, P., 524
Pine, F., 140
Pines, M., 223, 224
Piper, R. B., 89
Plato, 267
Polanyi, M., 8
Polivy, J., 149
Polonsky, S., 47, 53
Pomeroy, W., 490
Popper, K., 56
Powell, A., 389
Powell, R. A., 45
Preiswerk, E. See Jung, Emilie P.
Preiswerk, H., 61
Preiswerk, S., 61
Prentice, N. M., 224

Pryor, D. B., 223
Pyszczynski, T., 543

Q

Qualls, D. L., 515
Quinlan, D. M., 149
Quinn, S., 129, 157, 176
Quintana, S., 223
Quixote, D., 407

R

Rabinowitz, F. E., 521, 522
Rank, O., 457
Rattner, J., 97, 99
Rauschenbach, E. See Jung,
    Emma R.
Ray, J. J., 196, 197, 513
Rayner, R., 266, 269
Reeses, C., 546
Rehfish, J. M., 291
Reichman, F. See Fromm-
    Reichman, F.
Reitler, R., 21
Reizes, Emanuel, 128–29
Reizes, Emilie, 128
Reizes, L. D., 128
Reizes, M., 128, 129
Reizes, S., 128–29
Rest, J. R., 196
Richard, R. L., 515
Richards, P. S., 421, 422
Ridley, S. E., 89
Riklin, F., 85
Ritter, B., 319
Roazen, P., 21, 22, 59, 197, 230
Robb, Z., 513
Robinson, P., 56
Rodriguez, M. L., 358, 362
Rogers, C. R., 3, 10, 52, 100, 294,
    311, 312, 329, 405, 432,
    454–87, 489, 513, 522,
    524, 526, 540–42,
    552–58
Rogers, D., 456
Rogers, H. E., 456
Rogers, J. C., 455, 456
Rogers, J. D., 255
Rogers, M. See Cattell, M. R.
Rogers, M. E., 456
Rogers, N., 456
Rogers, W., 455, 456
Rohrer, G. E., 356
Romney, D. M., 446–47
Roodin, P. A., 196–97
Roosevelt, E., 503
Rosen, D. H., 91
Rosenberg, M., 480–83
Rosenthal, D. A., 253

Rosenthal, T. L., 319
Ross, C. A., 224
Ross, D., 318, 321
Ross, D. L., 52
Ross, J. M., 420–21
Ross, S. A., 318, 321
Rostal, S. See Eysenck, S. B. G.
Rotter, C. B., 328
Rotter, Jean, 329
Rotter, Julian B., 3, 13, 100, 322,
    327–45, 346, 355–62,
    430, 449, 491, 552–56
Rotter, R., 329
Rowan, D. G., 515
Royce, J. R., 389
Ruble, V. E., 90
Rudikoff, E. C., 480
Ruffins, S. A., 148
Runco, M. A., 514–15
Rushton, J. P., 396
Rust, J. O., 515
Rychlak, J. F., 321
Ryckman, R. M., 172–73

S

Sachs, H., 179
St. Clair, M., 154
St. John, C., 122
Salome, 73
Sapir, E., 204
Sartre, J. P., 521, 524, 525, 546
Savill, G. E., 121
Sayers, J., 128
Schacht, A., 90
Schacht, T. E., 223
Schaefer, C. E., 223, 224
Schlein, S., 232
Schmideberg, M. K., 129–30
Schmideberg, W., 130
Schneider, H. G., 355
Scholl, K. See May, K. S.
Schuerger, J. M., 383
Schuettler, A. See Cattell, A. S.
Schur, M., 20
Schurr, K. T., 90
Schweitzer, A., 503
Segal, E. M., 14
Segal, H. G., 148
Segal, Hanna, 128
Segal, J., 154
Seiffge-Krenke, I., 224
Serson, J. See Erikson, J. M.
Shadish, W. R., 8
Shakespeare, W., 99, 267
Shanklin, G., 90
Shapiro, S. I., 519
Shaver, P., 150
Sheffield, M., 514
Shelburne, W. A., 91
Shevrin, H., 53

Subject Index

Fromm's, 178–80
Horney's, 156–58
Jung's, 61–64
Kelly's, 429–31
Kernberg's, 142
Klein's, 128–30
Kohut's, 143
Mahler's, 139–41
Maslow's, 489–92
May's, 521–34
Mischel's, 346–47
Rogers's, 455–59
Rotter's, 328–29
Skinner's, 261–65
Sullivan's, 202–28
Biophilia, 189, 192, 196, 197
Birth order. *See* Family
    constellation
Birth, psychological, 140
Bobo doll, 318, 321
Body ego, 232–34
Borderline personality disorder,
    148–49
Bulimia, 149

C

Care, 246, 532–35
    love, will and, 532–35
Castration anxiety, 23, 39–40
Castration complex, 39–42, 239
Catharsis, 18
Causality, 12, 75, 104, 552
    vs. teleology, 12, 75, 104, 552
Center of Personal Construct
    Psychology, 430–31
Center for Studies of the
    Person, 458
Chance encounters, 297–98,
    301–2
Character, 187
Character Orientations (Fromm),
    187–90, 194
    nonproductive, 188–89
        exploitative, 188
        hoarding, 188–89
        marketing, 189
        receptive, 188
    productive, 189–90
Chicago College of Medicine and
    Surgery, 203
Chicago Psychoanalytic Institute,
    157, 180
Chicago Study, 477–80
Child Personality Questionnaire
    (CPQ), 378
Childhood, 82, 215–16
    early, 237–39
Choice corollary, 437–38
Choice, elaborative, 450

Client-centered therapy, 459,
    468–84
    effectiveness of, 473–77, 480
Clinical Analysis Questionnaire
    (CAQ), 378
Cocaine, 18, 289–90
Codependency, 164, 172
Cognition, 298–300
    levels of, 211–13
Cognitive-affective personality
    system, 349–55
Cognitive-affective units, 351–55
Cognitive mediation, 299–300
Cognitive social learning theory
    (Mischel), 327, 329,
    345–62
Cognitive social learning theory
    (Rotter), 327–45,
    355–62
Collective efficacy, 312–13
Collective unconscious, 23, 61,
    64, 65–74, 539
    phylogenetic endowment
        and, 23
Comfort, need for, 336
Commonality corollary, 440
Compensation for feelings of
    inferiority, 101–2
Competence, 241, 249
Competencies, 351–52
Competition, 216–17
Complexes, 65, 84–85
Comprehensive Early Memory
    Scoring System, 120–21
Compromise, 216–17
Compulsion, 239
Compulsion, repetition, 47
Conative needs, 496
Concept of Humanity, 11–12
    Adler's, 123–24
    Allport's, 424–25
    Bandura's, 323–25
    Cattell's, 398
    dimensions for a, 11–12
    Erikson's, 256–57
    Eysenck's, 398
    Freud's, 57–58
    Fromm's, 198–99
    Horney's, 174–75
    Jung's, 92–93
    Kelly's, 450–51
    Klein's, 151
    Maslow's, 516–17
    May's, 545–46
    Mischel's, 360–61
    Rogers's, 484–85
    Rotter's, 360–61
    Skinner's, 292–94
    Sullivan's, 226–27
    summary of, 551–54

Conditioning
    operant, 268–77
    respondent, 268–69
Conflicts, intrapsychic, 165–69
Conformity, 187
Congruence, 468–70
Conscience, 28
Conscious, 24–25, 58, 64–65,
    105–6, 552
    perceptual, 24
    vs. unconscious, 12, 552
Consistency paradox, 348–49
Constructing obstacles, 115
Construction corollary, 435
Constructive alternativism, 429,
    432–33
Contingencies, describing, 284
Contingency management, 289
Cooperation, 216–17
Core pathology, 237–49
Correlation coefficient, 367
Cosmology, 267
Countercontrol, 286–87
Countertransference, 88–89, 193
Creative Personality Scale,
    514–15
Creative power, 101, 110
Creative scientists, 395–96
Creativity, 282, 395–96, 507–8,
    514–15

D

D-love, 509
Dasein, 525–26. *See also* Being-in-
    the-world
Death, 31–32, 131, 527
Decay, syndrome of, 190–92,
    194–96
Defense mechanisms, 27, 33–36,
    58, 288, 307–8
    disengagement of internal
        control and, 307–8
    psychic, 134–36
    safeguarding tendencies and,
        112–13
Defensiveness, 466
Defining Issues Test, 196
Delay of gratification, 328, 357–59
Denial, 463, 466
Dependency, 164, 172, 336
Depreciation, 113
Depression, 149, 191
Depressive position, 133–34
Depressive reactions, 316–17
Deprivation, 284–85
Desensitization, systematic, 319
Destiny, 535, 537–38
    defined, 537
    freedom and, 535–38

William Alanson White Institute
    of Psychiatry,
    Psychoanalysis and
    Psychology, 180, 204,
    522, 534
Willoughby Emotional Maturity
    Scale (E-M Scale), 478
Wisdom, 246, 247–48
Withdrawal, 114–15
    as a coping strategy, 161

Wizard of Oz, 71
Word association test, 84–85
Worth, conditions of, 464–65

Y

Yang, 73, 74
Yin, 73, 74
Young adulthood (Erikson's stage
    of), 245–46

Youth, 82
Yuork tribe, 231, 233,
    248–50

Z

Zen Buddhism, 180
Zodiac group, 157, 204